W9-CHI-114

RESEARCH METHODS IN SOCIAL RELATIONS

CLAIRE SELLTIZ • MARIE JAHODA

MORTON DEUTSCH • STUART W. COOK

EDITORIAL READERS

ISIDOR CHEIN • HAROLD M. PROSHANSKY

PUBLISHED FOR THE SOCIETY FOR THE

PSYCHOLOGICAL STUDY OF SOCIAL ISSUES

Holt, Rinehart and Winston

New York - Chicago - San Francisco
Toronto

RESEARCH METHODS IN SOCIAL RELATIONS

Revised One-Volume Edition

ACKNOWLEDGMENTS

Grateful acknowledgment is made to the following for the use of copyrighted materials:

University of Minnesota Press for the paragraphs from *Interracial Housing: A Psychological Evaluation of a Social Experiment* by Morton Deutsch and Mary Evans Collins. 1951

Harper & Brothers for quotations from *The Authoritarian Personality* by T. W. Adorno, Else Frenkel-Brunswik, Daniel J. Levinson, and R. Nevitt Sanford.

From *On The Witness Stand* by Hugo Münsterberg. Copyright 1908, 1923 by Doubleday & Co., Inc. Reprinted by permission of the publisher.

Robert F. Bales and Addison-Wesley Publishing Company, Inc., for the reproduction of a chart from *Interaction Process Analysis* by Robert F. Bales.

Free Press for a passage from *The Focused Interview* by Robert K. Merton, M. Fiske, and P. L. Kendall.

Harper & Brothers for permission to quote from *Public Opinion and the Individual* by Gardner Murphy and Rensis Likert.

The University of Illinois Press for a diagram from *The Measurement of Meaning* by Charles E. Osgood, G. J. Suci, and P. H. Tannenbaum.

Personnel Psychology, Inc., for permission to quote from an article, "The Validity of Direct and Indirect Questions in Measuring Job Satisfaction," by Joseph Weitz and R. C. Nuckols, 1953, 6.

Teachers College, Columbia University for a passage from *Measurement of Fairmindedness* by Goodwin B. Watson, Teachers College, Columbia University Contributions to Education No. 176.

Cambridge University Press for an extract from *Scientific Explanation: A Study of the Function of Theory, Probability and Law in Science*, by R. B. Braithwaite.

The University of Chicago Press for a paragraph from "Fundamentals of Concept Formation in Empirical Science" by Carl G. Hempel, *International Encyclopedia of Unified Science*, Vol. II, No. 7.

Yale University Press for a selection from *Communication and Persuasion: Psychological Studies of Opinion Change*, by Carl I. Hovland, I. K. Janis, and H. H. Kelley.

Columbia University Press for material from *Negro Intelligence and Selective Migration* by Otto Klineberg.

The authors also are indebted to Professor Sir Ronald A. Fisher, Cambridge, and to Messrs. Oliver and Boyd Ltd., Edinburgh, for permission to reprint an extract from their book *The Design of Experiments*.

PREFACE TO THE FIRST EDITION

ALTHOUGH THERE HAVE BEEN many technical publications on specific aspects of research methods for the study of social relations, few books bring together on an introductory level the considerations which enter into every step of the research process. This is what we have set out to do.

Research methods can be presented in many different ways. The special emphasis of our presentation arises from a growing concern among social scientists that their work should contribute to the solution of practical problems as they arise in the contemporary world. Experience has demonstrated that research conducted without concern for immediate application is neither easily nor promptly put to use. Research concerned with immediate application requires throughout the research process a collaborative effort between social scientists and those who are to act upon their findings. Such collaboration creates problems of its own, for which neither partner is fully prepared by his specific training. This book, therefore, includes a treatment of such problems.

Wherever possible we have chosen the illustrative material from an area in which such collaboration is particularly needed and where it has already been attempted with some success: the area of prejudice. Hostilities between persons of different racial, religious, or national background present one of the major problems of our times. To the extent to which we learn to understand the factors which promote or obstruct harmonious relations among such groups, we may hope to contribute to the solution of this problem.

The book is divided into two parts. Part I, *Basic Processes*, deals consecutively with the major steps of a scientific inquiry into social relations, as well as with the interrelationships between the steps. Part II, *Selected Techniques*, deals in more technical detail with some specific methodological problems.

In Part I we have aimed at two groups of readers—those who are preparing to conduct social research and those who are to use its results. The former will find in Part I an introduction to the methods of social research. The latter reader will find in Part I an orientation to research procedures which will, we hope, prevent him from expecting either too little or too much from research. If he expects too little, he will be disinclined to collaborate, to the detriment of further research; if he expects too much, collaboration must end in disappointment.

Parts I and II together are organized as a text for courses in research methods. We have experimented with their use as a text in a graduate course on research methods at New York University and hope that others will have equally encouraging experiences with its use. In addition, the social scientist here and abroad who has not specialized in conducting research in social relations will, we hope, find useful the systematic account of the research process in Part I and the more technical elaborations of some methodological problems in Part II.

This book is in many ways the outcome of group effort. The idea of producing it arose in a group; its production was financed by several groups; it had the editorial guidance of a group; and it was produced by a group.

The Society for the Psychological Study of Social Issues (S.P.S.S.I.), under whose auspices this book is presented, conducts much of its scientific and professional activities through committees; one of them, the Committee on Intergroup Relations, in 1948 received from Gordon W. Allport a suggestion to produce a book on the measurement of prejudice. A subcommittee was established under the chairmanship of Robert Chin to investigate whether such a book was needed and whether its production was feasible. Both questions were answered in the affirmative, and the subcommittee prepared a first outline of the material to be covered in such a publication. The following members of the subcommittee participated actively in the preparation of the outline: Gordon Allport, Robert Chin, Harold Kelley, Bernard Kramer, Bernard Kutner, M. Brewster Smith, Nancy Starbuck, and Babette S. Whipple.

After the Council of S.P.S.S.I. decided to adopt the project and support it financially, an editorial committee was appointed consisting of the following members: Hadley Cantril (Princeton), Robert

Chin (Boston University), Stuart Cook, chairman (New York University), Eugene Hartley (City College of New York), Samuel Flowerman (American Jewish Committee), Herbert Hyman (National Opinion Research Center), Donald McGranahan (United Nations), Irwin Shannon (National Conference of Christians and Jews), Leo Srole (Anti-Defamation League of B'nai B'rith), Frank Trager (Anti-Defamation League of B'nai B'rith), and Goodwin Watson (Teachers College, Columbia University). The editorial committee reviewed the outline on several occasions and selected the contributors. The reading of the final manuscript was delegated by the Council of S.P.S.S.I. to Theodore Newcomb and Goodwin Watson.

The first planning conferences among the editors resulted in a recommendation for a shift in focus, based on two considerations. First, the measurement of prejudice is not fundamentally different from the measurement of other social relations; secondly, a discussion of measurement techniques alone runs the risk of being misleading unless it is placed into the broader context of the entire research process. With the concurrence of the editorial committee, this shift was made: the plan was modified from one for a book of techniques for the measurement of prejudice to one on research methods in the study of social relations with especial emphasis on prejudice. This led to the conception of Part I in its present form. This part was produced by the three authors. Although Marie Jahoda and Morton Deutsch were primarily responsible for writing the drafts of the various chapters, cooperation among all three was so close and continuous that it would be impossible to specify the contribution of any one individual. The chapters in Part II were written, with few exceptions, especially for this book by experts in various special fields.

In the conviction that the production of a book on methods of research in the study of social relations would serve the interests of many other organizations, the Council of S.P.S.S.I. approached several other groups to enlist financial support for the undertaking. The production of the book might not have been possible without the prompt and generous response of the Anti-Defamation League of B'nai B'rith. This was followed by a grant from the National Conference of Christians and Jews and a contract with the United Nations Educational, Scientific and Cultural Organization.

We are indebted to a number of colleagues for their generous contribution of time and thought. Gordon Allport has never lost touch with the development of this perhaps somewhat wayward child of his imagination. He has carefully and constructively criticized our early efforts and suggested many helpful avenues of approach. Robert Chin and M. Brewster Smith collaborated in a two-day conference with the editors during which the original outline was transformed into the one underlying this book. M. Brewster Smith and Harold Kelley have given intensive assistance in reviewing drafts of most of the chapters in Part I. Both have made many helpful critical suggestions. Isidor Chein has reviewed several chapters and in addition contributed much to the final editorial work. Claire Selltiz has collaborated with us in the last revision of Part I. She has, through her suggestions, much improved the general organization and clarity of presentation. To her and to Alicia Hemler we are also indebted for much editorial assistance with the final manuscript of the entire book. Robert Lee has given valuable assistance in the preparation of the bibliography. The secretarial personnel of the Research Center for Human Relations, especially Miss Sally Cohen, Mrs. Virginia Revere, and Mrs. Anita Walkley, have borne patiently with the typing and retyping of many revisions of the text. Their cheerful cooperation has helped to reduce the tensions which so often arise in the attempt to meet a deadline and coordinate the work of several contributors.

We acknowledge with thanks the permission of the following organizations for reprinting material originally produced by them: The United Nations for permission to reprint a condensed version of *The Main Types and Causes of Discrimination* in Appendix B; The Bureau of Applied Social Research, Columbia University, for permission to reprint a condensed version of *Training Guide on Constructing Questionnaires and Interview Schedules* in Chapter 12; and the Princeton Press for permission to reprint a slightly modified version of Chapter I of *Measurement and Prediction* in Chapter 21.

Research Center for Human Relations
at New York University   MARIE JAHODA
March 1951   MORTON DEUTSCH
                                              STUART W. COOK

PREFACE TO THE REVISED EDITION

IN REVISING *Research Methods in Social Relations*, we have had two main goals: to bring the book up to date, and to organize it as a one-volume text suitable for use in undergraduate courses as well as in introductory graduate courses in research methods in social psychology and sociology.

In the years since the first edition was prepared, there has been a considerable increase in the number of colleges offering undergraduate courses in research methods in the social sciences. Teachers who have used the earlier edition in such courses have reported that students had difficulty with some parts of Volume One and much of Volume Two. It seemed to us that the trouble in Volume One sprang from occasional complications of style and from an occasional taking-for-granted that readers were familiar with certain concepts, rather than from any formidable difficulty in the subject matter. On the other hand, some sections of Volume Two were highly technical and demanded, for their understanding, background beyond what could be expected of an undergraduate student or what could be provided within the text. In the present version we have tried to clarify the material that was in Volume One by simplifying the language and by expanding some of the discussion; and we have incorporated some material from Volume Two that seems to be within the grasp of students without extensive technical background. Although we have tried to make the volume more easily understandable, we have not "talked down," nor have we omitted the discussion of any concepts or methods that seem to us important for a basic understanding of research methods in social psychology and sociology.

In bringing the book up to date, we have taken account of new developments in both concepts and methods. For example, since the first edition was written, there have been new formulations of the concepts of validity and reliability of measuring instruments; the discussion of these concepts has taken account of these new formulations. At the same time, new measuring techniques have come into general use —for example, the semantic differential and the Q-sort—and brief explanations of these techniques have been added. In addition, we have, of course, included illustrations from research carried out since the earlier writing.

One other feature of the revision should be mentioned: to the illustrations used in the first edition, which were taken largely from the area of intergroup relations and prejudice, we have added examples from research dealing with other social phenomena, in order to make more clear the applicability of the discussion to a whole range of problems of social relations.

As with the first edition, this revision has been very much a group enterprise. It has again been carried out under the auspices of the Society for the Psychological Study of Social Issues. Major responsibility for the revision has been carried by Claire Selltiz, in close cooperation with the authors of the earlier edition. Again, we owe thanks to many colleagues for their help. Isidor Chein, Mary Evans Collins, John Harding, Robert R. Holt, Irwin Katz, Robert S. Lee, Harold M. Proshansky, Lillian C. Robbins, and M. Brewster Smith have each read and commented on one or more chapters. There is not space to acknowledge in detail the contributions of each of them. We want, however, to express especial gratitude to Drs. Chein, Harding, and Proshansky, and to Mrs. Robbins, for their many helpful suggestions. Mrs. Robbins and Drs. Chein and Proshansky—the two latter in their capacity as the review committee for S.P.S.S.I.—have read the entire manuscript. Dr. Chein drafted parts of Chapters 4, 6, 8, and 10, and wrote Appendix B; Dr. Harding drafted parts of Chapters 1, 2, 6, and 10; and Dr. Proshansky drafted parts of Chapters 7 and 8. Arthur Kornhauser, Donald V. McGranahan, Paul B. Sheatsley, William Foote Whyte, and Alvin Zander kindly gave us permission to incorporate in this volume material they had contributed to Volume Two of the earlier edition. In addition to the help of these professional colleagues, we had the assistance of a number of undergraduate students, who read several chapters and not only pointed out passages that were ambiguous or unnecessarily complicated, but made many helpful suggestions. They were: Patricia Buchalter, Marilyn Charney, Jane Wiener

Einhorn, Ira Latto, and Stephen Silverman, of the Washington Square College of New York University, and Alan Guskin and Naomi Litt, of Brooklyn College. Mary Insinna and Gloria Greaves have typed and re-typed the various drafts with patience and care. To all of these collaborators we express our thanks.

February 1959

CLAIRE SELLTIZ
MARIE JAHODA
MORTON DEUTSCH
STUART W. COOK

Einhorn, Ira Lairo, and Stephen Silverman, of the Washington Square College of New York University, and Alan Gitkin and Naomi Litt, of Brooklyn College. Mary Institue and Gloria Graves have typed and re-typed the various drafts with patience and care. To all of these collaborators we express our thanks.

February 1959

Claire Selltiz
Marie Jahoda
Morton Deutsch
Stuart W. Cook

CONTENTS

RESEARCH METHODS IN SOCIAL RELATIONS

1

THE RESEARCH PROCESS

The Importance of Knowing How Research Is Done

Major Steps in Research

An Illustration

Organization of the Text

It cannot be that axioms established by argumentation can suffice for the discovery of new works, since the subtlety of nature is greater many times over than the subtlety of argument. FRANCIS BACON

T HE PURPOSE OF RESEARCH is to discover answers to questions through the application of scientific procedures. These procedures have been developed in order to increase the likelihood that the information gathered will be relevant to the question asked and will be reliable and unbiased. To be sure, there is no guarantee that any given research undertaking actually will produce relevant, reliable, and unbiased information. But scientific research procedures are more likely to do so than any other method known to man.

Research always starts from a question or a problem of some sort: Why is the sun visible for more hours each day in summer than in winter? Why do apples regularly fall to the ground instead of floating off into space? How does it happen that a book appears to be about the same size whether it is fifteen feet away or two feet away, even though the image on our retina is much smaller when it is farther away? Is the desire to own private property inherent in "human nature"? Are the efforts of a settlement house to reduce juvenile delinquency in its neighborhood having the desired effect? Will sponsorship of a quiz program on television increase the sales of a given brand of cigarettes more than sponsorship of a telecast of a baseball game? Is it true that property values fall when a Negro family moves into a formerly all-white neighborhood? Will training foremen in "human relations" lead to a reduction in absenteeism on the part of workers?

The nature of the question varies. Starting from observation of an event or a series of events, one may ask whether events of this sort always follow the same pattern, or whether there are circumstances in

2

which the outcome may be different. Or one may seek an explanation of the process by which certain conditions lead to certain outcomes. Questions may take the form "What happens when . . .?" or "What would happen if . . .?" or "Which is the more efficient way of accomplishing . . .?" They may be concerned with filling in a gap in knowledge, or with testing a hypothesis, or with checking whether some proposition which is generally believed is in fact tenable.

In order to be answerable by research, questions must have one characteristic in common: They must be such that observation or experimentation in the natural world (including, in the case of the social sciences, the behavior of human beings) can provide the needed information. Many questions of choice or decision cannot be answered on the basis of information alone, since they involve *values* as well as information. "Should the government establish a compulsory system of health insurance?" is a question of this type. The answer depends not only on factual information, such as the incidence of disease, the cost of medical care, etc.; it also involves values about individual initiative, the "welfare state," etc. However, it is often possible to transform what seems to be a question of value into a question of fact. For example, opposition to compulsory health insurance may be based on values having to do with the freedom of patients to choose their doctors, the freedom of doctors to practice without bureaucratic interference, etc. But whether health insurance does or does not limit the freedom of patients to choose their doctors, does or does not introduce bureaucratic controls over medical practice, are questions of fact, and therefore open to answer by research. Here, however, further values have been specified—namely, freedom to choose one's doctor and freedom from bureaucratic control—and the question of the desirability of a given course of action becomes transformed into whether or not it is likely to lead to the valued outcomes. This latter question can be answered by research. But the further values imply other questions—for example, "Is the freedom of patients to choose their doctors so important that it outweighs all other considerations?" This question, in turn, can be answered by research only if some other value is specified, so that the importance of freedom of choice in reaching this other goal can be determined.

There are other questions which *could* be answered on the basis of information alone but cannot be answered by research at the present time because adequate procedures for gathering the relevant information have not yet been devised. Issues calling for universally applicable scales of psychological measurement are a case in point.

Many questions, however, *can* be approached by scientific methods at the present time. This does not mean that research will always emerge with an answer, let alone a definitive answer. Research is oriented toward seeking answers; it may or may not find them. Characteristically, modern science, and especially social science, is an unfinished process. To quote Jaspers (1950): "Whereas ancient science had the appearance of something completed, to which the notion of progress was not essential, modern science progresses into the infinite." More often than not, social research results in the raising of new questions or the reformulation of old ones.

The reasons for asking research questions are of two general kinds: *intellectual*, based on the desire to know or understand for the satisfaction of knowing or understanding; and *practical*, based on the desire to know for the sake of being able to do something better or more efficiently. The investigations to which these two types of question lead—sometimes labeled "pure" (or "basic") and "applied" research— are at times discussed as if they were somehow opposed or mutually exclusive, and frequently as if one were better than the other. Such an approach is misleading. Historically, the scientific enterprise has been concerned both with knowledge for its own sake and with knowledge for what it can contribute to practical concerns. This double emphasis is perhaps especially appropriate in the case of social science. On the one hand, its responsibility as a *science* is to develop a body of principles that make possible the understanding and prediction of the whole range of human interactions. On the other hand, because of its *social* orientation, it is increasingly being looked to for practical guidance in solving immediate problems of human relations. Even this statement—"On the one hand . . . on the other"—suggests that the two aspects are distinct. But in the long run, neither goal can be fully realized without the other. Only as general principles are developed can social science offer sound guidance for immediate action, and only to the extent that it *can* make predictions about the results of action in specific situations does it justify its claim of providing an adequate systematic body of knowledge about social interactions. Moreover, the starting point of a study does not necessarily determine what the nature of its contribution will be. Both in the social sciences and in the physical sciences, research on practical problems may lead to the discovery of basic principles, and "basic" research often yields knowledge that has immediate practical usefulness. And whether the motivating purpose of a given investigation is primarily intellectual or primarily practical, the requirements of sound research procedure are essentially the same.

The general scientific enterprise, then, must be concerned both with the development of general principles and with practical problems in specific situations. This does not mean, however, that every study must have both goals. An investigation may be concerned with a practical problem or with "pure" research, or with some combination of these interests. Not only may any given piece of research quite properly be concerned with only one aspect or the other; any given investigator may choose to concentrate more or less exclusively on one or the other aspect. The condition that is required for the healthy development of science is that each aspect be adequately represented in the collective research enterprise.

Throughout this book, we have tried to keep both emphases in mind. This means that, in addition to concerning ourselves with the basic requirements of good research, we have devoted considerable attention to ways of making research relevant to the solution of social problems and to increasing the likelihood that its findings will actually be used.

The Importance of Knowing How Research Is Done

Even though research cannot provide any final answers to the questions with which it is concerned, there has been a constant effort to devise procedures that will increase the probable accuracy of research answers. Why is it important to be familiar with these procedures? For the student who is preparing for a career of carrying out research in social psychology or sociology, the answer is obvious: Research techniques are the tools of his trade. He needs not only to develop skill in using them but also to understand the logic behind them.

But it is not only the student who intends to carry out research who needs to know about research methods. The positions for which social science students are likely to be preparing themselves—teaching, administration in government or business, community consultation, social work—increasingly call for the ability to evaluate and to use research results: to judge whether a study has been carried out in such a way that one can have reasonable confidence in its findings and whether its findings are applicable to the specific situation at hand.

Even if one does not expect to make specific use of research findings in his job, in our scientific age all of us are in many ways "consumers" of research results. To use them intelligently, we need to be able to judge the adequacy of the methods by which they have been obtained. As a student, for example, you will find that many of the "facts" presented in your courses rest on the results of research. But you may discover that the "facts" reported by one study are quite different from those produced by another study on the same point. One investigator, for example, may report that children who are weaned early grow up to be more independent and better adjusted than those who are nursed for a longer time; another investigator turns up with just the opposite finding. Or several studies may conclude that when Negroes and whites live near each other, each group is likely to become more favorably inclined toward the other; but other studies may conclude that interracial hostility is likely to be especially intense in neighborhoods where Negroes and whites live in close proximity. In order to be able to make a tentative judgment about which conclusion merits more confidence, you need to be able to judge the adequacy of the studies. Later sections of this book will consider the criteria of good research in detail. Here we may suggest simply that you will want to ask such questions as: How do the investigators define their terms? Are they really both talking about the same things, or have they used the same words for different phenomena? Was the evidence they gathered relevant to the problem? Were there any obvious sources of bias in the way the data were gathered? Were there different conditions in the studies that might account for the difference in findings?

Even in the course of daily living, the average citizen increasingly needs to be able to evaluate research in order to make intelligent decisions. This is perhaps most clear at the present time with respect to medical research and decisions based on it: Should I have my child inoculated with "flu" vaccine? Should I vote for fluoridation of the local water supply? Should I stop smoking in order to lessen the risk of getting lung cancer?[1] With the rapid increase in social science research, it seems likely that the average citizen will increasingly be presented with social science findings. At the present time, he has relatively little occasion to evaluate these findings as a basis for his own actions. But the person who knows how research is carried out is better able to judge the probable accuracy of opinion polls or election predictions and to view with appropriate skepticism the claims that "9 doctors out of 10 approve . . ."

Besides all these practical advantages of familiarity with research methods, there is the satisfaction of acquiring a new intellectual tool. And it is a tool with much broader uses than the specific purposes for which it was devised. It can become a way of looking at the world, of judging everyday experience. The person who really understands the basic elements of research method is in a position to ask, with respect to every statement he reads or hears: What is the basis for that view? Is it supported by evidence? Under what conditions is it likely to hold true? Of course, he will not necessarily question all statements in this way. As has already been pointed out, not all matters are appropriately considered in this way. If a friend admires a beautiful sunset, or expresses a preference for spending his vacation in the mountains, it is irrelevant to question the factual basis or the "objective truth" of his opinion. It may often be inappropriate to change the tone of a social situation by demanding evidence for a statement lightly made. But if one reads that public opinion, as reflected in mail to members of Congress, is opposed to foreign aid, or that a legislator has proposed

---

[1] Any individual's decisions will be determined not only by the facts as discovered by research but also by his values, which determine the import of the facts for him. With respect to health matters, since there is nearly universal agreement on the desirability of good health, the importance of values as well as fact in determining action is often overlooked. However, the importance of values in social issues is indicated by considering the question: "Should there be racial integration?" The fact that integration is conductive to friendly association between Negroes and whites may be taken by some as a basis for supporting segregation and by others as a basis for supporting integration.

curing juvenile delinquency by fining the parents of delinquents; or if one hears a neighbor say that he will not sell his home to a Jewish family because it would spoil the neighborhood—in such situations one may well want to raise, at least in his own mind, such questions as: How do you know that? What are the facts on which you base your conclusion? Is the interpretation warranted by the facts?

Major Steps in Research

The object of this book is to describe in detail the procedures necessary to discover answers to questions through research. But since concern with detail often obscures perception of the whole, it is well, before embarking on the examination of specific procedures, to point out some over-all aspects of the research process.

The research process consists of a number of closely related activities that overlap continuously rather than following a strictly prescribed sequence. So interdependent are these activities that the first step of a research project largely determines the nature of the last. If subsequent procedures have not been taken into account in the early stages, serious difficulties may arise and prevent the completion of a study. Frequently these difficulties cannot be remedied at the time they become apparent because they are rooted in the earlier procedures. They can be avoided only by keeping in mind, at each step of the research process, the requirements of subsequent steps.

To be sure, as research proceeds from the conception of a theme for a study through the gathering of data to the production of a report and the application of the findings, the focus of attention will necessarily shift from one activity to the next. This shift reflects a difference in emphasis, however, rather than an exclusive concentration on one step. A mechanically consecutive sequence of procedures, in which one research step is entirely completed before the next is begun, is rarely, if ever, the experience of social scientists.

The usual pattern of *reporting* research creates an oversimplified expectation of what is involved in *doing* research. Customarily, a report on completed research, when it appears as an article in a technical journal, resembles, with minor modifications, the following model:

1. A statement of purpose is made in the form of *formulating the problem;*
2. A description of the *study design* is given;
3. The *methods of data collection* are specified;
4. The *results* are presented;
5. Frequently, there follows a section on *conclusions and interpretation.*

Whatever the individual variations from this model, published research strongly suggests the existence of a prescribed sequence of procedures, each step presupposing the completion of the preceding one. Although this model is entirely justified in the interest of economy of scientific reporting, it must not be mistaken for a model of the research process, which differs from it in two respects: (1) The research process almost never follows the neat sequential pattern of activities suggested in the organization of research reports; and (2) the process involves many additional activities which are rarely mentioned in published studies.

Some of these additional activities are related to the scientific requirements of the study; others to its practical demands. The apparently simple reporting of the methods of data collection, for example, summarizes decisions about the kinds of data needed and the most efficient way of collecting them, and the activities carried out in the development and pretesting of the data-collection instruments. In addition to these steps, related to the scientific requirements of the study, there are other, more "practical," demands: the budget must be planned; funds must be obtained and administered; personnel must be allocated and, in some cases, specially trained; the setting within which the data are to be collected must be explored and the cooperation of the people in it must be gained; etc. In addition, if the study is one designed to solve an immediate, practical problem, the anticipated application of the findings must be considered from the outset.

An Illustration

The manner in which each step influences, and is influenced by, others is perhaps best demonstrated by a brief case history of a research project. As an illustration, we shall use a study of interracial housing projects carried out by Deutsch and Collins (1951). To a considerable extent we shall use the authors' own words, as they appear in the report of the study. But since, like all reports, this one suggests that the study was carried out in a neat series of separate steps, we shall intersperse comments about activities carried on in the course of the study which are not mentioned in the formal report. The account of this study will give an over-all view of the research process; each of the steps within the process will be discussed in detail in later chapters.

The investigators were members of a research group that had as a primary concern the study of relations between members of different racial and religious groups within the United States. As a further specification of its general area of interest, the group had chosen to concentrate on the study of situations in which members of different groups are in face-to-face contact. Clearly, these decisions mapped out a very general area of interest; the focus had to be specified much more sharply before a study could be undertaken.

In this case, the next step was somewhat atypical; it was the selection of a general *setting* for the research, even before the problem to be studied had been identified. This setting was to be large-scale interracial housing. Since no member of the research group had any real familiarity with such housing, the group had little basis for selecting a specific problem to be studied within that setting. Accordingly, they drew up a proposal which called for research to be carried out in two stages: (1) six months to be devoted to an exploratory study, consisting of interviews with housing experts, on the basis of which a specific question would be selected for more systematic study; (2) a year to be spent in a systematic study of the research question selected on the basis of the exploratory study. A foundation interested in research in the field of intergroup relations granted them the necessary funds.

One member of the research team took primary responsibility for the exploratory study. Preliminary work involved reading material about public and private interracial housing, compiling a list of housing experts whose experience and insights might make a valuable contribution, and arranging to interview them. In conferences with the director of the research group and with other colleagues, plans for these interviews were drawn up. Next, the investigator visited housing projects and housing officials in the eastern, midwestern, and far-western United States. Forty-two interviews, with managers of housing projects, race relations officials of public housing agencies, and other persons with relevant experience in housing, were carried out. The interviews lasted from two to eight hours. They covered the respondents' views about factors important in influencing relations between Negro and white tenants, problems on which research was especially needed, and suggestions about the feasibility of research on various problems.

These interviews strengthened the belief that the housing setting would be a useful one for study of the effects of personal association between members of different racial groups, pointed to the choice of public housing because of the scarcity of private interracial housing projects, and suggested a number of research questions, one of which the investigators selected for the systematic study. They explain both their choice of setting and their choice of a specific question on grounds of implications for social action, theoretical interest, and opportunities for research:

> Public housing has existed for more than ten years. It has had a chance to develop standard patterns and variations with respect to racial occupancy. The common pattern is complete segregation—Negroes and whites live in separate housing projects—but there are important exceptions. These exceptions and the variations among them, in effect, provide a natural social experiment which permits those engaged in carefully controlled social research to gather valuable information about conditions which make for wholesome race relations. Such research can, by providing scientifically grounded knowledge in the place of current uncertainties, aid policy makers in their efforts to live up to the principles of the democratic ethos in their official functioning.
>
> . . .
>
> Not only may such research be socially useful . . . but it might also have theoretical significance. Most of the studies of attempts to change prejudice have, by and large, been limited to influences which were relatively minor in relation to other

influences in the subject's social milieu. . . . there is reason to believe that the housing community . . . provides one of the few opportunities for interracial contact of a sufficiently intimate and extended nature to result in large attitudinal change. In light of the crudity of most attitude measurement techniques, changes of relatively large magnitude are necessary to make possible identification and measurement of significant theoretical relationships.

. . .

With a census of problems and issues in the field of interracial housing before us, our task was to select a problem for more definitive research. Many studies were suggested by our survey [of housing officials]: the effects of different policy decisions, the effects of different management procedures, the effects of different kinds of tenant activities. All of these and many more would be useful. From these possibilities, we selected for study the impact of different occupancy patterns: *the integrated interracial* pattern (families are assigned to apartments without consideration of race) and the *segregated bi-racial* pattern (Negro and white families live in the same project but are assigned to different buildings or to different parts of the project).

We make no claim that the occupancy pattern is the only important influence on racial relations in projects that house both white and Negro families. Quite on the contrary, our survey indicated that the state of racial relations in a project would be affected by many factors . . .: the neighborhood in which the project is located, the racial composition of the tenants, the attitudes of the management staff, project facilities, etc. The effects of the occupancy pattern would, of necessity, be colored by the influence of these other factors. . . .

Yet our decision to investigate the effects of the occupancy pattern, as our first systematic study in this area, was not a matter of whim. We had several reasons for the choice. From our survey of housing officials and from our theoretical expectations . . . it was apparent that the occupancy pattern would very probably prove to be one of the most crucial influences on race relations in housing projects. . . .

It is not often that social research executed without the

instigation of an administrator will be useful in affecting administrative decisions. Nevertheless, a further important reason for our interest in the occupancy pattern is our belief that, under the present circumstances, *something can be done about it* and that research can offer guidance in the doing. Unlike many of the factors which affect the state of race relations in a housing project, the occupancy pattern is directly determined by an administrative decision, a decision which is responsive primarily to the "social climate" rather than to economic and physical limitations. . . . With the political atmosphere such as it is, with the alternative occupancy policies each having its pros and cons with respect to political feasibility, these decisions are particularly apt to be influenced by knowledge of the consequences of the different patterns for tenant relations.

Actually, it had not seemed feasible within the exploratory study to examine in detail the practical possibilities for research on each of the topics suggested; the investigators therefore did some further "scouting" before they settled on the effects of occupancy patterns as the focus of the second stage of the research. The purpose of this scouting was to determine whether it would be possible to find appropriate projects in which to carry out research on this topic and to secure permission from housing officials to do so. Preliminary inquiries suggested that it would be feasible; accordingly, the decision was made to study the effects of occupancy patterns.

For much of the next fourteen months, both investigators worked on the study full time. Their efforts were supplemented from time to time by conferences with a consultant and with colleagues, by a staff of interviewers, a group of coders, an organization which specialized in the machine processing of data, a secretary. But before these more specialized services were needed, it was necessary to formulate the research question more precisely, and to consider its relation to existing knowledge.

Our statement of the problem . . . needed much additional formulation before it could serve as a guide to research. In effect, we had to develop hypotheses about the possible effects of the occupancy pattern from our knowledge of the essential differences between the two types of project we were studying and from a knowledge of basic socio-psychological principles. Otherwise research efforts would be dissipated on the investigation of factors not likely to be related to the occupancy pattern.

. . . In the development of hypotheses, it is always simpler to deal with imaginary, idealized phenomena rather than with events as they occur in the real world. So, for the sake of convenience, let us conjure up two projects exactly alike except for their occupancy pattern. In one project, Negro and white families are assigned to apartments without consideration of race; in the other project, though Negro and white families live in the same project, they are assigned to different buildings or to different parts of the project. . . .

From the point of view of race relations, what . . . are the essential differences between the two projects? . . . it seems to us that the two types of projects differ mainly with respect to (1) the physical and functional proximity of Negro and white families, (2) the social norms regarding racial relations implicit in the policy decision of the occupancy pattern by an official public authority, and (3) the relationship of the project to the broader community.

These are the differences, but what are their effects? The answer to this question requires a further specification of interest. Effects upon what? Our original interest directs us to inquire about the effects of the occupancy pattern upon (1) social relations across racial lines, (2) the social standards for behavior with people of the other race, (3) the general pattern of social relations in the project, and (4) interracial attitudes.

As it became clear what the research question was to be and what type of evidence would be relevant to the answer, the investigators began to consider how to collect this evidence most economically and with least chance of being led to an incorrect conclusion—i.e., they began to develop their research design. The essential feature of the design was a comparison of the responses of residents in the two types of project. The development of a satisfactory research design is likely to be particularly difficult when the research is to be carried out in a real-life setting. In the case of this study, it required that the two types of project be alike in all relevant respects except occupancy pattern, and that the tenants in the two projects should have comparable initial attitudes. It was not easy to satisfy these conditions.

In the abstract, the research design called for by the hypotheses is relatively uncomplicated. It simply requires a comparative study of a number of segregated and integrated interracial housing projects which are equated in all relevant respects other than the occupancy pattern. Practically speaking, however, the phrase "equated in all relevant respects" introduces enormous complications and difficulties. As any housing administrator will point out, "No two housing projects are alike."

. . .

We designed our study to overcome as many as possible of the difficulties which would otherwise distort our findings. First of all, we carefully selected the segregated and integrated interracial projects we were to study so they were as equivalent as possible in all relevant respects other than the occupancy pattern. Second, we decided not to limit our study to one project of each type; we stretched our funds so as to study two of each kind. And third, in our method of investigation we carefully collected data about factors other than the occupancy pattern, to determine whether our results could be explained in terms of these other factors.

Compromises with the ideal of projects "equated in all other relevant respects" had to be made. In the course of the preliminary scouting, it had been learned that the number of integrated projects was limited. At the time of the study, there were some fifty-odd cities throughout the United States that had public housing projects officially described as integrated; however, in most of these projects the great majority (over 90 per cent) of the families were of one race. It seemed reasonable to suppose that the effects of occupancy pattern would show up more clearly in projects where the numbers of white and Negro families were more evenly balanced. But such projects existed in less than ten cities. While the research question was being sharpened and the design of the study worked out, the search for appropriate projects continued. It was finally decided that New York City presented the best setting for selection of integrated projects; neighboring Newark provided matching segregated bi-racial projects. But interviewing could not be conducted in the projects without the consent of the housing officials. Although officials in both cities were interested and cooperative, several conferences were needed to complete arrangements with them.

The fact that the integrated and the segregated projects were in different cities introduced a problem; so too did certain characteristics of the projects. New York and Newark are different. Since the research funds did not provide for studying the attitudes of a sample of citizens of each city not living in public housing projects, it was not possible to work out a study design that would make it possible to judge to what extent observed differences between tenants in the two types of project might reflect differences in atmosphere in the two cities rather than the impact of occupancy pattern. Further, it developed that the projects that could best be matched on other grounds all had a high proportion of Negro tenants—from 40 to 70 per cent. This meant that the findings could properly be generalized only to projects with a similarly high proportion of Negroes. Finally, the projects in Newark were of a type known as area-segregated, with Negro and white families living in different sections of the project. Although this had the advantage of giving a clear-cut pattern of segregation, it meant that the findings might not hold for projects with less extreme patterns of segregation, such as those in which separate buildings occupied by Negro families and by white families are scattered throughout the project.

During the same period that the projects were being selected, the staff considered the selection of subjects within the projects and the method of collecting data. Here again there were limitations and compromises:

> From our preliminary survey and the theoretical analysis, it became clear that the focus of the study would be the tenants themselves. Since there was, by and large, little evidence of much organized or observable group activity, it was evident that the main source of our information must come through interviewing.

> . . .

> Because of the limited number of interviews that our resources made possible, it seemed advisable to concentrate on some segment of the tenant population. We decided to collect

our data primarily from white housewives. We made this choice mainly on the ground that the home is largely the domain of the woman. She spends more time in it than anyone else; she is, by and large, the initiator of activities and contacts that develop directly out of the home. Whether or not she "wears the pants in the family," she is the key person in activities centered in the place of residence.

It was not financially feasible to interview both Negro and white housewives in equal proportion. We decided to interview more white housewives as a result of our conviction that prejudiced interracial attitudes are more socially crucial among whites than among Negroes. Segregation and discrimination are, after all, enforced by the white, and not by the Negro segment of the population.

A more serious problem was that of determining whether the white housewives in the two types of project had had similar attitudes toward Negroes before they moved into the projects. Since all the projects had been occupied for several years, it was impossible to get measures of attitudes the tenants had held before moving in. Instead, the investigators drew on their knowledge of other studies, which had shown that such characteristics as religion, political attitudes, education, and previous experiences with Negroes are frequently related to attitudes toward Negroes. Accordingly, they included in the interview schedule questions on these points. If it turned out that the women in the integrated and in the segregated projects were similar in these respects, there would be some reassurance—though by no means certainty—that they were similar in their initial attitudes toward Negroes. Unfortunately, it developed that there were differences between the two groups in religion, political attitudes, and education; thus these factors had to be taken into account throughout the analysis.

Decisions such as this, about what information was needed, led naturally to consideration of the interview schedule, the instrument by which the data were to be collected. The process of developing questions was simplified by the fact that much research on attitudes toward Negroes had already been carried out. The interview as finally developed covered five major areas: the attitudes of the housewives toward living in the project, attitudes toward Negroes, the amount and intimacy of contact with other women in the project, the social supports for attitudes, and the characteristics of the housewives.

While the interview schedule was being developed, the samples of women to be interviewed were being drawn from the lists of tenants in the projects. During this same period, one of the staff members began taking steps to recruit the number of skilled interviewers who would be needed to collect the data within a reasonable time. The interviewers were graduate students in social work and psychology. As soon as the interview schedule was in a form that seemed reasonably satisfactory, a "pilot test" was carried out; two or three of the most experienced interviewers, and the investigators themselves, carried out interviews with a small number of white housewives in other housing projects similar to those that had been selected for the study. As was expected, these pilot interviews pointed up questions that were not clear, those that needed especially careful handling to avoid antagonizing the respondents, those that did not seem to elicit the information they were intended to get. Changes were made in the interview schedule to overcome these difficulties. After another set of pilot interviews had been checked, all interviewers were trained in use of the schedule. Each interviewer spent approximately twelve hours in training sessions and conducted two practice interviews with residents of projects not included in the study.

Finally, the actual interviewing got under way. Five hundred interviews were conducted: four hundred with white housewives, one hundred with Negro housewives. The interviews lasted, on the average, from an hour to an hour and a half. There were nineteen interviewers, and all the interviews were completed within a month. During the interviewing, the investigators spent time in each of the projects, supervising the assignments and inspecting the interviews as they were completed.

Once data collection had taken place according to the specified research design, a number of irreversible decisions had been made which largely determined the next step—analysis and interpretation. In this study, the plan of data collection made it possible to compare the white housewives in the area-segregated and the integrated projects in terms of: (1) their extent of association with Negroes, (2) their perception of the social norms concerning association with Negroes,

(3) the relation between perceived social norms and extent of associa-tion, (4) their attitudes toward Negroes living in the project and Negroes in general, and (5) their attitudes toward living in an inter-racial project.

The limitations and compromises that have already been pointed out meant that it was not possible to be entirely sure that the differ-ences found between the housewives in the two types of project repre-sented the effect of occupancy pattern rather than general differences in attitude in the two cities or differences in attitude between the two groups of white housewives that existed before they ever moved into the projects. Nor was it possible to say whether the findings would hold for projects with smaller proportions of Negroes and for projects where the pattern of segregation was less marked—for example, in projects segregated by buildings rather than total sections.

Finally, the pattern of area-segregation in the Newark projects meant that, even if it was found that the white housewives living in integrated projects had more favorable attitudes toward Negroes than those in the segregated projects, it would be difficult to draw inferences about the processes that contributed to the difference in attitudes. In thinking about the ways in which different occupancy patterns might be expected to lead to differences in attitudes, the investigators con-sidered two major factors: (1) the extent to which Negro and white tenants had occasion to see and to meet each other and thus had natural opportunities to become acquainted, and (2) the implications of the integrated and segregated arrangements in terms of social ap-proval or disapproval of association between white and Negro families. The pattern of segregation in the Newark projects, with white and Negro families living in separate sections of the project rather than in separate buildings scattered throughout the project, made it impos-sible to disentangle the effects of perceived social standards from those of simple physical proximity, since in these area-segregated projects not only did white and Negro families live relatively far from each other but the segregated arrangement suggested social disapproval of interracial association. This was a limitation primarily on the potential contribution of the study to theoretical knowledge of the dynamics of attitude change; it did not interfere with the possibility of gathering evidence on the practical question of the effects on attitudes of living in an integrated or an area-segregated project.

In order to provide answers to those questions which could be answered by a study having this particular design, it was necessary, of course, to analyze the replies to the interviews. The function of the analysis was to make possible a comparison of the women in the integrated projects with those in the segregated projects in terms of the possible effects (or dependent variables) which had been specified in the formulation of the research problem and in the construction of the interview schedule.

The first step in the analysis was to derive from the answers to the interview questions an indicator of each dependent variable with which the study was concerned, or sometimes several indicators. For example, in the general area of social relations within the projects, the main dependent variable with which the investigators were concerned was intimacy of contact with Negroes on the part of white housewives. The interview provided three indicators of this variable: (1) whether the housewife reported knowing any Negro residents "pretty well"; (2) whether she included at least one Negro among the five people in the project whom she knew best; and (3) the number of different types of neighborly contact she reported with Negro women in the project.

In the general area of interracial attitudes, the investigators distinguished eleven different variables, such as degree of esteem for Negroes in the project, degree of esteem for Negroes in general, degree of friendly feeling toward Negroes in general, etc. For each of these variables, one or more indicators were derived from the answers to the interview questions or from ratings by the interviewers.

The second step in the analysis was to prepare tables showing the distribution, on each index, of respondents in each of the four projects. These tables were then examined and subjected to tests of statistical significance to determine whether the differences between housewives in the segregated projects and housewives in the integrated projects on a particular variable were so large that they could not be reasonably interpreted as resulting simply from accidents in the random selection of subjects.

Almost all the tables showed large differences between housewives in the two types of project, and the differences were consistently in the direction of more social contacts with Negroes and more favorable attitudes toward Negroes in the integrated projects. Most of the differences were far too large to be reasonably attributed to sampling fluctuations.

The next step in the analysis was to investigate the distribution of respondents on each of the *background variables*, or characteristics of respondents thought to be related to attitudes toward Negroes. As we have previously noted, there were substantial differences between respondents in the two types of project in religion, political attitudes, and education. It was consequently necessary to prepare additional sets of tables showing, for each index, the scores of Protestant women in each of the four projects, of Catholic women, and of Jewish women. From these tables it was possible to determine that the previously found relationships between occupancy pattern and the dependent variables remained approximately the same when Protestant, Catholic, and Jewish women were examined separately—that is, when religion was "held constant." Similar tables were prepared "holding constant" education and political attitudes, with similar results.

On the basis of this analysis it was concluded that the differences in attitudes and social relations with Negroes between housewives in the two types of project could not be accounted for by the differences in religion, education, or political views. Similar analyses indicated that these differences could not be accounted for by differences in initial attitudes toward Negroes (as reported by the respondents themselves), or by differences in expectations regarding the occupancy pattern at the time of moving in. It was not possible to rule out the possible effect of differences in the "social climate" of New York City and Newark, or of other uncontrolled variables that were not tapped by the interview schedule; but it was tentatively concluded that the differences in the dependent variables were due to the differences in occupancy pattern in the two types of project.

Interest then turned to the question of *how* the difference in occupancy pattern might produce the observed differences in attitudes toward Negroes. The investigators had included in their interview schedule a question on the ways in which someone living in the project might get to know the Negro women in the project. The most common ways mentioned by housewives in the integrated projects were meeting the Negro women as neighbors in the building, or on benches outside the building. In the segregated projects only half as many women mentioned any ways in which one would be likely to get to know the Negro women, and the contacts that were most frequently mentioned, such as meeting in stores or in streets around the project, did not provide natural opportunities for extended conversation.

Another analysis was made comparing the housewives in the integrated projects who reported that their attitudes toward Negroes had become more favorable since living in the project with those who reported no change in their attitudes. This showed, among other things, that the women whose attitudes had changed tended to be those who had more intimate contact with the Negro women in the project and who believed that their white friends in the project approved of their friendly association with the Negro women. As was pointed out earlier, the study design did not make possible an evaluation of the relative influence of association with Negroes and of perceived social approval of such association on the process of attitude change.

Because of this and other uncertainties of interpretation mentioned earlier, plans were made almost immediately for another study, which would build on this one and carry its findings still further (Wilner, Walkley, and Cook, 1955). This new study was carried out in four cities (all of them outside the New York metropolitan area). The projects all had a quite small proportion of Negroes, and the segregated projects took the form of scattered Negro and white buildings rather than separate areas. These two latter characteristics made it possible to examine separately the influence of physical proximity and of implied official standards, since some white women in the building-segregated projects lived closer to Negroes than did some white women in the integrated projects. The findings of this study indicated that physical proximity was the more important influence.

This illustration can indicate only in barest outline the nature of the research process. As would be the case with any illustration, it does not cover all the possibilities of interrelation and interdependence of research steps. The pattern of interaction among the various procedures that constitute a scientific inquiry will, of course, vary from study to study. The point of this illustration is to show not only that early steps influence subsequent ones—an obvious matter—but also that the interaction of each step with others is a major consideration in its selection, and that subsequent steps often lead to a reconsideration of preceding ones. Social research is not a deductive process, in which everything follows from some clearly defined premises; it is a continuous search for truth, in which tentative answers lead to a refinement of the questions to which they apply and of the procedures by which they were obtained.

Organization of the Text

This volume describes the major steps in the process of social research. The demands of organization require that these steps be discussed separately and consecutively, but it should always be kept in mind that the steps are not so clearly demarcated from one another as an organized discussion makes them appear to be.

Chapter 2 discusses the problems and considerations arising in the selection and formulation of a research question. Chapters 3 and 4 deal with research design and its function in a scientific inquiry. Variations in design are discussed, from the relatively unstructured exploration of a problem to the rigorous testing of hypotheses by means of controlled experiments.

Chapter 5 presents some general problems of measurement in the social sciences. It provides a background for the next five chapters. Chapters 6, 7, and 8 discuss three broad groups of data-collection methods—observational methods, questionnaires and interviews, and projective techniques. Chapter 9 treats the use of data already available, such as statistical records and the content of communications and personal documents. Chapter 10 discusses techniques for placing individuals on scales on the basis of data collected by any of the methods considered in the preceding chapters.

Chapter 11 deals with the analysis and interpretation of data; Chapter 12 with the writing of a research report; and Chapter 13 with the application of research. Finally, Chapter 14 discusses the continuous and close interrelationship between empirical research and theory, and points to the significance of theoretical development for the practical application of social science.

There are three appendices. Appendix A discusses the need for careful planning of time and personnel requirements, and presents time budgets of three studies. Appendices B and C consider certain technical problems in greater detail than seems appropriate in the body of the book. Appendix B discusses sampling procedures; Appendix C discusses questionnaire construction and interview procedure.

2

SELECTION AND FORMULATION OF A RESEARCH PROBLEM

The formulation of a problem is often more essential than its solution.   A. EINSTEIN AND L. INFELD

Selecting a Topic for Research

THE RANGE OF POTENTIAL TOPICS for social research is as broad as the range of social behavior itself. The range of topics that have actually been selected for inquiry is, of course, much narrower. Yet even in one research area—for example, in the relations among groups of different ethnic or religious origin—investigations have covered a vast field, including studies of how such groups act toward one another and feel and think about one another; how they differ in their traditions, beliefs, personalities, culture, and the way they treat their children; how they grow to be what they are; how they respond to attempts at changing their relation to another group; and so on. These inquiries have been conducted in many parts of the world; they have involved members of many ethnic and religious groups in many walks of life.

As we noted in Chapter 1, the general topic of a study may be suggested by some practical concern or by some scientific or intellectual interest. A wide variety of *practical concerns* may present topics for research. For example, one may want information as a basis for deciding whether there is need for some new facility or service. Thus, the director of a state or city department of health and welfare may want a survey of all people over 65 to determine whether additional services are needed for this age group, and, if so, what kind—more extensive financial aid, case work services, social and recreational centers, special housing, hospitals, etc.

Or, one may want to evaluate the effects of a settlement house program on the mental health of its participants, the effects of a leaflet campaign in influencing votes, the effects of a movie about Jackie Robinson on attitudes toward Negroes.

Still another type of practical issue that may lead to research is one in which information about the probable consequences of various courses of action would be helpful in deciding among proposed alternatives. Thus, toward the end of World War II, the United States Army carried out an extensive survey among its men to find out what system of deciding on priorities for discharge would generally be viewed as fair.

A slightly different practical concern requires the prediction of some future course of events in order to plan appropriate action. For example, in 1945 the United States Treasury requested a study that would permit a prediction of the course of war bond redemptions during the following year, as a guide to policy and action related to problems of inflation control. A builder who is considering the construction of a development in which homes will be sold without regard to the race of the purchaser may want an estimate of the probable market and the extent to which it will be affected by the interracial character of the development.

Scientific or *intellectual interests* may suggest an equally wide range of topics for research. Perhaps the major difference between topics suggested by practical concerns and those dictated by scientific interests is that the latter are less likely to involve the study of a specific situation primarily for the sake of knowledge about that particular situation. Scientific and intellectual interests are more likely to lead to general questions, and to a concern with specific situations as examples of general classes of phenomena rather than as objects of interest in their own right.

The investigator who is prompted by scientific curiosity may be interested in exploring some general subject matter about which relatively little is known. For example, when Piaget began his studies on children's thinking, this was a relatively unexplored area.

Or he may be interested in phenomena that have already been studied to some extent; in this case he is likely to be interested in such matters as specifying more exactly the conditions under which the given phenomenon appears, and how it may be affected by other factors. For example, let us say that he is interested in the extent to which the judgments of individuals are influenced by the expressed opinions of their associates. This is a question on which a good deal of work has been done; it has been quite clearly established that individuals' judgments are frequently influenced by the expressed judgments of others. The investigator may want to establish differentiations within this general finding. He may want to ask, for example: Are judgments on questions to which there is no single factually "correct" answer more likely or less likely to be influenced by the stated opinions of others than judgments on questions to which there is an objectively correct answer? As an example of the first type of question, he might ask his subjects whether they consider Tennessee Williams or Arthur Miller a better playwright; as an example of the second, he might ask them to judge the length of lines. His research problem would be answered by comparing the extent to which the subjects' judgments were influenced by those of other people in the two situations.

Or, if he happens to be working in a field in which there is a highly developed theoretical system, he may want to test specific predictions based on that theory. Thus Hunt (1941), interested in experimental testing of psychoanalytic theory, chose to test the prediction that deprivation in infancy leads to "miserly" behavior as an adult. He reared three groups of rats: one was fed normally during the developmental period; the second was fed normally in infancy, scantily during the prepubertal period, then normally again; the third was fed scantily during infancy, but adequately later. In adulthood, all groups were subjected to feeding deprivation; the one which had been deprived in infancy reacted by hoarding food.

Given such a variety of sources that may suggest topics for research, how does the investigator select a problem to study? Among the important factors determining his choice are his own personal inclinations and value judgments. In Whitehead's words:

> Judgments of worth are no part of the texture of physical science, but they are part of the motive of its production. . . . There has been conscious selection of the parts of the scientific fields to be cultivated, and this conscious selection involves judgments of value. (Quoted from Cantril, Ames, Hastorf, and Ittelson, 1949).

The role that values inevitably play in the selection of a subject for research is not, however, always recognized. In this connection, Cook (1949) reports the following incident:

> I once described to another psychologist a study in which our staff was trying to assess the effect of a certain experience in changing the attitudes of non-Jews toward Jews. This psychologist, however, did not feel these attitudes should be changed. My interest in measuring the success of efforts to bring about change, it became apparent, implied to him endorsement of a goal with which he strongly disagreed. Moreover, it brought up the possibility that my endorsement would be interpreted by others *to mean endorsement by psychologists in general* [italics supplied].

If the fact that values are involved in the selection of every research topic had been recognized in this instance, the fear that the values leading to the selection of one study might be assumed to be values common to psychologists in general might not have arisen. If it is recognized that every investigator, in his selection of a topic for research (whether it be racial or religious prejudice or the development of children's spatial concepts), is expressing his judgment or feeling about what is important to study, then the great variety of research undertaken makes it clear that no one study represents a common agreement by social scientists on appropriate research emphases.

Social scientists with different values choose different topics for investigation. The social scientist who knows which of his personal preferences have entered into the selection of his topic will be better able to guard against biases they might introduce into his research than the one who works under the illusion that he is guided by scientific considerations only. Since personal values inevitably influence the choice of topic, the only means by which the rationality of scientific procedure can be maintained is the awareness of where and how they enter.

It would be erroneous, however, to assume that personal values are or could be the only determinant in selecting a topic for inquiry. Not only do social conditions under which science is pursued shape the preferences of investigators in a subtle and often imperceptible way, but there are also a number of powerful and overt inducements for pursuing research on one topic rather than another. Different societies place premiums on work on different research topics. It may bring more prestige to do research on cancer than to try to find a cure for the common cold; more research funds may be available for noncontroversial experiments with animals than for the investigation of topics that may have political repercussions; better-paid positions may be available for the market researcher than for the educational psychologist. There are few social scientists who can afford to ignore prestige, research funds, and personal income. This state of affairs is likely to result in reducing the effective freedom of choice of research topics unless a variety of agencies with different interests, views, and values support research, so that the individual research worker can choose among them. In the United States at the present time, although the number of different sources of research funds is fairly large, a considerable proportion of the money available for research is concentrated in a few government agencies and a few large foundations. As a result, these organizations determine to a considerable extent the problems on which research shall be done. This is true for both the physical and the social sciences.

Formulating the Research Problem

The selection of a topic for research does not immediately put the investigator in a position to start considering what data he will collect, by what methods, and how he will analyze them. Before he takes these steps, he needs to formulate a specific problem which can be investigated by scientific procedures. Unfortunately, it happens not infrequently that an investigator attempts to jump immediately from the selection of a topic to the collection of observations. At best, this means that he will be faced with the task of formulating a problem after the data collection; at worst, that he will not produce a scientific inquiry at all.

> [For] it is an utterly superficial view, that the truth is to be found by studying the facts. It is superficial because no inquiry can ever get under way until and unless some *difficulty* is felt in a practical or theoretical situation. It is the difficulty, or problem,

which guides our search for *some order among the facts* in terms of which the difficulty is to be removed (Cohen and Nagel, 1934).

Scientific inquiry is an undertaking geared to the solution of problems. The first step in the formulation of research is to make the problem concrete and explicit.

Although the selection of a research topic may be determined by other than scientific considerations, the formulation of the topic into a research problem is the first step in a scientific inquiry and, as such, should be influenced primarily by the requirements of scientific procedure. However, there is no foolproof rule which will guide the investigator in formulating significant questions about a given research area. Here, the training and gifts of the individual are of major importance. As Cohen and Nagel (1934) point out:

> The ability to perceive in some brute experience the occasion for a problem, and especially a problem *whose solution has a bearing on the solution of other problems*, is not a common talent among men. . . . It is a mark of scientific genius to be sensitive to difficulties where less gifted people pass by untroubled by doubt.

Yet it is possible to enumerate some conditions that experience has shown to be conducive to the formulation of significant problems. Among these conditions are systematic immersion in the subject matter through firsthand observation, the study of existing literature, and discussion with persons who have accumulated much practical experience in the field of study.[1] Important as these conditions are in the formulation of a research project, they contain a danger. In social science, as elsewhere, habits of thought may interfere with the discovery of the new and the unexpected unless preliminary firsthand observation, reading, and discussion are conducted in a constantly critical, curious, and imaginative frame of mind.

The first step in formulation is the discovery of a problem in need of solution. Without this step, research cannot proceed, as the following episode demonstrates. Every summer an educational institution in

[1] See Chapter 3 for a detailed discussion of study designs that involve these procedures. The primary value of such exploratory inquiries is that they may lead to the asking of more significant questions than would otherwise have been possible.

this country brings together for six weeks about two hundred young men and women from all walks of life. Every region of the country, every creed, and every race is represented. Some of the young people are workers or farmers; others are clerks or students. They are selected for this summer school because of the promise of leadership they have shown in their unions, social organizations, or colleges. The sponsoring agency aims at giving these young people information about the world they live in, an experience in living together, and skills to enable each of them to meet the demands of a leadership role in his own sphere of life even more effectively than before. The organizers of this voluntary venture invited a team of social scientists to discuss the possibility of doing research on the school. The reason for the invitation was one that prompts many agencies to seek help from social scientists—the institution hoped to obtain reassurance about the value of the program and was convinced that science could establish this value beyond doubt. The topic of the envisaged research was clearly, then, the value of the educational venture. The discussion between sponsors and social scientists had the purpose of transforming this topic, step by step, into a research problem.

As is customary in such discussions the social scientists started with the question: What would you like to find out about your enterprise? This was followed by the equally customary counter-question: What can social science tell us about it? The remainder of the session demonstrated to both parties the difficulties of research formulation.

After the original impasse had been overcome, the representatives of the institution explained in complete detail their long-term objectives. They already had considerable knowledge of the typical problems and short-range effects of their pioneering effort, but their own high goals and their educational outlook prevented them from accepting as a trustworthy yardstick of success the obvious enjoyment of the experience by the young people. What they sought was something that would show itself outside the confines of the educational setting and throughout the later life of each participant. The immediate problems of administering the school—recruitment, program, organization, etc.—were apparently well in hand.

Although the discussion of long-term effects was of considerable interest, it was agreed that research on these effects was not feasible short of a twenty-year research program, which neither the institution nor the social scientists could contemplate at the moment. All agreed, too, that the educators' competence and experience were a better guide in planning a program aimed at long-range goals than the results of research efforts on minor questions could possibly be. In other words, although there was a topic, it was not possible to formulate an achievable project on the long-term effects of the school's work; had there been interest in a study of short-range effects, the outcome undoubtedly would have been different. However, in spite of the largely negative outcome, the discussion yielded a valuable if unanticipated by-product in the form of clarification of the objectives and assumptions underlying the institution's program.

Although this example demonstrates that not every topic can readily be transformed into a feasible research project, it is, fortunately, somewhat atypical in its failure to arrive at any basis from which research could proceed. More frequently, it is possible to identify some aspect of the topic which can be formulated into a specific research question which it is feasible to investigate with the resources available.

As an example of the process of formulating a research problem within a general subject-matter area, let us consider a study by Morris and Davidsen (forthcoming) of foreign students in the United States. In deciding that they wanted to study some aspect of the experience of being a student in a foreign country, the investigators had selected a general topic. But a large number of specific questions might be investigated within this area. Exploratory studies already carried out had provided a number of interesting leads. For example, they suggested the possibility that students in a foreign country go through a regular sequence of stages of adjustment, starting with a "spectator" phase and ending with a stage of preparation for the return home. Another idea derived from earlier exploratory studies was the possibility that a student's attitude toward his host country is colored to a considerable extent by the position he occupies in his home country, in combination with the general attitude toward the host country held by various groups in his home country. Still another suggestion from these earlier studies was the idea that a student's attitude toward the host country may be strongly affected by his estimate of the regard that members of the host country have for his home country.[2]

Clearly, it was not feasible to consider all these possibilities within the limits of a single study. One of the first steps, then, was to select a topic that would yield a *task of manageable size*. This is frequently a necessary step in the initial stages of problem formulation. The topic selected for investigation—whether it be evaluation of the program of an action agency, or a diagnostic survey of a community, or a public opinion survey of attitudes and opinions on international affairs, or the development of cooperation within small groups—is usually of such scope that not all aspects of the problem can be investigated simultaneously. The task must be reduced to one that can be handled in a single study or divided into a number of subquestions that can be dealt with in separate studies.

Morris and Davidsen chose to focus on the question of how students' attitudes toward the host country are influenced by their perception of the regard members of the host country have for their home country. Having thus narrowed the problem to one that could reasonably be handled within a single study, they proceeded to several interrelated steps: formulation of hypotheses; clarification and formal definition of the concepts used in the study; specification of the kinds of evidence that could serve as indicators of the various concepts (that is, the establishment of "working definitions"); consideration of methods of relating this study to others using similar concepts so that it would make the greatest possible contribution to general knowledge in this field.

These steps are so closely tied together that they cannot be worked on one at a time. As an investigator formulates his hypotheses, he must define the concepts that enter into them, and in this definition he is likely to consider the relation of his studies to other studies and to a general body of theory. Nevertheless, for the sake of clarity in presentation, the various steps must be discussed separately, and in some order. We shall start with the formulation of hypotheses—not because this is always the aspect that receives attention first, but because, when it is

[2] For a brief description of one of the studies that led to this latter suggestion, see Chapter 11, pages 400–401.

feasible to start with this aspect, it provides considerable guidance for the other steps.

Formulating Hypotheses

A hypothesis is "a proposition, condition, or principle which is assumed, perhaps without belief, in order to draw out its logical consequences and by this method to test its accord with facts which are known or may be determined" (*Webster's New International Dictionary of the English Language*, Second Edition, Unabridged, 1956). The role of hypotheses in scientific research is to suggest explanations for certain facts and to guide in the investigation of others. The importance of hypotheses in research has been emphasized by Cohen and Nagel (1934), who state:

> We cannot take a single step forward in any inquiry unless we begin with a *suggested* explanation or solution of the difficulty which originated it. Such tentative explanations are suggested to us by something in the subject matter and by our previous knowledge. When they are formulated as propositions, they are called *hypotheses*.
>
> The function of a hypothesis is to *direct* our search for the order among facts. The suggestions formulated in the hypothesis may be solutions to the problem. Whether they are, is the task of the inquiry. No one of the suggestions need necessarily lead to our goal. And frequently some of the suggestions are incompatible with one another, so that they cannot all be solutions to the same problem.

It seems to us that this is an accurate statement of the nature and value of hypotheses in scientific investigation, but we believe it to be too sweeping in its assertion that research *cannot* begin until a hypothesis has been formulated. As we shall argue later, a very important type of research has as its goal the formulation of significant hypotheses about a particular topic.

A hypothesis may assert that something is the case *in a given instance*, that a particular object, person, situation, or event has a certain characteristic. For example, Freud's book *Moses and Mon-*

otheism begins with the hypothesis that Moses was actually an Egyptian, not a Jew. Or a hypothesis may have to do with the frequency of occurrences or of association among variables. It may state that something occurs a certain proportion of the time, or that something tends to be accompanied by something else, or that something is usually greater or less than something else. A great many social science investigations are concerned with such hypotheses. For example, psychologists have investigated the correlation between different kinds of ability; sociologists have studied the ecology of crime and of mental illness; anthropologists have investigated the relation between religious beliefs, marriage customs, and other practices in a society.

Still other hypotheses assert that a particular characteristic or occurrence is one of the factors which *determine* another characteristic or occurrence. For example, psychoanalytic theory involves the hypothesis that experiences in infancy and early childhood are important determinants of adult personality. Hypotheses of this type are referred to as *hypotheses of causal relationship* or simply as *causal hypotheses.* They will be discussed in more detail in Chapter 4.

Hypotheses may be developed from various sources. A hypothesis may be based simply on a hunch. It may rest on the findings of another study or studies and the expectation that a similar relationship between two or more variables will hold in the present study. Or it may stem from a body of theory that, by a process of logical deduction, leads to the prediction that if certain conditions are present, certain results will follow. Regardless of the sources of a hypothesis, it performs an important function within a study: It serves as a guide to (1) the kind of data that must be collected in order to answer the research question and (2) the way in which they can be organized most efficiently in the analysis.[3]

But the sources of the hypotheses of a study have an important bearing on the nature of the contribution the research will make to the general body of knowledge. A hypothesis that arises simply from intuition or a hunch may ultimately make an important contribution to science. However, when it has been tested in only one study, there

[3] The importance of hypotheses in planning the analysis of a study is discussed in Chapter 11.

are two limitations on its usefulness. First, there is no assurance that the relationship between two variables found in the given study will be found in other studies. To go back to the example of Morris and Davidsen's study—suppose these investigators had just "guessed" that foreign students who believe Americans think highly of the country from which they come are likely to have more favorable attitudes toward the United States than students who believe Americans look down on their home country. Even though this proved to be the case in their study, there would be no way of judging whether the difference in attitudes between the two groups of students really stemmed from the difference in their perception of the attitudes of Americans toward their home country, or whether some other factor within the situation accounted for the difference. Secondly, a hypothesis based simply on a hunch is likely to be unrelated to other knowledge or theory. Thus the findings of a study based on such a hypothesis have no clear connection with the larger body of social science knowledge. They may raise interesting questions, they may stimulate further research, they may later be integrated into an explanatory theory. But unless these developments take place, they are likely to remain isolated bits of information.

A hypothesis that arises from the findings of other studies is freed to some extent from the first of these limitations. If the hypothesis is based on findings of other studies, and if the present study supports the hypothesis, then the result has helped to confirm this relationship as a regularly recurring one. Continuing with our example—if two or more studies find a relationship between perception of Americans' view of one's home country and one's attitudes toward the United States, we have greater confidence in the proposition that a foreign student's perception of the regard in which Americans hold his home country does in fact influence his attitudes toward the United States. The possibility that the apparent relationship is due to some special condition in a given situation is reduced, though of course not eliminated.

A hypothesis that stems not simply from the findings of an earlier study but from a theory stated in more general terms is freed from the second limitation—that of isolation from a larger body of knowledge. Suppose, for example, that Morris and Davidsen based their prediction on a theory of social stratification which holds that individuals who are rising in status are likely to be favorably inclined toward individuals and objects that are seen as aiding their upward movement, while those who are falling in status are likely to be unfavorably inclined toward individuals and objects that are seen as contributing to their downward movement. In order to establish a relationship between their study and the general theory, they must be able to argue convincingly that their measures could be considered as indicators of change in status and that it could reasonably be inferred that the students saw Americans as contributing to this change.[4] If the connection between the specific data of the study and the general theory has been satisfactorily established in this way, and if the results of the study confirm the prediction, the investigators have made a double contribution. On the one hand, the study findings help to confirm the general theory by demonstrating that it holds in this situation as well as in others where it has been applied. On the other hand, the application of the general theory to the specific case helps us to understand how it comes about that the foreign student's perception of American views of his country influences his attitude toward the United States.[5]

In the case of Morris and Davidsen's study, the investigators were able to draw both on previous research findings and on existing sociological theory to formulate specific hypotheses, of which the major one was a more complex version of the one stated in the preceding paragraphs. The fact that there were in existence both relevant research findings and a relevant theory simplified the task of formulating hypotheses; having clearly formulated hypotheses simplified the task of planning what kinds of data to gather and how to analyze them. The major hypothesis was supported by the findings of the study. The relation to earlier research strengthened confidence in the regular occurrence of the relationship between estimate of Americans' views of one's country and one's attitude toward the United States. The fact that the study was planned in terms of a sociological theory

---

[4] How the investigators developed this argument is discussed in more detail on pages 41–42.

[5] For a more detailed discussion of the relation between empirical research and theory, see Chapter 14.

about the effects of upward and downward status mobility meant that the findings contributed to confirmation of the general theory. At the same time, the theory provided an explanation of the study's findings as an instance of the more general psychological process stated in the theory.

Whether or not the nature of the anticipated relationships can be stated explicitly—i.e., whether or not they can be expressed as hypotheses in the formulation stage of an inquiry—depends largely on the state of knowledge in the area under investigation. Scientific research can begin with well-formulated hypotheses, or it can formulate hypotheses as the end product of the research.

It goes without saying that the formulation and verification of hypotheses is a goal of scientific inquiry. Yet there is no short cut to this goal. In many areas of social relations, significant hypotheses do not exist. Much exploratory research, therefore, must be done before hypotheses can be formulated. Such exploratory work is an inevitable step in scientific progress.

For example, not very much is yet known about the influence of planned communities on the behavior, feelings, and outlook of the people living in them. When Merton and his colleagues (forthcoming report) undertook to investigate this topic in the case of public housing projects in the United States, there existed no set of well-established hypotheses with which they could start. There were, at the time, few descriptive studies available that would permit the formulation of hypotheses applicable to this new phenomenon on the American physical and social landscape. Merton's studies were conceived on a broad basis; a whole series of interrelated research problems was formulated and a variety of ways in which the impact of public housing would manifest itself were anticipated.

One of these problems had to do with the extent of political participation. Tenants in public housing have, as a rule, an opportunity to share responsibility in the administration of the projects and to elect local representatives, much as in municipal government. At the stage of problem formulation, little was known about this aspect of behavior and its implications. Two opposite effects of participation in the administration of the projects seemed equally possible. On the one hand, concern with local self-government might lead the tenants to become so absorbed in the small matters of the housing project that they were not interested in larger political issues. On the other hand, participation in the operation of a small community, where the workings of political forces could easily be observed, might serve as a training ground for participants and thus lead to a heightened interest in and understanding of political forces on a national plane.

However, since it was not even known whether and to what extent the tenants availed themselves of the opportunity to participate in self-government, it would have been premature for the investigators to base the plan of their work on any hypothesis concerning the effects of this participation. In the course of the investigation, it became evident that participation was the rule. Moreover, it was discovered that in two vastly different housing projects, concern with local politics did not replace but rather initiated and reinforced concern with national affairs. In view of this evidence, it may now be possible to begin an investigation in public housing—or in any other setting, for that matter—in order to verify this hypothesis in different circumstances.

On the other hand, in the area of prejudice, where a great amount of research has already been done, investigations are possible in which hypotheses can be formulated in advance. This was demonstrated in the study of public housing (Deutsch and Collins, 1951) which was discussed in Chapter 1. It will be remembered that in this study the problem was the impact of occupancy pattern on relations between Negro and white tenants. In the light of previous research, the investigators were able to formulate in advance a number of interrelated hypotheses about the effects of the occupancy patterns on the attitudes of the tenants.

These examples make it clear that it is pointless to regard a study which sets out with hypotheses as more "scientific" than one which ends with hypotheses. The time for formulation of hypotheses varies with the nature of the problem and the extent of prior knowledge about it. Formulation and reformulation of research questions is a continuing process. As the German sociologist Max Weber said, "Every scientific fulfillment raises new questions; it asks to be surpassed and outdated."

Defining Concepts

Any investigator, in order to organize his data so that he may perceive relationships among them, must make use of concepts. A *concept* is an abstraction from observed events or, as McClelland (1951) puts it, "a shorthand representation of a variety of facts. Its purpose is to simplify thinking by subsuming a number of events under one general heading." Some concepts are quite close to the objects or facts they represent. Thus, for example, the meaning of the concept *dog* may be easily illustrated by pointing to specific dogs. The concept is an abstraction of the characteristics all dogs have in common—characteristics that are either directly observable or easily measured. Other concepts, however, cannot be so easily related to the phenomena they are intended to represent; *attitudes, learning, role, motivation* are of this sort. They are inferences, at a higher level of abstraction from concrete events, and their meaning cannot easily be conveyed by pointing to specific objects, individuals, or events. Sometimes these higher-level abstractions are referred to as *constructs*, since they are *constructed* from concepts at a lower level of abstraction.

The greater the distance between one's concepts, or constructs, and the empirical facts to which they are intended to refer, the greater the possibility of their being misunderstood or carelessly used, and the greater the care that must be given to defining them. They must be defined both in abstract terms, giving the general meaning they are intended to convey, and in terms of the operations by which they will be represented in the particular study. The former type of definition is necessary in order to link the study with the body of knowledge using similar concepts or constructs. The latter is an essential step in carrying out any research, since data must be collected in terms of observable facts.

As an illustration, let us go back to Morris and Davidsen's study of foreign students. Their hypothesis had to do with the effects of the student's estimate of the regard in which Americans hold his country on his attitudes toward the United States. Actually, as we have noted, the hypothesis was more complex than this. It involved the constructs of "national status gain" and "national status loss" through coming to the United States. *National status* was defined as "the relative valuation placed upon one's own country in an international scale of comparison." The hypothesis involved a distinction between two estimates of national status: "perceived national status"—the student's own valuation of his country—and "perceived accorded national status"—the student's estimate of how Americans would evaluate his country.[6] The difference between these two valuations gave a measure of "national status discrepancy." This construct was linked to the general theory of social stratification and status mobility by the assumption that a student who believed Americans rated his home country higher than he himself did had experienced "national status gain," and that one who believed Americans rated his country lower than he did had experienced "national status loss." These key constructs were given formal definition in terms of the meaning of *status gain* and *status loss* in general sociological theory. A start was made on a working definition for this particular study by defining *national status gain* and *national status loss* in terms of a comparison between two ratings made by the student—his own rating of his country's position, and his estimate of Americans' ratings. Let us now consider how the working definitions were further spelled out.[7]

Establishing Working Definitions[8]

No matter how simple or how elaborate an investigator's formal definition of his concepts, he must find some way of translating them into observable events if he is to carry out any research. It is not possible to study "national status gain" or "loss" as such, since these constructs have no direct counterparts in observable events. The investigator

---

[6] "Actual accorded national status"—the valuation actually made by Americans —was also taken into account, as a check on the student's perception.

[7] A number of other constructs were involved in the hypotheses of this study, among them *identification* and *attitude*. Since we are concerned with the study for purposes of illustration only, we shall not consider how these terms were defined.

[8] The reader may notice a similarity between our concept of *working definitions* and the more commonly used term *operational definitions*. We have avoided this more usual term because it carries with it certain philosophical connotations that we do not wish to go into here.

must devise some operations that will produce data he is satisfied to accept as an indicator of his concept. This stage of project formulation may require considerable ingenuity, especially if the constructs are far removed from everyday events and if little research using these constructs has been carried out.

In the case of the foreign student study, although there had been considerable research on status gain and loss in other contexts, no previous study had worked systematically with the concept of "national status gain or loss," and thus no operations that would constitute working definitions of these terms had been devised. Morris and Davidsen had already made a start on their working definition when they decided that their basic measure would be the discrepancy between the student's own rating of his country and his estimate of Americans' ratings. But in what terms should these ratings be made? Could students be given a list of countries and asked simply to arrange them in order of the regard in which they held them? This seemed too ambiguous a task; from their own reactions, the investigators concluded that countries would be arranged differently on the basis of different criteria. They finally settled on three criteria in terms of which countries were to be rated: standard of living, cultural standards, and political standards. On the basis of these ratings, an index of "national status" would be constructed. (It will be obvious from this example that the step of establishing working definitions is very closely related to decisions both about the data-collection instruments to be used and the pattern of analysis. This is another instance of the way in which earlier steps determine later ones, and of the necessity for anticipating later steps in earlier stages.)

Working definitions are adequate if the instruments or procedures based on them gather data that constitute satisfactory indicators of the concepts they are intended to represent. Whether this result has been achieved is often a matter of judgment. An investigator may feel that his data provide reasonably good indicators of his concepts; a critic of the study may feel that they do not. It frequently happens that the investigator himself is aware that his data constitute only a very limited reflection of the concept he has in mind, but, especially in the early stages of research on a problem, he may not be able to devise a more satisfactory one. In any case, although the investigator will usually report his findings in terms of his abstract concepts in order to relate them more readily to other research and to theory, he and his readers must keep in mind that what he has actually found is a relationship between two sets of data that are intended to represent his concepts. Thus, what Morris and Davidsen actually found was that the discrepancy between two ratings of the home country was related to the answers to certain questions about the United States. Although they may quite properly interpret this as indicating a relationship between national status gain or loss on the part of a foreign student and his attitude toward the host country, one should remember that this interpretation depends on the assumption that the answers to the interview questions are adequate working definitions of the concepts *national status gain, national status loss,* and *attitude toward the host country.*

Relating the Findings to Other Knowledge

Scientific research is a community enterprise, even though single studies are frequently carried out by individual investigators working alone. Each study rests on earlier ones and provides a basis for future ones. The more links that can be established between a given study and other studies or a body of theory, the greater the probable contribution.

There are two major ways of relating a given study to a larger body of knowledge. One, obviously, is to examine the research and the thinking that has already been done on the given research problem or problems related to it, and to plan the study so that it ties in with this existing work at as many points as possible. The second is to formulate the research problem at a level sufficiently abstract so that findings from the study may be related to findings from other studies concerned with the same concepts.

The study of foreign students which we have been considering was formulated at a very high level of abstraction, and thus could readily be related to other studies of status mobility in different situations and with different populations. In studies that take their impetus from some scientific question, it is usually not difficult to formulate the research problem at a useful level of abstraction, since scientific questions, by their very nature, are likely to be stated in general terms. But studies that arise from the need to answer a practical question may remain at such a specific level that they make no real contribution to knowledge unless the investigator takes pains to transpose the question to a higher level of abstraction.

Let us consider the example of an investigator who is asked by an agency concerned with the improvement of intergroup relations to carry out a survey for the purpose of evaluating the effectiveness of a series of cartoons about prejudice. If he sets up the problem in such a way that he cannot generalize beyond the specific cartoons in question, he will fail in both his scientific and his practical assignment. The cartoons he is about to investigate are unique products and to some extent different from all other cartoons in content and form. If he sets the research process in motion in order to determine the effectiveness of these few cartoons, which may be topical today and forgotten tomorrow, he is involved in a task that will have to begin all over again as soon as it is finished. If he discovers, for example, that a specific cartoon attracts and amuses a part of its audience but is misunderstood by the majority, he has learned little that deserves to be classified as scientific knowledge. Nor can such results provide much guidance for the cartoon producer. In order to remove this limitation on his work, the investigator, before he proceeds to data collection, must reformulate his concrete problem in a manner that will ultimately permit him to draw conclusions about the more general aspects of both the cartoon itself and the response of persons exposed to it. In other words, his concern, in this stage of problem formulation, must be with the generalizability of his results. It is not enough to ask whether one particular cartoon is understood. Rather, he must ask: What aspects of the cartoon are understood—and by whom? To be able to answer the first part of the question, he must analyze the general features of the cartoon. He may emerge with categories such as "satire," "caption required for understanding," etc. If he can then demonstrate through his inquiry that this type of cartoon is misunderstood because it is taken literally instead of satirically, he is in a position to advise the artist to experiment either with nonsatirical cartoons or with ways of making the satire clearer.

Only when a problem is formulated in generally meaningful terms can the social scientist hope to transfer to other problems the knowledge gained from the study of a unique event. Generalizing from the study of unique occurrences requires that the research problem be formulated in more abstract terms than might be necessary if one were concerned only with answering a question about the single event. Every event in human life, when regarded in its full concreteness, is, of course, unique. Yet, however rare and atypical, it becomes a legitimate problem for scientific inquiry *if underlying processes that may occur in other unique configurations are specified.* In this sense an earthquake, the bombing of Hiroshima, or the execution of Mussolini by enraged Italians—unique events in every sense—are subject matter for research,[9] provided the problem is formulated in terms that refer to processes potentially observable on other occasions.

To formulate a research problem in this manner permits the repetition of studies under different unique conditions. This process of repetition is known as the *replication* of research. It is essential to the development of confidence in research findings. For example, Morris and Davidsen's finding of a relationship between national status gain or loss and attitude toward the host country is interesting and suggestive, and its congruence with the general theory of status mobility lends credence to the finding. But it can be accepted as generally true only after it has been repeated with other students, attending different universities, studying in countries other than the United States. Such replication of research will in the end show whether the underlying process that the social scientist had in mind accounted for the relationship between the two sets of observed events, or whether it was accounted for by some as yet undiscovered conditions that characterized the specific study. Although it is essential to search for more general processes, the investigator must maintain a careful balance between his attention to the unique configuration and to the general aspects of his observations. To neglect the unique configuration may lead to false and premature generalizations; to neglect the general aspects may lead

---

[9] Of course, a major difficulty in investigating such events is that of managing to be in a position where one can obtain trustworthy information about the event, its initiating conditions, and its consequences.

to failure to develop principles that can be used in understanding situations other than the specific one studied.

Summary

Many considerations—and many difficulties—arise in selecting a research topic and formulating it as a research project. Basically, these processes demand that the social scientist be aware of the choices open to him and that he understand the rules governing problem formulation.

The formulation of a research project proceeds in several steps:

First, *a problem demanding solution must be perceived* within the area circumscribed by the selected topic.

Second, *the research task must be reduced to manageable size* or divided into a number of subtasks, each of which can be handled in a single study.

Next come a number of steps which are so closely interrelated that their order cannot be specified. If relevant knowledge exists concerning the research problem, the formulation will contain *hypotheses*, both as a guide to the collection and analysis of data and as a means of relating the study to other studies or to a body of theory. If there is not enough knowledge to provide a basis for setting up hypotheses at this stage, the formulation of the problem will indicate the areas in which an exploratory study aims to establish hypotheses.

Whether or not hypotheses are established at this stage, the study will require the *definition of the concepts* that are to be used in organizing the data. These definitions will include *formal* ones, designed to convey the general nature of the process or phenomenon in which the investigator is interested and its relation to other studies and to existing social science theory. They will also include *working definitions*, which make possible the collection of data the investigator is satisfied to accept as indicators of his concepts.

Throughout these processes, there will be concern with the *generalizability* of the findings and their relation to other knowledge. This involves careful study of work already done in the field, and formulation of the research problem in terms general enough to make clear its relation to other knowledge and to permit replication of the research.

In formulating the research problem, *subsequent steps in the research process must be anticipated* to ensure that the problem can be tackled by available techniques. This anticipation should include both scientific and practical steps.

3

RESEARCH DESIGN
I. Exploratory and Descriptive Studies

Formulative or Exploratory Studies

Descriptive Studies

Summary

ONCE THE RESEARCH PROBLEM has been formulated clearly enough to specify the types of information needed, the investigator must work out his *research design*. A research design is the arrangement of conditions for collection and analysis of data in a manner that aims to combine relevance to the research purpose with economy in procedure. It follows that research designs will differ depending on the research purpose.

Each study, of course, has its own specific purpose. But we may think of research purposes as falling into a number of broad groupings: (1) to gain familiarity with a phenomenon or to achieve new insights into it, often in order to formulate a more precise research problem or to develop hypotheses; (2) to portray accurately the characteristics of a particular individual, situation, or group (with or without specific initial hypotheses about the nature of these characteristics); (3) to determine the frequency with which something occurs or with which it is associated with something else (usually, but not always, with a specific initial hypothesis); (4) to test a hypothesis of a causal relationship between variables.

In studies that have the first purpose listed above—generally called *formulative* or *exploratory* studies—the major emphasis is on discovery of ideas and insights. Therefore, the research design must be flexible enough to permit the consideration of many different aspects of a phenomenon.

In studies having the second and third purposes listed above, a major consideration is accuracy. Therefore a design is needed that will minimize *bias* and maximize the *reliability* of the evidence collected. (*Bias* results from the collection of evidence in such a way that one alternative answer to a research question is favored. Evidence is *reliable* to the extent that we can assert confidently that similar findings would be obtained if the collection of evidence were repeated. For a detailed discussion of bias and reliability in connection with measurement procedures, see Chapter 5.) Since studies with these second and third purposes present similar requirements for research design, we can treat them together; we shall call them *descriptive* studies.

Studies testing *causal* hypotheses require procedures that will not only reduce bias and increase reliability but will permit inferences about causality. Experiments are especially suited to meeting this latter requirement. However, many studies concerned with testing hypotheses about causal relationships do not take the form of experiments.

In practice, these different types of study are not always sharply distinguishable. Any given research may have in it elements of two or more of the functions we have described as characterizing different types of study. In any single study, however, the primary emphasis is usually on only one of these functions, and the study can be thought of as falling into the category corresponding to its major function. In short, although the distinctions among the different types of study are not clearcut, by and large they can be made; and, for the purpose of discussing appropriate research designs, it is useful to make them.

Formulative or Exploratory Studies

Many exploratory studies have the purpose of formulating a problem for more precise investigation or of developing hypotheses. An exploratory study may, however, have other functions: increasing the investigator's familiarity with the phenomenon he wishes to investigate in a subsequent, more highly structured, study, or with the setting in which he plans to carry out such a study; clarifying concepts; establishing priorities for further research; gathering information about practical possibilities for carrying out research in real-life settings; providing a census of problems regarded as urgent by people working in a given field of social relations.

Our discussion will focus on studies that are directed primarily toward the formulation of problems for more precise investigation or toward the development of hypotheses. The points made and the procedures described are, however, applicable to exploratory studies having other goals.

The relative youth of social science and the scarcity of social science research make it inevitable that much of this research, for a time to come, will be of a pioneering character. Few well-trodden paths exist for the investigator of social relations to follow; theory is often either too general or too specific to provide clear guidance for empirical research. In these circumstances, exploratory research is necessary to obtain the experience that will be helpful in formulating relevant hypotheses for more definitive investigation.

Suppose, for example, that one is interested in obtaining insight into the process by which social environment influences mental health. Although there has been much speculative writing on this topic and some research that is incidentally related to it, the research worker entering this area is not in a position to advance any precise hypothesis for investigation. Indeed, it would be foolhardy for him to try to do so. Without some knowledge of the scope of the area, of the major social variables influencing mental health, of the settings in which these variables occur, any hypothesis that is set forth is likely to be trivial. In the case of problems about which little knowledge is available, an exploratory study is usually most appropriate.

Occasionally there is a tendency to underestimate the importance of exploratory research and to regard only experimental work as "scientific." However, if experimental work is to have either theoretical or social value, it must be relevant to broader issues than those posed in the experiment. Such relevance can result only from adequate exploration of the dimensions of the problem with which the research is attempting to deal.

Although, for the most part, we are discussing the exploratory study as an entity, it is appropriate to consider it also as an initial step in a continuous research process. In practice, the most difficult portion of an inquiry is its initiation. The most careful methods during the later stages of an investigation are of little value if an incorrect or irrelevant start has been made. As Northrop (1947) has pointed out:

> Again and again investigators have plunged into a subject matter, sending out questionnaires, gathering a tremendous amount of data, even performing experiments, only to come out at the end wondering what it all proves. . . . Others, noting the success of a given scientific method in one field, have carried this method hastily and uncritically into their own, only to

end later in a similar disillusionment. All such experiences are a sign that the initiation of inquiry has been glossed over too hastily, without any appreciation of its importance or its difficulty.

For whatever purpose an exploratory study is undertaken, ingenuity and good luck will inevitably play a part in determining its productiveness. Nevertheless, it is possible to suggest certain methods that are likely to be especially fruitful in the search for important variables and meaningful hypotheses. These methods include: (1) a review of the related social science and other pertinent literature; (2) a survey of people who have had practical experience with the problem to be studied; and (3) an analysis of "insight-stimulating" examples. Most exploratory studies utilize one or more of these approaches.

Whatever method is chosen, it must be used flexibly. As the initially vaguely defined problem is transformed into one with more precise meaning, frequent changes in the research procedure are necessary in order to provide for the gathering of data relevant to the emerging hypotheses.

THE SURVEY OF THE LITERATURE

One of the simplest ways of economizing effort in an inquiry is to review and build upon the work already done by others. In a study of the type we are discussing here, the focus of review is on hypotheses that may serve as leads for further investigation. Hypotheses may have been explicitly stated by previous workers; the task then is to gather the various hypotheses that have been put forward, to evaluate their usefulness as a basis for further research, and to consider whether they suggest new hypotheses. More frequently, however, an exploratory study is concerned with an area in which hypotheses have not yet been formulated; the task then is to review the available material with sensitivity to the hypotheses that may be derived from it.

In many areas a bibliographical survey will undoubtedly be more time-consuming than rewarding; often one will find that no research of significance has been done in one's area of interest. This is perhaps less often true, however, than is assumed by those who fail to build upon the work of previous investigators. In any case, the conclusion that there is no relevant material would be unjustified without a thorough search of journals which are likely to carry articles on the given topic, and of such publications as the *Psychological Abstracts*, the *Child Development Abstracts and Bibliography*, the *Sociological Abstracts*, the bulletin of *Current Sociological Research* issued by the American Sociological Society, the listing of *Doctoral Dissertations Accepted by American Universities* compiled for the Association of Research Libraries, and the *Dissertation Abstracts* available in microfilm from University Microfilms, Ann Arbor, Michigan. In addition to these general sources, some government agencies and voluntary organizations publish listings or summaries of research in their special fields of interest. For example, the Children's Bureau of the U. S. Department of Health, Education, and Welfare publishes a bulletin of *Research relating to Children*; the Anti-Defamation League of B'nai B'rith issues *Research Reports*, summaries of research relevant to intergroup relations. Professional organizations, research groups, and voluntary organizations are sources of information about unpublished research in their specific fields.

It would be a mistake to confine one's bibliographical survey to studies that are immediately relevant to one's area of interest. Perhaps the most fruitful means of developing hypotheses is the attempt to apply to the area in which one is working concepts and theories developed in completely different research contexts. Thus, the theory of adaptation level developed in work on psychophysical problems may provide stimulating analogies for work on factors influencing, for example, the perception of characteristics of members of an ethnic group other than one's own; level-of-aspiration theory may provide a parallel for studying changing community goals; learning theory may give insights into the process of attitudinal change; the concepts of *role*, *social norm*, *psychological need*, *frustration*, *group structure*, etc., may direct attention to important variables in any new situation to be studied.

The sensitive descriptions to be found in the works of creative writers are also a fertile ground of hypotheses for study. Although the social scientist does not aim at capturing the richness of the novelist's descriptions, he may find in the world's literature many stimulating suggestions about important variables in the situations he wishes to study. For example, Paton's *Cry the Beloved Country* and *Too Late the Phalarope,* Sartre's *Portrait of the Anti-Semite,* Wright's *Native Son,* and E. M. Forster's *A Passage to India* are laden with penetrating analyses of the causes and consequences of prejudice.

THE EXPERIENCE SURVEY[1]

Probably only a small proportion of existing knowledge and experience is ever put into written form. Many people, in the course of their everyday experiences, are in a position to observe the effects of alternative decisions and actions with respect to problems of human relations. The director of a settlement house, and the group workers on his staff, are likely to develop insights into the characteristics of young delinquents and the probable effectiveness of various approaches to them. The psychiatric social worker may acquire sensitivity to the environmental conditions that impede the adjustment of patients released from a mental institution and, on the other hand, to factors that support adjustment. Such specialists acquire, in the routine of their work, a reservoir of experience that could be of tremendous value in helping the social scientist to become aware of the important influences operating in any situation he may be called upon to study. It is the purpose of an experience survey to gather and synthesize such experience.

THE SELECTION OF RESPONDENTS. Research economy dictates that the respondents in an experience survey be carefully selected. The aim of the experience survey is to obtain insight into the relationships between variables rather than to get an accurate picture of current practices or a simple consensus as to best practices. One is looking for provocative ideas and useful insights, not for the statistics of the profession. Thus the respondents must be chosen because of the likelihood that they will offer the contributions sought. In other words, a *selected* sample of people working in the area is called for.[2]

In an experience survey it is a waste of time and effort to interview people who have little competence, or little relevant experience, or

---

[1] Much of the following is based on an unpublished article by C. Selltiz, S. W. Cook, and R. Hogrefe entitled "The Experience Survey: A Step in Program Design for Field Research on Unexplored Problems."

[2] In terms of the different kinds of sample discussed in Appendix B, this is a *purposive* sample.

who lack ability to communicate their experience. An individual may have worked in a field for a number of years and not necessarily be a good informant. Perhaps the most direct method of selecting informants is to ask strategically placed administrators working in the area one desires to study to point out the most informative, experienced, and analytical people. Although this does not guarantee insight-stimulating respondents, one does obtain through this method people with a reputation for good experience and good ideas. The likelihood of their being useful informants is, of course, increased if they are recommended by more than one source, particularly if the different sources are known to have dissimilar points of view.

Although a random sample of practitioners may not be of value in an experience survey, it is nevertheless important to select respondents so as to ensure a representation of different types of experience. Wherever there is reason to believe that different vantage points may influence the content of observation, an effort must be made to include variation in point of view and in type of experience. Thus, for example, in an experience survey of factors affecting employee morale in industry, it is advantageous to interview representatives of both management and labor. It is also desirable to interview people at different levels in each group—workers, foremen, personnel managers, shop stewards, educational directors of unions, etc., to obtain a varied perspective.

Apart from interviewing enough people to ensure adequate representation of different types of experience, there is no simple rule for determining the number of informants who should be interviewed in an experience survey. At a certain point, the investigator will find that additional interviews do not provide new insights, that the answers fall into a pattern with which he is already familiar. At this point, further interviewing becomes less and less rewarding.

THE QUESTIONING OF RESPONDENTS. Before any systematic attempt is made to collect the insights of experienced practitioners, it is, of course, necessary to have some preliminary ideas of the important issues in the area. One source of such ideas, as we have previously indicated, is a bibliographical survey. Before an interview schedule for the systematic questioning of informants is developed the information from such a survey almost invariably must be supplemented by a number of unstructured interviews[3] with people who have had extensive experience in the field to be investigated.

Even in the more systematic interviewing of the later informants, it is essential to maintain a considerable degree of flexibility. The purpose of providing the interview with structure is to ensure that all people interviewed respond to the questions the researcher wishes to have answered; however, the formulative and discovery functions of the experience survey require that the interview always allow the respondent to raise issues and questions the investigator has not previously considered.

In formulating questions for an interview schedule with social practitioners, it is generally useful to orient inquiries to "what works." That is, the questions should usually be of the following form: "If (a given effect) is desired, what influences or what methods will, in your experience, be most likely to produce it?" There are several reasons for focusing primarily on change-producing influences. First, the social practitioner, necessarily heeding the imperatives of his work, is oriented toward producing change, toward "what works." He is more likely to understand and to be able to respond to a practically phrased question than to one that is worded abstractly. Second, the emphasis on change allows the investigator to collect insights into processes operating over a period of time, which the practitioner is in a uniquely favorable position to observe. Third, if the investigator's concern is not only with the theoretical relationships among variables but also with their implications for social action, he needs to know how these variables tend to cluster in everyday life and how these commonly found clusters of variables promote or hinder socially desirable objectives.

Where possible, in order to stimulate the informant to compare the major alternative methods for accomplishing a specific end, it is desirable to probe beyond a mere statement of general principles about producing a given change. Concrete illustrations, from the respondent's own experience, of successful and unsuccessful attempts to achieve a specific effect are of particular value. They enable the investigator to collate experiences of different people in diverse circumstances and

[3] For a discussion of "structured" and "unstructured" interviews, see Chapter 7, pages 255–268.

thus to form tentative conclusions and generalizations which go beyond the observations of any one informant.

To illustrate one type of question that has been found particularly useful in experience surveys, we present the following questions from such a survey of intergroup relations in industry.[4]

Some people believe that a non-discriminatory employment policy requires that minority group members with average qualifications for a particular job be brought into the job on a first-come-first-served basis. Other people believe that in introducing members of a minority group it is important for the first member of the group to have certain special qualifications. The assumption is that this will make it easier to get acceptance for other members of that minority group in this situation later.

Question: Should special qualifications be set for the first members of a minority group to be introduced into a new situation?

If the first members of a minority group introduced into a new situation are specially selected, there are several bases upon which the selection may be made.

Alternative A: Some people believe that the first members of a minority group introduced should be very high in ability for the particular job they are to fill.

Alternative B: Other people believe it is more important that the minority group members should be very pleasant and agreeable personally.

Alternative C: Still other people believe the main consideration is that the first minority group members be as similar as possible to the people they are to work with in physical appearance, manners, speech, education, interests, and previous experience.

Question: What are the relative advantages and disadvantages of these three principles for selecting the first members of a minority group to be introduced into a new situation?

In general, an experience-collecting interview is likely to be quite long, frequently lasting several hours. In view of the nature of the information wanted, it is desirable to prepare the respondent a week or

---

[4] This survey was conducted by J. Harding and R. Hogrefe of the Commission on Community Interrelations of the American Jewish Congress.

so before the interview is to take place by sending him a copy of the questions to be discussed. This gives him an opportunity not only to do some advance thinking, but to consult his colleagues and to add the knowledge to be gained from their experiences.

SOME BY-PRODUCTS OF EXPERIENCE SURVEYS. An experience survey, as well as being a good source of hypotheses, can provide information about the practical possibilities for doing different types of research. Where can the facilities for research be obtained? Which factors can be controlled and which cannot in the situations one might wish to study? What variables tend to be clustered together in community settings? How ready are agencies, professional workers, and ordinary citizens to cooperate in controlled research studies of the problem in question? The answers to these and similar practical questions may be one of the by-products of a carefully planned experience survey. In addition, such a survey may provide a census of the problems considered urgent by the people working in a given area. This census may be extremely useful in establishing priorities in a program of research.

The report of an experience survey also provides a summary of the knowledge of skilled practitioners about the effectiveness of various methods and procedures in achieving specified goals. In lieu of more definitive knowledge, this information may be of enormous value as a guide to "best" practices in a given field. Of course, in presenting such a summary, it should be made clear that the survey was in no sense based on a random sample of workers in the field. Its usefulness comes from the presentation of insights and effective practices rather than from the presentation of the "typical."

THE ANALYSIS OF "INSIGHT-STIMULATING" EXAMPLES[5]

Scientists working in relatively unformulated areas, where there is little experience to serve as a guide, have found the intensive study of selected examples to be a particularly fruitful method for stimulating insights and suggesting hypotheses for research. The remarkable theoretical insights of Sigmund Freud were, of course, stimulated by

[5] Much of the following discussion is based on an unpublished paper by J. P. Dean, "The Method of Unstructured Pilot Inquiry." A condensation of this paper may be found in Dean (1954).

his intensive studies of patients. So, too, profound changes in our conception of the relationship between man and society have been brought about largely by anthropological studies of primitive cultures.

From these examples it should be clear that we are not describing what is sometimes called the "case-study" approach, in the narrow sense of studying the records kept by social agencies or psychotherapists, but rather the intensive study of selected instances of the phenomenon in which one is interested. The focus may be on individuals, on situations, on groups, on communities. The method of study may be the examination of existing records; it may also be unstructured interviewing or participant observation or some other approach.

What features of this approach make it an appropriate procedure for the evoking of insights? A major one is the *attitude* of the investigator, which is one of alert receptivity, of seeking rather than of testing. Instead of limiting himself to the testing of existing hypotheses, he is guided by the features of the object being studied. His inquiry is constantly in the process of reformulation and redirection as new information is obtained. Frequent changes are made in the types of data collected or in the criteria for case selection as emerging hypotheses require new information.

A second feature is the *intensity* of the study of the individual, group, community, culture, incident, or situation selected for investigation. One attempts to obtain sufficient information to characterize and explain both the unique features of the case being studied and those which it has in common with other cases. In the study of the individual, this may entail an extensive examination of both his present situation and his life history. In the study of a group, an incident, etc., individuals may be treated as informants about the object, rather than being themselves the objects of intensive analysis.

A third characteristic of this approach is its reliance on the *integrative* powers of the investigator, on his ability to draw together many diverse bits of information into a unified interpretation. This last characteristic has led many critics to view the analysis of insight-stimulating instances as a sort of projective technique, in which conclusions reflect primarily the investigator's predisposition rather than the object of study. Even if this reproach is appropriate to many case studies, the characteristic is not necessarily undesirable when the purpose is to evoke rather than to test hypotheses. For even if the case material is merely the stimulus for the explicit statement of a previously unformulated hypothesis, it may serve a worth-while function.

Social scientists who work with this approach have frequently found that the study of a few instances may produce a wealth of new insights, whereas a host of others will yield few new ideas. Although here, as elsewhere, no simple rules can be established for the selection of the instances to be studied, experience indicates that for particular problems certain types are more appropriate than others. We list below some of these types, together with the purposes for which they have been found most useful. The list is not exhaustive, nor are the types mutually exclusive.

1. The reactions of *strangers* or *newcomers* may point up characteristics of a community that might otherwise be overlooked by an investigator reared in the culture. A stranger is likely to be sensitive to social customs and practices that are more or less taken for granted by the members of a community. His curiosity or surprise or bewilderment may call attention to features of community life to which members of the community have become so accustomed that they no longer notice them.

2. *Marginal individuals*, or groups, who are moving from one cultural grouping to another and are on the periphery of both groups, are similar in some respects to strangers or outsiders. Because they are "in between," exposed to conflicting pressures of the groups from and to which they are moving, they can often reveal dramatically the major influences operating in each group. For example, in the field of intergroup relations, the study of emigrants, of displaced persons, of Jews who are trying to be assimilated into local cultural groups, of Negroes who are trying to "pass" as whites, of people who are in the process of conversion to or from Catholicism, of people in areas of disputed national sovereignty, is likely to be highly rewarding.

3. Study of individuals or groups who are in *transition* from one stage of development to the next has been fruitful, particularly in anthropological investigations of the influence of culture upon personality. In his investigation of any culture, the anthropologist is necessarily limited by time to a cross-sectional study rather than one that would trace individuals from birth to death. The study of indi-

viduals who are at a point of transition helps overcome, to some extent, the limitations of a cross-sectional investigation. For example, intensive study of babies who are being weaned, or of adolescents, or of women in the period of menopause, is likely to give considerable insight into the process of change and into the socio-psychological characteristics of contiguous stages of development (see Mead, 1946). Similarly, the study of groups or societies in transition may be of value in understanding the processes of social change.

4. *Deviants, isolates,* and *pathological* cases may, by indirection, throw light on more common cases. The study of deviants (for example, individuals who are interested in world government although most of their associates hold nationalistic and isolationist views) may serve to highlight the social norms and practices from which they are deviating. It may indicate the types of pressure to conform and the socio-psychological consequences of nonconformity; it may perhaps even help to reveal the methods by which social changes may be produced. In a similar manner, the analysis of isolates may accentuate the factors making for cohesiveness in a given group or community. It may also reveal much about the way in which attitudes and information are transmitted in a social group (see, for example, Festinger, Schachter, and Back, 1950). The contributions of psychoanalysis to the understanding of personality are a striking illustration of the insights that may be uncovered by a study of pathological cases, which frequently serve to underscore, through exaggeration, basic processes in nonpathological cases. Thus, for example, Ackerman and Jahoda (1950), in a study based on reports of psychoanalysts about cases under treatment, found that depressed patients are rarely prejudiced. This finding, with its implication that individuals who have turned their aggression against themselves do not need prejudice as a channel for aggression, provides an interesting hypothesis about the psychodynamics of prejudice. Extreme cases may also be enlightening when the interest is in social dynamics. The study of the breakdown of social controls and their reinstatement, as illustrated in natural disasters or a race riot—see, for example, Lee (1943)—may result in worth-while insights into the processes of social control.

5. "*Pure*" cases are often productive. For example, Levy (1943), in his study of maternal overprotection, was interested in three ques-

tions: What leads a mother to be overprotective, what effects does maternal overprotection have on the child, and how can the difficulties that may result from overprotection be prevented or remedied? Reasoning that he could best find clues through the study of cases of marked overprotection, he examined many records of cases treated in a child guidance clinic. There were two major criteria for selecting cases for intensive study. First, they must show extreme overprotection by the mother, as evidenced by inseparability of mother and child, the mother's treating the child as a baby, and the mother's prevention of independent behavior on the part of the child. Second, they must be "pure" cases, in the sense that the mother's behavior was consistently overprotective and also in the sense that there was no evidence of rejection of the child. (This latter criterion was introduced on the ground that the combination of overprotection and rejection differs from overprotection per se and may have different origins and consequences.) Of the cases that met these criteria, only those were retained that contained enough information about the mother to make possible some inferences about the factors producing overprotective behavior, enough information about the child to yield insight into the kinds of problems produced by such behavior, and enough information about treatment of the case to give clues as to the effects of therapy. Of the more than five hundred cases examined, only twenty met all these criteria; these formed the basis of Levy's study.

6. The characteristics of individuals who fit well in a given situation and those who do not fit well provide valuable clues about the nature of the situation. Thus, the knowledge that the people who feel at home in a given community, who seem to fit best, are either highly dependent or authoritarian in personality provides some insight into the characteristics of the community. Similarly, discovery that those who feel thwarted by a given situation are the young and ambitious and those who have considerable personal initiative would provide a clue to the nature of the situation.

7. Selection of individuals who represent different positions in the social structure helps to produce a rounded view of the situation they are reflecting. In almost all social groups, one finds variations in social status and specialization of social roles or functions. Individuals occupying these different positions are likely to see any given situation

from different perspectives, and this diversity is productive of insights. Thus, interviewing the porters in a housing project may be as important for understanding relations within the project as interviewing the manager. The discrepancies as well as the similarities in the social perceptions of people holding different positions or fulfilling diverse functions are frequently revealing.

8. A review of the *investigator's own experience* and a careful examination of his reactions as he attempts to "project" himself into the situation of the subjects he is studying may be a valuable source of insights. After all, the "case" with which an investigator is likely to have the greatest familiarity (though also the most bias) is himself. As Jones's biography (1953) of Freud makes clear, many of Freud's most valuable insights came from his efforts to understand himself. To be sure, there probably are few persons with the qualities of a Freud; we cannot expect that analysis of one's own experience will often have such fruitful results. But, even so, here is a source of ideas that ought not to be neglected. That the point needs to be made at all stems from the fact that scientists are often so preoccupied with the importance of objectivity that they actively strive to maintain as great a distance as they can between themselves and the objects of their study. In the stages of research in which one is looking for *ideas* rather than *conclusions*, such objectivity may be inappropriate.

Our listing of "insight-stimulating" cases is inevitably incomplete. The type of cases that will be of most value depends largely, of course, on the problem with which one is concerned. Nevertheless, it is generally true that in an explanatory study, cases that provide sharp contrasts or have striking features are most useful, since in exploratory work the discernment of minute differences is likely to be difficult.

It is important to remember that exploratory studies merely lead to insights or hypotheses; they do not test or demonstrate them. In selecting cases that have special characteristics, one has by definition taken cases that are not typical. Although marginal, deviant, or "pure" cases are likely to be fruitful sources of ideas about processes that may occur in more typical cases, one cannot assume that these processes do in fact occur in cases other than those one has studied. Pressures on marginal individuals may be quite different from those on individuals who are well integrated in a group; deviant cases may be deviant not only in their behavior but in the psychological processes underlying it. An exploratory study must always be regarded as simply a first step; more carefully controlled studies are needed to test whether the hypotheses that emerge have general applicability.

Descriptive Studies

An enormous amount of social research has been concerned with describing the characteristics of communities. One may study the people of a community: their age distribution, their national or racial background, the state of their physical or mental health, the amount of education they have had—the list could be extended indefinitely One may study community facilities and their use: the condition of housing, the extent to which libraries are used, the amount of crime in various neighborhoods—again, the list is endless. One may undertake to describe the structure of social organization in the community, or the major patterns of behavior.

Another vast body of research has been concerned with estimating the proportion of people in a specified population who hold certain views or attitudes or who behave in certain ways: How many favor admitting Communist China to the United Nations? How many believe that Negroes and whites should live in separate neighborhoods? How many think capital punishment should be abolished? How many watched which television programs last week?

Still other studies are concerned with specific predictions: How many people will vote for a certain candidate? How many will cash their government bonds during a given period? In what neighborhoods is the growth of population likely to be great enough to require new schools or new transportation facilities within the near future?

Others are concerned with discovering, or testing, whether certain variables are associated: Do more Catholics than Protestants vote Democratic? Do people who spend a good deal of time reading go to the movies often? Are people who are prejudiced against Jews also likely to be prejudiced against Negroes? Do girls, on the whole, learn to talk at an earlier age than boys? Note that none of these questions, as they have been presented, involves a hypothesis that one of the variables *leads to* or *produces* the other; questions embodying such hypotheses pose different requirements for research procedures.

This is a considerable array of research interests, which we have grouped under the heading of *descriptive* studies. We have grouped them together because, from the point of view of research procedures, they share certain important characteristics. The research questions presuppose much prior knowledge of the problem to be investigated, as contrasted with the questions that form the basis for exploratory studies. The investigator must be able to define clearly what it is he wants to measure and must find adequate methods for measuring it. In addition, he must be able to specify who is to be included in the definition of "a given community" or "a given population." In collecting evidence for a study of this sort, what is needed is not so much flexibility as a clear formulation of *what* and *who* is to be measured, and techniques for valid and reliable measurements.[6]

Descriptive studies are not limited to any one method of data collection. They may employ any or all of the methods to be presented in subsequent chapters. Thus Lundberg, Komarovsky, and McInery (1934), in their study of leisure, collected information through interviews, questionnaires, systematic direct observation, analysis of community records, and participant observation:

> More than two hundred formal interviews lasting from one to three hours were secured with ministers, school officials, and women in their homes. There were many more interviews incidental to the circulation of schedules, and a very large number through casual contact and association of living in a community. In addition to the customary analysis of secondary material such as histories, annual reports of organizations, and newspapers, we studied the mobility of the population through the analysis of telephone and other directories of fifteen villages and cities, involving a checking of more than two hundred thousand names and addresses. Among the projects of formal direct observation was the recording of a schedule of the activities of some 6800 commuters on trains. Constant traveling throughout the county,

---

[6] For a discussion of validity and reliability of measurement, see Chapter 5.

visits to homes, schools, playgrounds, all major recreational resorts and all the contacts incidental to daily living complete the story of observations upon which this study of leisure of a people is based.

Although descriptive studies may use a wide range of techniques, this does not mean that they are characterized by the flexibility that marks exploratory studies. The procedures to be used in a descriptive study must be carefully planned. Because the aim is to obtain complete and accurate information, the research design must make much more provision for protection against bias than is required in exploratory studies. Because of the amount of work frequently involved in descriptive studies, concern with economy of research effort is extremely important. These considerations of economy and protection against bias enter at every stage: formulating the objectives of the study; designing the methods of data collection; selecting the sample; collecting, processing, and analyzing the data; and reporting the findings. The following paragraphs point out some of the ways in which economy and protection against bias are taken into account in the design of a descriptive study.[7] As an illustration, we shall consider a study of the treatment of Negro patrons in New York City restaurants (Selltiz, 1955).

FORMULATING THE OBJECTIVES OF THE STUDY

The first step in a descriptive study, as in any other, is to define the question that is to be answered. Unless the objectives are specified with sufficient precision to ensure that the data collected are relevant to the question raised, the study may not provide the desired information.

In our example, the research question was: Do restaurants in New York City discriminate against Negro patrons? But before data could be gathered to answer this question, it was necessary to specify what was meant by *discrimination*. It was defined as any inequality between the treatment accorded white and Negro diners, unless there seemed

[7] For a more detailed discussion of descriptive studies, and especially those that take the form of surveys of opinion, attitudes, etc., see Hyman (1955, Part II), and Parten (1950).

reason to believe that the difference in treatment was due to some factor other than the difference in race. This general concept was translated into a working definition by specifying the kinds of behavior on the part of restaurant personnel that might be taken as indicative of discrimination: outright refusal to serve prospective Negro diners; indirect refusal to serve Negroes, by keeping them waiting indefinitely or by stating that reservations were necessary; evidence of confusion at the appearance of Negroes in the restaurant, such as a hasty conference between headwaiter and waiter; direction of Negroes to an undesirable table or to one that placed them out of view of other diners; poor service; inferior food; overcharges. Each item in the working definition included the basic concept of inequality of treatment; thus, poor service in itself was not to be considered evidence of discrimination.

The focal point of the study was the question: Do restaurants in New York City discriminate against Negro patrons? Discussions with various people who might be expected to have a good basis for estimating the probable extent of discrimination showed such wide divergence of opinion that there seemed little basis for advancing a prediction about the existence or the extent of discrimination. A number of subsidiary questions were also formulated: Would discrimination occur more frequently in relatively high-priced restaurants? Would discrimination be more likely in restaurants with headwaiters? In "American" rather than "foreign" restaurants? These subsidiary questions pointed to the need for collecting certain kinds of information about the restaurants studied.

Considerations of economy also entered into the specification of the research question. The study was undertaken by a voluntary group with limited resources. Looking forward to later stages of the study— selection of a sample of restaurants, collection of data, reporting of findings—the planners considered whether they were likely to be able to test a large enough sample of all types of eating places throughout New York City to provide reliable findings. The obvious negative answer led to a restriction both of the geographical area to be covered (about 150 square blocks in east midtown Manhattan) and of the price range of restaurants to be included (eliminating the most and the least expensive).

Designing the Methods of Data Collection

After the problem has been formulated specifically enough to indicate what data are required, the methods by which the data are to be obtained must be selected. Techniques for collecting the information must be devised if, as is likely, no suitable ones already exist. Each of the various methods—observation, interviewing, questionnaires, projective techniques, the examination of records, and so forth—has its advantages and limitations, which are discussed in detail in later chapters.

In the study we are using for illustration, the specific method of collecting data was somewhat unusual: teams of Negro and white diners went to restaurants, ate, and reported their experiences. This was an expensive procedure, but it was considered the one most likely to give trustworthy evidence about restaurant practices. Basically it was an observational technique; as such, it was especially appropriate for the study of behavior in its natural setting. Had the study been concerned with the feelings of restaurant owners about serving Negroes, or with the opinions of the white population about whether Negroes are or should be served in all restaurants, other techniques, such as interviewing, questionnaires, or projective methods, would have been more appropriate. Had it been concerned with a question such as the volume of business done by restaurants, it might have been possible to obtain the information by examining records.

The stage of developing data-collection procedures is one of the major points at which safeguards against bias and unreliability are introduced. In the study of restaurant discrimination, they were directed against two major possible sources of bias: differences in treatment of white and Negro diners due to some factor other than the difference in race, and distortions in the reporting of experiences.

Elaborate precautions were taken to rule out other possible reasons for differences in treatment, such as the possibility that those arriving first would be given the most desirable table, that better-dressed people would be given better service, that men or older people would be given better service than women or younger ones, etc. First, the pairs of diners going to a given restaurant were matched in sex and age. It the Negro team consisted of two men, the white team going to the same restaurant consisted of two men; with few exceptions, both teams were of about the same age. Since the entire group was relatively homogenous in socioeconomic level, in dress, and in general social behavior, no special matching of teams in these respects was needed. Next, the testers were given instructions to ensure that their behavior would be alike in certain respects, such as the number of courses ordered and the approximate price of the meal. Above all, they were instructed to accept without protest any behavior on the part of restaurant personnel, and not to give any indication that they had any purpose for going to the restaurant other than eating.

Efforts to guard against bias in reporting entered into both the construction of the report form and the training of the testers. Most of the questions in the report form called for short factual answers: "When did you enter the restaurant?" "When were you seated?" "Did you pick your own table, or were you assigned by a restaurant employee?" It seemed unlikely that replies to such questions would be greatly distorted by the testers' feelings. Moreover, they made it possible to identify cases in which the Negro team was given better treatment than the white team as well as those in which it was treated less well. Thus the possibility that the over-all findings would be biased by undue attention to instances of discriminatory treatment of the Negro team was reduced. In an intensive training session, the testers were given detailed instructions about procedures and an opportunity to practice in imaginary situations.

Analogous safeguards must be introduced in any study, whatever the method of data collection. Questions must be carefully examined for the possibility that their wording may suggest one answer rather than another; interviewers must be instructed not to ask leading questions or express their own opinion; observers must be trained so that they all record a given item of behavior in the same way.

Once the data-collection instruments have been constructed, they must be pretested before they are used in the study proper. Questions that seem clear and straightforward to the research staff may, in a trial testing, prove difficult to comprehend, or ambiguous, or simply not productive of useful information. Observational categories, statistical forms, etc., may be awkward or inappropriate to the material being studied.

In the survey of restaurant discrimination, there were two pre tests: one by members of the committee planning the study, covering only a few restaurants; the second, by volunteers similar to the testers in the final study, covering a sample of cafeterias and luncheonettes. In this case, the pretests indicated need for only minor revisions in the testing instructions and report form, but they revealed serious organizational and administrative problems—in recruiting testers, making assignments, filling out and returning report forms, supervising progress, etc.—and led to much more careful planning of these aspects in the survey proper. Much difficulty can be avoided by carefully pretesting the techniques to be used, to ensure that they will collect the information needed.

SELECTING THE SAMPLE

In many—though by no means all—descriptive studies, the investigator wishes to be able to make statements about some defined group of people or objects (in our example, restaurants). It is rarely necessary to study all the people in the group in order to provide an accurate and reliable description of the attitudes and behavior of its members. More often than not, a sample of the population to be studied is sufficient.

Much work has been done on the problem of designing samples in such a way that they yield accurate information with a minimum amount of research effort. At this point, it may be profitable to illustrate how an awareness of statistical considerations may result in considerable research economy. Rowntree (1941), in his classic study of poverty in York, England, investigated every working-class household. To check the accuracy of sampling methods, he selected, according to a systematic procedure, every tenth interview schedule and compared the results obtained thereby with those obtained from all the cases. Similar calculations were based on samples of 1 in 20, 1 in 30, 1 in 40, and 1 in 50. The table below shows his results for one type of information—the proportion of income spent on rent by families in five different income groupings. It is apparent that the various samples, regardless of their size, gave results fairly close to those found for all the households in each income class. Thus, comparing the extreme right-hand column (figures based on a sample of 1 in 50 families) with the left-hand column (figures based on the complete survey), we see that

PERCENTAGE OF INCOME SPENT ON RENT

Income Class	Complete Survey	Sample Surveys				
		1 in 10	1 in 20	1 in 30	1 in 40	1 in 50
"A"	26.5	26.6	25.9	27.0	28.3	27.1
"B"	22.7	22.9	23.5	23.3	22.3	22.6
"C"	19.8	18.1	17.2	18.3	17.2	18.0
"D"	15.8	16.0	14.4	15.8	17.1	16.9
"E"	11.3	11.0	10.1	10.7	11.2	11.5

the sample shows families in income class "A" spending 27.1 per cent of their income on rent, while the total survey shows that such families spent 26.5 per cent of their income on rent; in income class "B," the sample shows 22.6 per cent of income spent on rent, while the total survey shows 22.7 per cent; and so on. For no income group does the figure shown by the sample based on 1 family in 50 differ by more than 2 percentage points from that shown by the complete survey. In other words, by taking a sample of 1 in 50 instead of every working-class household in the city, essentially the same results would have been obtained. That is, a substantial saving in time and effort could have been effected without significantly impairing the results.

Even very slight differences between figures—for example, the difference between 26.5 per cent and 27.1 per cent—may be statistically significant. In deciding whether a difference is worthy of attention, two kinds of considerations are relevant: statistical ones and practical ones. Whether a difference between two figures is *statistically* significant involves precisely the question being discussed here—the probable deviation of figures based on samples from those for the total population from which the samples are drawn.[8] If a particular difference is

[8] The concept of statistical significance is discussed in Chapter 11, pages 414–422. For more detailed discussion, consult any standard statistics textbook.

statistically significant, the decision whether it has practical significance is, of course, a matter for judgment in terms of the consequences of the different figures. If some major decision—as, for example, a general increase in wages—is to be made on the basis of the findings, then a difference of as little as one percentage point between the sample findings and the true state of affairs for the total population may be serious. However, in most surveys it seems unlikely that a difference as small as those shown in the table above would lead to any major change in interpretation or in recommendations for action, if such recommendations were among the goals of the study.

It is, of course, important that the study findings based on a sample (that is, on only part of the group about which statements are to be made) should be a reasonably accurate representation of the state of affairs in the total group (referred to, in sampling terminology, as the "population"). This means that the sample should be selected in such a way that findings based on it are likely to correspond closely to those that would be obtained if the population were studied. To bring this about, considerable attention has been paid to problems and methods of sampling. These are discussed in Appendix B.

In the restaurant survey, a systematic stratified sample was used. (See Appendix B for definition of these terms). The units in the sample were, of course, restaurants. A complete list of restaurants in the area had been compiled by volunteers who walked through every block, recording each eating place—its name, address, price range, and other relevant information. Since one of the questions to be investigated was whether the occurrence of discrimination was related to the price level of restaurants, the sample was stratified on that basis. The cards on which the data about each restaurant had been entered were arranged in order of the estimated price of an average meal. It was not known in advance exactly how many testers would be available, and therefore how many restaurants could be included in the sample. In view of the decision to concentrate on restaurants in a middle price range, the median card was selected as the first case in the sample; the other cases were selected by taking, alternately, every fourth card above and every fourth card below the median. This meant that, whatever the final size of the sample, it would constitute 25 per cent of the restaurants within a specifiable price range in the given geographical area. The final sample consisted of 62 restaurants, constituting 25 per cent of the 248 restaurants with average prices from $1.30 to $3.75.[9]

The research purpose determines the appropriate sampling unit. In an election study, the sampling units would be eligible voters; in a study of family budgets, families; in a study of infant behavior, they might be time periods. Whatever the sampling unit, it is important to have a basis for identifying the total population of such units and a specified method of selecting units from that population (see Appendix B).

COLLECTING AND CHECKING THE DATA

To obtain consistent data free from the errors introduced by individual interviewers, observers, and others, it is necessary to supervise the staff of field workers closely as they collect and record information. Checks must be set up, for example, to ensure that interviewers are honest and that the data they collect are unbiased.[10] As data are collected, they should be examined for completeness, comprehensibility, consistency, and reliability.

In the restaurant survey, all testers, immediately after leaving the restaurants, returned to the study headquarters to fill out their report forms. The two members of each team filled out the form together, but without any discussion with the other team that had gone to the same restaurant. After the two reports for a given restaurant had been completed, a member of the supervisory committee checked both, to make sure that they were complete and to see whether the two teams agreed. If there was any discrepancy, it was discussed with the two teams

[9] As pointed out in Appendix B, *systematic* sampling procedures such as this have certain limitations that are not present when samples are *randomly* selected. However, given the decision that the sample should constitute 25 per cent of the restaurants within the price range covered by the study, *plus* the uncertainty about how many restaurants could be tested, systematic sampling was more appropriate because the boundaries of the price range to be covered could be expanded as arrangements were made for additional tests. A random sampling procedure, on the other hand, would have necessitated an advance decision as to the "population" of restaurants to be sampled—i.e., the price range to be covered.

[10] For a discussion of "cheating" by interviewers and methods of detecting it, see Blankenship et al. (1947).

jointly. In most cases it became apparent that the discrepancy did not represent genuine disagreement, but rather an oversight by one team in filling out the report, or a physical inability on the part of one team to observe behavior visible to the other. In the two or three instances of genuine disagreement, the supervisor wrote a detailed report of the versions given by the two teams. Such checking at the time reports are turned in prevents much difficulty at later stages and ensures the usability of data that might otherwise have to be discarded.

ANALYZING THE RESULTS

The process of analysis includes: coding the interview replies, observations, etc. (placing each item in the appropriate category); tabulating the data (counting the number of items in each category); and performing statistical computations. These procedures are discussed in considerable detail in Chapter 11. Here we may simply note that both considerations of economy and the need for safeguards against error enter into each of these steps. In general, considerations of economy require that the analysis be planned in detail before actual work on it is started. In this way, the investigator may avoid unnecessary labor, such as working out tables for which he later finds he has no use or, on the other hand, re-doing some tables because he failed to include relevant data. To be sure, complete planning of the analysis in advance is not always possible or even desirable; new ideas occur to the investigator as he examines his preliminary findings. But, except in exploratory studies, it is always possible and desirable to work out in advance the basic outlines of the analysis.

Safeguards against error in coding ordinarily take the form of checking the reliability of the coders—that is, determining the extent to which they agree in assigning a given item to a given category. If the code requires complex judgments, the usual procedure is to have two or more coders independently code a sample of the material, continuing—with additional training or, if necessary, modifications in the code—until they have achieved a satisfactory degree of reliability. In the case of simple codes, one coder may process the entire group of cases without advance determination of reliability; a second person may then code, say, every twentieth case, in order to provide a check on accuracy.

If the material is to be tabulated by machine, it must be entered on appropriate cards; this is usually done by punching holes corresponding to a given code. It is advisable to check the accuracy of punching; again, it is usual to check only a sample of the cards.

The accuracy of tabulation may also be checked by having a sample of the tables re-done. However, at this stage it is possible to make a rough check by comparing figures from different tables. For example, the figures in each table should add up to the total number of cases, unless there is reason to omit some from a given table. Moreover, certain classifications are likely to be used in more than one table, and these figures provide a partial check on accuracy. For example, in the restaurant survey, in addition to the basic table showing the number of restaurants in which discrimination was found and the number in which it was not, there were tables showing the number of restaurants in which a given kind of discrimination was encountered, the occurrence of discrimination in restaurants at different price levels, in American and "foreign" restaurants, etc. If any of these more detailed tables had shown a different number of restaurants as discriminatory than the basic table, this would have been evidence of error.

Finally, statistical computations are needed in a study of any complexity; averages, percentages, correlations must be computed. Again, these operations may be checked by having a second person re-do a sample of them.

Statistical operations of another sort are introduced for the purpose of safeguarding against drawing unjustified conclusions from the findings. These involve such procedures as estimating from the sample findings the probable occurrence of some characteristic in the population the sample is intended to represent, and estimating the probability that differences found between subgroups in the sample represent differences between the corresponding subgroups in the population rather than simple chance differences due to sampling. (The logic underlying such procedures is discussed briefly in Chapter 11; the procedures are discussed in detail in standard statistics texts).

The process of analysis in the restaurant survey was relatively simple. The number of cases was not large; the only complex coding judgment required was the decision whether or not a given restaurant was to be classified as having shown discrimination against the Negro diners; and the number of characteristics of restaurants that were to be examined in relation to the occurrence of discrimination was small. In view of the small number of cases, the importance of the decision whether or not discrimination had occurred, and the structure of the organization that carried out the survey, an unusual and uneconomical procedure was followed in coding restaurants as having shown or not shown discrimination. Eight persons served as coders. Preliminary classification of each restaurant as discriminatory or nondiscriminatory was made by a pair of coders working together. Finally the whole group, working as a committee, reviewed all the tests and made the final decisions as to whether or not there had been clear inequality of treatment that could not reasonably be considered accidental.

The small number of cases and the few variables to be examined in relation to the occurrence of discrimination made tabulation a simple process.

The appropriate statistical operations to safeguard the drawing of conclusions were carried out. Thus, from the finding that 42 per cent of the restaurants tested gave the Negro diners clearly inferior treatment, it was estimated, by means of the formula for the standard error of a percentage, that probably between 36 per cent and 48 per cent of all restaurants in the given area and price range discriminated against Negroes.[11] Similarly, appropriate tests of significance were used to determine whether differences in frequency of discrimination in restaurants of different price levels, different nationality, with and without headwaiters, etc., probably represented true differences or merely chance variations. Of the variables examined, only price proved to be significantly related to discrimination. When the restaurants were divided into three price ranges, it was found that a far smaller proportion of those in the lowest range were discriminatory in their treatment of Negroes.

[11] Another survey of the same area two years later, in 1952, after a campaign to induce nondiscrimination, found discrimination in only 16 per cent of the restaurants tested. Computing the standard error of this percentage led to the estimate that at this time probably between 12 per cent and 20 per cent of all restaurants in the given area and price range discriminated against Negroes.

Summary

In this chapter we have pointed out that the function of research design is to provide for the collection of relevant evidence with minimal expenditure of effort, time, and money. These considerations are important in any study, whatever its purpose. But *how* they can best be achieved depends to a considerable extent on the research purpose. When the purpose of a study is exploration, a flexible research design, which provides opportunity for considering many different aspects of a problem, is appropriate. When the purpose of a study is accurate description of a situation or of an association between variables, accuracy becomes a major consideration; a design is needed that minimizes bias and maximizes the reliability of the evidence collected. Designs appropriate to exploratory and descriptive studies have been discussed in this chapter.

When the purpose of a study is to test a hypothesis of a cause-and-effect relation between variables, other requirements are introduced. Research designs appropriate for such studies are discussed in the following chapter.

4

RESEARCH DESIGN
II. Studies Testing Causal Hypotheses

*The Logic of Testing Hypotheses about
Causal Relationships*

Causal Inference from Experiments

Causal Inference from Other Study Designs

Summary

> *Experimental observations are only experience carefully planned in advance, and designed to form a secure basis of new knowledge.*   R. A. FISHER

The Logic of Testing Hypotheses about Causal Relationships[1]

A HYPOTHESIS of causal relationship asserts that a particular characteristic or occurrence (X) is one of the factors that determine another characteristic or occurrence (Y). Studies designed to test such hypotheses must provide data from which one can legitimately infer that X does or does not enter into the determination of Y. Before we consider the kinds of research procedures that can provide grounds for inferences of this sort, some discussion of the concept of "causality" is needed.

THE CONCEPT OF "CAUSALITY"

The concept of causality is complex, and a thorough analysis of it would be far beyond the scope of this book. We shall limit our discussion to those points that seem essential to understanding the requirements for research procedures in studies designed to test causal hypotheses.

"Common-sense" thinking about causality tends to be along the line that a single event (the "cause") always leads to another single event (the "effect"). In modern science, the emphasis is rather on a multiplicity of "determining conditions," which together make the occurrence of a given event probable. Both common-sense and scientific thinking are concerned with discovering *necessary* and *sufficient* conditions for an event. (We shall define these terms in the

---

[1] For a more detailed discussion of this topic, see Churchman (1948), and Cohen and Nagel (1934, Chapter 13).

following paragraphs.) But while common sense leads one to expect that one factor may provide a complete explanation, the scientist rarely if ever expects to find a single factor or condition that is both necessary and sufficient to bring about an event. Rather, he is interested in *contributory* conditions, *contingent* conditions, *alternative* conditions —all of which he will expect to find operating to make the occurrence of the event probable, but not certain. (Further explanation of these terms, too, follows.)

A *necessary* condition, as the term implies, is one that *must* occur if the phenomenon of which it is a "cause" is to occur. If X is a necessary condition of Y, then Y will never occur unless condition X occurs. *Example:* Prior experimentation with drugs is a necessary condition of drug addiction, since it would be impossible for addiction to occur if the individual had never used drugs.

A *sufficient* condition is one that is *always* followed by the phenomenon of which it is a "cause." If X is a sufficient condition of Y, then whenever X occurs, Y will always occur. *Example:* Destruction of the optic nerve is a sufficient condition of blindness, since no one whose optic nerve has been destroyed can see.

A condition may be both *necessary and sufficient* for the occurrence of a phenomenon. In such a case, Y would never occur unless X occurred, and whenever X occurred, Y would also occur. In other words, there would be no instance in which either X or Y appeared alone. Clearly, neither of our examples fits this pattern. Although drug addiction (Y) can never occur unless the person has experimented with the use of drugs (X), it is nevertheless true that an individual can experiment with drugs without becoming addicted; thus experimentation with drugs is a *necessary but not sufficient* condition of addiction. In order to understand the occurrence of drug addiction, we must find other contributory conditions.

On the other hand, although destruction of the optic nerve (X) will always lead to blindness (Y), blindness may come about in other ways even though the optic nerve is undamaged; destruction of the nerve is a *sufficient but not a necessary* condition of blindness. To understand all the "causes" of blindness, we must seek alternative conditions that may produce it.

We shall use our drug-addiction example to illustrate the search for *contributory, contingent,* and *alternative* conditions. A *contributory* condition is one that increases the likelihood that a given phenomenon will occur, but does not make it certain; this is because it is only one of a number of factors that together determine the occurrence of the phenomenon. Thus, research on drug addiction is not satisfied with recognizing that experimentation with drugs is a necessary condition of addiction, but goes on to consider what personal, family, and neighborhood factors are conducive to such experimentation and what factors make it more likely that an individual who has experimented will become addicted (Chein, 1956). Studies comparing adolescent male addicts and non-addicts may find, for example, that a considerably higher proportion of those who have become addicts grew up in homes from which the father was missing; in other words, these studies suggest that the absence of a father figure from the home during childhood is a contributory influence in the development of drug addiction in adolescent males.

But the behavior with which social science deals is extremely complex; the interaction of factors must be taken into account. A factor that operates as a contributory condition of a phenomenon under one set of circumstances may not do so under another. The conditions under which a given variable is a contributory cause of a given phenomenon are called *contingent* conditions. Much research in social science is concerned with identifying such conditions. In our drug-addiction example, further studies may be directed toward discovering whether the relationship between father's absence and drug addiction holds under a variety of conditions. They may find that in neighborhoods where drug use by adolescents is rare or nonexistent, boys brought up without a father in the home do not turn to drugs. The hypothesis may then be refined as follows: In neighborhoods where the use of drugs is common (contingent condition), absence of a boy's father contributes to the probability that the boy will become an addict.

Awareness of the multiplicity of contributory causes leads also to an interest in *alternative* conditions that may make the occurrence of a phenomenon more likely. Thus, it may be found that, in neighborhoods with a high rate of drug use, the rate of addiction is especially high not only among boys who have been brought up without a father but among boys whose fathers have been present in the home during their childhood but have treated them with hostility or indifference. The hypothesis would then be reformulated to take account of these alternative contributory conditions: *Either* the absence of a father figure or the occurrence of hostile or indifferent treatment by the father contributes to the probability of addiction in neighborhoods where the use of drugs is common. The social scientist may then seek a hypothesis that includes a factor common to *both* the alternative contributory causes—for example, that in neighborhoods where drugs are easily available, the lack of opportunity for identification with a father figure during childhood makes drug addiction more likely in adolescence.

Bases for Inferring the Existence of a Causal Relationship between Two Variables

Most hypotheses in social science are concerned with contributory or alternative conditions and the contingencies under which they operate. However, it is impossible to *demonstrate directly* that a given characteristic or occurrence (X) determines another characteristic or occurrence (Y), either by itself or in combination with other characteristics or occurrences (A, B, C, etc). Rather, we are always in the position of *inferring* from observed data that the hypothesis that X is a condition for the occurrence of Y is or is not tenable with some specified degree of confidence. What evidence is necessary to justify such inferences?

concomitant variation. One type of relevant evidence concerns *concomitant variation*—that is, the extent to which X and Y occur together or vary together in the way predicted by the hypothesis. Let us say we wish to test the hypothesis that X is a contributory condition of Y. Unless we find that the proportion of cases having the characteristic Y is greater among cases having the characteristic X than among those not having the characteristic X, we will ordinarily conclude that the hypothesis is not tenable. Moreover, if our hypothesis also specifies that the *amount* of Y is determined by the amount of X, we should also find that, on the whole, those cases that show a higher amount of X also show a higher amount of Y.

An example may help to make this clear. Suppose that physicians in a northern town notice a sudden increase in the number of patients who come to them with severe digestive upsets. Suppose it also happens that a tropical fruit—let us say, the mango—has recently become available in the markets of this town. One of the doctors thinks these two sets of events may be related; he advances the hypothesis that eating mangoes (X) may lead to severe digestive upsets (Y) in people who are not accustomed to the fruit (contingent condition). For a period of time, several doctors ask all patients with digestive upsets whether they have recently eaten any mangoes. If none of them has, the hypothesis that eating mangoes is a cause[2] of the digestive upsets would be rejected.

But suppose some of them *have* eaten mangoes. We would then ask a number of people *without* digestive disturbance whether *they* had eaten any mangoes. If it turned out that the proportion having eaten the fruit in this group was as great as the proportion in the group with digestive upsets—say, 30 per cent in each group—we would infer that eating mangoes did not have much to do with developing digestive disturbances; in other words, we would reject the hypothesis that it was a cause of the upsets. It is important to note, however, that we may be wrong in rejecting the hypothesis. It may be that those who ate the mangoes and became ill had a slight malfunctioning of the liver, which was aggravated by eating the mangoes and thus led to the digestive upsets; while those who ate the mangoes and did not become ill did not have this liver difficulty. In other words, eating mangoes may be a *contributory* condition of digestive upset under the *contingent* condition of malfunctioning of the liver. By neglecting the possibility of a contingent condition under which eating mangoes leads to digestive upsets, we may have made an incorrect inference from the fact that equal proportions of people with and without digestive upsets had eaten the fruit.

Suppose, on the other hand, that 90 per cent of patients with digestive upsets *had* eaten mangoes, and that only 30 per cent of the

2 Since, as has been pointed out, modern science approaches causality in terms of multiple determining conditions rather than with the expectation of finding a single factor that always leads to a given event, the word "cause" must be understood, throughout this book, as meaning "one of a number of determining conditions which together make the occurrence of a given event probable."

people without digestive upsets had done so. We would conclude that the hypothesis that eating mangoes leads to digestive disturbances was tenable.

Evidence of whether X and Y vary together in the predicted way may be sought from the other direction. We might locate a group of people who had eaten mangoes and another group who had not, and compare the incidence of digestive upsets in the two groups. If similar proportions of people in the two groups showed symptoms of the disease, we would again conclude that eating the fruit did not lead to development of the disease. Suppose, however, that 70 per cent of those who had eaten mangoes had digestive upsets, while only 10 per cent of those who had not eaten them showed such symptoms; we would conclude that the hypothesis of a causal relationship between mangoes and digestive upsets was tenable.

But it would be simply *tenable*, not *proved*. Three other possible explanations of the relationship would, at this point, be equally tenable: (1) having digestive disorders in some way led people to crave mangoes, so that the direction of the relationship was the opposite of that hypothesized; (2) some other condition led to *both* eating mangoes and having digestive disturbances; (3) some other condition, which merely happened to be associated with eating mangoes, was responsible for the upsets.

TIME ORDER OF OCCURRENCE OF VARIABLES. The alternative hypothesis that digestive disturbances lead to a craving for mangoes and thus to eating them brings us to a second type of evidence relevant to inferences about causality—the time order of the two events. One event cannot be considered the "cause" of another if it occurs *after* the other event. The occurrence of a causal factor may precede or may be simultaneous with the occurrence of an effect; by definition, an effect cannot be produced by an event that occurs only after the effect has taken place. However, it is possible for each term in the relationship to be both a "cause" and an "effect" of the other term. Many of the basic relationships of physical science are of this sort. For example, Boyle's law asserts that, under conditions of constant temperature, the pressure of a gas is inversely related to its volume. This means that any change we are able to produce in the volume of the gas will simultaneously result in a change in its pressure, and also that any change we are able to produce in the pressure will simultaneously result in a change in its volume. The two variables in the relationship function interchangeably as causal factor and as effect, so the relationship is said to be *symmetrical*.

An example of a symmetrical causal relationship in the social sciences is Homans' hypothesis that "*the higher the rank of a person within a group, the more nearly his activities conform to the norms of the group. . . .* The relationship is strictly mutual: the closer the person's activities come to the norm, the higher his rank will tend to be, but it is also true that, rank being taken as the independent variable, the higher the person's rank, the closer his activities will come to the norm." (Homans, 1950.)

Although symmetrical causal relationships are frequently found in social phenomena, it is often useful and convenient to focus upon the influence of one factor on the other. Thus, in testing Homans' hypothesis, one might wish to see whether one could cause a deviant member of a group to conform more closely to the group norms by increasing his rank within the group. One would not conclude that increasing an individual's rank in the group was a cause of greater conformity unless the increase in rank was followed by an increase in conforming behavior. In distinguishing between cause and effect, it is useful to establish which of the two events came first, assuming they did not occur simultaneously. Knowing that an increase in rank, in a specific instance, preceded an increase in conformity, we know that the increase in conformity was not the causal factor. (The finding that in this instance an increase in rank has led to greater conformity does not, of course, rule out the possibility that the reverse would also hold true.) However, knowledge of temporal priority is not in itself sufficient ground for inferring causality; other factors than the presumed cause may have produced the effect.

In our digestive-upset example, if people ate mangoes *after* they had developed digestive upsets, rather than before, then eating mangoes would not be considered a cause of digestive upsets. Let us say, however, that questioning showed that every patient suffering from digestive upset who had eaten mangoes had eaten the fruit before the symptoms developed. The hypothesis that eating mangoes is a contributory condition of the disease would remain tenable, and we would have ruled out one of the alternative hypotheses—that having digestive disorders led people to crave mangoes. But we must still consider the remaining alternative hypotheses: that some other condition led to *both* eating mangoes and digestive disturbances; and that some other condition, which merely happened to be associated with eating mangoes, was responsible for the upsets.

ELIMINATION OF OTHER POSSIBLE CAUSAL FACTORS. We might consider the possibility that some chemical imbalance led both to a craving for mangoes and to digestive disturbances. Such a hypothesis might be tested by examining a sample of people, identifying those with the specified type of chemical imbalance, and tracing both subgroups over a period of time to discover whether a larger proportion of those with the chemical imbalance ate mangoes and developed digestive upsets.

Or we might search for factors accidentally associated with eating mangoes which might be responsible for the digestive upsets. Let us say that mangoes were sold in only four stores in the town. Suppose that in three of these stores, the mangoes were sprayed with a certain preparation to improve their appearance, while in the fourth they were not. Suppose further that it was found that all those who had eaten mangoes and had developed digestive upsets had bought the fruit in one of the stores where it was sprayed, while all those who had eaten the fruit and had *not* developed such symptoms had bought it in the store where it was not sprayed. The hypothesis that eating mangoes was in itself a cause of digestive upset would be discarded, and attention would be turned to the effects of the spray; for example, did the spray lead to digestive upsets when it was used on other fruit, or was there some interaction between the spray and the chemical composition of mangoes that produced the toxic effects?

SUMMARY OF TYPES OF EVIDENCE RELEVANT TO CAUSAL INFERENCE. Let us briefly summarize the three major types of evidence that are relevant to testing hypotheses about causal relationships:

1. Evidence of concomitant variation—that is, that X (the assumed *causal*, or *independent*, variable) and Y (the assumed *effect*, or *dependent*, or *criterion*, variable) are associated in the way predicted by the hypothesis. In the case of a hypothesis that X is a *contributory* condition of Y, this would mean that Y should appear in more cases

where X is present than in cases where X is absent. Other types of causal hypotheses (that X is a necessary or sufficient cause of Y, or a contingent cause in association with A, or an alternate cause with B) would call for other specific patterns for association between X and Y.

2. Evidence that Y did not occur before X.

3. Evidence ruling out other factors as possible determining conditions of Y.

It must be stressed that such evidence merely provides a reasonable basis for inferring that X is or is not a cause of Y; it does not provide absolute certainty. On the one hand, if the evidence does not support the hypothesis of a causal relationship, it may be that we have neglected some condition under which X *is* a determinant of Y, and thus that we have been wrong in completely rejecting the possibility that X is a determining condition of Y. On the other hand, if the evidence supports the hypothesis, it may still be that we have neglected some other factor associated with X which is, in fact, the determining condition of Y. In short, we may conclude that it is reasonable to believe that X is or is not a cause of Y, but we can never be certain that the relationship has been conclusively demonstrated. The cumulation of studies that point to one or the other conclusion helps to increase our confidence in its probable correctness, but still does not constitute absolute proof.

ADEQUACY OF DIFFERENT RESEARCH DESIGNS AS SOURCES OF EVIDENCE

Some types of study design provide more convincing grounds for drawing causal inferences than do others. In our example, all the procedures suggested so far for testing the hypothesis that eating mangoes is a cause of digestive upsets have made use of situations that occurred in the ordinary course of events: comparison of individuals who had become ill with those who had not; comparison of those who had eaten mangoes, for whatever reasons, with those who had not; etc. Such an approach called for a number of different studies, any one of which provided only tenuous grounds for testing the hypothesis because it left alternative hypotheses untested. For example, an investigation focused on whether eating of mangoes had preceded or followed the digestive upset would provide no evidence as to the possible operation of other factors.

An experimental design provides both greater certainty and greater efficiency by making possible the simultaneous gathering of various lines of evidence. In an experimental test of the hypothesis about the relation between mangoes and digestive upset, the investigator would arrange for a number of subjects to eat mangoes and for a number of comparable subjects not to eat any of the fruit during the period of the experiment. In other words, he would select the subjects to be assigned to different "treatments," and would in one treatment expose the subjects to the presumed causal variable and in the other treatment not expose them to it (technically referred to as "manipulating the independent variable"). He would assign the subjects to the different treatments in such a way as to ensure that the two groups did not differ except by chance before eating the mangoes. Comparison of the incidence of digestive upsets in the two groups after one group had eaten mangoes and the other had not would provide evidence of whether eating mangoes and having digestive upsets varied together. By keeping careful records of the time of eating mangoes and the time of onset of digestive disturbances, he would gain evidence as to which of the variables came first. Equating the two groups before they ate the mangoes would lend assurance not only that they did not differ in incidence of digestive upsets before eating the mangoes (thus contributing further evidence about the time relation between the two variables) but that they did not differ in some other way or ways that might lead to a subsequent difference in incidence of digestive upsets. In addition, the experimenter might introduce "controls" to protect against the possibility that different experiences during the experiment, other than the eating or not eating of mangoes, might be responsible for a difference in occurrence of digestive upsets; for example, he might see to it that all the other food eaten by all the subjects was the same. Moreover, he might build into his experiment provision for testing hypotheses about specific alternative causal factors. For example, he might simultaneously test the hypothesis about the effects of the spray used on the mangoes by having some subjects eat mangoes that had not been sprayed, some eat mangoes that had been sprayed, others eat other fruits that had been sprayed, etc. Thus, in a single study, he could gather evidence of the three kinds needed to provide a basis for inferring a causal relationship: concomitant variation, time order, and the possible influence of other factors.

When an experiment is possible, it is the most effective method of testing a hypothesis that one variable, X, causally influences another variable, Y. Many questions of causal relationship lend themselves easily to experimental study. For example, the investigator who is interested in the relative effectiveness of group discussion and decision versus reading a pamphlet or listening to a lecture as a method of changing behavior can set up a situation in which one or more groups of individuals discuss a certain issue and come to a decision about it, while comparable individuals read a pamphlet or listen to a lecture on the subject. Similarly, the influence of subliminal stimuli on the perception of subsequent supraliminal stimuli can be investigated by exposing subjects to such stimuli. Or the effects of "packaging" on the evaluation of a product can be tested by giving one sample of people a product in a container of a given style, a comparable sample the same product in a different container. In such cases, the investigator himself manipulates the independent variable.

In other problems, however, manipulation of the independent variable by the experimenter, or assignment of subjects to different treatments, is not feasible. Suppose one wishes to study the effects of different methods of child-rearing on the personality structure of children. He is not likely to be able to assign certain children to be brought up in one way, others in another. (He might be able to do something of this sort in the case of children in institutions, but his findings could not well be generalized to children in family settings.) He must proceed by locating children who have been brought up in different ways and assessing their personalities. If he finds a correlation, he has secured evidence of concomitant variation. In order to provide a basis for inferring that the child-training practices (X) are a cause of the personality structure (Y), he must gather evidence that Y did not precede X and that other possible factors are not the determining ones. Ordinarily, the evidence on these points will be less convincing than that provided by an experiment.

Hypotheses about the effects of attributes of individuals (rather than of the situations in which they are placed) often are not amenable to experimental investigation in the sense of manipulation of the "independent" variable by the investigator. To be sure, a hypothesis that hungry subjects will be more likely to interpret ambiguous pictures as representing food than will subjects who are not hungry can be tested experimentally; the degree of hunger can be controlled reasonably well by specifying the length of time subjects must go without eating before viewing the pictures. Many attributes of individuals, however, cannot be manipulated in this way. Non-manipulatable attributes are involved, for example, in such hypotheses as: Brain damage impairs the ability to think abstractly; or, People will tend to remember those parts of a message that are consistent with their own views and to forget those that are contrary. The investigator working with human subjects will not manipulate the variable of brain damage willfully by destroying portions of the brain; he must seek existing cases of brain damage. And he cannot assign certain views to certain individuals: they bring their views with them. The investigator achieves the variation he wants, not by direct manipulation of the variable itself, but by selection of individuals in whom the variable is present or absent, strong or weak, etc. He presents brain-damaged and non-damaged subjects with the same task; he asks individuals with different views to read the same passage; etc.

The logic of testing hypotheses about the presumed effects of an attribute of a person, such as brain damage, which is not created experimentally, is essentially the same as that of testing hypotheses in any other nonexperimental study. The nonexperimental study, in its design, does not allow one to rule out in advance, with any confidence, the possibility that the effect was created by some other factor that is correlated with the presumed causal factor. Hence, one is faced with the necessity of ruling out on an ex post facto basis (i.e., after the presumed causal variable has already occurred) the possibility that other factors correlated with the presumed causal factor may have produced the observed effect. For example, if we exposed patients with brain damage and patients without brain damage to a test, differences in their test performance might reflect the effects of brain damage or they might reflect such other factors as differences in anxiety that are associated with different types of illness, differences associated with socioeconomic variables (e.g., brain damage occurs more frequently in certain types of occupations), etc. Hypothetically, if we felt free to create brain damage (as is done with lower animals), we might assign people to the treatment of "being brain-damaged" or to the treatment of "not being brain-damaged" in such a way as to rule out in advance the possibility that test differences would be explainable by other factors. One could then rule out known possible alternative explanations such as anxiety and socioeconomic variables by assigning subjects to the "brain-damaged" and "not brain-damaged" conditions in such a way that the two groups would be similar in the types of illness represented, the degree of anxiety, the variety of occupations, etc. Moreover, in the *ideal* experiment, one is able to eliminate alternative explanations that may not have been thought of in advance. For example, one might not consider, in advance, the possibility that the presumed differences due to "brain damage" might reflect sex or age differences. Even so, if one were experimentally creating the "brain-damaged" and "not brain-damaged" conditions and assigning subjects to the treatments *randomly*, the subjects in the two treatments should not differ in their sex or age distribution except by chance. Hence, the random assignment of subjects to experimentally created conditions would automatically eliminate these alternative explanations whether or not they had been considered beforehand. Obviously, however, investigators are *not* going to inflict brain damage on humans in the interest of getting more certain knowledge about its effects. Instead, they will concentrate on finding substitute methods for ruling out the possible effects of other variables.

Occasionally, natural situations may provide both the desired contrasting conditions and the opportunity for sufficiently rigorous procedures to make possible a reasonably firm basis for inferences. For example, suppose that a social scientist has an inside track on the deliberations of a labor union concerned with some important service to consumers. He learns that the union leaders consider a drawn-out strike inevitable in the near future. He is interested in several hypotheses concerning the effects of suffering personal discomfort on attitudes toward the person or group seen as responsible for the discomfort. He quickly takes advantage of the pending situation by organizing a study in two comparable cities, one where the strike will occur and one where it will not occur. As a result of his alertness, he gets measures of attitudes toward labor unions, procedures for settling industrial disputes, etc., in two comparable groups (*i.e.*, the residents of the two cities), one of which undergoes the critical experience and one of which does not. Does it matter that he himself has not instigated the strike? Clearly it does not, provided he can assume that the two cities are really comparable before the strike and that the decision to strike in the one city and not the other has not been influenced by characteristics of the cities that might be related to their potential reactions to the strike.

Ordinarily, however, natural situations are complicated and do not permit the investigator to assume, with any confidence, that the groups to be compared differ only by chance. As Greenwood (1945) has stated:

> . . . the created situation gives us better control power over our phenomenon. We can determine at our own discretion the circumstances which shall be present, and thus arrive at more conclusive evidence of causality. . . . The ability to produce the necessary changes permits the test of hypotheses otherwise not amenable to verification.

No matter how carefully controlled the study, however, there is no way to be *completely* certain of the validity of inferences that may be drawn. There is always the possibility, for example, that later research will reveal the influence of some factor not taken into account in the study; or that the evidence collected was not critical to the hypothesis under scrutiny (in other words, that the working definitions did not provide adequate indicators of the concepts in the hypothesis); or it may be that the research procedures did not meet the logical requirements for the making of inferences. Certainly in the social sciences, where there is little knowledge of what factors should be controlled, and where many of the relevant factors (such as individual characteristics, or life events outside the experimental situation) are difficult or impossible to control, these possibilities are ever present; but the principle applies to the physical sciences as well, especially at the frontiers of knowledge.

This possibility of fallacious inference makes it necessary to evaluate experimental findings in the context of other knowledge. Confidence in a research result requires not only statistical evidence of its reliability (for example, that the effects of X and X′ are significantly different statistically)[3] but, in addition, evidence that the interpretation is in keeping with the interpretations of other "facts" about which one has considerable confidence. This is why the establishment of confidence in the imputation of any causal relationship between events requires repetition of research and the relating of the findings to other research.

Causal Inference from Experiments

The basic outline of an experiment is simple: an "experimental" group is exposed to the assumed causal (or independent) variable while a "control" group is not; the two groups are then compared in terms of the assumed effect (or dependent variable). This pattern makes possible the collection of the three major types of evidence relevant to testing hypotheses about causal relationships: (1) evidence of concomitant variation—that is, that the causal variable and the dependent variable are associated; (2) evidence that the dependent variable did not occur before the causal variable; and (3) evidence ruling out other factors as possible determining conditions of the dependent variable.

Evidence of the first type—concomitant variation—is provided very simply in an experiment. The investigator knows which subjects have been exposed to the assumed causal variable (X); he measures all subjects in terms of the assumed dependent variable (Y). He then determines whether Y occurs more frequently among the subjects who have been exposed to X than among those who have not, or whether those who have been exposed to X show a greater amount of Y than those who have not, or whatever specific relationship between X and Y is predicted by his hypothesis. For example, suppose an investigator is testing the hypothesis that the use of televised instructional programs in eighth-grade general-science classes will lead to greater gains in information than more conventional teaching methods. He will arrange for the use of television in some classes (the experimental

[3] For a discussion of the concept of statistical significance, see Chapter 11, pages 414–422.

group, exposed to X, televised programs) but not in others (the control group, not exposed to X). At the end of the semester he will compare the scores of the experimental and control groups on a test of general-science information. If children in the classes where television was used score higher, on the average, than those in the regular classes, he will have evidence that televised instructional programs and information about the subject matter are related.

Evidence of the second type—that the assumed effect did not occur before the assumed cause—is secured in one or both of two ways: by setting up the experimental and control groups in such a way that it is reasonable to assume that they did not differ in terms of the dependent variable before exposure to the independent variable, or by measuring their position on the dependent variable before exposure to the independent variable. In our television example, the investigator might assign classes to the television and non-television "treatments" in such a way that it was reasonable to assume that they were comparable in general-science information before taking the course; or he might administer a test of information at the beginning of the course; or he might do both. (Various procedures that might be used, and some of their advantages and limitations, will be discussed later in this chapter.) Note that the requirement that X cannot be considered a cause of Y if Y occurred before X does not mean, in the case of a hypothesis such as the television one, that the students must have had no prior general-science knowledge. Since the hypothesis asserts that the use of television will lead to acquisition of more information than conventional teaching methods, what is required is that the experimental group should not have had more information than the control group before the start of the course.

Evidence of the third type—ruling out other factors as possible determining conditions—may be secured in several ways. A variety of factors need to be considered as possible determining conditions. Among the major ones are: (1) factors that have occurred in the past or are relatively enduring characteristics of the subjects, (2) contemporaneous events other than exposure to the experimental variable, (3) maturational or developmental changes, and (4) the influence of the measurement process itself. Somewhat different procedures are appropriate for ruling out each type of factor as a possible determining condition.

1. In order to rule out factors that have occurred in the past or are relatively enduring characteristics of the subjects, the investigator may set up his experimental and control groups in such a way that it is reasonable to assume that they do not differ systematically in terms of characteristics or past experiences that might be relevant; or he may measure them before the experiment in terms of such factors; or he may do both. For example, in the case of the television hypothesis, another factor that immediately suggests itself as a possible determining condition of acquiring general-science information is intelligence. In order to rule out difference in intelligence as the cause of a difference in information between the experimental and the control group after the experiment, the investigator will set up the two groups so that it is reasonable to assume that they are comparable in IQ, or he will administer intelligence tests before the experiment, or both. (Again, procedures will be discussed later.)

2. In attempting to rule out contemporaneous events other than exposure to the experimental variable as causes of differences in position on the dependent variable, the investigator may arrange for certain conditions to be the same in the experimental and the control groups, or he may deliberately vary them within his experiment. He may, for example, make sure that the same subject matter is covered in the classes with and without television instruction, that the teachers using the two methods are approximately equal in teaching ability, that the courses involve the same amount of time, etc. On the other hand, he may deliberately select teachers of different degrees of competence. In this case, he will assign both some of the more skillful and some of the less skillful to the television classes as well as to the classes in which television is not used. Thus he is in a position to assess the effects not only of television instruction but also of the teacher's ability, and to determine whether televised programs are more helpful to relatively skillful or relatively unskillful teachers.

Some contemporaneous events that may affect the outcome of experiments in the social sciences cannot be controlled, either in the sense of holding them constant or of deliberately manipulating them. For example, a headline-making scientific event occurring during the experiment may lead to an increase in information regardless of the general-science course. If such an event affects the experimental and the control group in the same way, no problem is created, since an effect common to the two groups could not be a cause of differences between them in terms of the dependent variable. However, one may not be justified in assuming that the event affects the two groups in the same way; its impact may be different in the group exposed to the experimental variable than in the control group. Complex designs—discussed later in this chapter—have been devised to take account of this possibility.

3. Normal changes associated with maturation and development may also become confounded with the results of the experimental treatment. For example, whether or not they are taking science courses, it is possible that children growing up in a science-minded society such as ours may show an increase in general-science knowledge during the period of a year. Whenever an experiment extends over a long period of time, processes of growth and development must be considered as possible determining conditions of changes. Again, if maturational processes can be assumed to be the same in the experimental and the control groups, and if it can be assumed that the effect of the experimental variable is not specific to a given stage of development, the effects of maturation can be ruled out by comparing the two groups. More complex designs may be used if there is reason to believe that these assumptions are not justified.

4. The measurement process used in the experiment may itself affect the outcome. If people feel that they are "guinea pigs" being experimented with, or if they feel that they are being "tested" and must make a good impression, or if the method of data collection suggests responses or stimulates an interest the subject did not previously feel, the measuring process may distort the experimental results. Variations in experimental design have been worked out to take account of the effects of the measuring process; they will be discussed later in this chapter.

The entire design of an experiment has the function of providing for the collection of evidence in such a way that inferences of a causal relationship between the independent and the dependent variables can legitimately be drawn. However, certain aspects are especially im-

portant in this respect: the method of selecting experimental and
control groups; the points in time when the dependent variable is
measured, and the pattern of control groups used; and the number of
possible causal variables systematically included in the study. Each of
these is discussed in the following sections.[4]

SELECTING EXPERIMENTAL AND CONTROL GROUPS

In any design that involves comparing two or more groups of
subjects who have been exposed to different experimental treatments,
there is an underlying assumption that the groups being compared
are equivalent before the introduction of the treatments. However,
the investigator cannot simply *make* this assumption; he must take
steps to see that it is met.

Clearly, the task of creating or of unearthing groups that are
equivalent in all respects is an impossible one. Before considering how
one gets around this problem, it is necessary to distinguish two different reasons for wanting equivalent experimental and control groups.
The first is to provide a basis for inferring that differences which may
be found on the dependent variable do not result from initial differences between the two groups, in terms either of position on the
dependent variable or of other factors. The goal here is to ensure, as
far as possible, the *validity* of the inferences made on the basis of the
experiment. But there is a second goal, that of increasing the *sensitivity* of the experiment—i.e., increasing its ability to register small
effects of the experimental treatment that might be obscured by the
effects of other factors.

These two goals call for somewhat different procedures in establishing the equivalence of groups. The goal of protecting the validity of
the experiment by ensuring that experimental and control groups differ
initially only by chance is achieved by procedures termed *randomization*. The goal of increasing the sensitivity of the experiment, so that
the effects of the causal variable will be apparent even if they are
relatively small or if there are relatively few subjects, is achieved by

---

[4] For a fuller discussion of factors that may affect the outcome of an experiment, and of the ways in which different experimental designs deal with them,
see Campbell (1957).

matching procedures. These two types of procedure are discussed more fully below. It is important to realize that all well-conducted experiments involve randomization, since experimental inference presupposes randomization; hence, whenever matching procedures are used, randomization procedures should, ideally, also be employed. It is not necessary, however, that randomization be supplemented by matching, although this is often desirable.

RANDOMIZATION. Randomization provides the basic safeguard against differences between experimental and control groups that might lessen the validity of inferences about the effects of the experimental treatment. Random assignment of members of a pool of subjects to experimental and control groups entails the same principles and procedures as those involved in selecting a simple random sample for a descriptive study (see Appendix B). The assignment procedures must give each subject the same chance as that of any other subject of being assigned to any given condition. The procedures are such that any selection based, either consciously or unconsciously, on the investigator's judgment is ruled out. For example, one may flip a coin for each subject, assigning him to the experimental group if it comes up "heads," to the control group if it comes up "tails." Or one may number each person and then, by using a table of random numbers (see Appendix B), select as many cases as are wanted for the experimental group and assign the remaining ones to the control group.[5] The chance assignment of individuals to the different conditions precludes the possibility of *systematic* or nonrandom differences between the groups selected. This does not mean that the experimental and control groups will be exactly alike, but rather that whatever differences exist before the introduction of the experimental variable are the result of chance alone. The rules of probability make it possible to specify the extent of differences that might be expected by chance in the long run (that is, if the selection were repeated a large number of times). If, after one group has been exposed to the experimental treatment, the two groups are found to

[5] In most experiments, groups of equal size are used. However, when the cost of introducing the experimental variable is very high, it may be more economical to use more cases in the control than in the experimental group. See McNemar (1940) for a more detailed discussion.

differ more than would be expected by chance, one may infer that the experimental variable led to the difference. This inference, of course, must always be made tentatively, subject to the possibility that some other factor may have led to the difference.

R. A. Fisher (1951), one of the outstanding figures in the development of experimental design, has pointed out that:

> . . . the uncontrolled causes which may influence the result [of an experiment] are always strictly innumerable. When any such cause is named, it is usually perceived that, by increased labour and expense, it could be largely eliminated. Too frequently it is assumed that such refinements constitute improvements to the experiment. . . . whatever degree of care and experimental skill is expended in equalising the conditions, other than the one under test, which are liable to affect the result, this equalisation must always be to a greater or less extent incomplete, and in many important practical cases will certainly be grossly defective. . . . the simple precaution of randomisation will suffice to guarantee the validity of the test of significance, by which the result of the experiment is to be judged.

To go back to our television-teaching illustration: Let us say that our subjects are to be all the eighth-grade children in a given school, half of whom (the experimental group) will be assigned to a class in which television will be used, half (the control group) to a class using the conventional methods. But the children will certainly not all have the same IQ; some of them may already have more science information than others; some will be more interested than others in the subject matter; some will have better eyesight than others; etc. From the point of view of the *validity* of the inferences to be drawn, it is necessary that the experimental and the control groups shall not differ on any of these variables to such an extent that it leads to a difference in science information, as measured at the conclusion of the experiment, which will be incorrectly interpreted as resulting from the difference in teaching methods. Since all tests of statistical significance are based on the assumption that cases have been randomly assigned to the groups being compared, they are specifically designed to take account of chance differences in the initial characteristics of the two groups. Therefore the statistical test of significance[6] offers protection against the possibility that differences on the dependent variable that result from chance initial differences between the experimental and the control group will be incorrectly interpreted as effects of the experimental treatment.

The social scientist, however, is not always in a position to assign cases randomly to different conditions. Compromises with the ideal of random selection are often necessitated by practical circumstances. In our television-teaching example, for instance, it may not be feasible to select randomly from among all eighth-grade children those who are to be assigned to the experimental class. In order not to disrupt school routines, it may be necessary to assign existing classes to one or the other treatment. In this case, the classes may be randomly assigned to one or the other treatment, but this does not afford as much protection as the random assignment of individuals. Sometimes such compromises may be made without invalidating the bases for inference within the study (though, in terms of our definition, a study in which cases are not randomly selected does not constitute an experiment). One extreme form of nonrandom assignment, however, does seriously impair the grounds for inference. This is assignment on the basis of self-selection. For example, if an investigator wishes to test the hypothesis that social case work with the families of delinquent children reduces the delinquent behavior, he would be ill advised to draw his experimental sample from families who have voluntarily come to social agencies and his control sample from families with similarly delinquent children who have not sought such help. The reason is obvious: Families who seek help of this sort may have certain characteristics that either directly affect the probability that the delinquent behavior would be reduced even without the case work service or that make the service effective with them although it would not be with other families. We might suppose, for instance, that a mother who seeks the help of a social agency in dealing with her child's delinquency is both more concerned about the delinquent behavior and more aware

---

[6] For a brief discussion of the meaning of statistical tests of significance, see Chapter 11, pages 414–422. For a fuller discussion, consult any standard statistical text.

of community facilities for dealing with it than a mother who does not. Either of these characteristics might mean that she would be likely to take steps intended to change her child's behavior even if she did not have the help of a social case worker. And the fact that she applied for case work help might mean that she would be more receptive to it, and thus that it would be more likely to have an effect on the delinquent behavior, than if she had been assigned involuntarily to receive such help. The same principle applies whenever subjects place themselves in the "experimental" or the "control" group.[7]

MATCHING. Although random assignment, where it is feasible, is generally considered to provide adequate protection against interpreting differences on the dependent variable as resulting from the independent variable when in fact they stem from prior differences between the two groups, it is not the most effective procedure from the point of view of increasing the sensitivity of the experiment. In the interest of research efficiency, it is desirable that the experiment reveal true differences brought about by the experimental treatment, even if they are small in relation to differences produced by other variables. In our television example, teaching method may have less influence than IQ on science information. Random assignment of children to groups being taught by one or the other method would not be likely to lead to exact matching of the two groups in terms of IQ. This difference in IQ might lead to a difference in information at the end of the study. As already noted, statistical tests of significance based on the assumption of random sampling would provide protection against attributing this difference to the difference in teaching methods. However, there might be a small difference in the effectiveness of the two teaching methods which would be obscured by the difference in information related to IQ. The more such "extraneous" differences are reduced, the more chance there is for the effects of the experimental treatment to show up.

An oversimplified hypothetical example may help to make this point clear. Suppose, in our study of the effects of teaching science with

---

[7] This is a frequent problem in studies designed to test causal hypotheses that do not follow the pattern of controlled experiments. Methods of dealing with it are considered in the section of this chapter which discusses such studies.

the help of television, we took existing classes rather than individual students as our sampling units. Suppose further that eight classes were to be used in the experiment—four to receive the televised instruction, four to serve as controls. Let us say these classes differed in average IQ; four had a mean IQ of over 100 (these will be called the "highs" in the table below), and four of under 100. If the classes were randomly assigned to the television or no-television treatments, we might have a pattern such as that shown below, with grades on the final test shown in the right-hand column.

Class	Television	Mean IQ	Mean Grade on Test
1	Yes	High	90
2	No	High	80
3	Yes	Low	70
4	No	High	80
5	Yes	Low	70
6	No	Low	60
7	Yes	Low	70
8	No	High	80

In this example, the mean score of all classes on the final test is 75. The mean score of the high-IQ classes is 82.5; that of the low-IQ classes, 67.5. But both those with television and those without have mean scores of 75, even though it is apparent from inspection of the table that high-IQ classes with television instruction score higher than high-IQ classes without, and that low-IQ classes with television instruction score higher than low-IQ classes without it. But the fact that random assignment has led to an arrangement whereby three of the four classes receiving television instruction are of low IQ, while three of the four without television are of high IQ, obscures the effect of television when the average score of all classes receiving the experimental treatment is compared with that of all the control classes.

To illustrate the effect of matching, let us suppose that the television and no-television treatments had had equal numbers of high- and low-IQ classes. Making the same assumptions as in the preceding table about the relative contribution of intelligence and teaching method to scores on the final test, the results would be as follows:

Television	Mean IQ	Mean Grade on Test
Yes	Low	70
Yes	High	90
Yes	Low	70
Yes	High	90
No	Low	60
No	High	80
No	Low	60
No	High	80

Now the mean score of the classes with television is 80; that of those without television is 70. By equating the groups in terms of intelligence, the effects of teaching method have been permitted to appear.

It should be noted that in the matching procedure it is important not to sacrifice randomization. In our example, randomization might have been incorporated in the procedure in a number of ways; for example, by tossing coins to determine which two of the four high-IQ classes, and which two of the low-IQ classes, should receive the television treatment. Or, if there were a large number of classes from which to select, they might be divided into two groups—high- and low-IQ's; then, by means of a table of random numbers, two classes from each group might be selected for the television treatment and two from each group to serve as controls.

The fact that matching may make an experiment more sensitive by controlling the effects of other variables which might obscure that of the variable in which the investigator is interested often leads experimenters to supplement randomization by matching procedures. Two methods are commonly used: *precision control* and *frequency distribution control*.[8] Both, when combined—as they should be—with randomization procedures, are methods of stratified random sampling (see Appendix B).

The equating of groups by *precision control* involves matching the *individuals* in the groups, case by case. To take a complicated problem —suppose we wish to determine the effect of psychoanalytic therapy of a certain sort upon the attitudes of prejudiced people. We would try

[8] For a more detailed discussion of these methods of matching, as well as of the method of random assignment, see Greenwood (1945).

to set up two groups of persons who are matched, individual for individual, in attitudes and in factors that might be relevant to their predisposition to attitude change. That is, for person A who is highly prejudiced, who is exposed to pressures from his social group to be prejudiced, who is intelligent, who has no strong unconscious needs that motivate his prejudices, etc., we would try to find an exact counterpart, A'. A would be assigned to one group and A' to the other. For B, who is moderately prejudiced, who is exposed to social pressures not to be prejudiced, who is of average intelligence, and who has underlying insecurities that find an outlet in his prejudices, etc., we would try to find a B'. And so on until for every individual in the experimental group we had a matched individual in the control group.

The matching of individuals is obviously a very difficult task for several reasons. First, if matching is to be precise and if individuals are to be matched on several factors, there must be a large number of cases to select from in order to achieve an adequate pairing. All of these cases have to be measured in the relevant factors, but only a few will be used. The more precise the matching, and the greater the number of factors on which matching is to take place, the greater the number of cases for which no match is available. Secondly, it is frequently difficult to know which factors, of the many possible relevant ones, are the most important to use in obtaining precision control. Matching on more than two or three factors with any degree of precision is rarely possible. Fortunately, however, relevant factors are often so interrelated that matching on one factor brings with it partial matching on other factors; there is a "diminishing return" as additional factors are controlled. Third, it is often difficult to obtain adequate measures of the factors on which it may be important to match; consider, for instance, our suggested experiment on the effects of psychoanalysis. If no adequate measures of the assumed relevant factors are available, then obviously matching is not likely to be very accurate.

Successful matching can greatly increase the efficiency of an experiment by decreasing the size of the differences on the dependent variable that would occur between the experimental and the control groups by chance alone. When the chance differences are small, it is easier to demonstrate a difference that is due to the effect of the experimental variable. If one is able to match the members of each pair in terms of initial position on the dependent variable or on some attribute that is highly correlated with it, one would need considerably fewer cases to be confident that an obtained difference was not due to chance than would be required with unmatched groups. However, if the matching is in terms of some other characteristic that in fact has no relation to the dependent variable, then the matching procedure, no matter how elaborate, provides no experimental or statistical advantage. Suppose, in our effect-of-therapy-on-attitudes example, instead of being able to match cases on all the characteristics we suggested, we were able to match them only on intelligence. If intelligence were unrelated to prejudice, we would not have succeeded in matching cases for their initial degree of prejudice, and thus we would not have eliminated such initial differences as one of the causes of the differences observed after therapy. In such a situation, not only does matching provide no advantage; for reasons that are too technical to discuss here, unsuccessful matching may even lead to a statistical disadvantage.[9]

As has already been emphasized, matching is not a substitute for random assignment, but a supplement to it. Matching procedures can take account of only a few variables; those that are unaccounted for should be randomly distributed between the experimental and the control groups. Thus, if our matching procedure in the therapy experiment has given us a number of pairs of matched individuals (A and A', B and B', C and C', etc.), we must use some random procedure for determining whether A or A' is to go into the experimental group, whether B or B' is to go into that group, etc.

One further point should be emphasized: If one is experimenting with social groups that have some psychological unity, if the interest is in a functioning collective (a club, a factory, a class) rather than in the separate individuals, it is appropriate to match group with group rather than individual with individual. The interactions of the individuals, their attitudes toward one another, their complementary skills and interests—all of these require that, if groups are the object of study, groups rather than individuals be matched (see Deutsch, 1949).

[9] For a detailed discussion, see Edwards (1950, Chapter 14.)

Frequency distribution control is an attempt to reap some of the advantages of matching without paying the price of losing as many cases as one usually does in precision control. As the name implies, frequency distribution control attempts to match an experimental and a control group in terms of the over-all distribution of a given factor or factors within the two groups rather than individual by individual. For example, if age were considered relevant to the effects being studied, one would attempt to see that the *average* ages in the two groups were alike and that the *distributions* of ages in the two groups were similar. For each of the other factors considered relevant, one would try to equate the distributions in the two groups. It may be necessary to eliminate cases to equate the distributions, but compared to the method of matching individual by individual, relatively few cases are lost.

Matching by distribution rather than by precision control has a potential disadvantage of some importance. Although distributions on single factors are equated, the groups may actually be badly mismatched on combinations of these factors. Suppose, for example, that we were matching two groups in terms of income and age. Despite the fact that the distributions of income and of age separately were equated in the two groups, it would be possible to have in one group young people with high income and older people with low income and in the other group just the opposite combination.

Two other points must be noted in considering whether matching by frequency distribution has in fact yielded equated groups. First, one should not assume that the distributions in two groups are similar simply because their averages are similar. This may not be the case; one group may range widely about the average, the other may have a narrow range of variation. These differences will, of course, affect research results. In addition to the average, other statistical measures (such as the standard deviation, skewness, kurtosis—see Chapter 11, pages 412–413) which provide an indication of the nature of the distribution of cases are relevant to the equating of distributions. Second, even though a statistical test indicates that the two distributions do not differ significantly (i.e., that the two samples could have been drawn from the same population), one is not necessarily justified in concluding that they are equivalent. It is a logical fallacy to assume that if you have not conclusively demonstrated things to be unequal, you have demonstrated them to be equal. The differences between the two groups should be as small as it is possible to make them with the available resources. Again, it should be remembered that, ideally, randomization should always be used to equate the unmatched factors whenever precision or frequency distribution control is employed.

Types of Experimental Design

If one wishes to test the hypothesis that X is a cause of Y, by comparing a group that has been exposed to X with one that has not, it is obviously essential to measure the two groups with respect to Y either during or after exposure to X. Sometimes it is desirable or even essential to have, in addition, measures of their position with respect to Y before they have been exposed to X. The time at which the dependent variable is measured provides a basis for classifying experiments in two main groupings: "after-only" and "before-after." The pattern of control groups used provides a basis for further subdivision.

"AFTER-ONLY" EXPERIMENTS. In studies of this type, as the name implies, the experimental and the control groups are observed or measured with respect to the dependent variable (Y) only during or after the exposure of the experimental group to the assumed causal variable (X).[10] As in all experimental designs involving control groups, the experimental and the control groups are selected before the introduc-

---

[10] Usually the "control group" is exposed only to the "absence of X" rather than to some contrasting variable, X', whose influence is to be compared with X. However, it is possible to expose the "control group" to X' and thus to have it constitute a second experimental group. In such a case, it is sometimes feasible to use only one group of subjects, who "serve as their own controls." For example, in testing the hypothesis that people will tend to remember unfinished tasks better than finished tasks, one group of subjects might be allowed to finish all their tasks and another group might be prevented from finishing all their tasks. Here, one would be using two groups of subjects—one of which is exposed to X ("finished tasks"), another to X' ("unfinished tasks"). It is possible to test the same hypothesis using one group of subjects, all of whom would be exposed to both X and X', that is, they would be allowed to finish some tasks and not others. In doing so, it is necessary to consider carefully the sequence of finished and unfinished tasks, in order to avoid complications which might arise from such factors as a tendency to remember the first task, or the last task, etc.

tion of the experimental variable (X), and the variable is introduced either specifically for the purpose of the experiment or at a specified time and in a specified manner known in advance to the experimenter. As discussed in the preceding section, subjects are randomly assigned to the two groups, with or without supplementary matching procedures.[11] If one of the matching techniques is used, the matching is in terms of characteristics other than initial position on the assumed dependent variable (Y), since this is not measured before the experimental treatment. The two groups are observed or measured with respect to Y only *during* or *after* the exposure of the experimental group to the assumed causal variable, X. Column 1 of the table on page 110 shows a schematic representation of this type of study.

In this design, one concludes that the hypothesis is or is not tenable simply by comparing the occurrence of Y (or its extent, or its nature, etc.) in the experimental group after exposure to variable X, with the occurrence (etc.) of Y in the control group, which has not been exposed to X. Thus, in Column 1, we would compare Y_2 with Y'_2. Clearly, this provides evidence as to whether X and Y vary together.

What about evidence that Y did not precede X in time? This is inferred from the method used in setting up the two groups. If they were randomly selected, probability theory tells us to what extent they might have been expected to differ by chance in terms of their position on Y before the introduction of the experimental treatment, and the test of significance takes account of such chance differences. If, in addition, they have been matched in terms of some variable or variables that are related to position on Y, the probable initial differences on Y will be even less than might otherwise have been expected by chance. The randomization procedures used in setting up the groups (whether or not they are supplemented by matching) also provide a basis for concluding that differences between the groups in other past factors or relatively enduring characteristics that might influence their position on Y after the experimental treatment are no

[11] Studies in which groups that have not been randomly selected are exposed to different conditions and then compared do not, strictly speaking, constitute experiments. Such studies are discussed later in this chapter.

TYPES OF EXPERIMENTAL DESIGN

Condition	1 "After-only" — Experimental group	1 "After-only" — Control group	2 "Before-after" with single group — Experimental group	3 "Before-after" with interchangeable groups — Experimental group	3 "Before-after" with interchangeable groups — Control group	4 "Before-after" with one control group — Experimental group	4 "Before-after" with one control group — Control group
Prior selection of groups	Yes	Yes	Yes	Yes	Yes	Yes	Yes
"Before" measurement	No	No	Yes (Y_1)	No	Yes (Y'_1)	Yes (Y_1)	Yes (Y'_1)
Exposure to experimental variables	Yes	No	Yes	Yes	Perhaps	Yes	No
Exposure to uncontrolled events	Yes	Yes	Yes	Yes	Yes	Yes	Yes
"After" measurement	Yes (Y_2)	Yes (Y'_2)	Yes (Y_2)	Yes (Y_2)	No	Yes (Y_2)	Yes (Y'_2)
Change	$d = Y_2 - Y'_2$		$d = Y_2 - Y_1$	$d = Y_2 - Y'_1$		$d = Y_2 - Y_1$	$d' = Y'_2 - Y'_1$

Condition	5 "Before-after" with two control groups — Experimental group	5 — Control group I	5 — Control group II	6 "Before-after" with three control groups — Experimental group	6 — Control group I	6 — Control group II	6 — Control group III
Prior selection of groups	Yes	Yes	Yes	Yes	Yes	Yes	Yes
"Before" measurement	Yes (Y_1)	Yes (Y'_1)	No ($Y''_1 = \dfrac{Y_1 + Y'_1}{2}$)	Yes (Y_1)	Yes (Y'_1)	No ($Y''_1 = \dfrac{Y_1 + Y'_1}{2}$)	No ($Y'''_1 = \dfrac{Y_1 + Y'_1}{2}$)
Exposure to experimental variables	Yes	No	Yes	Yes	No	Yes	No
Exposure to uncontrolled events	Yes	Yes	Yes	Yes	Yes	Yes	No
"After" measurement	Yes (Y_2)	Yes (Y'_2)	Yes (Y''_2)	Yes (Y_2)	Yes (Y'_2)	Yes (Y''_2)	Yes (Y'''_2)

greater than the chance differences taken account of by the test of significance.

Although this design shares a problem of all social research, that the measurement procedures used may alter the characteristic they are intended to measure, the problem is less serious here than in "before-after" studies. (The difficulties introduced by measurements made before exposure to the experimental variable will be discussed later, in connection with "before-after" designs.)

What about the effects of other contemporaneous events or maturation? The assumption is made that both groups are exposed to the same external events and undergo similar maturational processes between the time of selection and the time at which Y is measured. If this assumption is justified, the position of the control group on the dependent variable (Y'_2) at the close of the experiment includes the influence of the external events and maturational processes that have affected both groups. Thus the difference (d) between Y_2 and Y'_2 may be taken as an indication of the effect of the experimental treatment, provided that neither external events nor maturational processes interact with the experimental variable to change its effects. (The possibility of interaction between the experimental variable and other factors will be discussed later.)

The "after-only" design may be illustrated by a study of the effects of a film, The Battle of Britain, carried out by the Experimental Section of the Research Branch in the War Department's Information and Education Division (Hovland, Lumsdaine, and Sheffield, 1949). In this study, the experimental group was shown the film, the control group was not. In assigning men to the two groups, random selection of individuals did not seem feasible, since this would have required pulling specified men out of their regular units to see the film. Such an unusual procedure would not only have made for administrative difficulties but would presumably have raised questions in the men's minds about the purpose of the operation. Therefore selection of cases for the sample was on the basis of company units rather than individuals. In view of evidence that companies differed in certain ways, two groups of companies were set up which were comparable in characteristics such as average score on the Army General Classification Test, education, age, region of birth, stage of training, etc. Randomization took the form of tossing a coin to decide which of the matched groups should see the film, which should not. [12]

The experimental group was shown the film during their weekly orientation hour, as part of the regular training procedure. The control group did not see the film. Approximately a week later, the men in both groups were asked to fill out a questionnaire as part of a War Department survey "to find out how a cross-section of soldiers felt about various subjects connected with the war." Mixed in with "camouflage" items were a number of factual and opinion items that might have been expected to be influenced by the film but were not so specifically related to it as to suggest a connection between the "survey" and the film. The measure of the effects of the film was the difference (in excess of chance difference) between the proportion of the experimental and the control groups who responded to each of the relevant items in a given way.

"BEFORE-AFTER" EXPERIMENTS. In addition to the measures of Y *after* exposure to the experimental variable, an investigator may wish to have measures of Y *before* such exposure, for a variety of reasons:

1. As discussed in the section on selecting experimental and control groups, he may wish to increase the sensitivity of his experiment by matching cases in terms of their initial position on the dependent variable. As pointed out in that section, such matching should be accompanied by procedures of random assignment.

2. He may want to check whether there is "room" for the experimental variable to have an effect. For example, suppose one were studying the effectiveness of an advertising campaign to induce women to use perfume. If, by chance, one selected an experimental and a control group of women such that 100 per cent of them were already using perfume before the onset of the advertising campaign, it would

[12] This procedure of establishing two matched groups and making use of randomization only to determine which one should be exposed to the experimental treatment is, of course, a rather marked departure from the recommended procedure of deciding on a random basis which individual or which unit of each matched pair should be assigned to the experimental group. Strictly speaking, an estimate of the probable chance differences between the two groups which is arrived at on the assumption that *individuals* have been randomly assigned does not provide an appropriate estimate of the probable chance differences between two groups set up in this way. This fact was recognized by the investigators. The study illustrates the point that realistic requirements sometimes necessitate compromises with ideal procedures.

be impossible to determine the effectiveness of the advertising, since a "ceiling effect" would be operating. A "before" measure makes it possible to determine the possibility for change in the dependent variable and to take it into consideration in evaluating the effects of the experimental variable.[13]

3. The hypothesis with which the study is concerned may specify initial position on the dependent variable as one of the determining conditions, or as one of the conditions on which the effect of some other variable is contingent. For example, the hypothesis may state that a film carrying a message of interracial friendliness will have a greater effect on persons who are already neutral or favorable toward Negroes than on those who are prejudiced. In such a case, an initial measure of prejudice, as well as another measure after the film, is obviously required by the hypothesis.

4. Even though the major hypothesis of the study does not refer to initial position on the dependent variable, the investigator may wish to analyze the data in such a way as to see whether the experimental treatment has different effects on persons who were initially at different positions on the dependent variable. If he is to do this, he must of course have a measure of position on the dependent variable before subjects are exposed to the experimental treatment.

5. In the event that he has not been able to assign subjects on a completely random basis to the different conditions, he may wish to check their initial comparability. As pointed out earlier, failure to assign subjects to experimental and control conditions on a completely random basis is a departure from the requirements of an ideal experiment, but compromises in this respect are sometimes necessary, especially in studies carried out in real-life settings. In such cases, evidence from a "before" measure that the experimental and the control groups were initially equated on the dependent variable helps to increase confidence that a difference on the "after" measure is due to the effects of the experimental variable. However, in the absence of randomization, the possibility remains that the two groups may have differed in other characteristics or past experiences that may interact with the experimental variable to lead to final differences on the dependent

[13] See Hovland, Lumsdaine, and Sheffield (1949) for a discussion of the problem of "ceiling effects" and proposed solutions.

variable. Thus evidence that the two groups were initially comparable in their position on the dependent variable is only a partial substitute for random assignment.

Studies using "before" as well as "after" measures of position on the dependent variable may follow various arrangements with respect to control groups. (1) Only one group may be used in the study, with the "before" measure serving as a "control" in the sense that it is assumed to represent the level of the dependent variable in the absence of the experimental treatment. (2) The "before" measure may be taken on one group and the "after" measure on a different but presumably equivalent group. (3) "Before" and "after" measures may be taken both on the experimental group and on one control group. (4) There may be two or more control groups. These four patterns will be discussed below.

Whatever the pattern of control groups, the "before-after" experiment, like the "after-only," provides evidence of concomitant variation between the independent and the dependent variables by comparing the occurrence (or the extent, or the increase) of Y in the group that has been exposed to X with the occurrence (etc.) of Y in the group that has not been exposed to X. That Y did not occur before X is inferred from the assurance provided by randomization that the groups are not likely to have differed initially in their position on Y by more than the specified chance amount taken account of in the test of significance. This initial equivalence with respect to Y may be checked by comparison of the "before" measures of the two groups. In the event that random assignment has not been possible, the "before" measures still provide evidence of whether there were differences in Y that preceded differences in X. But if random assignment has not been possible, there is no basis for ruling out the possibility that there were greater-than-chance differences on other factors that might account for a difference in position on Y after exposure to the experimental treatment.

The variations in control group arrangements are concerned with attempts to take account of contemporaneous events, maturational processes, and the effects of the initial measurement. Although the measuring process itself may affect the characteristic being measured in any type of social research, the "before-after" design is especially subject to this difficulty. For example, the attempt to measure the subjects' attitudes before the experiment begins may crystallize the attitudes; it may exhaust the good will of the subjects; etc. The second, or "after," measurement may introduce other problems: the subject may be bored and therefore unwilling to respond; he may try to give responses that are consistent with his previous responses (thus minimizing the apparent change); or he may try to make his responses "interesting" by varying them from one interview to the next (thus increasing the apparent change). The process of repeated measurement may also affect the "measuring instrument"; for example, in the course of repeated measurements, an observer may become bored, fatigued, more sensitive or less sensitive to the phenomena he is recording.

The different control group arrangements differ in the extent of protection they offer against mistakenly attributing to the independent variable differences on the dependent variable that may really be due to other contemporaneous events, to maturation, or to the effects of the initial measurement

The "before-after" study with a single group. Barker, Dembo, and Lewin (1941), in their study of the effects of frustration on young children's play, used a "before-after" design without a control group. Each child was taken into a room where there were simple toys with which he was allowed to play for half an hour; during this time his play was rated by an observer on a scale of "constructiveness." Next a partition was raised; in the part of the room now exposed was an elaborate and attractive set of toys. When the child had become thoroughly involved in playing with these, the experimenter took him by the hand, led him back to the part of the room in which he had been playing earlier, and locked the new toys behind a wire-net partition through which the child could still see them. The child's play with the original toys was again rated for constructiveness during a half-hour period. The difference in ratings of constructiveness of play during the "pre-frustration" and "post-frustration" periods was taken as evidence of the amount of regression induced by the frustrating experience. (At the end of the experiment, the child was allowed to play as long as he wished with the more attractive toys, in order to undo the frustrating effects of the experiment).

In this design, each subject "serves as his own control." The difference between his position on the dependent variable before and after exposure to the independent variable is taken as a measure of the effect of the independent variable. (See Column 2 of table on page 110). But other influences may have operated between the "before" and "after" measures. External events unrelated to the experimental treatment may lead to a change in position on the dependent variable; so may processes of growth and development. The initial measurement itself (in this case, the period of play on which the initial rating was made) may lead to changes. This design does not make it possible to separate such effects from those of the experimental treatment. Thus its use is justified only when one has good reason to believe (as did Barker, Dembo, and Lewin): (1) that the "before" measure itself will not in some way affect either the response to the experimental treatment or the "after" measure; and (2) that there are not likely to be any other influences, besides the experimental treatment, during the course of the study that might affect the subjects' response at the time of the second measurement. In order to be reasonably sure that such assumptions are justified, one must have considerable knowledge of the probable effects of his measurements and of the conditions other than the experimental treatment that are likely to influence the dependent variable. This may be true of many problems in such fields as learning and sensory perception, where much experimental work has been done; it is much less likely to be so, at the present time, in social psychology and sociology.

The "before-after" study with interchangeable groups.[14] One approach to ruling out the effects of the initial measurement is to measure one group before the introduction of the experimental factor, a different group after exposure to the experimental factor. The two groups are selected in advance from the population that is to be exposed to the experimental variable; as in other designs, random selection provides assurance that the groups probably did not differ by more than a specifiable amount before introduction of the experimental variable, and thus that they may be treated as interchangeable. Again, matching may be used to supplement randomization. The difference

---

[14] In the earlier edition of this book, this was called the "simulated before-after" design. D. T. Campbell, in a forthcoming paper ("Quasi Experimental Designs for Use in Social Science Settings"), refers to it as the "offset before and after" design.

between the "before" measure taken on the first group (Y'_1) and the "after" measure taken on the second group (Y_2) is assumed to be a measure of the effect of the experimental factor. (See Column 3 of the table on page 110).

This design was used in a study of a publicity campaign about the United Nations in the city of Cincinnati (Star and Hughes, 1950). Two equivalent samples, of a thousand persons each, were drawn from the city's population. One was interviewed before the start of the publicity campaign, the other two months later. To determine the effectiveness of the campaign, the responses of the two groups were compared. As it turned out, there was very little difference between them.

The "before-after" study with interchangeable groups eliminates the possibility of confounding an effect of the initial measurement with that of the experimental variable. Suppose the same group of respondents had been interviewed before and after the campaign. The initial interview might have aroused their interest in the United Nations and thus made them especially sensitive to the publicity campaign. If this were true, a simple "before-after" study, in which the difference between the "before" and "after" responses of a single reinterviewed group was taken as the measure of the effect of the experimental variable (the publicity campaign), would have been misleading.

On the other hand, the "before-after" study with interchangeable groups provides no protection against the effect of other events that may occur between the two measurements. Suppose a difference had been found between the "before" response of the one group and the "after" response of the other; suppose also that world events in which the U.N. played a prominent role had occurred between the two measures. This design would give no way of determining whether the change in response was due to the publicity campaign, to the world events, or to a combination of the two.

The "before-after" study with one control group. In an attempt to take account of the effects both of the initial measurement and of contemporaneous factors, a control group is frequently included in the "before-after" design. This design is shown in Column 4 of the table on page 110. In such a study, both the experimental and the control group are measured at the beginning and at the end of the experimental period. The experimental variable, of course, is introduced in the experimental group only. Since the control group as well as the experimental group is subjected both to the initial measurement and to the contemporaneous influences, the difference between the scores of the two groups should constitute a measure of the effectiveness of the experimental variable alone. For this purpose, either the final scores of the two groups (Y_2 and Y'_2), or their change scores (d and d'), may be compared.

Another study of the effects of the *Battle of Britain* film, parallel to the "after-only" study described on pages 111–112, provides an example of a "before-after" study with one control group. In a different camp, the effects of the film were tested by this design. The procedure was the same as that already described, except that about two weeks before the film was shown to the experimental group, members of both groups were asked to fill out the questionnaire as part of " a survey." Then the film was shown to the experimental group in the course of its regular training procedures; it was not, of course, shown to the control group. About a week after the showing of the film, the men in both groups were again asked to fill out a questionnaire, which repeated the essential items of the "before" measure, but which was presented as a "revised" version of the survey instrument that had been changed on the basis of the earlier administration. To support this explanation, the format had been changed, and some "camouflage" items omitted while others were added. The differences between the "after" replies of the experimental and the control groups were taken as the measure of the effects of the film.

If the "before" measure and the events other than the experimental treatment affect experimental and control groups in the same way, a "before-after" design with one control group provides adequate safeguards against attributing to the experimental variable a difference on the "after" measure that is really due either to the effects of initial measurement or to contemporaneous events. However, it may happen that either the initial measurement or external events *interact* with the experimental variable in such a way that its effect is changed. For example, comparison of the two *Battle of Britain* studies showed an interaction between the initial measurement and the experimental variable; there was less difference between the "after" replies of the experimental and the control groups in the "before-after" than in the "after-only" study. The investigators suggested that an effort to be consistent in replies to the two versions of the survey questionnaire might have lessened the changes in opinion that might otherwise have been produced by the film, or that the explicit taking of one position or another on the first questionnaire might have tended to crystallize views that would otherwise have been more fluid.

When there is such an interaction between the initial measure or contemporaneous events and the experimental variable, a "before-after" study with one control group does not provide a firm basis for inferences about the effect of the experimental variable, since this design does not provide any way of discovering the interaction and thus separating out the effect of the experimental variable alone. Solomon (1949) devised more elaborate designs that make it possible to take account of such interactions. They involve the use of additional control groups.

The "before-after" study with two control groups. This design, shown in Column 5 of the table, makes it possible to separate the influence of the experimental variable from that of the initial measurement, even if there is interaction between them. It involves adding a second control group, which is *not* pre-measured but which *is* exposed to the experimental variable and to an "after" measurement. As in the "before-after" design with one control group, the first control group is given the "before" measure and the "after" measure, but is not exposed to the experimental treatment. The three groups (the experimental and the two control) should, of course, be selected in such a way that they differ only by chance at the beginning of the experiment. As in other experimental designs, this means that they should have been constituted by random assignment or by some matching procedure supplemented by randomization. If this has been done, we may assume that the pre-measure for control group II would have been similar to the other pretest scores; i.e., the average initial score for the experimental group and control group I. This inferred initial score for control group II is indicated by Y''_1 in Column 5. This produces a group with both a "before" (assumed) and an "after" measure, which has received the experimental treatment but in which there is no possibility of interaction between experimental treatment and effects of the "before" measure.

It may be noted that the treatment of the second control group in this design (no pre-measure, but exposure to the experimental variable, and a post-measure) is the same as the treatment of the experimental group in the "after-only" design and of the group that is measured only after exposure to the experimental variable in the "before-after" design with interchangeable groups. The two-control-group design, however, not only provides a group in which there is no possibility of interaction between the pre-measure and the experimental treatment, but also gives a measure of the extent of that interaction, through comparison of the experimental group and the two control groups.

If one has reason to believe that contemporaneous events and developmental processes are not likely to be important influences in a given study, the "before-after" design with two-control groups may be interpreted as follows: (1) the change of control group II (d'') is due to the experimental variable alone; (2) the change of control group I (d') is due to the effects of the pre-measurement alone; (3) if the change score of the experimental group (d) is different from the sum of the change scores of the two control groups ($d' + d''$), this is a reflection of *interaction* between the pre-measure and the experimental variable. Such interaction may either enhance or reduce the effects of the experimental variable.

Although it is generally recognized that Solomon's solution is a sound one, his design has not often been used. However, a few studies in which it has been employed have suggested that interaction effects are frequently large enough to have marked effects on experimental results. For example, Canter (1951) used this three-group design in a study of the effectiveness of a human relations training course for supervisors. The members of the experimental group were given various tests of information and opinion before the training course, took the course, and were then again given the questionnaires. The first control group was given the tests at the same times as the experimental group (that is, before and after the training program), but was not given the training program. The second control group was not pre-measured, but was given the training program and the "after" measurements. Comparing the changes in scores of the three groups, Canter found that each of the tests in the pre-measure interacted in some way with the experimental variable: some of the initial tests seemed to make the supervisors more receptive to relevant aspects of the training course; others seemed to make them less responsive.

The "before-after" study with three control groups. Solomon has suggested a still further elaboration of this design, to provide safeguards when contemporaneous events or developmental changes may be expected to influence experimental results. This involves the addition of a third control group, as shown in Column 6 of the table. Here again, all the groups should be selected in such a way that they differ only by chance. In this design, the experimental group and control group I are pre-measured. Control groups II and III are not pre-measured; it is assumed that their pre-measure scores would be the same as the average of the combined scores of the experimental group and control group I. The experimental variable is introduced in the experimental group and in control group II; it is absent in control groups I and III. All four groups are assumed to be equally exposed to contemporaneous events, and all four are measured after the experiment.

In such a design, the change in control group III (that is, the difference between the post-measure and the inferred pre-measure) represents the effect of contemporaneous events or of developmental processes, since neither the pre-measure nor the experimental variable was present in this group. The change in control group II represents the effects of the experimental variable and of contemporaneous events or developmental processes; change in control group I, the effects of the pre-measurement and of contemporaneous events or developmental processes. The effect of the experimental factor alone can be determined by subtracting the change in control group III (the result of contemporaneous events and maturational processes) from the change in control group II (the result of contemporaneous events, maturational processes, and the experimental variable). The extent to which the change in the experimental group reflects the effects of the pre-measure, of the experimental variable, of uncontrolled events, or of interaction between the factors can be determined by comparison of the change in this group with those in the other groups.

It may be observed that this four-group design amounts to doing the experiment twice, once with a "before-after" design with one control group (experimental group and control group I), and once with an "after-only" design (control groups II and III). If the results of these two experiments are consistent, we have greater assurance that the outcome is not an artifact than we would with either version alone, since we have replicated the finding within the study.

TESTING THE EFFECTS OF TWO OR MORE EXPERIMENTAL TREATMENTS

All the examples we have considered so far involve the comparison of an experimental group subjected to a given treatment with a control group not subjected to that treatment. Some of them, as has been pointed out, provide for disentangling the effects of that treatment from the effects of initial measurement, of maturation, or of contemporaneous events. However, the designs as described so far are not adequate for testing hypotheses about the joint contribution of two or more independent variables in influencing a dependent variable, or for comparing the effects of two or more experimental treatments with no experimental treatment. For example, they can provide an answer to such a question as: Does a publicity campaign about the United Nations change attitudes toward that organization? But in their simple form, they do not efficiently provide answers to such questions as: Which are most effective in changing attitudes—lectures, movies, television programs, or group discussions? or, Is a publicity campaign most likely to change the attitudes of persons who were initially unfavorable, initially neutral, or initially favorable? However, each of the basic designs can be adapted to answer such questions efficiently if the experiment is planned in such a way as to permit an *analysis of variance*.

Let us suppose that we are interested in finding out which of three techniques in answering bigoted remarks is most effective in influencing bystanders: (1) an appeal to intelligence, calling prejudice a display of ignorance and stupidity; (2) an appeal to "fair play" and democratic tradition; (3) an appeal to the notion of individual differences—i.e., that there are "good and bad" individuals in all groups. We may decide to include also a situation in which no answer is made; this is equivalent to adding a control group. Although it is possible to dispense with control groups in some comparative experiments, since the groups being contrasted can be considered as "controls" for each other, this procedure is not recommended. The use of control groups in comparative experiments establishes a base line against which it is possible to assess the various methods being studied. For example, a comparison of two advertising techniques may reveal that one produces more sales than the other. This "fact" might take on entirely new significance if it were found that a control group not subjected to advertising buys more than either of the two experimental groups.

Going back to the answers to bigoted remarks, let us further suppose that we suspect that each of the techniques of answering may have different results under different circumstances; for example, one answer may be best when the answerer reacts in a highly indignant and emotional manner, another when his manner is calm and dignified.

Eight groups of people are needed for the experiment. The members of the pool of subjects are randomly assigned to the eight groups. Each group is shown a scene in which a bigoted remark is made, but the answer presented before each group involves a different

Group	Content of Answer	Manner of Answer
1	Intelligence	Indignant
2	Intelligence	Calm, dignified
3	Fair play	Indignant
4	Fair play	Calm, dignified
5	Individual differences	Indignant
6	Individual differences	Calm, dignified
7	No answer	Angry turning away with an expression of disgust
8	No answer	Acting as if nothing has been said

combination of "content" and "manner," as shown in the preceding table (p. 123). Suppose that we use an attitude scale to measure the response of the audience. If the study is set up as an "after-only" experiment, the differences among the groups in scores on this one administration of the scale will be used as a measure of the effects of the experimental variables. If it is set up as a "before-after" experiment, the effect of the experimental variables may be evaluated by comparing either the final scores of the different groups or the differences in extent of change between "before" and "after" measures.

With such a design, one can answer a number of research questions in a single study by comparing different groupings of subjects. In order to measure the relative effectiveness of appealing to intelligence, to fair play, or to the concept of individual differences, or of saying nothing at all, one computes the average score of subjects in groups 1 and 2 (intelligence), in groups 3 and 4 (fair play), in groups 5 and 6 (individual differences), etc., and compares them. Similarly, to measure the relative effectiveness of answers made with different manners, the average score of individuals in groups 1, 3, 5, and 7 (indignant manner) is compared with that of individuals in groups 2, 4, 6, and 8 (calm manner). In order to determine whether the effectiveness of the various contents is influenced by the manner in which they are delivered, one compares the scores of the eight separate groups. If the differences among them are greater than can be accounted for by the differences in content and in manner considered separately, one concludes that the effectiveness of the various contents is influenced by the manner of delivery. For example, it may be found that the "fair play" argument is especially effective when made in a calm manner, the "intelligence" argument in an indignant manner. The statistical technique which makes possible the investigation of these three questions in a single study is known as an *analysis of variance*.[15]

It is apparent that a design which permits an analysis of variance makes possible a study of complex interrelationships. It also results in an efficient design; that is, it permits more reliable conclusions about

[15] Designs of this type and the statistical techniques for their analysis were developed by R. A. Fisher and are discussed in his book, *The Design of Experiments* (1951). Simpler discussions may be found in Cochran and Cox (1957), Edwards (1950), Lindquist (1953), and other statistical texts.

more hypotheses with fewer cases than if the hypotheses were tested in separate studies.

REPRESENTATIVE DESIGN

A radical criticism of the types of experimental design that we have described in this chapter has been advanced by Brunswik (1956). He expresses the view that the classical experimental designs have the unwitting consequence of artificially "untying" or "tying together" variables in a manner that is not representative of the way they exist in reality. Thus, he points out (Brunswik, 1955), classical experimental designs in medicine have sometimes led to harmful practices. For example, the research which demonstrated that boiling of liquids would destroy bacteria led to the practice of boiling milk to make it germ-free. Boiling of milk, however, not only destroys bacteria but also results in a vitamin loss. Brunswik's thesis here is that the usual systematic experimental design, which attempts to relate an independent variable with a dependent variable, throws the picture of the interplay of factors out of balance: the connection between the boiling of milk and its devitaminization is ignored if the study focuses only on the connection between boiling and antisepsis.

Similarly, in the social sciences one could cite investigations in which different kinds of leadership style, or different types of visual display, etc., have been studied in highly controlled laboratory experiments with considerable precaution to keep other variables constant. Brunswik's criticism of these experiments would be that leadership style, or a given type of visual display, or any other variable one might wish to study, occurs in a variety of contexts; and that to understand, for example, the relationship between "permissive leadership" and "membership participation in group affairs," one must study a representative sample of situations in which leadership occurs. There may be many different ways in which the effect of a high degree of membership participation may be achieved. Permissiveness may produce it in one context (e.g., with a highly motivated and intelligent membership) and fail to produce it in another context; authoritarian leadership may be effective or ineffective in differing circumstances.

Brunswik, in effect, calls for a survey type of research design in which a representative sampling of situations is made. This type of design means that the variables being studied can be investigated in the context of the naturally occurring concomitant variation of other factors. The use of this design entails the abandonment of customary notions of experimental control; we must take the interaction among variables as we find it in the situations included in the sample. The essential tools of analysis are partial and multiple correlational procedures. The fruitfulness of Brunswik's proposed methodology has been demonstrated in perceptual experiments (Brunswik, 1956) and in some investigations in clinical psychology (Hammond, 1955).

Brunswik's criticisms of systematic experimental design have the salutary effect of highlighting some of the misinterpretations and faulty overgeneralizations that are commonly made from traditional experiments. Further, he has stressed the need for an adequate sampling of experimental conditions and situations as well as an adequate sampling of people, if appropriate interpretations and generalizations are to be made. However, there are limitations in his methodology, which become apparent when we attempt to answer some of the questions necessary to the fulfillment of a "representative design." For example, if one wanted to study the conditions that lead to "active membership participation in group affairs," one would have to compile a complete list of group situations in which membership participation may occur and study a representative sample of this universe, taking measurements of all relevant variables in each situation that appeared in the sample. The theoretical difficulties of compiling such a list and of identifying the variables relevant to membership participation, plus the practical difficulties of studying a representative sample of such group situations, are, of course, insuperable in any one investigation.

Practically speaking, the research investigator must always settle for less than an investigation of all of the relevant conditions of the phenomena he wishes to understand. Part of the art of experimental investigation lies in having a "feel" for one's subject matter, in being sensitive to the nature of the phenomena which one is investigating so that the significant dimensions are taken into consideration. Scientific research, as well as any other meaningful human activity, requires judgment. There are, of course, no guarantees that even well-tutored judgment will be correct or fruitful.

Causal Inference from Other Study Designs[16]

The investigator may not be in a position to test a hypothesis by assigning subjects to different conditions in which he directly controls the presumed causal variable. Consider, for example, the research that has been done on the relationship between cigarette smoking and lung cancer in humans. The extent of smoking has not been controlled, as it would be in an experimental study, by *assigning* different individuals to smoke different numbers of cigarettes; for many reasons, such an experiment is not likely to be performed on humans. Rather, a record (or a retrospective estimate) is secured of how much an individual has smoked, and of whether he has lung cancer; the relation between extent of smoking and occurrence of lung cancer is then computed.

But, as has been pointed out, the existence of a correlation between two variables does not necessarily demonstrate that one is a "cause" of the other. We must, therefore, at least consider the possibility that the kinds of people who become smokers are also, for some as yet unknown reason, the kinds of people who develop lung cancer. We might remember that, before smoking became common among college students, it was found that smokers made poorer grades than nonsmokers. Eventually it became clear that, at least in those days, the students who smoked were also the students who were especially likely to neglect their studies.

Whatever the form of a study, if it is to provide a test of a causal hypothesis, it must provide grounds for making inferences about causality and safeguards against unwarranted inferences. Nonexperimental studies cannot provide safeguards as adequate as those given by random assignment of subjects to experimental and control groups, direct manipulation of the experimental variable, and control over some of the extraneous variables that might operate during the course

---

[16] For a detailed and enlightening discussion of the testing of causal hypotheses by means of nonexperimental studies, see Hyman (1955, Part III). Our discussion of this subject is very much indebted to Hyman's presentation.

of the experiment. What substitute safeguards are available? For direct manipulation of the experimental variable, the investigator may substitute one or more of several lines of evidence: comparison of people who have been exposed to contrasting experiences, attempts to determine the time order of variables that are associated, examination of the relationship between variables in terms of the pattern of relationships that might be anticipated if one or the other were the causal factor. For assignment of subjects to experimental and control groups, the investigator may substitute evidence which provides a basis for inferring that groups of people who have undergone contrasting experiences were or were not similar before those experiences; or he may select from his total group subsamples matched in terms of certain characteristics but with contrasting experiences; or he may restrict his sample to persons with certain characteristics. For direct control over extraneous variables, either past or contemporaneous, he substitutes the gathering of data on other characteristics or experiences of his subjects which he believes may be relevant to position on the dependent variable, and makes use of these data in his analysis. This latter operation will be discussed in Chapter 11. Various procedures intended as substitutes for direct manipulation of the assumed causal variable and for random assignment of subjects to experimental and control groups will be discussed in the remainder of this chapter.

SUBSTITUTES FOR DIRECT MANIPULATION OF THE ASSUMED CAUSAL VARIABLE

COMPARISON OF GROUPS EXPOSED TO CONTRASTING EXPERIENCES. If an investigator is not in a position to assign subjects to different groups, one of which will be exposed to a given treatment and one of which will not, an obvious substitute solution is to locate groups of people who are about to be, or have been, exposed to experiences that differ with respect to the assumed causal variable in which he is interested. For example, Cook, Havel, and Christ (1957), in planning a study of the effects of a summer orientation program for foreign students in the United States, knew in advance what students were to attend the orientation centers, although they had no part in selecting them. They compiled from all available sources a list of foreign students who were to begin their formal studies in the United States at the same time as these "orientation" students, but without receiving the prior orientation. Students in both groups were similar in that they were coming to the United States under some form of grant or scholarship made available by the United States government. Starting with the list of students who were to attend the orientation centers, these investigators selected students from the comparable non-orientation list on the basis of frequency distribution control, roughly matching the two samples in terms of such characteristics as nationality, age, and field of study. Since the students were identified in advance, it was possible to secure initial measures early in their stay in the United States, and thus to check whether the two groups were initially similar in their position on the dependent variables. This study approximated a "before-after" experiment with one control group: the students attending the orientation centers represented the "experimental" group; those not attending the centers, the "control" group. However, there was an important limitation: the "experimental" group and the pool of subjects available for the "control" group were constituted on the basis of administrative considerations having to do with the type of scholarships they received, and they may therefore have differed from each other in some systematic way. In a "pure" experiment, the total group of students would have formed a pool from which individuals were randomly assigned (with or without supplementary matching procedures) to attend or not to attend an orientation center.

The investigator often is not in a position to know in advance, as Cook, Havel, and Christ did, which individuals will be exposed to a given experience and which will not. He may instead locate a group of people who have been exposed to the type of experience in which he is interested and a group, similar in other respects, who have not been exposed to such an experience; he compares the groups on an *ex post facto* basis. The Deutsch-Collins (1951) study of the attitudes of white tenants toward Negroes in public housing projects (described in Chapter 1) followed this procedure. The investigators selected housing projects that differed in the independent variable in which they were interested—occupancy pattern. Within these projects, they selected white housewives on a random basis. Thus they approximated an "experimental" group, which had been exposed to the experience of living with Negroes as neighbors in an unsegregated occupancy pattern, and a "control" group, which had not had this experience. By selecting as their "control" group residents of bi-racial housing projects within which whites and Negroes were segregated, rather than other residents of the city, they controlled certain extraneous variables, such as the socioeconomic level of the subjects and the experience of living in a housing project. Studies using this *ex post facto* pattern have an even more serious limitation than those resembling the foreign student study just described; not only are subjects not randomly assigned to the different conditions, but there is no possibility of prior measurement to check whether the two groups were initially similar in their position on the assumed dependent variable or in certain characteristics believed to be relevant to it. For this reason, such studies must provide for the collection of data from which it can be *inferred* whether the two groups were or were not initially similar. Kinds of evidence that may provide a basis for such inference are discussed later in the chapter.

EVIDENCE OF THE TIME ORDER OF VARIABLES. As we have said, one kind of information that may help to provide grounds for an inference that a specified variable (X) is the cause of another (Y) is evidence that Y did not occur before X. In some cases the temporal relationship of two variables is so clear that no supplementary evidence is needed. For example, if one finds that individuals born in different countries differ in their views on some political issue, there is no question as to which variable, nationality or political views, is prior in time. Often, however, the time relationship between two variables is not so clear. Even though one appears to be prior to the other, it may not actually be so. For example, in a study of the effect of childhood experiences on adult adjustment, an investigator may rely on his adult subjects' accounts of their childhood. Obviously, childhood experiences are prior, but the selection and interpretation of events may be colored by present mood, with the result that the apparently earlier variable, in the form in which it is measured, is really a reflection of the later variable. In other cases, there may be no basis at all—not even a deceptive one—for making a judgment of time relationships; this is likely to be the case, for example, when one is dealing with two attitudes that are related.

The investigator may introduce various procedures in an attempt to secure evidence of the time relationship between the occurrence of variables. Two such procedures—asking people about time relationships and gathering evidence over a period of time—are discussed in the following paragraphs.

Asking respondents about time relationships. The investigator may include in his questionnaire or interview questions about when certain things happened, or how the respondent felt about something before a certain event took place, or whether there have been any changes in his feelings. Thus, Deutsch and Collins asked such questions as: "Before you moved into [the project], how did you feel about coming to live here? . . . Since you've moved into [the project], have you come to like the idea of living in a project where there are colored and white families more, about the same, or less? . . . Can you remember what you thought colored people were like before you moved into the project? . . . How much have your ideas about colored people changed since you have lived in the project? . . . (If some change) In what ways have they changed?"

There is, of course, always the danger that replies to such questions may be inaccurate. People may not remember; their present attitudes may distort their recollections; etc. While it is not possible to check conclusively the accuracy of such retrospective reports, the investigator can sometimes devise indirect checks on the probability of distortion. For example, Deutsch and Collins compared the replies of respondents in the four projects they studied to the question about prior attitudes toward Negroes. Other questions in their interview showed striking differences between tenants of integrated and segregated projects in attitudes at the time of the study. If current attitudes were distorting recall, the investigators reasoned, this should lead to consistent differences between the tenants in the two types of project in their reports of the attitudes they had before moving in. As it turned out, although the two segregated projects were very similar in the proportion of tenants reporting favorable, neutral, and unfavorable attitudes toward Negroes before moving in, there was no such similarity between the two integrated projects. In one, more tenants than in the segregated projects reported initially favorable attitudes; but the other had the highest proportion reporting initially unfavorable attitudes. From the fact that the reports of tenants in the integrated and the segregated projects about their initial attitudes did not differ consistently, whereas their current expressions of attitude did, the investigators concluded that recall was not being systematically distorted by attitudes at the time of the study. Further, they found that women who were similar in education, religion, and political attitudes gave similar reports of their initial attitude toward Negroes, regardless of which project they lived in; this consistency was taken as further evidence against distortion of recall by present attitudes.

Gathering evidence through studies extended over time. In studies which are limited to a single interview or observation or other measurement of each respondent, and in which the investigator does not have supplementary information about individuals' experiences, there is little possibility of getting evidence about time sequences except by asking the respondent to recall when things happened. But in studies that focus on the same people over a period of time, the investigator may secure direct evidence of time relationships among variables. Such longitudinal studies may take the form of repeated observations of the same subjects, or repeated interviews with them,[17] or of different measurement procedures at different times.

Stouffer et al. (1949a) provide an example of a study using different kinds of data about the same subjects at different times. The investigators were interested in the relation between acceptance of the official value-system of the Army and promotion. Had they simply interviewed a cross-section of Army personnel and found that those of higher rank expressed attitudes and opinions more in line with official Army values, they would have had no grounds for inferring whether acceptance of the official value-system was conducive to promotion or whether being promoted increased acceptance of the system. To avoid this dilemma, they interviewed a group of newly inducted soldiers, using questions from which an index of "acceptance of Army value-system" could be constructed. Four months later, they examined the Army records of these same men, and found that a higher proportion of those who had expressed views in keeping with the Army's values had become privates first-class than of those who had not. Thus it was clear that conformity with the Army's value-

[17] For a detailed discussion of studies using repeated interviews with the same respondents ("panel studies"), see Rosenberg, Thielens, and Lazarsfeld (1951).

system was conducive to promotion. (It is, of course, entirely likely that the relationship between these two variables is a mutually reinforcing one; further research might well have shown that after promotion, views were even more in line with official Army position.)

SEARCH FOR PATTERNS OF RELATIONSHIP INFERRED FROM COMPETING CAUSAL ASSUMPTIONS. Sometimes one can infer which of two factors that vary together is the "causal" one on the ground that the two variables would show a certain pattern of association if X were the "cause," a different pattern if Y were the "cause." For example, it is sometimes reasonable to expect that if X were the cause, it would affect Y cumulatively—that is, that individuals who had been exposed to X for a longer time would show a higher degree of Y—but that this would not be so if Y were the causal factor.

Such an inference was central to the plan of a study by Newcomb (1943, 1947), which focused on the question of what kinds of people accept certain kinds of social change. One of the hypotheses of the study was that "values come to be values largely through the mediation of the groups with which an individual has direct contact." Studying students at Bennington College, Newcomb considered the college community as a group with which the students had direct contact, and attitude toward public affairs as a relevant value. This attitude was selected because the college was characterized by a high degree of concern with public affairs and a "liberal" attitude on controversial issues. The investigator reasoned that if group membership were indeed the causal variable, then those who had been exposed to the group atmosphere for longer periods should show attitudes more in keeping with those characteristic of the group (in this case, more liberal attitudes). If, on the other hand, it was the possession of liberal attitudes that led to attending the college, there would be less reason to expect an increase in liberalism with increased years of attendance.[18] Using a variety of measures, Newcomb found that length of exposure to the Bennington community, as indicated by college class, was accompanied by increased information about public issues and increased liberalism

[18] Again, of course, there is the possibility that attending the college might further have strengthened initial liberal attitudes, but presumably this would not have led to such marked differences between longer-exposed and shorter-exposed students as would be expected if college membership were the major causal factor.

of views. On all his measures, freshmen were most conservative, seniors least so.

Similarly, in an earlier study, Klineberg (1935a) reasoned that the comparatively low IQ's of Negroes in the South and in rural areas might be attributable to poor environments. This led him to expect that the IQ's of Negro children should increase with length of residence in a city such as New York. Investigations of twelve-year-old Negro children in New York City supported this expectation.

However, the fact that scores on Y differ with different lengths of exposure to X does not provide a clear-cut basis for an inference of causality. Not only may X and Y be mutually reinforcing, as we have noted. Other factors may be associated with differences in length of exposure to the independent variable, and it may be these other factors which account for differences in the dependent variable. For example, selective processes may be different at different times. In the Bennington illustration, it might have happened either that increased prestige of the college (which had been founded only a few years before the study) or a change in admissions policy led to a change in the type of students entering in different years, and this change, rather than the influence of the college atmosphere, might have accounted for the differences between freshmen and seniors. Similarly, it is conceivable that more intelligent Negroes might have migrated to New York City earlier, and that the higher IQ's of children who had been in New York longer reflected this characteristic of their parents.

A variety of checks for such possibilities have been used. One is repetition of the study at another time. Newcomb repeated his measures of attitudes of Bennington students for four consecutive years (1935–1939). Each year, he found that juniors and seniors were more liberal than those in lower classes; thus the inference was strengthened that it was the college experience rather than some other factor which accounted for the change in attitudes and information. Klineberg also used the repetition procedure, conducting parallel investigations in two successive years, 1931 and 1932. He reasoned:

> If the findings [of the 1931 study—that Negro children who have been in the North longer have higher IQ's] are due to a progressive deterioration in the quality of the migrants rather than to an environmental effect, the results obtained . . . in

1932 should be consistently *below* those obtained . . . in 1931. A specific example will make this reasoning clearer. The twelve-year-old boys in the 1931 study who have been in New York four years, for example, arrived in 1927; those in the 1932 study who have been in New York for a similar period arrived in 1928. If the migrants are becoming inferior as time goes on, the four-year group in the later study ought to be inferior to the corresponding group in the earlier one.

Comparison of the 1931 and 1932 results, however, showed, for each length-of-residence group, a slight but consistent superiority in the 1932 study. For example, the average IQ of students who had been in New York for three or four years in 1931 (that is, who had migrated in 1927 or 1928) was 66.86, while the average IQ of those who had been in New York for three or four years in 1932 (that is, who had migrated in 1928 or 1929) was 79.06. In other words, the differences, although slight, were consistently in favor of the more *recent* arrivals. Klineberg commented:

> This difference may be due to improvement in the schooling in the South; in any case there is no evidence that the more recent arrivals are inferior. The conclusion is therefore justified that the superior showing of those subjects who have had a longer period of residence is due to this longer residence, and not to any regular change in the quality of the migrants.

There are, of course, methods other than repetition of the study to determine whether other factors may be responsible for the differences found on the dependent variable. For example, Klineberg provided two other checks on the hypothesis that differences in the intelligence of Negroes who left the South at different times might account for differences in IQ related to length of residence in New York. He investigated reasons for migrating from the South, and found nothing in these reasons to support the hypothesis that factors leading to migration might be expected to correlate with intelligence. He also studied records of southern schools attended by Negro children, and found no systematic difference in the relative class standing of children who subsequently migrated and of those who did not. Both these lines of evidence suggested that, at least during the period covered by these interlocking investigations, intelligence was not a selective factor in Negro migration from the South.

Another factor that may be confounded with length of exposure to a variable is age. It is likely that those individuals who have been exposed to a given experience for a longer time are older, and it may be the difference in age rather than in exposure to the assumed causal variable which accounts for differences in the dependent variable. The solution here is to "control" for age—that is, to compare individuals of the same age who differ in length of exposure to the variable. Newcomb did not use this approach, presumably because of the slight age differences within a college population. In the Klineberg study, where all of the children were twelve years old, age was not a factor. However, in a study that covers a wide age range, this is an important point to check; and it is relatively easy to do so.

SUBSTITUTES FOR RANDOM ASSIGNMENT OF SUBJECTS TO EXPERIMENTAL AND CONTROL GROUPS

As we have pointed out, one of the ways in which the experimenter protects himself against fallacious inferences is by random selection of his experimental and control groups, with or without supplementary matching. Probability theory makes it possible to determine to what extent groups randomly selected from the same population are likely to differ by chance, either in initial position on the dependent variable or in characteristics or past history that might be expected to influence subsequent position on the dependent variable. Tests of statistical significance, which take into account the probability of chance differences, make it possible to say, with a specified degree of certainty, whether a difference between the two groups on the dependent variable after exposure of one of them to the experimental treatment is greater than would be expected by chance, and thus can legitimately be attributed to the effects of the experimental variable. The investigator using a nonexperimental design has a variety of substitute ways of trying to achieve this objective.

EVIDENCE OF INITIAL COMPARABILITY OF GROUPS. The investigator may gather data from which he can infer whether individuals who have undergone different experiences and who now show differences on the dependent variable were comparable *before* they were exposed to the experiences in question. Newcomb used this procedure, among others, in the study referred to earlier. He compared Bennington students with students at two other colleges which did not have the same general atmosphere of liberalism and of concern with public affairs. He found Bennington seniors markedly less conservative than those at the other two colleges. Before he could infer, however, that this difference resulted from differences in college atmosphere, he had to check on the possibility that students who attended Bennington might have been less conservative even before they entered college. Comparison of attitudes of freshmen at the three colleges served this function, and indicated that Bennington students at the beginning of their college life were only slightly less conservative than freshman at the other colleges; thus he could conclude that the groups of students had initially been quite similar.

Frequently it is impossible to obtain measures of individuals in the early stages of the experiences whose effects one wishes to determine. However, if enough is known about other factors likely to influence or at least to be associated with the dependent variable with which the investigator is concerned, he may be able to make tentative estimates of initial position on the dependent variable by gathering information about these related characteristics. This was one of the checks used by Wilner, Walkley, and Cook (1955) in their study of the attitudes of white tenants toward Negroes in public housing projects with different occupancy patterns. Earlier studies had indicated that such characteristics as education, general political ideology, religion, and previous experience with Negroes are related to attitudes toward Negroes. Accordingly, these investigators included questions on these matters in their interview. On the basis of the replies, they constructed for each respondent an estimate of her probable degree of favorable attitude toward Negroes at the time she moved into the project; they then compared tenants in integrated and segregated projects in terms of this estimate of initial attitude. Obviously, evidence of this sort is far from conclusive unless the customary correlation between the dependent variable and the characteristics on which the investigator has information is known to be sufficiently high for the purpose.

There is usually a possibility that people who have undergone different experiences chose them. Such self-selection almost certainly means that the groups being compared were not initially equivalent; they may have differed in ways that would strongly influence their position on the dependent variable. Therefore it is important, whenever possible, to check on the likelihood of self-selection. Thus, Wilner and his associates included among their checks evidence on this point: some from the tenants themselves, some from other sources. They asked white tenants whether, at the time they applied for admission to the projects where they were living, they knew that the projects also had Negro tenants. If an individual did not know that a project was biracial, there was little chance that his attitude toward Negroes would enter into his decision about moving in. From housing officials they obtained the following information: whether all housing projects in the community had the same racial occupancy pattern, thus reducing the opportunity for choice; records of refusals by white applicants of apartments next door to Negroes, or of moving out of such apartments; records of refusal and move-out rates in apartments not near a Negro family; etc.

Occasionally an investigator will be fortunate enough to find a situation in which there was no possibility of self-selection. For example, the Information and Education Division of the U. S. War Department (1947) found that white soldiers in units that had companies made up of white and Negro platoons were much more favorable toward having white and Negro platoons in the same company than were white soldiers in all-white units. Given the nature of military assignments, there was no possibility that white soldiers who were initially more favorable toward Negroes had placed themselves in mixed units.

COMPARISON OF MATCHED SUBGROUPS. Suppose that the evidence collected indicates that the groups which have undergone different experiences were not initially comparable. This was the case in the Deutsch-Collins (1951) study of attitudes of public housing tenants. These authors found that the residents of their integrated and segregated projects differed in religion, education, and political attitudes—characteristics which other studies had found to be related to attitudes toward Negroes. Moreover, the nature of the differences was such that the tenants in the integrated projects might be assumed to have been somewhat less prejudiced before moving into the projects than were those in the segregated ones. The authors state:

> . . . it is clear that in the analysis and presentation of our results it will be necessary to eliminate or control the effects of these population differences in order to attribute causal significance to the effects of the occupancy pattern.

To do this, they compared matched subgroups within the projects. For example, considering separately the politically liberal tenants interviewed, they examined the proportion within the integrated and the segregated projects who showed friendly feelings toward Negroes in the project. They found that 31 per cent and 72 per cent of the political liberals in the two integrated projects, as compared with 0 per cent and 17 per cent of the political liberals in the two segregated projects, were classified as having friendly feelings toward Negroes in their project. Separate examination of "middle-of-the-road" respondents, of conservatives, of those of different religions and different amounts of education, all showed the same results: among respondents matched in these other characteristics, those in integrated projects consistently showed more friendly feelings toward Negroes in the project.[19]

RESTRICTION OF THE SAMPLE. Rather than taking a heterogeneous sample and comparing matched subgroups within it, the investigator may ensure that his subjects are matched in certain respects by including in his sample only persons with certain characteristics. This procedure may be used in experimental studies also; there it is done usually for reasons of administrative convenience or to increase the sensitivity of the experiment by ruling out factors that might influence the dependent variable so strongly as to obscure the effects of the independent variable in which the investigator is interested (see pages 102–104). In nonexperimental studies, restriction of the sample has another function: disentangling of the independent variable in which the investigator is interested from other variables with which it is commonly associated, so that any effects that are found can justifiably be attributed to that variable. In experiments, of course, this separation is achieved

---

[19] Procedures used in analysis to compare such subgroups are discussed in Chapter 11.

by random assignment of cases to experimental and control groups and by control over some of the other contemporaneous variables.

For example, suppose we wish to investigate whether having a quiet place at home in which to study affects high school students' grades. Having a quiet place to study is likely to be part of a cluster of factors. Overcrowding is greater among low-income families; thus there is less possibility of quiet study space in their homes. At the same time, lower-class families are likely to put less emphasis on scholastic achievement than are the parents of middle- and upper-class children. Moreover, in lower-class homes there is likely to be less opportunity for children to gain the type of knowledge that would contribute to academic achievement. If one simply selects a cross-section of high school students, asks each of them whether or not he has a quiet place to study at home (or gets this information in some other way), and then compares the grades of those who have a quiet study place and those who do not, he may come to a quite misleading conclusion. The difference in grades may be due not to the difference in study arrangements but to the difference in emphasis on scholastic achievement, in opportunities for gaining scholastically relevant knowledge, or to some combination of all these factors associated with socioeconomic class.

If the problem were amenable to experimental investigation, the experimenter might select a cross-section of students and arrange for some of them (randomly selected) to have a quiet study place, others (also randomly selected, but perhaps also matched in socioeconomic status) not to. Lacking this possibility, the investigator may rule out the effects of class differences by limiting his study to students of only one socioeconomic level. He might study only lower-class children, or only middle-class ones, comparing the grades of those with and without quiet study arrangements. In thus limiting his sample, he would have disentangled his independent variable from certain class-linked variables with which it is usually associated. He would not, of course, have ruled out such complications as the possibility that within the lower class, or within the middle class, parents who are most concerned with academic success provide quiet study arrangements for their children. In other words, if he found a relationship between quiet study space and school grades within his restricted sample, he could feel confident that the differences in grades were not due to differences in socioeconomic status, though they might be due to some other factor or factors which he had not controlled.

A simple logical point is relevant here. The phrase "not due to differences in . . ." means, quite literally, "not due to *differences* in . . ." It does not mean that socioeconomic status plays no part in the observed relations. Thus, if his study included only lower-class children, a finding that children who had a quiet place to study received higher grades might hold only for that socioeconomic group; among middle-class children, it is possible that some other relationship, or no relationship, would be observed. The point is worth making because it is commonly, albeit incorrectly, assumed that holding certain variables constant in a study *eliminates* their effect. Consider, for instance, the following example: One member of a pair of identical twins is raised in an underprivileged socioeconomic environment, the other under much better circumstances. At the age of twelve, a difference of twenty IQ points is found between them. It is now asserted that, since their heredities were identical, the IQ difference is due to the difference in environment—and, by implication, that the common heredity had nothing to do with it. Yet it is conceivable that, if that common heredity had been different in some significant respect from what it actually was, the two children might have reacted differently than they actually did to their respective environments, and a different IQ difference, or even no difference, might have been found.

While this procedure of restricting the sample has the advantage of ruling out variations in other specified characteristics as contributory conditions of the observed variations in the dependent variable, it has the corresponding disadvantage of limiting the population to which the findings can be generalized. Thus, in our example of the relation between study space and school grades, if we limit the subjects to lower-class children attending public schools, any findings about the effect of study space on grades cannot with any confidence be presumed to hold for middle-class children, etc. In order to have confidence in the generalizability of the findings, the study must be repeated with groups of subjects who have other characteristics. This process of repetition with other groups has, of course, an additional function: it helps to specify the *contingent* conditions under which a relationship between two variables obtains.

USING A COMBINATION OF APPROACHES

Since none of these substitutes for experimental procedures provides as much protection as does random assignment of subjects to situations in which the investigator controls the application of the independent variable, it is always advisable to plan as many different approaches as possible to provide a basis for making inferences of causality. Most of the studies we have mentioned used several checks; we have not described them all. The subject matter of a study will often determine which checks are most relevant and most feasible.

Most of the devices for making possible causal inferences in non-experimental studies introduce specific requirements in the analysis of the data. Therefore a section of Chapter 11, which deals with analysis of data, is devoted to a discussion of analytic procedures useful when one wishes to draw inferences about causality from such studies.

Summary

In these two chapters we have been concerned with the requirements for research procedure posed by different kinds of research problems. We have stressed the fact that not even carefully controlled research will give knowledge with absolute certainty. Yet despite its limitations, scientific method, more than any other procedure known to man, can minimize misinformation. The skepticism, the alert self-criticism, the constant testing of hypotheses by empirical research, the awareness of its own limitations which characterize scientific endeavor, make research results, if intelligently used, the most dependable source to which one can turn for information.

In Chapter 3 we pointed out that research is not simply a matter of experimentally testing well-formulated hypotheses. The development of fruitful hypotheses does not occur in a vacuum, nor is it solely a matter of good fortune or ingenuity. It can be aided by carefully planned exploratory and descriptive studies, which have the purpose of accumulating the background information necessary to a pertinent formulation of the problem. We have indicated that such studies, particularly in a young science, call for the most imaginative efforts the scientist has to offer and are not to be scorned because they lack the elegant rigor of the experimental study. The function of descriptive studies in assessing the characteristics of a given situation and in testing hypotheses that do not involve causal relationships has also been examined. In the present chapter we have discussed in detail studies designed to test causal hypotheses. In this context we have presented the logical considerations involved in drawing inferences about causality, and have described various procedures for gathering data that can provide a basis for such inferences.

It is now appropriate to turn our attention from the structure of a research study to the methods of giving substance and body to the research design—the data-collection procedures. In the next chapter, we shall discuss some general considerations of measurement that affect all data collection. Chapters 6, 7, and 8 will then discuss methods for the collection of primary data—observational methods, questionnaires and interviews, and projective techniques. In Chapter 9, the use of secondary sources of data—statistical records, personal documents, communication content—will be treated. Chapter 10 will consider techniques for placing individuals on scales on the basis of data collected by any of these methods.

5

SOME GENERAL PROBLEMS
OF MEASUREMENT

⁓

Variations in Scores on Measuring Instruments

The Validity of Measurements

The Reliability of Measurements

Scales of Measurement

Summary

> *Measurement . . . is more than the pedantic pursuit of a decimal place. Its vital and absorbing aspect emerges most clearly perhaps when it becomes a question of measuring something that has never been measured. Or better still, something that has been held to be unmeasurable.*   s. s. stevens

T HE QUALITY OF RESEARCH depends not only on the adequacy of the research design but also on the fruitfulness of the measurement procedures employed. Basic to any meaningful measurement are an adequate formulation of the research question and clear definitions of the concepts involved. In other words, one must first know *what it is* he wants to measure.

Suppose that we are faced with the problem of determining the effects of a visit to the United States on the attitudes of British tourists. In order to secure relevant data, we must know what questions we want to investigate. Specifying these questions requires, among other things, consideration of the concept *attitude*. One may include in his definition of *attitude* various aspects—for example, beliefs about the nature of an object, person, or group; evaluations of it; tendencies to behave toward it in a certain way; views about appropriate policy with respect to it. One may also include in his definition such other characteristics of an attitude as the salience of the object for the individual, the extent of differentiation in his view of the object, his time perspective with respect to it, etc. Having thus specified his definition of *attitude*, the investigator is in a position to formulate his research problem more clearly by deciding which aspects he wishes to focus on. He may wish to determine whether a stay in the United States changes the British visitors' beliefs about the nature of life in America, or whether it leads to changes in the extent to which they are willing to generalize about

146

Americans, or to changes in the degree of their liking and respect for Americans, or in their evaluation of American foreign policy.

Such specification of what is to be measured is a prerequisite to deciding how it is to be measured—that is, to the establishment of measurement procedures. A measurement procedure consists of a technique for collecting data plus a set of rules for using these data. The purpose of the various data-collection techniques is to produce trustworthy evidence that is relevant to the research questions being asked. (As we have noted in the preceding chapters, a period of exploratory research is often needed in order to find out what kinds of data actually bear on the question or constitute adequate indicators of the concepts.) The purpose of the accompanying rules is to facilitate the use of these data in making specific statements about the characteristics of the phenomenon to which the data are believed to be relevant. The measurement procedures constitute the "working definitions" of the concepts being used in the study, as discussed in Chapter 2.

Data may be collected in many different ways: by observation of behavior, by questionnaires or interviews, by projective techniques, by examination of existing records. The rules for using these data to make statements about the phenomenon in which one is interested may be built into the data-collection technique, or they may be developed as a supplement to it. An attitude questionnaire that yields a score placing an individual along a favorable-unfavorable scale not only provides for collection of the data necessary for an estimate of the individual's position, but also includes the rules for making that estimate. On the other hand, an unstructured interview on the same subject may gather the necessary data, but a coding system (that is, a set of rules for using the data) is necessary in order to estimate the degree of the individual's favorable or unfavorable attitude. The discussion in this chapter and subsequent ones will clarify this distinction.

The data-collection techniques and the rules for using the data, to be useful, must produce information that is not only relevant but free of systematic errors; that is, they must produce valid information. Suppose that the study of British visitors is to focus on their evaluations of Americans. A study using techniques which, for example, led to a substantial proportion of persons with favorable feelings being classified as unfavorable could not emerge with sound conclusions.

A good measurement procedure must also be *reliable*; that is, independent but comparable measures of the same object (or attitude, or whatever) should give similar results (provided, of course, that there is no reason to believe that the object being measured has in fact changed between the two measurements). A measuring stick, for example, is a highly reliable instrument. Under ordinary circumstances, a table which it shows to be 30 inches long on one day will appear 30 inches long the next day and the next; the variations are likely to be negligible for most practical purposes. However, a measuring tape made of elastic would be extremely unreliable; the table might appear 28 inches long one day and 32 the next, depending on how taut the elastic was stretched. Similarly, an instrument established to measure feelings toward Americans would be considered unreliable if persons who were classified as "favorable" on one measurement were classified as "unfavorable" on a second measurement made at such a time and under such circumstances that there was no reason to believe their feelings had in fact changed.

In addition to being valid and reliable, a research instrument should be capable of making distinctions fine enough for the purpose it is to serve. Instruments differ in the specificity or exactness with which they attempt to localize the position of any individual in respect to the characteristic being measured. For example, a very crude measuring instrument might distinguish only two positions in the British visitors' evaluations of Americans: "favorable" and "not favorable." A somewhat more finely graduated instrument would distinguish "favorable," "neutral," "unfavorable"; an even more finely graduated measuring technique would distinguish varying degrees of "favorable" and "unfavorable." If our measuring instrument could distinguish only two categories, our study would be unable to reveal many socially important shifts in attitudes; for example, from "unfavorable" to "neutral" or vice versa, or from "slightly favorable" to "markedly favorable."

In addition to demanding the ability to make fine distinctions, research objectives often call for data-collection procedures that permit us to state *how much* people differ in a given characteristic. In a later section of the chapter it will become clear that such statements can be meaningfully made only if the measurement procedures involve scales that have equal units as well as certain other characteristics.

One further point should be noted. Measurement of an individual, object, event, etc., in terms of a given attribute presupposes that the individual or object can appropriately be described in terms of that attribute. An attempt to measure a given attribute may be irrelevant for some people, objects, etc. For example, it would not make much sense to ask how favorable a person is toward logical positivism if he is not aware of such an approach to the philosophy of science. Unfortunately, it is not always readily apparent whether measurement in terms of a given attribute is or is not relevant for a given individual. Especially in the case of questions of opinion or attitude, many people can be induced to give answers on matters about which they really have no opinion or attitude. Clearly, the results of such measurements have little or no meaning. There is no simple solution to this difficulty. By being alert to it, however, the investigator either may incorporate into his measuring instruments provision for ascertaining whether the measurement is or is not relevant for a given subject, or he may decide to omit measures that seem likely to be irrelevant for a considerable number of subjects. Again, a period of exploratory research may help to provide a basis for judging whether measurement of a given attribute is relevant for a given group.

Variations in Scores on Measuring Instruments

Measurement always takes place in a more or less complex situation in which innumerable factors may affect both the characteristic being measured and the process of measurement itself. One attempts to control or keep constant the more important of these variables and hopes that the variation of uncontrolled factors will operate so as to cancel out one another's effects. The statement that a body has a certain length, for example, is accurate only in relation to an assumed set of conditions among other characteristics of the system (temperature, velocity, etc.) of which length is an attribute. To the extent that these characteristics are related to length and to the extent that they change, one would, of course, expect both the measuring rod and the length of the object being measured to change. Similarly, the measurement of any psychological or social characteristic presupposes a constant set of known conditions among the factors relevant to it and to the process of measuring it. Unfortunately, one's knowledge and one's attempts at control are seldom completely adequate. As a consequence, the results of measurement reflect not only the characteristic being measured but also other unknown factors that affect both the characteristic being measured and the process of measurement.

Thus the variation among individual scores on a measuring device administered to a group of subjects arises from a number of different contributing factors. Some of the variation may be conceived of as being due to true differences among the individuals in the characteristic being measured; some of it represents "errors" in measurement. The basic problem in evaluating the results of any measurement is that of defining what shall be considered true differences in the characteristic being measured and what shall be considered as variations due to error in measurement.[1]

Let us briefly consider some of the possible sources of differences in scores among a group of individuals:

1. *True differences in the characteristic which one is attempting to measure.* In the ideal measuring situation, all of the differences in scores among individuals would be due to their differences in the characteristic one is attempting to measure. For example, if one were attempting to measure attitude toward religion, all of the differences in scores would be due to the individuals' differences in this attitude; none of the differences would reflect chance variations or the effects of other attitudes.

2. *True differences in other relatively stable characteristics of the individual which affect his score.* Few of the techniques available to the social scientist provide "pure" measures of any given characteristic. Such general variables as intelligence, education, information, social status, and various personality characteristics frequently "contaminate" the results of an attitude questionnaire or of an observer's ratings. Hence the scores of the individuals in a group will reflect not only differences in the characteristic being measured but also differences

[1] For a more detailed discussion of this approach to the sources of variations in scores, see Thorndike (1949).

in other characteristics. For example, Edwards (1957b) has shown that the number of people who accept or agree with a given statement on a questionnaire is highly correlated with the "social desirability" of the position presented in the item. Thus, differences in scores on instruments which ask the respondent to indicate his agreement or disagreement with statements that are subject to considerations of social desirability may reflect differences in willingness to admit holding "undesirable" positions, as well as differences in the characteristic the instrument is intended to measure. For example, scores on an attitude test may be influenced not only by individuals' attitudes toward the object in question, but also by their willingness or unwillingness to admit holding opinions they know to be unpopular. Similarly, differences in scores on tests of "personality" may reflect differences in willingness to admit having feelings that are generally considered "neurotic" or behaving in ways that are socially disapproved, as well as true differences in the feelings and behavior asked about.

3. *Differences due to transient personal factors.* Various personal factors such as mood, state of fatigue, health, mental set, distractibility, etc., may vary even within a short period of time. For the most part, one would expect the state of the person to exert its influence on his responses primarily through the way he defines the situation of measurement. For example, if he is fatigued, his response to the measurement situation may be: "I'll get it over with as quickly as possible; it's too much of a bore to bother with." Under appropriate conditions of motivation and rapport, these transient personal factors often have negligible effects.

Measuring instruments differ in the extent to which performance on them is affected by transient personal factors. The usefulness of an instrument for measuring some characteristics other than these transient ones is, of course, decreased to the extent that scores on it are influenced by such factors.

4. *Differences due to situational factors.* Variations in the situation in which measurement takes place often play a large role in contributing to the differences in scores among a group of individuals. For example, an interview with a housewife may be markedly affected by the presence of her husband. The anonymity or lack of anonymity provided by the situation, the rapport or lack of ease, the seriousness or playful-

ness, the various distractions, etc., all tend to affect responses of the subject. If the situations of measurement vary from individual to individual or from one measurement to another, a considerable variation in scores is likely to result from such factors quite apart from the true differences among individuals with respect to the attribute being measured.

5. *Differences due to variations in administration.* Inadequate and nonuniform methods of administering a measuring instrument may contribute to variations in scores. Interviewers may add questions, change wording, revise the order, omit questions, etc., in such a way as to make one interview noncomparable with another. A bored test administrator may improvise his own instructions; a satiated coder may glance at rather than read the item to be coded; a tired observer may not be able to keep recording the constantly changing group process. All of these variations in the use of a measuring instrument may markedly affect both the consistency with which a given coder, observer, etc., rates the responses of various individuals and the consistency of rating from one coder, observer, etc., to another.

Both the situation in which the measurement is made and the method of administration may influence the orientation with which the subject answers—for example, whether he responds in terms of what he believes to be true, of what he thinks the measurer considers the "right" answer, etc.

6. *Differences due to sampling of items.* Any measuring instrument necessarily taps only a sample of items relevant to the characteristic being measured. Thus, an attitude questionnaire contains only a relatively few items from the universe of relevant items that might have been included. If we conceive of a score broadly, as a measure of attitude, rather than narrowly, as the score on a specific questionnaire, it is apparent that the variations in attitude as measured by different questionnaires will be, in part, dependent on the nature of the sample of items included in the questionnaires. For example, in one questionnaire dealing with attitudes toward Negroes, the particular items included may happen to be those on which a given individual is more likely to respond favorably than he would on another questionnaire consisting of a different sample of items.

It is obvious that, if other things are equal, a one-item questionnaire is likely to be a less adequate sample of the total universe than a questionnaire with thirty items. Similarly, ratings based on a few observations or made by a single observer are not as trustworthy as ratings based on many observations by several observers. Increasing the number of items (provided the added items are equally appropriate to the purposes of the given questionnaire), or the amount of relevant material on which a score is based, makes it likely that the variation in scores attributable to this source will decrease.

7. *Differences due to lack of clarity of the measuring instrument.* If individuals understand the items in a measuring instrument differently, variations in their responses may reflect these differences in interpretation rather than true differences in the characteristic one is attempting to measure. Frequently the categories in a coding or observational instrument are complex and ambiguous; different coders or observers may interpret the categories differently and assign similar responses to different categories. Interview questions may be so long, or phrased in such a complex way, that some respondents do not understand them; the responses of these subjects can hardly constitute an adequate indication of the characteristic or attitude at which the questions were aimed. Words such as *free enterprise* or *liberty*, which are emotionally colored or which have special connotations not common to all people measured, may set off differential reactions not directly related to the characteristic which the instrument aims to measure. Even apparently simple questions may be unclear if their context is ambiguous. Take, for example, the following question used in a survey of a college community: "During the last week, did you visit the home of any faculty member?" If the interview took place immediately after a week of vacation, some respondents might interpret the question to mean "during the last regular week of classes," others as "the preceding week—i.e., during the vacation." Simplicity, concreteness, and a high degree of specificity are to be desired in measuring instruments.[2]

8. *Differences due to mechanical factors.* Circumstances such as broken pencils, check marks in the wrong box, poorly printed instructions, lack of space to record responses fully, play their role in preventing the most effective functioning of a measuring instrument. Many

---

[2] This statement does not apply when the characteristic the investigator is trying to measure is the way in which a subject interprets an ambiguous situation —as is the case in most projective techniques (see Chapter 8).

sources of error may be eliminated by adequate attention to mechanical factors in the presentation of stimuli and the recording of responses. It is impossible to list the many mechanical details that must be given thought; they range from the layout of a questionnaire to the handwriting, or typing, of an interviewer.

9. *Differences due to factors in the analysis.* Commonly overlooked is the possibility of errors in the processes of scoring, tabulation, machine analysis, statistical computation, etc. These processes can be easily checked, but unless they are, large differences in scores due to such errors may be introduced into the data.

These, then, are some of the major factors that influence the results obtained from any measurement process. An examination of the list above indicates many sources of "error"—i.e., many influences on the score other than the influence of the characteristic one is trying to measure. It is customary to classify errors as *constant* (systematic, or biasing) or *random* (or variable). A *constant* error is one introduced into the measurement by some factor that systematically affects the characteristic being measured or the process of measurement. Factors such as those discussed in (2) above are of this type. When such a factor is unnoticed, its effects are not taken into consideration in evaluating the results of the measurement. *Random* error is due to those transient aspects of the person, of the situation of measurement, of the measurement procedure, etc., that are likely to vary from one measurement to the next, even though the characteristic one is trying to measure has not changed. A random error reveals itself in the lack of consistency of repeated or equivalent measurements of the same person, object, or event, or of the same group of persons, objects or events. As will be seen in the following sections of this chapter, estimates of *validity* are affected by both types of error; estimates of *reliability* usually take into account random errors only.

The Validity of Measurements

Certain basic questions must be asked about any measuring instrument: What does it measure? Are the data it provides relevant to the characteristic in which one is interested? Do the differences in scores represent true differences on the characteristic one is trying to measure, or do they reflect also the influence of other factors?

The *validity* of a measuring instrument may be defined as the extent to which differences in scores on it reflect true differences among individuals, groups, or situations in the characteristic which it seeks to measure, or true differences in the same individual, group, or situation from one occasion to another, rather than constant or random errors.

Several of the factors discussed in the preceding section as contributing to variations among individual scores may lead to constant errors. It is obvious that true differences among individuals on enduring characteristics other than that measured by the test, which affect scores on the measuring instrument, will produce constant errors. So, too, may factors in the instrument itself or in the situations in which it is administered. For example, measurement procedures that rely heavily on the complex intuitive processes of observers frequently have constant errors introduced by selective perception, recall, or recording.

Note that the constant errors under discussion apply to individual scores and, by implication, to comparisons of averages of groups of scores. For instance, suppose that we administer a test of racial prejudice to children in a setting where prejudice is frowned upon. There is, in this situation, comparatively little pressure on the unprejudiced children to distort their answers to the test but a good deal of pressure on the prejudiced children to give unprejudiced answers. Thus the score of an unprejudiced child may reflect his true attitude quite accurately, while that of a prejudiced child may be shifted to some unknown degree from his true position. As a consequence, both the prejudiced and the unprejudiced children will tend to come out alike —equally unprejudiced. Repeated administrations of the test or of parallel forms of it under the same conditions will not cause the distortion of the replies of the prejudiced children to show up as random error, since there will again be distortion in the same direction. Suppose now that we want to use the test to evaluate the effectiveness of a course in human relations, by comparing the scores of children who have had the course with a control group who have not. If both prejudiced and unprejudiced children give unprejudiced answers, the test cannot reveal any effects which the course may have had.

Since we usually do not know an individual's true position on the variable we are attempting to measure, there is no direct way of determining the validity of the measure. (If there were some other source of information as to true position on the variable, there would often be no need for another measure of the variable, unless the available method of measurement was extremely cumbersome or expensive or in some other way impractical or inappropriate to use.)

In the absence of direct knowledge of individuals' true position on the variable being measured, the validity of an instrument is judged by the extent to which its results are compatible with other relevant evidence. What constitutes relevant evidence depends on the nature and purpose of the measuring instrument. The purpose of some tests is to provide a basis for specific predictions about individuals; for example, whether they will be successful in a certain type of job, whether they need psychiatric care or are likely to need it in the future, etc. Other tests, however, are not used in this way. Although they are designed to measure specific characteristics of individuals, they do not—at least in the present state of our knowledge—lead to definite predictions about how individuals will function in given situations. This difference in the purpose of tests leads to a difference in the type of evidence considered relevant for estimating validity. In the case of tests intended as a basis for predictions in terms of some specific criterion (such as success on a particular job), evidence about individuals' position on that criterion provides a basis for estimating the validity of the test. Investigation of validity in these terms may be described as *pragmatic*; validity is judged in terms of the accuracy of predictions made on the basis of the test's results.

Instruments designed to measure characteristics that do not lead to specific predictions cannot be evaluated so directly. Other evidence must be sought to provide a basis for judging whether the instrument adequately measures the concept it is intended to measure. This less direct approach has been described as *construct* validation. These approaches to validation are discussed in the following sections.[3]

[3] For somewhat different, but related, ways of describing approaches to validation, see Cronbach (1949), Cronbach and Meehl (1955), and *Technical Recommendations for Psychological Tests and Diagnostic Techniques* (1954).

PRAGMATIC VALIDITY

One approach to validation is to ask: Does this measuring instrument work? Can I make decisions better with its help than without it? Does it help me to distinguish individuals in terms of some criterion? The investigator may wish, for example, to distinguish between individuals who, at the time of measurement, are "well adjusted" and those who are in need of psychiatric care. A test that helps him distinguish individuals who differ in their *present* status is said to have *concurrent validity*. On the other hand, the investigator may wish to predict which individuals are likely, in the future, to need psychiatric care. The adequacy of the test for distinguishing individuals who will differ *in the future* may be called its *predictive validity*. In both instances, the approach to validation is a pragmatic one.

In the pragmatic approach to validity, the interest is in the usefulness of the measuring instrument as an indicator or a predictor of some other behavior or characteristic of the individual. For example, tests that require the individual to reproduce a complex design by means of blocks have been shown to be useful in identifying individuals with organic brain disorders. The test-user is not interested in the individual's design-reproducing ability per se; he is interested in performance on the test only as an indication of possible brain damage. He does not need to know why the test performance is an efficient indicator of the characteristic in which he is interested.[4]

What *is* essential in this approach to validation is that there be a reasonably valid and reliable criterion with which the scores on the measuring instrument can be compared. In general, the nature of the predictions and the techniques available for checking them will determine what criteria are relevant. In validating the design-reproduction test as an indicator of brain damage, for example, the obvious criteria would be other well-established indicators of brain damage, or postmortem examinations, to the extent that these can feasibly be used. In the problem suggested earlier, of identifying individuals in need of psychiatric care or likely to need such care in the future, the most adequate criterion presently available is probably that of independent

---

[4] However, from the point of view of advancing scientific knowledge, as distinct from the ability to make useful predictions, he is likely to be interested in discovering why his test works. This point will be discussed in more detail later.

diagnoses by competent psychiatrists, but this is not an infallible criterion. If the purpose of a test is to predict success in college, the criterion is likely to be college grades. If the aim is prediction of job success, one may have to rely on supervisors' ratings as a criterion, unless the job is one in which more objective records of quantity and quality of output can be secured.

Ideally, of course, the criterion with which the scores on the measuring instrument are compared should itself be perfectly valid and reliable. Checking predictions against a criterion which may be irrelevant, inaccurate, or unreliable provides a dubious evaluation of the measurement procedure. In practice, however, the investigator frequently finds that no thoroughly tested criterion is available; he selects the one that seems most adequate and tries to keep in mind its limitations and, if possible, to supplement it by additional criteria.

The development of an adequate criterion for checking predictions and thus evaluating the usefulness of measuring instruments is an important part of research, which seldom receives the time or attention it deserves. Frequently, even though no perfect criterion is available, the reliability and validity of available criteria can be improved. In a study in which supervisors' ratings are to be used as the criterion for validating a test predicting success in a given job, for example, different supervisors may use such different bases of judgment that their ratings are not comparable. The reliability and validity of their ratings can be increased by careful specification of the kinds of behavior that are to be considered in rating job performance, by clarity in defining points on the rating scales, by providing a training period in which two or more supervisors rate the same individuals and then discuss discrepancies in their placement, etc. Generally, pooling of ratings by two or more observers who are rating the same subjects tends to increase both reliability and validity.[5]

CONSTRUCT VALIDITY

Frequently, however, the investigator is interested in the test performance not as a simple predictor of behavior but as a basis for infer-

[5] For further discussion of methods of improving the reliability of ratings, see Chapter 10, pages 352–353.

ring the degree to which the individual possesses some characteristic presumed to be reflected in the test performance. The presumed characteristic being reflected is not something which can be pointed to or identified with some specific kind of behavior; rather, it is an abstraction, a construct.[6] Therefore the process of validating this kind of measuring instrument is referred to as *construct validation.*

Many of the measures used in the social sciences deal with constructs. Measures of intelligence, of attitudes, of authoritarianism, of introversion-extroversion, of anxiety, or of more global personality patterns, are of this sort. Cronbach and Meehl (1955), who first made explicit the concept of construct validity, pointed out that the definitions of such constructs consist in part of sets of propositions about their relationships to other variables—other constructs or directly observable behavior. Thus, in examining construct validity, it is appropriate to ask such questions as: What predictions would one make, on the basis of these sets of propositions, about the relationships to other variables of scores based on a measure of this construct? Are the measurements obtained by using this instrument consistent with these predictions?

Three closely related points should be noted in connection with these questions. First, the predictions are of a somewhat different nature, and serve a somewhat different function, from those involved in determining pragmatic validity. Consider a prediction of how individuals will vote in a national election. A measuring instrument may have the specific aim of making this prediction possible. In this case, the interest is in the accuracy of the prediction, and there need be no concern about the psychological attributes involved in the relation between an individual's behavior on the test and his voting behavior. But a prediction about voting may also be made in connection with examining the construct validity of a test of political conservatism. Here the reasoning runs: "I believe that this test measures political conservatism (a construct). Given the generally accepted view of the position of American political parties, I should expect that people who score as less conservative on this test will be likely to vote Democratic; those who score as more conservative, to vote Republican."

[6] See Chapter 2, pages 41–42, for a discussion of *concepts* and *constructs*, terms which we have used interchangeably

But there is no necessary expectation that the correlation between test score and voting behavior will be very high, because it is recognized that voting for one or the other party is not *equivalent* to being less conservative or more conservative. The Democratic and Republican parties do not clearly represent lesser or greater conservatism; in some respects official Republican stands are less conservative than those of Democrats. Moreover, even if the two parties were unequivocally identifiable in this respect, one would expect other influences in addition to the individual's conservatism to enter into the determination of his vote: family tradition, religion, socioeconomic status, voting intentions of his friends, expectations of specific gains if one or the other party wins.

Second, in the case of pragmatic validation, the ability of the measure to distinguish in terms of the single criterion toward which it is directed is *the* test of its validity; in the case of construct validation, *all* the predictions that would be made on the basis of the set of propositions in which the construct is involved (or as many of them as possible) enter into the consideration of validity. Thus, in the case of the conservatism measure, besides predicting whether an individual will vote Democratic or Republican, one might predict preferences for candidates *within* a given political party; for example, one might predict that Republicans who score as less conservative on the test will favor a given candidate, those who score as more conservative, another candidate. One might also make and test predictions about relationships to socioeconomic status, to education, to stands on specific issues. Failure to confirm any one of the predictions would, of course, call into question the validity either of the measure or of the underlying hypotheses. However, even if each of the correlations proved to be quite low, their cumulative effect would be to support the validity of the test and its underlying theory.

Third, examination of construct validity involves validation not only of the measuring instrument but of the theory underlying it. If the predictions are not supported, the investigator may have no clear guide as to whether the shortcoming is in the measuring instrument or in the theory. Consider, for example, a study focused on the hypothesis that personal association with members of an ethnic group other than one's own is likely to lead to more favorable attitudes toward that group. Suppose that the findings do not show the predicted relation between extent of personal association and attitude change. Shall the investigator conclude that his measure of attitude was not valid, or shall he conclude that, under the conditions of the study, the hypothesis was incorrect? He will probably be led to re-examine the construct *attitude* and the network of propositions that led to his specific prediction. The result may be a refinement of the construct, with more detailed hypotheses about its relation to other variables, and changes in the measuring instrument. For example, a number of investigations focusing on the hypothesis that personal association with members of an ethnic group other than one's own is likely to lead to more favorable attitudes have come out with quite different results. Analysis of a number of these studies indicates that the differences in results may be accounted for partly in terms of the specific aspects of attitude tapped by the different measuring instruments, and suggests that the hypothesis might be refined to specify which aspects of attitude are most likely to be affected by personal association.

Campbell and Fiske (1959), have suggested that the investigation of construct validity can be made more rigorous by increased attention to the adequacy of the measure of the construct in question, before its relationships to other variables are considered. They propose that two kinds of evidence about a measure are needed before one is justified in examining relationships to other variables: (1) evidence that different measures of the construct yield similar results, and (2) evidence that the construct as thus measured can be differentiated from other constructs. In order to secure such evidence, one must measure the construct in question by two or more different methods; one must also measure the characteristic or characteristics from which he wishes to differentiate his construct, using the same general methods he has applied to his central construct.

For example, Burwen and Campbell (1957) were interested in an assumption common to several different psychological theories—that, on the basis of early experiences within the family, an individual develops a generalized attitude toward authority figures. Before attempting to study the relation between "attitude toward authority figures" and early family experiences, they concentrated on developing a number of measures of "attitude toward authority figures." Ratings of attitude toward authority figures were made on the basis of each of the following methods: interview questions about father and present superior officers (the respondents were Air Force trainees); a list of traits to be checked as descriptive of father and of immediate superior; written character descriptions of photographs of middle-aged and older persons (intended as symbolic authority figures); stories about scenes containing symbolic authority figures; an autobiographical inventory; an attitude survey; and a sociometric questionnaire.

Each of these methods was also used to measure a second characteristic: attitude toward "nonauthority figures" (present colleagues, a past fellow worker, "symbolic peers" represented by pictures of young persons). This second characteristic—attitude toward nonauthority figures—was measured in order to determine whether the attitudes expressed toward authority figures were indeed specific to persons in authority or whether they were expressions of attitudes toward people in general. If there were a high positive correlation between attitudes expressed toward authority figures and toward nonauthority figures— that is, if individuals favorable toward authority figures were also favorable to nonauthority figures and those who were unfavorable toward one were also unfavorable toward the other—one would conclude that what was being tapped by the first group of measures was not a specific attitude toward authority figures but a more general attitude toward people. On the other hand, if there were little or no correlation, or a negative correlation, between the measures of the two types of attitudes, one would conclude that the first set of measures was indeed getting at attitudes specifically directed toward authority figures.

As it turned out, the measures of attitude toward authority figures showed so little agreement that there seemed no basis for believing that any consistent attitude had been tapped; thus there was no point in trying to determine whether these measures were getting at a specific attitude that could be distinguished from attitude toward nonauthority figures. Ratings made on the basis of the interviews showed a high correlation between attitude toward father and attitude toward superior officers; had this been the only method used, the investigators might have concluded that they had successfully measured a generalized attitude toward authority figures. However, the ratings based on different methods showed little agreement with one another; moreover, techniques other than the interview showed little correspondence between attitude toward father and attitude toward superior officers. In such a situation, one faces the question whether the measuring instruments are invalid or whether the construct one is attempting to measure (in this case, "attitude toward authority figures") is somehow faulty. In this study, the investigators reasoned that the number of different methods they had used provided a basis for concluding that the difficulty was with the construct rather than the measuring instruments. Although they recognized that any one or more of the measures might have been invalid, they thought it unlikely that all of them were inadequate indicators of the construct "attitude toward authority." In view of the fact that no two of their measures showed high agreement, they concluded that their findings required a modification of the assumption that each individual has a generalized attitude toward authority which reflects his attitude toward his father.

From this discussion, it is apparent that construct validity cannot be adequately tested by any single procedure. Evidence from a number of sources is relevant: correlation with other tests and with other behavior, internal consistency of items, stability over time, etc. How evidence from each of these sources bears on estimation of the validity of the test depends on the relationships predicted in the theoretical network in which the construct is embodied. The more different relationships tested and confirmed, the greater the support both for the measuring instrument and for the underlying theory.

RELATIONSHIPS BETWEEN DIFFERENT APPROACHES TO VALIDATION

The "pragmatic" and "construct" approaches to validation are not mutually exclusive. A single test or measuring instrument may be used for a number of different purposes, and for each purpose the appropriate method of testing validity must be employed. As already pointed out, estimates of pragmatic validity may enter into the evaluation of construct validity. On the other hand, although many measures shown to have pragmatic validity have been arrived at purely on a trial-and-error basis, there is no reason for not investigating why these measures work—that is, considering the constructs involved and their relation to the criterion variables. Such investigations may lead to the clarification of concepts and eventually to the construct validation of these measures or to the development of alternative measures which have both construct and pragmatic validity.

In fact, there are good reasons for not remaining content with a measurement procedure that has been validated only pragmatically. As long as the *why* of its working is not understood, one has no assurance that the conditions of its working still hold for any particular application, and with every application one can only proceed with a naive faith that it will still work *this* time. Moreover, to the extent that the pragmatic approach limits itself to discovering empirical correlations without any concern for an underlying theoretical explanation of the relationships, it is an uneconomical procedure. It permits no generalization to other problems; it results in knowledge which is isolated and barren rather than interconnected and logically fertile (Margenau, 1950).

Is the Validity of a Measure Ever Self-evident?

In the examples we have been discussing, the data provided by the measuring instruments have been used as an indicator of some attribute of the individual which is not itself directly measured. Thus, scores based on answers to a questionnaire may be used to diagnose or to predict mental illness, or to infer the extent to which the individual possesses some characteristic not directly revealed in the test. But sometimes measures are based directly on behavior of the kind in which the investigator is interested. Performance tests are frequently of this sort: reading speed is measured by computing how much of a passage a person reads with comprehension in a given time; ability to solve arithmetic problems by success in solving a sample of such problems; job performance by rating the quantity and quality of the work produced. Observations of behavior may also have this characteristic, if they are used descriptively rather than as a basis for inferences about underlying dynamics. Thus, an investigator interested in studying the behavior of a group leader may record a sample of his behavior; one interested in interaction among group members may record the exchanges among them.

Such measures, which focus directly on behavior of the kind in which the tester is interested, are often said to have "face validity"; that is, the relevance of the measuring instrument to what one is trying to measure is apparent "on the face of it." Whether such an assumption is justified in any given case is ultimately a matter of judgment. But in making this judgment, two major questions must be considered: (1) whether the instrument is really measuring the kind of behavior that the investigator assumes it is, and (2) whether it provides an adequate sample of that kind of behavior. Frequently, in the case of achievement and proficiency measures—where consideration of "face validity" is most appropriate—one is justified in the assumption that the behavior which appears to be involved in the test is the behavior it actually measures. For example, if one is interested in evaluating the adequacy of an individual's performance as a stenographer, analysis of the letters she types, from the point of view of accuracy, spelling, neatness, speed, etc., would seem to provide clearly relevant evidence. However, it may occasionally happen that a test which appears to measure one kind of behavior is in fact measuring another. Suppose, for example, that we give a set of arithmetic problems to a group of eighth-graders and obtain a wide range of scores. We think that we have measured performance in arithmetic. But it may happen that the arithmetical operations involved can be performed by all members of the group; the differences in scores may stem from differences in ability to understand the language in which the problems are presented. The investigator must always be alert to possibilities of this sort.

The second consideration—whether the test provides an adequate sample of the kind of behavior with which it is concerned—requires, in principle, a complete specification of the universe of behavior in question and of all possible test items that might be used to measure it. Frequently this is impossible, since the number of potential test items may approach infinity. What is possible, and essential, is careful consideration of exactly what the behavior is that one wishes to measure, and of the variety of ways in which it might be measured. Suppose, for example, that one wishes to test reading comprehension. Obviously, one cannot assemble all the material that has been written in a given language and select a sample, either randomly or on any other basis. The investigator must make a selection without knowing the total universe. But he can, and should, consider whether the passages included in his test refer to topics which may be more familiar to some individuals than to others, and which may thus test knowledge of the topic rather than reading comprehension; whether they involve peculiarities of style that may present more difficulty to some individuals than to others; etc.

The Reliability of Measurements[7]

As pointed out earlier in this chapter, scores on measuring instruments usually reflect not only the characteristic which the instrument is attempting to measure, but a variety of constant and random errors. The evaluation of the *reliability* of any measurement procedure consists in determining how much of the variation in scores among individuals is due to inconsistencies in measurement. When independent but comparable measures of the same thing are obtained, they will yield the same results to the extent that the measurements are free from random or variable errors.

If we knew that a measuring instrument had satisfactory validity for the purpose for which we intended using it, we would not need to worry about its reliability. If an instrument is valid, it is reflecting primarily the characteristic which it is supposed to measure, with a minimum of distortion by other factors, either constant or transitory; thus there would be little reason to investigate its reliability—that is, the extent to which it is influenced by transitory factors.

However, an investigator is seldom in the position of knowing in advance that his measure has satisfactory validity, unless this has been demonstrated in earlier studies concerned with the same characteristic. Moreover, it rarely happens that an instrument can be shown to have such high validity that no improvement is needed. In the case of pragmatic validity, the coefficient of correlation with the criterion measure is usually substantially below 1.00; the lack of complete correlation may be due to the fact that the instrument does not measure exactly the characteristic reflected by the criterion measure, or to variable errors in the criterion, or to variable errors in the measuring instrument. In

---

[7] For more detailed discussions of reliability, see Gulliksen (1950), Guilford (1954), and Tryon (1957b).

these circumstances, it is important to determine the extent of variable error in the measuring instrument—and also in the criterion measure, if that is possible. In the case of construct validity, no simple direct determination of validity is possible; in these circumstances, evidence of the extent of variable error is a necessary part of the evidence concerning validity.

Unless satisfactory validity or reliability has already been demonstrated, the reliability of a measuring instrument should be determined before it is used in a study, rather than after. If a research instrument is plagued by variable error, the likelihood of achieving significant results is minimized. Rather than go ahead with unreliable instruments, it may be prudent to delay the research and try to increase their reliability.

METHODS OF DETERMINING THE RELIABILITY OF MEASUREMENT

Evaluation of the reliability of a measuring instrument requires a determination of the consistency of independent but comparable measures of the same individual, group, or situation. Clearly, it would be desirable to have many repeated measurements of the same individuals, under the same conditions, as a basis for estimating random errors of measurement. In the study of human behavior, however, this is not often feasible. Not only may oft-repeated measurement create annoyance; it may also affect the characteristics one wishes to measure. When this is likely to be the case, reliability may be estimated on the basis of as few as two measures for each individual in a sample of the population on which the measurement device will be used—or even on the basis of one measure if it can be subjected to internal analysis. Enough measurements to provide an adequate basis for evaluation are obtained by increasing the number of individuals measured rather than the number of measurements of each individual. The usual procedure in computing reliability involves calculating some index of agreement between the results of the repeated measurements.

Different methods of estimating reliability focus on different sources of variation in scores. Some are concerned with the *stability* of individuals' position from one administration of the measure to another; in other words, they focus primarily on fluctuations in the characteristic being measured or on change in transient personal or situational factors. We shall use tne term *stability coefficient* to refer to this type of estimate. Others are concerned with the *equivalence* of individuals' position on different instruments intended to measure the same characteristic, or on a given instrument as administered by different people at essentially the same time or as scored by different judges. In other words, they focus primarily on unreliability due to sampling of items or to variations in administration or analysis. Still others are concerned with both *stability* and *equivalence*.[8]

STABILITY. The stability of results of a measuring instrument is determined on the basis of the consistency of measures on repeated applications. It is important, however, to distinguish between inconsistency due to genuine changes in the characteristic being measured and inconsistency due to changes in extraneous factors. The characteristic being measured may fluctuate from one application of the measure to another. This is true of such physical phenomena as temperature, blood pressure, the weight of individuals. Many of the phenomena with which social science is concerned—for example, leadership behavior, attitudes, morale—show such variation. Inconsistency of this type should not be interpreted as unreliability of the measuring instrument, but it complicates the problem of determining the stability of the instrument itself.

Even though there are genuine fluctuations in the characteristic we are attempting to measure, it is often reasonable to assume that there is some "typical" position for a given individual, object, etc., around which the fluctuations center. Such an assumption is made, for example, in computing the mean temperature in a given city during a given season, or in determining an individual's weight. It is a frequent assumption in dealing with social and psychological characteristics of individuals or groups. When we are interested in determining this "typical" position, we must consider the extent to which any given measurement is likely to deviate from it and how many measurements may be needed to yield a stable average estimate. In this sense we

---

[8] The consideration of reliability in terms of *stability* and *equivalence* of scores was suggested by Cronbach (1951). Earlier terminology (test-retest method, etc.) reflects the fact that procedures for estimating reliability originated, for the most part, in connection with the development of intelligence and aptitude tests.

may be concerned with the stability of measures even though the issue is not one of unreliability of the measuring instrument.

Inconsistency in repeated measurements may also, of course, be due to inadequacies of the measuring instrument. A scale that shows an individual's weight as 120 pounds and two minutes later shows the same individual as weighing 140 pounds probably has some mechanical defect. An observer may on one occasion categorize a long answer by a teacher to a student's question as "discussion," on another as "lecture." An individual may reply differently on two occasions to the same item on an attitude scale, even though his "attitude" has not changed.

The appropriate method for determining stability is comparison of the results of repeated measurements. This is true whether the source of instability is genuine fluctuation in the characteristic being measured or random error due to inadequacies of the measuring procedure. When the measuring instrument consists of observations, a considerable number of repeated observations may be made. When it consists of an interview, questionnaire, or projective test, usually only two administrations are used.

Let us illustrate both of these procedures. Suppose we are interested in the percentage of time which a particular group leader spends in lecturing, as compared with other possible activities. A single observer may be assigned with a stop watch to observe the leader for a fifteen-minute period while he is in charge of the group and record the amount of time he spends lecturing during this period. From this record the percentage of time spent in lecturing may be easily calculated. Then the same observer may make a similar record of the group leader's behavior on another occasion when he is in charge of the same group. When the process is repeated several times we have a series of numbers, each representing the percentage of time which this group leader devoted to lecturing on a particular occasion, according to this observer. We may take as our index of the *stability* of this percentage the range of percentages, their standard deviation, or some other measure of the variability of the series. Lack of stability may be due to variations in the leader's behavior or in the observer's recording of it, or both.

We may also be interested in the lecturing proclivities of a number of group leaders. If each one is observed for fifteen minutes by the same observer under comparable conditions, it is possible to order them in terms of the proportion of time which each spends in lecturing. How stable is this ordering? We could follow the procedure described in the last paragraph to determine the stability of the percentage of time spent in lecturing by each of the group leaders, but this would not tell us anything directly about the extent to which the *order* of the group leaders remained the same in this particular characteristic from observation to observation. The stability of ordering of individuals in a group is usually measured by a coefficient of correlation or some other index of agreement between the scores or ratings received by these individuals on the first administration of a measure and the scores or ratings received by the same individuals on a second administration of the same measure. In the particular example we are discussing, the "score" of an individual would be the percentage of time he was observed lecturing.

In the case of an interview, questionnaire, or projective test, essentially the same procedure is used to estimate the stability of the measure, except that it is usually applied only twice, in what is known as the *test-retest* procedure. The identical interview, etc., is given to the same individuals at different times under equivalent conditions, and the results of the two measurements are compared. However, in the case of measuring procedures such as these, which require a great deal of participation by the individual subject, there are additional complications. The very process of remeasurement may intensify differences in transient factors; for example, anxiety, interest, and motivation may be lower during the second administration of the test simply because the individual is already familiar with it. To the extent that such changes occur, the test which is given on the second administration, although objectively identical with the earlier one, may actually represent a quite different test situation. Moreover, the subject may remember the responses he gave to the first test (particularly if the time interval between the two tests is short) and, in the second test, may give again the responses he remembers (or misremembers) having made earlier rather than responses which are spontaneous or thought through anew in the second situation.

There is the further possibility that the initial measure has actually changed the characteristic being measured. (The reader is reminded of the discussion of the "before-after" experimental design in the preceding chapter.) An interview, a situational test, an attitude questionnaire may raise questions a person has never thought about and may heighten interest and stimulate the development of definite opinions; thus, for example, a "don't know" response may be replaced by a definite agreement or disagreement.

In addition to the possibility of changes brought about by the initial measurement, there is—as with all types of measurement—the possibility of genuine change between the two administrations of the test. As a result of influences unrelated to the testing, some subjects may have acquired more information, or undergone a shift in attitude, during the interval between the two administrations of the test.

When there is both the possibility that the initial measure may affect the results of the second measurement and the possibility of genuine changes brought about by other factors, the common practice is to try to steer a course between waiting long enough for the effects of the first testing to wear off and not long enough for a significant amount of real change to take place. If the second measurement is administered before the effects of the first have worn off, the estimate of stability will not be trustworthy because the results of the two measurements will not be independent; the error is likely to be in the direction of an overestimate of stability. On the other hand, if genuine changes have occurred, the resulting coefficient will be an underestimate of the stability of the instrument itself. No hard and fast rules can be offered for judging the optimal interval; much depends on the specific nature of the test. Fortunately, one can expect the effects to wear off most rapidly at the beginning, with a decreasing rate as time goes on.[9] In other words, there are diminishing returns for waiting over longer and longer periods of time. Two weeks to one month is commonly considered to be a suitable interval for many psychological tests. If in doubt, however, it is better to wait a longer rather than a shorter period of time, since with increasing time such errors as occur are likely to be in the direction of underestimation of the stability of the instrument rather than overestimation. One is safer with an underestimate than an overestimate: in the former case, the investi-

---

[9] See the curves of forgetting in any standard textbook of psychology.

gator knows that his instrument is *at least* as stable as the coefficient indicates; in the latter case, he does not know where he stands.

In summary: The stability coefficient indicates the extent to which the measure reflects relatively enduring differences among individuals in characteristics that affect the measure.[10] To the extent that the coefficient is below the maximum value possible, it is assumed either that there are genuine fluctuations in the characteristic being measured or that the measure is subject to random errors due to transient personal factors or other conditions that have changed from one administration to the next. The stability coefficient does not take into account the sampling of items as a source of unreliability. If the personnel administering and scoring the test are the same on the repeated applications, the stability coefficient does not take account of possible variations in the use of the instrument by different administrators or analysts.

EQUIVALENCE. Estimates of equivalence concern the extent to which different investigators using the instrument to measure the same individuals *at the same time*, or different instruments applied to the same individuals *at the same time*, yield consistent results.[11] We shall illustrate the first condition (different investigators using the same instrument) by our earlier example of the behavior of group leaders; the second (different instruments) by the example of a test of information, ability, or attitude made up of a number of items.

In our earlier discussion of the measurement of lecturing proclivities among group leaders we assumed a single observer who was responsible for all the measurements made. But what if this observer is biased, or otherwise unreliable? The notion of a reliable measurement procedure requires that it yield comparable results from administrator to administrator, provided each has been properly trained; in other

[10] Note that these "relatively enduring differences" may be in characteristics other than those the test is attempting to measure; i.e., they may involve constant errors.

[11] It is convenient to use the phrase "at the same time"; however, the two measures are not necessarily administered simultaneously. In fact, in the case of different instruments, it is often impossible to administer them literally at the same time. What is meant is that, in estimating equivalence, the time interval between the measures is short enough so that there is no reasonable expectation that the characteristic may have changed.

words, the sources of variation discussed in item (5), page 152, should be minimized. We can estimate the extent of variation by having different trained observers watch our group leaders at the same time, and by having each record independently the time during which he thinks the group leader is lecturing.

From such records, indices of equivalence can be calculated in several different ways. If we have a number of observers watching a single group leader, and each reports independently the percentage of time the leader spends in lecturing, we can use the range or the standard deviation of these percentages as our index of the degree of equivalence of the different observers. Another possibility is to divide the period of observation into time units of equal length; 15 seconds might be a convenient time unit for an observation period 15 minutes long. Each observer would record for each time unit whether the major activity of the group leader during that unit was or was not lecturing. The index of equivalence for two observers would be the percentage of time units for which they agreed that the group leader was or was not lecturing.

If our major interest lies in the extent to which different observers agree on the ordering of several group leaders (each observed for only one session) with respect to proportion of time spent lecturing, we would use a correlation coefficient as an index of the equivalence of any pair of observers.

Estimates of equivalence of individuals' position on different in-struments intended to measure the same characteristic focus on varia-tion in scores due to differences in sampling of items. There are many possible items we might select to measure any given characteristic; to what extent is the measure of the characteristic we would derive from one set of items equivalent to the measure we would derive from another possible set? In discussing such estimates, we shall use as illustration a test made up of a number of different items to which the subjects respond.

The construction and selection of test items is a fairly arbitrary procedure, and there is a great range of possible items for measuring a given characteristic; consequently there is usually little interest in knowing the extent to which a single individual's responses vary from item to item of a particular test. Indeed, most tests are constructed to ensure a great range of responses for each individual; e.g., in an attitude test it is expected that every individual will find some items with which he agrees and some with which he disagrees, and in an achievement or ability test it is expected that every individual will find some items that he can pass and some that he will fail. Interest centers on the extent to which the *ordering* of individuals is the same from one sample of items to another sample, and the index of equivalence which is calculated is typically a correlation coefficient or some closely related statistic.

The principles involved in estimating the effect of item sampling on equivalence are most easily seen in the case of *alternate forms administered at the same time*. In this procedure, supposedly equivalent forms of the same test are given to the same individuals at the same testing session. Although the two forms contain different items, the items are intended to measure the same underlying characteristic. The correlation between scores on the two forms of the test indicates the extent to which the two forms are actually measuring the same characteristic in a consistent fashion.

Obviously, this procedure does not take account of day-to-day fluctuations in the person or in the situation of measurement, since both forms of the test are administered during a single session. Some transient differences, however, undoubtedly enter. There may be shifts in attention during the testing period; increasing boredom or fatigue may influence the responses to the second test; responses to items in the first test may affect responses to items in the second test. Nevertheless, unless the measuring devices are extremely long, these changes are likely to be less than the random changes that would occur over a longer period of time; thus coefficients computed on this basis do not fully take into account the effect of variable errors of this sort. On the other hand, since there is little likelihood of genuine change in the characteristic during one testing session, this method of computing reliability avoids the problem of confusing real change with random error.

The *split-half method* may be thought of as a special case of the method of alternate forms administered at the same time. In this procedure, a single form of a test is administered once to a group of individuals; the items on the test are then divided into two halves, and the scores on the two halves are correlated to provide an estimate of the extent to which they are equivalent. In other words, the two halves are treated as alternate forms of the same test. The resulting coefficient is an indication of the internal consistency of the test; again, a high coefficient of equivalence is taken as indicating that the individual's position is not affected by the particular sampling of items in either half of the test but would be substantially the same on any test made up of items from the same universe. As in the alternate-forms approach, a coefficient of less than 1.00 may reflect random errors in responses to individual items as well as nonequivalence of items.

Traditionally, it has been held that in the split-half method the test or measurement should be split into *equivalent* halves, each of which represents the total test in all significant respects.[12] The usual method of obtaining presumably equivalent halves is to assign the even-numbered items to one half, the odd-numbered to the other. The correlation between the scores on the two parts is then regarded as an estimate of the equivalence coefficient of a test half as long as the original test. From this, an estimate of the coefficient of equivalence for the entire test—known as the *corrected split-half reliability*—can be computed by means of the Spearman-Brown formula. (This procedure is discussed in greater detail on page 183.)

More recent thinking holds that, if all items in the test are intended to measure the same characteristic, *random* rather than supposedly equivalent halves should be compared, and a new method of computing a coefficient of equivalence has come into use.[13] The index resulting from this method, called *coefficient alpha*, has, among its other properties, that of being the average split-half correlation for all possible ways of dividing the test into two parts. This satisfies the requirement of randomness with respect to the items composing the halves of the test. Coefficient alpha gives an exact coefficient of equivalence for the full test. The rationale of the method cannot be developed here, but the interested reader may consult the references cited.

[12] See Thorndike (1949) and Guilford (1954).
[13] See Cronbach (1951) and Tryon (1957b).

Whatever the procedure used for estimating split-half equivalence, this approach, like that of alternate forms administered at the same time, does not take into account the day-to-day fluctuations in the person and in the conditions of administration.

In summary: The coefficient of equivalence indicates the extent to which measurements of the same individuals at the same time agree. The measurements may be made by different observers using the same instrument, or by different instruments intended to measure the same characteristic. To the extent that the coefficient is less than the maximum value possible, it is assumed, in the case of different observers using the same instrument, that there are variations in the use of the instrument by different observers. In the case of different instruments made up of a number of items, it is assumed that the items are not equivalent measures of the same characteristic or that there are random errors in responses to individual items, or both. In either case, the coefficient of equivalence does not take into account instability over time as a source of unreliability.

STABILITY AND EQUIVALENCE. As we have pointed out, indices of the stability of scores take account primarily of fluctuations in personal and situational factors as sources of unreliability, while indices of equivalence take account primarily of variations in the administration, content, and circumstances of the measurement procedures. The method of *alternate measurement procedures administered at different times* is an attempt to take account of the combined effect of these various sources of unreliability. A group of individuals receive one form of a test at one time (or are rated by one observer in a particular situation); after a lapse of time they receive a *different* form of the test (or are rated by a different observer in another situation). Correlation of scores or ratings on the two occasions provides an over-all index of the reliability of the measurement procedure.

In the case of questionnaires, interviews, etc., this procedure has the advantage over the test-retest method of being less affected by memory and practice. Nevertheless, the fact that the items in the two forms are different does not mean that the results of the second testing are completely independent of the first. Having taken the first, one's attitude and approach to the second may be different; one has had the impact of practice with or of stimulation by items that resemble the new items; and even effects of remembering or misremembering may enter as a consequence of the similarity of items. As a precaution against distortion of the results by the specific effects of taking a given form of the test first, the administration of the two forms is usually counterbalanced; that is, half of the group is given Form A first and Form B on the second administration, while the other half takes Form B first. However, this does not rule out the more general effects of having taken one form, whichever it is. The problem of setting a suitable time interval between the two testings is not essentially different, therefore, from that encountered in estimating stability by the test-retest method.

As in the repeated-observation or test-retest method, there is the possibility that genuine changes in the characteristic being measured have occurred in the interval between the two test administrations. But again, provided that the results of the two testings are reasonably independent, the effect of this possibility is to make the obtained coefficient an estimate of the minimal reliability of the measuring instrument.

Since the method of alternate measurement procedures administered at different times takes into account more sources of variation than the other methods we have described, it will ordinarily give a lower—but a more accurate—estimate of reliability than either a coefficient of stability or a coefficient of equivalence.

Which method of estimating reliability an investigator will use in any given research depends not only on the value of different techniques for his purposes but also on the practical possibilities open to him and the resources that can be devoted to the development of the measurement procedures. Sometimes it is not possible for him to reach the same group of subjects twice, or the cost of doing so may seem prohibitive; in such a case he has no choice but to base his estimate of reliability on the equivalence of scores. Sometimes the measuring instrument does not lend itself to the internal analysis that may be needed for a measure of equivalence. Whatever the method an investigator uses, he should be aware of its implications and its limitations.

What Is a Satisfactory Reliability?

There is no simple answer to the question of satisfactory reliability. It depends both on one's purpose and on the method by which reliability has been estimated. In general, any lack of reliability in a test lessens its validity; correspondingly, it lessens one's ability to demonstrate relationships between variables or to make precise distinctions among individuals who are similar in the characteristic one is trying to measure.

RELIABILITY AND VALIDITY. To the extent that scores on a measuring instrument are influenced by random errors, they are not accurate indicators of an individual's position in terms of the characteristic one is trying to measure. In other words, to the extent that a measure is unreliable, it lacks validity. An exception must be noted, however. When the estimate of reliability consists of a split-half equivalence coefficient, low reliability does not necessarily detract from validity; paradoxically, it may even increase validity. In order for split-half equivalence to be high, all items of the test must be highly correlated; that is, they must all provide a measure of essentially the same characteristic or of characteristics that vary together. To use the technical term, they must be *homogeneous*. But for some purposes, a test that taps a number of different characteristics may be more valid than one that measures a single characteristic.

Suppose, for example, that we are concerned with selecting candidates for training as nurses. Assume that we have eliminated by other methods those who are clearly not equipped for the profession, on such grounds as low intelligence, poor physical stamina, gross personality disturbances, etc. We want a test that will help us select, from those who have met the basic requirements, the ones who are most likely to be successful as nurses. It seems obvious that a number of characteristics are likely to be relevant; these may include, for example, ability to withstand strain, ability to accept and follow directions, perhaps such characteristics as insight into self and others, sympathy, or optimism. We might, of course, develop a test for each characteristic that we believe, or know, to be relevant. But for practical use in selecting candidates, such a battery of tests might not be feasible; we might prefer to combine into a single test of "Probable success in nursing" items that measure a number of the relevant char-acteristics. In such a test, the correlations among different items would probably be quite low; thus the estimate of equivalence computed by a split-half technique would be low. Nevertheless, the test might be very effective in identifying candidates who will do well as nurses. How can this come about?

From the point of view of predicting a particular behavioral out-come, the ideal test consisting of a number of items should have the following properties: Every item should have a reasonably high cor-relation with the criterion and a zero correlation with every other item. If we were able to construct such a test and measure its reliability by the split-half or related methods, it would turn out to have ex-tremely low reliability. Thus, it would seem that the specifications for maximal pragmatic validity require *low* reliability, a seeming contradic-tion of the proposition stated earlier, that reliability is a necessary condition of validity. It should be noted, first of all, that our ideal test would still have to have reasonably high test-retest reliability to be useful—i.e., to have pragmatic validity. In the second place—and there is an important lesson here about what good pragmatically valid tests measure—the low split-half reliability is not what it seems. Our ideal test is not really one test at all, but a battery of one-item tests. The pragmatically valid test, thus, does not measure a characteristic, but a composite of many characteristics. The determination of a split-half reliability coefficient for a test so set up is meaningless. If one-item tests are themselves not likely to be very reliable, this is compensated for by touching on the many facets of the complex. An error of under-estimation of one facet would tend to be counterbalanced by an error of overestimation of another. In principle, if each item were expanded into a more reliable multi-item test and the scores from each com-ponent test assigned optimal rather than equal weights, the pragmatic validity of the total battery would increase.

DISCOVERING RELATIONSHIPS BETWEEN VARIABLES. Random errors in measurement of a variable—that is, unreliability of the measuring in-strument—obviously reduce the possibility of discovering how that vari-able is related to another.[14] Suppose that we have constructed a ques-

---

[14] Again, we must note that this does not apply to measures where low split-half equivalence does not reduce pragmatic validity.

tionnaire to measure worker morale in the hope that it will help us make predictions about the rate of absenteeism under specified conditions. If the questionnaire were completely unreliable—for example, if workers whom it classified as having low morale were just as likely to show up as having high morale on a second administration ten minutes later— it would be impossible to observe a relationship between morale and absenteeism, even if the two were in fact closely related. If the questionnaire is not completely unreliable, we may be able to demonstrate that some relationship exists between morale and absenteeism. However, if we hope to discover how close the relationship between the two variables is, it is necessary to have highly reliable measuring instruments.

DISTINGUISHING AMONG INDIVIDUALS AND AMONG GROUPS. All the methods of estimating reliability that we have described, and most of the others in common use, consist basically in determining whether measurements at different times or by different forms of the instrument place individuals in the same position in relation to the total group tested. No matter what the subject matter of the test or the method of estimating reliability, the question being asked is essentially: Do the results of the two testing situations agree in where they place Charlie (and Joe and Mary and each of the others) in relation to the average score of the group? Charlie and Joe and Mary and each of the others may score ten points higher in one testing situation than in the other, but this will not show up as unreliability if each is in the same position relative to the others on both measures. Nor will different changes in scores for different individuals affect the estimate of reliability unless they change the position of the individuals in relation to one another. Suppose that on the first measure Charlie scored 30, Joe, 40, and Mary 50; and that on the second measure Charlie scored 33, Joe 40, and Mary 47. Since the relative position of the three would not be changed, these shifts would not appear as unreliability. But suppose that on the first measure Charlie has scored 39, Joe 40, and Mary 41. If Charlie again gained three points on the second measurement and Mary again lost three points, their relative position would change; thus the changes in scores between the two testing situations would appear as unreliability.

From the nature of these operations used in estimating reliability follow several consequences:

1. *The reliability of a measurement procedure is always contingent on the degree of uniformity of the given characteristic within the population being measured.* Small shifts in individual scores may lead to changes in relative position in a group where the scores of many individuals are close to one another, whereas the same shifts may not lead to changes in relative position in a group where individuals differ markedly from one another. Thus, a test with a low reliability in a very homogeneous population may have a high reliability in a very heterogeneous population. Tests are sometimes published with deceptively high estimates of reliability, computed on the basis of administration to very heterogeneous populations, whereas the application of the test may require the ability to distinguish among individuals in relatively homogeneous groups.

2. *High reliability is more important if we wish to make fine discriminations among individuals than if we merely wish to identify people who are at the extremes.* To demonstrate a significant difference between two scores, the difference between them would have to be approximately three times as great if the reliability coefficient were .10 than if it were .90; twice as great if it were .60 rather than .90; and about 1.4 times as great if it were .80 rather than .90. Reliability is obviously important for precise discrimination, and without it the fine gradations of a measuring instrument are illusory.

3. *Estimates of reliability apply to the average reliability of scores of individuals in a group.* They provide no estimate of the different reliabilities of the scores of each individual within the group. It is, of course, an approximation of unknown degree to assign the same reliability coefficient to scores of all individuals. Frequently, the reliability of a score at one point on a continuum is different from that at another point; for example, individuals who have more intense attitudes may be more consistent than individuals who are less intense (see Cronbach, 1949). The reliability of an average score is higher than the reliability of the individual scores that go into the computation of that average. If we are interested in group results, therefore, we can afford to operate with measuring instruments of relatively low reliability,

compensating for the low reliability by increasing the size of the sample. However, if we are interested in making statements or predictions about particular individuals on the basis of their scores, reliabilities below .90 are risky.

METHODS OF INCREASING RELIABILITY

The reliability of measurement procedures can often be increased by taking appropriate steps with respect to the sources of error. Thus, the conditions under which the procedure is applied can sometimes be highly standardized, with attention to illumination, noise level, temperature, presence of observers, etc., if these are considered relevant. Undesired variations in the administration of the procedure can be minimized by using only sufficiently trained, instructed, and motivated personnel. One may specify that subjects are to be interviewed only while they feel in the best of health, are sufficiently relaxed, and after appropriate steps have been taken to assure rapport. The greater the control desired over these sources of unreliability, the greater the resources one needs to have at one's command.

There are two very powerful methods of increasing the reliability of a measurement procedure that involve the selection and accumulation of measurement operations rather than any change in the conditions under which the measurement operations are made. These methods can be illustrated most clearly when the "measurement operation" is the administration to a subject of a particular test item which he either passes or fails; but the same principles apply when the measurement operation is the administration of another kind of test item, or the rating of some aspect of the subject's behavior by a particular observer.

The first method of increasing reliability is to *add measurement operations of the same type as the ones with which we started,* and assign the subject a score based on the sum of the results of all the measurement operations. In the testing situation, this means increasing the length of the test. In the observational situation, it means increasing the number of observers, or the number of occasions on which each subject is observed, or both. If the correlation between the results of any one measurement operation and any other measurement operation is approximately the same within the series of operations we are using, there is a very simple formula, known as the Spearman-Brown formula, which enables us to predict approximately the effect of increasing the number of measurement operations:[15]

$$r_{NN} = \frac{Nr}{1+(N-1)r}$$

A close examination of this formula shows that we can make the reliability of a measurement procedure approach as closely to 1.00 as we wish, provided that we are able to add measurement operations indefinitely without changing their nature in any important way. If the correlation between the proportion of time spent lecturing by a group leader during one fifteen-minute period and the amount of time spent lecturing during another fifteen-minute period is .10, a measure of lecturing proclivities based on observation during only one such period will be of little use. But if we can base the measure on the average results of observation during five fifteen-minute periods, its reliability can be expected to increase to around .36. If we can average the results for ten fifteen-minute periods (of the same sort as we have been using), the reliability of our measure will probably increase to around .53, while if we can use as many as 100 such periods of observation, we can expect to attain a reliability of more than .90. Exactly the same principle applies when we add individual items to a psychological test.

The Spearman-Brown formula assumes that the correlation between any one measurement operation, or "item," and any other item is approximately the same for all pairs of items being considered; to the extent that we add items or measurement operations that do not correlate with the others, our actual results will fall short of those predicted by the formula.

An alternative method of increasing reliability starts by assuming

[15] In this formula r is the correlation between any one measurement operation and any other, N is the number of measurement operations, and r_{NN} is the correlation between the sum or average of N measurement operations of this particular sort and the sum or average of another N operations of the same sort. Essentially, r is the measure of reliability for a "test" consisting of one measurement operation, while r_{NN} is the predicted reliability for a "test" consisting of N measurement operations of the same sort. The Spearman-Brown formula is discussed in most textbooks on mental measurement. See, for example, Gulliksen (1950) or Guilford (1954).

that there are sizable differences in the correlation of items with one another. The problem then is to select from the possible available items or measurement operations those that correlate most highly with one another, and to increase the reliability of the measurement procedure as a whole by increasing its *internal consistency*.

This method has rarely been used outside the field of psychological testing (including attitude measurement), but in this field it has been quite successful. The most common practice is to begin with a fairly large collection of items, calculate a score based on each item, and another score based on responses to the total set of items. Then the score for each item is correlated with the total score, and those items are selected that correlate most highly with this score. These items are divided into two equivalent groups; two new scores are calculated based on the two groups of selected items; and these scores are correlated to provide a measure of the reliability of the "purified" test. If the new reliability is not satisfactory, the test may be further purified in the same manner as before, or additional items may be added of the type represented by the selected items.

Rather than correlating the score for each item with that for the total test, the goal of increasing internal consistency may be approached by the following procedure: The subjects are divided into two groups —a high-scoring and a low-scoring one—on the basis of their total scores. If the number of subjects is quite large, as it properly should be, one takes extreme groups—say, the top and the bottom twenty per cent. If an item is consistent with the complete set of items, then the proportion of high scorers who answer the item in a specified way should be significantly different from the corresponding proportion of low scorers. Those items are most consistent with the total set which yield the largest differences in the appropriate direction.

As an example, let us consider the procedure used in constructing a scale of anti-semitism for use in the *Authoritarian Personality* investigation (Adorno *et al.*, 1950). A questionnaire consisting of 52 items referring to Jews was administered to a group of female college students. Let us consider the results for five of the items on the test:

A. One trouble with Jewish businessmen is that they stick together and connive, so that a Gentile doesn't have a fair chance in competition.

B. Colleges should adopt a quota system by which they limit the number of Jews in fields which have too many Jews now.

C. Anyone who employs many people should be careful not to hire a large percentage of Jews.

D. The trouble with letting Jews into a nice neighborhood is that they gradually give it a typical Jewish atmosphere.

E. Most hotels should deny admittance to Jews, as a general rule.

The respondents were asked not simply to agree or disagree with each item, but to indicate the strength of their opinion, from "strong support, agreement" to "strong opposition, disagreement." The reply to each item was scored on a scale ranging from 1 (strong opposition to anti-semitism) to 7 (strong anti-semitism), with a neutral point of 4. For each item, the mean scores of the 25 per cent who scored highest and the 25 per cent who scored lowest on the total test were computed; the difference between the two means was taken as the "discriminatory power" of the item. The figures for our five items are given in the following table:

Item	Mean Score		Discriminatory Power	Mean for Total Group
	Upper 25%	Lower 25%		
A	5.86	1.38	4.48	3.45
B	2.89	1.00	1.89	1.67
C	5.30	1.19	4.11	2.84
D	5.28	1.32	3.96	3.23
E	2.22	1.05	1.17	1.46

It is apparent that items A, C, and D distinguished sharply between the high and low scorers. On these three items, those who scored high in anti-semitism on the total test took a mean position of slight to moderate agreement, while those who scored low on the total test took a mean position between moderate and strong disagreement. Items B and E, on the other hand, showed much less difference between the high and low scorers; the entire group tended to disagree with these items. Items A, C, and D were kept; items B and E were dropped.

It is important to recognize that the process of eliminating items from a test or attitude scale by the criterion of internal consistency always results in a change in the working definition of what is being measured (see Chapter 2). This change is always in the direction of narrowing and restricting the working definition. How far to carry this process depends on the purpose of the research and the specificity of the characteristic the investigator is trying to measure. The extreme limit of the purification process would be represented by a set of items that correlated perfectly with one another and differed only in difficulty or "acceptability." Such a set of items corresponds to the conception of a completely *homogeneous test* or *unidimensional scale*, which will be discussed further in Chapter 10.

Another important thing to remember about the method of internal consistency is that it is concerned solely with the *equivalence* of two sets of items or measurement operations. It can reduce unreliability resulting from lack of equivalence of items, but it does nothing to reduce unreliability resulting from instability of a subject's responses or variations in the conditions of measurement. The method of increasing the number of measurement operations can be used to reduce these sources of unreliability if it is possible to spread the measurement operations out in time or to distribute them over a number of different conditions of measurement. If either of these procedures is feasible, the investigator should ask himself: "Is what I really want to measure the average level of this characteristic in a variety of situations, even if there may not be much consistency in the characteristic from one situation to another; or do I want to measure something more specific?" The answer to this question will determine the approach he adopts for increasing the reliability of his measurement procedure.

Scales of Measurement

The effectiveness of our behavior both in science and in everyday life depends on our ability to distinguish among objects and to make differential responses to them. Many of our activities require no more than the distinguishing of objects possessing qualities that are rather sharply demarcated from those of others. To take obvious examples from daily life, it is both useful and simple to notice the differences between a pear and an apple, between an infant and an adult, between a tennis court and a swimming pool, between the ringing of a telephone and a Beethoven sonata.

Similarly, in the social sciences many of the distinctions that are made are *qualitative* in nature. For example, we distinguish different languages, different types of social system, different nationalities, and so forth.

However, both in the sciences and in everyday life, it is often desirable to make distinctions of *degree* rather than of *quality*. In daily life we are frequently faced with the problem of selecting among alternatives: Which person is *more intelligent?* Which type of cloth is *sturdier?* Which teacher is *more interesting?* In the interest of both accuracy of judgment and the discovery of constant relationships among characteristics that vary in *amount* as well as in *kind*, science pursues the objective of replacing statements that simply affirm or deny differences by more precise statements indicating the *degree* of difference.

Although there is little doubt that quantification facilitates the establishment of scientific laws, it should be recognized that measurement exists in a variety of forms. Sometimes measurement has been defined so as to exclude methods of data collection that permit only qualitative discriminations. For example, McGregor (1935) defined measurement as "the process of assigning numbers to represent quantities." Other writers, such as Weyl (1949), Stevens (1946, 1951), and Coombs (1953), have included in their concept of measurement any empirical procedure that involves the assignment of symbols, of which numerals are only one type, to objects or events according to rules.

Measurement is possible only because there is a certain correspondence between the empirical relations among objects and events, on the one hand, and the rules of mathematics, on the other. We use empirical procedures to determine the relations among objects and events. In the case of physical objects, these empirical procedures may take the form of direct manipulation. Suppose that one has a number of bars of iron and sticks of wood, which he wishes to distinguish from one another. On the basis of criteria we need not go into here, he identifies some of them as being wood (that is, as being *equivalent* to one another in composition) and others as being iron (that is, as being equivalent to one another, but *not equivalent* to the sticks).

Now he wants to know more about the relationships among the sticks in terms of their length. He wants to *arrange them in order*, with the longest at one end, the shortest at the other. He wants to find out whether *the differences between pairs are equal*; for example, whether stick A is as much longer than stick B as B is than C. He wants to *determine ratios among them*; for example, whether A is twice as long as B. All these relationships can be determined by empirical operations of placing the sticks next to each other in certain ways and making certain observations.

In practice, of course, the measurer would be likely to use a yardstick rather than to carry out these operations directly with the pieces of wood. He is able to do this, however, because the properties that can be ascertained by the empirical operations correspond to the properties of the numerical system in terms of which the yardstick is set up. For example, if his empirical operations have shown that stick A is twice as long as B, and if the yardstick shows B to be four inches long, it will show A to be eight inches long. In other words, numbers yield to mathematical operations which are analogous to the empirical ones by which we can determine relationships among objects. This correspondence between properties of the numerical system, when the various rules are laid down, and certain empirical relations among objects, permits the use of the numerical series as a model to represent characteristics of the empirical world.

The same correspondence between empirical relations and properties of the numerical system is basic to measurement in the social sciences. Suppose that one is interested in studying attitudes toward the United Nations. If one wants simply to assert that two people differ in their attitudes toward the U.N., without specifying how great the difference is or whether one is more favorable than the other, he must at least be able to distinguish different types of attitude; that is, he must be able to identify certain attitudes as equivalent, others as not equivalent. If one wishes to state that the attitude of one person is more favorable than that of another (without, however, specifying how much more favorable), he must be able to rank different attitudinal positions as being more favorable or less favorable than other positions.

If one wishes to make the statement that A is as much more favorable than B as B is than C, or that two experiences have produced equal changes in attitudes, he must be able to determine whether the difference between two attitudinal positions is equal to the difference between two other attitudinal positions. And if one wishes to make some such assertion as "A is twice as favorable as B," he must be able to determine the existence of an *absolute* zero of favorableness for the given attitude, as well as equal units above the zero point.

These four types of statement correspond to four types of measurement scales described by Stevens (1946, 1951):[16] nominal, ordinal, interval, and ratio scales.[17] Let us indicate, briefly, the formal rules and empirical operations that distinguish these various scales. The scales are listed in ascending order of power. The "stronger" scales presuppose the ability to perform the empirical and mathematical operations of the "weaker" ones; thus, the ratio scale implies all the operations of the nominal, ordinal, and interval scales as well as those that are unique to itself, and it contains all of the types of information contained in the preceding scales as well as certain information unique to itself.

NOMINAL SCALES

One of the dictionary definitions of *nominal* is "of, pertaining to, or consisting in a name or names." A nominal scale is one that consists of two or more named categories, into which objects or individuals or responses are classified. The basic requirement for a nominal scale is that one be able to distinguish two or more categories relevant to the attribute being considered and specify criteria for placing individuals, etc., in one or another category. The only specified relationship between the categories is that they are different from each other; there is no implication that they represent "more" or "less" of the characteristic being measured. The empirical operation is the decision that a given object, individual, or response belongs in a given category or that it does not; in other words, it is the determination of *equivalence*

[16] Our discussion of measurement scales is directly indebted to Stevens.
[17] Coombs (1950, 1953) has described, in addition, the "partially ordered scale," which falls logically between the nominal and the ordinal scale, and the "ordered metric," which falls logically between the ordinal and the interval scale.

or *nonequivalence*, with respect to the attribute in question, between the given object and other objects placed in a given category.[18] Classification of individuals according to nationality, for example, constitutes a nominal scale.

For convenience, numbers may be used to identify the categories in such a scale, but they are used only in the way that letters or words would be; there is no empirical relation among the numbered categories that corresponds to the mathematical relation between the numbers assigned. Therefore statistical techniques that make use of mathematical relations among numbers (such as the computation of means or correlation coefficients, for example) are inappropriate; one may use only such statistics as are appropriate to counting; for example, the number of cases, the mode, the coefficient of contingency, and the chi-square.[19] Thus, in a study of the relationship between personality and nationality, one might establish some criterion or criteria on the basis of which he would categorize people according to personality types, and would then determine whether a given personality type tends to be associated with a given nationality more frequently than the other types by counting the number of cases of each personality type which fall into each nationality grouping.

Use of nominal scales is characteristic of exploratory research, where the emphasis is on uncovering a relationship between two characteristics rather than on specifying, with some degree of precision, the mathematical form of the relationship; or where the focus of the study is on the *pattern* of relationship among several characteristics of the person. However, if the data permit the ordering of people in terms of a characteristic, it is uneconomical to use a nominal scale, since such a scale severely limits the nature of the conclusions that can be drawn.

---

[18] The relation of *equivalence* (or *equality*) has the logical characteristics of being *transitive* and *symmetrical*. In a *transitive* relation, if A stands in a certain position with respect to B, and B stands in a similar position with respect to C, then A also stands in that position with respect to C. For example, if A equals B and B equals C, then A equals C; if A and B are placed in the same category on a nominal scale, and B and C are placed in the same category, then A and C are placed in the same category. In a *symmetrical* relation, if A stands in a certain position with respect to B, B stands in the same position with respect to A. For example, if A equals B, then B equals A; if A is placed in the same category as B, B is placed in the same category as A.

[19] The procedures used in computing these statistics may be found in any standard statistics text.

ORDINAL SCALES

An ordinal scale defines the relative position of objects or individuals with respect to a characteristic, with no implication as to the distance between positions. The basic requirement for an ordinal scale is that one be able to determine, for each individual or object being measured, whether that individual has more of the attribute in question than another individual, or the same amount, or less; in other words, one must be able to determine the order of positions.[20] This presupposes that one must be able to place each individual at a single point with respect to the attribute in question. If the attribute or the measuring procedure is such that one can say, "In some respects John has more of this attribute than Bill, but in other respects he has less," the two men cannot be placed in relation to each other on a single ordinal scale. Difficulties of this sort are not uncommon in the social sciences. Take, for example, the attempt to order people in terms of degree of favorable or unfavorable attitude toward some minority group. John may have more negative stereotypes of the group than Bill does, but less hostile feelings; they may engage equally in discriminatory behavior. In such a case, in order to meet the requirements for ordinal scaling, it is necessary either to rank the men on each of the three dimensions separately, or to have some rationale for combining positions on the three dimensions into a single score representing degree of favorable or unfavorable attitude toward the group.[21] The ability to place a given individual at a single position is a prerequisite for the more powerful scales as well.

An ordinal scale is like an elastic tape measure that is being stretched unevenly; the scale positions as indicated by the numbers on the tape are in a clearly defined order, but the numbers do not provide a definite indication of the distance between any two points.

[20] The relation of order has the logical characteristics of being *transitive* and *asymmetrical*. Transitivity has been discussed in the preceding footnote; in this case, if A is greater than B and B is greater than C, then A is greater than C. In an asymmetrical relation, if A stands in a certain position with respect to B, then B does not stand in that position with respect to A; if A is greater than B, then B is not greater than A. The relation of ancestor to descendant, for example, is both transitive and asymmetrical.

[21] This issue is discussed in more detail in the section on attitude scales in Chapter 10.

The distance between 8 and 9 may be equal to, less than, or greater than the distance between 1 and 2. *With ordinal scales we are limited to statements of greater, equal, or less; we cannot undertake to state how much greater or how much less.*

An example of an ordinal scale in the physical sciences is the Mohs' scale of hardness, which is applied to minerals. The empirical relation in this case is the ability of minerals to scratch one another. A diamond is ranked highest on this scale, since it can scratch all other known minerals but none can scratch it; however, the scale does not assert anything about *how much* harder a diamond is than other minerals.

When the operation by which objects or individuals are placed on a scale involves direct comparison of the individuals in terms of the extent to which they possess the attribute in question, it is easy to see that the scale reflects only the order of positions and not the distances between them. This is the case, for example, in a spelling bee, or in a teacher's ranking of children in terms of cooperativeness, or in the judgment of the relative desirability of applicants for a job. Although the individual who is ranked highest is given the number 1, the next highest 2, etc., it is clear that there is no necessary assumption that #1 is as much higher than #2 as #2 is than #3, etc.

However, when the data needed for placing an individual are gathered by an instrument that yields a numerical score, the fact that one may still be dealing only with an ordinal scale is sometimes obscured. Suppose that three individuals taking a spelling test, or an attitude questionnaire, receive scores of 100, 80, and 60, respectively. Our knowledge of mathematical relations may dispose us to think that the person who scores 100 is as much higher than the one who scores 80 as the latter is above the one who scores 60. But unless we have reason to believe that the distance between 80 and 100 represents the same amount of the attribute being measured as does the distance between 60 and 80, these scores indicate only that the first person ranks higher than the second, and the second higher than the third.

The statistics applicable to data that permit only rank ordering are limited. In addition to those applicable to nominal scales, one may, strictly speaking, use only such statistics as medians, percentiles, and rank-order correlations. Within recent years there has been a rapid expansion of statistical tests appropriate to data that are simply ranked or ordered.[22]

INTERVAL SCALES

On an interval scale, not only are the positions arranged in terms of greater, equal, or less; the units, or intervals, of measurement are equal. In other words, the distance between the positions labeled 1 and 2 on the scale is equal to the distance between positions 2 and 3, etc. The basic empirical operation for the establishment of such a scale is a procedure for determining that intervals are equal. The Fahrenheit and Centigrade thermometers are examples of interval scales; the units represent equal amounts of change in the volume of a column of mercury under a certain pressure.

For many of the attributes with which the social sciences deal, procedures have not yet been devised that will give reasonable certainty about the equality of intervals. Attempts, however, have been made, particularly in connection with the measurement of attitudes. The most frequent approach to determining the equality of intervals has made use of the judgments of large numbers of people about the location of various positions. Intervals between adjacent positions have been considered equal either on the basis of a consensus of judgments that they appeared equal,[23] or on the basis of statistical calculations based on the distribution of judgments about the location of various positions.

If one has reason to believe that the units of his scale are equal, then he is justified in making use of mathematical relationships among numbers which correspond to this fact. For example, he may assert that an individual whose score changes from 3 to 5 has shown as much change as one whose score shifts from 5 to 7. He may appropriately compute means, standard deviations, and product-moment correla-

[22] For a presentation of a variety of statistical techniques applicable to data gathered by means of ordinal scales, consult Siegel (1956).

[23] For a more detailed account of this approach, see the discussion of Thurstone scales in Chapter 10.

tions; in fact, almost all the usual statistical methods are applicable to an interval scale.

As in the scales previously discussed, the zero point on an interval scale is a matter of convention. Its arbitrariness is indicated by the fact that a constant can be added to all scale positions without changing the form of the scale. The arbitrariness of the zero point is apparent when one compares the Fahrenheit and Centigrade scales of temperature. In the latter, zero corresponds to the point at which water freezes; in the former, zero is well below that freezing point. Because the zero point is arbitrary, multiplication and division are meaningless; although relations between positions can be stated in terms of the distance (i.e., number of scale points) between them, they cannot be stated in terms of ratios. Thus, with data that meet the assumptions of an interval scale (but not of a ratio scale—see below), one cannot state that a person's attitude is twice as favorable as that of another person, just as one cannot state that 20° F. is twice as hot as 10° F., or 20° C. twice as hot as 10° C. However, *differences* between values on an interval scale can be treated in terms of ratios. Thus, we can say that an individual who shifted from a score of 3 on an interval scale to a score of 7 has changed twice as much as one who shifted from a score of 3 to a score of 5. This is because the point of *no difference* provides an absolute zero.

RATIO SCALES

A ratio scale, in addition to having the characteristics of an interval scale, contains an absolute zero. The empirical operations necessary to establish a ratio scale include methods for determining not only equivalence-nonequivalence, rank order, and the equality of intervals, but the equality of ratios. Since ratios are meaningless unless there is an absolute zero point, it is only with this type of scale that one is justified in making assertions such as: "A is *twice* as heavy as B," or "I spent *half* the amount that you did."

This type of scale, often called "fundamental measurement," is most commonly found in physics. Measures of weight, time intervals, length, area, angles, etc., all conform to ratio scales. So does the scale of cardinal numbers itself—the scale we use when we count people, dollars, eggs.

For most of the subject matter of the social sciences, we are far from having devised procedures that satisfy the requirements of a ratio scale. However, attempts have been made to construct such scales in connection with the judgment of psychophysical attributes such as loudness and pitch (see Stevens, 1951, 1957). As in the case of attempts to construct interval scales for the measurement of attitudes, the judgments of people have been used as the basis for determining positions on the scale. For example, a tone of a given magnitude is sounded, and subjects are asked to select a tone that is half as loud, another tone that is twice as loud, etc. The absolute zero point is established by the threshold between no perception of sound at all and the barest perception of sound.

If one's data conform to the criteria for a ratio scale, all the relations between numbers in the conventional system of mathematics obtain between the correspondingly numbered positions on the scale. Thus, as in an ordinal scale, an individual, object, or event which is placed at the position labeled 10 on the scale ranks higher on the attribute being measured than does one which is placed at the position labeled 5; as in an interval scale, the individual, etc., at position 15 is as much higher than the one at 10 as that one is above the one at position 5; and, in addition, the one at position 10 can be said to possess twice as much of the attribute as the one at position 5. With such a scale, all types of statistical procedures are applicable.

THE PRESENT STATUS OF MEASUREMENT IN THE SOCIAL SCIENCES[24]

Whether various techniques used in the social sciences yield data corresponding to one or another of these scales of measurement has been the subject of considerable controversy. Disagreement centers on whether a given measurement technique, or most techniques, or any techniques used in the social sciences meet the criteria for an interval scale. There is little argument about nominal scales. A nominal scale is usually recognizable as such, and there is little temptation to

[24] For more detailed discussion, see Coombs (1953), Green (1954), Gulliksen (1950), Stevens (1946, 1951, 1957), and Torgerson (1958).

use inappropriate statistics since, in the absence of distinctions of degree, the mathematical rules governing order and distance are clearly inapplicable. At the other extreme, there is general agreement that except for the scale of number itself, which is used in counting frequencies, none of the measurement techniques used in the social sciences, with the possible exception of the procedures for measuring certain psychophysical phenomena referred to on the preceding page, correspond to ratio scales.

There is, however, considerable disagreement over whether an ordinal or an interval scale provides the most appropriate model for most measurement techniques currently used in the social sciences. This disagreement manifests itself both in explicit statements and implicitly, in the choice of statistical techniques. Some writers have taken the view that few, if any, of the techniques now in use provide data that can be considered as appropriate to more than ordinal scales. Others have taken the position that data from certain measurement procedures—for example, those used in measuring IQ, or in certain types of attitude scales—may properly be treated as conforming to interval scales. Still others have taken the position that, although most of the measurements used do not go beyond ordinal scales, probably little harm is done in applying to them statistics that are, strictly speaking, appropriate to interval scales.

Statistics appropriate to interval scales continue to be widely used in the analysis of social science data, with or without the assumption that the data actually meet the requirements of such scales. However, there is also an increasing use of statistics that are specifically appropriate to ordinal scales.

If the experiences of the natural sciences may be taken as a guide, the discovery of precise relationships among characteristics, as expressed in numerical laws, is largely dependent upon the existence of ratio scales. Without knowledge of such relationships, the measurement of characteristics by indirect or derived procedures is difficult. But indirect measurement may be more efficient than direct measurement. For example, it is rather simple to measure the density of liquids on the basis of the law that expresses density as a constant function of the ratio between the weight and the volume of the particular liquid, but it would be tedious and less precise by direct procedures. By a direct procedure we might, for example, use a standard set of solid bodies, which we would place in the various liquids. We would agree to call one liquid more dense than another if we could find a solid body which would float in one but not in the other. Following this procedure systematically for all liquids, we would assign the numbers 1, 2, 3, 4, 5, etc., to designate the position of the liquids in the density scale. Clearly, the direct procedure is more cumbersome and less precise than the indirect procedure.

Only by the aid of indirect procedures can we measure the temperature of the distant stars or the blood pressure in the arteries of living things. Similarly, it seems probable that much of social science measurement will always be indirect, and thus will depend on the development of knowledge of regular relationships among characteristics. The development of this knowledge is in turn partly dependent upon the development of fundamental measurement. The history of science attests to the fact that the development of measurement processes is dependent upon the constant interaction of both empirical procedures for measurement and theoretical concepts about what is being measured. Exclusive concern with either the empirical procedures or the theoretical concepts is likely to be unproductive.

The opinion is sometimes expressed that the social sciences can never hope to reach the precision of measurement achieved in the physical sciences, because the very nature of the material with which the social sciences deal does not permit such refinements as, for example, the establishment of an absolute zero point. This may prove to be a correct prediction, but it seems premature at this early stage of the development of the social sciences. As Stevens (1951) has pointed out, the measurement of many physical qualities has progressed from scale to scale:

> When men knew temperature only by sensation, when things were only "warmer" or "colder" than other things, temperature belonged to the ordinal class of scales. It became an interval scale with the development of thermometry, and after thermodynamics had used the expansion ratio of gases to extrapolate to zero, it became a ratio scale.

Summary

In this chapter we have discussed some general problems of measurement that must be considered in connection with any procedure for gathering data. We have indicated that scores on any measuring instrument are determined not only by the characteristic it is intended to measure but also by a variety of other factors, some relatively stable, some transitory. A measurement procedure is considered *valid* to the extent to which scores reflect true differences among individuals, groups, or situations in the characteristic which it seeks to measure, or true differences in the same individual, group, or situation from one occasion to another, rather than constant or random errors. A measurement procedure is *reliable* to the extent that independent applications of it yield consistent results.

It has been pointed out that measurement rests on the correspondence between empirical relations among individuals, objects, etc., and properties of the numerical system. In this connection, four types of scale have been described: the *nominal* scale, consisting simply of distinguishable categories, with no implication of "more" or "less"; the *ordinal* scale, on which positions can be identified in terms of "more" or "less" but with no implication as to the distance between positions; the *interval* scale, on which the distance between any two adjacent positions is the same as that between any other two adjacent positions; and the *ratio* scale, which has not only equal intervals but an absolute zero.

In the next few chapters we shall discuss specific approaches to the collection of data: observation, interviews and questionnaires, projective and disguised techniques, and the use of data already available.

6

DATA COLLECTION
I. Observational Methods

Unstructured Observation

Structured Observation

> *How odd it is that anyone should not see that all observation must be for or against some view, if it is to be of any service.* CHARLES DARWIN

WE ARE ALL CONSTANTLY OBSERVING—noticing what is going on around us. We look out the window in the morning to see whether the sun is shining or whether it is raining, and make our decision about carrying an umbrella accordingly. If we are driving, we look to see whether the traffic light is red or green. We see a child dash into the street in front of a car, and watch whether the driver manages to stop or swerve to avoid hitting him. There is no need to multiply examples; as long as we are awake, we are almost constantly engaged in observation. It is our basic method of getting information about the world around us.

Observation is not only one of the most pervasive activities of daily life; it is a primary tool of scientific inquiry. Observation becomes a scientific technique to the extent that it (1) serves a formulated research purpose, (2) is planned systematically, (3) is recorded systematically and related to more general propositions rather than being presented as a set of interesting curiosa, and (4) is subjected to checks and controls on validity and reliability.[1]

---

[1] The fact that observation as a research technique must be purposefully integrated with other steps in the research process does not, however, preclude the possibility that observations of great scientific significance can occasionally be made by chance. The history of science is replete with discoveries based on haphazard observations that were unrelated to an established research purpose; the discovery of radium and of penicillin are two of many available examples. For a discussion of the role chance observations have played in scientific discoveries and many interesting examples, see Beveridge (1950). The significant chance observation, however, is largely a gift of the gods. Moreover, we must distinguish between the chance observation that points to a hitherto unsuspected phenomenon or suggests some important hypothesis and the systematic follow-up observation that makes something of this gift.

Many types of data required by the social scientist as evidence in research can be obtained through direct observation. Suppose that he is interested in how members of different groups behave toward one another when some activity brings them into contact; or in the manner in which mothers rear their infants; or in comparing the quality of housing occupied by different social strata of the population; or in describing religious ceremonies and rituals. To obtain these and many other types of data, he proceeds best by observing the appropriate situations.

Direct observation of behavior is, of course, not the only method by which the scientist can obtain data; interviews and questionnaires, projective techniques, and available records can be substituted for the scientist's own observation.[2] Compared with these other methods of data collection, observation has some advantages and some disadvantages.

Perhaps the greatest asset of observational techniques is that they make it possible to record behavior as it occurs. All too many research techniques depend entirely on people's retrospective or anticipatory reports of their own behavior. Such reports are, as a rule, made in a detached mood, in which the respondent is somewhat remote from the stresses and strains that influence what he does or says in the ordinary course of events, while he may be influenced by other stresses and strains peculiar to the research situation. The degree to which one can predict behavior from interview data is at best limited, and the gap between the two can be quite large. In contrast, observational techniques yield data that pertain directly to typical behavioral situations— assuming, of course, that they are applied to such situations. Where the social scientist has reason to believe that such factors as detachment or distortions in recall may significantly affect his data, he will always prefer observational methods. Sometimes a study demands that what people actually do and say be compared with their account of what they did and said. Obviously, two methods of collecting data must be employed in such inquiries—observation and interviewing.

Many forms of behavior are so taken for granted by the subjects

[2] See Chapters 7, 8, and 9.

under investigation, are so much "second nature," that they escape awareness and resist translation into words. Anthropologists, for instance, in observing foreign cultures, often note facts that their best local informants would never have thought of reporting. Not only rituals and ceremonies but also everyday occurrences, such as the treatment of a small child by his mother, are often of the kind that have to be seen if their characteristic features are to be discovered.

Moreover, some investigations deal with subjects (infants, for example, or animals) who are not able to give verbal reports of either their behavior or their feelings for the simple reason that they cannot speak. Such investigations necessarily use observation as their method of data collection. Spitz and Wolf (1946), through the observation of behavior of babies in a nursery, were led to the conclusion that prolonged separation of a child from a previously attentive mother may lead to a severe depression, starting with weepiness and culminating in rigid withdrawal. Observations of chimpanzees at the Yerkes Laboratories have provided data on the social behavior of animals. For example, a study (Hebb and Thompson, 1954) in which the experimenter played at some times the role of a "timid man," at other times the role of a "bold man," showed both marked individual differences in the reactions of different chimpanzees and striking common features of their behavior. The apes behaved in ways interpreted as indicating fear much more often when the "bold man" appeared (for example, they moved to a far corner of the cage); toward the "timid man" they behaved much more often in ways interpreted as teasing (or, as the investigators describe it, "behavior which . . . enticed an innocent close just to scare the hell out of him").

In addition to its independence of a subject's *ability* to report, observation is also independent of his *willingness* to report. There are occasions when social research meets with resistance from the person or group being studied. People may not have the time, or they may not be inclined, to be interviewed; they may resent being singled out or being asked questions whose purpose is obscure to them; they may object to being tested, out of fear that they may not come up to the standards of their group; and so on. Although observation cannot always overcome such resistance to research, it is less demanding of active cooperation on the part of the subjects. To be sure, people under observation may, if they know they are being observed, deliberately try to create a particular impression; but, even so, it is probably more difficult for them to alter what they do or say in a life-situation than to distort their memory or report of what they have done or said.

On the other hand, observation has its specific limitations. We have listed as an asset the possibility of recording events simultaneously with their spontaneous occurrence. The other side of the coin is that it is often impossible to predict the spontaneous occurrence of an event precisely enough to enable us to be present to observe it. If an anthropologist wishes to learn about marriage ceremonies by observation rather than through interviews, he has to wait until a wedding to which he has access takes place. If a social psychologist wishes to observe behavior in extreme situations (such as during a disaster), his physical and emotional endurance as well as his patience may be put to a severe test. Even the observation of regular daily occurrences may become difficult because of the possibility that unforeseeable factors will interfere with the observational task. An observer attempting to collect data on the games played by children in a playground is at the mercy of the weather, alternative attractions in the street which may interrupt the games, the possibility of fights, etc. Unless there are good reasons for engaging in direct observation, the method of interviewing is often more economical in such cases.

Furthermore, the practical possibility of applying observational techniques is limited by the duration of events. Life histories, for example, can hardly be obtained in this way. Moreover, some occurrences that people may be able and willing to report are rarely, if ever, accessible to direct observation. Sexual behavior, a family crisis, or an undisturbed family breakfast are examples of events that, as a rule, are not open to direct observation by an outsider.

One prevalent notion about a limitation of observational techniques, however—the idea that observational data cannot be quantified—is a misconception. Historically, observational data have, it is true, most frequently been presented without any attempt at quantification. Pioneering work in the use of observational techniques was done by anthropologists who were studying small, isolated cultures and did not feel a need for quantifying their observations. The richness of their data, based as it was on their subtle and perceptive approach, has tempted other social scientists to adopt similar methods. In so doing, they have frequently taken over not only the subtlety of the approach but the neglect of the possibilities for quantification as well. This is not to imply that all observational data must be quantified, but it is important to note that they can be.

Observation may serve a variety of research purposes. It may be used in an exploratory fashion, to gain insights that will later be tested by other techniques; its purpose may be to gather supplementary data that may qualify or help to interpret findings obtained by other techniques; or it may be used as the primary method of data collection in studies designed to provide accurate descriptions of situations or to test causal hypotheses. Observation may take place in "real-life" situations or in a laboratory. Observational procedures may range from almost complete flexibility, guided only by the formulation of the problem to be studied and some general ideas about aspects of probable importance, to the use of detailed formal instruments developed in advance. The observer may himself participate actively in the group he is observing; he may be defined as a member of the group but keep his participation to a minimum; he may be defined as an observer who is not part of the group; or his presence may be unknown to some or all of the people he is observing.

In general, the degree of structure and the degree of participation tend to vary with the purpose of the study. In an exploratory study, the observational procedures are likely to be relatively unstructured, and the observer is more likely to participate in the group activity than he is in a study focused on accurate description of a situation or on testing a causal hypothesis. However, these characteristics do not necessarily vary together. The investigator in an exploratory study may be clearly identified as an observer watching the group, or his presence may be unknown to the group. For example, an investigator interested in developing hypotheses about young children's social behavior may watch a nursery school group from behind a one-way screen; or he may be present with the group, may openly take notes, but may refrain from any interaction with the children. Participant observers may use highly structured observational instruments; for example, in an investigation of some aspect of psychotherapy, both patients and therapists may fill out formal rating scales. And, of course, there are degrees of structure, rather than a sharp distinction between "unstructured" and "structured" observation.

Whatever the purpose of the study, four broad questions confront the investigator: (1) What should be observed? (2) How should observations be recorded? (3) What procedures should be used to try to assure the accuracy of observation? (4) What relationship should exist between the observer and the observed, and how can such a relationship be established?

Since the ways of answering these questions differ somewhat depending on the nature of the study and the extent to which observational procedures can be structured, we shall discuss these questions separately for relatively unstructured and relatively structured observation. Because of the frequent use of unstructured observation in exploratory studies and in situations where the observer participates in the activity of the group, we shall consider problems specific to exploration and to participant observation in the section on unstructured observation.

One key issue, however—that of the need for attention to the correctness and adequacy of observation—is so basic, regardless of the degree of structure of the procedures used, that it seems appropriate to discuss it here.

Because all of us are constantly observing in the course of our daily lives, we may be inclined to think that no special training is needed in order to become a scientific observer. But the observation of everyday life is haphazard. We pay attention to some things, not to others. We may observe with a purpose, as in the case of the traffic light or the weather; we may observe out of curiosity; or we may observe simply because our eyes are open, our other sense organs are responsive, and stimuli are impinging upon them. Our observations may agree with those of other people who have observed the same event, or they may be quite different. The selectivity, the inaccuracies, and the omissions of observation have long provided interesting and instructive demonstrations for social science classes. One of the first such experiments was conducted by Münsterberg (1908) early in the twentieth century:

> I stood on the platform behind a low desk and begged the men [in a psychology class] to watch and to describe everything which I was going to do from one given signal to another. As soon as the signal was given, I lifted with my right hand a little revolving wheel with a colour-disk and made it run and change its color, and all the time, while I kept the little instrument at the height of my head, I turned my eyes eagerly toward it. While this was going on, up to the closing signal, I took with my left hand, at first, a pencil from my vest-pocket and wrote something at the desk; then I took my watch out and laid it on the table; then I took a silver cigarette-box from my pocket, opened it, took a cigarette out of it, closed it with a loud click, and returned it to my pocket; and then came the ending signal. The results showed that eighteen of the hundred had not noticed anything of all that I was doing with my left hand. Pencil and watch and cigarettes had simply not existed for them. The mere fact that I myself seemed to give all my attention to the colour-wheel had evidently inhibited in them the impression of the other side. Yet I had made my movements of the left arm so ostentatiously, and I had beforehand so earnestly insisted that they ought to watch every single movement, that I hardly expected to make any one overlook the larger part of my actions.

On the basis of a number of similar experiments and of analysis of testimony presented in legal proceedings, Münsterberg commented:

> The sources of error begin . . . before the recollection sets in. The observation itself may be defective and illusory; wrong associations may make it imperfect; judgments may misinterpret the experience; and suggestive influences may falsify the data of the senses.

Innumerable subsequent experiments have confirmed these conclusions. They point to the need for careful training of observers and systematic procedures for checking the reliability of their observations. Since the nature of the training and checking procedures is somewhat different in two types of observation, they will be discussed separately in the following sections on *unstructured* and *structured* observation.

Unstructured Observation[3]

The technique of unstructured observation has been contributed mainly by social anthropology, where it has frequently taken the form of *participant observation*. In this form of observation the observer takes on, to some extent at least, the role of a member of the group and participates in its functioning. Later in this section we shall deal with some of the problems and isssues that are involved when the observer is a participant in the process he observes. However, much of the discussion is relevant to both participant and nonparticipant observation when the observer has no predetermined set of categories to use.

THE CONTENT OF OBSERVATION

The first question the observer must face is: What should be observed? "Everything" is an unachievable goal, since not even the best observer, or the best team of observers, can be expected to provide a *complete* record of even seemingly simple events. For example, in the course of an arithmetic lesson in a school classroom, a great deal is going on. The teacher is engaged in certain activities. Each of the thirty children is doing something slightly different. Presumably learning is taking place, but there are also movements and talk not directly related to the learning process. It is impossible to record all the details. From the start, one must face the difficult problem of selection. In more highly structured studies, the formulation of the research problem indicates what kinds of data will be most relevant. But in an exploratory study, where unstructured observation is most likely to be used, one does not know in advance which aspects of the situation will prove to be most relevant.

A meaningful answer to the question of what to observe is, indeed, difficult to give. Since unstructured observation is often used as an exploratory technique, the observer's understanding of the situation is

[3] For a more detailed discussion of many problems arising in this type of observation, with emphasis on situations where the observer participates in the group activity, see Whyte (1951). Much of the material in this section is taken verbatim from that source, with Dr. Whyte's permission.

likely to change as he goes along. This, in turn, may call for changes in what he observes, at least to the extent of making the content of observation more specific; and often the changes called for may be quite radical. These changes in the content of observation are not undesirable. Quite the contrary; they represent the optimal use of unstructured observation.

Suppose that an observer wishes to explore child-rearing practices in a foreign culture. He will probably begin by observing situations in which mother and child are together. In the course of his initial observations he may discover that such situations are much less frequent than he anticipated because mothers in the particular culture go out to work while fathers or older siblings take care of the infants. As soon as he has satisfied himself about this fact, the focus of his observational efforts, will of course, shift to the persons entrusted with the rearing of the young.

The shift in focus often goes hand in hand with narrowing the scope of observation. Suppose an observer wishes to explore social relations among the families in a suburban community. He may begin by observing street life, shopping centers, the local drugstore; he may attend club meetings and lectures, watch the crowds in front of the local theater, visit sessions of the local governing body, mix with parents waiting for their children at the close of the school day, etc. His initial observations may reveal that street life is hurried and unconducive to social interchange in the particular community; that the resident families give their shopping orders by telephone or send a maid to the store; that the drugstore is a center of activities only for adolescents; etc. Probably he will exclude these situations from his schedule after an initial period of observation and narrow the focus of attention to those more rewarding for his purpose.

However, although narrowing the range of situations to be observed facilitates observation, it still leaves the crucial part of the question—what to observe—unanswered. Among the features of a social situation that has been recognized as rewarding, which should be noted?

No hard and fast rules can be laid down; the observer must always be prepared to take his cues from unanticipated events. Nevertheless, it may be helpful to provide a check list such as the one which follows.

The list indicates significant elements of every social situation; it suggests directions of observation that may otherwise be overlooked.

1. *The participants.* Here one wants to know: Who are the participants, how are they related to one another, and how many are there? There are various ways of characterizing the participants, but usually one will want to know at least the following about any person who is being observed: age, sex, official function (e.g., "teacher," "doctor," "spectator," "customer," "host," "club president") in the situation being observed and in the occupational system of the broader community. One will also want to know how the participants are related to one another: Are they strangers or do they know one another? Are they members of some collectivity, and if so, what kind—e.g., an informal friendship group, a fraternity or club, a factory, a church? What structures or groupings exist among the participants—e.g., can cliques, focal persons, or isolates be identified by their spatial groupings or patterns of interaction?

2. *The setting.* A social situation may occur in different settings—e.g., a drugstore, a busy street intersection, a factory lunchroom, a nursery school, a slum dwelling, a palatial mansion. About the setting one wants to know, in addition to its appearance, what kinds of behavior it encourages, permits, discourages, or prevents. Or the social characteristics of the setting may be described in terms of what kinds of behavior are likely to be perceived as expected or unexpected, approved or disapproved, conforming or deviant.

3. *The purpose.* Is there some official purpose that has brought the participants together, or have they been brought together by chance? If there is an official purpose, what is it—e.g., to attend a funeral, to compete in a boat race, to participate in a religious ceremony, to meet as a committee, to have fun at a party? How do the participants react to the official purpose of the situation—e.g., with acceptance or with rejection? What goals other than the official purpose do the participants seem to be pursuing? Are the goals of the various participants compatible or antagonistic?

4. *The social behavior.* Here one wants to know what actually occurs. What do the participants do, how do they do it, and with whom and with what do they do it? With respect to behavior, one usually wants to know the following: (a) what was the stimulus or event that

initiated it; (b) what appears to be its objective; (c) toward whom or what is the behavior directed; (d) what is the form of activity entailed in the behavior (e.g., talking, running, driving a car, gesturing, sitting); (e) what are the qualities of the behavior (e.g., its intensity, persistence, unusualness, appropriateness, duration, affectivity, mannerisms); (f) what are its effects (e.g., what behavior does it evoke from others)?

5. *Frequency and duration.* Here one wants to know the answer to such questions as the following: When did the situation occur? How long did it last? Is it a recurring type of situation, or unique? If it recurs, how frequently does it occur? What are the occasions that give rise to it? How typical of such situations is the one being observed?

It should be emphasized that this list is not meant to apply in its entirety to every situation observed. Frequently it is impossible to obtain enough clues to permit such a comprehensive description. Or the course of events may be too rapid to permit consideration of all dimensions of a social situation. Or some aspect of an occurrence may need the entire attention of the observer, to the virtual exclusion of everything else. The list has its greatest advantage in planning the content of observational activities.

RECORDING UNSTRUCTURED OBSERVATION

In recording unstructured observation, two questions require consideration: When should the observer make notes? How should notes be kept?

The best time for recording is undoubtedly on the spot and during the event. This results in a minimum of selective bias and distortion through memory. There are many situations, however, in which note-taking on the spot is not feasible, because it would disturb the naturalness of the situation or arouse the suspicions of the persons observed. This is, of course, especially likely to be true in participant observation. Furthermore, constant note-taking may interfere with the quality of observation. The observer may easily lose relevant aspects of the situation if he divides his attention between observing and writing.

Some anthropologists have designed mnemonic devices that may be adapted by other investigators to their needs. E. J. Lindgren (1935), for example, says:

> I found a few simple devices for remembering things extremely useful in ethnographic work. Thus during a shaman ceremony which may go on for ten hours and presents, as I have said, peculiar difficulties, I associate the first outstanding incident which occurs with a word beginning with "A," the next with a word beginning with "B," and so forth. If I am not able to return to my tent before one or two o'clock in the morning, when I am generally too exhausted to record much, I can at least write down these key words to guide me when writing up a fuller account next day.

In situations in which immediate, detailed note-taking is not feasible, the memory of the observer may be too heavily taxed if recording is postponed until the observational period is over. For such situations it is well to acquire the habit of jotting down significant key words in an almost imperceptible manner, using a small sheet of paper, the back of an envelope, or other inconspicuous material. If the amount to be recorded is so great that this method does not satisfy the observer, he may well decide, if it is at all feasible, to retire from an on-going situation for a few minutes every hour or two to make more detailed notes.

However the observer records his immediate impressions, he should write up, as soon as possible after a period of observation, a complete account of everything in the situation that he wishes to remember. This write-up will ordinarily be in narrative form. Each record of a period of observation contains a great deal of information. As the records of observation accumulate, it will become difficult or impossible to remember which records contain information on a particular topic and which do not. Some *indexing* system is essential if the observer is to avoid wasting hours searching through his notes for items he remembers vaguely but cannot locate. The indexing system should be adapted to the purpose of the research, so no flat rules can be given here. However, the index should probably contain at least the following information: number or date of observation notes (or of interview, in the case of participant observation[4]); group chiefly in-volved (unless the study is confined entirely to one group); names of persons observed or interviewed, and perhaps also of persons discussed by them; and a brief summary of what is covered in the notes.

As the inquiry becomes more clearly focused, the investigator may develop a more elaborate indexing system. For example, during the course of a study of a street gang, he may tentatively decide that the analysis is likely to center around such topics as relations with other gangs, relations with adults, relations with girls, attitudes and be-havior concerning work, attitudes and behavior concerning the use of drugs. Each of these topics may then become a category in the index. If the observer has made carbon copies of his notes (always a sound procedure), he may wish to cut up one copy in order to file the various items under the relevant index categories. However, in order to avoid losing the context of a given item, which may be important in its interpretation, it is desirable to keep one copy of the observation in the original chronological narrative form. Notes may be made in the margin showing the index categories to which the various paragraphs are relevant.

Increasing the Accuracy of Observation

When one first observes in situations where immediate recording is not feasible, he is likely to find that by the time he has an oppor-tunity to write his observations, he remembers little of what has been said and done, or remembers it in a vague and confused way. With experience, however, the ability to remember increases, and the ob-server comes to *feel* that he is able to record significant parts of con-versations almost verbatim. However, such an impression is no substi-tute for an independent check. In order to check the accuracy and completeness of the observer's record, it would be interesting to com-

---

[4] An observer who participates as a member of a group will naturally talk with other members of the group. Some of these talks may serve the function of inter-views, in that the other members will give the observer information about past events, their reactions to present events, etc. Such interviews will usually be un-structured (see Chapter 7); the observer may combine them with more strictly observational notes in his records and in the analysis. For a discussion of the rela-tive advantages of observation and unstructured interviews, and of ways of com-bining the two, see Dean (1954).

pare it with a record made by sound-recording equipment. However, this is not often feasible; as far as we know, no such comparison has ever been made.[5] In any case, a sound recording captures primarily what is *said*; it cannot portray gestures and other nonverbal behavior. To supplement sound recording by a motion-picture record would ordinarily be prohibitively expensive, even if it were feasible on other grounds.

The next-best solution is to have two or more people observe the same event. When two or more observers are watching and recording in the same problem area, they have opportunities to compare their findings and check bias. It is desirable for them to make independent records first, so that the written records can be compared. This is an excellent way to discover one's blind spots. When both are participant observers in the situation, each will have opportunities to observe the other in action and to check on how people are reacting to him. This provides each observer with a valuable check on himself. Even if it is not possible to use more than one observer throughout the course of a study, it may be desirable to do so in the early stages, or at least during a pilot period in a setting similar to the one which is to be observed in the investigation.

The use of more than one observer, however, will in itself provide no clues to biases of interpretation that are common to all. When observers have a common cultural background and similar training— as is usually the case—it is inevitable that they will share certain general ways of perceiving and interpreting events. Whether these ways of perceiving and interpreting constitute a serious source of potential bias depends to a large extent on the nature of the data being collected. If, in observing a street gang, one is interested primarily in such questions as which members are central, which ones peripheral, the observer's point of view may make little difference. But if one is interested, for example, in the amount of aggression or friendliness the members show toward one another, the observer's point of view may have an important influence. Behavior that a middle-class observer

[5] Studies of *interviewing* in which tape recordings were used have shown that even when the interviewer is recording responses as they are made, omissions and distortions occur (see Hyman *et al.*, 1954). It seems reasonable to suppose that they would occur even more frequently when observations and conversations are recorded from memory.

interprets as aggression may seem like good-natured horseplay to one who has himself grown up in a street gang. Where interpretations of this sort are important to the study, it is desirable (though often not feasible) to have two observers from quite different backgrounds observe the same situation.

Whether an observer is working alone or as a member of a team, he may increase the objectivity of his observations by indicating, as he writes up his notes, which statements refer to actual events and which represent his interpretations. This is no easy task. Interpretation of the meaning of a situation must be present to some extent in the observer's mental set during the act of observation; otherwise it would be impossible for him to perceive the relationships among discrete movements, gestures, statements, and objective conditions of the situation. When the observer participates with the people he is observing, at least to the extent of asking them questions, his own tentative interpretation of a situation may lead him to ask certain questions. These questions, in turn, may channel and focus the informant's replies, possibly even suggesting to him certain interpretations of events that he might not otherwise have thought of.

Notwithstanding the difficulty of the task, efforts in the direction of trying to separate observations from interpretations can be made and will be rewarded by greater understanding of the situation. An overdose of interpretation in an observer's record may seriously interfere with the validity and reliability of his ultimate conclusions. One way of detecting the intrusion of interpretation is to have two observers record the same event according to the same system. If their accounts differ, it is not hard to determine whether the differences result from the inclusion of more detail by one or from the intrusion of interpretation on the part of one or both. (Agreement between them does not necessarily indicate that interpretation has not entered. They may both have made the same interpretation). In the case of reports by informants, the investigator may become more sensitive to the possible influence of his own tentative interpretations on the informant's statements if he records the questions he asked and his reasons for asking them.

The participant observer faces especially severe difficulties in maintaining objectivity. He is likely to develop friendly relations with some of the people he is studying. He may find himself personally concerned with a story told by a certain informant. Full recording helps to restore objectivity. As the story is recorded, the observer has something like a catharsis experience himself. He is still interested in the informant and his story, but he can now look at the record more objectively. Instead of feeling, with the informant, that the informant did the right thing and the other fellow was wrong, the observer begins asking: Why did the informant act as he did? He seeks to explain instead of defending or accusing. A full record of interviews and observations is as important in maintaining the objectivity of the researcher as it is in providing research data.

Becoming involved in a situation may lessen the sharpness of observation not only because the investigator identifies with his informants but also because he becomes accustomed to certain kinds of behavior. To get access to intimate data, the observer allows himself to become absorbed in the local culture, but then this very absorption process makes him take for granted behavior that he should be trying to explain. Whyte (1951) reports that, as he began the investigation which he reported in *Street Corner Society*, everything he saw and heard was new and strange, and all sorts of questions arose in his mind. But at this point he did not know enough or have enough data to ask good questions and get any answers. As he became part of the community, the richness of the data increased; yet he found in himself an increasing tendency to take for granted the sort of behavior that was taken for granted by the people he was observing.

How can this problem be met? The observer can hardly avoid becoming accustomed to the setting he is studying and thus becoming blind to valuable data. He can help himself to some extent simply by being aware of the tendency to take things for granted. If he writes progress reports at fairly frequent intervals, he will find, as he reads them over, points at which explanations are weak or at which they are needed and not provided. It is still more helpful to describe and explain his observations regularly to someone outside of the situation. The outsider does not take as much for granted, and his questions are a safeguard against growing blind spots.

Reference to a check list, such as the one on pages 209–210, may also be helpful in overcoming blind spots, especially if it is reviewed with the attitude, "Have I been overlooking anything about this item which is relevant in the context of this study?"

It is also possible to overcome blind spots by deliberately breaking up the perceptual field so that the factors that lead it to be seen in a particular way lose much of their force. The natural way of seeing a situation (and the most valid for most purposes) is to see the action centered around the principal characters. But sometimes the real center of the action is not the obvious one. For example, one of our associates has informally described a family that he has known fairly intimately for many years. It had always seemed obvious to him that the mother was the central character in the group. She was the manager, the disciplinarian, the one who gave direction and set limits to the activities of the children. The father seemed like a negative quantity. He rarely spoke. When he came home, no one seemed to notice him. There was never any exchange of greetings. He would be there, reading a book; then you would notice that he was no longer there, with hardly more than a softly closing door to mark his departure. The children developed certain behavioral disturbances, and it was in trying to understand these that our colleague eventually realized that he had totally misperceived the family constellation. Actually, that entire family gravitated around the person of the father. The mother was constantly interpreting the wishes of the father, regulating things so that they would fit in with the father's notions of how things should be. The children were very much aware that the ultimate source of approval and disapproval was the father. And both mother and children attributed a mystical power to the father's few words; they shared a belief that even his most casual remark was bound to come true.

Sometimes one discovers that a parent who has been dead or missing for many years is, nevertheless, the real center of a situation. In any group, important leadership functions are not necessarily vested in the manifest leaders; there may be a variety of behind-the-scenes sources of power without formal leadership status—individuals who crystallize opinion, individuals who take over the organization of actions in emergencies, individuals who can block particular lines of action, individuals who take the center of the stage on certain social occasions, etc. By deliberately refocusing on individuals who do not appear to be central in the group, one may gain new insights about important relationships.

A very different kind of check on the accuracy of observation and interpretation may come from the people who are being observed, if the investigator establishes the sort of relationship with them which make it possible for him to take them into his confidence about the research. Whyte reports, for example, (1951) that in gathering material for *Street Corner Society*, he had innumerable research discussions with "Doc," one of the key figures in the group he was observing, and that Doc read every page of the first draft of his manuscript. Usually, of course, the participants in the situation cannot check on the validity of theoretical interpretations, but they can tell the observer whether he has caught the meaning the situation and the behavior have *for them*.

Rosenfeld (1958) has suggested that the situation of being a participant observer is likely to create inner conflicts within the investigator which may interfere with objectivity. She points out that, especially if the group being observed is undergoing an emergency of some sort, there is strong pressure on the observer to become an active participant, to the extent of abandoning at least temporarily his detached position as an observer. If he does not do so, he may feel guilty about not helping when help is needed. On the other hand, if he does enter completely into the activities of the group, he becomes anxious about losing his identity as a scientist. In order to re-establish his position as an objective investigator, he may lean over backward to separate himself from the group he is observing; in doing so, he may become susceptible to sources of negative bias and distortion. Rosenfeld suggests that the first step in safeguarding against bias arising from inner conflicts is to be aware of the conflicts and of the nature of one's defenses. With this awareness, one can develop specific safeguards appropriate to the nature of the conflicts and the situation being studied.

THE RELATION OF OBSERVER AND OBSERVED

The need to prepare both oneself and the field carefully for observation in a real-life setting cannot be emphasized too strongly. For here, more than in many other techniques, mistakes in approach are heavily penalized. If, in an inquiry based on a sample, a faulty approach to a respondent leads to a refusal to be interviewed, another respondent can, as a rule, be substituted without much harm to the inquiry. (If there should be many such cases, one would, of course, become concerned about the possibilities of sampling bias.) In field observation, however, a faulty approach to a key person may have dire consequences for the entire inquiry. Since the method is applied in the actual life sphere of the subjects, where people are in contact with one another and exchange views or pass rumors, the observer is inevitably talked about, and his mistakes cannot remain isolated incidents.

Before he approaches anyone in the community or group he wishes to study, the observer-to-be must decide whether he will reveal the fact that he is a research worker or whether he will attempt to enter the situation under some other guise. Ordinarily, it seems preferable to make known the fact that one is doing research. First, this is often the simpler procedure; it is not easy to turn up suddenly as a member of a street gang, or as a skilled carpenter, or in some other role that provides a strategic vantage point for observation. Second, identifying oneself as a research worker frequently increases one's opportunities to get information. While one can learn much about the life of a factory worker by taking a job in a factory, introspecting on his own experience and watching the behavior of others, he may need to supplement this by getting people to explain what they are doing or why they are doing it. He needs to be able to ask questions—the sort of questions that would not be asked by a bona fide factory worker. Third, the investigator who proposes to enter a situation without revealing his research purpose has an obligation to ask himself whether there is any possibility that his disguised activities will harm any of the people in the situation and, if so, whether the potential results of his research are valuable enough to justify their acquisition under these circumstances.[6]

[6] This is only one of many ethical questions that may arise in connection with research in the social sciences. At every stage in the process—from the selection of a topic to the reporting and application of results—consideration of ethical implications may be relevant. In raising and answering such questions, the investigator would do well to turn to the publication of the American Psychological Association (1953) entitled *Ethical Standards of Psychologists*, especially pages 113–124; to the discussion by Rogers and Skinner (1956); and to the volume of the *Journal of Social Issues* devoted to "Values and the Social Scientist" (Benne and Swanson, 1950)

Sometimes, however, an investigator may decide that knowledge of his research interest would interfere with the behavior he needs to observe in order to answer his research problem, and that disguised observation would not have damaging effects on the people observed. For example, in a study of the sociopsychological effects of long-term unemployment in an Austrian village (Jahoda-Lazarsfeld and Zeisl, 1932), the study design required an observation of the standard of maintenance in the households of the unemployed. Because the Austrian unemployment allowance was linked to an official investigation of the actual needs of the unemployed, the families were understandably reluctant to admit curious strangers into their homes. To overcome this difficulty, a large collection of used clothing was brought to the village. On the pretext of having to establish the most urgent clothing needs of every family, research workers presenting themselves as members of a voluntary welfare group found entry into the homes, where they were welcomed with open arms when their mission of distributing clothing became known.

Two recent examples of data gathered by disguised observers that probably could not have been secured by any other means are presented by Sherif and Sherif (1953) and Festinger, Riecken, and Schachter (1956). In the former case, the gang activities of boys in a summer camp were observed by a research worker disguised as a laborer on the camp grounds. In the latter case, a sect that had predicted the end of the world was observed by investigators posing as converts to the sect.

Entrance into a community as an admitted research worker may require somewhat less ingenuity than entrance under some other guise, but nevertheless it requires careful staging. Depending on his specific task, the observer will wish to be in good rapport with many strata of the population. If he studies a factory, for example, he will have to be accepted by both management and workers. Unless he wishes to run the risk of being identified with one side in the industrial set-up, he must, so to speak, stage a simultaneous entry into both sides of the plant. The problem becomes even more complicated in community studies, in which there are, as a rule, many more than two sides to be approached simultaneously. The essential task here is to avoid premature identification with one side or faction of the community.[7]

[7] For a more detailed discussion of this problem, see Merton (1947).

The moment the observer enters the community, he must be prepared to provide a rationale for his presence which is understandable and acceptable to all members of the community. It may, on occasion, be better to let influential persons in the community handle the explanation of the investigator's work. Even in these circumstances, however, the investigator must have a hand in formulating the explanation of the role he is to play during his stay in the community. In conjunction with the explanation of his role, the observer must already have decided on the degree of his participation. This can vary from the bare minimum of answering when addressed to major activity in the community.

At first sight, it might seem that a high degree of participation could be justified only as an inevitable compromise with the practical demands of a situation. For a high degree of participation not only demands more effort on the part of the investigator, but introduces a new person into the community—the participant observer, whose presence may change it to an unknown extent. However, participation in community life can actually enhance the "naturalness" of the observer's position. There are many situations in which the observer might well be experienced as an inhibiting stranger unless he undertook a function meaningful to members of the community. Yet the importance of active participation for research is not limited to assuaging suspicions, establishing rapport, and enhancing the "naturalness" of the observer's position. Its main function for research consists in opening new avenues of understanding. Through intensive participation in community life, the observer exposes himself to experiences that give him a firsthand knowledge of the more subtle pressures and counterpressures to which the members of the community are exposed. His introspection about his own experiences as a participant represents one of the most fruitful means of understanding the community's characteristics.

Moreover, active participation opens the door to sources of information that might otherwise remain closed. Thus, it is natural for an active participant to enter into seemingly spontaneous and informal conversations through which he may learn a great deal that he might miss in more formal interviews.

The observer will usually be wise to establish relationships gradually, not to try to go too far too fast. Emotionally loaded topics should be avoided until the observer's relationship with an informant is very secure. Otherwise an informant may reveal very intimate information in an early interview but later regret having "given himself away" and so be reluctant to talk further with the observer.

In the interest of maintaining good rapport, active participation should never be forced on a resisting community or on any group within the community. Personal attributes of the observer, entirely unrelated to his scientific skills, will often be decisive factors in the community's tolerance of his active participation and observation. Depending on the situation, a man or a woman, a young or an old person, a white person or a Negro, a Moslem or a Hindu may be preferred. It is, of course, entirely in the interest of the study to comply, where possible, with such preferences.

Structured Observation[8]

Much of what has been said previously is applicable also to the more formal observational techniques that are often used in studies designed to provide systematic description or to test causal hypotheses. The major difference is that in these more systematic studies the investigator knows what aspects of the group activity are relevant for his research purposes and is therefore in a position to develop a specific plan for the making and recording of observations before he begins collecting data.

Structured observation focused on designated aspects of behavior may take place either in field settings or in controlled experiments within a laboratory setting. For example, a study of the effects of a training course for leaders of youth groups may call for the observation of meetings of a number of Boy Scout troops. Although the social scientist has little, if any, control over what happens at these meetings and cannot predict the course events will take, he can determine in advance what kinds of behavior should be observed if he is to get the information necessary to answer his research question. In laboratory

[8] Much of the material in this section has been taken verbatim from Zander (1951), with Dr. Zander's permission.

settings, the investigator can arrange the major aspects of the situation in such a way as to suit his research purposes and reduce the danger of unexpected interference from disturbing factors. Few of the problems that arise with observation in a community setting need trouble the observer if he can arrange and control the situation. Here his observational activity is often, but not necessarily, reduced to noting the presence, absence, or intensity of clearly specified types of behavior, much as the animal experimenter observes a rat's behavior in a specific way under controlled conditions. Of course, such control of the situation is appropriate only when the investigator already possesses a great deal of information about the phenomena he wishes to study.

Katz, Goldston, and Benjamin (1958), for example, created a series of controlled situations to test predictions about Negro-white social interaction. The hypotheses were suggested by findings in field studies of interracial contact and in experiments on the dynamics of small face-to-face groups. Male college students, white and Negro, were "hired" to work together in groups of four (two whites and two Negroes) for several three-hour sessions. Members of each group remained together throughout their employment and had no contact with other groups. The subjects were given various group tasks (ostensibly materials that were being developed for vocational aptitude tests), which included mental problems, mechanical construction, human relations problems, map drawing, and a game that required a high degree of coordination of effort among the four participants. Two types of hypothesis were tested. First, there were predictions having to do with the effect of the general difference in social status between Negroes and whites in our culture on the content and direction of communication between them: that the white students would tend to ignore the Negroes, and that the Negro students would speak less than the white participants and would direct most of their remarks to the latter. The second group of predictions concerned the effects on interracial behavior of two experimental variables: group reward versus individual reward, and high group prestige versus no prestige. It was hypothesized that group reward and group prestige would tend to reduce the divisive effects of disparity in social status—specifically, that these experimental conditions would bring about greater friendliness and cooperation between men of the two races, less behavioral restraint on the part of Negroes, less "bias" in the direction of communications of both Negroes and whites, and higher group productivity.

In order to measure amount and direction of relevant types of behavior, it was first necessary to develop a set of reliable categories for systematic observation and recording. Many weeks of preliminary work with pilot groups preceded the establishment of a satisfactory classification scheme. It consisted of twenty-eight interaction categories for describing such facilitative and disruptive behaviors as giving help, advice, information, and encouragement; rejecting another's suggestions, hoarding materials, disparaging another's contributions, expressing anger, and so on. Direction of behavior was recorded by noting the initiator and recipient of every social action. Specific categories were developed for the various tasks, so that the unique effects of each work situation could be ascertained. The observers were in a room adjoining that in which the subjects worked, behind a one-way screen; a recording device made it possible for them to hear what was being said. Although the subjects could not see the observers, they were told that they were being observed; the reason given them was that, in order to improve the aptitude tests, it was necessary to have a detailed record of how people went about working on them.

On the whole, the results of this rather elaborate investigation tended to support hypotheses about the effects of status disparity and of group reward; predictions about the effects of group prestige tended to be contradicted.

The Content of Observation

Structured observation, as has been indicated, is used mainly in studies starting with relatively specific formulations. Normally, therefore, there is much less freedom of choice with respect to the content to be observed than in unstructured observation.

Since the situation and the problem are already specified, the observer is in a position to set up in advance the categories in terms of which he wishes to analyze the situation. When he starts out, he is likely to have a considerable number of categories. As he tries out his instrument, he may find both mechanical problems in observation and failures in reliability. To meet these problems, categories are dropped or combined or formulated more clearly. By the time the "real" observations are to be made, either in a field setting or in an experiment, the categories will have been defined well enough to provide reliable data on the questions to be asked. For example, Bales (1950) at first used more than fifty categories in observing group situations. As his experience with reliability accumulated and as his theories developed, the number of categories gradually decreased. The final version, shown opposite, was a set of twelve standard behavioral categories applicable to a wide range of group situations. Behavior of any group member, or of the leader, is coded in terms of careful definitions for each category.

During the first attempts to use an observational instrument, it is useful to check, by means of interviews with the persons observed, whether, according to their own account, they are doing or feeling what the observer has described them as doing or feeling.

THE OBSERVER'S FRAME OF REFERENCE. An observer may categorize the behavior of a person in terms of the assumed reactions of other group members, or he may categorize it in terms of the intention the speaker probably had. The procedures developed by Bales instruct the observer to do the former. The method developed by Steinzor (1949) requires the observer to do the latter. Obviously either or both observer sets can be used. What is important is to make a decision about the appropriate frame of reference and to train observers accordingly.

Thelen and Withall (1949) reported substantial agreement among observations of the same classroom groups by three observer teams, each working within a different frame of reference. The observers categorized the behavior of a teacher according to whether it was "learner centered" or "teacher centered." Several observers concentrated on the objective behavior of the teacher. An equal number made inferences about the intents and attitudes of the teacher. The third group was made up of the class members themselves, who indicated how they felt at various points by pressing levers attached to their desks. (The lever pressings were recorded by a kymograph.) Observations made according to these different frames of reference were in close agreement in identifying the teacher's behavior as teacher-centered or learner-centered. It appears, then, that at some levels of data collection, the nature of the observer's set may make little dif-

THE BALES SYSTEM OF CATEGORIES FOR RECORDING GROUP INTERACTION[9]

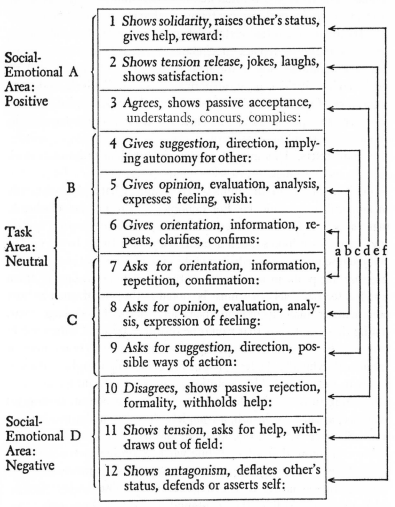

Social-Emotional A Area: Positive

1 *Shows solidarity*, raises other's status, gives help, reward:

2 *Shows tension release*, jokes, laughs, shows satisfaction:

3 *Agrees*, shows passive acceptance, understands, concurs, complies:

B

4 *Gives suggestion*, direction, implying autonomy for other:

5 *Gives opinion*, evaluation, analysis, expresses feeling, wish:

6 *Gives orientation*, information, repeats, clarifies, confirms:

Task Area: Neutral

C

7 *Asks for orientation*, information, repetition, confirmation:

8 *Asks for opinion*, evaluation, analysis, expression of feeling:

9 *Asks for suggestion*, direction, possible ways of action:

Social-Emotional D Area: Negative

10 *Disagrees*, shows passive rejection, formality, withholds help:

11 *Shows tension*, asks for help, withdraws out of field:

12 *Shows antagonism*, deflates other's status, defends or asserts self:

a b c d e f

KEY:

a Problems of Communication
b Problems of Evaluation
c Problems of Control
d Problems of Decision
e Problems of Tension Reduction
f Problems of Reintegration

A Positive Reactions
B Attempted Answers
C Questions
D Negative Reactions

[9] Reproduced from Bales (1950).

ference. The more one is interested in details, however, the more important the choice of the proper frame of reference may become.

It often happens that certain data can be coded only in retrospect. Whether or not a remark precipitates group tension, for example, can be determined only in the light of the events following that remark. To handle this type of categorizing, some studies have made tape recordings of the observed situation; others have demanded that the observer pause periodically to go back over his notes in order to make codings in the light of subsequent events.

TIME UNITS. The amount of time included in one notation by an observer may range from a few seconds to several hours. The central problem in setting up time units is to determine what a psychologically meaningful unit would be. For example, it may not be sensible to make a rating of the constructiveness of a child's play with a certain toy every two minutes. Such a rating may have to be based on the *complete* sequence of events in a child's use of a toy. A typical way of meeting this problem is to use more than one observer. One of them watches for those acts that must be noted as they occur, such as brief comments or small bits of motor behavior. Another takes a larger view, noting those behaviors that would be distorted by strict adherence to time or other sampling citeria, and codes these in terms of an index or rating scale whenever he feels that he has enough data for his purposes.

WHAT IS AN ACT? The definition of an act is difficult when one is attempting to categorize the verbal behavior of a person. Is an act a sentence, a pause for breath, a complete thought, or the least noticeable difference between one idea and another in a given speech? An act is even more difficult to define when recording motor behavior, since the person being observed seldom separates his movements one from another as neatly as the categories on the observation schedule. The problem is still further confounded when dealing with group phenomena. Is the act of a group a speech by one member, a decision reached, a function carried out, an event, a set of events, a program item, the completion of an item on an agenda, a mood shift, or what? The definition of an act will be determined by the frame of reference used as well as by the size of time units recorded.

The most frequent practice in coding verbal behavior is to code each complete thought separately. Thus, one sentence may include thoughts that fit several categories or none at all. The observation of motor behavior is usually concerned with the general nature of the behavior, such as sitting, walking, slouching, gesturing, handling, etc. The recorded acts of a group, on the other hand, are usually decisions, or the completion of items on an agenda or of certain phases of the meeting.

RATING SCALES VERSUS ALL-OR-NONE CATEGORIES. If the research purpose requires only a record of the objective facts of behavior, without any further qualification, all-or-none categories are usually adequate. "Speaking" versus "not speaking" is an example of an all-or-none category; the observer simply places a tally on his sheet when a given person speaks, and makes no tallies for this person until he speaks again. A series of discrete categories intended to describe the behavior of the speaker may take the form of all-or-none tallies. For example, in one study the observer noted, for each act of a youth-group leader, whether the leader was acting in the role of a comrade, a policeman, a referee, an educator, or a coordinator.

Often, however, observers are asked to describe the behavior of a group member by making ratings on scales. In watching the leader above, for example, the observer rated each leadership act in terms of the degree of freedom implied and the strength of the influence exerted on the group members by the act.

PRESERVING THE PATTERN OF THE PHENOMENA. The personal interactions or group phenomena in any situation make up a number of themes which it may be important to preserve in their original pattern. In many studies, of course, it is sufficient to get a record of acts apart from their context. An example is that of tallying the frequency of remarks addressed to a deviant group member. In other studies, however, the main function of the data is to specify the nature of some general pattern of behavior in the group, such as the teaching method being used, the rise and fall of group tension, or the establishment of group procedures for handling the feelings of members.

In part, this is a problem of analysis. However, a reliable observational device may turn out to provide only fragmented information, which cannot be combined into a meaningful picture. It is necessary, therefore, that the tryout stage of any instrument include attempts to code the data in order to make sure that information of the desired type can be obtained.

A study of leadership among nursery school children in Hungary (Merei, 1949) provides an example of how a complex set of observations recorded by a number of different observers can be combined to give a total pattern. Merei was interested in the relationship between leader and group, particularly in whether leadership at this early age is maintained when a child leader is put into groups which have various degrees of cohesiveness and with which he is not familiar. Some of the criteria Merei used for identifying leadership behavior were: giving orders more frequently than following orders; being imitated more frequently than imitating; attacking more often than being attacked. Categories for recording the behavior of each child were established according to these criteria. In addition, categories were developed to describe other dimensions of the group situation. It was decided that several observers were needed to note all of the relevant dimensions of behavior. Some of the observers concentrated on describing the activities of the group by five-minute intervals; others recorded the behavior of the leader, his relation to other children and to the on-going activity, for the same intervals. Others singled out the following dimensions of behavior: group formation and isolation; imitation; order-giving and response to orders; taking the initiative; ownership and change of ownership of toys; etc. Typical forms of behavior were itemized under each of these categories. In the ownership category, for instance, the following forms were distinguished: the child asks for something and receives it; the child asks for something and does not receive it; the child takes an object away from another child; etc. Each form of behavior was given a special written symbol to facilitate speed of recording. When the observers had mastered this symbol language, the actual recording could proceed at considerable speed. Synchronizing the various protocols at five-minute intervals made it possible to reconstruct the complete scene when the data were analyzed.

RECORDING OBSERVATIONS

There is no one best method of recording observations, although some procedures yield certain kinds of data that others cannot. The simplest and most economical device that will yield the required data is the one to use.

The most frequently used system of recording is one that provides the observer with a number of duplicated sheets containing the list of categories to be coded and the cells in which they are to be marked. An economical variation was used by Lippitt and Zander in an unpublished study that required field observations of group leadership. Each of the observers had a ring-binder notebook containing sets of cards of the type used in machine analysis, on which the observational categories had been printed. The observers made a pencil mark on the proper card opposite the appropriate category. These cards were then run through an automatic punch machine which was sensitive to graphite and which punched the cards wherever a mark had been made. The cards were then ready for machine sorting without the usual expense, time loss, and danger of error involved when a punch-machine operator transfers material from code sheets to a card.

Mechanical recording instruments have been used in some studies. Chapple (1949) has devised an "interaction chronograph," on which the observer indicates who is talking by pressing a button for the duration of each person's statement. The machine is so designed that it will automatically summate, at the end of the observation period, certain frequencies of interaction among group members. Thelen has developed an "audio-introspectometer," which allows observers or members of the group to record their feelings or other observations by placing a desk-lever at one of several precoded positions.

Bales and Gerbrands (1948) have described an "interaction recorder" which they have found useful in dealing with a large number of categories. This device consists of a box containing a roller mechanism. On top of the box, at the left, is fastened a sheet showing the categories in terms of which observations are being made. A roll of paper, as wide as the sheet showing the categories, is moved from right to left across the top of the box by a roller mechanism. At any given moment, a blank portion of this paper appears at the right of the category sheet; the observer makes the appropriate entries on this blank section of the paper. Suppose, for example, that he is observing a small group in terms of the categories shown on page 225. Let us say that member #1 makes a remark that the observer categorizes as "gives opinion"; he writes a "1" on the paper in the position next to this item on the category sheet. As the roller continues to move the paper, the portion with this mark now disappears into the box, and an unmarked portion of the paper is again available to the observer. Here he records the response of another member to #1's opinion— perhaps a "5" in the position corresponding to the item "disagrees." Since the strip of paper on which he records his entries is constantly moving, the final record shows the sequence of behavior.

Sound recordings and motion pictures have been used when it is necessary to describe the over-all nature of an event or to code certain actions of members or of the group in terms of the frame of reference provided by the entire event. Tape recordings have often been used for this purpose. Here, however, one loses the direction of the remark and the gestures, nods, and bodily postures which are often needed for a full comprehension of the behavior of the speaker as well as that of the recipient of the remark. Silent motion pictures have limited usefulness because remarks are omitted. Sound movies are so expensive that they have seldom been used.

Although such devices as tape recordings, motion pictures, and television may be very helpful in giving an over-all view of a social event, their use does not in itself solve the problem of gathering data for systematic purposes. Relevant categories for recording behavior must be established, time units decided upon, methods set up for recording who initiated an action and to whom it was addressed. Observations may be recorded either at the time the event occurs (that is, simultaneously with the making of the motion picture or the tape recording), or coding may be done from the movie or the recording. But at some point, if the data are to be used in a quantified way, they must be recorded in terms of such a formal scheme.

INCREASING THE RELIABILITY OF OBSERVATION

In one sense, all that has been said thus far is relevant to the problem of obtaining adequate reliability in the use of an observational instrument. That is, wise and consistent procedures in the development of such an instrument will greatly enhance reliability, assuming, of course, that the observers have been trained to interpret their instructions similarly and have practiced enough to develop the skills necessary for proper categorizing and recording. There are some special problems, however, in achieving reliable and valid observation that are worth separate consideration.

One problem grows out of inadequate definition of the kinds of behavior that are to be taken as corresponding to a given concept. Berkowitz and Guetzkow (1949), for example, have pointed out that in categorizing different groups in terms of "pleasantness of group atmosphere," one observer might be especially sensitive to the personal liking of the group members for one another, another to the informality of the relationships among members, another to still a different dimension of pleasantness of atmosphere.

Another factor that may lower the reliability of even well-trained and skilled observers is the degree of confidence one must have in one's judgment before marking a given category. If observers are required to rate the presence of "ego need" behavior (an example used by Berkowitz and Guetzkow) even when little behavior relevant to such a rating occurs, one observer may rate the extent of it as being greater than it "actually" is simply because he himself has a predisposition to perceive evidence of "ego need" behavior; another observer may rate it as lower than it "actually" is because he requires more evidence or, perhaps, greater confidence before making a decision about the presence of "ego need" behavior.

One of the greatest sources of unreliability is the constant error introduced by the observer because of distortion of his perceptions by his own needs or values. An observer who sharply disapproves of certain leadership practices, for example, will have difficulty in preventing a bias; he may code more of the leader's behavior as falling in the categories he disapproves of than would another observer who feels less strongly on the matter. Adequate training and practice can overcome this in most persons, though not in all.

Although research observers have been able to rate a group reliably on as many as fifty categories and even more, there is a point at which the load can seriously hamper reliability. The major result of overloading is that the observer cannot record all the relevant data and may unwittingly record some aspects more adequately than others, thus giving a biased account. This may result from fatigue, which causes the observer to slow down and later spurt; from avoidance of more difficult categories in order to keep up the pace; or from any of a number of other reasons. Overloading can be prevented by standardized rest periods, by distributing the job among several observers or by mechanically recording the session (if such recordings are suitable).

Obviously, one important method of increasing reliability is careful training of observers. A well-developed observational procedure can be spoiled by differences among users or by failure to understand the rules for its use. It is necessary, therefore, that the investigator plan to invest a good portion of time in training the observers. The elaborateness of the training depends on the complexity of the observer's task. One study, which used almost one hundred observers in several different parts of the country, determined the length of the training course by the amount of time it took the trainee to obtain adequate agreement with the observer-trainer. When he had achieved sufficient skill, he was allowed to begin observations.

A typical training program begins with an explanation of the purposes and theory involved in the given study and then moves on to an explanation of the categories and the rules for their use. The purpose of each category in relation to the theory and to specific hypotheses is pointed out. After the trainees have had an opportunity to ask questions, they try to use the schedule on a group that is attempting to demonstrate phenomena of the type the observers will be expected to code when the actual data collection begins. The trainee naturally encounters difficulty in selecting proper categories, sampling, keeping abreast, deciding how to categorize marginal cases, etc. These difficulties are ironed out by discussion and further practice. Next comes a tryout in a pilot study on a group similar to the one the trainee will later be expected to observe. Here again difficulties arise which can be corrected. At this point, or a little later, it may be helpful to use tape recordings or motion pictures in order to check events that were coded differently by different observers. Now the observers are ready for reliability tests, followed by subsequent practice and more reliability tests until the trainer is satisfied that the observers have become useful and comparable measuring instruments.

Here too, as in the case of less structured observation, checking and increasing reliability does not eliminate the possibility of a constant bias shared by two or more observers.[10] There are no simple techniques for dealing with this problem. If it seems likely that such constant biases may seriously affect the findings, it may be desirable to have two or more observers with different backgrounds record the same events, at least during a preliminary period.

THE RELATION OF OBSERVER AND OBSERVED

Unless he is concealed behind a one-way screen, his presence unknown to the group, the nonparticipant observer faces the same kinds of problems as the participant observer in establishing relations with the people he is observing. He, too, must carefully prepare his entry into the situation and make sure that all members of the group are willing to accept him. Since he is usually conspicuously engaged in recording behavior on prepared schedules, using a timing device and perhaps other technical aids, it is ordinarily not possible to disguise the fact that he is doing research. Hence, it is all the more important that he obtain the group's full agreement to the inquiry. In some situations, however, only the consent of the group leader is necessary, and a rather vague explanation may satisfy the group members. Whenever possible, investigators usually attempt to create an impression of the observer as a neutral, psychologically nonvisible person.

Conceivably, the entry of an observer into a group, however unobtrusive, may introduce another variable into the situation that may change the behavior being observed. In children's groups, for example, the presence of adult observers may be more potent than the particular experimental variable that is supposed to be operating. Deutsch (1949) found that college students who were in a competitive situation said that they were more aware of the observers than comparable students who were in a cooperative situation. It is important that some thought be given to ways in which the observer's presence may influence the outcome of the research, and to developing techniques that reduce this possibility.

On the whole, however, people seem to get used to observers if the behavior of the observers convinces the group members that they

[10] See pages 213–214.

are no threat. Deutsch also found that the members of small groups were much more aware of the observer's presence (as indicated on a rating scale marked after each weekly meeting by the group members) at the beginning of their experience with them than they were after they had been observed for three meetings. Many investigators believe that it makes little difference in the observed behavior of the group members whether the observer sits in the room with the group, behind a one-way screen with the group aware that he is there, or behind a one-way screen with the group left to wonder whether he is there or not.

7

DATA COLLECTION
II. Questionnaires and Interviews

Comparison of Interview and Questionnaire

Question Content

Types of Interviews and Questionnaires

The Sociometric Method

Visual Aids in Interviewing

A Concluding Note

If we want to know how people feel: what they experience and what they remember, what their emotions and motives are like, and the reasons for acting as they do—why not ask them?   G. W. ALLPORT

OBSERVATIONAL METHODS, as we have seen in the preceding chapter, are primarily directed toward describing and understanding behavior as it occurs. They are less effective in giving information about a person's perceptions, beliefs, feelings, motivations, anticipations, or future plans; and certainly they provide no information about past behavior or private behaviors, such as sexual activity or dreaming, which are, by their very nature, either unfeasible or impossible to observe. To obtain such information, the interview, the questionnaire, and the projective method have been devised.

In the interview and questionnaire approach, heavy reliance is placed on the subject's *verbal report* for information about the stimuli or experiences to which he is exposed and for knowledge of his behavior; usually the investigator has not observed the events discussed. The subject's report may or may not be taken at face value; it may be interpreted in the light of other knowledge about him or in terms of some psychological theory; inferences may be drawn about aspects of his functioning which he has not reported. Regardless of the amount and kind of interpretation, however, the starting point is the subject's self-report. Thus these approaches can ordinarily obtain only material that the subject is willing and able to report.

For many years now, a controversy has been raging in the psychological literature about the validity of verbal reports. The question is: How do we know a person is *really* hungry when he says, "I am hungry"? There are many weighty issues involved in this question, which we shall not discuss.[1] Let us point out, however, that in everyday life we accept many verbal reports as valid. For example, if we ask a friend what he thought of a certain play and he says "It's terrible," we ordinarily believe that his statement of *feeling* is correct; whether his feeling is appropriate to the play is, of course, another matter. However, in everyday life we also realize that in certain circumstances verbal reports are not to be trusted. For example, whenever we have reason to suspect that a person's truthful self-report would be embarrassing, humiliating, or degrading, or would in some way place him in an unfavorable light, we are likely to entertain some reservations about a report that shows him in favorable light. Or whenever we have reason to believe that a person is using a verbal report to ingratiate himself, to gain respect or prestige, to amuse or astonish, or in some other way to create a certain social effect, we are likely to place little confidence in it. In other words, when the circumstances in which the report occurs lead us to suppose that the subject's *motivation* or the pressures to which he is exposed are such as to prevent a candid report, we are not likely to give it much credence.[2]

Not only may people be reluctant to report openly their beliefs, feelings, motivations, plans, and so on; they may be *unable* to do so. As psychoanalysts have pointed out, we are not aware of many of our important beliefs and motivations, and hence cannot report them. Moreover, self-report frequently requires *self-diagnosis*. Even such seemingly simple questions as "Are you shy with strangers?," or "Would you rather go to a party or stay home and read a good book?" require the individual to make a judgment about himself on the basis of many past events. Feelings, beliefs, and motivations become appar-

---

[1] For an excellent discussion of these issues, see the "Symposium on Operationism" in the *Psychological Review*, 1945, 52, 241–294.

[2] The research of Parry and Crossley demonstrates how the answers even to factual questions may be influenced by the desire to appear "respectable." As summarized by Katz (1951), "They found that people consistently exaggerated their registration and voting behavior. The exaggeration varied from thirteen percent who falsely claimed to have voted in the 1948 election to twenty-eight percent who made fictitious claims to voting in local elections. One third of those who reported contributing to the Community Chest were speaking of pious intentions, not actual contributions. Telephone and home ownership were accurately reported. Similarly, car ownership was not appreciably inflated, but ten percent of those reporting a driver's license did not have one. Again, ten percent claimed to have library cards when in fact they had none."

ent to the self in an intellectually comprehensible form only as the end result of an involved process of inference. With respect to complex social attitudes, many people have never learned to make the inferences necessary to an adequate verbal report; they cannot indicate, in any systematic or analytic manner, their attitude toward their husband or wife, for example, or toward "progressive education," or toward a minority group.

Nevertheless, every person has a unique opportunity to observe himself. To the extent that he can and will communicate his knowledge about himself, he provides the investigator with information that could otherwise be obtained, if at all, only by more time-consuming methods. Despite the limitations of self-report, it is frequently both possible and useful to get an individual's own account of his feelings toward a psychological object, his image of the object, his views of appropriate behavior toward it, etc.

Comparison of Interview and Questionnaire

Although both interviews and questionnaires place heavy reliance upon the validity of verbal reports, there are important differences between the two methods. In a questionnaire, the information one obtains is limited to the written responses of subjects to prearranged questions. In an interview, since the interviewer and the person interviewed are both present as the questions are asked and answered, there is opportunity for greater flexibility in eliciting information; in addition, the interviewer has the opportunity to observe both the subject and the total situation to which he is responding. Let us detail further some of the general characteristics of the questionnaire and interview approaches, with their respective advantages and disadvantages.

ADVANTAGES OF QUESTIONNAIRES

By its very nature, the questionnaire is likely to be a less expensive procedure than the interview. It requires much less skill to administer than an interview; in fact, questionnaires are often simply mailed or handed to respondents with a minimum of explanation. Further, questionnaires can often be administered to large numbers of individuals simultaneously; an interview, on the other hand, usually calls for questioning each individual separately.[3] Questionnaires can be sent through the mail; interviewers cannot.[4] With a given amount of funds, it is usually possible to cover a wider area and to obtain information from more people by means of questionnaires than by personally interviewing each respondent.

The impersonal nature of a questionnaire—its standardized wording, its standardized order of questions, its standardized instructions for recording responses—ensures some uniformity from one measurement situation to another.[5] From a psychological point of view, however, this uniformity may be more apparent than real; a question with standard wording may have diverse meanings for different people, may be comprehensible to some and incomprehensible to others. Nevertheless, much can be done to ensure meaningful uniformity of questions by careful pretesting and by helping the subjects to understand the questionnaire during its administration. The interviewing situation, on the other hand, is rarely uniform from one interview to the next. Not only do the personalities of different interviewers affect the measurement situation differently; each interviewer is bound to vary somewhat from interview to interview. Moreover, in some types of interview, the

[3] This is not true, of course, of group interviews, where as many as eight to ten people may discuss the subject matter of an investigation under the direction of an interviewer. However, such interviews are more satisfactory as a source of hypotheses or as a way of gathering information about the group; they do not ordinarily yield systematic information from every individual in the group on each point covered in the interview schedule.

[4] Interviewing by telephone may, in certain circumstances, cost less per return than the mail questionnaire. The telephone interview is particularly useful in obtaining information about what an individual or a family is doing (e.g., what television program he is watching) at the time of the call. Usually, telephone interviewing has to be brief and superficial to obtain the cooperation of the respondent. Another serious limitation is that telephone surveys cannot reach a random sample of the total population, since not all people have telephones, and people who work away from home are hard to reach by telephone. For a further discussion of telephone surveys see Blankenship (1946) and Parten (1950).

[5] This is not true for mailed questionnaires, where there is likely to be considerable variation from home to home in the conditions under which the questionnaire is filled out. In one home, for example, the questionnaire may be filled out by the head of the family, in another by some other member; in one the questionnaire may be given time and attention, in another it may be competing with a television broadcast or a crying baby.

interviewer has no standard set of questions to ask. As a result, interviews may be less easily comparable with one another than questionnaires.

Another advantage of questionnaires is that respondents may have greater confidence in their anonymity, and thus feel freer to express views they fear might be disapproved of or might get them into trouble. Although an interviewer may assure the respondent that he will not be identified in any way, the respondent may doubt his good faith; since, in most interviewing situations, the interviewer knows either the respondent's name or his address or other identifying information, it is always possible that he may include this information in the completed interview. If a questionnaire is presented as anonymous and there is no apparent identifying information, the respondent may feel greater confidence that his replies will not (or cannot) be identified as coming from him. Studies that have used both methods have sometimes found rather marked differences between the replies to the interview and those to the questionnaire. Edwards (1957a), for example, in a survey of attitudes of residents of Seattle toward a proposed state bill providing a cash bonus to war veterans, had interviewers question half of the respondents; the other half were given a sheet marked "Secret Ballot," which they checked, folded, and inserted into a box labeled "Secret Ballot Box." (This was, of course, an unusually vivid way of emphasizing anonymity.) The interviews showed many more "don't know" replies and fewer unfavorable responses than the ballots. A referendum vote in an election held a few weeks later provided a check; the proportions obtained from the secret ballot were much closer to those of the actual vote than the results of the direct interview. It should be noted, however, that anonymity is not always the best method of inducing frank answers. On more complex questions, where there may be strong emotional involvement—as, for example, questions of marital adjustment—an understanding and permissive manner on the part of an interviewer is likely to be more successful than the anonymity of a questionnaire in eliciting frank responses.

Another characteristic of the questionnaire that is sometimes, though not always, desirable is that it may place less pressure on the subject for immediate response. When the subject is given ample time for filling out the questionnaire, he can consider each point carefully rather than replying with the first thought that comes to mind, as often happens under the social pressure of long silences in an interview.

Advantages of Interviews

It has been estimated that, for purposes of filling out even simple written questionnaires, at least 10 per cent of the adult population of the United States is illiterate. For complex questionnaires, the percentage would undoubtedly be considerably higher.[6] Thus, one of the major drawbacks of the usual questionnaire is that it is appropriate only for subjects with a considerable amount of education. Complicated questionnaires requiring extended written responses can be used with only a very small percentage of the population. Even many college graduates have little facility for writing, and of those who do, few have the patience or motivation to write as fully as they might speak. Hence, questionnaires are not an appropriate method for large segments of the population; for those for whom they are appropriate, the burden of writing or of maintaining interest is great enough to limit the number of questions that may be asked and the fullness of the responses. On the other hand, interviews can be used with almost all segments of the population; in fact, in contrast with the questionnaire, a frequent problem in interviewing is that of limiting the responses of the verbose individual.

Surveys conducted by personal interviews have an additional advantage over surveys conducted by mailed questionnaires in that they usually yield a much better sample of the general population. Many people are willing and able to cooperate in a study when all they have to do is talk. When questionnaires are mailed to a random sample of the population, the proportion of returns is usually low, varying from about 10 to 50 per cent. There are many factors that influence the percentage of returns to a mailed questionnaire. Among the most important are: (1) the sponsorship of the questionnaire; (2) the attractiveness of the questionnaire format; (3) the length of the questionnaire; (4) the nature of the accompanying letter requesting coopera-

---

[6] Subjects with limited education may be able to fill out questionnaires with the help of questionnaire administrators. However, in such cases the questionnaire loses much of its advantage over the interview with respect to economy.

tion; (5) the ease of filling out the questionnaire and mailing it back; (6) the inducements offered to reply; (7) the nature of the people to whom the questionnaire is sent. Attractively designed questionnaires that are short, easy to fill out, simple to return, sponsored by a group with prestige, and presented in a context that motivates the respondent to cooperate are most likely to be returned. However, even under the best of circumstances a sizable proportion do not return questionnaires. The people who *do* return them are usually the less mobile (and thus the more likely actually to receive the questionnaire), the more interested, the more literate, and the more partisan section of the population.[7]

Another advantage of the interview is its greater flexibility. In a questionnaire, if the subject misinterprets a question or records his responses in a baffling manner, there is usually little that can be done to remedy the situation. In an interview there is the possibility of repeating or rephrasing questions to make sure that they are understood or of asking further questions in order to clarify the meaning of a response. Its flexibility makes the interview a far superior technique for the exploration of areas where there is little basis for knowing either what questions to ask or how to formulate them.

In addition, the interviewing situation offers a better opportunity than the questionnaire to appraise validity of reports. The interviewer is in a position to observe not only *what* the respondent says but also *how* he says it. He can, if he wishes, follow up contradictory statements. If need be, the interviewer can directly challenge the subject's report in order to see how consistent his answers will be.

The interview is the more appropriate technique for revealing information about complex, emotionally laden subjects or for probing the sentiments that may underlie an expressed opinion. If a verbal report is to be accepted at face value, it must be elicited in circumstances that encourage the greatest possible freedom and honesty of expression. Although, as already noted, an anonymous questionnaire may sometimes be the most effective way of producing such a permissive atmosphere, its usefulness is limited to issues on which respondents have rather clearly formulated views that can be simply expressed. The more or less rigid structure of questionnaires, the inability to explain

[7] For a fuller discussion, see Parten (1950, Chapter 11).

fully in writing one's asocial or antisocial feelings and behavior, and the solemnity and permanent nature of a response that is put on paper in one's own handwriting or (if the questionnaire is not anonymous) under one's own name—all work against frank discussions of socially taboo or socially controversial issues in response to a questionnaire. With respect to many questions, an interview is likely to be more successful in creating an atmosphere that allows the respondent to express feelings or to report behaviors that are customarily disapproved.[8]

In the interview situation, the "social atmosphere" can be varied in other ways. Behavior in real life occurs in situations that are seldom free from social pressures. The interview, more than the questionnaire, allows one to approximate in the measurement situation these varying social pressures, since the interviewer can, within limits, vary the nature of the atmosphere as he questions the respondent. He can, for example, point out objections to the position of the person being interviewed, and observe how the latter responds.[9] This is a very useful flexibility, especially if the ultimate objective of the measurement is to predict behavior in varied situations.

Question Content

In both questionnaires and interviews, information is obtained by asking questions. Questioning is particularly suited to obtaining information about what a person *knows*, *believes* or *expects*, *feels* or *wants*, *intends* or *does* or *has done*, and about his *explanations* or *reasons* for any of the preceding. These major types of question content are discussed below. It should be recognized, however, that questions do not always fall neatly into one or another "content type." The distinctions among types are a matter of custom and convenience rather than theoretical rigor.

[8] For an interesting discussion of the flexible use of the interview method to obtain information about a socially taboo subject, see Kinsey et al. (1948).

[9] As a rule, this would constitute very bad interviewing practice. However, in interviews designed to measure responses under varying degrees of social pressure, such procedures on the part of the interviewer are an essential part of the measurement process.

Content Aimed Mainly at Ascertaining "Facts"

Often the simplest and most economical method of obtaining "facts" is to go directly to the people who are in a position to know them and to ask for the desired information. It is reasonable to assume that people who have access to information, who are sufficiently intelligent to absorb it, and who are motivated to acquire and retain it are able, if they are willing, to provide the investigator with reports of many interesting and valuable "facts." We may expect, for example, that the people who are responsible for the execution of a policy know what it is. Similarly, we should expect every individual to know a variety of facts about himself and his environment. A sizeable proportion of most questionnaires and interviews is directed toward obtaining such facts. Questions about the person's age, education, religion, income, nationality, marital status, occupation, etc., are of this type. So, too, are questions about the characteristics (behavior, beliefs, feelings, desires, intentions, etc.) of persons who are known to the respondent, such as family, friends, and colleagues. Questions about events, circumstances, policies, etc., known to the respondent are also of this nature.

Reported "facts" must, of course, always be evaluated in terms of credibility. The rules of evidence that have developed through the centuries in judicial procedure are a good source of insight into factors affecting credibility. Thus, it is always pertinent to raise such questions as: How did the respondent obtain knowledge of the "fact"— through direct observation, through inference, through hearsay, etc.? What motives may the respondent have in reporting the "fact"? How accurate is the respondent's memory of the "fact" likely to be? Any one of these factors may affect, for example, even such an apparently clear-cut piece of information as a housewife's report of her husband's income. Her knowledge may be based only on her husband's statement, and he may be deceiving her; or she may wish to impress the investigator and therefore claim a higher income; or she may not be interested enough in her husband's income to remember it precisely. The fallibility of memory for nonrecurring events, for events in the distant past, for events of little interest, and for events difficult to comprehend; the ephemeral quality of memory and its dependence on situational factors; the corruptibility of memory in relation to events of significance to the self—all of these factors require caution in accepting as true the remembrance of things past (see McGeoch, 1942).

When the focus is on description or understanding of an event, a situation, or a community, rather than on information about the individual respondent, it is frequently possible to check accuracy through comparison of the reports of several respondents. If respondents occupying widely different positions in the community agree on a statement, there is much better ground for accepting it as true than if only one of these respondents makes the statement. On the other hand, contradictions between the reports of apparently reliable informants provide important leads for further investigation. Rapkin, Grier, and Grier (1957) used this method of checking in a survey of race relations in an urban community. The study was exploratory in nature, the purpose being to identify problems on which research was needed as a basis for policy decisions. The investigators interviewed a variety of individuals in the community: city officials, representatives of Negro organizations, white persons known to be concerned with problems of interracial relations, other community leaders. The respondents were asked about such matters as the extent of employment of Negroes, police treatment of minority groups, etc. On some points the reports were almost unanimous; on others there was wide discrepancy. Almost all informants, for example, agreed in their accounts of the policy and practices of the Public Housing Authority with respect to racial integration, though there was some disagreement about the wisdom of that policy. This impressive agreement led the investigators to conclude that there was no need to study further the nature of the Housing Authority's policy and practices, though there might well be need for research directed toward finding ways of solving the problems the agency was encountering in carrying out its policy. At the other extreme, reports about police treatment of Negroes were contradictory; they ranged from the statement that Negroes were arrested for even the most minor infractions, which would go unnoticed if committed by whites, to the view that law enforcement in Negro neighborhoods was so lax that only the most serious offenses brought police action. On the basis of this striking lack of agreement about the actual state of affairs, investigation of the practices of the

Police Department with respect to Negroes was included in the recommendation of research priorities.

Often, however, contradictions can be cleared up within a given study. Whenever possible, statements should be checked against statistical records. Comparison of contradictory statements may provide a clue to the accuracy of one of them. For example, Rapkin and his associates were told by a representative of a minority group organization that the local breweries did not employ Negroes. Checking with the appropriate union brought the explanation that no new brewery personnel of any kind had been hired within the past ten or twelve years; employment had been at a peak during World War II, and when additional workers were needed in the subsequent period, former employees were called back. Thus, if there was discrimination against Negroes, it was a reflection of a situation that had existed some years before, not necessarily of present policies. Several other informants supported the union's version; the person who had originally made the statement about discrimination, when presented with the union's explanation, agreed that it was correct.

CONTENT AIMED MAINLY AT ASCERTAINING BELIEFS ABOUT WHAT THE FACTS ARE

Instead of asking questions to find out the objective facts from people in a position to know, the investigator may wish to learn what people believe to be the "facts." This is the purpose, for example, in asking a respondent to indicate whether the following statement is true or false: "No Negro has ever made a worth-while contribution to the arts." The respondent's answer is not used to establish what is objectively true but rather to provide a picture of his beliefs. Frequently, before asking questions about the *nature* of a person's beliefs, it is desirable to find out whether he *has* any beliefs or information relevant to the topic under investigation. For example, it makes little sense to inquire, except "projectively," about a person's beliefs about the United Nations if he does not know that the organization exists.

The distinction between an inquiry into "facts" and an inquiry into beliefs must be kept clearly in mind by the investigator. If, for example, he wishes to know objectively how much delinquency there is in a community, he will interview people who have been carefully selected for their knowledge about the topic—members of the police force, for example, workers in settlement houses or recreation centers, group workers assigned to street gangs (if there is such a program in the community)—and will consult court, police, and school records, etc. On the other hand, if he wishes to know what people *believe* about the extent of delinquency in the community, he will interview a general sample of the population rather than selected "experts," and he may simply ask about their beliefs rather than pressing for objective evidence. To use a simple analogy, one does not measure the temperature of a room by asking the people in it how hot they believe it is. But if one is interested in the subjective experience of temperature under varying conditions, one may follow precisely this procedure of asking people how hot they believe the room is. In the field of social attitudes, the relationship between objective reality and a person's beliefs is frequently of considerable interest. Distortions in perception and beliefs, as well as gaps in knowledge, are very often clues to a person's desires or fears.[10]

In addition to discovering the content of a person's beliefs, a questionnaire or interview may provide information about the characteristics and interrelationships or structure of the beliefs. In other words, the purpose of questioning may be to investigate such aspects of belief as: What are the person's most important beliefs? Which beliefs are relatively private, and which are accessible to the public? How specific is a given belief? How clear is it? How strongly held?[11]

CONTENT AIMED MAINLY AT ASCERTAINING FEELINGS

A person's beliefs about what the facts are will often give very clear indications of his feelings and his desires. The converse is also true; an emotional reaction will sometimes reveal beliefs that a subject is unable to verbalize. To understand a person's behavior, knowledge of his feelings may be at least as fruitful as knowledge of his beliefs.

In questionnaires, perhaps the most common method of investi-

---

[10] For a discussion of techniques that employ distortions in perception and memory as a method of measuring social attitudes, see Chapter 8.

[11] For a discussion of the measurement of the various characteristics of beliefs, see Krech and Crutchfield (1948).

gating feelings is to include items that bear directly on various possible emotional reactions—fear, distrust, disgust, contempt, hate, envy, sympathy, admiration, etc. Some examples follow:[12]

> When prize fights are held between Negroes and white men,
>   I want the Negro to win.
> The sight of a Negro almost always frightens me.

Feelings and motives are probably investigated better, however, by questions that allow the subject considerable freedom in response. Emotional reactions are frequently too complex to report in a single phrase. Moreover, the words used to identify an emotional reaction may not have the same meaning for the investigator and for the respondent.

Questions that call for simple unitary responses assume that a subject reacts with the same emotion toward members of a given group regardless of the specific situation or of his relationship with specific members of the group. Clearly, this is a dubious assumption. For example, a highly prejudiced plantation owner in the United States is likely to feel somewhat benign toward Negroes who are self-abasing and "Uncle Tom-ish" but hostile toward Negroes who refuse to consider themselves his inferiors. An investigation of emotional reactions, if it is to provide a full picture, must uncover not only the individual's feelings but also the circumstances in which the feelings are likely to be aroused. Both can be studied most concretely by linking them to specific events in the subject's past. Thus, instead of asking, "How do you feel about walking through Negro neighborhoods alone at night?," one would ask, "Did you ever walk through a Negro neighborhood alone at night? (If yes) How did you feel?"[13] Of course, if the investigator is interested in the subject's response to an abstract "Negro neighborhood," the former phrasing may be preferable.

Content Aimed Mainly at Discovering Standards of Action

An individual's definitions of appropriate behavior in various social situations are of interest both as a reflection of the prevailing

---

[12] For further illustrations, see Kramer (1949).
[13] For further illustrations, see Kramer (1949).

climate of opinion and as a basis for predicting his probable behavior in such situations. Definitions of appropriate action frequently have two components: ethical standards of what *should* be done, and practical considerations of what it is *feasible* to do. Questions may be directed toward either of these components.

The following are examples of questions focused on what *should* be done (Kramer, 1949):

For years ＿＿＿＿＿＿ College, a privately endowed college in New England, had followed the policy of admitting Jewish students in numbers no greater than eight percent of the Freshman class. When a new president took office he dropped this policy and proposed to admit Jews on the same basis as other students. Do you approve or disapprove of the action of the new president? Why?

In your opinion should Negro and white children go to the same public schools, or to separate ones? Why do you think this?

The "should" or "ought to" question—whether phrased in terms of "I," "he," "we," or "they"—provides an indication of the idealized policies of the individual, of the actions he would favor in a situation free from all but moral imperatives. These policies are, for the most part, the product of the idealistic social expectations to which the individual has been exposed in the teachings of societal surrogates— parents, clergy, teachers, government spokesmen. When there is a large discrepancy between social ideals and practices, the ideals, for most adults, tend to function as a guide to what to say on formal occasions rather than what to do in everyday behavior (see Lee, 1949); they may also be the source of "twinges of conscience" with respect to everyday behavior.

A person's behavior toward any person or group is determined not only by his beliefs, feelings, and social conscience but also by what he considers to be feasible behavior in the existing social situation. Thus, in parts of the United States or of South Africa, an unprejudiced person in the face of existing social pressures against being friendly with Negroes may act in a manner resembling that of a prejudiced person. Conformity needs, as well as beliefs and feelings about the individual or group that is the ostensible "object" of the behavior, are likely to be important determinants of action. Thus it is useful to inquire not only into beliefs and feelings about what is "right" but also into the "realistic" policies that serve to guide the individual's actions in specific situations.

For example, Stouffer (1949), in a study of conflicting social norms, asked students to imagine that they were proctoring an examination and saw a fellow student cheating. A questionnaire listed possible steps the proctor might take, ranging from "Take away his notes and exam book, dismiss him and report him for cheating," to "Act as if nothing had happened and not report him for cheating." Each student was asked to indicate which of these actions he, as proctor, would be most likely to take, next most likely, etc., under a number of specific conditions: If he did not know the student who was cheating; if the student were a good friend of his; if the authorities but not his student friends were likely to hear about his action; if his student friends but not the authorities were likely to hear about his action.

The "would" question involves a personal prediction with respect to one's behavior in a given situation. Unless the respondent has been in a comparable situation at some time, he may have little basis for making such a prediction. His response in this case may be no more than an expression of his desires or of his moral standards. Behavior in a real-life situation is influenced by many momentary social pressures that are difficult to imagine unless they have been previously experienced. Personal prediction by a respondent may thus be a hazardous affair unless it is solidly based on past behavior.

As a matter of fact, even when a respondent has in the past been faced with a situation of the type described, his reply about what he would do may be at variance with his actual past behavior or his probable future behavior. The classic investigation of the discrepancy between actual behavior and response to a question of the "what would you do" type is that of LaPiere (1934). LaPiere traveled throughout the United States with a young Chinese couple, stopping at 66 hotels, auto camps, and tourist homes, and eating in 184 restaurants and cafes. Only once were they refused service. Six months later, LaPiere sent a questionnaire to all of the places at which they had eaten or slept, asking, "Will you accept members of the Chinese race as guests in your establishment?" Responses were received from half of the establishments; of these, over 90 per cent said "No."

On the other hand, Pace (1939) found a high correspondence between answers to a series of "what would you do" questions on social, economic, and political issues, and actual behavior as indicated by voting and group membership. He presented college students with 37 questions, of which an example is given here:

> Your state needs an additional tax so that its budget can be balanced. If you could vote, and a tax bill which provided for a widely distributed general retail sales tax was submitted to the people of the State for approval, what would you do?
> _____ not vote at all
> _____ vote for the bill
> _____ vote against the bill
> _____ vote for the bill and try to persuade others to vote for it too
> _____ vote against the bill and try to persuade others to vote against it too

In a pretest, Pace administered this questionnaire to 25 known "radicals" and 25 known "conservatives." The "radicals" included members of the Young Communist League, Trotskyites, Farmer-Laborites, liberal New Dealers; they had all been seen frequently at partisan meetings and at addresses by such speakers as Earl Browder and Norman Thomas; they had all voted Communist, Socialist, or Farmer-Labor in 1936. None of the "conservatives" had ever been seen by the investigator at such meetings; 23 of them had voted for Landon in 1936. Scores on the questionnaire distinguished between the two groups with no overlap. Moreover, on all but three of the 37 items, the mean scores of the two groups differed significantly.

Interesting differences have been found between answers to "should" and "would" questions. In a study by Blankenship (1946), at a time when an amendment to permit horse racing and parimutuel betting was under consideration, alternative question wordings were used with two equivalent samples. One set of respondents was asked: "Is it desirable to permit or to prohibit horse racing and parimutuel betting in New Jersey?" The other was asked: "Would you vote for or against the amendment to permit horse racing and parimutuel betting in New Jersey?" The first received more "don't know" and more opposed answers. This suggests that the "is it desirable" form was answered from a social or moral point of view, whereas the "would you vote" form was answered in terms of personal preference.

In a study of reactions to prejudiced remarks (Selltiz et al., 1950), subjects were shown a skit representing an informal situation in which an anti-semitic remark was made before a group of people. In interviews following the skit, the subjects were asked a series of three questions: "What do you think is the right thing to do or say? What do you think you yourself really would have done in a situation like this? What do you think most people would do or say in a situation like this?" More than half (56 per cent) of the respondents replied that the *right* thing would be to answer the anti-semitic remark in some way (that is, verbally express disagreement with it); only 35 per cent said *they themselves* would have answered the remark; and only 15 per cent said *most people* would answer the remark.[14]

CONTENT AIMED MAINLY AT PRESENT OR PAST BEHAVIOR

The present or past behavior of any person is a type of "fact" that he himself is in a uniquely favorable position to observe. We single out this type of "fact" for special notice because of the value of knowledge of past and present behavior in predicting future behavior. How a person has behaved in the past in a certain type of situation is, in the absence of contradictory evidence, an indication of what his future behavior will be in similar situations.

In asking about present or past behavior, experience has demonstrated that the most valid answers are obtained by specific rather than general questions. For example, it is preferable, in a study of consumer behavior, to ask, "Which brand(s) of coffee do you have in the house at the moment? May I see it? Do you usually buy this brand?" than to ask, "Which brand of coffee do you usually use?" Specifying a concrete instance and then asking whether this instance is typical or atypical provides the subject with more cues for recall

---

[14] For further discussion of questions that ask directly about the respondent's own reactions compared with those asking for estimates of other people's reactions, see Chapter 8, pages 290–292.

and, in a sense, binds him to a reality that acts as an obstacle to distortion in response. Similarly, in the study of prejudice, questions about
past behavior in specific situations are likely to elicit a more accurate
report than general inquiries about previous behavior. Thus it is
preferable to ask, "For whom did you vote in the last mayoralty election? What made you vote for him? Did you know the religion of the
candidates? Were you influenced for or against any candidate by
knowledge of his religion? Do you usually tend to consider a candidate's
religion in deciding for whom to vote?" than to ask only the general
question, "Do you usually tend to consider a candidate's religion in
deciding for whom to vote?"

Content Aimed Mainly at Conscious Reasons for Beliefs, Feelings, Policies, or Behavior

Finally, questions may be designed to obtain the reasons the
respondent is able to offer for his beliefs, feelings, policies, or behavior.
In effect, the investigator is interested in finding out *why*. "Why?" may
seem like a simple question, but, as Lazarsfeld (1935) has pointed out,
the answer to it is seldom simple. Consider merely the problem of
determining why one student selects one college, another a different
one. A full answer to the question would require knowledge of their
information about various colleges, of their needs and interests, of their
ability to meet the entrance requirements or the financial cost of different colleges, and perhaps of still other factors.

In order to secure a full answer to the question "Why?" it is well
for the investigator to consider the various possible factors that may
influence the belief, behavior, etc., in which he is interested, and to
provide for consideration of each factor by asking a number of specific
questions rather than a single "Why?" Although the specific influences
that are relevant depend on the question being studied, it is possible
to identify certain broad classes of considerations that are likely to enter
into the determination of *why*. They include: (1) The *history* of the
act or feeling: e.g., "What were the circumstances when you started
to . . .?" (2) The *characteristics in a given entity* that provoke a given
reaction: e.g., "What is there about_____that leads you to (feel,
believe, act, etc., in a given way)?" (3) The *supports* for the beliefs,

feelings, etc., about a given entity: e.g., "What do your friends, relatives, clubs, etc. (feel, believe, etc.) about _____ ?" "What evidence is there to support your beliefs, feelings, etc., about _____?" (4) The *personal desires, motives, values, or interests* involved in a given reaction: e.g., "Is there anything about yourself that makes you want to (believe, feel, or act in a given way)?" (5) The *specific situations and circumstances* in which a given reaction occurs: e.g., "In what types of situation are you most likely to (feel or act in a given way)?"

In addition to these reasons for a given belief, feeling, action, etc., it may be relevant to inquire into the reasons *against* alternative beliefs, actions, etc. It may also be important to distinguish between past and present influences; for example, between reasons for starting on a given course of behavior and reasons for continuing it.

Once the investigator has decided which kinds of influences are likely to be relevant to his particular question, he sets up an "accounting scheme" (see Zeisel, 1957), mapping out, in preliminary fashion, the various kinds of reasons in which he is interested and providing questions to tap each of them. The following illustration of a set of questions to serve as a guide in an interview aimed at learning why an individual selected a particular college is adapted from Zeisel. Note that it starts with the general question, "Why?," permitting the investigator to find out what is salient in the mind of the respondent, and then provides specific questions to cover the history of the choice and the kinds of influences in which the investigator is interested but which the respondent may not have mentioned in his spontaneous reply:

1. Why, when planning your college years, did you decide to go to _____ college?
2. (Supplementary questions clarifying the history of the decision. Ask only those that were not answered in 1.)
   a. When did you first seriously consider going to _____ college?
      (Probe for answer in terms of circumstances rather than dates.)
   b. Did you seriously consider any other colleges you might go to?
   c. How did you come to your decision?

3. (Supplementary questions about reasons for the choice. Ask only those that were not answered in 1 or 2.)
   a. Was there anything about the college itself (and/or the alternatives) that influenced your decision? What? How did you learn about these particular qualities of the college?
   b. Did you feel that any of your own particular needs would be particularly well taken care of by this choice? (Needs while at college? Postgraduate needs?)
   c. Did your parents, friends, teachers or any other persons help you to come to your decision? In what way? Did your own decision in any way depend on the decisions made by your friends? Did you work it out together?
4. In the light of your actual experience would you now make a different choice? Would you make the same choice on a different basis?

Types of Interviews and Questionnaires

The form of interviews and questionnaires may vary widely. Interviews may range all the way from the rigidly *standardized*, in which both the questions and the alternative responses permitted the subject are predetermined, to the completely *unstructured*, in which neither the questions to be asked nor the responses permitted the subject are determined before the interview. Although the possible range of questionnaire structure is more limited, there too some variation is possible

STANDARDIZED INTERVIEWS AND QUESTIONNAIRES

In the standardized interview or questionnaire, questions are presented with exactly the same wording, and in the same order, to all respondents. The reason for standardization, of course, is to ensure that all respondents are replying to the same question. If one interviewer asks, "Would you like to see taxes reduced next year?" and another asks, "Do you think a tax reduction next year would be desirable?," the answers may not be comparable. Differences in question order can also influence the meaning and implications of a given question. The question about the desirability of a tax cut might well be answered differently if it followed a question about the need for developing intercontinental missiles than if it followed a question about the respondent's budget.

Standardized interviews and questionnaires may differ, however, in the amount of structuring of the questions used. They may present fixed alternative answers, or they may leave the respondent free to answer in his own words.

"FIXED-ALTERNATIVE" QUESTIONS. A "fixed-alternative" (or "closed") question is one in which the responses of the subject are limited to stated alternatives. These alternatives may be simply Yes or No, or they may provide for indicating various degrees of approval or agreement, or they may consist of a series of replies of which the respondent picks one as being closest to his position. The following are examples of fixed-alternative questions:

To what social class would you say you belong—middle class, lower class, working class, or upper class?

For the purpose of our survey, we need to have a rough indication of the income of your family. Would you mind telling me in which of these classes it falls:

Below $1,000 a year	From $3,000 to $4,000
From $1,000 to $2,000	From $4,000 to $5,000
From $2,000 to $3,000	Over $5,000 a year

Put a 1 in front of the thing that is most important to have or do in order to get ahead in the world. Put a 2 before the next most important, etc.

_____ pull	_____ brains
_____ good luck	_____ hard work

Do you own an automobile? _____ Yes _____ No

As you probably know, the Governor of Arkansas has called out the National Guard to prevent Negro children from attending a formerly all-white high school in Little Rock. How do you feel about this action? Would you say you:

_____ strongly approve
_____ mildly approve
_____ are undecided
_____ mildly disapprove
_____ strongly disapprove

Questions of this type are essentially the same whether they are used in interviews or in questionnaires. The only reason for using interviews rather than written questionnaires with this type of material is to reach subjects who are either not willing or not able to fill out questionnaires.

"OPEN-ENDED" QUESTIONS. The "open-ended" question is designed to permit a free response from the subject rather than one limited to stated alternatives. The distinguishing characteristic of open-ended questions is that they merely raise an issue but do not provide or suggest any structure for the respondent's reply; the respondent is given the opportunity to answer in his own terms and in his own frame of reference.

Examples of open-ended interview questions follow:

Now that you have been living in _____ for _____ years,
I wonder if you'll tell me how you feel about it?
    a. What do you like *most* about it?
    b. What do you *dislike* most about it?
    c. How about the neighborhood? What do you think of it?
    d. How about living in a public housing project?

When used in questionnaires, both the questions and the order in which they are presented are predetermined; it is impossible to ask any supplementary questions. When open-ended questions are used in standardized interviews, the questions and their order are predetermined, but the interviewer is given freedom to repeat the question if the reply is not to the point and to use at his discretion such nondirective probes as, "Won't you tell me more? What makes you think . . .? Why? In what way . . .?," etc. The task of the interviewer is to encourage the respondent to talk freely and fully in response to the questions included in the interview schedule and to make a verbatim record of his replies. Generally he has no freedom to raise new questions except to clarify the meaning of the subject's responses, and these must be nondirective.

ADVANTAGES AND DISADVANTAGES OF OPEN-ENDED AND FIXED-ALTERNATIVE QUESTIONS. Fixed-alternative questions have the advantages of being "standardizable," simple to administer, quick and relatively inexpensive to analyze. The analysis of responses to open-ended questions is often difficult and expensive. Categories for analysis must be built up, coders must be trained, and the responses must be coded into one of the categories before they can be tabulated and statistically analyzed. Compared to the simple process of tabulating the precoded responses to closed questions, the analysis of open-ended questions is complex and often troublesome.[15]

From the point of view of obtaining the information needed for a given investigation, however, each type of question has certain advantages and certain disadvantages. A closed question may help to ensure that the answers are given in a frame of reference that is relevant to the purpose of the inquiry and in a form that is usable in the analysis. For example, to the question, "About how often do you go to the movies, on the average?," if no alternative answers are supplied, one respondent might answer, "Not very often"; another, "When I have a date"; still another, "Only when there's something I especially want to see." If the investigator is interested in frequency of movie attendance, such answers are not usable. Provision of a check list with specific estimates ("more than once a week," "about once a week," "about three times a month," etc.) requires the respondent to frame his reply in terms that will be usable.

Sometimes the provision of alternative replies helps to make clear the meaning of the question. Respondents are more likely to understand the question, "Are you married, single, widowed, or divorced?" than the question, "What is your marital status?" This function of clarification may be important not only in relation to words whose meaning may not be generally known but in relation to concepts that may not be familiar to the respondent. A study by Gross, Mason, and McEachern (1958) of the school superintendency role provides an example. One aspect of this study concerned superintendents' perception of role conflicts (defined by the investigators as exposure to incompatible expectations on the part of different groups). Open-ended questions failed to bring replies relevant to the investigators' concept of "role conflict"; experimentation with different wording brought no success. Finally, they changed to a procedure of opening the interview with descriptions of situations involving problems that all superintendents face (criteria for the hiring and promotion of teachers, for ex-

15 For a further discussion of the analysis of interview material, see Chapter 11.

ample), including a number of fixed alternative actions that might be taken. The respondent was asked which of these actions various specified people or groups (e.g., his school board) would expect him to take. This procedure seemed to make the concept clear; the interviewers could then get meaningful answers to open-ended questions about *other* role-conflict situations that the superintendent had encountered.

A similar function of alternative responses is to make clear the *dimension* along which answers are sought. Consider the question, "Are you satisfied with your present wages?" One subject may answer, "No; I'd like to earn $100,000 a year." Another may say, "Yes, I think the wage scale at our plant is fair; I'm earning as much as other fellows who do the same kind of work in other places." The question involves neither words nor concepts that are difficult. But one subject has answered in terms of his level of aspiration (or fantasy), while the other has answered in terms of a judgment about the equity of his pay. To code the first respondent as dissatisfied and the second as satisfied might be misleading; if both of them had replied along the two dimensions, both might have said "No" in terms of level of aspiration but "Yes" in terms of fairness of wage scale. More precise wording of open-ended question might eliminate this difficulty by indicating more clearly which dimension was intended or by asking separately about both. However, the dimension along which answers are sought can frequently be indicated more clearly by a series of alternative responses than by the wording of the question itself.

Finally, the closed question may require the respondent himself to make a judgment about his attitude, rather than leaving this up to the interviewer or coder. This may or may not be desirable, depending on the nature of the question. On some issues the respondent may be in a better position to make the judgment. Suppose, in answer to the question, "How well satisfied are you with your job?," a respondent says: "Well, some things about it I like, some I don't. My boss is a nice guy; he doesn't chew us out for every little thing. And they're fair about promotions and things like that. But it's awfully dirty work, and it's a crummy old building; no decent place to eat, either." Let us say the plan of analysis calls for categorizing attitudes in terms of the following scale: definitely dissatisfied, more dissatisfied than satisfied, about half and half, more satisfied than dissatisfied, definitely satisfied. The coder may find it difficult to decide in which of the three middle categories to place this man. The man himself, however, might have little difficulty in making the judgment if he were presented with the alternative positions.

Most of these advantages of fixed-alternative questions have, however, corresponding disadvantages. One of the major drawbacks of the closed question is that it may force a statement of opinion on an issue about which the respondent does not have any opinion. Many individuals have no clearly formulated or crystallized opinions about many issues; this important characteristic is not likely to be revealed by a closed question. Inclusion of a "Don't know" alternative may help to provide an indication of a lack of crystallized opinion, but the tendency in much interviewing with questions of this sort is to press for a definite response and to accept a "Don't know" only as a last resort. Under such pressure, the answer chosen by a respondent may be an artifact of the specific wording or phrasing of the question or of the stated alternative responses. Suppose one were to ask, "Do you approve or disapprove of the Eisenhower Doctrine for aid to Middle Eastern countries threatened by Communist aggression?" It is easy to say "Approve" or "Disapprove," and many respondents may find this less embarrassing than admitting that they don't know what the Eisenhower Doctrine is, much less have an opinion about it. In the closed question, the reply is taken at face value. Open-ended questions, especially when they are used in an interview and can be followed by probes, provide a much better indication of whether the respondent has any information about the issue, whether he has a clearly formulated opinion about it, and how strongly he feels about it.

Even when a respondent has a clear opinion, a fixed-alternative question may not give an adequate representation of it because none of the choices corresponds exactly to his position, or because they do not allow for qualification. Take such a question as, "Which of the following considerations are most important to you in choosing a job? Interesting work; opportunity to assume responsibility; pleasant surroundings; congenial associates; opportunity for advancement; high salary; security. Place a 1 next to the one most important to you, 2 next to the one that is next most important, etc." Let us suppose that the items cover the range of relevant considerations for a given respondent, and that he has a fairly clear view. But his view may involve interrelations among the factors. In general, interesting work may be more important to him than a high salary. However, given a choice between two jobs, one of which pays twice as much as the other but is slightly less interesting, he may choose the higher-paying. Or there may be some lower limit of salary beyond which he feels he cannot afford to go, no matter how interesting the work. Such qualifications can be expressed in reply to an open-ended question; a closed question not only makes no provision for them, but even discourages the respondent from thinking about them.

Omission of possible alternative responses may lead to bias. Even when a space is provided for "other" replies, most respondents limit their answers to the alternatives provided. Omission of an alternative may seriously change the replies to even a factual question such as what magazines people read. In a study of applicants who were accepted by a certain college but did not actually enter, the subjects were presented with a check list of reasons for not attending. These reasons included such factors as the location of the college, its cost, the fact that it was not coeducational, the fact that specific desired courses were not offered, etc. However, the possibility that the applicant had in the end entered another college because it had a generally higher academic reputation was not included. Although a few respondents added this in the space provided for "other reasons," there was no way of estimating how many would have checked it had it been included among the suggested alternatives. Unless one can be reasonably certain, on the basis of either the logical possibilities or prior investigation, that the alternatives presented adequately cover the complete range of probable responses, it is safer to use an open-ended question, which does not bias the responses by suggesting some but not others.

The fact that the wording of questions is the same for all respondents may conceal the fact that different respondents make different interpretations, some of which may be quite different from those intended by the interviewer. This possibility exists, of course, in both closed and open questions, but it is much more likely to go undetected in the former. An instance of interpretations made from such varying frames of reference as to make the meaning of the obtained replies unclear has been reported by Crutchfield and Gordon (1947). A national survey used the following question: "After the war, would you like to see many changes or reforms made in the United States, or would you rather have the country remain pretty much the way it was before the war?" Most of the respondents replied that they wanted the country to remain "pretty much as it was." In a follow-up study, the same question was asked, but then followed by probes to ascertain what the respondents had in mind when they answered the question. The investigators identified seven different frames of reference: domestic issues (employment conditions, standards of living, etc.); technical improvements (better transportation, communications, etc.); political affairs; and so on. It seemed clear that no single interpretation of the responses to the closed question was justified.

From this discussion of the relative advantages and disadvantages of open and closed questions, it is apparent that the two differ in the purposes for which they are appropriate. Closed questions are more efficient where the possible alternative replies are known, limited in number, and clear-cut. Thus they are appropriate for securing factual information (age, education, home ownership, amount of rent, etc.) and for eliciting expressions of opinion about issues on which people hold clear opinions. Open-ended questions are called for when the issue is complex, when the relevant dimensions are not known, or when the interest of the research lies in the exploration of a process or of the individual's formulation of an issue. The closed question has the advantage of focusing the respondent's attention on the dimension of the problem in which the investigator is interested; by the same token, it does not provide information about the respondent's own formulation of the issue, the frame of reference in which he perceives it, the factors that are salient for him, the motivations that underlie his opinions. When these matters are the focus of interest, open-ended questions are essential.

Lazarsfeld (1944) has proposed that the development of a closed-question interview schedule be preceded by more intensive, freer interviews with a subsample of the population in order to discover the range of probable responses, the dimensions that are seen as relevant, and the various interpretations that may be made of the question wording. On the basis of such preliminary exploration, more meaningful closed questions can be formulated. He has also suggested another method of using the two types of question to supplement each other: after a survey using closed questions, more intensive interviews might be held with a subsample in order to delve more deeply into areas that appear significant. For many purposes, a combination of open and closed questions is most efficient; an interview or questionnaire need not consist entirely of one type or the other.

LESS STRUCTURED INTERVIEWS

For some research problems, a still more flexible approach than that provided by a standardized interview with open-ended questions is appropriate. Largely as a result of the influence of clinical interviewing and anthropological field work, a varied assortment of interviews has been developed in which neither the exact questions the interviewer asks nor the responses the subject is permitted to make are predetermined. Such interviews take various forms and go under various names—the "focused" interview, the "clinical" interview, the "depth" interview, the "nondirective" interview, etc. They are commonly used for a more intensive study of perceptions, attitudes, motivations, etc., than a standardized interview, whether with closed or open questions, permits. This type of interview is inherently more flexible, and of course it requires more skill on the part of the interviewer than do the standardized types. Obviously, this approach is impossible in a questionnaire.

The flexibility of the unstructured or partially structured interview, if properly used, helps to bring out the affective and value-laden aspects of the subject's responses and to determine the personal significance of his attitudes. Not only does it permit the subject's definition of the interviewing situation to receive full and detailed expression; it should also elicit the personal and social context of beliefs and feelings. This type of interview achieves its purpose to the extent that the subject's responses are spontaneous rather than forced, are highly specific and concrete rather than diffuse and general, are self-revealing and personal rather than superficial.

The freedom which the interviewer is permitted is, at once, both the major advantage and major disadvantage of interviews of this type.

The flexibility frequently results in a lack of comparability of one interview with another. Moreover, their analysis is more difficult and time-consuming than that of standardized interviews. There can be little doubt of their usefulness, in the hands of a skilled investigator, as a source of hypotheses that can later be submitted to a systematic test. Partially structured interviews are also used, on occasion, in studies *testing* hypotheses. However, the lack of comparability from interview to interview and the complexity of analysis usually make them less efficient for this purpose than standardized interviews.

Let us briefly discuss several of the major types of partially structured and unstructured interview.

In the *focused interview*, as described by Merton, Fiske, and Kendall (1956), the main function of the interviewer is to focus attention upon a given experience and its effects. He knows in advance what topics, or what aspects of a question, he wishes to cover. This list of topics or aspects is derived from his formulation of the research problem, from his analysis of the situation or experience in which the respondent has participated, and from hypotheses based on psychological or sociological theory. This list constitutes a framework of topics to be covered, but the manner in which questions are asked and their timing are left largely to the interviewer's discretion. He has freedom to explore reasons and motives, to probe further in directions that were unanticipated. Although the respondent is free to express completely his own line of thought, the direction of the interview is clearly in the hands of the interviewer. He wants definite types of information, and part of his task is to confine the respondent to discussion of the issues about which he wants knowledge.

Merton, Fiske, and Kendall (1956) have described this type of interview:

> First of all, the persons interviewed are known to have been involved in a *particular situation*: they have seen a film, heard a radio program, read a pamphlet, article or book, taken part in a psychological experiment or in an uncontrolled, but observed, social situation (for example, a political rally, a ritual or a riot). Secondly, the hypothetically significant elements, patterns, processes and total structure of this situation have been provisionally analyzed by the social scientist. Through this *content or sit-*

uational analysis, he has arrived at a set of hypotheses concerning the consequences of determinate aspects of the situation for those involved in it. On the basis of this analysis, he takes the third step of developing an *interview guide*, setting forth the major areas of inquiry and the hypotheses which provide criteria of relevance for the data to be obtained in the interview. Fourth and finally, the interview is focused on the subjective experiences of persons exposed to the pre-analyzed situation in an effort to ascertain *their definitions of the situation*. The array of reported responses to the situation helps test hypotheses and, to the extent that it includes unanticipated responses, gives rise to fresh hypotheses for more systematic and rigorous investigation.

The focused interview has been used effectively in the development of hypotheses about which aspects of a specific experience (a radio broadcast, a moving picture, a lecture, etc.) lead to changes in attitude on the part of those exposed to it. The interviewer, being equipped in advance with a content analysis of the stimulus experience, can usually distinguish the objective facts of the case from the subjective definitions of the situation. Thus, he is alerted to the possibility of "selective perception" and prepared to explore its implications. Suppose, for example, that one is concerned with reactions to a series of newspaper pictures portraying housing conditions in a slum neighborhood, intended for use in connection with a campaign for more stringent housing laws or for slum clearance and urban redevelopment. The pictures show broken stairs, wallpaper peeling off, holes in walls through which rats are reported to enter—in general, conditions that may reasonably be attributed to inadequate maintenance on the part of the landlord rather than slovenliness on the part of tenants. A respondent, in discussing the pictures, may say, "They show how these low-class people don't take care of their places; there's no use trying to give them decent housing, they just knock it to pieces anyway; you know, like they always say, if you give them bathtubs they just put coal in them." The interviewer, knowing that the content of the pictures is not intended to give this impression, can follow up the respondent's interpretation, trying to discover whether there are unconsidered aspects of the pictures that form a basis for this impression, whether it stems from the subject's stereotyped views, etc.

The definition of a focused interview may be broadened to include any interview in which the interviewer knows in advance what specific aspects of an experience he wishes to have the respondent cover in his discussion, whether or not the investigator has observed and analyzed the specific situation in which the respondent participated. For example, in a study of the functioning of a program of part-time work for high school students, one may prepare a set of questions to be covered even though he is not familiar with the specific job setting of each of the students. Such a list might include questions such as the following: "Does the student feel that he was given an adequate picture of the job before he started? Does he feel that his job is at a level appropriate to his skills?," etc.

Obviously, the more detailed the investigator's knowledge of the situation in which the person being interviewed has participated, and the more specific his hypotheses, the more precisely he can outline in advance the questions to be covered in the interview.

Somewhat similar to the focused interview is the *clinical interview*, the primary difference being that the clinical interview is concerned with broad underlying feelings or motivations, or with the course of the individual's life experiences, rather than with the effects of a specific experience. In this type of interview, too, the interviewer knows what aspects of feeling or experience he wants the respondent to talk about, but again the method of eliciting the information is left to his discretion. The "personal history" interview, used in social case work, prison administration, psychiatric clinics, and in social research using individual life histories, is perhaps the most common type of clinical interview. The specific aspects of the individual's life history which the interview is to cover are determined, as in all data-collection instruments, by the purpose for which the information is gathered.

For example, Lee (1957) was interested in the possibility that adolescents who become heroin addicts may be predisposed to addiction by family experiences that lead to certain personal characteristics. On the basis of earlier work with juvenile addicts, he and colleagues conducting related studies hypothesized that among boys living in the same neighborhood and thus exposed to roughly the same opportunities for using heroin, addicts are likely to differ from non-addicts in the following ways: they have relatively weak ego functioning, defective superego functioning, inadequate masculine identification, lack of realistic middle-class orientation, and distrust of major social institutions. Next, the investigators asked themselves what types of family environment might be expected to stimulate or enhance such characteristics. On the basis of theoretical considerations, largely drawn from psychoanalytic thinking, they constructed a list of circumstances or events of family life that might be expected to contribute to each of the five characteristics. For example, it was considered that factors such as the following might be conducive to weak ego functioning: inappropriate handling of childhood illnesses, discordant relationship between parents, the mother figure either passionate or hostile toward the boy, either parent's having unrealistically high or low aspirations for the boy, etc.

It seemed clear that relatively unstructured interviews would be a more appropriate method of getting the needed information than would a standardized series of questions. Accordingly, the interviewers visited the parents of the boys included in the study—a sample of addicts and a control group of non-addicts—and encouraged them to talk freely about their sons. The interviewers had no set questions to ask. They were instructed to cover the following major topics: the physical characteristics of the neighborhood and the house, the composition of the family and the household, the health history of the family, the present and early adolescent life situation of the subject, childhood training and socialization, relationships within the family, and relationships between the family and the "outside world." The interview guide indicated a number of subtopics to be covered under each of these major ones; for example, under "childhood training and socialization," the interviewer was to get information about early development, discipline and patterns of handling by parents, early socialization experiences, early school experiences, etc. Under each of these subtopics, the interview guide listed more specific points to be covered.

In the *nondirective interview*, the initiative is even more completely in the hands of the respondent. The term *nondirective* received its currency from a type of psychotherapy in which the patient is encouraged to express his feelings without directive suggestions or questions from the therapist. In a more limited sense, nondirection is implicit in most interviewing; that is, although the interviewer is expected to ask questions about a given topic, he is instructed not to bias or direct the respondent to one rather than another response.[16] In nondirective interviewing, however, the interviewer's function is simply to encourage the respondent to talk about a given topic with a minimum of direct questioning or guidance. He encourages the respondent to talk fully and freely by being alert to the feelings expressed in the statements of the respondent and by warm, but noncommittal, recognition of the subject's feelings. Perhaps the most typical remarks made by the interviewer in a nondirective interview are: "You feel that . . ." or "Tell me more" or "Why?" or "Isn't that interesting?" or, simply, "Uh huh."

The nondirective interviewer's function is primarily to serve as a catalyst to a comprehensive expression of the subject's feelings and beliefs and of the frame of reference within which his feelings and beliefs take on personal significance. To achieve this result, the interviewer must create a completely permissive atmosphere, in which the subject is free to express himself without fear of disapproval, admonition, or dispute, and without advice from the interviewer.[17]

The Sociometric Method[18]

Sociometry is concerned with the social interactions among any group of people. The data collection is geared to obtaining information about the interaction or lack of interaction among the members of any group (or among subgroups, or among groups, or among sub-

[16] In "stress interviews," this statement does not hold. Here, the interviewer tries to see how well the respondent can function under the stress of baiting, disparagement, expressed hostility, etc. The term may also be applied to interviews in which the interviewer tries to see how much pressure or stress is required to change the respondent's expression of views.

[17] For a more detailed discussion of nondirective interviewing see Roethlisberger and Dickson (1939) and Rogers (1945).

[18] Sociometry is most closely identified with the work of J. L. Moreno. For a discussion of its origin, see his Who Shall Survive? (1953). For numerous articles, consult the journal Sociometry. For a survey of research using sociometric techniques, and a discussion of the values and shortcomings of this approach, see Lindzey and Borgatta (1954).

groups and individual members, etc.). The interaction that is investigated may be behavioral, or it may only be desired, or anticipated, or fantasied. The content or type of interaction studied may be any one of a variety of social behaviors—sitting next to, eating with, buying from, lending to, visiting, playing with, having as a friend, talking to, living next to, etc.

Sociometric studies most commonly use questionnaires, although observational data or other kinds of records may provide the grist for a sociometric analysis. Essentially, sociometry is not so much a data-collection procedure as a focus on a certain type of subject matter and a related method of analysis.

When interest is in actual behavior, one may observe the participants in an action, the nature of the action, and the relationship of the participants to one another; both the *initiation* and the *reception* of social behavior are of interest. When interest is in desired or fantasied interaction, or in feelings about interaction with specified individuals, verbal reports are called for. The sociometric questionnaire or interview, as most commonly used, involves simply asking each member of a group to indicate which other members he would like to have as a companion in some activity (e.g., "eat lunch with") and which ones he would not like to have as a companion. Sometimes the individual is allowed to name as many members as he wishes; more frequently he is limited to naming a specific number. It is assumed that preferences are more likely to be stated honestly when the subject believes that they will really determine subsequent social arrangements; that is, that he will be assigned to sit next to (work with, etc.) the individuals he has named. Therefore, when it is feasible, sociometric questionnaires are usually given with a statement that the investigator will arrange circumstances to permit the fulfillment of the individual's preferences if possible.

Sociometric questionnaires are easy to administer and are adaptable to many different types of setting. Studies of the reliability of sociometric data, on the basis of repeated tests, indicate that although there may be considerable variation in specific choices, patterns of group interaction and various scores or indices derived from the data are quite stable. Despite the ease of administration, however, the analysis of sociometric data is frequently more complex than one anticipates.[19]

Sociometric data can provide information about an individual's position in the group, the social subgroupings within the group, the relationships among the subgroups, the group's cohesiveness, etc. Data of this type have been used in studies of leadership, of relations among ethnic groups, of the effect of experimental treatments on group structure, of the effect of variations in group structure on the behavior of group members, of characteristics of individuals who are frequently chosen and those who are seldom chosen.

One of the first studies of leadership that made use of sociometric techniques was that of Jennings (1943). Girls in a state training school were asked to indicate which girls in the school they would want to live with and which ones they would want to work with; for each of these activities, they were asked to list also which girls they would *not* want as companions. A "choice score" was computed for each girl on the basis of the selections and rejections she received; in terms of these scores, each girl could be described as "over-chosen," "average-chosen," or "under-chosen." It was found that choice score was closely related to leadership in the community; of the twenty members of a Community Council selected a few months before the sociometric measures were taken, eighteen were "over-chosen," and the other two were just below the "over-chosen" point. Study of the reasons given for the sociometric choices and rejections led to the conclusion that leadership is not explainable by any particular personality characteristic or constellation of traits, but rather on the basis of the interpersonal contribution an individual makes in a specific group.

Festinger, Schachter, and Back (1950), in a study of the effect of the location of dwellings on friendship formation, used reports of actual social behavior rather than statements of preference. Studying a relatively self-contained community of married veteran students, they asked each of the wives, "What three people in Westgate or Westgate West do you see most of socially?" (Westgate consisted of 100 single-family houses arranged in nine courts; Westgate West consisted of

---

[19] For a discussion of methodological problems in the analysis of sociometric data, see Proctor and Loomis (1951).

seventeen two-story buildings with five apartments on each floor.) They found that 65 per cent of the people named by Westgate West residents lived in the same building as the chooser, 44 per cent of them on the same floor. Moreover, people living in the immediately adjacent apartment were named more often than those living two doors away, who in turn were named more often than those living three doors away, etc. A similar pattern was found in the Westgate community. Thus it was clearly demonstrated that in this community, consisting of new residents homogeneous in age, interests, socioeconomic status, etc., and relatively isolated from the larger community, ecological factors were an important determinant of friendships.

Among the earliest applications of sociometric techniques to the study of relations between racial or ethnic groups were the studies of Criswell (1937, 1939). She asked children in mixed Negro-white classes, from kindergarten through the sixth grade in a public school, to choose two classmates beside whom they would like to sit. She found that, in this school and within this age range, cleavage between the sexes was far more marked than cleavage between Negroes and whites. The white children did not begin to withdraw from the Negro children until the fourth grade and did not form a "racial" group until the fifth grade—a finding previously reported by Moreno (1934).

Although such studies are extremely useful in revealing interrelationships among members of a given group, one must be cautious about interpreting cleavages as evidence of prejudice. Preference for members of one's racial or ethnic group may simply indicate greater familiarity. For example, the white students in a racially mixed school class may live in the same neighborhood and know one another well, but they may have little acquaintance with the Negro students, who live in a different neighborhood. If this is true, a nonrandom choice (more white students choosing other white students than would be expected by chance) does not necessarily indicate an avoidance of the Negro students. This is not to deny that prejudice may be involved somewhere, historically, in the chain of causation—as in the creation of the segregated neighborhoods. But this is different from asserting that the nonrandom choice patterns of the children are necessarily indications of prejudice among the children.

Visual Aids in Interviewing

Occasionally visual aids—photographs, line drawings, dolls, etc. —are introduced into the interviewing situation. We shall discuss here the use of such techniques in the course of direct interviewing; that is, in situations where the visual material is used simply as a substitute for a verbal statement or to make clear what is being asked about, and the respondent is asked directly for his reaction to it. Such use has been rather limited; more frequently, visual materials are used in indirect, or "projective," questioning. This latter use will be discussed in the following chapter.

Perhaps the most common use of visual materials has been in studies of racial awareness and racial attitudes of young children. The device was first used in this way by E. L. Horowitz (1936). He presented children with pictures of groups and of individuals, and asked questions similar to those used in many of the sociometric procedures. One of his tests uses a set of paired photographs depicting identical activities and settings. One photograph in each pair shows five white children participating, whereas the matched photograph shows the same group with a Negro boy substituted for one of the whites (for a portion of the study, three of the five boys were Negroes). The subjects are shown each picture and are asked to indicate whether they would care to join in the activity with the children depicted in the picture. From their responses ("Yes," "No," "Undecided"), it is possible to compute a "willingness to join in" score for the series of all-white pictures and for the series of racially mixed pictures; the difference between the scores is taken as a measure of bias.

Another approach developed by Horowitz is the "faces test," consisting of twelve photographs of boys—four white, four "light" Negro, and four "dark" Negro. In one use of these photographs (the "ranks" test), the children are asked to indicate which one of the twelve they like best, next best, and so on until the twelve pictures are ranked in order. A second use is the "show me" test, in which children are asked: "Show me all those you want to come to your party," etc., for twelve different activities. A later revision of the "show me" test also attempts to get at stereotypes by including such items as: "Show me which children live in a dirty house," "Show me which are most stupid," etc. For each test, the individual is scored in terms of the extent to which his pattern of responses differs from that which would be expected if the racial identification of the pictures were not a factor in his choice. For example, if choices for companions in the twelve activities were made without regard to race, one would expect that the total choices would include roughly equal numbers of the white boys, the "light" Negroes, and the "dark" Negroes. A child who consistently chose only the pictures of white boys as those he wanted to share in activities with him would deviate markedly from the random pattern to be expected if race were not a factor.

A number of other investigators have used the Horowitz pictures. In one study (Mussen, 1950) an attempt was made to estimate their validity by comparing scores on the "ranks" and "show me" tests with actual sociometric choices of cabin-mates in an interracial camp. Scores on the tests correlated significantly with the proportion of choices of white and Negro boys as cabin-mates, and changes in test scores from beginning to end of the camp period were correlated with changes in proportion of whites and Negroes in the sociometric choices.

Picture tests have been used by Helgerson (1943), by Horowitz and Horowitz (1938), and others to discover whether race or other characteristics, such as sex, age, socioeconomic status, facial expression, etc., are more important in determining an individual's preferences. The technique consists of pairing pictures in which several variables are contrasted. In a study contrasting the effects of sex and race on preference, for example, the individual would be presented with the following pairs of pictures: a Negro boy and a white girl, a white girl and a white boy, a Negro girl and a white boy, a Negro boy and a Negro girl. With respect to each pair of pictures, he would be asked, "Which one would you rather play with?"

Picture tests have also been employed by R. E. Horowitz (1939) and by Clark and Clark (1939) to study young children's awareness of their own race. The technique consists mainly in showing the children a series of pictures (varying in race, sex, age, etc.) and asking the child, "Which one is you?" or "Which one is most like you?" or "Is this you?"

White and brown dolls have been used in a similar fashion by Clark and Clark (1950) and by Goodman (1952). In both of these studies, the dolls were used not only in connection with questions directed toward the child's awareness of his own racial identification but toward his attitudes: "Which doll do you like best?," "Which doll is prettier?," etc.

Clark and Clark (1950) used an interesting variation of a pictorial technique to get at children's awareness of their own racial identification and their feelings about it. They presented Negro children with a box of crayons, including a range of shades of brown as well as the colors usually included in children's crayon sets, and two line drawings. The child was asked first to color one figure "the color that you are," then to make the other one "the color that you like little girls (boys) to be."

The use of pictorial techniques has not been limited, however, to studies of children or of intergroup attitudes. Murphy and Likert (1938) made use of both photographs and motion pictures in a study of the attitudes of college students. The photographs, borrowed from news services, all showed conflict situations—strikes, war, race riots. In connection with each picture, the subjects were asked to answer such questions as: "Describe briefly in outline form your reaction to this photograph. . . . In this situation, with whom do you sympathize? . . . What do you like or dislike in this photograph? Why?" Three motion pictures were shown: one portraying the aftermath of a race riot; another, the attempt of a mob to storm a courthouse with the intent of lynching a Negro who was in custody there; and the third, fleet maneuvers. After seeing each film, the student was asked to write briefly what he thought about it, and then to express his agreement or disagreement with a number of statements related to it (e.g., "Riots of this kind are a tragedy for both the white and black races").

Visual aids are sometimes helpful in inducing people to discuss matters about which they may feel awkward or embarrassed when questioned directly. Thus, Whyte (1957) reported that in a study of the meaning of work, he had difficulty in getting respondents (skilled glass workers) to talk about certain aspects of their work. They talked freely about working conditions, the union, fellow workers, foremen, and higher management people. But when he tried to get at their reactions to mental and physical processes involved in the work itself —for example, esthetic satisfactions, feelings of creativity—they became embarrassed and inarticulate. Therefore he made line drawings of a number of different products on which the men had worked, and asked each respondent to arrange the cards in the order of his preference for the different jobs. Then the respondent was asked to explain why he had ranked the cards as he did. The resulting comments revealed much more about feelings toward the work process itself than had been elicited in the earlier, purely verbal interviews.

Collier (1957) carried out a small-scale experiment to discover the relative effectiveness of a purely verbal interview and one using photographs. In a study of migration and acculturation of French-Acadians to an English industrial town in one of the Canadian maritime provinces, he was especially interested in the areas of work, home, and community relationships. Two respondents were each interviewed twice by purely verbal techniques in partially structured interviews, a third time with the addition of photographs. In interviews with two other respondents, photographs were used throughout. The photographs were of industrial plants in the town in which the respondents worked, houses and street scenes in the communities in which they lived, and activities in and around the home of the particular respondent; these latter pictures were taken with the cooperation of each respondent and his family. Collier found much greater interest in the interviews with the photographs, much more specific information given in the interview, greater ease of keeping the interview on the topics in which the investigator was interested, and greater ease of judging the extent of a respondent's information about certain matters.

Whether or not visual techniques are likely to be an effective aid in interviewing depends on the circumstances and the research purpose of a given study. Pictorial methods are particularly useful in the study of attitudes of children or of those with limited literacy. Verbal comprehension is needed only to the extent of understanding the general test instructions; since these can frequently be given orally, reading ability is not required. The usefulness of pictorial methods, however, is not restricted to respondents with limited reading ability. Pictures are of value in depicting many types of situation that are difficult to describe; thus they permit the uncovering of reactions that are difficult to obtain by other methods. Another advantage is that a pictorial test, because it usually has more inherent interest than a written questionnaire, is likely to meet with less resistance.

Against these assets must be counterposed certain liabilities. A picture presents a concrete situation; if one is interested in investigating general attitudes, he may find that responses are influenced by specific details of the pictures he presents. Thus, Murphy and Likert (1938), in the study described above, found that responses to the pictures dealing with unions and strikes seemed to depend on the respondent's interpretation of which side had started the violence shown in a given picture. A related limitation is the difficulty of using pictures to study attitudes toward groups that have no distinguishing visual characteristics (for example, Catholics, socialists, psychologists). Though it is possible to use symbols or names to identify members of different religions, nationalities, or other groupings, the symbols may not have a clear-cut meaning for the respondents; or the respondents may react to the symbols rather than the groups they represent. There is a further difficulty in studies whose design calls for comparison of responses to pictures or photographs that supposedly differ only in the racial (or other) identification of the individuals portrayed. A score based on deviations from random choice assumes that the pictures, for example, of Negro and white children are of equal attractiveness apart from their racial characteristics. To be sure that this condition has been met is no easy matter if unretouched photographs are used; on the other hand, dubbing in color on equated "white" pictures may create an artificial effect.

A Concluding Note

From this survey of questionnaire and interview procedures, it is apparent that the investigator interested in individuals' self-reports has a choice of many different ways of eliciting them. In making such decisions as whether to use a questionnaire or an interview, whether to use a standardized or a less structured form, and whether to supplement the verbal material by visual aids, he needs to consider the advantages and disadvantages of each approach in the light of the purpose of his study.

The investigator should be concerned, of course, with the reliability and validity of his measures. Although it seems likely that most investigators are concerned with these matters in the sense of hoping that their measures are reliable and valid, this concern has not often been expressed in attempts to determine the reliability or validity of the instruments used. This is at least as true of interviews and questionnaires as of other types of measuring instruments—perhaps even more so, since most interviews and questionnaires are specifically designed for the purpose of a single study, and thus do not have the benefit of testing by repeated use.

An occasional investigator has tested the reliability of his instruments by having two different interviewers interview the same individuals, or by repeating a questionnaire or interview with the same individuals after a lapse of time. To be sure, this procedure is time-consuming, and it is not always easy to secure the cooperation of subjects for a repetition of the same interview or questionnaire to which they have already responded. This latter difficulty can be lessened somewhat by changing parts of the instrument, repeating only certain selected questions for the test of reliability.

In connection with a few of the measurement techniques described in this chapter, the investigators reported evidence about validation; for example, Pace's testing of his measure of political-economic-social attitudes on known "liberal" and "conservative" groups, and Mussen's comparison of scores on the "faces test" with sociometric choices. Many other investigators have attempted to find ways of assessing the validity of their measures. Nevertheless, it remains true that many—probably most—questionnaires and interviews have been used without evidence of their validity. Again, the reasons are not hard to find. It is not always easy to determine what would be appropriate criteria of validity. Even if one can identify what would constitute appropriate evidence, it may not be feasible to gather the necessary data. But without such evidence, one can only hope that his instruments are actually measuring what he believes they are measuring. Thus it would seem desirable to devote more time than is usually given to investigation of the reliability and validity of questionnaires and interviews, as well as of other instruments for collecting data.

It has been found in many public opinion surveys that even slight differences in question wording may lead to considerable differences in the proportion of people who answer in one or another way. Obviously, too, the behavior of an interviewer may influence responses. A good deal is known about common sources of bias in question wording and in interviewer behavior. Even if an investigator decides that he cannot invest the time, effort, and expense that would be needed to test the reliability and validity of his questionnaire or interview, he can and should examine carefully both his questions and the instructions to his interviewers to make sure that he has avoided obvious sources of bias. A more detailed discussion of the construction of questionnaires and interviews and of interviewing procedure, from this point of view, is given in Appendix C.

8

DATA COLLECTION
III. Projective and Other Indirect Methods

Projective Methods

Structured Disguised Tests of Social Attitudes

Substitute Measures

A Note on Validation

TECHNIQUES that rely on the individual's own report of his behavior, beliefs, feelings, etc., presuppose, as has already been pointed out, that the person is willing and able to give such information about himself. But this is not always true. People may be unwilling to discuss controversial topics or to reveal intimate information about themselves. They may be reluctant to express their true attitudes if they believe that such attitudes are generally disapproved. Or they may be unable to give the desired information, either because they cannot easily put their feelings into words or because they are unaware of their feelings about the matter in question.

To get around these limitations, techniques have been devised that are largely independent of the subject's self-insight and of his willingness to reveal himself. These indirect techniques may be grouped in two broad classes, differing in their degree of structure. The less structured ones are commonly referred to as *projective methods*; among the more structured techniques we may identify *disguised methods* and *substitute measures*.

Projective Methods

Frank (1939), the originator of the term, has given the following definition of a projective technique:

> A projective method . . . involves the presentation of a stimulus situation designed or chosen because it will mean to the subject not what the experimenter has arbitrarily decided it should mean . . . but rather whatever it must mean to the personality who gives it, or imposes upon it, his private, idiosyncratic meaning and organization.

The assumption is made that the individual's organization of the relatively unstructured stimulus situation is indicative of basic trends in his perception of the world and in his response to it.

Projective Methods in the Study of Personality

Projective methods were first devised by psychologists and psychiatrists concerned with the diagnosis and treatment of patients suffering from emotional disorders, and this has continued to be their major use. Tests for this purpose attempt to give a comprehensive picture of the individual's personality structure, his emotional needs, his conflicts, etc. To discuss either the theory underlying these tests or the methods of interpreting them is beyond the scope of this book. They are primarily tools of the clinical psychologist rather than the social psychologist or sociologist; moreover, their use requires intensive specialized training. However, in view of their great usefulness in the investigation of certain types of problems in social psychology, sociology, and anthropology, we shall briefly describe their general characteristics, mention some of the more frequently used tests, and indicate the kinds of social relations research in which they have been used.[1]

It will be sufficient, for our purposes, to note the following characteristics of these techniques: The stimuli are capable of arousing many different kinds of reaction: for example, an ink blot, which can be perceived in different ways; a picture, which can elicit a variety of stories; a set of dolls, which can be made to behave in many ways. There are no "right" or "wrong" answers; nor is the respondent faced with a set of limited alternatives. The emphasis is on *his* perception of the material, the meaning he gives to it, the way in which he organizes or manipulates it. The nature of the stimuli and the way in which they are presented do not clearly indicate the purpose of the test or the way in which the responses will be interpreted. The individual is not asked to talk directly about himself. The ostensible subject matter is the ink blot, the picture, the dolls, or whatever, not the individual's own experiences or feelings. However, the responses are interpreted as indicating the individual's own view of the world, his personality structure, his needs and feelings, his ways of interacting with people.

In a projective test, the individual's responses are not taken at face

[1] The student who is interested in pursuing the subject of projective techniques in the study of personality should consult one of the volumes that give descriptions of the various methods—for example, Abt and Bellak (1950), Anderson and Anderson (1951), and Bell (1948).

value—that is, with the meaning that the subject presumably would expect them to have—but are interpreted in terms of some pre-established psychological conceptualization of what his responses to the specific test situation mean.[2] This underlying conceptualization provides the framework for interpreting the responses. Usually the system of interpretation provides for considering responses not in isolation but in terms of patterns. In effect, the clinician attempts to arrive at a psychologically coherent picture of the individual by deriving the full meaning of any particular response tendency from the total record of his replies.

One of the most frequently used projective techniques in the clinical setting is the Rorschach Test, consisting of ten cards, on each of which is a copy of an ink blot. The subject is asked, "What might this be?" Another commonly used technique is the Thematic Apperception Test, or T.A.T. This test consists of a series of pictures about which the subject is asked to tell stories. In some of the pictures the persons or objects are quite clearly represented, in others they are not; some of the pictures deal with ordinary or usual events, some with situations that are unusual or bizarre.

Techniques such as these are designed to elicit a rich sample of behavior, from which a great variety of inferences can be drawn. Some inferences may have to do with adaptive aspects of the person's behavior; that is, how well he carries out the task posed by the test (to tell what an ink blot looks like, to make up a story, etc.). Others have to do with expressive aspects. The way the person deals with the materials of the test is taken as reflecting the "style" of his personality; for example, his approach to the test may show constriction or expansiveness, intellectual control or impulsiveness, etc. Inferences about adaptive and expressive aspects are generally considered relevant to a description of the individual's personality structure. In addition, from the content of what the individual says, inferences may be drawn about

[2] Some authors (e.g., Deri et al., 1948, Proshansky, 1950) consider this the essential characteristic of projective techniques. We do not share this view because we believe that all data-collection methods which attempt to measure the characteristics of a person—for example, his attitudes—except those which assume an a priori validity in self-report, involve an interpretation of responses in terms of some psychological formulation. What is distinctive about projective tests in this respect, perhaps, is the extent of inference involved—that is, the lack of apparent relevance of the responses to the characteristics about which inferences are drawn.

his needs, attitudes, values, conflicts, ideologies, and conception of himself. Such inferences rest on the assumption that what the individual perceives in the test materials represents in some way (though not necessarily in terms of direct correspondence) an externalization or projection of processes within himself.

Other projective tests have somewhat more specific focus. A relatively new technique, the Tomkins-Horn Picture Arrangement Test, is designed for group administration and machine scoring. It consists of twenty-five plates, each containing three sketches that may be arranged in various ways to portray a sequence of events; the subject is asked to arrange them in the most reasonable sequence. The responses are interpreted as providing evidence concerning the following dimensions of personality: conformity; social orientation (sociophilia, sociophobia, aggression, dependence, etc.); optimism-pessimism; level of functioning (relative emphasis on thinking, fantasy, affect, overt behavior); and work orientation.

Other commonly used tests are: word association, sentence completion, doll play, and figure drawing. In the word-association test, the subject is presented with a list of words; after each one, he is to respond with the first word that comes to his mind. Both the rate and the content of his responses may indicate areas of emotional disturbance. In the sentence-completion test, the first few words of a possible sentence are given, and the individual is asked to complete it. Like the word-association test, the sentence-completion method may provide clues to areas of emotional disturbance; any given area may be investigated by presenting the respondent with relevant sentence beginnings. In doll-play procedure, the subject is given a set of dolls, usually representing adults and children of both sexes, and is either encouraged to play freely with them or to show how they would act in various circumstances. This procedure is, of course, especially appropriate for use with children; it is well suited for eliciting feelings about family relationships. In the figure-drawing test, the subject is asked to "draw a person," to "draw a man," or to "draw a woman," etc. The assumption is that the drawing represents the person's image of himself, and that unusual features represent areas of conflict, strain, etc. In addition to the relatively specific function ascribed here to each of these tests, each of them may be used as a basis for broader interpretations about the individual's personality.

Many of these techniques have been subjected to much investigation; standardized methods of administration, scoring, and interpretation have been published. Nevertheless, questions have been repeatedly raised about their validity, and the research evidence on this point is far from conclusive. This matter will be discussed in more detail in the summary section of this chapter.

Despite these questions about validity, projective tests from which inferences about personality structure may be drawn have been used fruitfully not only in clinical research and practice but in studies concerned with the relation of individual personality to various social and cultural factors. A number of studies concerned with the relation of social attitudes to the individual's broader personality structure have made use of projective tests. For example, Adorno et al. (1950), in their study of The Authoritarian Personality, used T.A.T. pictures as well as partially structured interviews in assessing the personalities of individuals who scored high and those who scored low on questionnaires designed to measure anti-semitism and ethnocentrism. In comparing the T.A.T. stories of these prejudiced and unprejudiced people, they found that the unprejudiced identified more closely with the heroes in their stories, expressed aggression in more sublimated forms, tended to emphasize autonomous behavior based on inner rational decision rather than on external forces, and described status relationships between men and women, parents and children, or Negroes and whites as more nearly equal than did the prejudiced individuals.

Another area in which projective tests of personality have been widely and fruitfully used is the study of the relationship between culture and personality. An example is DuBois' study (1944) of The People of Alor. DuBois, an anthropologist, spent some time in a small village in what was then the Netherlands East Indies, making observations about the behavior and beliefs of the people and their cultural practices, and reconstructing the biographies of several individuals. From these materials a psychoanalyst, Kardiner, drew a picture of the "modal personality" of the people of Alor. However, in order to study relationships between culture and personality, it is important to have evidence about personality patterns which is secured independently of the description of cultural behavior. Accordingly, Rorschachs were administered to a number of the villagers; the records were analyzed by a specialist in this technique, Oberholzer, who had no knowledge of the cultural descriptive materials. The similarity between the personality sketches obtained in the two ways was striking.

Some investigators (Henry and Guetzkow, 1951, and Horwitz and Cartwright, 1953) have experimented with adaptation of the Thematic Apperception Test for the *diagnosis of characteristics of small groups*. Pictures are used which are believed especially likely to elicit responses indicative of group functioning; the group as a whole, rather than each individual member, is asked to make up a story about each picture. The assumption is that a small group develops a "group personality" which is revealed in the response to the pictures in a way analogous to the revelation of an individual's personality through his response to a projective technique.

PROJECTIVE METHODS IN THE STUDY OF SOCIAL ATTITUDES

When the focus of an investigation is on the specific content of an individual's attitudes toward some social object, rather than on his general personality structure, the projective techniques designed for the study of personality are not very helpful. Yet a projective approach frequently seems desirable as a way of encouraging freedom and spontaneity of expression. This is especially likely to be the case when there is reason to believe that respondents may hesitate to express their opinions directly for fear of disapproval by the investigator, or when respondents are likely to consider direct questions as an unwarranted invasion of privacy or to find them threatening for some other reason.

A considerable variety of ingenious techniques have been developed for use in such situations. These techniques share some of the characteristics of the projective methods already described: they have the capacity of arousing many different reactions, they encourage a free response on the part of the individual, they do not ask him to talk directly about himself or his own views or feelings, yet his responses are taken as reflecting his own attitudes. In line with the purpose of tapping specific attitudes, the test materials or instructions usually provide a more specific subject-matter focus than do those used in tests designed to yield information about broad personality patterns; for example, the individual may be presented with a picture in which some of the characters are white and others Negro, or with a photograph which he is told represents a union meeting, or with a cartoon in which a leader is giving orders to a group.

Of course, if no precautions are taken, the general purpose of the test, or at least the topic with which it is concerned, may be quite apparent. However, two procedures may be used in the construction of a projective attitude test in order to make its objective or the topic involved less patent: a fictitious purpose may be ascribed, which appears plausible in the light of what is demanded of the subject; and, in addition to the stimuli relevant to the investigator's objective, "neutral" or unrelated stimuli may be included, so that the subject's suspicions are not aroused by having the same "theme" or "issue" occur in every stimulus situation presented to him. For example, suppose that we were interested in measuring attitudes toward Negroes by means of a series of pictures showing Negroes and whites in a variety of social settings. By having each picture exposed for a brief period of time (which incidentally makes for greater ambiguity and hence increases the influence of inner determinants) and having subjects describe what was seen, it is not at all difficult to get subjects to accept the idea that the purpose of the test is to see how much people can recall of stimuli presented very briefly. If the subject is allowed to keep the picture in front of him as he makes up a story or gives his opinion of what is happening, then the purpose of getting at "imaginative ability" or "how different people see different situations" can be ascribed to the test procedure. If, in addition to the pictures showing Negroes and whites together, we also employ pictures involving only whites, country scenery, animals, etc., the likelihood that the subject will correctly perceive the purpose of the test is reduced.

When limited time prevents the inclusion of "neutral" stimuli, or with highly sophisticated respondents, it may not be possible to conceal the purpose of a projective attitude instrument. Yet the transparency of the purpose is not necessarily a serious disadvantage. While the subject may be motivated to distort his responses in the direction of creating a favorable impression, this is not as easily done as one might suppose. In the process of telling a story about a Negro-white social situation with the intention of appearing unbiased, the subject may still reveal his beliefs or feelings by automatically assigning Negroes to inferior roles or by unwittingly attributing behavior to Negroes along stereotyped lines.[3] The subject may not even realize that some of the beliefs and views he has about Negroes are indicative of bias; he may assume that most people see Negroes as "lazy" or "unintelligent" because that is the way they are. Of course, it is still true that conscious attempts to distort may reduce the extent of valid information obtained.

When it seems likely that the purpose of a projective test will be apparent, one may ask: Why bother with such a test, in view of the time and effort involved in its construction and application? Why not simply use a direct interview or questionnaire? There are several possible reasons for preferring the projective test, even though the latter may be transparent, which must be evaluated for each particular situation:

1. The subject may find it easier to express himself if he is not explicitly talking about his own feelings and attitudes, even though he knows that what he says will be so interpreted. He may have a certain measure of distance from the topic if he can ostensibly talk impersonally, and a certain measure of security in not having to say in so many words that this is how he himself feels.

2. With the best intentions in the world, the subject may be unable to describe his feelings and attitudes as accurately as they may be discerned in the projective test situation. Suppose one asks a subject, "When you meet a person for the first time, what do you notice first, the person's sex or race?" The subject may well have been totally insensitive to this aspect of his behavior. He may literally not know. But suppose one asks him to describe the persons represented in a series of pictures, mentioning whatever occurs to him as he looks at the pictures. One may readily determine what is remarked upon first, and one may even determine this analytically by presenting pictures of individuals representing the various possible combinations of sex and race along with age, manner of dress, and situational context. That is,

---

[3] We do not wish to suggest that there is a simple correspondence between a person's beliefs or feelings and the characters he depicts in a story. A subject may depict a Negro as being in an inferior social role in a story without feeling that this is the only appropriate role for Negroes.

from the responses to the entire series of pictures, one may be able to make such statements as, "In describing white females, the subject remarks upon their sex before he remarks upon their race, but in describing white males the reverse is true; in describing Negroes, he consistently remarks upon race first, regardless of sex." And one can compare the patterns with those available from normative data. Can one generalize from such a test? This is a problem of validation.

3. Sometimes access to certain populations of potential subjects (e.g., school children, workers in a factory, etc.) may be withheld if the topic under investigation is made explicit to the subjects, but granted if it remains tacit even though obvious.

4. Even though the purpose of a projective attitude test is apparent, it may produce more extensive information than a questionnaire or even an interview with open-ended questions would. In the descriptions of the pictured situations, for example, we may see how attitudes color perception, or what aspects of attitude (feelings, beliefs, etc.) are significant for the individual, and so on.

The projective techniques that have been devised for the study of social attitudes vary in the effectiveness with which they mask their purpose, in the richness of personality material they reveal, in the ambiguity of the stimulus presented to the subject, and in the expenditure of skill and effort necessary to the collection and analysis of responses. Few of the specific adaptations of these techniques have been employed in more than one investigation; none is supported by a wide body of experience. Nevertheless, we shall briefly describe the major techniques, since they are directly relevant to the study of social relations and since they do not usually require the complex skills demanded by the projective methods for the study of personality. Caution in their use and interpretation, however, is indicated.

We shall group the many specific adaptations of projective tests for the study of social attitudes in terms of certain general materials and methods of approach: verbal, pictorial, play, and psychodramatic techniques.

VERBAL TECHNIQUES. Perhaps the simplest method is based on the classic technique of word association employed many years ago by Carl Jung in the study of abnormal behavior. As employed in the study of social attitudes, the technique is essentially the same: a number of words are presented to the subject, one by one, and he is asked to indicate the first thought that he associates with each word. Some of the words used as stimuli are neutral; some relate to the social attitudes being investigated. The speed of response and its emotional concomitants, as well as its content, may constitute valuable indicators of attitude. This technique has been used frequently in market research, to discover, for example, associations to a given brand name or to a proposed name for a new product.[4] It has also been used in several studies of the relation of specific attitudes to broader personality patterns. Murray and Morgan (1945), for example, used a modification of the word-association technique, asking the subject to respond to such words as *communism*, *religion*, *Negro*, by giving the most descriptive adjective he could think of.

Somewhat similar to the word-association method is the *sentence-completion* technique. The individual is presented with a series of incomplete sentences which he is asked to complete, usually under some time pressure to ensure spontaneity of response. The content of responses, if the items are carefully selected, may provide considerable insight into the person's attitudes. However, for sophisticated subjects it is unlikely that the purpose of the task is effectively masked, even though neutral or irrelevant items are included. On the other hand, time pressure may do much to prevent concealment of attitudes.[5]

This technique has been used for studying attitudes of many kinds. For example, Kerr (1943) used it in a study of national stereotypes held by English people. Some of the sentence beginnings were:

> The thing I do admire America for is . . .
> The trouble with America is . . .
> When I think of the Russians I think of . . .
> If the British and Soviet armies fight side by side they . . .
> If you invite an American to your home he may . . .

The technique has been used frequently in market research; for example, a study of attitudes, motives, and behavior of subscribers to

[4] Smith (1954) gives a comprehensive review of the use of projective techniques in marketing research. For a discussion from a different point of view, raising questions about the ethics of using projective techniques, see Packard (1957).

[5] For detailed discussion of the method, see Rohde (1946), Rotter and Willerman (1947), Rotter (1951), and Stein (1947).

Better Homes and Gardens (Smith, 1954) used the following sentence beginnings, among others:

> To own your own home . . .
> The ads in *Better Homes and Gardens* . . .
> Most fiction magazines . . .

Sometimes the items are phrased in the first person ("When I am asked to be in charge, I generally tend to . . ."), sometimes in the third person ("When they asked him to be in charge, he . . ." or "When they asked Bob to be in charge, he . . ."). As yet, there is no clear evidence about which phrasing is more successful in eliciting the respondent's own attitudes. Two studies directed to this point have reached contradictory conclusions. Sacks (1949) found that interpretations based on the first-person form agreed better with psychiatrists' diagnoses, and that respondents, comparing the two forms, reported that their responses to the first-person items corresponded more frequently to their own feelings. However, Getzels (1951) found that third-person items discriminated better between a group previously classified as "maladjusted" and one classified as "adjusted." He also found that the third-person items yielded more expressions of hostility to Negroes, more expressions of conflict with parents, and more "neurotic" answers to personality-relevant questions than did the first-person items. He found little difference between the two forms on topics permitting a variety of acceptable responses—that is, on topics not generally subject to social pressure. His subjects reported that in responding to the third-person items, they usually thought of the person as "someone like myself." However, when the item refers to "most people" rather than some mythical third person, it appears that respondents frequently make a serious attempt to estimate other people's views rather than expressing their own.

Similar to the sentence-completion technique are the *story-* and *argument-completion* techniques. The subject is given enough of the story or argument to focus his attention on a given issue but not enough to indicate how it will turn out. He is then asked to supply a conclusion. For example, a subject might be asked to complete the following argument (Murray and Morgan, 1945):

X, who has grown up in the belief that war never settles anything, is contemplating with some misgivings the probability of being drafted. He meets his friend Y, and they stop to have a beer together.

Y has been accepted, and is on his way to camp. He tells X that he expects to be sent to the Pacific. He is buoyant at the prospect, and says that he will be glad to take his shirt off and get into it all.

"How is it possible," asks X, "that . . ."

Similar in some respects to the open-ended question (discussed in the preceding chapter) is the so-called *projective question*. The subject is asked to respond to a vague question (e.g., "What are you?"), and the response is taken not at face value but rather from the point of view of the perceptions, beliefs, sentiments, and motives that predispose the individual to answer in the way he does. Such questions frequently take the form of asking about a possible event in the future ("What would you do if you inherited a large fortune?"), or about an imaginary event ("Suppose a man from Mars came down to this planet and you were the first person he saw and he asked what kinds of people there were in the world; what would you tell him?"), or about something the subject clearly is not in a position to know.

Sometimes projective questions take the form of asking about *other people's* views. The assumption here is that a respondent may hesitate to express critical or unpopular views as his own, but will put them into the mouths of other people. Smith (1954) gives the following illustration from the field of market research. Instead of asking housewives, "What do you think are the objectionable features of this cleanser?," the interviewer said: "Some women who use this cleanser find a lot of faults with it. I wonder if you can guess what they are objecting to."

Again, as in the case of sentence completion, it must be noted that one cannot always safely assume that a person's answer to a question of this sort really reflects his own feelings, especially if the question is of the "most people" form. Maccoby and Maccoby (1954) give the following striking example:

. . . a young woman being interviewed about her attitudes toward her job situation was asked: "How do most of the girls in the office feel about the supervisor?" She answered: "They think he's wonderful. They'll do anything for him." At which point the interviewer followed with: "And how about you—how do you feel about him?" with the reply: "I really detest him. I'm trying to transfer out of the unit."

Weitz and Nuckols (1953), in a study of the relationship between job satisfaction of insurance agents and continuance in the job, used both direct questions and those asking for estimates of the reactions of others. The indirect questions were introduced with the explanation:

We want to get your opinion about the attitudes of other agents toward their job. Below are a number of questions which can be answered by a percentage. Circle the per cent figure you believe best answers the question. If you don't know, guess.

The questions were of the form:

Approximately what per cent of the agents in your company think that: The training they received was good.
0%, 10%, 20%, 30%, 40%, 50%, 60%, 70%, 80%, 90%, 100%.

The direct questions were introduced with the explanation:

Now we'd like to get your attitude about your own job. Check the word or phrase which you feel best completes the statement for you.

The questions were of the form:

The training I received for my present job was
——poor
——adequate
——excellent

Although neither the score based on the direct questions nor that based on the indirect questions correlated very highly with job survival at the end of a year, these investigators found that the direct questions about the person's own reactions provided a better basis for prediction than did those asking for estimates of other people's reactions.

Another verbal technique is that of asking the respondent to describe the kind of person who would behave in a specified way. This approach has been used most frequently in market research, to elicit respondents' "images" of a given product, but it would seem easily adaptable to the investigation of attitudes of other kinds. Smith (1954) gives an example of this approach in a study of attitudes toward small cars. The person being interviewed is asked to imagine that a new family has moved into his block. Before he sees any members of the family, he sees their car parked outside the house; it is a Burton (a small car). He is asked, "What kind of people would you guess they are?"

One use of this approach in market research (Haire, 1950) has become almost a classic. In a conventional survey of attitudes toward Nescafé, an instant coffee, women were asked, "Do you use instant coffee?" If the answer was "No," they were asked, "What do you dislike about it?" Most of the replies were along the line, "I don't like the flavor." The investigators, suspecting that this was a stereotype that did not express the underlying reasons for rejection of instant coffee, switched to an indirect approach. Half of the sample of housewives interviewed were presented with the following shopping list made out by a hypothetical woman:

> pound and a half of hamburger
> 2 loaves Wonder bread
> bunch of carrots
> 1 can Rumford's Baking Powder
> Nescafé instant coffee
> 2 cans Del Monte peaches
> 5 lbs. potatoes

The other half of the sample were presented with the same list, except that "1 lb. Maxwell House Coffee (Drip Ground)" was substituted for the Nescafé. Each respondent was asked to read the shopping list and then to write a brief description of the personality and character of the woman who had made it out. The differences between the descriptions of the woman who bought Nescafé and the one who bought Maxwell House coffee were striking. Almost half of the women who read the list containing instant coffee described its writer as lazy and failing to plan her household purchases well; the woman who bought the drip-ground coffee was hardly ever described in these terms. In addition, the woman who bought instant coffee was more often described as a spendthrift and a poor wife. A check of the pantries of the respondents showed that most of the women who described the buyer of instant coffee in these unfavorable terms did not have instant coffee on their shelves; those who did not describe her unfavorably were much more likely to have instant coffee. In other words, it seemed clear that the decision to buy or not to buy instant coffee was influenced at least as much by attitudes about what constitutes good housekeeping as by reaction to the flavor of instant coffee, but these attitudes could not easily have been elicited by direct questioning.

A variation of this approach is the *matching* technique, in which the respondent is given a list of various brands of the same kind of product and another list of different kinds of people (e.g., doctors' wives, electricians' wives, stepmothers, career women) and is asked to match each kind of person with the brand she would be likely to buy. Gardner and Levy (1955) report striking differences in the "images" of different brands elicited by this technique.

PICTORIAL TECHNIQUES.[6] Pictorial techniques, many of them borrowed from well-established clinical procedures, have long been popular in the projective study of social attitudes. The Thematic Apperception Test (T.A.T.) has been the stimulus for several ventures.

Proshansky (1943) was one of the first to employ the T.A.T. type of picture in the study of social attitudes. Ambiguous pictures of situations involving labor were intermingled with regular T.A.T. pictures and exposed to a group for five seconds each. The subjects were asked to write briefly what they thought the pictures represented. On the basis of these stories, three judges rated the subjects' attitudes toward labor on a five-point scale. The pooled ratings of the three judges correlated .87 for one group of subjects and .67 for another group with a standard scale for measuring attitude toward labor.[7]

Sayles (1954) used pictures somewhat differently in a study of attitudes of union members toward grievance procedures. Finding that many questions seemed threatening to his respondents, or too personal,

---

[6] The pictorial techniques discussed here differ from those discussed in Chapter 7 in that they use pictures to stimulate indirect expression of the respondent's attitudes, whereas those discussed in the preceding chapter ask direct questions about the subject's response.

[7] The construction and use of non-disguised attitude scales are discussed in Chapter 10.

he decided to use a projective approach. On the basis of exploratory interviews, he identified seven stages in the grievance process; for example, informal discussion with fellow workers on what to do about a complaint, informal meeting of the foreman and union official and the worker involved, etc. He took photographs of such situations in other plants, with personnel unknown to his respondents. These photographs were then shown to the respondents, with an accompanying explanation—e.g., "This person has a grievance, something bothering him, but before taking it to the union he's discussing it with his fellow workers." The respondent was then asked such questions as, "How do you think this guy is feeling right now? What has happened just before this picture was taken? What do you think is going to happen next?" Sayles reports that the responses elicited by this technique were very similar to those obtained in the intensive interviews conducted in the exploratory stage of the research. The pictorial technique had a number of advantages: It took only about ten minutes to administer, compared with an average of two hours for the intensive interviews; it could be administered in the factory, whereas the interviews had to be conducted at home in order to assure free responses; it could be administered by someone unknown to the respondents, whereas the interviews had to be preceded by a six-week period of developing rapport before respondents were willing to talk freely.

Pictures of the T.A.T. type have been used in several studies of attitudes toward minority groups. In the *Authoritarian Personality* study (Adorno et al., 1950), ten pictures were presented to each subject: six pictures from the T.A.T. and four especially aimed at uncovering attitudes toward minority groups. The latter were of "Jewish-looking people in a poor district," "an older Negro woman with a younger Negro boy," "a young couple in zoot suits," and "a lower-class man accosted by a policeman wielding a nightstick." Subjects were asked to construct a complete story about each picture, and their stories were recorded verbatim by the examiner. Stories were analyzed quantitatively, in terms of the strength and frequency of expression of various needs, and qualitatively, in terms of the theme expressed in the various stories. Interestingly enough, the pictures designed to distinguish between those with high and low ethnocentrism were less effective for this purpose than the pictures from the regular T.A.T. series.

The "Human Relations Test" developed by the staff of the College Study in Intergroup Relations (Cook, 1950) offers another example. It consists of ten drawings, each depicting an ambiguous situation of intergroup contact. One picture shows a basketball scene with a white player lying on the floor and a Negro player standing above him; another shows a couple applying for a room in a hotel, with a sign on the wall indicating that the hotel has a restricted clientele; a third portrays a scene in a restaurant in which three Negro men are at the entrance talking to the headwaiter, who has his hand upraised; etc. Each scene can be interpreted as one of conflict or of amity. The subjects are asked to construct a short story about each scene. Their stories are evaluated in terms of whether or not conflict is portrayed, of how the subject allocates the blame for conflict, of how the conflict turns out, etc.

T.A.T.-type pictures have also been used in market research (see Smith, 1954). In a study of magazine readership, for example, respondents were shown a picture of a family sitting in a living room reading, and were asked to tell a story about it. In a study of factors influencing purchases of consumer items, respondents were asked to tell stories about such pictures as one of a woman walking down the street with money in her hand; there is a store on one side of the street, a bank on the other.

Fromme (1941) presented to subjects political cartoons, each with four alternative captions judged by the author to represent a full range of favorable and unfavorable attitudes, and requested the subjects to choose the one that best fitted each cartoon. Although Fromme used the cartoons and their captioning primarily to stimulate discussion and to obtain qualitative insights into political attitudes, it seems probable that the use of cartoons has fruitful possibilities for the quantitative study of social attitudes.

J. F. Brown (1947) modified the Rosenzweig Picture-Frustration Test for use in the study of ethnic attitudes. The Rosenzweig Test uses a cartoon format, in which one character is represented as saying something; there is a blank balloon for the other character, and the respondent is asked what this second character would probably say. In the clinical form of the test, all the pictures portray situations of frustration for the second character; the responses given for him are scored in terms of whether they indicate a tendency to place blame on others, or on oneself, or not to react in terms of blame. The Brown adaptation of this test includes a number of pictures in which (a) Negroes or Jews frustrate whites or non-Jews and (b) whites or non-Jews frustrate Negroes or Jews. In one picture, for example, a "Jewish-looking" moneylender refuses a loan to a "non-Jewish–looking" man, saying: "Sorry, sir, but we cannot see our way clear to make the loan." The subject has to fill out a blank space indicating what the frustrated person replies. The type of reply is considered by Brown to be indicative of the subject's attitude toward the minority group in question. As with many of the pictorial techniques, the visual cues necessary to elicit the attitude toward the different ethnic groups make the purpose of the test manifest to any but the most naive subjects.

A similar format has been used in other studies, with different content. In a study of reactions to leadership and authority (Sanford, 1950; Sanford and Rosenstock, 1952), several drawings were used. One showed two men sitting and talking; the first is saying, "You were telling me about something that's been bothering you. What was the problem?" Another showed a man saying to a group of people, "Since I'm head of this group you'd better do as I say." This study, unlike many of those in which projective devices have been used, was a large-scale survey, in which interviewers questioned a cross-section of the population of a large city. The investigators reported that respondents were interested and cooperative; the use of the pictures seemed to break the monotony of the interview, and made readily comprehensible situations and problems that it might have been difficult to present verbally. The reliability of coding was reported to be equal to that generally achieved in coding interview questions, and repetition of the interview with part of the sample after a month's lapse showed repeat reliability comparable with that in conventional surveys. As evidence of validity, it was reported that the pictures discriminated between groups rated as authoritarian or equalitarian on an authoritarianism-equalitarianism scale included in the interview.

Pictures of this sort, too, have been used in market research. For example, one used in a study of attitudes toward cigar smoking showed a man saying to a woman (presumably his wife), "I've decided to take up smoking cigars, dear" (Smith, 1954). A picture used in a study carried out for a grocery store whose sales were declining showed two women sitting at a table drinking coffee. One woman said, "Well, I feel I have to buy food where the price is lower—that's the main thing as far as I'm concerned." The other woman was shown as saying, "Art and I agree that I should shop where . . ." The respondent was asked to fill in the rest of the answer (Zober, 1956).

The device of asking the respondent to describe the kind of person who would behave in a certain way, described in the preceding section on verbal techniques, has also been used in conjunction with pictorial material. Smith (1954) gives an example from a study testing proposed ads for a new perfume. One of the ads featured a Gauguin picture of South Sea girls; the other, a picture of a young American girl clasping a bouquet of flowers. The interviewer said: "A good many women prefer this picture; others prefer this one. I wonder if you could say anything about these two types of women—the sort of people they are." The responses made it clear that the Gauguin picture would not appeal to the market for whom the perfume was intended.

PLAY TECHNIQUES. Techniques involving the manipulation of dolls have been used in investigating the attitudes of young children. Hogrefe, Evans, and Chein (unpublished study) gave their subjects a number of "white" and "colored" dolls and asked them to play out specific scenes, such as "going to school" or "arranging a party," as though they were producing a movie. The inclusion or exclusion of the colored dolls, as well as the role assigned to them, provided a simple, objective score which was taken as a measure of the child's attitude toward Negro children. The majority of the children they tested showed a striking *avoidance* of segregated patterns; that is, they created mixed situations far more often than would be expected by chance. This was in keeping with the children's reports of their own play activity; in answer to the question, "Do you ever play with Negro children?," four fifths of the white children said "Yes." But observation of their actual behavior in an interracial recreation center showed a striking contrast; on repeated occasions, when children were asked to pick partners for some activity, the number of *segregated* pairs was far greater than would be expected by chance.

Hartley and Schwartz (1948) combined doll play with pictorial material in the investigation of intergroup attitudes of children. Pictorial backgrounds carried characteristic symbols of the Catholic religion in one set, the Jewish religion in another, and middle-class surroundings (without religious identification) in a third. Identical family sets of dolls were placed on the three backgrounds and the child was allowed to use them in playing out situations such as a birthday party, school bus, etc.

PSYCHODRAMATIC AND SOCIODRAMATIC TECHNIQUES. Although psychodrama and sociodrama have not been used systematically in the study of social attitudes, the fact that they are methods of considerable flexibility makes it reasonable to examine the possibility that they might be used in this way. The methods require that the subject act out a role, either as himself (psychodrama) or as somebody else (sociodrama), as he would in a real-life situation. For example, a white subject may be presented with the problem of acting out the role of a Negro factory worker who has been absent from work several times and who has just been called into the foreman's office to explain his absenteeism. The manner in which he plays his role, the history that he creates for the role, etc., may provide considerable insight into his attitudes. The investigator, in much the same way as an observer, can record the behavior for later analysis, can categorize it on the spot, or can rate it in terms of various scales, etc. Psychodrama and sociodrama, it should be noted, are among the few tools available for the systematic investigation of social *skills*. They enable one to place a person in situations in which one can observe how skillfully he behaves in relation to other people.[8]

Structured Disguised Tests of Social Attitudes

Investigators of social attitudes have been interested in developing tests that would have some of the advantages of the projective techniques—notably that of not making apparent to the subject the investigator's purpose—but that would be simpler to administer, score, and interpret than most projective tests are. Accordingly, a number of

---

[8] For a discussion of the research uses of psychodrama, see Franz (1940).

structured disguised tests have been devised. Campbell (1950) describes such measures as "approximating the objective testing of attitudes."[9]

Most tests of this kind are based on the fact that a person's attitudes are likely to influence his perceptions, beliefs, judgments, memory, etc. That this is so has been demonstrated in a number of studies. For example, Bartlett's classic experiment (1932) on the recall of pictorial materials and stories revealed the influence of social attitudes on memory. In one of these experiments, students at Cambridge University read twice a story drawn from the folklore of a culture foreign to them and dealing with matters with which they had little familiarity. After varying periods of time, the subjects were asked to repeat the story as accurately as possible. Bartlett found that the reproductions all showed systematic changes, increasing with time, which could partly be accounted for by the cultural frame of reference of the subjects.

Similarly, Newcomb (1946), in his study of the effects of social climate on attitudes and information, showed the nonrandom character of right and wrong answers to factual questions. On a questionnaire about the Spanish Civil War, pro-Franco students tended to know those items of information that favored Franco, but not those that were anti-Franco; the reverse was true for anti-Franco students. Newcomb commented that on difficult items "the direction of guessing is altogether likely to be weighted toward the subject's attitude. If this reasoning is correct, the . . . test tends to become an attitude test."

Findings of this nature have given rise to the development of apparently objective tests difficult or complex enough to allow the subject's attitudes to influence his performance. To the respondent, the situation of measurement is similar to that of an achievement or ability test. In contrast with most projective tests, in which the individual is encouraged to believe that there are no objectively "correct" answers, the subject is led to believe that there are "right" and "wrong" responses, and the attempt is made to motivate him to do as well as possible on the test.

[9] In this section we have drawn heavily on Campbell's review (1950) of such tests.

However, the rationale underlying the use of such tests is essentially the same as that underlying the use of projective techniques: When there is no clear, objectively verifiable basis for choosing among alternative responses to a situation, an individual's response tends to reflect his predispositions. Of course, the stronger the individual's predispositions, the more likely they are to be reflected in his responses.

Campbell (1950) provides a formula for constructing such tests:

> Find a task which all your respondents will take as objective, and in which all will strive to do well. Make the task sufficiently difficult, or use a content area in which respondents have had little experience or opportunity for reality testing. Load the test with content relative to the attitude you study. Look in the responses for systematic error, or for any persistent selectivity of performance. If such be found, it seems an adequate basis for the inference of an attitude.

Let us briefly indicate some of the disguised "objective" techniques that have been used to measure social attitudes.

INFORMATION TESTS

Hammond (1948) employed an "information test" to measure attitudes toward labor-management relations and toward Russia. His questionnaire included three types of question. The first type, of which there were eight items, forced the respondent to choose between two alternative answers, both of which were, by intent, equally wrong, but in opposite directions from the correct answer—e.g., "Average weekly wage of the war worker in 1945 was (1) $37.00, (2) $57.00." The second type, of which there were twelve items, required the subject to respond to a question about which the facts could not be determined—e.g., "Russia's removal of heavy industry from Austria was (1) legal, (2) illegal." The third series of questions consisted of twenty genuine information items, which were interspersed among the twenty items mentioned above. These items, all relating to the same general fields as the "test" items, were introduced in order to increase the apparent authenticity of the test as one of information. Despite the limited number of items, Hammond's scales differentiated a labor-union group from two business clubs, with practically no overlap, on attitudes toward both Russia and labor-management relations.

Weschler (1950) also used this technique in a test of attitudes toward labor and management. He found that, within a group of college students, scores on this indirect test correlated highly with self-ratings of attitude. In addition, representatives of unions and of management attending a course in labor relations differed markedly in their scores on the test.

REASONING TESTS

In laboratory investigations of the process of reasoning it has been apparent for many years that syllogistic inference does not always proceed logically; frequently it is affected by the content of the syllogism. G. B. Watson (1925) included as part of his "Measurement of Fair-Mindedness" an inference test composed of statements of fact followed by several conclusions that might be drawn. For example, one statement was:

Statistics show that in the United States, of one hundred men starting out at an age of 25, at the end of forty years, one will be wealthy, while fifty-four will be dependent upon relatives or charity for support.[10]

This statement was followed by several possible conclusions:

The present social order cheats the many for the benefit of the few.

The average young man, under present conditions, cannot count on being wealthy at the age of 65.

Most men are shiftless, lazy, or extravagant, otherwise they would not need to be dependent.

The one man is living upon luxuries ground out of the bones of the masses of common people.

Some day the workers will rise in revolt.

No such conclusion can fairly be drawn.

[10] To the student of today, this may not appear to be a factual statement. But at the time the test was devised—before the introduction of social security programs —statistics *did* show that 54 percent of 65-year-old men were dependent on relatives or charity for support.

The subjects were asked to check only conclusions established by the facts given in the statement, drawing upon no other evidence. They were cautioned to check only those inferences that were certain, none that were merely probable. Checking anything other than "No such conclusion can fairly be drawn" or the alternative that simply rephrased the original statement (in this case, item #2) was taken as evidence of bias.

In a study of attitudes toward the Japanese, Morgan (1945) used a test made up of pairs of syllogisms. One syllogism in each pair was stated either in abstract form or with neutral content; the other, roughly parallel, used statements about the Japanese. For example, one pair read as follows:

No A's are B's. Some C's are B's. From these statements it is logical to conclude:
1. All C's are A's.
2. Some C's are A's.
3. Only a few C's are A's.
4. Some C's are not A's.
5. Most C's are not A's.
6. No C's are A's.
7. No logical conclusion can be drawn from the given statements

A trustworthy man does not engage in deceitful acts. The bombing of Pearl Harbor by the Japanese was a deceitful act. From these statements it is logical to conclude:
1. All of the Japanese are trustworthy.
2. Some of the Japanese are trustworthy.
3. Only a few of the Japanese are trustworthy.
4. Some of the Japanese are not trustworthy.
5. Most of the Japanese are not trustworthy.
6. None of the Japanese are trustworthy.
7. No logical conclusion can be drawn from the given statements.

The difference between the response to the abstract form and the form referring to the Japanese was used as an indicator of attitude toward the Japanese. The two syllogisms forming a pair were not, of course, placed next to each other in the questionnaire as it was presented to the subjects.

TESTS OF PERCEPTION, MEMORY, AND JUDGMENT

It has long been recognized that perception, memory, and judgment can be markedly influenced by one's predispositions and past experiences. E. L. and R. E. Horowitz (1938), in their studies of the development of race attitudes, designed a number of techniques based on this fact. In one, the Aussage test, a complicated picture was exposed for two or three seconds; then a series of standardized questions testing perception and memory were asked. For example, after exposure of a picture that did not include a Negro, the question was asked. "What is the colored man on the corner doing?" With increasing age, the children were more likely to "perceive" or "recall" the Negro in a menial role. The Perception-Span Test consisted of a series of posters, on each of which were mounted pictures of ten items. Each poster was exposed for ten seconds; after it had been removed, the children were asked to "tell all the pictures you can remember." Among younger children, Negroes were less well remembered than would be expected by chance; among older children there was a selective awareness of them. The Pictorial Recognition Test involved exposing sets of Negro and white faces and testing for recall by asking that the previously exposed pictures be picked from a larger group. Using this test, Seeleman (1940–41) found that the discrepancy between memory for white and for Negro faces correlated about .70 with a questionnaire measuring prejudice. An unfavorable attitude tended to obliterate recognition or recall of individual differences among Negro pictures.

Following the lead of the Horowitz studies, there has been increasing interest in the relation between attitudes, on the one hand, and perception and memory, on the other. Illustrative of this development is a series of techniques developed by Cattell and his co-workers (1949, 1950). One test, Immediate Memory, required the subject to recall statements from sets of twelve presented at one-second intervals. Selective recall of statements relevant to a given attitude was taken as a measure of the strength of the attitude. Another technique, the Misperception method, involved a one-second tachistoscopic exposure of attitude statements with misspellings. The subject was required to recall the statement and note the misspellings; overlooking of the latter was regarded as a sign of a strong attitude. Although Cattell's results, in terms of correlation with other tests designed to measure attitude toward the same objects, are not particularly encouraging, his tests are cited as examples of the range of possibilities in the objective but disguised measurement of attitude.[11]

Levine and Murphy (1943) found that both the learning and the forgetting of controversial material were related to attitude. Strongly pro-Soviet and anti-Soviet groups of American college students were asked to learn two passages about the Soviet Union, one of which was very favorable, one very unfavorable. Each group learned more rapidly, and remembered longer, the passage in harmony with its own attitude.

Jones and Kohler (1958) introduced a qualification of the finding that people learn best those statements which are in favor of their position by suggesting that this is true only if the statement is sufficiently plausible and effective to permit the individual comfortably to endorse both the position implied by the statement and the supporting reasons given. They hypothesized that people would be most likely to remember plausible statements that agree with their own position and implausible statements opposing their position; and conversely, that they would tend to forget implausible statements in favor of their own position and plausible ones opposing it. In testing this hypothesis, they presented subjects with six statements favoring and six opposing segregation; within each type of statement, three were "plausible," three were "implausible." For example, a plausible pro-segregation statement was, "Southerners will have to pay the price of lowered scholastic standards if they yield to the pressures to integrate their schools"; an implausible pro-segregation statement was, "If Negroes and whites were meant to live together, they never would have been separated at the beginning of history." As predicted, subjects who were rated as pro-segregation (on the basis of other attitude scales administered at a different time) were most successful in learning the plausible pro-segregation arguments and the implausible anti-segregation ones; those who were anti-segregation were most successful in learning the plausible anti-segregation arguments and the implausible

[11] It is possible that the Misperception procedure gets at a dimension of attitude not tapped by other tests—something like "mental alertness or flexibility in the presence of attitude-entangling stimuli." Note the possibility of getting comparative data by using favorable, unfavorable, neutral, and irrelevant statements of equal difficulty.

pro-segregation ones; for each type of argument, the neutral group made scores intermediate between the two extreme groups. Using an index representing the difference between learning of plausible pro-segregation and implausible anti-segregation arguments, on the one hand, and implausible pro- and plausible anti- arguments, on the other, they found no overlap between subjects who scored as pro- or anti-segregation on their criterion attitude scale. On the basis of this finding, these investigators suggested the possibility of constructing an indirect test of attitude in terms of the learning of relevant material in which both direction and plausibility were varied.

A number of investigators have employed tests of "judgment" in the study of social attitudes. Murphy and Likert (1938) showed respondents pictures labeled as a union president, a railroad magnate, a pacifist, a Negro champion of Negro rights, etc., and asked them to judge the character of the pictured person in terms of courage, selfishness, intelligence, conceit, etc. They found no relationship between these ratings and attitudes as measured in a variety of paper-and-pencil tests. However, since photographs do not usually provide significant clues to character, it is reasonable to suppose that such judgments would be influenced by reaction to labels (e.g., union president). Thus this approach seems worth further exploration.

Several investigators have used discrepancies in judgments of comparable situations as measures of social attitudes. Watson (1925), in a test of "moral judgment," asked for judgments of approval or disapproval about a variety of situations, sets of these situations being identical except for the specific persons or groups involved. For example, unwarranted search is made of a suspected "radical" headquarters in one item, and of a business corporation suspected of dishonesty in a parallel item. The discrepancy in judgment between the two parallel situations formed the basis for scoring.

Seeman (1947) employed a similar technique in the study of attitudes of white persons toward Negroes. He presented college students with brief descriptions of relations between men and women, involving such issues as extramarital sexual relationships, divorce, etc., and asked for judgments about the behavior of the characters. For example:

Bob and Helen want to get married soon. They have been engaged for a year. So far as they can foresee, it will be impossible for the marriage to take place for another two years at least. Bob and Helen have already had complete sexual relations upon a number of occasions. Helen says she can see nothing wrong with this "as long as people marry eventually" and "do not feel guilty about it."

a) Is this wrong for Helen? Yes ____ No ____ Uncertain ____
b) Is this wrong for Bob? Yes ____ No ____ Uncertain ____
Any remarks?

In half the copies of the test, each story was accompanied by a picture of a white couple; in the other half, by a picture of a Negro couple.

Since it would have been immediately apparent that the test was concerned with attitude toward Negroes if each student received both forms, each was given only one; the Negro and white forms were distributed randomly among the sample. The results were analyzed by comparing the replies of the group of students who received the Negro form with those of the group who received the white form. As expected, the responses to the two forms of the test differed. Subjects who had the form with the white illustrations more often judged the unconventional behavior as being wrong; there were more "No" and "Uncertain" answers to the form with the Negro illustration.

The more detailed results of this study provide a vivid illustration of the problems involved in the use of indirect techniques. Seeman had hypothesized that prejudiced subjects would be more likely than unprejudiced ones to make different judgments for Negroes and for whites. In order to test this hypothesis, he administered the Likert scale of attitude toward Negroes[12] and divided the sample into a "more prejudiced" and a "less prejudiced" group on this basis. To test his hypothesis, he compared the replies of the "more prejudiced" subjects who had received the Negro form with those of the "more prejudiced" subjects who had received the white form, and the replies of the "less prejudiced" subjects who had received the Negro form with those of the "less prejudiced" subjects who had received the white form. Contrary to his hypothesis, he found that the replies of the "less prejudiced"

[12] Attitude scales of this type are discussed in Chapter 10.

subjects who received the Negro form differed significantly from those of the "less prejudiced" subjects who received the white form, whereas among the "more prejudiced" subjects the distributions of responses to the two forms were essentially the same. This finding led Seeman to question what was actually being measured by the indirect test and by the Likert scale, and which one was more valid for what purposes. He concluded by pointing to the "need for extreme care in interpretation of projective and semi-projective techniques for the study of specific attitudes."

Other investigators have employed changes in judgment of literary merit, changes in evaluation of the quality of mottoes, and changes in level of aspiration as indicators of attitudes. The general technique is always essentially the same. The item to be evaluated is presented as a product or as a characteristic of a given person or group, and the same or an equivalent item as originating with a different person or group. The discrepancy in judgment is taken as a measure of the attitude toward the given group. Note, however, that the discrepancies in judgment are more complex than may appear on the surface, since changes in meaning go along with changes in imputed origin.[13]

Hovland and Sherif (1952) have suggested another way in which judgments might be used as an indication of attitude. In a study discussed in more detail in Chapter 10, these investigators found that people's judgment of the degree of favorableness or unfavorableness of a given statement about Negroes was influenced by their own attitude toward Negroes. This finding led to the suggestion that attitude might be assessed indirectly through study of the way an individual places items in terms of his judgment of their favorableness or unfavorableness toward the object. Individuals with strongly "pro" attitudes would be expected to perceive relatively many items as unfavorable; those with strongly "anti" attitudes to perceive relatively many as favorable; and those with neutral attitudes to see the items as being rather evenly spaced over the entire range. Hovland and Sherif point out that such a test should include a large number of ambiguous items, since it is the judgment of these items that is most affected by the individual's attitude.

Just as the perception of other types of stimuli may be affected

13 See, for example, Lewis (1941).

by attitudes, so may perception of social facts. Saenger and Birch, for example (cited in Saenger and Proshansky, 1950), asked respondents to estimate the number of Communists in the country; they found that the average figure given by Republicans was five times as great as that given by Democrats. Merton et al. (forthcoming) found that, in a mixed housing project, white residents who were prejudiced against Negroes overestimated the proportion of Negroes in the project and underestimated the average amount of education the Negro residents of the project had had.

Many people tend to overestimate the size of the group that agrees with their opinions. For example, in a study of attitudes toward Negro sales personnel in department stores, Saenger and Gilbert (1950) found a striking correspondence between subjects' own attitudes, as rated on the basis of their replies to a number of interview questions, and their estimates of the proportion of people who would object to the hiring of Negro sales clerks. Of those who were rated as showing no prejudice, only 13 per cent said "most people" would be opposed to the employment of Negroes, while 52 per cent said "a few" or "none." At the other extreme, of those who were placed at the most prejudiced end of the rating scale, 92 per cent said "most people" would object to the employment of Negroes, and none said "a few" or "none" would object. Findings such as these have led several investigators to attempt to measure social attitudes indirectly by asking subjects to estimate the percentage of a group that would agree with specific opinions.

Although such "estimating" techniques have been used successfully in showing that groups with different attitudes differ in their perception of social facts, as measures of attitude they must be used with extreme caution. First of all, in order to determine the extent and direction of distortion, the investigator must have some independent measure of group composition or opinion. Second, different individuals within the group may have had different experiences that provide objectively different bases for their estimates. For example, if, in Merton's mixed housing project, the proportions of Negroes were different in different buildings, tenants in buildings with relatively many Negroes might be expected to overestimate the proportion of Negroes in the total project simply on the basis of their everyday observation of the people around them. Third, in the absence of firm theoretical or empirical support, it is frequently not clear whether distortion in a given direction reflects a favorable or an unfavorable attitude. For example, Saenger and Birch, in addition to finding different estimates of the number of Communists, found that individuals were likely to exaggerate the size of their own group. Thus, people who described themselves as "liberal Republicans" gave higher estimates of the size of this group than did people who described themselves as "conservative Republicans," and so on. In other words, distortion in estimation may reflect either wishes or fears; not enough research has been done to know the conditions under which distortion indicates one or the other.

Substitute Measures

Still another indirect approach to the measurement of a characteristic involves measuring something else, or some combination of other things, that is sufficiently highly correlated with the characteristic one wants measured to enable it to serve as a satisfactory substitute. We may call this approach the *substitute measure*.

The F-scale (Adorno *et al.*, 1950) was constructed on this principle. It was reasoned that authoritarian attitudes should correlate highly with anti-semitism, so that a measure of the former should also yield a satisfactory measure of the latter. To increase the substitutability of the F-scale for a measure of anti-semitism, items were selected for inclusion in the F-scale not only on the basis of the criterion of internal consistency, but also on the basis of how well they correlated with a scale of anti-semitic attitudes.

Wilner, Walkley, and Cook (1955) used a different type of substitute measure in their effort to establish *post hoc* whether two groups of white tenants in housing projects (one living relatively close to Negroes in the project, the other relatively far from them) had held similar attitudes before moving into the project. Working from the fact that a number of socioeconomic characteristics (for example, religion and education) are known to be correlated with attitudes toward

Negroes, they constructed an index of "probable initial attitude" on the basis of such characteristics.

Ideally, the method of substitute measurement calls for the combination of a number of indices, each of which has a relatively high correlation with the characteristic for which one needs a measure, and a relatively low correlation with each of the other indices in the combination. In principle, such a measure involves an application of the logic of pragmatic validation. It should be noted, however, that such a measure cannot be used as an "after" measure in an attitude-change experiment. The experimental factor is designed to change the attitude, not necessarily the variables which were initially correlated with it. If successful, the experimental factor may change the basis of the relationship and, among other things, lower the pragmatic validity of the substitute measure.[14]

A Note on Validation

As we indicated earlier, many questions have been raised about the validity of indirect techniques, and relatively little research evidence is available to answer them. Actually, as noted in the preceding chapter, there is not much evidence of the validity of direct techniques depending on self-report, such as interviews and questionnaires. The validity of such instruments is less often questioned, however, probably because of the "obvious" relevance of the questions to the characteristics they are intended to measure. It is the degree of inference involved in indirect tests—the gap between the subject's response and the characteristic it is presumed to indicate—that intensifies questions about validity.

In the case of projective techniques, there are additional reasons for questions about validity: the great variety of aspects about which inferences may be drawn and the heavy reliance on the interpretive

[14] This consideration points to the grave weakness of pragmatic validation without support in a body of theory or knowledge of the conditions on which the correlation between test and criterion depends. Under these circumstances, we never know whether the underlying conditions may not have changed so that the test no longer has the pragmatic validity we think it has. That is, we can only hope that since the test has worked until now, it will continue to work in any given application.

skill of the individual analyst. For most of the projective techniques, the rules by which the data are to be transformed into scales of measurement are not specified in detail; nor, for that matter, are the dimensions one is attempting to measure. As a consequence, each investigator is forced to some extent to develop his own rules. Moreover, the very flexibility of the tests means that they do not always cover the same aspects in the same detail. In other words, at least in their present form, projective tests sacrifice precision and reliability in the interest of breadth and depth.

This variability both in the detail with which various aspects are covered and in the interpretations made by different users introduces a question of the extent to which one can speak of validating "the Rorschach" or "the T.A.T." Rather, specific inferences made by specific interpreters using these techniques can be validated. Cumulation of evidence of validity in specific respects contributes, of course, to validation of the technique as a whole.

To a considerable extent, projective techniques intended to measure broad aspects of personality must rely on construct validation (see Chapter 5) rather than on evidence of high correlation with any single criterion. All studies in which scores or qualitative descriptions based on projective techniques are found to be related to some other variable —and there are many such—contribute to the construct validation of the given technique. Thus, the finding in the *Authoritarian Personality* study that the T.A.T. stories of prejudiced and unprejudiced individuals tended to differ in specified ways helps not only to confirm the basic hypothesis of the study (that prejudice is a function of deep-lying personality trends) but to validate the T.A.T. as an instrument for uncovering such personality trends.

In estimating the validity of indirect measures of social attitudes, both those of the projective type and the more structured tests, an investigator may administer the test to two or more groups that may be expected to differ in the characteristic the test attempts to measure, and compare their scores. If the test differentiates between the groups, this is contributory evidence of its validity. Thus, Hammond's finding that there was almost no overlap between scores of union members and of members of business clubs on his "information test" provides some assurance that the test is a valid measure of attitudes toward labor-management relations. A number of other investigators have used this approach.

Or the user of an indirect test may attempt to validate it by comparing scores on it with those on a non-disguised test designed to measure the same attitude. Proshansky used this procedure with respect to his projective test of attitude toward labor, with positive results. Seeman used it, with respect to his indirect "moral judgment" test of attitudes toward Negroes, with negative results. It has been used by a number of other investigators in estimating the validity of an indirect technique.

This use of an undisguised test as a criterion may seem a rather odd procedure, considering the fact that the major reason for using indirect techniques is to get at information that might not be revealed in response to a direct technique. However, two points should be considered in this connection. One is that an indirect technique may be used simply as a more effective way of getting information that the individual could give in response to a direct question if he were willing to. When this is the case, it is appropriate to use responses to a non-disguised instrument as a criterion for the validity of the indirect technique, provided that the non-disguised test is administered under circumstances that make it reasonable to expect minimal concealment of true attitudes. For example, it would be reasonable to use scores on a non-disguised test of attitudes toward labor as a criterion against which to compare the results of an indirect test only if the non-disguised test were administered under circumstances that assured the subjects of anonymity or if the rapport between investigator and subjects were such that they would feel free to reply frankly; it would not be reasonable to use as a criterion scores on a test administered to workers by their supervisor.

Another point in evaluating the use of a non-disguised test as a criterion for a disguised one is that the purpose of the disguised test may be to gain more *extensive* insight into the nature of an individual's attitude. This more extensive knowledge may not mean a different estimate of how favorable or unfavorable an individual is toward a given object, but rather some understanding of how his attitude is related to other factors. It is not unreasonable to assume that if a projective technique gives evidence of measuring some aspect of an attitude validly (as indicated by its consistency with the results of a validated undisguised technique), it may also measure other aspects of an attitude validly; nevertheless, the consistency should not be taken as conclusive evidence of validity in measuring these other aspects.

Another approach to validation is to compare the results obtained by a measuring instrument with observations of actual behavior. That this approach has not often been used is undoubtedly due in part to the difficulty of determining what kinds of behavior in what situations would provide an adequate criterion, in part to the difficulty of securing measures of such behavior. Nevertheless, a few of the studies mentioned in this chapter have used this approach. Haire used it in the instant coffee study, and found high correspondence between responses to his indirect measure and actual behavior. Hogrefe, Evans, and Chein, in their study of relations between white and Negro children, found high correspondence between scores on their indirect measure and children's reports of their own behavior, but little correspondence with observation of actual behavior in test situations.

In summary: Much more investigation of the validity of indirect tests is needed. Some of the studies carried out to date have given encouraging evidence of correspondence between the results of an indirect test and those provided by an independent criterion; others, however, have revealed discrepancies between different measures that raise questions about what the various tests are in fact measuring. Investigation of the validity of indirect tests—and especially of projective tests which attempt to measure more than one dimension—is hampered by the difficulty of finding appropriate criteria. Nevertheless, more attention needs to be paid to validation of tests of this type before they can make their full contribution to social research.

9

THE USE OF AVAILABLE DATA
AS SOURCE MATERIAL

Statistical Records

Personal Documents

Mass Communications

Summary

Statistical Records

ACONSIDERABLE AMOUNT of statistical data on the behavior of its members is available in every literate community. Although these data have been accumulated primarily for purposes of administration and historical description, social science research can make good use of them. To neglect their existence often involves either a disregard of relevant information or, if the investigator laboriously collects data that already exist, a waste of effort.

The range of subject matter covered in available records, and the treatment a subject receives in such records, varies with the administrative needs for which they were originally collected. Many available statistical data refer to socioeconomic attributes of individuals. Thus, the census of a population contains information about age, sex, family size, occupation, residence, etc. Health statistics give birth and death rates and the like; federal, state, municipal, and private economic institutions collect and publish data on wages, hours of work, productivity, absenteeism, strikes, financial transactions, and so on. Many voluntary organizations have records not only of their own membership but of groups of people whom they serve. In addition, a small but steadily increasing body of data is being collected by various institutions on the psychological level proper. For example, schools, hospitals, social service agencies, personnel departments in industry, and similar institutions nowadays frequently administer psychological tests of various kinds to their entire populations.

Data collected in the course of such other activities have a number of advantages in social research, in addition to that of economy. A major one is the fact that much information of this sort is collected periodically, thus making possible the establishment of trends over time. Another is that the gathering of information from such sources does not require the cooperation of the individuals about whom information is being sought, as does the use of questionnaires, interviews, projective techniques, and, frequently, observation. Moreover, since such data are collected in the ordinary course of events, the measurement procedure is less likely to reveal the investigator's purpose or to change the behavior in which he is interested than are some of the other data-collection techniques.

Guiding Principles for Using Statistical Records

The use of available statistical records requires that the social scientist be familiar with the better known sources of such data and that he display some ingenuity in discovering less well known material.

The study by Kenesaw M. Landis, *Segregation in Washington* (1948), is based exclusively on the analysis and interpretation of available data. Among other sources, Landis used publications by the Bureau of the Census to indicate the pressure on Negroes to live together in great numbers in a small area and to illustrate the poor conditions of housing available for Negroes; official health statistics to demonstrate the consequences of these conditions in terms of a higher death rate, especially from tuberculosis; official employment data and records from a private industrial concern to point up discrimination in work; and the city-wide figures collected by the Department of Research of the Washington Council of Social Agencies to illustrate the relation between overcrowding and the arrests of juveniles made by the metropolitan police. Landis' contribution in this study consisted in discovering the sources of these data and in extracting from them information relevant to his topic.

Other research questions demand a greater investment of energy or ingenuity in obtaining relevant records. Leo Srole, while at work on the study of status and prestige in the *Yankee City* series of investigations (Warner et al., 1941–1947), discovered an unusual source of data relevant to his problem—cemetery records.[1] Apparently it had become the practice in Yankee City for residents who had risen to a social status higher than that of their dead relatives to have the remains of their family members transferred from a lower-status cemetery to one of higher social standing.

These examples could easily be multiplied. They demonstrate

---

[1] Reported in a personal communication to the authors.

that systematic searching and ingenuity will uncover many more available data than are often assumed to exist.

Another requirement for the use of statistical records has to do with the formulation of research hypotheses. In essence, the use of such data demands *a capacity to ask many different questions related to the research problem*. By definition, the purpose for which available records have been collected is different from the purpose for which the social scientist wishes to use them. (If that were not the case, research would be superfluous, since the records would answer the research questions.) A research problem can, as a rule, be translated into a wide variety of questions; a hypothesis can be verified in many different ways. *The guiding principle, then, for the use of available statistics consists in keeping oneself flexible with respect to the form in which research questions are asked.* If a research idea or hypothesis can be formulated in such a manner that the available recorded material bears on the question, the use of such material becomes possible.

Perhaps the outstanding example of how the superior flexibility of a great intellect resulted in the testing of a social theory by available statistics is Durkheim's *Le Suicide*. As Talcott Parsons (1937) said about Durkheim, he "possessed to a remarkable degree the faculty of persistence in thinking through the consequences of a few fundamental assumptions . . . his empirical observation is of the nature of the crucial experiment. . . ." Durkheim's basic concern was with the relation of an individual to a group and to the prevailing norms and values in the group. He started with the hypothesis that the causes of suicide are to be found in social conditions. To test this theory, he studied records of suicide rates in all European countries for which they were available. Some of these statistics had already been collated by other investigators; others were readily available in public documents; still others Durkheim compiled from official files. With great ingenuity, he examined these statistics for their bearing on a number of different hypotheses. In his book, he examines first a number of alternative hypotheses: that suicide is the result of psychopathic states, of imitation, of racial or hereditary factors, of cosmic factors. He demonstrates that the statistics are not in accord with any of these hypotheses. For example, in considering the hypothesis that suicide is influenced by climatic factors, he starts with the observation that in all the countries for which statistics are available over a period of years, the incidence of suicide increases regularly from January until about June and then declines until the end of the year. This observation had led other writers to conclude that temperature has a direct effect on the tendency to suicide. Durkheim examines this possibility in great detail and demonstrates that the data do not support it. He argues, for example, that if temperature were the basic cause, suicide would vary regularly with it; but this is not the case. There are more suicides in spring than in autumn, although the temperature is slightly lower in spring. Moreover, suicide reaches its height not in the hottest months (July and August), but in June. By a series of such analyses, he demonstrates that the seasonal regularities in suicide rates cannot be accounted for by temperature, and suggests the alternative hypothesis that social activity is seasonal and that the rate of suicide is related to the extent of social activity.

Turning to the hypothesis that a basic cause of suicide is lack of integration into a social group, he examines three major social influences: religion, family, and political atmosphere. He finds suicide rates lower among Catholics than among Protestants, lower among married than among single people, lower among those with children than without, lower during periods of national fervor. All of these findings, he argues, support the hypothesis that belonging to a cohesive social group is a deterrent to suicide. As he analyzed the data in more and more detail, he continuously modified and refined his theory.

Some studies, such as Durkheim's research on suicide and Landis' account of segregation in Washington, rely entirely on the analysis of data collected for purposes other than those of the particular study. In others, such data are used in conjunction with other procedures. Data regularly collected for other purposes may be used to measure the effects of an experimental treatment. For example, the effects of an election appeal may be measured by a study of voting rcords, the effects of various personnel procedures by records of productivity. Thus, in the "Hawthorne studies," Roethlisberger and Dickson (1939) found that changes in such conditions as illumination, rest periods, and hours of work could not account for a consistently rising rate of productivity in their experimental groups over a period as long as one year; they concluded that changes in the social organization of the work groups and in their relationship to management were responsible for the rise in productivity.

Available data may be used at other points in a study. They are frequently helpful in selecting cases with specified characteristics for intensive study, or a random sample for interviewing in a survey. A study of worker morale in war industries by Katz and Hyman (1947) illustrates both these uses of available data. First, production records were used as a basis for selecting five shipyards which differed in productivity; within each of these yards, a sample of workers to be interviewed was selected by taking every nth name from the payroll lists. These investigations found a circular relation between morale and production, with high production giving a feeling of accomplishment which led to increased effort, while low production reduced motivation, which in turn reduced productivity. They concluded further that factors directly associated with the job were more important determinants of worker morale than more general community conditions such as housing, transportation, and recreational facilities.

Available records may also be used to supplement or to check information gathered specifically for the purposes of a given investigation. For example, in a study of the psychological impact of long-term unemployment in an Austrian village (Jahoda-Lazarsfeld and Zeisl, 1932), the accounts of their experience given by several unemployed men suggested that they felt much worse at the onset of unemployment than after three years, in spite of the gradual deterioration of their economic condition. This "shock" effect of unemployment was checked against such records as the accounts of the local grocer, which showed a sudden drop in sales in the months immediately after the onset of unemployment, followed by a slight recovery and a steady decline thereafter.

In many of these examples, the investigator's interest was in behavior or characteristics of the sort directly reflected in the statistical records—segregation, suicide, voting, productivity. Like other types of data, however, records of specific behavior may be used as an indicator of some more general concept. A series of studies by Tryon (1955) illustrates both these uses of existing data. Tryon was concerned with the problem of identifying subcultural groups in more meaningful and reliable ways than the usual ratings of "social class." He was interested in two related hypotheses: (1) that *demographic social areas* can be identified on the basis of census data; and (2) that a demographic social area is also a *psychosocial area*—that is, that residents of a common demographic social area will experience certain common socially relevant situations and certain common psychological states elicited by those situations, and will behave in certain common ways. In connection with the first hypothesis, he examined thirty-three items in the 1940 U. S. Census for the 243 census tracts in the San Francisco Bay Area; the items included, for example, the percentage of detached single-family homes, the percentage of women not in the labor force, the percentage of managerial or professional workers, etc. By a statistical technique known as cluster analysis,[2] he found that these thirty-three items fell into three main groupings, which could be described as: socioeconomic independence, having to do with wealth and social independence; assimilation, or the incorporation of persons into standard white-collar American culture; and orientation around the family. Each of the census tracts could be described in terms of its position on each of these three basic variables. Many tracts, of course, showed the same pattern; for the entire area, eight basic patterns were found. These could be given descriptive labels as well as index scores; for example, "the exclusives"—above average in assimilation, in orientation around family life, and especially in socioeconomic independence; "the workers"—average in orientation around family life but somewhat below average in assimilation and socioeconomic independence; "the segregated"—low in assimilation, socioeconomic independence, and family life as defined in the study.

As evidence to test his second hypothesis—that demographic areas are also psychosocial areas—Tryon used voting records. His interest was not in voting per se, but as an indicator of social attitudes. He found a high correspondence between demographic pattern and voting in the 1940 presidential election. In most of the "exclusive" tracts, about a quarter of the votes were cast for Roosevelt, and in none were

[2] For procedures involved in cluster analysis, see Tyron (1957a).

more than a third for him; at the other extreme, in most of the "worker" and "segregated" tracts, three quarters or more of the votes went to Roosevelt, and in none did he get less than half the votes. Analysis (as yet unpublished) of election results fourteen years later showed a continued relationship between demographic pattern (as determined in 1940) and social attitudes as revealed in 1954 votes on such issues as bonds for a hospital, tax exemption for welfare institutions, and pensions for needy aged.

SOME PITFALLS IN USING STATISTICAL RECORDS

THE DEFINITION OF TERMS. The definitions of categories used in available statistical material frequently do not coincide with those used in social research, a fact often hidden by the use of similar terminology. For example, the social scientist may be interested in family composition. When he consults census reports, he may find material under the category "household composition." Although family composition includes blood relations only, household composition extends to lodgers, servants, and other employees who may share the residence of their employer.

An even more striking invitation to confusion is provided by some statistics on criminal offenses. For example, in all the forty-eight states of the United States, a distinction is made between a felony and a misdemeanor; however, an act which is a felony in one state may be classified as a misdemeanor in another.

In view of such differences, the use of available records may be more misleading than enlightening unless the precise definition on which the statistics are based is known.

METHODS OF DATA COLLECTION. To know what the original collector of available data set out to gather is not enough; one must also inquire into the adequacy of his methods. Many records are collected with the intention of covering an entire universe of events, and not merely a sample. However, many obstacles stand in the way of realizing this ideal. First, the informants from whom the original collecting agency drew the information may not have been willing or able to provide it. There is a well-grounded suspicion, for example, that income statistics based on individual tax declarations tend to be under-estimates, whereas expense accounts tend to be overestimates of expenditures. For equally understandable reasons, statistics concerning illegitimacy are somewhat less accurate than those on births in wedlock.

It is quite possible that the degree of inaccuracy in official records due to these reasons is negligible from the point of view of the social scientist's purposes. But there are other methodological errors that may lead to serious inaccuracies. This should be kept in mind, especially when using data collected over many years. For example: The Prussian suicide statistics (see Halbwachs, 1930) go back to 1816. Until 1883 the duty of keeping suicide records was the responsibility of the local police. Then, in 1883, the task was transferred to the civil service. In view of this change, one would hesitate to interpret the fact that official Prussian suicide figures show an increase of 20 per cent between 1882 and 1883 as anything but a reflection of the change in techniques.

Occasionally, it is possible to correct available records in the light of what is known about the methods by which they have been gathered. More often, this is not possible. In any case, the proper qualifications of such data when used for research purposes can be made only if the social scientist is aware of the possible errors inherent in the particular method employed.

Personal Documents

In speaking of personal documents for research purposes we refer to autobiographies, letters, diaries, certain types of school essay, prize essay, and the like. Other authors[3] have used the term in a much broader way to include such additional material as questionnaire data, interviews, art forms, projective productions, records of social agencies, etc. In our limited usage we refer only to items that meet the following criteria: They are (1) written documents; (2) documents that have

[3] See especially the very illuminating publications by the Social Science Research Council: Allport (1942), and Gottschalk, Kluckhohn, and Angell (1945).

been produced on the writer's own initiative or, if not, in such a way that their introspective content has been determined entirely by the author; and (3) documents that focus on their author's personal experiences. These criteria exclude interview material, however informal the interview situation may have been. They exclude also those literary efforts that can be used as personal documents only through projective interpretation. This more limited definition of personal documents has the advantage of bringing to the fore their most distinctive characteristic: they permit us *to see other people as they see themselves.*

Augustine, who produced one of the greatest personal documents of all times, fully realized the unique contribution they can make in this respect. In Book X of his *Confessions* he explains why he wrote this personal document. He starts from the assumption that "men are a race curious to know of other men's lives," an assumption which is as valid now as then; and he argues that nothing but what a man says about himself can fully satisfy this curiosity:

> As to what I now am while I am writing my Confessions, there are many who desire to know—both people who know me personally, and people who do not, but have heard from me or about me. Yet they have not their ear at my heart, where I am what I am. They wish, therefore, to hear from my own confession *what I am inwardly where they cannot pierce with eye or ear or mind* [italics supplied].

It is true that the social sciences have developed modern techniques that aim at piercing through outward appearance and behavior to inner experiences. Depth interviews, projective techniques, and psychoanalysis aim at just this. Successfully applied, they can often penetrate even beyond what a man knows of himself.[4] But these techniques, although they are able to discover the nature of *selected* inner experiences, can hardly ever reconstruct the *entire structure* of a person's self-image, with its spontaneous emphases and complexities.

Gordon Allport (1942), in his defense of the value of personal documents for psychology, stresses the importance of aiming for a view

---

[4] Augustine realized the limitation of personal documents in this respect: " . . . yet there is something of man that the very spirit of man that is in him does not know."

of the whole before details of inner experience are subjected to more
systematic scrutiny:

> Acquaintance with particulars is the beginning of all knowl-
> edge—scientific or otherwise. In psychology the font and origin
> of our curiosity in, and knowledge of, human nature lies in our
> acquaintance with concrete individuals. To know them in their
> natural complexity is an essential first step. Starting too soon with
> analysis and classification, we run the risk of tearing mental life
> into fragments and beginning with false cleavages that misrepre-
> sent the salient organizations and natural integrations in personal
> life. In order to avoid such hasty preoccupations with unnatural
> segments and false abstractions, psychology needs to concern
> itself with life as it is lived, with significant total processes of the
> sort revealed in consecutive and complete life documents.

By and large, the rationale for the use of personal documents is
similar to that for the use of observational techniques. What the latter
may achieve for overt behavior, the former can do for inner experiences:
to reveal to the social scientist life as it is lived without the interference
of research. However, although the number of situations that can be
observed is considerable, personal documents are relatively rare; hence
the scope of their usefulness for research is rather limited.

Even when they are available, personal documents have to be used
with some caution. Augustine pointed to one of the basic reservations
—the doubt about authenticity: "And when they hear me confessing
of myself, how do they know whether I speak the truth . . . ?" He
saw clearly that there was no completely satisfactory answer to such
skepticism, for "I cannot prove to them that my confession is true."

There are two possible kinds of falsification with which a social
scientist who uses personal documents has to be concerned. In its
crudest form, falsification amounts to conscious, deliberate deceit. A
document can be produced in the form and manner of a personal document by someone else and be presented to the world as the genuine
article. The motives for such falsification are various: material gain,
malice, practical joke, literary exercise. The most outstanding example
in the psychological literature was an extremely skillfully presented
falsification of the diary of an adolescent girl, which deceived even
Freud, who called it a "gem." Hug-Helmuth, who originated this

Tagebuch eines halbwüchsigen Mädchens,[5] asserted that it was the diary of a young girl and that it had not been edited or altered. It took several years for this falsification, which was gaining wide recognition as a demonstration of the development of sexual consciousness, to be unmasked for what it was.

The incident is worth noting because of the manner in which it was finally proved to be a falsification. Critics had asserted that the style of the document was too mature to be credited to a girl between the ages of 11 and 14 years. Yet the content was not exaggerated, and was similar enough to much that enters authentic diaries of early adolescents. Finally, however, a check on various casual references to the weather on given days, the mention of a visit to a place that was nonexistent at the date on which the entry appeared, and similar small inconsistencies convinced the psychological world that the diary was not authentic. Historians, who are perhaps more often exposed to deliberate falsifications than other social scientists, have developed techniques of detection similar to those mentioned above which might well be applied whenever the use of personal documents is considered (see Gottschalk et al., 1945).

However, Augustine, when he raised the question as to the truth-fulness of a personal document, obviously had in mind a less crude form of falsification. He was concerned not with deception about the authorship but with the possibility of the author's misrepresenting what he knew about himself. If such misrepresentation is due to self-deception, it does not impair the value of the document. If one is interested in the author's self-image, the question of whether or not the self-image agrees with the image other persons have of the author is of secondary importance. To be sure, a confrontation of self-image and images that others have of a person would be highly illuminating. Yet even if a discrepancy appears between two such descriptions, the decision as to which is right and which is wrong cannot easily be made.

There is still another possible reason for an author's misrepresentation of himself in a personal document. All personal documents are produced for some purpose. Letters are written to communicate with someone else; school essays are submitted to teachers, prize essays to

[5] Translated into English by E. and C. Paul as *A Young Girl's Diary* (1921).

judges; the writers of even the most intimate diaries probably keep an eye on a potential future reader. Augustine wanted to "stir the hearts of the sinners and the just"—the sinners to find courage from his *Confessions* that a way of life can be changed, the just to rejoice in his conversion. Many autobiographical statements are produced for purposes such as this—in cruder form, for propaganda purposes. The social scientist using personal documents will do well, whenever possible, to inquire into the motives that induced their production.

The disadvantages of using personal documents in research have been amply discussed in the literature (see especially Allport, 1942), particularly in the prolonged debate about the scientific value of Thomas and Znaniecki's *The Polish Peasant in Europe and America* (1918), which relied heavily on letters and diaries for data. The use of personal documents has been criticized on the grounds that they are rarely suited for treatment by statistical techniques; that their validity is hardly ever beyond doubt; that they can be the result of deception or self-deception; that they are subject to errors of memory and are at the mercy of passing moods. In addition, they are by no means easy to come by.

By and large, these arguments carry weight. It should be pointed out, however, that the applicability of statistical techniques is not determined by the nature of the data but rather by the type of question with which the social scientist approaches his data. Unique as Augustine's *Confessions* and other autobiographical writings are, they can be treated by quantitative content-analysis techniques if such procedure is in accord with the research problem.

Two types of personal document have added considerably to our knowledge of inner experiences: (1) descriptions of rare and extraordinary events in human life, and (2) diaries and letters dealing with the inner aspect of more frequent and ordinary events.

In 1907, the first edition of C. W. Beers' autobiography appeared. This book, written soon after the author recovered from a manic-depressive breakdown, was largely responsible for the foundation of the mental hygiene movement in the United States. It stands as a model for self-descriptions of mental states, not easily obtained by any other method. Helen Keller's famous book on her conquest of life as a blind deaf-mute, and the *Confessions*, also belong to the first group.

Among the most frequently used documents of the second type are diaries of adolescents. Charlotte Bühler (1934), in developing her psychology of adolescence, conducted and sponsored a series of interrelated studies based on the use of such diaries. Bühler's interest led to the establishment of a collection of diaries of adolescents at the Psychological Institute of the University of Vienna; in a relatively short time almost one hundred specimens were assembled. Their availability in such number permitted a more systematic comparison than is ordinarily possible with unique documents.

At least two of Bühler's studies involved comparison of individuals at very different periods in time—something difficult to achieve by other methods of data collection. One study was based on three diaries of girls from three successive generations. Bühler demonstrated that in spite of the considerable cultural change between 1873 and 1910 (the years in which the oldest and the youngest of the three diary writers were born), some basic desires of adolescence, such as the need for intimate personal relationships, remained the same. Yet in other respects, such as the girls' relations to their parents, cultural changes were reflected in the diaries.

The second study was based on diaries of two girls of the same generation who, at the time of the study, were about twenty years older than at the time they had produced the diaries. A comparison between "then" and "now" revealed considerable similarities between the two girls during adolescence and considerable differences in later life.

Bühler's studies illustrate how a considerable gap in time can be bridged by the use of personal documents. Occasionally it becomes possible to use personal documents, especially letters, to bridge the gap in space which often separates the investigator from his subjects. Several studies have used the mail received by political representatives as a basis for gauging the climate of political opinion among the letter writers; others have used the fan mail of film, radio and television stars in attempts to analyze their attractiveness to the public. The study of such mail, is, of course, not free from ambiguities. Letters vary in length, in information about their authors, and in the degree of their apparent spontaneity. Nevertheless, they often provide the only feasible approach to an otherwise unreachable group of the population.

It must be kept in mind, however, that the study of personal documents permits generalization only to the universe of document-producers, not to the population at large. The inner life of individuals who keep diaries may be different in important respects from that of individuals who do not; the opinions of constituents who write to their Congressmen may be quite unrepresentative of the opinions of other citizens. It is one thing to study personal documents for the sake of understanding the particular individuals who produced them, or for clues about psychological processes that may be common to other individuals. It is quite another matter to assume that such documents provide a basis for conclusions about persons other than their writers. A striking example of this point was provided in the *New York Times* of March 17, 1957, under the headline, "5 Surveys Dispute Mail Opposing Aid." The story reported that analysis of Congressional mail had led to the belief that public opinion in the United States was strongly opposed to the continuation of foreign aid; "most" of the letters received on this subject recommended outright elimination or heavy cuts. However, five nation-wide surveys carried out by the National Opinion Research Center, from January 1956 to June 1956, using a variety of question wordings, all found substantial proportions of respondents favoring the continuation of foreign aid. The proportions expressing approval varied with the specific question wording. On the question of economic aid "to some countries like India, which have not joined us as allies against the Communists," opinion was about evenly divided; the proportions favoring aid to such nations ranged from 43 per cent to 52 per cent at different times. However, on the question of continuing "economic aid to countries which have agreed to stand with us against Communist aggression," as many as 90 per cent of the respondents expressed support. It should be noted that such survey data do not discredit the study of Congressional mail; they supplement it, as they are supplemented by the mail analysis.

These examples reveal both the values and the limitations of personal documents as sources of data. They suggest that better use is made of the peculiar nature of data contained in personal documents when they are employed for exploratory and descriptive rather than statistical purposes; for the development of insights and for illustrations rather than the verification or refutation of hypotheses; in conjunction with other methods rather than by themselves.

Mass Communications[6]

In addition to statistical records and autobiographical documents, every literate society produces a variety of material intended to inform, entertain, or persuade the populace. Such material may appear in the form of literary productions, newspapers, and magazines or, more recently, motion pictures and radio or television broadcasts.

Mass communication documents are not produced for the benefit of the investigator, and in this respect (although not in others) are free from the influence of his theoretical or personal bias. Like available statistical records, they enable one to deal with the historical past as well as with contemporary society, an advantage that can hardly be overestimated in view of the considerable methodological difficulties standing in the way of a historical perspective in social science. Even more than statistical records, documents of mass communication reflect broad aspects of the social climate in which they are produced.

PURPOSES OF ANALYSIS

Mass communications provide a rich source of data for investigating a variety of research questions. They may be used to throw light on some aspect of the culture of a given group, to compare different groups in terms of some aspect of culture, to trace cultural change. For example, Lowenthal (1943), in a study of cultural changes in American society in the course of the twentieth century, analyzed biographies appearing in popular magazines from the beginning of the

---

[6] In this section we have drawn heavily on McGranahan (1951); in fact, some of the material is taken verbatim from that source, with Dr. McGranahan's permission.

century until 1941 in terms of the profession of their subject. The following table summarizes some of his main findings:

PERCENTAGE DISTRIBUTION OF BIOGRAPHIES ACCORDING TO PROFESSIONS IN "SATURDAY EVENING POST" AND "COLLIER'S" FOR SELECTED YEARS BETWEEN 1901 AND 1941

	1901–1914	1922–1930	1930–1934	1940–1941
Political life	46%	28%	31%	25%
Business and professional	28	18	14	20
Entertainment	26	54	55	55
Number of cases	177	395	306	125
Yearly average of biographies	36	66	77	125

In analyzing further the sphere of entertainment, Lowenthal points out that in the earliest period covered by his study (1901–1914) 77 per cent of the persons described were engaged in the fine arts; in the latest period (1940–1941) the corresponding figure was 9 per cent.

In Lowenthal's study the communication content, taken at face value, was analyzed for clues to cultural changes. Other communication studies, especially those that aim to throw light on the entire communication process from sender to receiver, often deal with the ambiguity of meaning of communication. An example is the study by Wolfenstein and Leites (1950) of an American anti-prejudice motion picture, *No Way Out*:

> [The film] revolves around the difficulties of a young Negro interne in a county hospital of a large Northern city. On his first assignment to the prison ward, he is called upon to treat a hoodlum who has been wounded in the leg during a robbery. Led by various signs to suspect a brain tumor, the doctor performs a spinal puncture. The patient dies immediately, while his brother, also wounded and handcuffed to the adjoining bed, screams: "That nigger killed my brother!" The doctor wishes to have an autopsy to prove that his diagnosis and treatment were correct. But permission must be obtained from the surviving brother, the Negro-hater, who has gruesome fantasies about what

they would do to his brother's body and refuses. He gets word to his friends that his brother has been "murdered" by a Negro, and they plan to avenge the "murder" by a race riot. The Negro community is forewarned and by a well-organized strategy surprises and beats its white enemies, but without the participation of the Negro doctor, who disapproves of resorting to violence. The doctor forces the issue of the autopsy by "confessing" to the "murder" of his patient. The autopsy exonerates him. The hoodlum, to whom the physician who has performed the autopsy gives an explanation of his brother's death, remains unconvinced: "That's medical double-talk—I tell you I saw him kill my brother." The hoodlum escapes, lays a trap for the Negro doctor, and is about to murder him when he is stopped at the last moment.

It seems clear that the intention of the producers was to demonstrate the dangerous irrationality of color prejudice. The task which the investigators set themselves was to view the correspondence between intent and probable reception. This involved an interpretation of the major scenes in the light of what is known about irrational elements in color prejudice and the functioning of the unconscious. The application of this frame of reference revealed certain "negative" elements in the film. To quote from the study:

> In the death of the patient under treatment by the Negro doctor, we are shown one thing and told another. We are shown that the doctor is unsure of himself. He has come to the prison ward for the first time; the guards do not know him, are uncertain whether he should be there, and increasingly puzzled at the seemingly irrelevant instruments he requires for what everyone supposes to be a simple leg wound. Moreover, the doctor is already visibly shaken by the insults of the patient's brother. What we see is that an inexperienced, insecure Negro doctor, whose procedure looks dubious to everyone present, treats a man with a seemingly minor injury in such a way that he immediately dies.

> Likewise, the sequence of the race riot contains images which tend to confirm the fantasy of the Negro as a dangerous attacker. We know that the Negroes in stealing a march on the white gang who are preparing to attack them are acting in justified self-defense. But at the moment when the Negroes rush in, we see

standing beside the brutal bully who has been organizing the white gang a clean-cut young girl who does not appear before or after in the film. And as the fight begins, there is a close-up of another white girl, who also has no other part in the film, screaming in anguish. These two images would seem very likely to evoke the fantasy of "white womanhood" assaulted by the "bestial Negroes."

Whether the hypotheses about audience perception of meaning which are inherent in this interpretation are correct is a question to be tested by audience research and is outside the scope of analysis of communication content.

Another type of question that can be answered by analysis of mass communications has to do with the type of information made available to the public, or the light in which various issues are presented. For example, Davison (1947) took samples of newspapers from the Soviet, United States, and French zones of Berlin during December 1946. He analyzed the front-page news items in terms of whether references to "United States," "Great Britain," "U.S.S.R.," "France," "United Nations," "Communist Party," "Pro-Soviet States," "Greece," and "Iran" were favorable, unfavorable, or neutral. If, for example, the news item as a whole depicted the United States favorably, as in a story of United States assistance to starving Europe, then a positive tally was made for "United States"; if the news item described or implied, say, United States military imperialism, then a negative tally was made. Davison's results showed a wide divergence between the content of the Soviet- and non-Soviet–controlled Berlin press, and demonstrated the extent to which "news" conforms to the ideas of those who issue it.

Mass communications have been analyzed also for such purposes as identifying propaganda techniques or describing the appeals of political leaders to their followers. For example, R. K. White (1949), in a study of the values to which Hitler and Roosevelt appealed in their public speeches prior to the outbreak of World War II, used two books: My New Order, English translation by De Sales of Hitler's speeches, and Nothing to Fear, selected addresses of Franklin D. Roosevelt, edited by Zevin. Within each speech White classified every value statement. His tables are based on 4,077 value statements by

Hitler and 1,249 by Roosevelt. The following table, a simplified version of that published by White, summarizes his main findings:

PERCENTAGE DISTRIBUTION OF VALUES APPEALED TO BY HITLER AND ROOSEVELT IN SPEECHES BEFORE WORLD WAR II

	Hitler	Roosevelt
Strength values	34.8%	15.2%
Moral values	38.0	28.3
Economic values	10.8	27.7
Other values	16.4	28.8
Total	100.0	100.0

These are only a few examples of the kinds of research questions that can be investigated by analysis of mass communications. A survey of the field by Berelson (1952) enumerates the following specific purposes for which communication content has been analyzed:

Questions concerned with characteristics of content
To describe trends in communication content.
To trace the development of scholarship.
To disclose international differences in communication content.
To compare media or "levels" of communication.
To audit communication content against objectives.
To construct and apply communication standards.
To aid in technical research operations.
To expose propaganda techniques.
To measure the "readability" of communication materials.
To discover stylistic features.

Questions concerned with producers or causes of content
To identify the intentions and other characteristics of the communicators.
To determine the psychological state of persons and groups.
To detect the existence of propaganda (primarily for legal purposes).
To secure political and military intelligence.

Questions concerned with audience or effects of content
To reflect attitudes, interests, and values ("cultural patterns") of population groups.

To reveal the focus of attention.

To describe attitudinal and behavioral responses to communications.

A given study may, of course, pursue several of these purposes.

TECHNIQUES OF ANALYSIS

Stimulated by the rapidly increasing volume of material produced by the mass media, a special technique—*content analysis*—has been developed within the last few decades for describing in systematic form the content of communications.[7]

Many of the concepts and assumptions underlying this technique are, however, much older than its name. Long before content analysis became established as a technique with a name of its own, students of society used records of communication for a variety of purposes. Historians examined them in order to reconstruct the period in which they were produced. Literary critics studied the productions of writers to discover the message they wanted to convey, their peculiarities of style, the values they propagated, and many other aspects of creative work. The arguments about whether Shakespeare actually was the author of all the works associated with his name, for example, were supported largely by what today would be called content analysis.

It is true that modern content analysis has added a new feature to the exploitation of communication content for research purposes— namely, the development of elaborate techniques for quantification of the material. Indeed, in recent methodological publications, quantification is, as a rule, regarded as a necessary element. Berelson (1952), for instance, defines content analysis as "a research technique for the objective, systematic, and quantitative description of the manifest content of communication."[8]

---

[7] Although the technique of content analysis has been worked out primarily in relation to the mass media, it is applicable to other materials as well. For example, personal documents, unstructured interviews, protocols of responses to projective tests, records of patient-therapist interactions, etc., may all be subjected to content analysis.

[8] For other discussions of content analysis, see Bruner (1941), Goldsen (1947), Janis (1943), Kaplan (1943a), Kaplan and Goldsen (1943), Lasswell (1942a, 1942b, 1946), Lasswell, Leites, and associates (1949), and Sargent and Saenger (1947).

This emphasis, due largely to the work of Lasswell and his associates during the late 1930's, has advanced the study of communication content considerably by adding precision to insight. The analysis proceeds under certain controls that render it systematic and objective in comparison with a conventional review or critique of communication content. (1) The categories of analysis used to classify the content are clearly and explicitly defined so that other individuals can apply them to the same content to verify the conclusions; (2) the analyst is not free to select and report merely what strikes him as interesting but must methodically classify all the relevant material in his sample; (3) some quantitative procedure is used in order to provide a measure of the importance and emphasis in the material of the various ideas found and to permit comparison with other samples of material. If we take a systematic sample of, say, newspaper editorials, and count the relative number of editorials expressing favorable, unfavorable, and neutral attitudes toward a given foreign nation, we are carrying out a simple form of quantification that has proved feasible and reliable. We shall come out with a more exact summary of the situation than would be possible if only general impressions and memory were relied upon, since, without mathematical aid, there is a very clear limit to the amount of material that can be digested and recalled in balance and in detail by the human mind.

Yet—and this is the other side of the coin—concern with quantification has become so dominant that it often overshadows concern with the unique content of communications. Definitions of content analysis tend to emphasize *the procedure of analysis* rather than *the character of the data* available in recorded communications. In addition, they imply a somewhat arbitrary limitation of the field by excluding from it all accounts of communications that are not in the form of the number of times various themes or other elements appear in the material being analyzed. It is indeed difficult to see why quantification should be regarded as a *requirement* in content analysis when it is not so regarded in the analysis of data obtained by interviews or observation. Whatever the nature of the data, quantification is always a more precise procedure than qualitative description or exploration. Yet it is not always feasible; as we shall see in Chapter 11, both quantified and unquantified data have their legitimate place in contemporary social science.

By and large, the technical problems of analysis arising in the study of communication content are simply specific instances of general problems of analysis and interpretation in the social sciences, which will be discussed in Chapter 11. Here, as elsewhere, the execution of a study demands that the research problem be formulated; that a study design be developed; that categories be established for the classification of data; and that the data be systematically tabulated and summarized in terms of these categories. However, the character of communication material requires some modification of these customary procedures, especially if a study aims at quantitative analysis.

DRAWING A SAMPLE OF THE MATERIAL.[9] Suppose that one wishes to analyze the concern of the press of a given country or countries with the question of disarmament. The first task of the analyst—one of considerable difficulty—is to define his universe, the national press. The techniques of sampling from the mass media are not well developed. We are concerned with newspapers as potential molders of reader opinion; for our purposes it is not satisfactory to list all the newspapers published in a given country and draw every tenth or twentieth one, even if we also introduce controls to ensure that newspapers representing different geographical areas, political orientations, economic groups, ethnic groups, etc., are included in the proportion in which they are represented in the total population of newspapers. The difficulty arises from the fact that newspapers vary tremendously in size and influence, and a realistic sample should not weigh an obscure journal equally with a giant metropolitan daily. The situation is not the same as that of drawing a representative sample of a voting population, each member of which has equal influence at the polls—namely, one vote.

To take account of the size problem, one might divide the newspapers into a series of classes according to their circulation, each class having a total circulation value equal to that of every other class, and then draw from each such class a random sample covering a given number of readers. Another way of approaching the problem would be to view the population under study as the population of total news-

---

[9] General principles and procedures of sampling are discussed in Appendix B.

paper copies issued (a paper with a circulation of 1,000 would have 1,000 units in this population) and to draw a random sample from such a population rather than from the population of newspaper titles. So far as items concerning disarmament are concerned, however, we cannot assume that the circulation figure of a newspaper correctly reflects its influence upon the population. One paper may be concerned almost exclusively with local news, whereas another may feature many items dealing with international relations.

In view of the problems involved, we may use samples that do not pretend to be fully representative of the mass medium in question but that can be objectively defined and systematically drawn. One possibility is a "popularity sample," based only on circulation or audience figures—e.g., a sample that would use the ten largest newspapers in the country. Or, if we are interested in comparing the press of different countries in their handling of items concerning disarmament, and if resources permit the study of only one newspaper from each country, it may be appropriate to select the paper that is commonly quoted as the organ with the greatest authority or prestige in the nation concerned—e.g., the New York Times in the United States, the London Times in England, and Pravda in the Soviet Union.

There is another problem in sampling from the mass media that must be considered—the time problem. It would be easy to get a distorted impression of the general policy of newspapers if the editions for only a single day were studied, or even a single month. The impact of a particular current event may be such as to obscure a paper's usual policy. If the analyst elects to cover a period of several months, the task will be unmanageable unless he draws a sample of issues of the newspaper during that period. Before he knows how many issues he can handle, he will have to decide whether he wishes to analyze the entire issue of each paper on the sampling days, or to concentrate on specific aspects, such as headlines, editorials, news reporting, position of prominence within the paper (page-one articles, for example), or the like. In other words, he will have to decide on the nature and size of the units that are to compose his sample.

Frequently, then, the sampling procedure in communication analysis consists of three stages: sampling of sources (which newspapers, which radio stations, which films, etc., are to be analyzed);

sampling of dates (which period is to be covered by the study); and sampling of units (which aspects of the communication are to be analyzed). With respect to the sampling of units, decisions are often arbitrary and based on tacit assumptions about which feature of a medium best characterizes it. For example, is it the headline, the human-interest story, the editorial, or some other feature that best indicates the policy of a newspaper?

To avoid such arbitrariness, content analysts frequently follow one of two possibilities: They analyze on the basis of several different units (for example, they take samplings of headlines, of human-interest stories, of editorials, and count how many times a given subject is mentioned in each); or they disregard these "natural" units completely, dividing the issue of a newspaper mechanically into lines or inches of space from which they draw a sample. Much more work on readership habits is necessary before it will be possible to decide whether the apparent accuracy of a procedure that yields units of equal size compensates for the neglect of context and inherent organization.

ESTABLISHING THE CATEGORIES OF ANALYSIS.[10] Suppose that our analyst has decided in favor of a sample of two types of unit—editorials and front-page stories. His next task is to establish the categories in terms of which every unit can be classified. As elsewhere in social research, he has two sources for the establishment of relevant categories: the formulated research purpose, including any hypotheses he may have put forward; and the material itself. It is, of course, the material that suggests categories peculiar to communication analysis.

A newspaper's concern with disarmament can find expression in a variety of ways. The paper can either emphasize or ignore the issue or its controversial nature; it can restrict itself to straight reporting on the issue or it can produce much editorialized comment on it, playing up certain themes more than others; it can use certain key words, such as peace, frequently or rarely; it can treat the matter lightly or seriously; it can appeal to commonly accepted values or omit the moral implications of the issue. Each of these categories of analysis, and many more, have been used by content analysts.

The most extensive work in the content analysis of newspapers

[10] A more general discussion of establishing categories of analysis will be found in Chapter 11.

has been carried out by Harold D. Lasswell and his associates (1949). Lasswell developed a system of "symbol analysis," which was employed during World War II in several branches of the United States government. In this system, newspaper content is studied for the appearance of certain symbols, such as "England," "Russia," "democracy," "Jews," "Stalin," etc. The frequency with which these symbols appear is noted, as well as whether their presentation is favorable, unfavorable, or neutral (or "indulgent," "deprivational," "neutral.") Favorable references are sometimes further divided into those stressing "strength" and those stressing "goodness" or "morality"; negative references into "weakness" and "immorality" categories.

Davison's analysis of Berlin newspapers, described on page 333, made use of this type of analysis. The symbols he considered were the names of the countries; the favorable, neutral, or unfavorable quality of each reference was noted. Davison did not use the dimensions of strength-weakness and morality-immorality, but he made an additional analysis in terms of "themes," another widely used method of content analysis. In this approach, the analyst immerses himself in the material until its recurrent ideas or propositions become evident and then counts the frequency with which these propositions occur. For example, some of the major themes Davison found in news items in the Soviet-controlled Berlin newspapers were: the United States is torn by economic unrest and industrial strife; the United States is in the grip of reactionaries; the United States is pursuing policies of militarism, imperialism, and dollar diplomacy.

Wright and Nelson (1939) employed a more complicated method of content analysis of newspapers. Using a sample of editorials concerning Japan and China in the New York Times, the Chicago Tribune and the Chicago Daily News for the period January 1937 to March 1938, they selected a "representative statement" from each editorial and then asked judges to classify these statements in eleven piles, ranging from pile 1 (most hostile toward the country concerned) through pile 6 (neutral) to pile 11 (most favorable). Over-all scores for the different newspapers and for different periods of time were obtained by averaging the score values of specific statements. The results showed, among other things, that the bombing of Nanking had more influence in promoting unfavorable references to Japan than did the Panay incident, and considerably more than the juridical act of the League of Nations in branding Japan the aggressor.

RELIABILITY OF CLASSIFICATION. Reliability of responses and of classifications is, of course, a universal problem in social science. Methods of ascertaining, and of increasing, the reliability of measurement were discussed in Chapter 5. More specific discussion of problems of reliability of coding appears in Chapter 11. Ideally, our methods of analysis and quantification should be so clearly defined that different judges would arrive at exactly the same results when analyzing the same material. Perfect reliability, however, is something that can be achieved at the present time only when the more superficial kinds of analysis are made, such as counting the number of times a particular word turns up in a given amount of material. As soon as some degree of interpretation enters the analysis, judges tend to differ to some extent in their results.

White's study of the values stressed by Hitler and by Roosevelt, described on pages 333–334, provides an example of difficulties that may arise when complex judgments must be made. In the category "other values" White included the value *safety*, which is illustrated by the following statement from a Hitler speech: "It is quite unimportant whether we ourselves live, but it is essential that our people live, that Germany shall live." It is obvious that the assignment of the value *safety* to this statement involves an interpretation of the meaning of the sentence in the context within which it was used. The primary method of increasing reliability of classification is to specify clearly the characteristics of statements that are to be placed in a given category, and to use many examples drawn from the material being analyzed to illustrate what kinds of statements are to be considered as belonging in a given category. But it is obviously much more difficult to give a definition of the value *safety* which will be both sufficiently comprehensive and sufficiently specific to serve as a guide for the coder, than to give an adequate definition of a category such as "mentions racial groups" in coding an interview question about "what kinds of people live in this neighborhood." The difficulty is increased by the variety of material to be considered in content analysis, which is limited only by the interest or intention of the communicator, without the restricting influence of a specific interview question. To increase reliability of content analysis there is no other way but patient experimentation with the refinement of definitions and careful training of the persons entrusted with their use in classifying the data.

Summary

In the last four chapters we have discussed various ways of gathering data needed to answer research questions: observation, interviews and questionnaires, projective and other indirect techniques, and the use of available data in the form of statistical records, personal documents, and mass communications. We have pointed out that each method has its advantages and limitations, and that each is more appropriate for answering certain types of research questions than it is for others. Moreover, we have noted that no matter what technique an investigator uses, he must be alert to problems of reliability and validity of his data.

In the next chapter we shall consider procedures for placing individuals on scales on the basis of data collected by any of the methods discussed in these last four chapters.

10

PLACING INDIVIDUALS
ON SCALES

I N OUR DISCUSSION of measurement in Chapter 5, we noted that it is frequently desirable to make distinctions of degree rather than of quality. We wish to be able to assert, for example, that Mr. Brown is more prejudiced than Mr. Smith rather than being limited to the statement that their prejudices are different. Making these distinctions of degree may be thought of as a function of analysis rather than data collection. However, the desire to be able to make such distinctions influences the form in which the data are collected. At the very least, it means that the questions asked must be such as to give information on which judgments of degree can be based. Frequently, the distinctions of degree are introduced into the measuring instruments themselves.

Techniques for registering differences in degree are of two broad types. In one type, someone makes a judgment about some characteristic of an individual and places him directly on a scale defined in terms of that characteristic. Let us say that the characteristic in question is "attitude toward school desegregation"; the rater places the individual on a *rating scale* set up in such a way that it indicates various degrees of favorable or unfavorable attitude toward school desegregation. The person making the judgment may be the individual himself, someone who knows him, an observer, an interviewer, a coder, etc. He may make the judgment on the basis of his entire experience with the individual, or after observation of the individual in a specified situation or situations, or on the basis of the individual's responses to interview questions, projective techniques, etc. Different types of rating scale are discussed in the following section.

The other broad type of technique for registering differences in degree consists of questionnaires constructed in such a way that the score of the individual's responses places him on a scale. If the investigator is interested in an individual's attitude toward school desegregation, for example, he does not ask either the individual himself or anyone else to make a direct judgment about his attitude. Rather, the individual is asked to reply to a series of questions relevant to desegregation or to indicate his agreement or disagreement with a series of statements—for example, "I would be willing to sit next to a Negro in class; I believe the academic standards of my school would be lowered if Negroes were admitted," etc. From his replies to these questions or statements, a score is computed that is taken as indicating his position on a scale of favorable or unfavorable attitude toward desegregation. This technique has been used most often in the measurement of attitudes. Various types of *attitude scale* are discussed in a later section.

Both rating scales and attitude scales have the same purpose: to assign individuals to numerical positions in order to make distinctions of degree possible. The scale positions, generally, indicate only the order of positions with respect to the characteristic being measured. Although there have been attempts to construct interval scales, most rating scales and attitude scales do not provide more than ordinal measurement (see Chapter 5, pages 186–197).

Rating Scales

A number of types of rating scale have been employed; the number of types distinguished and the names given to them tend to vary with the measurement theorist.[1]

One feature is common to all types: the rater places the person or object being rated at some point along a continuum or in one of an ordered series of categories; a numerical value is attached to the point or the category. Scales differ in the fineness of the distinctions they permit and in the procedures involved in assigning persons or objects to positions. These differences will become apparent in our discussion of several of the more common types of rating scale.

Graphic Rating Scales

Perhaps the most widely used is the graphic rating scale. In this type, the judge (the subject himself, the interviewer, observer, coder,

[1] For more detailed discussions of rating scales, see Cronbach (1949), Guilford (1954), Freeman (1955), and Krech and Crutchfield (1948).

etc.) indicates his rating by simply placing a check at the appropriate point on a line that runs from one extreme of the attribute in question to the other. Scale points, with brief descriptions, may be indicated along the line; their function is to serve as a guide to the judge in localizing his rating rather than to provide distinct categories.

The following example is a scale checked by interviewers of respondents living in interracial housing projects (Deutsch and Collins, 1951):

RESPECT FELT FOR NEGROES IN THE PROJECT
(Place check on appropriate position on line, or circle X or Y.)

Thinks highly of Negroes in project without qualification	Generally respects Negroes living in project	Is ambivalent; partly respects, partly feels they are inferior	Generally feels they are inferior	Strongly feels they are inferior

1	2	3	4	5	6	7	8	9

X: Is indifferent to Negroes as a group; doesn't think about them.
Y: Doesn't think of Negroes as group; considers them as individuals.

In this example, the X and Y items were introduced to avoid forcing the interviewer to make a rating he considered inappropriate and to allow him to explain why a rating could not be made.

One of the major advantages of graphic rating scales is that they are relatively easy to use. Guilford (1954) has pointed out that "the graphic scale provides opportunity for as fine discrimination as that of which the rater is capable, and the fineness of scoring can be as great as desired." Yet, for the effective use of graphic rating scales, experience has shown that certain precautions must be taken in their design and use: end statements so extreme that they are unlikely to be used should be avoided; descriptive statements should be placed to correspond as closely as possible with numerical points on the scale; etc. For a more detailed discussion of practices to be followed in the construction and use of graphic rating scales, the reader is referred to Guilford (1954).

ITEMIZED RATING SCALES

Itemized rating scales have also been referred to as "specific category scales" (Krech and Crutchfield, 1948) and "numerical scales" (Guilford, 1954). In this type of scale, the rater selects one of a limited number of categories that are ordered in terms of their scale position. The number of scale positions or categories used has varied, depending on the research problem and the kinds of judgments required. Scales with five or seven categories are most frequently employed, but many investigators have used as many as nine or eleven points.

Itemized rating scales, like graphic ones, can be used in connection with data gathered by any of the methods discussed in the preceding chapters. Barker, Dembo, and Lewin (see pages 115–116), for example, in their study of the effect of frustration on constructiveness of play of young children, set up a seven-point scale for rating "constructiveness" in analyzing their detailed narrative records of the children's activities. From a detailed analysis of a few of these records they drew specific illustrations of activities that were judged to fall at various points on the scale; a different set of illustrations was provided for each of the toys available to the children. The descriptions of the scale points for constructiveness of play with a truck are given below, with one concrete example under each:

1. The toys are examined superficially.
   Ex: Sits on floor and takes truck and trailer in hand.
2. The truck is moved to a definite place or from one place to another.
   Ex: Bends over to truck and trailer, pushes back and forth.
3. Somewhat more complicated manipulation of truck.
   Ex: Truck and trailer backed under chair.
4. Definitely more complicated and elaborate manipulation of truck.
   Ex: Truck and trailer unloaded, detached; pulled in circles; reattached, detached, reattached . . .
5. The truck is used as a means to haul other things.
   Ex: "This is a fire truck." Pushes truck to middle of room, around in middle. "You can load things in it. Mr. Duck! I'll haul Mr. Duck."

6. The meaning of the play is an extensive "trip" or another elaborated story in which the handling of the truck is merely a part of a larger setting.

Ex: "Here's a car-truck, and it's going out fishing, so we have to take the trailer off. First, we have to go to the gas station. . . ." Gets gas; now back for the trailer and the fish pole; attaches motor boat to truck and trailer. . . .

7. Play showing more than usual originality.

Ex: Detaches truck, has it coast down trailer as an incline.

When the characteristic being rated can be thought of as extending on either side of a neutral point, the scale usually provides a central neutral point, with an equal number of categories on each side. For example, in the analysis of an open-ended interview question in a study of attitudes toward international relations, the Survey Research Center of the University of Michigan used a five-point itemized scale extending from "Emphatic approval or agreement" (scale value 1) to "Emphatic disapproval or disagreement" (scale value 5). The coding instructions included, for each category, a rather elaborate description of the kinds of responses that were to be assigned to it. Thus, the descriptions for the first two scale positions were as follows:

1. *Emphatic approval or agreement.* Included in this category are the people expressing agreement or a favorable attitude without equivocation or doubt and supporting it with a reason ("I think we should lend money to England. Their country is so torn up and lots of people need help") and the people giving an emphatic answer, regardless of whether it is supported by a reason ("Absolutely, it's the thing to do").

2. *Approval or agreement, with qualifications or uncertainty.* Included here are people expressing a qualified opinion, generally in such ways as "if . . ." "as long as . . ." ("It is a good thing for us to do as long as we get it back some day"), and those expressing a generally favorable attitude containing one negative or unfavorable argument ("It's a big load for us to take on with our country so in debt. But we didn't have the destruction the way England did, so I guess we have to do it"), and those expressing a favorable attitude without certainty or conviction by using ex-

pressions like "maybe," "perhaps," "I guess," "I suppose," etc., or expressing a simple affirmative answer with no reason.[2]

The verbal descriptions used to identify the scale positions may vary from brief statements indicating only degrees of the attribute to more elaborate descriptions including illustrations of behavior appropriate to the category. The two examples just given provide relatively detailed definitions and illustrations. At the other extreme, Proshansky (see page 294), in the analysis of descriptions of pictures in a projective test of attitude toward labor, instructed his judges to rate the descriptions in terms of a five-point scale on which the two end categories were defined simply as "very favorable" and "very unfavorable," and the middle category as indicating that it was impossible to classify the respondent as either favorable or unfavorable; the second and fourth positions were given no specific definition other than that they were to be used for subjects who fell between the extreme and the middle position.

The more clearly defined the categories, in general, the more reliable the ratings are likely to be. How much definition is needed depends on such considerations as the nature of the material, the familiarity of the coders with the concepts involved, the fineness of distinctions required for the study, etc.

The problems involved in the construction and application of itemized rating scales are for the most part similar to those that characterize other types of rating scales. These problems are treated later in this section.

Comparative Rating Scales

In using graphic and itemized rating scales, the rater makes his judgment of the individual without direct reference to the positions of other individuals or groups with which he might be compared. On the other hand, comparative rating scales—as their name suggests—

---

[2] Adapted from Cottrell (1947). This rating scale was used by coders in the analysis of interviews. However, similar ratings may be made directly by interviewers or by observers of group discussion.

clearly imply such relative judgments. The positions on the rating scale are expressly defined in terms of a given population or social group or in terms of people of known characteristics. For example, a questionnaire used in selecting applicants for admission to a graduate school may ask the rater for an estimate of the given applicant's ability to do graduate work "as compared with the total group of graduate students you have known"—is he more capable than 10 per cent of them, 20 per cent, 30 per cent, etc. Or the rater may be asked to indicate, for example, whether an individual's leadership skill most closely resembles that of person A, of person B, of person C, etc. (all of whom are known to the rater and all of whom have been assessed in terms of their leadership skill). In the first example above, in order to make a valid rating the judge must have a clear conception of the range and distribution of the abilities of the total graduate student group. Scales of the second type are often difficult to construct, since there may not be sufficient variation in leadership behavior (or whatever attribute is being rated) among the people known to the judges to serve as examples for the various points on the scale.

Another comparative or relative rating procedure is the *rank-order scale*. Here the judge is required to rank individuals specifically in relation to one another; he indicates which person is highest in terms of the characteristic being measured, which is next highest, etc., down to the one who is lowest. Ranking in this fashion is used only when the investigator is concerned with a limited group of individuals. The rating an individual receives indicates simply his relative rank or position in the group being studied; it would not necessarily be of any usefulness apart from the specific group whose members are being compared.

Self-Ratings versus Ratings by Others

All these types of scale may be used to secure an individual's rating of himself or someone else's rating of him. *Self-ratings* have the same advantages and limitations as self-reports, discussed at the beginning of Chapter 7. It seems reasonable to assume that the individual is often in a better position to observe and report his beliefs, feelings, etc., than anyone else is. This assumption is valid, however, only if the individual is aware of his own beliefs and feelings and is willing to reveal them to others. If the individual is unaware, for example, of the fact that he has hostile feelings toward a particular minority group, or if he is aware of such feelings but is afraid of the consequences of revealing them, then the self-rating procedure is of little value. Another difficulty arises from the fact that even if the individual is capable of reporting his beliefs or feelings objectively, his conception of what constitutes a moderate or an extreme position may be quite different from that of others making comparable self-ratings.

Despite the hazards involved, self-ratings have proved useful in the measurement of social attitudes. For beliefs and feelings that the individual can be expected to be aware of and willing to report—for example, attitudes toward television programs—self-ratings are a useful source of information. With respect to certain attributes of attitudes—for example, intensity, importance, etc.—self-ratings have so far proved to be the only satisfactory source of information. Attention by the investigator to such matters as clearly specifying the dimension to be rated and defining the frame of reference or standards against which the ratings are to be made may serve to reduce the possibilities of distortion in self-ratings and increase their usefulness.

Construction and Use of Rating Scales: Some Cautions

Since a large element of judgment enters into the use of rating scales, there is considerable room for systematic errors to be introduced by the personal bias of the rater or raters. One rather common systematic error is the "halo effect." If more than one characteristic of a person is to be judged, raters frequently carry over a generalized impression of the person from one rating to the next, or they try to make their ratings consistent.[3] Thus, if a rater considers a person to be shy and he believes shy people to be poorly adjusted, he is likely to rate

---

[3] The tendency to make ratings consistent is not unlike what Newcomb (1931) has described as a "logical error"; i.e., judges often give similar ratings on traits that seem to them to be logically related.

the person poorly adjusted as well as shy. It is apparent that the halo effect reduces the validity of the ratings of some traits and introduces a spurious degree of positive correlation among the traits that are rated.

Another frequent type of constant error is the "generosity error." Here the tendency of the rater is to overestimate the desirable qualities of subjects whom he likes. Still other frequent errors have been identified. Thus, raters tend to avoid making extreme judgments and to assign individuals to the more moderate categories. Murray et al. (1938) have identified the "contrast error," in which there is a tendency on the part of the rater to see others as opposite to himself in a trait. They found, for example, that raters who were themselves very orderly rated others as being relatively disorderly, whereas raters who were themselves less orderly tended to see others as more orderly.

Obviously, one way of reducing constant errors such as those described above is to train the raters carefully and, especially, to make them aware of the possibility of such biases. Specific steps may be taken to reduce the likelihood of specific types of error. For example, the tendency to avoid using the extreme positions may be counteracted by giving somewhat less-than-extreme labels to these positions. People are more likely to check "I am well satisfied with my job" than "I am completely satisfied with my job"; at the other extreme, they are more likely to check "There are many things about my job that I do not like" than "There is nothing about my job that I like." The "generosity error" may be reduced by using relatively neutral descriptive terms for the scale positions rather than evaluative ones; for example, "does not readily accept new opinions or ways of doing things" rather than "rigid." Halo effects may be reduced, or eliminated altogether, by having the various ratings of a given person made independently— either by different raters, or by the same rater at different times without awareness that he is rating the same person. Obviously, this latter condition can be met only when the ratings are made on the basis of recorded material, such as responses to interview questions, accounts of behavior, etc., from which identifying information can be removed.

Systematic errors, of course, reduce the validity of ratings. There may also be random errors that reduce their reliability. One frequent source of unreliability among different raters is the fact that some frame of reference is implicit in any rating; different raters may use different frames of reference in describing individuals in terms of the characteristic in question. For example, the rating of a person as "conservative" or "radical" takes its meaning from the rater's reference groups—the group norms he has in mind as he makes his rating. Lack of correspondence between ratings by different observers is frequently due to the fact that they make ratings with different reference groups in mind.

Reliability can be increased not only by careful training of raters but also by attention to the construction of the rating scale. Clear definitions of the characteristic being measured and of the various positions on the scale, as well as clear specification of the reference group, help to reduce unreliability. Whenever possible, the definitions of the scale points should include concrete illustrations of question responses, types of behavior, or communication content. Careful consideration should be given to distinguishing between adjacent positions on the scale; for example, to the difference between "favorable" and "very favorable." The example given on pages 348–349 illustrates this procedure.

In constructing a rating scale, one must decide how many scale positions or categories are to be used, unless one is using a graphic scale on which the rater is free to check any point on a continuous line. There is no simple rule for determining the optimal number of positions. A basic consideration, of course, is the degree of differentiation wanted in the measurement. But regardless of what is demanded by the research problem, other factors must be taken into account: (1) the discriminative ability of the judges or raters, including the extent to which they are trained and experienced; (2) the kind of characteristics to be judged; e.g., whether they are complex "inner" attributes or more manifest "outer" attributes; (3) the conditions under which the ratings are to be made; e.g., whether they are based on extensive data (long periods of observation of the subject or a great deal of communication content) or on limited data (brief observation or limited communication content). These factors interact in their effect on the degree of fineness possible in the rating scale. If relatively manifest behaviors are to be rated, then a more differentiated scale may be used even with relatively unsophisticated judges, provided they are trained appropriately. On the other hand, if complex attributes are to be judged and experienced judges are not available, it may be necessary to use a less differentiated scale in order to obtain reliable ratings. In any case, all of these factors must be considered in determining the number of distinctions to be included in the rating scale. Very often preliminary testing is necessary before a final decision can be made.

Reliability of ratings is usually enhanced considerably by having several raters working as a team—making independent judgments, comparing their ratings and discussing discrepancies, and making second independent judgments that are then pooled or averaged to give a final score (see Murray et al., 1938). Much research has demonstrated the superiority of the average, or consensus, of the judgments of several people over that of one individual (see Murphy, Murphy, and Newcomb, 1937). Poffenberger (1942) has written:

> From the studies of judgment that are available, it would seem that three independent estimates of the traits commonly judged is the minimal requirement for satisfactory work. In many cases where the variables affecting the judgments are numerous, the number should be even larger.

Obviously, the pooling of independent ratings is more feasible when the rating is being done by coders working from recorded material or by observers of a behavioral situation; it is often not feasible to have more than one rater (interviewer) present in an interviewing situation.

In many studies ratings are made in the process of analysis by coders who have studied the recorded material. Often, however, ratings are made on the spot by an interviewer, observer, etc., since there may be overtones in the subject's manner or behavior that cannot be recorded adequately and therefore cannot be taken into account in a rating made by an analyst who has not had direct contact with the subject. Little systematic evidence of the relative merits of these two procedures is available. However, Maccoby and Maccoby (1954) suggest that, at least in the case of interviewing, the advantage of the interviewer in being able to observe additional cues may be more than offset by two disadvantages: (1) interviewer ratings are especially susceptible to halo effects, since the interviewer necessarily knows that it is the same individual he is rating and since all the ratings of a given individual must be made at the same time; (2) each interviewer tends to develop his own frame of reference for his ratings, based on the particular sample of respondents he has interviewed, whereas the standards of coders working in the same office and subject to frequent checking, if necessary, can be kept more consistent.

It would be rather fruitless to attempt to discuss in any detail what constitutes a good rater, since there is very little definitive research on this topic. However, several general conclusions seem warranted. First of all, not only do individuals differ in their ability as raters, but the same individual differs in his ability to rate different characteristics. A good rater with respect to one characteristic may be poor with respect to another. In other words, the ability to judge is not general; it is a highly specialized function within the individual. Second—contrary to common expectation—acquaintance with the person to be rated does not lead to increasing validity of ratings. Guilford (1954) has pointed out that long acquaintance often results in substantial "generosity errors." Third, confidence in one's judgment is not necessarily an indication of its *validity*. At least one investigation (Kelly and Fiske, 1950) has reported an inverse relation between confidence and the validity of predictions. However, Guilford (1954) cited an early study by Cady, which indicated that judgments of which the rater is confident are much more *reliable* than those of which he is less confident. Fourth, most of the studies of validity of ratings seem to indicate that people who are high on a characteristic generally considered undesirable are poor judges of that characteristic both in others and in themselves.

The simplicity of rating scales commends their use to many. Their simplicity, however, may be more apparent than real. Often so much time is required to establish adequate reliability that the procedure becomes uneconomical. Yet it is also true that, despite the difficulties involved, a rating scale may be the only instrument available for a given purpose, at least in the present stage of development of research techniques. Furthermore, as we indicated earlier, rating-scale methods have a wide range of application; they can be used in connection with communication content, observed behavior, responses to questionnaires, or data collected by almost any other method.

Perhaps the most significant problem in the use of rating scales has to do with their validity. Even a cursory examination of the relevant literature reveals that, whereas evaluation of the reliability of rating scales is common, measures of validity are rarely reported. The reason, of course, is the dearth of available external criteria against which ratings can be compared. As a matter of fact, ratings themselves have often been used as criteria for checking the validity of other types of measuring instrument, such as personality tests.

This does not mean, of course, that investigators have completely ignored the question of the validity of their rating scales. In effect, they have assumed that their scales were valid when the following conditions obtained: (1) the attributes being measured were relatively "objective," so that their meaning would be uniformly understood by the raters using the scales; (2) the ratings themselves were obtained under optimal conditions, including carefully constructed scales, trained judges, and specified common frames of reference. Under these conditions, one may not go too far wrong in assuming that if the obtained ratings are reliable, they are probably also valid. However, if either one of these conditions is not met, then the assumption of validity is hazardous. The first condition has been overlooked by some investigators. There is little reason to assume that intuitive judgments about complex attributes are inherently valid, even when the judgments are made by highly trained and intelligent people.[4] If the concept of what is being measured is vague, as it is in some rating scales, it is unlikely that the ratings will be clear in meaning. When the concept of what is being measured is ambiguous, the ordering of individuals may actually be quite arbitrary, and even distinctions of greater or less become meaningless.

---

[4] For example, Kelly and Fiske (1950) found that ratings by experienced clinical psychologists based on unstructured interviews had little value in predicting performance in situations that were not clearly specified.

Questionnaires that Form Scales[5]

As we have pointed out, a large element of judgment enters when a rater (whether it be the individual himself or someone else) places an individual on a rating scale on the basis of his observed behavior, his answers to open-ended questions, etc. In an effort to devise procedures that would make it possible to place individuals on a scale with less likelihood of error, carefully standardized questionnaires have been constructed. In this approach, the individual does not directly describe himself in terms of his position on the dimension in question. Rather, he expresses his agreement or disagreement with a number of statements relevant to it; on the basis of these responses, he is assigned a score. In the process of standardizing the questionnaire, the investigator has established a basis for interpreting scores as indicating positions on the dimension. Since this technique has been used most often in the measurement of attitudes, our discussion will focus on attitude scales.[5]

Attitude scales differ in method of construction, method of response, and basis for interpreting scores. Different types of attitude scale will be discussed in this section.

The separate items or questions in an attitude scale are usually not of interest in themselves; the interest is, rather, in the total score or in subscores that result for each individual from the combination of his responses to various items. In effect, any set of items works as well as any other set provided they give the same final scores on the particular attitude being measured.

In selecting items for inclusion in a scale, two criteria are commonly used. First, the items must elicit responses that are psychologically related to the attitude being measured. For example, in a scale measuring anti-semitism, the following item has a *manifest* relation to the attitude being measured: "Anyone who employs many people should be careful not to hire a large percentage of Jews" (Adorno et al., 1950). However, the relationship does not necessarily have to be so

[5] For more detailed discussions of attitude scaling, see Edwards (1957a), Green (1954), and Peak (1953).

evident. In fact, there is a considerable advantage to using items that, on the surface, have no bearing on the attitude being measured. This may prevent the respondent from concealing or distorting his attitude. Thus, in their study of anti-democratic ideology, Adorno *et al.* used many items that have no apparent relationship to this attitude—e.g., "When a person has a problem or worry, it is best for him not to think about it, but to keep busy with more cheerful things." This item is one of several that indicate an individual's readiness or lack of readiness to adopt a psychologically insightful view of other people and of himself. The theory is that people who are lacking in psychological insight and understanding have a personality structure (e.g., greater repressed hostility, weaker ego, etc.) that predisposes them to an anti-democratic ideology.[6]

The second criterion requires that the scale differentiate among people who are at different points along the dimension being measured. To discriminate not merely between opposite extremes in attitude but also among individuals who differ slightly, items that discriminate at different points on the scale are usually included. Thus, a test of opinions about child-rearing practices, along the dimension "permissiveness-strictness," would contain not only items representing a very strict approach and others representing a very permissive approach, but intermediate items representing moderate strictness, moderate permissiveness, etc. Some types of scale, however, provide for the identification of moderate positions by permitting the expression of various degrees of agreement or disagreement with extreme items rather than by the inclusion of intermediate items.

The way in which a scale discriminates among individuals depends on the construction of the scale and the method of scoring. In some

[6] Such indirect items cannot, of course, be used as measures of the attitude being studied simply on the basis of theoretical assumptions about their relation to the attitude. Before they are accepted as adequate measures, their relation to the attitude must be demonstrated. (This statement is equally true for items that seem to have a *manifest* relation to the attitude being studied.) Thus, in the study of anti-democratic ideology, the hypothesis that items such as the one quoted were related to anti-democratic ideology was tested—and borne out—by analysis of the difference between responses to such items made by people known on other grounds to have a democratic ideology and those made by people known to have an anti-democratic ideology.

scales the items form a gradation of such a nature that the individual agrees with only one or two, which correspond to his position on the dimension being measured, and disagrees with statements on either side of those he has selected. Such scales, in which a person's response localizes his position, are sometimes called *differential* scales. In other scales, the individual indicates his agreement or disagreement with each item, and his total score is computed by adding the subscores assigned to his responses to all the separate items; such scales are sometimes called *summated* scales. Still others are set up in such a way that the items form a *cumulative* series; theoretically, an individual whose attitude is at a certain point on the dimension being measured will answer favorably all the items on one side of that point and answer unfavorably all those on the other side. Each of these types of scale is discussed in more detail in the following paragraphs.

DIFFERENTIAL SCALES

Differential scales for the measurement of attitudes are closely associated with the name of L. L. Thurstone. The methods he devised represent attempts to approximate interval scales. An interval scale, it will be recalled from Chapter 5, is one on which the distances between points on the measuring instrument are known, and on which equal numerical distances represent equal distances along the continuum being measured. Such a scale enables one to compare differences or changes in attitude, since the difference between a score of 3 and a score of 7 is equivalent to the difference between a score of 6 and a score of 10 and to the difference between any other two scores that are four points apart.

A differential scale consists of a number of items whose position on the scale has been determined by some kind of ranking or rating operation performed by judges. Various methods of securing judgments of scale position have been used: the method of *paired comparisons* (see Thurstone, 1927, 1928); the method of *equal-appearing intervals* (see Thurstone, 1929, 1931, and Thurstone and Chave, 1929); and the method of *successive intervals* (see Saffir, 1937). It is beyond the scope of this volume to give the details of these procedures; we shall only present in broad outline the method of *equal-appearing intervals*, which is the most commonly used.

In selecting the items for the scale and assigning values to them, the following procedure is used: (1) The investigator gathers several hundred statements conceived to be related to the attitude being investigated. (2) A large number of judges—usually from 50 to 300—working independently, classify these statements into eleven groups. In the first pile the judge places the statements he considers most favorable to the object; in the second, those he considers next most favorable; and in the eleventh pile, the statements he considers most unfavorable. The sixth, or "neutral," position is defined as the point at which there is neither "favorableness" nor "unfavorableness."[7] (3) The scale value of a statement is computed as the median position (or pile) to which it is assigned by the group of judges. Statements that have too broad a scatter are discarded as ambiguous or irrelevant. (4) A final selection is made, taking items that are spread out evenly along the scale from one extreme position to the other. It is often possible to construct duplicate forms of the scale from items not used on the original form.

The resulting Thurstone-type scale is a series of statements, usually about twenty; the position of each statement on a scale of favorable-unfavorable attitude toward the object has been determined by the judges' classification. The subjects, in filling out the questionnaire, are asked either to check each statement with which they agree or to check the two or three items that are closest to their position.

The following illustration of items from a Thurstone-type scale is taken from MacCrone's study of attitudes toward natives in South Africa (1937):

---

[7] Throughout this section, for the sake of simplicity, the discussion is worded in terms of scales measuring favorableness-unfavorableness toward some object. A scale may, of course, be concerned with some other dimension; for example, liberalism-conservatism of social, political, or economic views; permissiveness-strictness of views on child-rearing, etc. In developing Thurstone scales, the instructions to the judges specify the dimension along which the items are to be placed. Thus, in developing a scale to measure liberalism-conservatism, the judges would be instructed to place in the first pile the items they consider most liberal, in the eleventh those they consider most conservative. The same principles and procedures apply whether the dimension to be measured is favorableness-unfavorableness or some other.

Scale *Item*
value *no.*

10.3   1. I consider that the native is only fit to do the "dirty" work of the white community.

10.2   2. The idea of contact with the black or dark skin of the native excites horror and disgust in me.

8.6   15. I do not think that the native can be relied upon in a position of trust or of responsibility.

8.4   17. To my mind the native is so childish and irresponsible that he cannot be expected to know what is in his best interest.

3.8   22. I consider that the white community in this country owe a real debt of gratitude to the missionaries for the way in which they have tried to uplift the native.

3.1   3. It seems to me that the white man by placing restrictions such as the "Colour Bar" upon the native is really trying to exploit him economically.

0.8   11. I would rather see the white people lose their position in this country than keep it at the expense of injustice to the native.

The scale values, of course, are not shown on the questionnaire, and the items are usually arranged in random order rather than in order of their scale value. The mean (or median)[8] of the scale values of the items the individual checks is interpreted as indicating his position on a scale of favorable-unfavorable attitude toward the object.

Theoretically, if a Thurstone-type scale is completely reliable and if the scale is measuring a single attitude rather than a complex of attitudes, an individual should check only items that are immediately contiguous in scale value—e.g., items 15 and 17 above. If the responses of an individual scatter widely over noncontiguous items, his attitude

[8] Thurstone, on the assumption that scales constructed by this method were true interval scales (see Chapter 5), advocated the use of statistics appropriate to interval scales—the mean and the standard deviation. Other investigators, operating on the more cautious assumption that the intervals are not truly equal, have favored the use of the median as appropriate to ordinal scales. For a discussion of whether the assumption that these are true interval scales is justified, see pages 363–365.

score is not likely to have the same meaning as a score with little scatter. The scattered responses may indicate that the subject has no attitude or that his attitude is not organized in the manner assumed by the scale. There is no *a priori* reason to expect that all people have attitudes toward the same things or that attitudinal dimensions are the same for all.

The Thurstone method of equal-appearing intervals has been widely used. Scales have been constructed to measure attitudes toward war, toward the church, toward capital punishment, toward the Chinese, toward Negroes, toward whites, etc. In addition, an attempt has been made by Remmers and his colleagues (1934) to develop generalized Thurstone scales that might be used to measure attitudes toward any group, social institution, etc. For example, the Kelley-Remmers "Scale for Measuring Attitudes Toward Any Institution" consists of forty-five statements, ranging from "The world could not exist without this institution," through such items as "Encourages moral improvement" and "Is too radical in its views and actions," to "Is the most hateful of institutions." In applying this generalized scale to the measurement of attitudes toward a given institution (war, the family, the church, advertising, or whatever), the subject is instructed to check each of the statements with which he agrees in reference to the given institution, or the statements may be reworded to include mention of the specific institution being considered (e.g., "War is the most hateful of institutions").

The Wright-Nelson study of editorial positions of newspapers concerning Japan and China (see pages 340–341) illustrates an application of Thurstone-type scaling to the analysis of available data. In this study, the sorting of statements by the judges served simultaneously to establish the position of each item on a scale of favorableness-hostility and to determine the scores of the various newspapers. In effect, each newspaper was treated as having "checked" all the statements selected from its editorials; its score was obtained by averaging the score values of the specific statements.

Several objections have been raised against the Thurstone-type scale. First, many have objected to the amount of work involved in constructing it. Undoubtedly, the procedure is cumbersome. However, Edwards (1957) has expressed the opinion that, in view of recent developments in time-saving techniques, the amount of time and labor involved in constructing a scale by the method of equal-appearing intervals is not substantially different from that involved in constructing a summated scale. In any case, it is doubtful that simple methods for the rigorous construction of scales will ever be developed. The precise measurement of attitudes is perhaps inevitably a complex affair.

A second criticism has been that, since an individual's score is the mean or median of the scale values of the several items he checks, essentially different attitudinal patterns may be expressed in the same score. For example, on the scale of attitudes toward natives of South Africa given earlier, an individual who checks the two moderately "anti" items 15 and 17 receives a score of 8.5 (the median of their scale values). Another individual, who checks items 1, 15, 17 and 22 (perhaps because 22 has a meaning for him which is different from that which it had for the judges), also receives a score of 8.5 (the median of the scale values of these items). The two individuals are rated as having the same degree of prejudice, even though the latter checked the most unfavorable item in the scale and the former did not. Dudycha (1943), after six years' use of the Peterson test of attitude toward war (a test constructed by the method of equal-appearing intervals) with college students, reported that the average student, instead of checking only two or three contiguous items, covered more than a third of the scale; some students endorsed statements ranging from those placed at the "strongly favorable" end of the scale to statements at the "strongly opposed" end. (One must, of course, consider the possibility that such students had no clear attitude toward war and that it was therefore inappropriate to try to measure their attitude by any technique.) Dudycha questioned the meaning to be given to a median derived from such a range of responses. However, the criticism that identical scores do not necessarily indicate identical patterns of response is not unique to the Thurstone-type scale; it applies at least as strongly, as we shall see, to summated scales.[9]

A still more serious question has to do with the extent to which the scale values assigned to the items are influenced by the attitudes of the judges themselves. Do the attitudes and backgrounds of the

---

[9] The fact that different patterns may lead to identical scores is not necessarily as serious a limitation as it might seem. This point is discussed on pages 369–370.

judges affect the position of the various items on the scale? This obviously is a matter that is open to experimental inquiry. A number of early studies supported the view that the scale values assigned did not depend on the attitude of the judges. Hinckley (1932) found a correlation of .98 between the scale positions assigned to 114 items measuring prejudice toward Negroes by a group of Southern white students in the United States who were prejudiced against Negroes and those assigned by a group of unprejudiced Northern students. Similarly, MacCrone (1937), in the study of race attitudes in South Africa referred to earlier, found that the scale positions assigned various items by South Africans of European background and by educated Bantus, natives of South Africa, were similar except for a few items. Studies of the construction of scales measuring attitudes toward a particular candidate for political office (Beyle, 1932), toward war (Ferguson, 1935), toward "patriotism" (Pintner and Forlano, 1937), and toward Jews (Eysenck and Crown, 1949) all found correlations of .98 or higher between the scale positions assigned to the items by groups of judges with opposed attitudes toward the object of the scale.

More recent research, however, has sharply challenged the conclusions of these studies. Hovland and Sherif (1952), using the items employed in the Hinckley study mentioned above, found marked differences between the scale values assigned to items by anti-Negro white judges on the one hand, and those assigned by pro-Negro white judges and Negro judges, on the other. Items rated as "neutral" or moderately favorable by Hinckley's subjects were likely to be seen as unfavorable by the pro-Negro white judges and the Negro judges. This discrepancy between the earlier and the later findings can be accounted for by the different procedures used. Hinckley followed a rule suggested by Thurstone, that any judge who placed more than one fourth of the statements in a single category should be eliminated as "careless." Hovland and Sherif, however, found that judges with extreme attitudes tended to place many statements in the same category; checks within their procedure convinced these investigators that this was not a matter of carelessness. Application of the rule followed by Hinckley would have eliminated over three fourths of their Negro judges and two thirds of their pro-Negro white judges; when they did eliminate these judges, they found that the scale values assigned by the remaining white judges were very close to those assigned by Hinckley's judges. These findings strongly suggest that Hinckley's procedure had the effect of ruling out judges with extreme attitudes.

A subsequent study by Kelley et al. (1955), using twenty of the Hinckley items, found marked differences between the scale values assigned to items by white and by Negro judges, with the statements fairly evenly distributed from "favorable" to "unfavorable" by the white judges, but bunched at the two ends of the continuum by the Negro judges.[10] Granneberg (1955), in constructing a scale of attitudes toward religion, found not only that a religious group and a nonreligious group differed significantly in the scale values they assigned to items, but that judges of superior and of low intelligence differed, and that there was an interaction between attitude and intelligence which affected the scale position to which items were assigned.

Such findings, of course, cast serious doubt on the meaning of the scale positions and the distances between them. It should be noted, however, that even those studies that found marked differences between groups of judges in the absolute scale values they assigned to items found high agreement in the *rank order* in which judges with differing attitudes arranged the items along the favorable-unfavorable continuum. Thus, although the assumption that Thurstone-type scales are true interval scales seems dubious, it is still possible for them to constitute reasonably satisfactory ordinal scales; that is, they provide a basis for saying that one individual is more favorable or less favorable than another. If in practice individuals agreed with only a few contiguous items, so that a given score had a clear meaning, the Thurstone methods would provide highly satisfactory ordinal scales. But, as noted above, individuals may agree with items quite widely spaced on the scale, and in such cases the median of the items checked may not provide a meaningful basis for ranking the individual in relation to others.

---

[10] These investigators found that other methods of constructing Thurstone-type scales were less subject than the equal-interval technique to the effect of extreme attitudes on the part of the judges. The method of successive intervals showed less difference between white and Negro judges, and the method of paired comparisons eliminated the differences almost entirely.

SUMMATED SCALES

A summated scale, like a differential scale, consists of a series of items to which the subject is asked to react. However, no attempt is made to find items that will be distributed evenly over a scale of favorableness-unfavorableness (or whatever dimension is to be measured). Rather, only items that seem to be either definitely favorable or definitely unfavorable to the object are used, not neutral or "slightly" favorable or unfavorable items. Rather than checking only those statements with which he agrees, the respondent indicates his agreement or disagreement with each item. Each response is given a numerical score indicating its favorableness or unfavorableness; often, favorable responses are scored plus, unfavorable responses, minus. The algebraic summation of the scores of the individual's responses to all the separate items gives his total score, which is interpreted as representing his position on a scale of favorable-unfavorable attitude toward the object. The rationale for using such total scores as a basis for placing individuals on a scale seems to be as follows: The probability of agreeing with any one of a series of favorable items about an object, or of disagreeing with any unfavorable item, varies directly with the degree of favorableness of an individual's attitude. Thus, one could expect an individual with a favorable attitude to respond favorably to many items (that is, to agree with many items favorable to the object and to disagree with many unfavorable ones); an ambivalent individual to respond unfavorably to some and favorably to others; an individual with an unfavorable attitude to respond unfavorably to many items.

The type of summated scale most frequently used in the study of social attitudes follows the pattern devised by Likert (1932) and is referred to as a *Likert-type scale*. In such a scale, the subjects are asked to respond to each item in terms of several degrees of agreement or disagreement; for example, (1) strongly approve, (2) approve, (3) undecided, (4) disapprove, (5) strongly disapprove.[11] Reproduced below are several items, with directions, from a Likert-type scale, the so-called "Internationalism Scale" used by Murphy and Likert (1938).

---

[11] Although Likert used five categories of agreement-disagreement, some investigators have used a smaller and some a larger number of categories. Many summated scales call simply for an expression of agreement or disagreement, without indication of degree.

Directions: The following list of sentences is in the form of what should or should not be done. If you strongly approve of the statement as it stands, underscore the words "strongly approve," and so on, with regard to the other attitudes (approve, undecided, disapprove, strongly disapprove).

18. In the interest of permanent peace, we should be willing to arbitrate absolutely all differences with other nations which we cannot readily settle by diplomacy.

Strongly approve	Approve	Undecided	Disapprove	Strongly disapprove
(5)	(4)	(3)	(2)	(1)

19. A person who loves his fellow men should refuse to engage in any war, no matter how serious the consequences to his country.

Strongly approve	Approve	Undecided	Disapprove	Strongly disapprove
(5)	(4)	(3)	(2)	(1)

22. We must strive for loyalty to our country before we can afford to consider world brotherhood.

Strongly approve	Approve	Undecided	Disapprove	Strongly disapprove
(1)	(2)	(3)	(4)	(5)

The numbers under the scale positions do not appear on the questionnaire given to the respondents. They are shown here to indicate the scoring system.

The procedure for constructing a Likert-type scale is as follows: (1) The investigator assembles a large number of items considered relevant to the attitude being investigated and either clearly favorable or clearly unfavorable. (2) These items are administered to a group of subjects representative of those with whom the questionnaire is to be used. The subjects indicate their response to each item by checking one of the categories of agreement-disagreement. (3) The responses to the various items are scored in such a way that a response indicative of the most favorable attitude is given the highest score. It makes no difference whether 5 is high and 1 is low or vice-versa. The important thing is that the responses be scored consistently in terms of the attitudinal direction they indicate. Whether "approve" or "disapprove" is the favorable response to an item depends, of course, upon the content and wording of the item. (4) Each individual's total score is computed by adding his item scores. (5) The responses are analyzed to determine which of the items discriminate most clearly between the high scorers and the low scorers on the total scale. For example, the responses of those subjects whose total scores are in the upper quarter and the responses of those in the lower quarter may be analyzed in order to determine for each item the extent to which the responses of these criterion groups differ (see Chapter 5, pages 184–185 for an illustration of this procedure). Items that do not show a substantial correlation with the total score, or that do not elicit different responses from those who score high and those who score low on the total test, are eliminated to ensure that the questionnaire is "internally consistent"—that is, that every item is related to the same general attitude.

The Likert-type scale, like the Thurstone scale, has been used widely in studies of morale, of attitudes toward Negroes, of attitudes toward internationalism, etc. It has several advantages over the Thurstone scale. First, it permits the use of items that are not manifestly related to the attitude being studied. In the Thurstone method, the necessity of agreement among judges tends to limit items to content that is obviously related to the attitude in question; in the Likert method, any item that is found empirically to be consistent with the total score can be included. Second, a Likert-type scale is generally considered simpler to construct. Third, it is likely to be more reliable than a Thurstone scale of the same number of items. Within limits, the reliability of a scale increases as the number of possible alternative responses is increased; the Likert-type scale item permits the expression of several (usually five) degrees of agreement-disagreement, whereas the Thurstone scale item allows a choice between two alternative responses only. Fourth, the range of responses permitted to an item given in a Likert-type scale provides, in effect, more precise information about the individual's opinion on the issue referred to by the given item.[12]

[12] For a detailed comparison of the Thurstone and Likert methods, see Edwards and Kenney (1946) and Edwards (1957a).

The Likert-type scale does not claim to be more than an ordinal scale; that is, it makes possible the ranking of individuals in terms of the favorableness of their attitude toward a given object, but it does not provide a basis for saying *how much* more favorable one is than another, nor for measuring the *amount* of change after some experience. From the point of view of the level of measurement we would like our instruments to provide, this is, of course, a disadvantage. Whether it constitutes a disadvantage of the Likert scale in comparison with the Thurstone scale depends on one's judgment of whether Thurstone scales really meet the criteria for interval scales.

Another disadvantage of the Likert-type scale is that often the total score of an individual has little clear meaning, since many patterns of response to the various items may produce the same score. We have already noted that Thurstone-type scales are also subject to this criticism, but it applies even more strongly to the Likert scales since they provide a greater number of response possibilities. Using the three items in our illustration of the Likert-type scale, for example, an individual may obtain a total score of 6 by indicating: (a) disapproval of 18 and 19, approval of 22; (b) approval of 18, strong disapproval of 19, and strong approval of 22; (c) indecision on 18, disapproval of 19, and strong approval of 22; (d) other combinations of responses. It seems reasonable to suppose that, although the total scores are the same, their meanings may be markedly different. Thus one may raise a serious question whether the Likert-type scale actually conforms to the requirements of an ordinal, much less an interval, scale. Despite the lack of theoretical rationale for scalability, however, pragmatically the scores on the Likert-type questionnaire often provide the basis for a rough ordering of people on the characteristic being measured.

The fact that different patterns of response may lead to identical scores on either a Thurstone or a Likert scale is not necessarily as serious a drawback as it may at first appear. Some of the differences in response patterns leading to a given score may be attributable to random variations in response. Others may arise because specific items involve not only the attitude being measured but also extraneous issues that may affect the response. Thus some of the differences in response patterns leading to the same score may be thought of as error from the point of view of the attitude being measured, rather than as true differences in attitude that are being obscured by identical scores. The fact that the scale contains a number of items means that these variations on individual items unrelated to the attitude being measured may cancel each other out.

Moreover, different ways of getting to the same place may be equivalent from the point of view of the measurement goal that is being served. For example, if one weights addition and subtraction equally in a concept of arithmetic ability, it makes sense to score two individuals as equivalent in arithmetic ability, even though one is relatively strong in addition and the other relatively strong in subtraction. Similarly, it may make sense to say that the net degree of animosity toward a given attitudinal object is the same in two individuals even though the animosity expresses itself differently.

The problem is to determine when the fact that the same score can be arrived at in different ways has consequences for the meaningfulness of the score, and when it does not. In part, this problem is one of conceptual clarity; in part, it involves questions of fact. If the investigator is not clear about what he is trying to measure, and why, this will be only one of many problems with which he will be unable to cope. But even if his concepts are clear, he will still want to know (although, unfortunately, he may not be in a position to find out) the answers to such questions as: Do the response patterns of individuals remain stable over time? If alternate forms of the test are available, do individuals receive the same scores on different forms? Do different individuals achieving the same score in different ways react in the same way to particular stimuli, problems, incentives, etc.?

Ultimately what is involved is a question of the validity of the scale. Questions of validity always involve questions of fact, which cannot be settled by armchair argument. The problem of whether different combinations of responses can meaningfully be assigned the same score is one for empirical investigation.

CUMULATIVE SCALES

Cumulative scales, like differential and summated scales, are made up of a series of items with which the respondent indicates agreement or disagreement. In a cumulative scale, the items are related to one another in such a way that, ideally, an individual who replies favorably to item 2 also replies favorably to item 1; one who replies favorably to item 3 also replies favorably to items 1 and 2; etc. Thus, all individuals who answer a given item favorably should have higher scores on the total scale than the individuals who answer that item unfavorably. The individual's score is computed by counting the number of items he answers favorably. This score places him on the scale of favorable-unfavorable attitude provided by the relationship of the items to one another.

Sometimes the items as they appear in the scale are arranged in order of favorableness; sometimes they are randomly arranged. Ordinarily, no attempt is made to determine whether the intervals between items are equal; thus, in practice, cumulative scales are ordinal scales.

One of the earliest scales used in the measurement of attitudes, the Bogardus social-distance scale (see Bogardus, 1925, 1928, 1933) was intended to be of the cumulative type. The social-distance scale, which has become a classic technique in the measuring of attitudes toward ethnic groups, lists a number of relationships to which members of the group might be admitted. The respondent is asked to indicate, for specified nationality or racial groups, the relationships to which he would be willing to admit members of each group. His attitude is measured by the closeness of relationship that he is willing to accept. The Bogardus-type scale is illustrated below:

Directions: For each race or nationality listed below, circle each of the classifications to which you would be willing to admit the average member of that race or nationality (not the best members you have known, nor the worst). Answer in terms of your first feeling reactions.

	To close kinship by marriage	To my club as personal chums	To my street as neighbors	To employment in my occupation	To citizenship in my country	As visitors only to my country	Would exclude from my country
English	1	2	3	4	5	6	7
Negro	1	2	3	4	5	6	7
French	1	2	3	4	5	6	7
Chinese	1	2	3	4	5	6	7
Russian	1	2	3	4	5	6	7
etc.							

The items used in the Bogardus scale (that is, the column headings in the illustration above) were selected on logical grounds. It seems reasonable to expect that an individual who circles 4 in relation to Chinese, indicating that he would be willing to accept them to employment in his occupation, would ordinarily also circle 5 and not circle 6 or 7. (Here, as in other scales, the content of the item must be taken into account in deciding whether a "Yes" response is to be scored as favorable or unfavorable. Since 6 and 7 are essentially statements of exclusion, *absence* of a circle constitutes the favorable response to these two items. Thus, neither 6 nor 7 should be circled for a given group if any of the other numerals is circled.) If the individual did *not* circle 3 (willing to admit to my street as neighbors), one would expect, on logical grounds, that he would also not circle 2 or 1.

On the whole, the assumption that these items form a cumulative scale has been borne out. Nevertheless, in practice some reversals do occur. Some individuals, for example, who would object to living in a building with Puerto Ricans would not object to having Puerto Ricans in an informal social club (see Deutsch and Collins, 1951). Although individuals not infrequently show such reversals in replies on the social-distance scale, it is relatively uncommon to find an entire group reversing items. Thus, the social-distance scale has been used rather effectively in comparing the attitudes of different groups of people toward various nationalities. It may be noted that reversals can almost always be interpreted by postulating the intrusion of some factor other than the individual's own attitude toward the group in question—e.g., the respondent's image of how other people would interpret his living in a certain neighborhood, or his expectation concerning the impact on real estate values of admitting minority group members to residence on his street, etc.

With the appearance of the Thurstone and Likert scaling methods in the late nineteen-twenties and early thirties, attention shifted away from cumulative scales. However, the forties saw a revival of interest and a rapid development of techniques for determining whether the items of a scale do in fact have a cumulative relationship, regardless of whether they appear cumulative in common-sense terms. This renewed interest was linked to an emphasis on the development of unidimensional scales—that is, scales consisting of items that do not raise issues, or involve factors, extraneous to the characteristic being measured.

A number of investigators had pointed out that the Thurstone and Likert scales, although ostensibly measuring "an attitude," contained statements about various aspects of the object under consideration. Thus, Carter (1945) pointed out that Form A of the Peterson scale of attitude toward war (a Thurstone-type scale) had as its most favorable statement, "War is glorious"; as its most unfavorable statement, "There is no conceivable justification for war"; and as its mid-point, "I never think about war and it doesn't interest me." He commented that it is difficult to think of these statements as falling along a straight line. He suggested that such statements as, "The benefits of war rarely pay for its losses even for the victor" and "Defensive war is justified but other wars are not," belong on two different scales, one having to do with the economic results of war, the other with the ethics of war activity. It was argued that combining items referring to different aspects of the object made it impossible to specify exactly what the scale was measuring, and also accounted for the scattering of responses, which made it difficult to assign any clear meaning to the score based on the median of the items checked.

There have been several approaches to this problem. We shall discuss here only the technique developed by Guttman, commonly called scale analysis or the scalogram method. [13] One of the main purposes of this technique is to ascertain whether the attitude or characteristic being studied (technically termed the "universe of content" or the "universe of attributes") actually involves only a single dimension. In the Guttman procedure, a "universe of content" is considered to be unidimensional only if it yields a perfect, or nearly perfect, cumulative scale—that is, if it is possible to arrange all the responses of any number of respondents into a pattern of the following sort:

[13] For a more comprehensive discussion of the Guttman technique, see Stouffer et al. (1950). For critiques of it, and alternative approaches to the same problem, see Festinger (1947) and Loevinger (1948).

Score	Says "Yes" to item			Says "No" to item		
	3	2	1	3	2	1
3	x	x	x			
2		x	x	x		
1			x	x	x	
0				x	x	x

The important thing about this pattern is that, if it holds, a given score on a particular series of items always has the same meaning; knowing an individual's score makes it possible to tell, without consulting his questionnaire, exactly which items he endorsed. Consider, for example, the following items, with which respondents are asked either to agree or to disagree:

1. A young child is likely to face serious emotional problems if his parents get divorced.
2. Even if a husband or wife or both are unhappy in their marriage, they should remain together as long as they have any young children.
3 Divorce laws in this state should be changed to make it more difficult to get a divorce.

If these items were found to form a perfect cumulative scale, we would know, for example, that *all* individuals with a score of 2 on the scale believe that divorce of the parents presents serious emotional problems for a young child and that a couple with young children should remain together even if they are unhappy, but do *not* believe that the divorce laws should be made more stringent.

In practice, perfect cumulative, or unidimensional, scales are rarely or never found in social research, but approximations to them can often be developed. Scalogram analysis uses several criteria for deciding whether or not a particular series of items may be usefully regarded as approximating a perfect unidimensional scale. The most important of these is the *reproducibility* of the responses—the proportion of responses of a large number of subjects which actually fall into the pattern presented above.[14] This pattern contains all the responses to particular items that would be predicted from a knowledge of the individual's total score on the series of items (his "scale type"). Thus the proportion of actual responses which fall into the pattern provides a measure of the extent to which particular responses are "reproducible" from the total score. Guttman and his co-workers have set .90 as the minimal reproducibility necessary for a series of items to be regarded as approximating a perfect scale. Examples of such scales are presented in Stouffer et al. (1950).

The Guttman technique is a method of determining whether a set of items forms a unidimensional scale; as a number of writers have pointed out, it offers little guidance for selecting items that are likely to form such a scale. Edwards and Kilpatrick (1948)[15] have suggested a method of selecting a set of statements likely to form a unidimensional scale. Called the *scale-discrimination technique*, it combines aspects of the Thurstone and Likert approaches to scale construction, in the following steps: (1) A large assortment of items dealing with the issue of study is collected. Items that are ambiguous, irrelevant, neutral, or too extreme are eliminated by inspection. (2) As in the Thurstone method of equal-appearing intervals, a large number of judges place the remaining items in eleven piles, according to their judged favorableness or unfavorableness toward the issue. The extent to which the judges agree on the placement of each item is determined, and the half of the items on which there is greatest variability or scatter of judgments is eliminated. Each of the remaining items is assigned a scale value corresponding to the median position in which it has been placed by the judges. (3) These items are then transformed into a Likert-type scale by providing for the expression of five or six degrees of agreement-disagreement in response to each item. This scale is administered to a large group of subjects, and their responses are analyzed to determine which of the items discriminate most clearly between the high scorers and the low scorers on the total scale. The resulting "discriminatory coefficients" of the various items are then plotted against their scale values. From the total list of items, twice the

[14] For a detailed discussion of this and other methods of determining whether a scale is unidimensional, see White and Saltz (1957).

[15] This article appears also, with minor changes, in Edwards (1957).

number wanted in the final scale are selected. The items selected are those which have the highest discriminatory coefficients in their scale interval; for example, of all the items with scale values between 8.0 and 8.9, those with the highest discriminatory coefficients are selected. An equal number of items is selected for each interval. (4) The items in the resulting list are arranged in order of their scale value. The list is then divided into two equated forms of the questionnaire by assigning all the odd-numbered items to one form and all the even-numbered items to the other.

The Guttman and related techniques represent major contributions to the methodology of questionnaire construction and analysis. However, two qualifications related to the use of unidimensional scales should be kept in mind: (1) Such a scale may not be the most effective basis either for measuring attitudes toward complex objects or for making predictions about behavior in relation to such objects; (2) a given scale may be unidimensional for one group of individuals but not for another.

Let us consider the first reservation. Suppose we have devised a unidimensional scale to measure attitude toward the economic results of war, another to measure attitude concerning the ethics of war activity, still others to measure whatever other aspects of attitude toward war can be identified and measured by unidimensional scales. No single one of these scales may give an accurate reflection of an individual's attitude toward the complex concept "war," or provide a basis for predicting how he would vote on the question of his country's participation in a specific war. This is, of course, the same qualification noted in connection with the discussion of internal consistency in Chapter 5, pages 178–179; a complex measure may be needed as a basis for predicting complex behavior.

As for the second reservation, it is sometimes assumed that unidimensionality is a property of a measuring instrument, rather than of the patterning of an attitude among a given group of individuals. For one group, a number of items may be arranged unidimensionally in a given order; for another group, the same items may fall into a different order; for still another group, they may not form a unidimensional pattern at all. The way in which the experiences of different groups can lead to different patternings of items is illustrated in a study by Harding and Hogrefe (1952). These investigators interviewed three groups of white department-store employees. The members of Group 1 worked in departments in which there was at least one Negro in a job equal in status to their own, or of higher status than their own; those in Group II worked in departments in which all the Negroes were in jobs of lower status than their own; those in Group III were in departments where there were no Negroes. The interviews included six "social-distance" questions, having to do with: sitting next to Negroes in buses or trains, sitting at the same table with a Negro in a lunchroom, taking a job in which there were both Negroes and white people doing the same kind of work as you, working under a Negro supervisor, living in a building in which there were both white and Negro families, and having a Negro for a personal friend. The investigators found that these six questions formed satisfactory Guttman-type scales for each of the three groups, but that the question about taking a job in which there were both Negroes and white people doing the same kind of work as the respondent fell in a different position for each of the three groups. For Group I—the people who were actually in this situation— this question tied with the one about buses and trains for the "most acceptable" position. For Group II—those working in departments with Negroes, but in positions of unequal status—sitting next to Negroes in trains and buses was more acceptable than working with them on an equal status. For those in all-white departments, both sitting next to Negroes in buses and trains and sitting at the same table with a Negro in a lunchroom were more acceptable than working with them on an equal status.

In other words, as Coombs (1948) has pointed out:

> . . . in a highly organized social order with standardized education, there will tend to be certain traits generated which will be common to the population subjected to the same pattern of forces. There is, however, at the same time, opposition, contradiction, and interaction of these forces on organisms that are not equally endowed in the first place—with the result that the structuring of a psychological trait is less complete in some individuals than in others. . . . A psychological trait, in other words, may or may not be a functional unity and it may or may not be general, i.e., common to a large number of individuals.

Some Modifications of Scaling Techniques

Not all attempts to quantify attitudes fit into the classification of scales we have described. Especially within recent years, a number of approaches have been developed that use some aspects of scaling procedure but cannot properly be described as differential, summated, or cumulative scales. We shall discuss two such approaches: the Q-sort and the *semantic differential*.

THE Q-SORT[16]

The operations involved in a Q-sort are similar to the first steps in the construction of a Thurstone scale by the method of equal-appearing intervals. The subject is presented with a large number of statements believed to be relevant to the topic under investigation, and is asked to sort them into a specified number of piles—usually nine or eleven—according to some criterion. In the Thurstone technique, it will be remembered, this sorting process has the purpose of assigning scale values to statements; the criterion for sorting is not the sorter's agreement or disagreement with a statement but his judgment of its degree of favorableness or unfavorableness toward the object. In the Q-sort, the purpose of sorting is to get a picture of the individual's own view of, or attitude toward, the object being considered. The criterion for placing statements in the various piles is the extent of his agreement with them; the pattern into which he sorts the statements constitutes the data for analysis of his position. A restriction not present in the Thurstone sorting procedure is introduced into the Q-sort; this is specification of the number of cards to be placed in a given pile. In order to simplify the statistical analysis, the numbers are usually specified in such a way that the sort forms a roughly normal distribution.

Let us consider an example of the use of a Q-sort in the context in which it has most frequently been employed—the study of personality. More specifically, this was a study of changes in an individual's image of himself, of his ideal person, and of "the ordinary person," and

[16] For a detailed discussion of "Q methodology," see Stephenson (1953). For shorter discussions, see Cronbach (1953) and Mowrer (1953).

of changes in the relations among these images, as a result of psycho-therapy (Rogers and Dymond, 1954). Each subject was given a set of one hundred statements of personal characteristics, each printed on a separate card. The set consisted of such statements as: "I am a sub-missive person . . . I am a hard worker . . . I really am disturbed . . . I am afraid of a full-fledged disagreement with a person . . . I am likable." The subject was asked first to "sort these cards to describe yourself as you see yourself today, from those that are least like you to those that are most like you." The distribution was to be in nine piles, with one card in each of the two extreme positions, four cards in each of the next most extreme positions, and so on. Next the subject was asked to "sort these cards to describe your ideal person—the person you would most like within yourself to be." Finally, he was asked to sort them to describe "the ordinary person." The three sortings were carried out first before the person entered psychotherapy and again after a period of treatment.

The appropriate statistical techniques to be used in the analysis of data from Q-sorts are a matter of some controversy. Some authors have held that factor analysis[17] is essential; others have disagreed. (For a presentation and discussion of these points of view, consult the refer-ences cited on page 378.) In the study we are considering, factor analysis was not used. Rather, relations such as the following were in-vestigated by means of correlations: the correspondence between self-image and ideal image before and after therapy, with the finding that, on the whole, an individual's ideal and his self-image were more alike after therapy; differences in the extent of change in the self-image, the ideal image, and the image of the ordinary person, with the finding that the self-image changed more during therapy than the other images; etc.

In this study, the data yielded by the Q-sort were also summarized into a single score, as in a summated scale, to yield a score on "adjust-ment." This latter procedure made possible (although this was not its main purpose) estimation of the reliability and validity of the instru-ment used in this way. It was found that the "adjustment" scores of a

[17] Factor analysis is a method of finding the common element or elements that underlie a set of measures. For a discussion of factor analysis, see Cattell (1952) or Thomson (1946).

control group of individuals who did not receive therapy but who were tested several times showed a stability coefficient of .86 computed on the basis of two administrations of the instrument at least six months apart. Comparison of the "adjustment" scores with therapists' ratings of the success of therapy showed considerable, though by no means complete, agreement.

Although Q-sorts have been used most often in studies such as this, where the emphasis is on self-image and other person-images, the method is applicable to the study of other attitudes. Subjects might be presented with sets of statements about methods of child-rearing, or about labor-management relations, or about Negroes, and asked to sort them in terms of the extent of their agreement or disagreement with each statement. The resulting data might be used, for example, to compare a given individual's views about different ethnic groups, or to compare the views of different individuals about a given group or object.

THE SEMANTIC DIFFERENTIAL

Osgood, Suci, and Tannenbaum (1957), who developed the "semantic differential," describe it as a method for measuring the meaning of an object to an individual. It may also be thought of as an attitude scale. The subject is asked to rate a given concept (e.g., "Negro," "Republican," "wife," "me as I would like to be," "me as I am," "Picasso's Guernica") on a series of seven-point bipolar rating scales. Any concept—whether it is a political issue, a person, an institution, a work of art—can be rated. The seven-point scales include such bipolar scales as the following: (A) fair-unfair, clean-dirty, good-bad, valuable-worthless; (B) large-small, strong-weak, heavy-light; (C) active-passive, fast-slow, hot-cold.

One may use the individual's responses to determine whether, for him, two concepts are alike or different. For example, does his picture of "me as I am" coincide with his picture of "me as I would like to be," or are the two quite different? In this use, one draws a "profile" of the meaning of each concept to the individual simply by drawing lines between the points checked on each of the scales for a given concept. A technique for measuring the extent of similarity between the two profiles has been developed. Similarly, one may compare two individuals' concepts of a given object by measuring the similarity of the profiles provided by their checks on the various scales.

Used in this way, the semantic differential does not place individuals on an underlying scale representing some dimension of attitude; it simply provides a method of measuring the similarity or difference between their concepts of a given object. However, the responses to subgroups of the scales can be summated to yield scores that are interpreted as indicating the individual's position on three underlying dimensions of attitude toward the object being rated. These dimensions have been identified by using factor-analytic procedures in examining the responses of many individuals concerning many concepts or objects. It has been found that, more or less consistently, the scales labeled (A) on page 380 seem to group together; that is, an individual tends to place a given object in a similar position on each of these scales. Similarly, the scales labeled (B) seem to group together; so do the scales labeled (C). The manifest content of each scale does not clearly indicate the underlying attitudinal dimension to which it is relevant; what does it mean, for example, to rate Picasso's "Guernica" as hot or cold, as clean or dirty? But from the consistent grouping of the scales, Osgood and his colleagues have inferred that the three subgroups measure the following three dimensions of attitude: (A) the individual's *evaluation* of the object or concept being rated, corresponding to the favorable-unfavorable dimension of more traditional attitude scales; (B) the individual's perception of the *potency* or power of the object or concept; and (C) his perception of the *activity* of the object or concept.

The diagram on the following page is an adaptation of one given by Osgood and his colleagues, illustrating the use of the semantic differential in plotting the meaning of several different concepts to a group of Taft Republicans in a study that was made shortly before the 1952 presidential election. From the diagram one can see, for example, that to these subjects the concept of "Truman" is very different from the concept of "Taft" but is very similar to the concept of "socialism." The concept of "Stalin" is similar to the concept of "Taft" on the potency and activity dimensions but very different on the evaluative dimension.

Osgood and his colleagues suggest that the semantic differential makes possible the measurement and comparison of various objects

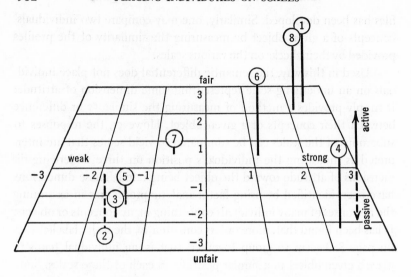

Model of the "Semantic Space" for Taft Republicans[18]

Each of eight concepts is numbered according to the key below. The point at which the line for a given concept starts shows the rating of that concept on the scales *fair-unfair* and *strong-weak*. The length of the line shows the rating on scale *active-passive*; a solid line indicates a rating toward the *active* end of the scale, a broken line a rating toward the *passive* end. Thus, for example, it can be seen that Stalin (4) was rated as very unfair, very strong, and very active; Truman (5) as somewhat unfair, somewhat weak, and somewhat active.

Key

1. Taft	5. Truman
2. Policy in China	6. Atom bomb
3. Socialism	7. United Nations
4. Stalin	8. Eisenhower

by diverse subjects; they imply that the measuring instrument is not grossly affected by the nature of the object being measured or by the type of person using the scale. If this is really true, the semantic differential would be a solution to many of the problems of attitude meas-

18 Adapted from Osgood *et al.* (1957).

urement. Osgood, Suci, and Tannenbaum provide some evidence that different types of subjects use the scales in similar ways. Thus, they indicate that Taft Republicans, Eisenhower Republicans, and Stevenson Democrats use the same underlying dimensions in their reactions; so do normals and schizophrenics; so do Korean exchange students, Japanese exchange students, and Americans. This is impressive evidence that the scales are comparable across different types of subjects, although it seems possible that if people with widely different educational backgrounds were compared, the same results might not obtain.

However, Osgood and his colleagues present considerable evidence indicating that the measuring instrument is not completely comparable across concepts. The meanings of scales and their relation to the other scales vary considerably with the concept being judged. What is good, for example, depends heavily on the concept being judged; "strong" may be good in judging athletes but not in judging women. The implication of this is that it may be quite difficult to develop rating scales that provide a consistent measurement of the underlying dimensions independently of the concepts being judged.

In concluding our discussion of attitude scales, it should be pointed out that the field of scale construction and analysis is in a period of rapid development and change. In addition to the work we have discussed, major contributions have been made in recent years by Coombs (1948, 1950, 1953), Lazarsfeld (1957), Loevinger (1947, 1948), Suppes and his co-workers at the Applied Mathematics and Statistics Laboratory of Stanford University (Davidson, Suppes, and Siegel, 1957), Torgerson (1958), and others.

A Concluding Note

In this chapter we have discussed various methods of scaling, that is, of distinguishing among objects or individuals in terms of the degree to which they possess a given characteristic. Here, as in connection with other measurement techniques, we have raised questions about reliability and validity. Although many users of scales have investigated the reliability and validity of their measures, it is probably still true, as one writer (Ferguson, 1957) has remarked, that there has been "more measurement than validation." As we have pointed out earlier, there are understandable reasons for the lack of attention to validity— notably the difficulty of determining what would be appropriate criteria of validity for measures of complex attributes and of gathering the necessary data. However, a number of investigators have demonstrated that, with ingenuity, one may develop useful criterion measures. It is perhaps to be expected that in relatively new research fields, such as the social sciences, more attention should at first be paid to the development of a variety of measuring techniques than to their validation. Nevertheless, it seems clear that research in the social sciences would now be advanced by greater attention to the validity of the instruments used.

Scaling procedures may either be built directly into the data-collection instruments or may be used in the course of analysis of data collected in other ways. In the next chapter we shall consider the problems and procedures of analyzing data collected by whatever method in order to abstract from them the relevant information for answering research questions.

11

ANALYSIS AND
INTERPRETATION

AFTER THE DATA have been collected, the social scientist turns his full attention to their analysis and interpretation, a process consisting of a number of closely related operations. It is the purpose of *analysis* to summarize the completed observations in such a manner that they yield answers to the research questions. It is the purpose of *interpretation* to search for the broader meaning of these answers by linking them to other available knowledge. Both these purposes, of course, govern the entire research process; all preceding steps have been undertaken in order to make their fulfillment possible.

The Influence of Anticipated Analysis and Interpretation on Previous Research Steps

Before we discuss the processes involved in analysis and interpretation, let us consider a specific study from the point of view of the ways in which concern for analysis and interpretation enters into the earlier stages of an inquiry. We shall use as an example a nonexperimental study designed to investigate the effects of association with Americans on attitudes of foreign students toward Americans and toward various aspects of life in the United States (Selltiz, Hopson, and Cook, 1956).

The study was planned against the background of a number of investigations which had suggested that, under certain conditions, when members of one racial or religious group within the United States are brought into face-to-face contact with members of a different group toward which they have been prejudiced, their attitudes are likely to become more favorable. The interest in this study was in finding whether association between individuals of different *nationality* or *cultural background* would also lead to favorable attitude changes. More specifically, the question was phrased: Do foreign students who have more, and more intimate, interaction with Americans tend to develop more favorable attitudes toward the United States than foreign students who have less, and less intimate, interaction with Americans?

The ideal study design would have called for selecting a random sample from the total number of foreign students entering this country in a given year and then randomly assigning these students to situations in which they would have varying degrees and kinds of associations with Americans. Obviously, this was not feasible. The compromise solution that was arrived at was to select educational settings that seemed likely to differ in the extent to which they would provide opportunities for interaction between foreign students and Americans. Specifically, it was hypothesized that small colleges in small towns would provide relatively many opportunities for frequent and intimate contact, for the following reasons: Students at such colleges typically live in dormitories or fraternity houses, where the daily opportunities for interaction are great; the social life is likely to be concentrated on the campus, again increasing opportunities for interaction between American and foreign students; there are likely to be relatively few other foreigners, either students or community members, so that there is little possibility for a foreign student to carry on all his social life within a foreign group. It was thought that large universities in metropolitan centers would provide considerably less opportunity for close association with Americans, and that large universities in small towns would fall between these two extremes.

Students attending these three types of educational institution were to be compared, then, in the following terms: (1) the extent to which the situations they were in encouraged interaction with Americans, (2) the extent to which they entered into interaction with Americans and the nature of these interactions, and (3) their attitudes toward Americans and the United States. However, the way in which the students were selected for the study—taking individuals who were attending institutions of these three types—left open the possibility that students might have chosen different types of educational institution because of the different possibilities they offered for association with Americans. In order to check whether the three groups were in fact comparable to begin with in their inclination to seek out association with Americans, it was decided to ask the students their reasons for coming to the United States, their reasons for attending the particular college or university, whether they had chosen their living arrangements or been assigned to them, whether they preferred being at a college with relatively many or few other students from their home country, and how many Americans they expected to get to know. In order to make sure that students in the three types of institution did not differ in their initial attitudes toward the United States, it was necessary to secure measures of these attitudes as soon as possible after the students' arrival in this country (ideally, before their arrival).

If comparisons on these measures showed that students in the three types of institution did not differ in their initial attitudes nor in their inclination toward association with Americans, they could then be compared in terms of the extent to which the situations they found themselves in favored interaction with Americans—that is, in terms of the *interaction-potential* of the situations in which they were placed. It was decided that two measures of interaction-potential would be used: the nature of the student's living arrangements, and the frequency with which he was in various situations in which there were Americans whom he knew well enough to speak to.[1]

If it turned out that students in different types of institution were in situations with different interaction-potential, it would then be legitimate to consider whether students in situations with relatively high interaction-potential do in fact interact more with Americans. This brought up the question of how interaction was to be measured: in terms of the number of Americans the student knew? the variety of situations in which he participated with them? the nature of the activities in which he engaged with them? his own judgment as to whether he had made any close friends? Earlier studies offered little guidance as to what would constitute the most satisfactory measure of interaction. Since one of the goals of the study was to try to analyze *what it is* about personal interaction that leads to attitude change (assuming a relation between interaction and attitude were found), it was decided that it would be desirable to have several different measures of interaction.

Next, if it was found that students in situations with greater interaction-potential also scored higher on actual interaction—thus permit-

[1] Note that these measures constituted the "working definitions" of the concept of *interaction-potential*.

ting the conclusion that differences in extent and nature of interaction were not primarily a matter of personal choice—it would be appropriate to consider whether students with different interaction scores differed in their attitudes toward the United States. When it came to measuring attitudes, a great deal of prior work was available as background. This helped in two ways: by suggesting aspects of the United States which are of special concern to foreign students; and by indicating that provision should be made for measuring various aspects of attitude—information, opinions, feelings, understanding.

The fact that the students came from a variety of countries, together with the impression based on earlier exploratory studies that students from different countries react differently to the United States, led to planning in advance for another aspect of the analysis. It was decided that it would be valuable not only to compare the total groups of students in the three types of educational institution, but to consider separately the responses of students from countries that were judged to be relatively similar in culture to the United States (that is, countries of Europe and English-speaking countries) and those of students from countries that were judged to offer relatively sharp cultural contrasts to the United States (countries of Latin America, the Near and Middle East, Asia, and Africa).

To a considerable extent, then, the analysis of this study was shaped before the data were collected; and the anticipation of the future task of analysis and interpretation determined what went before. Although the extent of early concern with these two subsequent steps will vary from study to study, it is safe to say that no scientific inquiry should be planned without anticipating what will be done when the data are in or without being concerned with the possible interpretation of findings. Otherwise the investigator is likely to discover when it is too late that he cannot perform the analysis he wants because relevant data are missing.

The process and direction of interpretation at various steps of an inquiry will undoubtedly bear the mark of the investigator's knowledge, imagination, and wisdom. No one study can ever plan to follow through on all interpretive ideas that emerge in the course of its conduct. But this situation is hardly improved by postponing concern with interpretation to later stages, when there is little chance for anything but speculation in attempts to circumscribe the meaning of one's results or to discover alternative explanations.

The relationship between analysis and interpretation, and the particular form they take separately and jointly, vary from study to study. Problems of analysis and interpretation differ in different study designs. As a rule, they present greater difficulties in exploratory than in experimental investigations. However, since the basic principles involved in analysis—even though not all the specific procedures—apply to studies of every type, we shall not discuss different research designs separately except in cases where a certain design presents special problems in connection with a given analytic operation.

Since interpretation is often inextricably interwoven with analysis, so that it becomes a special aspect of analysis rather than a distinct operation, it may be well to precede the discussion of analytic procedures with a clarification of the process of interpretation.

As noted earlier, interpretation is the search for the broader meaning of the research findings. This search has two major aspects. First, there is the effort to establish *continuity* in social research through linking the results of one study with those of another. In the study of the attitudes of foreign students which we have been describing, the attempt was made to establish continuity between findings about the effects of personal association between members of different racial or religious groups within the United States and findings about the effects of personal association between members of different national or cultural groups when the members of one of the groups are in a foreign country. In a somewhat different sense, interpretation is involved in the transition from exploratory to experimental work. The interpretation of the former often leads to hypotheses for the latter.

Secondly, interpretation leads to the establishment of *explanatory concepts*. Had it turned out that foreign students who engaged in greater interaction with Americans were more favorable in their attitudes or showed greater attitude change, the investigators hoped to be able to deduce something about the process by which personal association affects attitudes. Had the attitude differences been greatest between students who differed in the *variety* of their experiences with Americans, the investigators might have tentatively drawn the conclusion that association changes attitudes by breaking down stereotypes. Had the attitude differences been greatest between students who differed in the *intimacy* of the activities engaged in with Americans, the inference might have been that association influences attitudes by giving the individual an opportunity to observe qualities of people that are not apparent in more superficial contacts. Had the difference been greatest between students who said they had made a *close American friend* and those who had not, the deduction might have been that it is through increasing the warmth of personal feeling that association leads to attitude change. This function of interpretation is so closely linked to the function of theory for social research that it will be dealt with in Chapter 14, which is concerned with the relation between research and theory.

Our discussion of the procedures used in analysis and interpretation will cover the following topics: the *establishment of categories*, the application of categories to the raw data through *coding*, the *tabulation of responses*, *statistical analysis of the data*, *drawing inferences about causal relations*, and the use of *nonquantified data*.

The Establishment of Categories

CLASSIFICATORY PRINCIPLES AS THE BASIS FOR SETS OF CATEGORIES

In a neighborhood survey, a sample of the population was asked the following question: "What kinds of people live in this neighborhood?" The purpose of the question was not to obtain objective information about the neighborhood (which could have been obtained more accurately and with less effort from census figures), but rather to ascertain to what extent the people in the neighborhood thought in terms of ethnic group distinctions. Here are some of the answers:

Mostly poor people like myself.
Colored people and us.
Negroes and Italians and Jews and a lot of others.
There's plenty to say about the people around here. But I don't want to get into trouble. You have to live where you can.
Colored people.
It's a tough neighborhood. All kinds of people live here.

There are some Irish, I know.
Many Jews.
A lot of niggers.
I don't really know, I'm new around here.

Clearly, if several hundred such responses are to be organized so that they can be used in answering the research questions, they must be grouped into a limited number of categories. In order to decide on the relevant categories, some principle of classification must be selected. The research question, or the hypotheses if any have been formulated, provide the basis for selecting principles of classification. Suppose that this study was concerned with awareness of the Negro group; the appropriate principle of classification would be one based on explicit reference to Negroes. This classificatory principle immediately suggests two categories:

Mentioned Negroes
Did not mention Negroes

These two categories form a "category set." A category set must meet certain basic rules:

1. The set of categories should be derived from a single classificatory principle.
2. The set of categories should be exhaustive; that is, it should be possible to place every response in one of the categories of the set.
3. The categories within the set should be mutually exclusive; it should not be possible to place a given response in more than one category within the set.

A set may consist of more than two categories, provided these rules are not violated. For example, a perusal of the answers listed above soon reveals that "Did not mention Negroes" includes many diverse responses. The person who did not want to talk about the neighbors for fear of trouble, or the one who said he was new to the neighborhood, is quite different from those who mentioned groups other than Negroes. This suggests the need for subcategories to distinguish among the different types of response that did not mention Negroes. For example, it may seem psychologically meaningful to distinguish people who did not mention Negroes but did mention other groups from people who did not mention either Negroes or any other groups. The set would then consist of three categories:

Mentioned Negroes (with or without mention of other groups)
Did not mention Negroes, but mentioned other groups
Did not mention either Negroes or other groups

A decision has to be made about how far the extension should go. Reference to the actual answers suggests that this set of categories still does not do justice to their content. The groups other than Negroes that are mentioned vary in significant ways: some respondents describe the groups in economic terms (poor people); others refer to personal attributes (tough); still others mention religious or nationality groups (Jews, Irish). Each of these attributes selected by respondents to describe the groups of which they were aware presents a possible classificatory principle that could lead to another set of categories, much as we have demonstrated for Negroes. In principle it is, of course, possible to use all these attributes for the establishment of category sets. In practice this is often uneconomical and unrewarding, because not all of these classificatory principles bear on the purposes of the investigation.

If, as we have supposed, the study was concerned with awareness of Negroes, it might seem that all of these other classificatory principles are irrelevant. But such a view is based on too narrow a notion of the task of analysis. That a certain percentage mention Negroes is not yet a sufficient indication of awareness of Negroes. It may well be that any other ethnic group in the neighborhood would have been mentioned to the same extent. Whether or not there is a special awareness of Negroes can be decided only if the mention of other racial, national, or religious groups has been coded too. However, classification of the replies in terms of mentioning economic status or personal attributes of people in the neighborhood would probably not serve any function.

In order to provide for these additional classifications of references to other ethnic groups, additional sets of categories must be set up. Each of them, however, must obey the rules given on page 392. The following list, constituting the "code" for the question, might be the final result:

Racial groups
    1. Negroes: mentioned———; not mentioned———
    2. Other racial groups: mentioned———; not mentioned———
Nationality groups
    3. Irish: mentioned———; not mentioned———
    4. Italians: mentioned———; not mentioned———
    5. Other nationality groups: mentioned———; not mentioned———
Religious groups
    6. Jews: mentioned———; not mentioned———
    7. Catholics: mentioned———; not mentioned———
    8. Protestants: mentioned———; not mentioned———
    9. Other religious groups: mentioned———; not mentioned———
 10. *Mention of groups listed above*
    Mentioned one or more———; mentioned none, but mentioned other human grouping(s)———; mentioned none, stating "I don't know"———; did not answer question———

Notice that, although we are dealing with the answers to only one question, our specific research interests have led us to provide *ten* sets of categories in which to classify the respondents. Every respondent can be placed in one of the two categories of each of the first nine sets and in one of the four categories of the final set.

Since the failure to check a specific "mentioned" may be taken to imply the corresponding "not mentioned," the appearance of the code can be simplified by omitting all of the "not mentioned" categories; but each of the first nine sets will still remain a two-category set, one category indicated by a check mark and the other by the absence of a check mark. Such simplification is, however, not always wise. The failure to check a particular "mentioned" category may represent an oversight in coding. Such oversights can be discouraged (and certainly made detectable) by requiring that the placement of a respondent in a "not mentioned" category should call for as positive an act as his placement in a "mentioned" category. Also, to anticipate a bit, when coding such data for machine tabulation, it is highly desirable that all categories should have an explicit identification. The machines in most common use count the number of cases in each category separately. The sum of the counts in all of the categories in a set should equal the total number of cases; if the "not mentioned" as well as the "mentioned" category is explicitly coded, we can check whether all cases have been accounted for.

Several qualities of this code should be pointed out. First, four major classificatory criteria have been used in developing the ten sets of categories: racial groups mentioned *versus* racial groups not mentioned; nationality groups mentioned *versus* nationality groups not mentioned; religious groups mentioned *versus* religious groups not mentioned; any of these types of group mentioned *versus* none of these types of group mentioned. It should be noted that each of these four criteria of classification yields a number of sets of categories. Thus, "nationality groups mentioned *versus* nationality groups not mentioned" includes the following sets of categories: Irish mentioned *versus* Irish not mentioned; Italians mentioned *versus* Italians not mentioned; other nationality groups mentioned *versus* other nationality groups not mentioned.

Second, the categories within each set are mutually exclusive, and they also include all the possibilities relevant to that set of categories, so that each response can be unambiguously assigned to one or the other category; for example, a given respondent either mentioned Negroes or he did not mention Negroes. (He may also have mentioned other racial groups, and Irish and Jews as well. Each of these elements of his response is taken account of separately in this code, but each can be clearly placed within its relevant set of categories.)

Third, the total code is exhaustive in the sense that a place is provided for every possible response (mainly because of the residual "catch-all" category, number 10). But, fourth, it is not exhaustive in terms of all possible classificatory principles that could be applied to the answers. In addition to those already ruled out as irrelevant to the research problem, it does not, for example, provide for distinctions between the manner, derogatory or otherwise, in which groups are referred to.

Finally, the inclusion in the list of the categories "Catholics" and "Protestants" should be mentioned. Subsequent tabulation showed that 3 per cent of the respondents had named Catholics and 0 per cent Protestants. This was actually anticipated when the categories were established. The idea of including these two groupings came in part from knowledge of the actual composition of the neighborhood, in part from an expectation and an interest in demonstrating that these two groups, although they had many members in the neighborhood, were not considered as separate or distinct to the same extent as other groups.

In this case the "categorization of absent data"—i.e., the provision of a category for a response that is expected not to occur—may have led to an obvious result, the demonstration that members of dominant or socially accepted groups are often not perceived in terms of their group membership. The principle involved, however, is far from obvious and is all too often neglected. It is based on the notion that ideas for categorization should always come from two sources: an intimate acquaintance with the evidence in hand and general knowledge and anticipatory analysis of the possible types of response, based on theoretical, logical, or practical considerations. The application of this rule for the establishment of categories leads to the possible discovery of the significant absence of some response, which might otherwise have gone unnoticed.

There are types of studies and types of data for which the establishment of categories is even simpler than in this illustration. Where check-list questions have been used, or any form of rating scale, whether applied in an interview or in an observational situation, the analyst of the data need give virtually no attention to the problem of establishing categories. His data have been precategorized in previous stages of the inquiry. This is also true in all studies in which the observations are recorded in prescribed categories. Such precategorization, when undertaken as part of the development of research instruments, is, of course, very similar to the procedure employed in establishing categories after the data have been collected.

DEFINITION OF COMPLEX CATEGORIES

In some situations the establishment of categories is considerably more difficult and more time-consuming than in the neighborhood-study illustration. What made the establishment of a set of categories relatively easy in that case was that the answers were fairly simple and clear-cut; the categories could easily be defined in a completely un-ambiguous way. Although this is the way categories should always be defined, the task is much more difficult with some types of content than with others.

For example, Merton and his colleagues (forthcoming) asked white housewives, "How would you say the colored residents feel about living in the same community with whites?" and asked Negro house-wives, "How would you say the white residents feel about living in the same community with Negroes?" The answers ranged from imputations of highly favorable attitudes to imputations of highly unfavorable attitudes. Here are some examples:

> They want to live here so they can say they are equal.
> They seem very friendly to us.
> They like the idea.
> I don't think they mind; we get along.
> Some of them like it, some don't.
> They think it lowers them.
> I don't come in contact with them so I wouldn't know.
> They hate it.

According to the preceding discussion, it would not be difficult to evolve a simple set of categories based on the classificatory principle of favorable versus unfavorable attitude imputed to the other race. In that case one category would be needed for favorable attitude, one for unfavorable, one for neutral, plus a residual category. However, distinct shades of meaning appear among both the imputed favorable attitudes and the imputed unfavorable attitudes. A person who says, "They want to live here so they can say they are equal," conveys something different from the one who says, "They like the idea." Similarly, one who says, "They think it lowers them," may mean something different from one who says, "They hate it." What is the distinctive criterion? In both cases, it would appear, some of the respondents attribute the alleged feeling of the other race to a value believed to be held by that group. Hence, the imputation of such values was used as another classificatory principle. A set of categories was developed in which one category stood for attributing the favorable attitude of the other race to a material, social, or spiritual value or benefit they derived from the situation (or for attributing their unfavorable attitude to a corresponding loss or disadvantage), and another category stood for an absence of statements about values. For the sake of simplicity in the subsequent coding operation, the two sets of categories were combined, thus:

> Favorable attitude imputed to the other race, explained in terms of values or benefits they derive from living in the same project with respondent's race.
> Favorable attitude imputed to the other race, without explicit explanation in value terms.
> Neutral or accommodative attitude imputed to the other race.
> Unfavorable attitude imputed to the other race, explained in terms of values or benefits they derive from segregation.
> Unfavorable attitude imputed to the other race, without explicit explanation in value terms.
> Other answers, no answer, don't know.

Before a list of such categories is put into use, it is necessary to specify the content of each category as accurately as possible. This is done by adding an explanatory sentence or two to each category and illustrating the meaning by examples.

In the case of the first category in the list above, for example, the explanatory sentence read: "These answers imply that the other race gets something out of living with the respondent's race. E.g.: 'They want to live here so they can say they are equal.'"

Working with such complex categories requires considerable care and effort in classification. Even when the categories have been worked out carefully, their use will present more problems than the use of categories narrowly and exactly defined. If one respondent answers, for example, "They like it all right here, they know why," it is a moot question whether or not this statement implies a benefit. Additional rules have to be established to deal with such answers. In this case, an appropriate ruling for the first category might read as follows: "This category applies only to those statements which specify the nature of the value or benefit."

SELECTING CLASSIFICATORY PRINCIPLES FOR CATEGORIZING UNSTRUCTURED MATERIAL

Special problems arise in the categorization of unstructured material, such as observational protocols, case histories, speeches of agitators, unstructured interviews, etc. We have alluded to these difficulties in earlier chapters when discussing participant observation and the use of personal documents and communication content in research.

In a study using structured instruments for gathering data relevant to clearly formulated research questions or hypotheses, the appropriate principles for classification of responses are fairly clearly prescribed by the nature of the stimulus or of the questions and by the responses. In working with unstructured evidence, however, the first problem is to arrive at decisions about which aspects of the material are to be categorized—that is, what classificatory principles are to be used in establishing sets of categories.

The establishment of principles of classification is especially difficult in exploratory studies, since such studies, by definition, do not start with explicit hypotheses. At the time of data collection, the investigator does not know which aspects may turn out to be most important. Therefore he must usually collect a large amount of data; thus, in the analysis, he has the problem of dealing not only with unstructured material but also with a vast quantity of it, much of which may prove irrelevant to his purpose.

The first step in analyzing the data of an exploratory study is to develop working hypotheses that will yield classificatory principles. The investigator usually proceeds by reading carefully through all his material, keeping alert for clues in the data. There are several procedures that may help him in his task. One is to study, if it is available, material on a group that contrasts with the one he is investigating, in order to get ideas about the important differences between the two. In a study of delinquency, for example, it is appropriate to read social agency case records not only of delinquents but also of other juveniles under the care of an agency. That is, one contrasts cases that differ noticeably in the characteristic being investigated in order to see what other concomitant differences can be perceived in the contrasting cases.

Or the investigator may sort his cases into groups that seem to belong together, and then ask himself what led him to feel that those he has placed in a single group are alike. Thus, for example, Chein et al. (1952), in a study of views of prominent Jewish educators and group workers about a number of issues in Jewish education, found it appropriate first to sort their respondents into groups that could be characterized in terms of their total outlook on the meaning of being Jewish. The investigator may find that he has grouped his cases on the basis of common characteristics; he may then examine them to see whether those who have similar characteristics have undergone similar experiences. Or he may find that his grouping is on the basis of similar experiences; he may then re-read the cases to see if these similar experiences seem to have led to similar consequences.

Another approach that may stimulate the formulation of working hypotheses is to note matters that seem surprising in view of either common-sense or theoretical expectations, and then to search for possible explanations of the surprising phenomenon. For example, Lambert and Bressler (1957), in a study of Indian students in the United States, noticed that these students often seemed more disturbed by questions about Indian problems asked by relatively well-informed Americans than they were by the stereotypes or the ignorance of those who had no information about India; even when the questions were asked with no unfriendly intent, the students seemed to interpret them as hostile criticism. This observation led to the hypothesis that, for members of colonial or formerly colonial nations, certain "sensitive areas" develop. These "sensitive areas" are aspects of the nation's culture that have historically been the object of hostile criticism by the dominant country or countries and that have been used as an excuse for keeping the nation in a subordinate status. Any reference to these areas, no matter what the intention of the individual who makes it, carries with it the historical connotations of hostility. But the outsider (in this case, the American) must have some knowledge of the student's home country in order to be aware of these problem areas; thus the questions of relatively well-informed people are more likely to touch on one of the sensitive areas. Questions of totally uninformed people, which usually do not refer to these sensitive areas, are set down to ignorance; questions referring to sensitive areas, which can be asked only by persons with some information about the country, are interpreted as evidences of hostility.

Even with clear hypotheses, however, the analysis of unstructured material presents special problems. Since, by definition, the material is not of the kind in which the same question has been answered by all respondents or the same observations have been made on all subjects, there is always the possibility that information on a given point may be missing from some of the documents. On the other hand, there is likely to be a great deal of material that is not directly relevant to the hypotheses. Moreover, there is a problem of deciding on the size of the units of material to which the categories are to be applied. When data have been gathered through a structured instrument such as a questionnaire, ordinarily each question provides a natural unit for categorization, although some sets of categories may apply to larger units, such as the questionnaire as a whole. But when one is dealing with unstructured material, there are no such convenient "natural" units. For example, if the investigator is using case records kept by social service agencies, he may categorize every act or statement made by the client, or every session of the client with a case worker, or the entire case record. He must decide which of these units is most appropriate for providing answers to his specific research questions.

Coding: The Categorization of Data

Coding is the technical procedure by which data are categorized. Through coding, the raw data are transformed into symbols—usually numerals—that may be tabulated and counted. The transformation is not, however, automatic; it involves judgment on the part of a coder.

The judgment that assigns a response to a category is often made by someone other than the person who goes by the official title of "coder." Frequently, it is the respondent himself who assigns his response to a category. This is true for many poll-type and multiple-choice questions, for example, when the individual is limited to a response of "Yes," "No," "Don't know," or to "Agree," "Disagree," "Uncertain," or to indicating by a check mark his position on a rating scale. Or the person who collects the data may categorize as he collects them. This is, of course, what is being done when an interviewer or an observer employs a rating scale to describe a person's behavior.

There are a number of advantages to having the interviewer or the observer code the data. For one thing, he is in a position to notice the situation as well as the individual's behavior. Thus, he has more information upon which to base a judgment than the coder working from the written record. Another advantage is that categorization by the data collector saves both time and labor.

Notwithstanding these advantages, categorization of complex data is usually done by coders after the data have been collected. This procedure allows time for reflection; on-the-spot judgments of an interviewer or observer may not be as discerning as judgments made with more time for deliberation. The judgments of data collectors may be colored by irrelevancies such as the appearance and mannerisms of the respondent, his accent, responses to previous questions, etc. Moreover, if each interviewer or observer categorizes only the data he collects, unreliability is likely to be increased. There is a tendency to develop a frame of reference with respect to the material that one is coding. Even if the data collectors were all perfectly consistent with one another in their use of categories initially—an unlikely assumption —they would tend to develop varying frames of reference appropriate to their limited materials, which would make their categorizations unreliable after a time. A common frame of reference is easier to obtain and check in an office coding operation than in the field.

PROBLEMS OF RELIABILITY IN CODING[2]

There are many things that may operate to make the judgments of coders[3] unreliable. These factors may arise from the data to be categorized, from the nature of the categories that are to be applied, from the coders themselves, etc. Let us briefly consider some of these factors and possible safeguards against them.

DIFFICULTIES ARISING FROM THE DATA. Many of the difficulties that occur in coding result from the inadequacies of the data. Frequently,

[2] For a general discussion of problems of reliability, see Chapter 5.

[3] We are speaking here of persons who code the data after they have been collected, not of respondents or data collectors.

the data do not supply enough relevant information for reliable coding. This may be the consequence of inadequate data-collection procedures —poorly worded questions, untrained observers, etc. Perhaps more often, however, the difficulties are of a sort that can easily be corrected by careful editing of the data.

When the interviewer or the observer hands in his material, the possibility of eliminating many potential coding difficulties still exists. A careful examination of the data as soon as they are collected and, if necessary, a systematic questioning of the interviewer or observer will avert many coding problems. The process of scrutinizing the data to improve their quality for coding is commonly called editing.[4]

Not only does editing help to avoid later coding problems; it may also markedly improve the quality of data collection by calling attention to points at which the interviewers or observers have misunderstood instructions, are not recording data in sufficient detail, etc. To serve this function, editing should be done in the course of pretesting the interview or observation schedule and of training the interviewers or observers, as well as throughout the period of data collection. In any case, if editing is to remove coding problems, it must be done while the interviewers or observers are still available for questioning.

Each interview or observation schedule should be checked for:

1. *Completeness*. All items should be filled in. A blank next to a question in an interview schedule may mean "don't know," "refused to answer," or that the question was not applicable, that the question was omitted by mistake, etc. For many purposes, it is important to be able to distinguish among these potential meanings.

2. *Legibility*. If the coder cannot decipher the handwriting of the interviewer or observer, or the abbreviations and symbols he employs, then coding is impossible. It is a simple matter to check for legibility when the material is handed in and to have it rewritten if necessary, but it is often extremely time-consuming to have the coder attempt to decipher the handwriting or to track down the interviewer once coding has begun.

3. *Comprehensibility*. Frequently a recorded behavior or response seems perfectly comprehensible to the interviewer or observer but is

---

[4] For a detailed discussion of the process of editing in large-scale surveys, consult Parten (1950, Chapter 13).

not comprehensible to another. The context in which the behavior or response occurs is known to the interviewer but not to the coder, who thus cannot visualize exactly what the subject did or understand what his answer meant. Systematic questioning of the interviewer or observer to dispel confusions and ambiguities will considerably improve the quality of the coding.

4. *Consistency.* Marked inconsistencies within a given interview or observation schedule not only make for problems in coding; they may indicate errors in collecting or recording the data. For instance, if in an interview on Negro-white relationships the reply to one question is that the respondent does not know any Negro families but a later comment reports that the respondent visits back and forth with a Negro family, there is an obvious need to inquire immediately into this inconsistency. Often the interviewer, on questioning, clears up the inconsistency. If he is not able to do so, it may be desirable to get in touch with the respondent again if the point is important to the analysis of the data.

5. *Uniformity.* By and large, adequate instructions to the interviewers or observers will result in uniform procedures for collecting and recording the data; however, it is necessary to check the uniformity with which these instructions have been followed. For example, if income is recorded in units different from those specified in the instructions—say in terms of monthly rather than weekly income—and the units of recording are not clearly indicated, coding may be disrupted.

6. *Inappropriate responses.* Occasionally a response simply is not germane to the purposes of the investigation; this is particularly likely to occur if a question is not clearly worded or not intelligently asked. It is helpful to the coder to have such responses sorted out from the appropriate responses, since the categories developed to code the answers will probably not be applicable.

DIFFICULTIES ARISING FROM THE CATEGORIES. The value of the categorization of data depends entirely on the soundness of the categories employed. Categories must be well defined from a conceptual point of view and must be relevant to the purposes of the research. As pointed out on page 392, each set of categories must also meet certain formal requisites: it must be based on a single classificatory principle, the categories must be mutually exclusive, and they must be exhaustive. Even if the categories satisfy all these conditions, however, coding will be unreliable if the categories are not clearly defined in terms of indicators that are applicable to the immediate data. Usually the categories are defined by means of examples from the data. The examples should include not only responses that typify the category but also, if possible, responses that help to distinguish the boundary lines between similar categories.

TRAINING OF CODERS. It is obvious that the reliability of coding is affected by the competence of the coders. The training of coders usually proceeds by the following steps: (1) The various codes are explained and illustrated with examples from the material to be categorized. (2) The coders then all practice on a sample of the data. Problems that arise are discussed by the coders as a group with the supervisor in order to develop common procedures and definitions. (3) Frequently, as a result of the practice coding, the categories are revised to make them better applicable to the material and to put in writing the procedures and definitions that have evolved during the preliminary coding. (4) At the point in the practice period when relatively few new problems arise, the coders work on an identical portion of the data without consulting one another or the supervisor. The consistency or reliability of the coding is then computed to determine whether it is feasible to begin coding in earnest.

In computing the consistency of coding, one may use the coding of the supervisor as a criterion against which to test the various coders, or use some measure that reflects the consistency of the group as a whole, or compare each coder with every other coder. Depending on the results of the reliability checks, one may decide to eliminate categories that seem too unreliable to be of value, or to spend more time in training, or to eliminate the coders who are most inconsistent, or to use special procedures with more difficult items (such as having the more expert analysts work with the more difficult codes or having two or more people, in consultation, work with the more difficult codes). (5) After the coding of material has begun, periodic consistency checks are necessary to ensure that the coders do not become careless as they become more experienced and that they do not develop idiosyncratic methods of handling new problems in the material. The supervisor must insist that all new problems be discussed with him. To ensure uniformity, any decisions that are made after coding has begun in earnest have to be instantly communicated to all coders.

Computing the Reliability of Coding

Obviously, the consistency and appropriateness with which a given type of answer is assigned to a given category will have an important bearing on the outcome of the analysis. Therefore it is important to check the reliability of coding, and to increase the agreement among coders as much as possible. It is difficult to set any given level of reliability as a standard that should be achieved. Different types of material present different degrees of difficulty in achieving reliability; in general, the more highly structured the material to be coded and the simpler the categories used, the higher the reliability will be. Moreover, different research purposes may demand different standards of agreement. In any case, it is desirable not only to check the reliability of coding but to make this information available to the reader when the study is reported. Increasingly, this is becoming common practice.

There are various methods of computing the reliability of coding. Since the more carefully developed methods require a more detailed statistical presentation than is appropriate here, we shall refer the reader to representative articles.[5] It should be noted, however, that perhaps the most frequent error in reliability checks is the computation of reliability coefficients that are inappropriate to the use to which the data are to be put. Thus, it is a common but mistaken procedure to report only the reliability for the gross categories and to omit reliability checks on subcategories. For example, if in analysis one is going to employ subcategories of "initiating behavior"—say, "initiating behavior which is followed by other members of a group" and "initiating behavior which is not followed by other members of the group"—it would be misleading to perform or to report a reliability check on the over-all category of "initiating behavior" only.

Tabulation

Tabulation is a part of the technical process in the statistical analysis of data. The essential operation in tabulation is *counting* to

[5] See Guetzkow (1950); Lasswell, Leites and associates (1949); Robinson (1957); Schutz (1952); Scott (1955).

determine the number of cases that fall into the various categories. The term *marginals* is commonly used to refer to simple counts of the frequencies with which the various categories in each set occur in the data; for example, the number of people who have not gone beyond grammar school, the number who have attended high school but not graduated, etc. The terms *cross-tabulation* or *breakdown* are often employed to refer to the tabulation of the number of cases that occur jointly in two or more categories—for example, tabulation of the number of cases that are both high in education and low in income. Cross-tabulation is an essential step in the discovery or testing of relationships among the variables in one's data. Later in this chapter we shall discuss this use of cross-tabulation.

Tabulation may be done entirely by hand, or it may be done by machine. Each method has advantages and disadvantages. Briefly, manual tabulation is generally less expensive and less time-consuming when there is only a small or moderate number of cases, when the number of category sets to be counted is small, and when not many cross-tabulations are to be done. As the number of cases or the number of cross-tabulations increases, the use of machine tabulators becomes progressively more economical. The number of cross-tabulations is, perhaps, the most important factor in determining the relative efficiency of one rather than the other procedure in tabulation.

Generally, the efficiency of hand tabulation tends to be underestimated. With proper techniques, hand tabulation can be quite rapid and accurate. One of the most efficient techniques uses, for each case, a small (3 x 5) code card that can be easily sorted and counted. Scores from as many category sets can be placed on a card this size as on the 80-column punch card that is commonly used in machine tabulation. By use of such devices as colors, heavy lines, etc., the codes can easily be distinguished and the cards efficiently sorted. Parten (1950)[6] reports that a relatively unskilled clerical worker can sort 1,000 of these cards into six stacks in less than five minutes. Counting is also quite rapid if small cards are used; 1,000 cards can be counted in less than five minutes, if good technique is employed. At such a rate of speed, sorting and counting by hand is likely to rival, for short

[6] See her Chapter 15 for a detailed discussion of tabulation procedures.

periods of time, the efficiency of machine tabulation for even several thousand cases.

Both machine and hand tabulation presuppose that the data have been coded and that the coding has been checked. Scores for each individual are usually transcribed onto a card for hand tabulation or onto a sheet from which a card puncher punches them onto cards for machine tabulation. Machine tabulation actually involves more clerical and other specialized operations than hand tabulation does. Card punching, the checking of machine tabulations, the transposition of the results from machine tabulation forms to tables, are all steps that are not required in hand tabulation. With a large number of cases or with many cross-tabulations, however, the speed of the machines more than compensates for the time involved in these operations.

There are a number of types of machine available; developments in this field have been extremely rapid within recent years. Some machines simply sort and count cards; others sort, count, and print the results; still others are capable of performing the most complicated statistical operations. These latter machines are extremely complex; they must be "programmed" for a given operation by a specialist in this work. If a program is not already available, programming may be quite expensive.

The cost of using a machine is very high if one considers hourly rates. However, if there is a large amount of data requiring complicated statistical treatment, the speed of the machine may more than compensate for the expense; in some cases it makes possible analyses that would not otherwise be feasible. For example, with a few hundred subjects, the computation of all the intercorrelations among a hundred variables[7] is a job that might take a statistical clerk, using an ordinary calculating machine, many months; an electronic computer, once it has been properly set up for the operation, can complete the job in an hour or so.[8]

The rapidity of even the simpler machines presents a temptation

---

[7] For one hundred variables, there are 4,950 possible intercorrelations!

[8] For a more detailed discussion of the various machines, see Baehne (1935), Eckert (1940), Leahy (1931), Parten (1950), Paton (1935), Pease (1949), and Wrigley (1957); or consult representatives of the commercial agencies that rent the machines.

to "run wild" and simply cross-tabulate every variable against every other in the hope of finding some relationships rather than to plan the analysis by considering the probable value of each operation. This procedure is most undesirable. To say nothing of the expense, it has a number of fallacies which we shall discuss later in this chapter (page 421).

Statistical Analysis of Data

Let us suppose that we have asked a thousand people, who have been selected as a sample of the adult population of England, a series of questions to gather information about their movie-going habits. Assume that we have developed a number of sets of categories and have coded the responses of each individual. The coding may be considered a method of summarizing the responses of each individual; if we were concerned only about each individual, this might be as far as we would go in the analysis. However, the purposes of our research are broader than this. We wish to know more than that a given government clerk in London goes to the movies four times a month and that an innkeeper in Yarmouth goes only once a month. Our inquiry is directed toward providing information about the adult population of England.[9]

[9] Even if we were interested primarily in individual cases, we would still find a characterization of the total population useful for study of the individual. A fact about an individual frequently takes on its significance in relation to facts about the population of which the individual is a part. Thus, if one knows that it is customary behavior for members of a group to go to the movies twice a month, we have a frame of reference against which to interpret the individual who sees five movies a month. Our picture of this same individual might be different if the average member of the group went to the movies ten times a month. Such *normative* interpretation—the evaluation of the individual's behavior in the light of the group standard—is the most common type of interpretation. This is not to deny the value of *ipsative* interpretation, in which the frame of reference is the individual himself. Thus, the fact that an individual reports going to the movies five times a month may take on varying significance depending upon whether, in the past, it was customary for him to go ten times or not to go at all. Additional meaning may be given by other intra-individual comparisons—for example, by comparing the amount of time the individual spends at the movies with the amount of time he spends reading books. For a statistical approach to the ipsative study of the individual, see Baldwin (1950) and Cattell and Luborsky (1950).

As a necessary step in characterizing this population, we must describe or summarize the data we have obtained on the sample we have studied. Tabulation is a part of this step. In addition, we must estimate the reliability of generalizations from the obtained data to the total population. Statistical methods are used to fulfill both these functions. The term *descriptive statistics* is often applied to characterize the methods employed in summarizing the obtained data, and *sampling statistics* to characterize the methods utilized in making and evaluating generalizations from the data. Since the procedures are described fully in most statistics textbooks, we shall not discuss them in detail here. However, let us briefly indicate what is involved.

DESCRIPTION OF THE DATA

In giving an adequate description of a mass of data, we usually wish to do one or another, or several, of the following things:

1. *To characterize what is "typical" in the group.* We wish to know, for example, how many movies, *on the average*, the people in our sample attend, or, perhaps, we want to know what kind of movies most of them prefer. In the terminology of statistics, we wish to get some indication of the *central tendency*. There are various measures of central tendency, each of which makes assumptions about the nature of the data. If those assumptions are not met, then the measure of central tendency may be misleading. Thus, an *arithmetic mean* or average (the sum of individual scores divided by the number of individuals) implies equality of intervals, or an interval scale.[10] It is appropriate to such data as the number of times people go to the movies each month, since here the scale is that of number itself, with equal intervals between every two whole numbers.[11] On the other hand, suppose that we had asked the respondents to rate each of

[10] See Chapter 5 for a discussion of various types of scale.

[11] *Number of times* a person goes to the movies is, of course, on a ratio scale, and *a fortiori* on an interval scale. But, strictly speaking, even this scale violates one of the assumptions involved in the use of the arithmetic average. This scale is *discrete*; i.e., only integers are possible. What, for instance, does it mean to say that a person has gone to the movies 1.763 times? The arithmetic average presupposes a *continuous* scale; i.e., one in which all fractional values are possible. Sometimes, however, the attribution of continuity to a discrete scale is a convenient fiction.

several types of movie (comedies, documentaries, etc.) on a scale that attempted to gauge preference in terms of frequency of seeing such films; for example, "I go to see almost all the films of this type that are shown, . . . I occasionally go to see films of this type, . . . I seldom go to see films of this type, . . . I avoid films of this type." If we were to assign the numbers 1 to 4 to these four scale positions and average the rating for each type of film, the average would have no clear meaning, since there is no reason to believe that the scale positions are equally distant from one another. In such a case, it would be preferable to employ the *median* (the point on the scale above which— and correspondingly, below which—50 per cent of the cases lie). Or suppose that we had simply asked each respondent to check which of various types of film he preferred. Here the data would be in the form of a nominal scale, since various types of film have no relation of order to one another. In this case, the only appropriate method for measuring the central tendency would be the *mode* (the score that occurs with the greatest frequency—in this case, the type of film mentioned by the greatest number of respondents).

The various measures of central tendency not only make different assumptions about the nature of the data but provide somewhat different kinds of information. The arithmetic mean may be thought of as the point on the scale around which the cases balance: one case at one extreme of the distribution, for example, may be counterbalanced by one or more cases at the other extreme. If the cases are not symmetrically distributed around this point, the arithmetic mean may be very misleading in certain respects. Thus, it takes a very large number of cases of low income to counterbalance one case of a person whose annual income comes to over a million dollars; as a consequence, the arithmetic mean of income is far above the income of the vast majority of the population. It does not follow that knowledge of the mean income is pointless information; whether it has point depends on what you want to do with it. The median also implies a concept of balance, but, since it takes account only of the ordinal positions of scores rather than of their absolute values, one millionaire *is* counterbalanced by one pauper.

The use of the mode dispenses with the idea of a point of balance. In fact, it is possible to have several modes in one distribution; for example, frequency of movie-going may be *bimodal*, with a large number of people going once a week, another large number going less than once a month. As a rule, *multimodal* distributions such as this come about as a result of the intermingling of distinct populations. In our illustration, for example, going to the movies once a week may be the mode for people under 25; going less than once a month, the mode for an older group. However, it is not always easy to identify the basis of distinction.

It is also possible for a distribution of scores to have no mode at all, every score occurring about as frequently as every other. In this case, as in the case of bimodal and multimodal distributions, it is perhaps misleading to speak of *central tendency*, a term suggesting that the cases tend to cluster around some point more or less in the middle of the distribution. But even in these instances, the arithmetic mean and the median may be useful in bringing out aspects of the distributions which they describe.

2. *To indicate how widely individuals in the group vary.* We might wish to know, for example, whether the people in our sample are similar in their film preferences, so that most people prefer films of a given type, or whether there is great diversity. Or we might wish to know whether there is much variation in the frequency of movie-going among the sample being studied. There are many measures of interindividual variation. The purpose of each of them is to indicate how similar or how different the individuals in the group are with respect to a given characteristic. Some of the common measures are the range, the average deviation, the standard deviation, and the quartile deviation.

As with measures of central tendency, each of the measures of variability makes assumptions about the nature of the measurements and gives somewhat different kinds of information. The range shows the extremes of variation in the group; it might show, for example, that at least one person never goes to the movies, while at least one other goes every day. Obviously, the range is affected by extreme cases, and therefore may be misleading as a picture of the group as a whole. To avoid this difficulty, other measures of variation focus on the limits within which half of the group fall, or on the average distance of individuals from the group mean. The *quartile deviation* shows the points within which the central half of the cases fall; like the median, it assumes that the data correspond to an ordinal scale. The *average deviation* and the more frequently used *standard deviation* are measures of the average distance of individuals from the group mean; like the mean, they assume that the data correspond to an interval scale.

3. *To show other aspects of how the individuals are distributed with respect to the variable being measured.* For example, is the number of people who do not go to the movies at all about the same as the number who go three times a month? Or do relatively many people go three times a month, while relatively few do not go at all and relatively few go six or more times a month? If you plotted the figures on a graph, using the frequency of movie-going on the horizontal axis and the number of people reporting each frequency on the vertical axis, what would be the shape of the resulting graph? Is it rectangular (that is, are there equal numbers of people at each point on the scale, resulting in a graph that takes the form of a straight line across the page); or is it a bell-shaped or "normal" distribution; or is it an asymmetrical curve, with a piling up of cases at one side or the other; or does it have more than one mode (that is, is there a piling up of cases at two or more points along the scale, with relatively few cases in between)?[12]

Knowing the shape of the distribution curve is fundamental to the use of efficient statistical methods, since the more efficient methods make specific assumptions about the nature of the distribution curve. It is common to assume that the distribution curve for any variable is normal, but this may not be so. If it is not, one may see whether other known distribution curves fit the data or whether one can transform the raw data by mathematical manipulation to a known distribution.

4. *To show the relation of the different variables in the data to one another.* We wish to know, for example, whether, within our sample, the frequency of movie-going or the preference for different types of movies seems related to income, to sex, to age, etc. That is, we wish to know whether a variation in one characteristic is associated with or paralleled by variations in another characteristic. There are several methods of determining the relationship between variables.

[12] For a fuller discussion of these aspects of distribution, look up *skewness* and *kurtosis* in almost any statistics textbook. An unusually thorough and not overly technical discussion of various types of distribution may be found in Smith and Duncan (1945).

None of these methods in itself, however, permits the conclusion that an association or correlation between variables in one's data is indicative of a causal relationship. The imputation of causality requires an approximation to the logical model discussed in Chapter 4, pages 80–94. Later in this chapter we shall discuss the use of analytic procedures in drawing inferences about causal relationships in nonexperimental studies.

5. *To describe the differences between two or more groups of individuals.* For example, we may wish to compare the movie-going habits of those members of our sample who live in communities of less than 10,000 (whom we shall, for convenience, call rural residents) and of those members who live in communities of 10,000 or more (whom we shall call urban residents). This is, of course, a special case of showing the relationship between two variables. We distinguish it solely because in much social research interest is focused on the comparison of groups. Although such comparisons most commonly involve measures of central tendency, they need not be limited to this; they may include comparison of measures of variation within the groups or of the relations among variables in the two groups. It might be, for example, that the average frequency of movie-going is similar in the two groups but that there is greater variation among urban than among rural residents, or vice versa.

Generalization to the Populations from Which the Samples Were Drawn

Suppose that we have studied samples of rural and urban Englishmen and that our results show differences between the two samples. One may ask whether the differences that have been obtained reflect true differences between rural and urban Englishmen, or whether the two samples might have differed to this extent by chance even though the total rural and urban populations are alike in their movie-going habits. Through statistical procedures, one is able to answer such a question in terms of a statement of probability.

When we are contrasting samples or studying the differences between experimental and control groups, we usually wish to test some hypothesis about the nature of the true difference between the larger populations represented by the samples. Most commonly, in the social sciences, we are still concerned with relatively crude hypotheses (for example, that urban residents go to the movies more often than rural residents); we are usually not in a position to consider more specific hypotheses (for example, that they go to the movies *twice* as often). Suppose our data show that our sample of urban Englishmen attend an average of three motion pictures a month and that our sample of rural Englishmen attend an average of only two motion pictures. Clearly, the findings within our samples are in line with the hypothesis: urban residents attend the movies more often than rural residents. But we know that the findings based on our samples are not very likely to be exactly the same as the findings we would obtain if we had interviewed all the adults in England. (See Appendix B for a discussion of this point and of ways of estimating how much the findings for each of the samples are likely to differ from the true state of affairs in the population it represents.) Now we want to estimate whether, if we had interviewed the total population, we would still have found more frequent movie attendance on the part of urban residents. This we do, ordinarily, by testing the *null hypothesis*—in this case, the hypothesis that in the English population as a whole, rural and urban residents do *not* differ in frequency of movie-going. Various statistical techniques (called statistical *tests of significance*) have been devised, which tell us the likelihood that our two samples might have differed as much as they do by chance even if there were *no* difference between urban and rural Englishmen as a whole.[13]

It may seem odd that, when interested in one hypothesis (that there *is* a difference between the two populations represented by our samples), we should test its opposite (that there is *no* difference). But the reason is not too difficult to follow. Since we do not know the true state of affairs in the population, all we can do is make inferences about it on the basis of our sample findings. If we are comparing two groups,

[13] Which method of testing significance is appropriate depends on the nature of the measurements used and the distribution of the characteristic. Most of the tests commonly described in statistics textbooks assume that the measurements are in the form of at least interval scales and that the distribution of the characteristic is normal. These conditions, however, are seldom met in social research. In recent years, a number of statistical tests have been developed that do not rest on these assumptions; they are called *nonparametric* or *distribution-free* statistics. For a presentation of tests of this type, see Siegel (1956).

there are obviously two possibilities: either the two populations are alike, or they are different. Suppose that our *samples* from the two populations are different on a particular measure or attribute. Clearly, this would be likely to happen if the two populations from which the samples are drawn do in fact differ on that attribute. However, it does not in itself constitute evidence that they *do* differ, since there is always the possibility that the samples do not correspond exactly to the populations they are intended to represent. We must consider the possibility that the element of chance which is involved in the selection of a sample may have given us samples which differ from each other even if the two populations do not differ. Thus the crucial question is: Is it likely that we would have come up with samples that differ to this extent if the two populations were actually alike? This is the question the test of the null hypothesis answers; it tells us what the chances are that two samples differing to this extent would have been drawn from two populations that are in fact alike.[14] Only if the statistical test indicates that it is improbable that two samples differing to this extent could have been drawn from similar populations can we conclude that the two populations probably differ from each other.

Suppose, however, that our findings show no difference between the two samples; let us say that in our samples, both rural and urban Englishmen attend the movies, on an average, two and one-half times a month. Can we then conclude that the total populations of rural and urban Englishmen are alike in frequency of movie-going? Not with any certainty. Just as there is the possibility that samples may differ when the populations are alike, so there is the possibility that samples may be alike when in fact the populations differ. Thus, if our two samples are alike, all we can conclude is that we have no evidence that the populations differ—in other words, that the idea that the two populations are alike is tenable.

But to go back to the case where the two samples differ. We can affirm that the two populations they represent probably differ if we

[14] It should be kept in mind that all statistical tests of significance, and thus all generalizations from samples to populations, rest on the assumption that the samples are not biased—that is, that the cases to be included in the samples have been selected by some procedure that gives every case in the population an equal, or at least a specifiable, chance of being included in the sample. If this assumption is not justified, significance tests become meaningless.

can reject the null hypothesis—that is, if we can show that the obtained difference between the two samples would be unlikely to appear if the two populations were in fact the same. It is, however, in the nature of probability that even highly improbable events can sometimes happen. Thus, we can never be absolutely certain of our generalizations to the total population. Whenever we reject the null hypothesis, there is some chance that we are wrong in doing so.

However, since we are always dealing with inferences and probabilities, there is always also some chance that if we *accept* the null hypothesis, we are wrong in doing so. That is, even if our statistical test indicates that the sample differences might easily have arisen by chance even if the two populations are alike, it may nevertheless be true that the populations differ.

In other words, we are always confronted with the risk of making one of two types of error. We can reject the null hypothesis when, in fact, it is true; that is, we may conclude that there is a difference between the two populations when, in fact, they are alike. This is commonly referred to as the *Type I* error. Or, on the other hand, we can accept the null hypothesis as tenable when, in fact, it is false; that is, we may conclude that the two populations are alike when, in fact, they are different. This is referred to as the *Type II* error.

The risk of making the Type I error is determined by the *level of significance* we accept in our statistical testing. Thus, if we decide that we will conclude that the populations truly differ whenever a test of significance shows that the obtained difference between two samples would be expected to occur by chance not more than 5 times in 100 if the two populations were in fact alike, we are accepting 5 chances in 100 that we will be wrong in rejecting the null hypothesis. We can reduce the risk of a Type I error by making our criterion for rejecting the null hypothesis more extreme; for example, by rejecting the null hypothesis only if the statistical test indicates that the sample difference might have appeared by chance only once in a hundred times, or once in a thousand times, or once in ten thousand times. Unfortunately, however, the chances of making Type I and Type II errors are inversely related. The more we protect ourselves against the risk of making a Type I error (that is, the less likely we are to conclude that two populations differ when in fact they do not), the more likely we are to make a Type II error (that is, to fail to recognize population differences which actually exist). Once we have determined the degree of Type I risk we are willing to run, the only way of reducing the possibility of Type II error is to take larger samples and/or to use statistical tests that make the maximum use of available relevant information.[15]

The inverse relationship of the risks of the two types of error makes it necessary to strike a reasonable balance. In the social sciences, it is more or less conventional to reject the null hypothesis when the statistical analysis indicates that the observed difference would not occur more than 5 times out of 100 by chance alone. If the statistical analysis indicates that the difference between the two samples might have appeared by chance more than 5 times out of 100, the null hypothesis is not rejected. But these conventions are useful only when there is no other reasonable guide. The decision as to just how the balance between the two kinds of error should be struck must be made by the investigator. In some instances, it is obviously more important to be sure of rejecting a hypothesis when it is false than to fail to accept it when it is true. In other cases, the reverse may be true. This may be seen clearly in an example from everyday life, outside the sphere of statistical analysis. In many countries it is considered more important to reject a hypothesis of guilt when it is false than to fail to accept this hypothesis when it is true; a person is considered not guilty so long as there is reasonable doubt as to his guilt. In other countries, the acceptance of a false hypothesis of guilt is deemed less costly than the rejection of this hypothesis if it were true; a person charged with a crime is considered guilty until he has demonstrated his lack of guilt.

In much research, of course, there is no clear basis for deciding whether a Type I or a Type II error would be more costly, and so the investigator makes use of the conventional level for determining statistical significance. However, there are some studies in which one type of error would clearly be more costly than the other. Suppose that in a certain school it has been suggested that a new method of teaching arithmetic would be more effective; suppose also that this method would require expensive equipment for each arithmetic class. An

---

[15] For a discussion of the extent to which different types of statistical test offer protection against Type II errors, consult a statistics textbook that discusses this matter; for example, Dixon and Massey (1957, Chapter 14); or Walker and Lev (1953, pages 60–67).

experiment is set up to test whether the new method would in fact lead to better learning of arithmetic. Two groups of children are randomly selected; they may also be matched in arithmetic ability and achievement and in other relevant respects. One is taught by the new method, one by the old. Since the new method requires expensive equipment, the school system would not wish to adopt it unless there were considerable assurance of its superiority; in other words, it would be costly to make a Type I error and conclude that the new method is better when in fact it is not. On the other hand, if there were no difference in the expense of the two methods, a Type I error would not be especially costly, whereas a Type II error might lead to failure to adopt the new method when in fact it is superior.

Let us go back to the fact that any generalization from samples to populations is simply a statement of statistical probability, of the chances that a given difference between samples reflects a true difference between the populations. Let us say that we have decided to work with a 5 per cent level of confidence. This means that we will reject the hypothesis of no difference between the populations only if a sample difference as large as the one we have found can be expected to occur by chance 5 times or less in 100; if such a difference can be expected more than 5 times in 100, we will accept the null hypothesis. Is there any way of estimating whether or not our finding represents one of the 5 times that such a difference might have appeared by chance? On the basis of an isolated finding, there is not; but we can draw further inferences by examining patterns within our findings.

Suppose that we are interested in testing the effects of a series of lectures about the United Nations on attitudes toward that body. We have set up a careful study design, with randomly selected experimental and control groups, perhaps also matched in terms of initial attitudes, with precautions to assure the frankness of responses, etc. Now suppose that we use as our measure of attitudes toward the United Nations only one item—say, attitudes toward the establishment of a U.N. police force. We find that those who have attended the lectures are more favorable on this question than those who have not, and a statistical test indicates that the difference would not have appeared by chance due to random sampling fluctuations more than 5 times in 100. However, this has the corollary that it *might* have appeared by chance 5 times in 100, and we have no way of knowing whether this is one of those 5 times. Let us say, however, that we have asked 20 different questions that are reasonable indicators of attitude toward the United Nations. If we are using a confidence level such that we accept as significant a difference that might have occurred by chance 5 times in 100, then, if we had 100 questions, we might expect to find, by chance, statistically significant differences on 5 of them; out of 20 questions, we might expect to find, by chance, a difference on 1 of them. But suppose we find that on 12 of our 20 questions those who have attended the lectures are more favorable than those who have not. We may feel much safer in concluding that there is a true difference in attitudes, even though on each question the statistical test indicates that the difference might have arisen by chance 5 times in 100.

What if, out of the 20 questions, only the one about a U.N. police force shows a statistically significant difference between the two groups? This difference might well have occurred by chance; on the other hand, it may be that the lectures actually did influence opinions on this point though on no other. Unless our hypotheses specifically predicted that the lectures would be more likely to affect beliefs about an international police force than any of the other 19 items, we are not justified in making this latter interpretation, no matter how convincingly we may argue (after we have the finding) that the content of the lectures was such that they were especially likely to affect beliefs about an international police force. For if it had happened that the one item that showed a change dealt with the veto power in the Security Council, we might (in the absence of specific predictions about which items would be most affected) discover in the lectures material especially likely to change beliefs about the veto power. In other words, given any two variables that show a statistically significant relationship, an investigator usually finds it possible to propose an explanation for the relationship. However, the critical test of an obtained relation is not the ex post facto rationales and explanations for it, but rather the ability to predict it or to predict other relationships on the basis of it.[16] Thus, our unpredicted finding of a difference in

[16] As pointed out in Chapter 5, "prediction" in this context is not limited in meaning to the forecasting of future occurrences; it includes also the announcing of past or current events prior to knowledge of their occurrence.

attitudes toward a U.N. police force, even though "statistically significant," cannot be considered as established by the study we have carried out. It may, however, provide a fruitful hypothesis for a future study.

This point is clear enough as an abstract principle, but its implications are frequently ignored in analyzing and reporting data. Sometimes an investigator "runs wild" with an IBM machine and relates every variable to every other variable; it is then to be expected that a specified proportion of the relationships will appear statistically significant. Or he may first inspect the data for relationships and analyze only those that appear to be statistically significant. In either case, if he reports only those relationships that turned out to be statistically significant, the report may be entirely misleading, since the reader has no basis for judging whether these relationships form a consistent pattern within the findings or whether they are such a small proportion of the total number of relationships that it is more reasonable to assume their chance occurrence.

Since statistical statements are always statements of probability, we can never rely on statistical evidence alone for a judgment of whether or not we will accept a hypothesis as true. Confidence in the interpretation of a research result requires not only statistical confidence in the reliability of the finding (i.e., that the differences are not likely to have occurred by chance) but, in addition, evidence about the validity of the presuppositions of the research.[17] This evidence is necessarily indirect. It comes from the congruence of the given research findings with other knowledge about which there is considerable assurance. Even in the most rigorously controlled investigation, the establishment of confidence in the interpretations of one's results or in the imputation of causal relationships requires repetition of research and the relating of the findings to those of other studies.

It is important to recognize that even when statistical tests and the findings of a number of studies suggest that there is indeed a consistent difference between two groups, or a consistent relationship between two variables, this still does not constitute evidence of *the*

---

[17] Some of the common presuppositions are that the measures are relevant to the variables included in the hypothesis and that the effect of extraneous variables has been controlled or taken into account. These points were discussed in greater detail in Chapter 4.

reason for the relationship. If we want to make causal inferences—that is, to say that one variable or event has led to another—we must meet assumptions over and above those required for establishing the existence of a relationship. This point is discussed in detail in Chapter 4; analytic procedures that provide a basis for judging whether these assumptions have been met in nonexperimental studies are considered in the following section of this chapter.

One further point should be mentioned. The fact that a result is *statistically* significant does not necessarily mean that it is *socially* or *psychologically* significant. Many statistically significant differences are trivial. For example, given enough cases,[18] an average difference in intelligence between men and women of less than one IQ point may be statistically significant, but it is difficult to see any real import in the finding. On the other hand, there are cases where a small but reliable difference has great practical importance. For example, in a large-scale survey designed to give information about a population, a difference of one half of 1 per cent may represent hundreds of thousands of people, and knowledge of the difference may be important for policy decisions. One must constantly be concerned with the social and psychological meaning of one's findings as well as their statistical significance.

Inferring Causal Relations

As pointed out in Chapter 4, if one wishes to draw the inference that one variable (X) is the "cause" of another (Y), three types of evidence are necessary: (1) that X and Y vary together in the way predicted by the specific hypothesis; (2) that Y did not precede X in time; and (3) that other factors did not determine Y. It was pointed out that carefully controlled experiments provide evidence relevant to all these points. They do so by setting up randomly selected groups, one of which is then exposed to X while the other is not; the influence of other factors is taken into account more or less extensively, depend-

---

[18] The larger a sample, the less likely are findings based on it to deviate from the true state of affairs in the population. Tests of significance therefore take into account the number of cases in the sample. The larger the samples, the greater the likelihood that a given difference between them is statistically significant. For a more detailed discussion of this point, see Appendix B.

ing on the particular study design. Experimental studies present no special problems of analysis, since the precautions against invalid inference are built into the study design.

In nonexperimental studies designed to test causal hypotheses, however, the investigator must find substitutes for the safeguards that are built into experimental studies.[19] Many of these safeguards enter at the time of planning data collection, often in the form of providing for the gathering of information about a number of variables that might be alternative determinants of Y. By introducing these additional variables into the analysis, the investigator approximates some of the controls that are inherent in experiments. But the drawing of inferences of causality always remains somewhat hazardous in nonexperimental studies. In view of its many hazards, causal attribution in the analysis of studies not following an experimental design will be examined in some detail in the following pages.[20]

If a relationship or association between two variables has been established in a study that did not follow a rigorous experimental design, and if the research interest is in causal relationships rather than in the simple fact of association between the variables, the analysis has taken only its first step. The investigator must consider whether Y (or the variation in Y) might have occurred before X, in which case it cannot be an "effect" of X. Assumptions about the time relations between X and Y rest either on logical considerations, or on attempts to establsh (either by measurement before exposure to X or on an ex post facto basis) that the groups being compared did not differ in terms of Y before exposure to X, or on both. Several of the studies discussed in Chapter 4, pages 127–142, make use of assumptions and evidence of this sort.

In addition—and, sometimes, more important—the investigator must consider whether factors other than X may be the determinants of Y. In general, this is done by introducing additional variables into the analysis and examining how the relationship between X and Y is affected by these further variables. If the relationship between X and

[19] See Chapter 4 for discussion of nonexperimental studies designed to test causal hypotheses, and problems of drawing inferences from them.

[20] Much of the following discussion is indebted to Hyman (1955, Part III), and to Kendall and Lazarsfeld (1950). For a fuller discussion, consult these sources.

Y persists even when other presumably relevant variables are introduced, the hypothesis that X is a cause of Y remains tenable. The procedure followed in the Deutsch-Collins study of the effect of occupancy pattern in interracial housing projects on attitudes toward Negroes, described in Chapter 4, pages 138–139, provides an example. Here it was found that introduction into the analysis of the variables of political orientation, education, and religion did not affect the relation between X and Y; whatever their religion, education, or political views, white housewives living in integrated projects had more friendly feelings toward Negroes in the project than did housewives in segregated projects.

In other cases, however, introduction of additional variables may change the relation between X and Y: it may reduce or eliminate it; or it may enhance the relationship within one subgroup, reduce it within another. If the relationship between X and Y is enhanced in a subgroup characterized by Z and reduced in a subgroup not characterized by Z, we may conclude that Z is a *contingent condition* for the relationship between X and Y, or, in other words, that we have *specified a condition* under which the relationship holds. If Z reduces or eliminates the relationship between X and Y, we may conclude *either* that X is not a determining condition of Y (that is, that the relationship is *spurious*), or that we have *traced the process* by which X leads to Y. Let us consider first the circumstances under which we would conclude that an apparent relationship between X and Y has been shown to be spurious, next those under which we would conclude that the process of the relationship has been traced, and finally those under which we would conclude that a contingent condition has been specified.

Spurious Relationships

An apparent relationship between two variables, X and Y, is said to be *spurious* if their concomitant variation stems, not from a connection between them, but from the fact that each of them is related to some third variable or combination of variables that does not serve as a link in the process by which X leads to Y. The study of attitudes of foreign students described at the beginning of this chapter provides an example of a bit of analysis concerned with testing whether an apparent causal relationship might be spurious. One of the hypotheses of the study was that students who associated more with Americans would be more aware of differences among individuals and subgroups in the United States—that is, less likely to think of Americans in terms of stereotypes. Since the phrasing of the interview questions suggested that generalizations could be made (for example, "Which of the characteristics on this list would you say was most typical of Americans?"), the score on this variable was based on the number of times the student introduced into his replies the idea that a generalized answer must be qualified in terms of individual or subgroup differences.

Let us suppose that, when students were classified as low, medium, or high on an index of interaction with Americans, the findings were as shown in Table 1A; that is, that students who scored higher in interaction with Americans were more likely to qualify generalized statements about them.

TABLE 1A
(Hypothetical data)

	No.	% making qualifications
Low interaction	107	64
Medium interaction	101	72
High interaction	140	77
Total	348	72

Such a finding would have been in line with the hypothesis. Nevertheless, since the study was not an experimental one, in which students were randomly assigned to the different levels of interaction, it would be necessary to consider whether other factors might have accounted for this observed relationship between interaction with Americans and reluctance to generalize about them. One such factor might be the students' nationality. Suppose that it had already been found that students from Europe were more likely to score high in interaction with Americans than students from other parts of the world, and that European and non-European students differed in many of their views about the United States. A next step in the analysis would have been to "control for" nationality—that is, to examine the relationship between interaction with Americans and qualification of generalized statements about them separately within the European and the non-European group.

Suppose that the results were as shown in Table 1B. From this

TABLE 1B
(Hypothetical data)

	Students from Europe		Students from Other Parts of the World	
	No.	% making qualifications	No.	% making qualifications
Low interaction	17	84	90	63
Medium interaction	45	78	56	68
High interaction	90	82	50	68
Total	152	79	196	65

table, one would conclude that association with Americans does not lead to qualification of generalized statements about them, and that the observed relation between these two variables stemmed from the fact that European students were both more likely to associate with Americans and more likely to qualify their statements about them. The "No." *columns* show more than half the European students (90 out of 152) as scoring high on interaction with Americans, and almost half the non-European students (90 out of 196) as scoring low. The percentages in the "Total" row show European students as more likely to qualify their statements; according to these hypothetical figures, 79 per cent of them did so, compared with 65 per cent of the non-Europeans. The columns headed "Percentage making qualifications" indicate that neither among the European nor among the non-European students did the extent of interaction with Americans make any marked difference in the frequency with which students qualified their generalized statements. In other words, on the basis of such a pattern of findings, one would conclude that the relationship between amount of interaction with Americans and the likelihood of qualifying generalizations about Americans was *spurious*.

Tracing the Process Involved in a Relationship

The same study of foreign students provides an example of a piece of analysis from which it was concluded that part of the process by which X led to Y had been traced. The investigators had found, as they had predicted, that foreign students in three types of educational institution differed in their scores on a measure of "intimacy of association" with Americans. Mean scores of students in the three types of institution are shown in Table 2A.

TABLE 2A

	No.	Mean "intimacy" score
Students in small colleges	77	2.43
Students in non-metropolitan universities	139	2.17
Students in metropolitan universities	132	1.69

Such a finding suggests a question as to what about the three types of institution makes for greatest intimacy of association between foreign students and Americans in small colleges, least in metropolitan universities. This question had been considered in planning the study. It had been predicted that the three types of institution would differ in the opportunities they offered for association between foreign students and Americans, and especially in the extent to which the living arrangements provided for students would encourage such association. Therefore each student was given a score on the "interaction-potential" of his living arrangements—that is, the extent to which the circumstances under which he lived were likely to provide opportunities for association with Americans.[21] In order to check the hypothesis that it was largely through such differences in living arrangements that the three types of institution produced differences in interaction with Americans, type of institution and "interaction-potential" of living arrangements were considered together in relation to mean scores for

[21] For example, living in a fraternity house or having an American roommate were scored as situations of "high interaction-potential"; living, without an American roommate, in an apartment or a rooming house or other building not primarily occupied by American students was scored as a situation of "low interaction-potential."

"intimacy of association with Americans." The results are shown in Table 2B.

TABLE 2B

	Students in "Low Interaction-potential" Living Arrangements		Students in "Medium Interaction-potential" Living Arrangements		Students in "High Interaction-potential" Living Arrangements	
	No.	Mean "intimacy" score	No.	Mean "intimacy" score	No.	Mean "intimacy" score
Students in small colleges	7	1.43	20	2.45	50	2.56
Students in non-metropolitan universities	38	1.46	40	1.93	61	2.77
Students in metropolitan universities	64	1.16	34	1.79	34	2.59
All students	109	1.28	94	1.99	145	2.65

Reading across the rows, we see that the "interaction-potential" of living arrangements is strongly related to the student's score on intimacy of association with Americans. Whether we consider the row for small colleges, for non-metropolitan universities, for metropolitan universities, or for "all students," in every case there is an increase in the mean intimacy score with an increase in interaction-potential of living arrangements. Moreover, after reading the "No." entries across the rows, it becomes clear that type of institution and interaction-potential of living arrangements are highly related; approximately two thirds of the students in small colleges (50 out of 77) are in living arrangements with high interaction-potential, compared with less than half of those in non-metropolitan universites, and only about a quarter of those in metropolitan universities. Now, when we read the intimacy scores down the columns, we see that the relationship between type of institution and intimacy of association with Americans has been considerably reduced; in fact, for students in living arrangements with high interaction-potential, there is no relationship between type of institution and intimacy score. From this set of relation-

ships, the investigators concluded that their prediction had been correct
—that is, that one of the major ways in which a given type of educational institution encourages association between foreign students and
Americans is by providing living arrangements that offer considerable
opportunity for such association. Rather than concluding that the
relationship between type of educational institution attended and
intimacy of association with Americans was spurious, they felt that
they had *traced the process* by which the former variable influenced the
latter.

CRITERIA FOR DECIDING WHETHER A RELATIONSHIP IS SPURIOUS

What are the differences between these examples that lead us to
conclude, in the first, that the original relationship was spurious, and,
in the second, that we have traced the process through which the
relationship came about? In both cases, introduction of a third variable,
which was related to each of the variables in the initial relationship, reduced or eliminated the relation between them. One difference is apparent, however. In the former example, the third variable (nationality) was clearly *prior in time* to the other two (interaction with Americans, and qualification of generalized statements about them). In the
latter example, this was not the case. The third variable ("interaction-
potential" of living arrangements) did *not* occur before the assumed
causal variable (attending a given type of educational institution); it
was concurrent with it, and might be thought of as starting *after* the
student had begun attending the institution.

The time sequence (known or assumed) of the variables, then, is
an important consideration in deciding whether an apparent causal
relationship is spurious. If the third variable, Z, which removes the
relationship between the originally related variables X and Y, is assumed to have occurred before both X and Y, we usually conclude
that the apparent causal relationship between X and Y is spurious.
If, on the other hand, Z is known or assumed to have occurred at the
same time as X, or after X, we may conclude that what we have done
is trace the process by which X leads to Y, rather than showing the
apparent causal relationship between X and Y to be spurious.

However, the decision whether we have demonstrated a relationship to be spurious or have traced the process by which it comes about need not depend only on the *time* relationships among the variables; it may involve also a judgment about *logical* or *psychological* relationships. Take the relationship between type of institution attended and intimacy of association with Americans. Suppose the third variable, Z, which reduced the relationship between type of institution and intimacy of association was not "interaction-potential" of living arrangements but the way the student spent his Christmas vacation. Let us say that many students who were attending small colleges, and few of those attending metropolitan universities, spent their Christmas vacations with American families, and that it was this experience which led to the difference in intimacy scores. Whether we would consider that this bit of analysis showed the apparent causal relation between type of institution and intimacy of association to be spurious, or whether we would consider that it showed the process by which type of institution influenced intimacy of association, would depend on our judgment of the nature of the relationship between type of institution and manner of spending Christmas vacation. If we had reason to believe that those students who spent their Christmas vacation with American families were visiting with classmates, we would probably infer that attending a smaller college encouraged relationships that led to these invitations, which in turn led to greater intimacy of association with Americans. In this case, we would be inclined to feel that we had traced something of the process by which attending a certain type of institution influences intimacy of association with Americans. On the other hand, we might have reason to believe that invitations to spend Christmas vacation with American families came through some central organization and were distributed without attention to the type of institution; that it was a matter of *chance* that more students from small colleges spent their vacations with American families. In this case, we would probably conclude that the apparent causal relation between type of institution and intimacy of association was spurious. In other words, in instances where the third variable, Z, occurs simultaneously with or after the assumed causal variable, X, the inference that the apparent causal relationship between X and Y is or is not to be considered spurious depends on a judgment as to whether Z is or is not a consequence of X.[22]

In the analysis of nonexperimental studies, there is always a possibility of interpreting spurious relationships as causal. Thus, to have any confidence in causal relationships inferred from such studies, it is necessary to subject them to the critical test of eliminating other possibly relevant variables. For this reason it is important to collect, in the course of the study, data on possibly influential variables other than those with which the hypotheses of the study are centrally concerned.

SPECIFICATION OF A RELATIONSHIP

The inference that an assumed relationship is spurious or that one has traced the process through which it occurs is made only if the introduction of a third variable or combination of variables leads to the reduction or elimination of the initially found relationship. However, the introduction of a third variable may have still another effect; it may lead to an intensification of the relationship within one subgroup and its reduction within another. In this case, we say that we have *specified* a condition under which the relationship holds.[23]

Let us illustrate the process of specification. Suppose that, in a hypothetical study, we have found a relationship between income and educational level, such as that shown in Table 3A.

TABLE 3A
(Hypothetical data)

	Number	Percentage Earning Less than $3000	Percentage Earning $3000 or More
Graduated from high school	500	32	68
Did not graduate from high school	500	82	18
Total	1,000	57	43

The relationship is a fairly marked one. However, we may decide that it requires further specification; we may wish to know more about

[22] A number of procedures that may be built into the plan of data collection in order to provide a basis for judgments about the time sequence of variables and their logical connections are discussed in Chapter 4, pages 130–136.

[23] "Specifying a condition under which a relationship holds" is essentially the same process as demonstrating "interaction" between variables by means of an analysis of variance (see Chapter 4, pages 122–125).

the conditions under which it occurs. Suppose the thought strikes us that racial discrimination might severely curtail the advantages of education in the competition for remunerative employment. If so, we would "break down" Table 3A by race. Let us say that we now obtain Table 3B. The hypothetical data in Table 3B show a very different rela-

TABLE 3B
(Hypothetical data)

	Number	Percentage Earning Less than $3000	Percentage Earning $3000 or More
NEGRO WORKERS			
Graduated from high school	100	80	20
Did not graduate from high school	100	90	10
Total	200	85	15
WHITE WORKERS			
Graduated from high school	400	20	80
Did not graduate from school	400	80	20
Total	800	50	50

tionship between education and income for Negroes than for whites. For whites, it is somewhat higher than in the original relationship; for Negroes it is considerably lower. Thus, the breakdown of the original relationship by race has helped to specify some of the conditions under which it is more pronounced and some of the conditions under which it is less pronounced.

The Use of Nonquantified Data[24]
in Analysis and Interpretation

Every reader of social research publications is familiar with the fact that raw data,[25] in the form in which they were collected, are often

[24] It is customary to refer to data that are presented essentially in the form in which they were collected as "qualitative" data. The term is not too happily chosen, because it implies a contrast to quantitative data. Both qualities and quantities can, of course, be at least counted in social research. But not everything that can be quantified in principle is actually quantified in a study. In other words, nonquantified material is not necessarily nonquantifiable material.

[25] The term raw data is used synonymously with nonquantified data.

used in conjunction with data that have undergone analysis and are on a higher level of abstraction. For example, Jahoda and Cook (1952), in considering conditions that enhance or inhibit the effects of the United States loyalty and security procedures on freedom of thought among government employees, state: ". . . the work-relationship factor which seems, from our exploratory interviews, to influence most strongly the impact of the security measures is the relation of employees to their supervisors." This statement is almost immediately followed by a verbatim quotation from an interview, a response to a question about a hypothetical situation in which a loyal government employee believes that he may be suspected of disloyalty because a friend has been accused of being a Communist:

> In our department I'd advise him to stay and fight, and I'd be confident of a good chance of winning. I trust the head of the department; he would support me. But that's the only thing on which I base my advice. In every other case, no matter who the suspect is, however honest, outstanding and competent, I'd advise him to run as quickly as possible. In our place there is no need to change. But I don't believe in being a martyr. Everywhere else I might act differently.

There can be little doubt that the insertion of such material increases the readability of social science documents. Laudable as that is, increased readability in itself presents no compelling scientific reason for the inclusion of such anecdotes and verbatim quotations. Our purpose here is to discuss the scientific functions of using such material in the course of analysis.

Raw data can be used in analysis and interpretation whether or not they have been quantified in all aspects. Even if virtually every aspect of a statement has been converted into categories, recourse to the original makes it possible to see the whole context. More frequently, however, not every aspect of the material has been categorized. In these cases, recourse to the raw material has the additional advantage of bringing neglected aspects to the fore.

The use of raw data in the course of analysis fulfills two distinct functions: to illustrate the range of meaning attached to any one category, and to stimulate new insights. We shall deal with these two functions separately.

ILLUSTRATING THE MEANING OF CATEGORIES

As we pointed out earlier in this chapter, the sharpness with which categories can be defined varies according to the nature of the raw data, the type of problem under investigation, and the situations to which the data refer. Suppose that one wishes to study by observational methods the nature of the interaction between labor and management in a joint production committee, such as those established in British industry. Depending on the anticipated level of analysis, several types of categories for summarizing an observational session can be set up. One might count the frequency of spontaneous remarks exchanged between members of one group and members of the other, or one might observe the seating arrangements; categories of this kind are so easily given unambiguous definition that they need no illustration. But more complex categories can be established for the same purpose, such as interactions between the two groups that indicate feelings of equal status, subordination, or superior status. A worker opposing the point of view of management might say, "I beg to disagree"; a managerial representative might say to a worker, "You are wrong." To classify these two answers in different categories of status consciousness involves a considerable amount of judgment about both the implications of the statements and the exact meaning of the categories. In dealing with such data, illustrations are necessary for three purposes: to help the coder understand the meaning of the categories, to help keep the actual nature of the material assigned to each category clear in the investigator's mind as he carries out the analysis and interprets his findings, and to help the reader understand the nature of the variables described and the investigator's reasoning.

The use of illustrations in defining categories for coders has already been discussed; their use in aiding the reader's understanding is obvious. Let us consider their importance as guides for the analyst in keeping aware of the real nature of the material included in various categories.

In an analysis of reasons that prompted people to move into a housing project, Merton and his colleagues (forthcoming) introduced a distinction between those who *had to leave* their old residence and those who *wanted to leave* it. In these broad terms the two types of motivation appear to be clear-cut alternatives. However, illustration of both categories indicated that the dividing line, although sharp in some cases, was vague in others. One tenant explained, "The house was sold from under us." Clearly, he had to move. Another one commented, "I didn't like the people in the neighborhood." Obviously, he wanted to move. But one tenant said: "We lived with my in-laws. Sometimes I thought I'd go crazy with all the bickering. I had to get out sooner or later. I heard about this place here and I liked what I heard; so we moved right out." Did he have to move, or did he want to move? Whether the economic compulsion under which the tenant whose "house was sold from under us" acted is to be classified in the same category as the psychological compulsion under which the tenant who could not get along with his relatives acted depends largely on the purposes for which these categories are established. Whatever the decision, it is necessary to keep in mind the wide range of motivation covered by each category if the further use of the distinction between those who had to move and those who wanted to move is to be psychologically meaningful. This is facilitated by reference to examples from the raw data whenever the categories are used in a new context.

Stimulating New Insights

Whatever the design of a study, and no matter how refined its statistical procedures, inspection of the raw data may lead to important insights. These may bear on the course of the analysis, or they may help to make clear the nature of the relationships between variables that have been demonstrated statistically, or they may lead to hypotheses for further research.

The inspection of nonquantified data may be particularly helpful if it is done periodically throughout a study rather than postponed to the end of the statistical analysis. Frequently, a single incident noted by a perceptive observer contains the clue to an understanding of a phenomenon. If the social scientist becomes aware of this implication at a moment when he can still add to his material or exploit further the data he has already collected, he may considerably enrich the quality of his conclusions.

During the period of data collection in a study of the social and psychological effects of long-term unemployment in an Austrian village (Jahoda-Lazarsfeld and Zeisl, 1932), one of the field workers had a casual conversation with a small boy. This boy was at the age when the notion of becoming chieftain of an Indian tribe appeared a suitable vocational goal; "But," he added, "I'm afraid it will be hard to get the job." This incident suggested that the bitter reality of unemployment had affected even the realm of fantasy. The investigators were immediately confronted with the question whether this was a unique case or whether the relationship was a general one. It was decided to transform the hypothesis—that parental unemployment restricts the fantasies of children—into a situational context of wider applicability than the wish to become an Indian chieftain, and to test it statistically. The opportunity to do so arose just before Christmas. At that time a sample of children of unemployed parents and a sample of children of employed parents were asked for their Christmas wishes. The wishes of both groups transcended the possibilities of fulfillment, considering the budgetary conditions even of employed parents; bicycles, cameras, and other expensive articles were frequently mentioned. Yet when these unrealistic wishes were translated into current prices, it was found that those of children whose parents were unemployed would cost significantly less than those of children whose parents were employed. This statistical finding was regarded as bearing affirmatively on the hypothesis suggested by the qualitative account of the boy's vocational dream.[26]

Much of the analytical effort of social scientists is devoted to establishing relationships between objective characteristics of a group of people and their subjective reactions. However, the demonstration that a relationship exists does not in itself provide an understanding of the way in which the factors are related. The scrutiny of the raw data may be rewarding in the search for such understanding. Thus Merton et al. (1946), in a study of radio listeners' responses to a war bond drive, based their quantitative analysis on the hypothesis that people

[26] Since there was no corresponding measure from the time before the parents were unemployed, the hypothesis cannot be considered as conclusively demonstrated. It is possible—though unlikely—that even before the period of unemployment, children of the subsequently unemployed parents might have expressed more modest wishes than the other group. This is an example of the limitations of nonexperimental studies.

who had relatives in the armed forces would react differently to the themes of the drive than those without relatives in the armed forces. By and large, persons with relatives in the armed forces were, indeed, more impressed by and willing to respond to an appeal to make sacrifices. Yet the relationship was not as strong as the investigators had anticipated. Many persons with relatives in the armed forces remained unresponsive. In a search for explanatory variables, Merton turned back to the interviews. He reports:

> An analysis of the interviews provides the clue. The unresponsive persons had little basis for *acute fears and anxiety concerning the safety of sons or brothers in the service* [italics added] . . . their kin were stationed in this country. . . . Nor could a chief gunner's mate, the husband of another informant, be a source of anxiety, since at the time he was home on leave and listening with his wife. . . . Thus, the emotional context for selective listening was significantly different for the two categories of informants although both had close relatives in the Army or Navy.

Here, Merton discovered fear and anxiety—that is, the emotional context—as a possible explanatory variable for the different responses, through scrutiny of the actual interviews.

From what has been said so far, it should be clear that this use of nonquantified data as a source of clues for the explanation of relationships does not constitute a tracing of the process involved, in the sense discussed in pages 427–429. Unless the suggested explanation is one for which a measure can be found within the study, thus making possible the statistical testing of the suggested process, the insight provided by the raw data remains simply a promising suggestion as far as that particular study is concerned. But if research is regarded as a never-ending search for interrelationships, in which one study provides the basis on which another can build, the suggestion of plausible mediating variables becomes as important a step as the statistical demonstration of relationships.

The search for explanatory concepts through reference to the raw data often becomes the only possible way of dealing with cases that do not show the same trends or patterns of relationship as most of the cases in a study. Such cases, by the very fact that they are exceptions, occur in such small numbers as to preclude a refined statistical analysis. Yet study of the exceptions may make it possible to refine hypotheses so that the frequency of exceptions can be reduced. Thus, Bettelheim and Janowitz (1950), in their study of American war veterans, investigated the relationship of frustration to anti-minority feelings. Among other questions they asked the veterans, "Do you feel that you got a bad break in your army career?" Of those who were tolerant of minorities, 62 per cent[27] said that they had had a "good break," while of those who had outspoken and intense anti-minority feelings, only 43 per cent gave this reply. These figures establish a correlation between feelings of being fairly treated and lack of prejudice, but with a relatively high frequency of deviation. After turning back to their raw data in an attempt to explain the exceptions, the authors report:

> An examination of the interview records suggests interesting hypotheses which may partially explain why some of the men deviated from prevalent patterns. All three tolerant men who claimed that they had gotten a bad break in the army gave the same reason for their "bad break." In a general way they all resented the treatment they received from their officers. For example, a thirty-three year old air corps sergeant said: "I wasn't treated right by those damn officers. There was no respect due to an enlisted man from an officer." Thus, their feeling of having had a "bad break" was not due to an over-all attitude toward the army but rather to a specific resentment of officers.
>
> On the other hand, it is also striking that contrary grounds were offered by the intolerant men for their thinking they had gotten a good break in the army. . . . For example, one intolerant man stated that what he liked most was: "The discipline and the strong order. . . . If I were single I'd make a career out of it. I liked the physical culture, fitness. . . . "
>
> Clearly these . . . intolerant men felt that they had had a good break for reasons markedly different from the matter-of-fact attitude of having had a "good break" in the army which characterized tolerant veterans.

As the authors develop their argument, it becomes clear that the apparent deviation from the pattern established in the figures quoted

[27] Of 61 tolerant veterans, 38 (62 per cent) said they had had a good break, 12 (21 per cent) that they had had neither a good nor a bad break, 3 (5 per cent) that they had had a bad break, and 7 (12 per cent) made other remarks.

above is less of a deviation than originally suggested. One is led to conclude that the statement "I had a good break" or "I had a bad break" is only a crude indication of the basic relationship. The study of the concrete answers of those who deviate from this crude relation reveals that what is considered as a good or a bad break is more decisive than the phrase. And this concept of what constitutes a "good break" is, in turn, a function of characteristics of the person.

Thus, the concern with deviant cases through a study of their concrete responses may lead to a refinement of hypotheses so that they result in fewer exceptions than did the original hypothesis. As indicated before, this process of refinement is unending. And the refinement itself needs to be regarded with caution until it can be checked against new data. "Explaining away" the exceptions suffers from the weaknesses of all ad hoc reasoning (see pages 419–421).

The examination of nonquantified material often leads to ideas for further research by revealing aspects of the phenomenon that have not been sufficiently studied in the particular investigation. Recognition of those aspects needing further study may also help to point up limits to the generalizability of findings from the given study. An example will illustrate the latter point. One of the research purposes in *Patterns of Social Life* (Merton et al., forthcoming) was to discover whether living in a bi-racial housing project significantly influenced prejudiced attitudes. Several statistical indices suggested that for a considerable part of the tenant population, there had been a definite improvement in relations with the other race. For example, informal contacts, such as are implied in having friends and acquaintances among members of the other race, were more frequent among people who had lived in the project for a longer period. In the search for illustrations, the analyst used an excerpt from an interview with a white woman. This woman explained that originally she had been frightened by the idea of living in the same project with Negroes, that she had avoided them when possible, and that she had generally rejected the idea of informal contact with them. She went on to say that gradually she had realized how unfounded her fears had been, she had made friends with some Negro women, and now she regarded herself as a champion of good race relations in the project. By way of climaxing her account, she added: "I am friendly with the men too.

When I walk through the project, many a Negro man shouts from across the street, 'Hello, Helen.' "

So far, the excerpt has mainly an illustrative function. Following a table showing the frequency of such changes in the course of time, this vivid account would probably lead all readers to assume that race relations were considerably improved by living in the project, without any awareness of qualifications other than those indicated in the table. However, the excerpt continues: ". . . 'Hello, Helen.' [a pause]. Of course, I'd faint if they did this to me in the main street in front of everybody."

This afterthought introduces an important qualification of the results. It suggests that the relations of the white tenants to the Negro tenants are only in part a consequence of their own beliefs and feelings about Negroes; in part they are also a consequence of the white tenants' perception of social approval or disapproval of interracial association. Within the housing project, the white woman in the illustration apparently perceived approval of such association. Outside the project, "on the main street," she apparently perceived disapproval. Evidently her behavior toward Negroes varied accordingly. The illustration suggested not only a qualification of the findings but a lead for further research.

In the example given, the implication is so dramatically obvious that no analyst who examined the raw data would be likely to overlook it. In other cases, suggestions for further research are not so obvious; they must be deliberately sought in the raw data. Although the confirmation or refutation of hypotheses requires that a study be set up with these hypotheses in mind, the purpose of discovering promising leads for investigation is often served best by the painstaking inspection of nonquantified data.

12

THE RESEARCH REPORT

What the Report Should Contain

Modifications for Shorter Reports

The Style of the Report

A thing is not necessarily true because uttered badly, nor false because spoken magnificently. AUGUSTINE

T HE RESEARCH TASK is not completed until the report has been written. The most brilliant hypothesis, the most carefully designed and conducted study, the most striking findings, are of little import unless they are communicated to others. Many social scientists seem to regard the writing of a report as an unpleasant chore tacked on to the end of the research process but not really an inherent part of it. To be sure, this stage requires a set of skills somewhat different from those called for by earlier stages of research; and much of the excitement of discovery may have worn off by the time the investigator shifts the focus of his attention from analysis of his data to preparation of the report. Nevertheless, communication of the results so that they enter the general store of knowledge is an essential part of the investigator's responsibilities, which should receive the same careful attention that earlier stages do. Moreover, if sufficient time has been allowed for preparation of the report (which is seldom true), the investigator may even find himself enjoying the opportunity it presents to fit pieces together into a larger whole, to consider the implications of his findings, to mull over the gaps or new questions raised and to think about what kinds of future research might provide answers.

Perhaps the most important point to be kept in mind when writing a report is its function: *The purpose of a report is not communication with oneself but communication with the audience.* This statement may appear obvious. However, a perusal of social research documents will show that all too many bear the stamp of a struggle for clarification of the author's own thoughts; they are not designed to communicate with an audience about problems that it would find of interest.

Emphasis on communication with an audience demands that one be clear about the type of reader for whom a given report is intended. A report directed to fellow social scientists will be different in many ways from one addressed to administrators who may take action on the basis of the findings; both will differ in some respects from a report whose purpose is to inform the general public. Whatever the audience, two broad questions should be considered in planning the report: (1) What does this audience want or need to know about the study? (2) How can this information best be presented?

In this chapter, we shall discuss the writing of a report for a scientific audience.[1] The suggestions are directed primarily toward the preparation of a detailed report, such as a thesis or monograph.[2] Shorter reports—articles intended for publication in a social science journal, for example—involve somewhat different emphases; some of these differences will be pointed out.

What the Report Should Contain

The social scientist who reads a research report needs to be told enough about the study so that he can place it in its general scientific context, judge the adequacy of its methods and thus form an opinion of how seriously the findings are to be taken, and—if he wishes—repeat the study with other subjects. In order to give him the necessary information, the report must cover the following points:

1. Statement of the problem with which the study is concerned.
2. The research procedures: the study design, the method of manipulating the independent variable if the study took the form of an experiment, the nature of the sample, the data-collection techniques, the method of statistical analysis.

[1] The presentation of research results to audiences other than social scientists is discussed in the following chapter.

[2] For other discussions of the preparation of reports, see Good (1941), Ogburn (1947), or Parten (1950). Chapter 17 of the latter reference gives not only many practical suggestions but an extensive bibliography on the preparation of reports.

3. The results.

4. The implications drawn from the results.

This list provides the major headings for an outline of the research report. Each point is discussed in more detail below.

STATEMENT OF THE PROBLEM

It was pointed out in Chapter 2 that the first step in the research process is a precise formulation of the question to be investigated. Ordinarily, the research report also starts with this statement of the issue on which the study was focused. Enough background should be given to make clear to the reader why the problem was considered worth investigating. Since a social science audience is likely to be more interested in contributions to general knowledge of human behavior than in the solution of a specific practical problem, the report to such an audience usually stresses the relevance of the investigation to some aspect of psychological or sociological theory.[3] For example, a study undertaken at the request of an institution to ascertain reactions to a proposed change in personnel policy may be planned and carried out in such a way that it provides evidence on the manner in which an individual's role within the organization influences his perception of the new policy. The report to a social science audience would quite properly stress this latter aspect rather than the concrete issue with which the specific institution is concerned.

However, it should be recognized that not all studies have a direct bearing on theoretical issues, and that the relevance of a study to some theoretical point may become apparent only as one seeks to understand the findings. At the present time, in the social sciences, many studies are of necessity carried out without the guidance of a systematic theory. When this is the state of affairs, there is no reason to disguise it; attempts to invent theoretical relevance usually strike the reader as pretentious.

In addition to indicating the practical or theoretical importance of the question investigated, the statement of the problem should include

[3] For a discussion of the relation between research and theory, see Chapter 2, pages 44–47, and Chapter 14.

a brief summary of other relevant research, so that the study may be seen in context; the hypotheses of the study, if any were formulated; and definitions of the major concepts employed (see Chapter 2). The connections among these elements should be made clear; that is, the logical sequence of ideas leading from the existing theory and relevant research findings to the hypotheses and concepts of the study should be explicitly indicated.

THE RESEARCH PROCEDURES

The scientific reader needs to know in considerable detail how the study was carried out. What was its basic design? If the study was an experimental one, just what were the experimental manipulations? (For example, was "threat" established by telling the subjects that they were about to take a very difficult test, which would determine their grades in a course, or by shouting, "Fire!"?) At what point or points were the measurements taken?

If the data were collected by means of questionnaires or interviews , exactly what questions were asked? (The questionnaire or interview schedule is usually given in an appendix.) How much and what kind of experience had the interviewers had, and how were they trained for this particular study? If the measurements were based on observation, what instructions were given to the observers?

The reader also needs to know how the observations or replies to questions were translated into measures of the variables with which the study was concerned. (For example, which questions were taken into account in estimating "morale"; or what kinds of leader behavior were classified as "democratic"?)

Regarding the sample used in the study, he should be told: Who were the subjects? How many were there? How were they selected? These questions are crucial for estimating the probable limits of generalizability of the findings. Are elaborate conclusions being drawn on the basis of responses of ten college sophomores, selected because they happened to be friends of the investigator? Were only housewives interviewed? If so, is there any basis for extending the findings to people in general? Intensive study of a small number of cases that do not constitute a random sample of any specifiable population may be extremely valuable. Nevertheless, the number and characteristics of the subjects on which the findings are based should be clearly stated, so that the reader can draw his own conclusions about the applicability of the findings to other groups.

The scientific reader is also concerned with the statistical analysis of the data. What techniques were used to determine whether groups differing in certain background characteristics, or subjected to specified treatments, showed differences on a given measure that were significantly greater than might have been expected by chance? Ordinarily it is sufficient simply to name the technique used, and to indicate the level of confidence one has accepted in deciding whether differences are to be considered significant (see Chapter 11, pages 414–421). Only if the statistical technique is a new one need formulas be given. If one has used a technique that is, strictly speaking, not appropriate to the data, this fact should be noted, and explanations made. (For a brief indication of the kinds of data with which specific statistical tests may appropriately be used, see Chapter 5, pages 189–197; for more detailed discussion, see any statistics textbook.)

The Results

The basic rule in presenting findings is to give all the evidence relevant to the research question asked, whether or not the results are in accord with the investigator's views. This is the cardinal rule of scientific reporting. Unlike other writers, the scientific author is not free to choose what he will include and what he will leave out in terms of the effects he wishes to create.

Nevertheless, he must still make some selection in terms of what is relevant; not every table worked out in the course of the analysis can or should find a place in the report. How does one decide what is relevant? Guidance comes primarily from the research problem and from the hypotheses, if any, with which the study was concerned. Suppose one wishes to evaluate the effects of two different methods of selecting discussion leaders. The setting chosen might be a class of a hundred students, divided into discussion groups of five students each, with one of the students in each group serving as its leader. In half of the groups the leader is elected by the group from among its members; in the other half, he is appointed by the instructor on the basis of scores on an initial questionnaire. Let us say that the investigation was interested in the effects of the different methods of selecting leaders on the following aspects: (1) the satisfaction of members with the group's functioning, (2) the attendance of group members, (3) the extent of participation in group discussion, (4) the concern of members with having the group accept their views or with working out a position acceptable to the entire group, (5) grades in the course.

Whether or not explicit hypotheses were formulated, the investigator is obligated to report on each of these points—even if all he can say about a given one is that he was unable to collect the data needed to answer the question. He may have found, for example, that the ratings by which he had intended to get data relevant to point (4) were made so unreliably by different observers that they were not usable. This fact should be reported. If his data show differences between the two types of group on points (1), (2), and (3), but not on (5), this too should be reported.

But, as has been pointed out throughout this book, a study is not completely "jelled" at the time the research problem is formulated. During the course of the investigation, a more adequate statement of the problem itself may be developed, new hypotheses may emerge, unforeseen relationships may appear. Therefore, while the original formulation provides the basic point of reference for the report, there must also be room to include subsequent developments. For example, Selltiz, Hopson, and Cook (1956), in a study described in Chapter 11, pages 386–391, started out with hypotheses about the effects of association with Americans on the attitudes of foreign students toward the United States. Information about certain background characteristics of the students, including their nationality, was gathered primarily in order to check on conditions that might influence the relation between personal association and attitudes. As it turned out, the hypotheses about the effects of personal association were not supported, but it became clear that there were marked differences in attitude between students from different parts of the world. Therefore, although the initial plan of the study was not directly concerned with national background as a determinant of attitudes, it became appropriate to devote a section of the report to discussion of that relationship.

For every finding that involves a comparison between groups or a relationship between variables, the level of statistical significance should be reported. Suppose, for example, that in our group leadership study, attendance in the groups with elected leaders averaged 80 per cent, in those with appointed leaders, 75 per cent. Unless the reader is told the results of the test of significance, he is in no position to judge whether this finding indicates a slight superiority of elected leadership or whether the difference can reasonably be attributed simply to chance variations. Ordinarily, in a detailed report for a scientific audience, every finding that is considered sufficiently important to be stressed is accompanied also, either in the text or in an appendix, by a table or graph or chart showing the relevant data.

The guides suggested so far originate mainly in the initial formulation of the research problem and the hypotheses and in the statistical results of the analysis. However, not all studies begin with a research problem stated in sufficient detail to provide a basis for outlining the general points to be covered in the report, and not all studies make use of quantitative data. In an exploratory study, for example, the appropriate content and organization of the report are much less clearly suggested by the study design and analysis of the data; the investigator must rely more on his own judgment in deciding the outline of his report. Nevertheless, it is still necessary that he state clearly the problem with which he was concerned, the procedure by which he worked on the problem, the conclusions at which he arrived, and the bases for his conclusions.

DISCUSSION OF IMPLICATIONS

A bare statement of the findings is usually not enough to convey their meaning; usually the reader is interested in their implications for the general understanding of human behavior. Discussion of these implications is sometimes combined with the presentation of the data; sometimes it is placed in a separate section. Wherever the discussion appears, it usually includes three major aspects:

1. A statement of the inferences drawn from the findings in this

particular situation which may be expected to apply in similar circumstances. The inferences may be at a level quite close to the data, or may involve considerable abstraction. For example, in our group leadership example, if the investigator has found more satisfaction, better attendance, more participation, and higher grades in groups that elected their own leaders, he may simply conclude that in similar situations, election of the discussion leader will have similar effects. However, he may wish to carry his inference to some higher level of abstraction, especially if there is some partially developed theory to which he may link his findings, or if there have been other studies in which the specific phenomena are different but can be understood in terms of the same abstract principle. Thus, for example, he may treat election of the group leader as an example of the more abstract concept *autonomy*.

2. As a qualification of these inferences, the investigator should note conditions of his study that limit the extent of legitimate generalization. He should, for example, remind the reader of the characteristics of his sample and the possibility that it differs from a larger population to which one might want to generalize; of specific characteristics of his method that might have influenced the outcome; of any other factors he is aware of that might have operated to produce atypical results.

3. Finally, the discussion of implications of the findings will usually include relevant questions that are still unanswered or new questions raised by the study, perhaps with suggestions for the kinds of research that would help to answer them.

THE SUMMARY

It is customary to conclude with a very brief summary, restating in barest outline the problem, the procedures, the major findings, and the major conclusions drawn from them.

Modifications for Shorter Reports

Frequently, a detailed report such as that discussed above does not seem appropriate. The study may not seem important enough to warrant a great investment of time and money in writing and producing the report, or of the audience's time in reading it. In fact, the more usual report is one prepared for a psychological or sociological journal, which must ordinarily be kept to a few printed pages. Such reports must still give the reader the basic facts he needs to know, but in abbreviated form.

In an article written for publication in a social science journal, the discussion of previous research may be omitted except for reference to summaries that have appeared elsewhere. Or, if the significance of the study being reported stems in large part from its relation to certain other studies, these are mentioned and the crucial points on which they focus are briefly summarized, but the reader is referred to reports of those studies for additional details. Similarly, the relation of the study to theoretical issues is stated with the minimum of detail needed to make clear the general bearing of the study on social science theory.

Space is saved also by omitting the data-collection instruments, unless these are absolutely essential for understanding of the study. Ordinarily, in a journal article, the reader is told simply that the data were collected by a participant observer, or by an observer watching from behind a one-way screen, or by means of interviews or anonymous questionnaires. A few questions, observational categories, etc., may be included. If the method of data collection has been described in print elsewhere, reference is of course made to this description. If no published description is available, and the methodological innovations are of general import, the author may publish separately a description of his new techniques. He should send his methodological material to the American Documentation Institute of the Library of Congress, where it will be available to other investigators who wish to examine it.[4]

Limitations of space in a journal article require that one be much more selective about what aspects of the findings are to be reported. To be sure, the requirement that both positive and negative evidence be reported still holds. However, negative findings may be stated very briefly, and without supporting tables or graphs. In presenting the

---

[4] For a discussion of these and other procedures appropriate to the publication of articles in scientific journals, see the *Publication Manual* of the American Psychological Association, 1957 Revision.

findings, if the study is a fairly elaborate one, the investigator may have to decide which are most important, and present only those. Points that seem interesting and might warrant discussion in a longer report, but on which the data are only suggestive, must usually be omitted from a journal article. Tables, charts, and graphs will be used much more sparingly than in a longer report.

If the study has two or more aspects that can be discussed independently of each other, it may be advisable to write separate articles rather than to try to crowd too many different findings into a single article.

The Style of the Report

The basic qualities of good scientific writing are accuracy and clarity. A style that is pleasing from a literary or esthetic point of view is an "extra." The investigator reporting his research has no obligation to be colorful or elegant in his writing, or to hold the reader's interest by a lively style—though there is no reason why he should repel the reader by asking him to wade through long, involved, unclear, or pompous sentences.

The first step—and with it the battle is half won—is to decide just what information you want to convey and how the various points are related to one another. Writing a detailed outline is an invaluable aid at this stage. Some experienced writers can sit down with pencil or typewriter, with only a general notion of the final shape of the report, and produce a clear and well-organized account of their research. For most people, however—and especially for beginners—this is a very inefficient way to proceed. Writing "from scratch" relies on ideas somehow organizing themselves and appearing in the proper order. If they do not, the resulting draft of the report will be a garbled account requiring complete rewriting if it is to make sense.

Preparing a detailed outline allows one to concentrate exclusively, at first, on what is to be said, without worrying about how to say it. One constructs the skeleton of the report; looking at the bare bones, one can more easily see whether any important points have been left out. Moreover, the outline form, with its clear indication of major topics, subtopics, and still further subdivisions, almost forces attention to logical relationships within the material. If one is writing without an outline, he may write two or three paragraphs describing his sample, then go on to an account of his data-collection procedure, then add an afterthought about the sample, without noticing what has happened to the line of thought. The outline form clearly marks the shift from one topic to another and thus facilitates the grouping together of all the points about a given topic.

Once the outline has been written, it is a good idea to go back over it, to see whether anything important has been omitted and whether ideas that have been grouped together do logically belong together. It may be helpful to have someone else read and comment on it. Then, if changes in the basic structure of the report seem to be needed, they can be made before the actual writing starts.

Whether one worries about writing style in the course of producing the first draft is to some extent a matter of individual disposition. Some experienced writers spend a long time over each sentence, carefully choosing words that will best convey their meaning. However, when the purpose is to convey information rather than to achieve a literary production, it seems likely that in the long run time is saved by writing the first draft as quickly as possible. Once it is on paper, one can go back and rewrite sentences and paragraphs, fortified by the knowledge that he has produced at least a first draft of the report.

At some point, however, attention must be given to style. There is little that can be said about this, except to stress the value of simplicity and correct grammatical structure. A common fault is pretentiousness. It is, of course, entirely appropriate to use terms that have a technical meaning in social science. But the bulk of a social science report does not consist of technical language, and there is no good reason for consistently using four-syllable words instead of one-syllable words with essentially the same meaning. Similarly, two or three relatively simple sentences may convey an idea more clearly than one complicated sentence with a number of entangled clauses.[5]

Many students emerge from their language training with the view

[5] For examples of unnecessarily complex writing and ways of simplifying, see the *Publication Manual* of the American Psychological Association, 1957 Revision. For a more detailed discussion of "readability," see Flesch (1949, 1954), and Flesch and Lass (1955).

that the rules of grammar are an arbitrary construction of pedants, with which none but teachers of English need concern themselves. This is a serious misconception. One of the major functions of grammatical rules is to help us use language in such a way that it will convey our meaning with a minimum of ambiguity. The placing of commas around certain kinds of clauses and not around others, for example, is not an arbitrary matter; it is a way of specifying the relation of a clause to the word it modifies.

A good dictionary is an essential part of a writer's equipment. A good handbook of composition may also be helpful; for example, Woolley and Scott (1944) discuss words, sentence structure, punctuation, paragraphs, and organization. For specific problems in preparing a manuscript for publication, one may need to consult more specialized manuals; for example, the University of Chicago Press *Manual of Style* or the *Publication Manual* of the American Psychological Association.

The preparation of tables, graphs, etc., also requires care. This is not the place to discuss the preparation of such material in detail; however, a few general suggestions may be helpful. All tables and graphs should be clearly labeled. The title should state briefly the subject matter of the table; any necessary qualifications or explanations should be given in a footnote to the table. Row and column headings should be as short as is consistent with identifying the data being presented. Both axes of a graph should be clearly labeled to show both the variables being represented and the units of measurement. The number of cases on which the findings are based should be indicated in the table or graph as well as in the text; this is especially important when figures are given in percentages. Although the tabular or graphic presentation should be clear enough so that a reader can identify the major points it is intended to convey, it is customary to state the major findings in the text as well. In this way, the reader who does not want to take time to study tables can get all the necessary information simply by reading the text. (More detailed suggestions for the preparation of tables and graphs are given in the *Publication Manual* of the American Psychological Association and in a number of sources cited there.)

Once the report has been written and the tables and graphs prepared, the author should read it over, asking himself such questions as: Is this sentence clear? Is it grammatically correct? Does it say what I mean? Could the point be expressed more simply? Does the material given in the tables justify the conclusions I have drawn? Do the various points fit together logically?

Having at least one colleague read the report just before the final revision is extremely helpful. Sentences that seem crystal-clear to the writer may prove quite confusing to other people; a connection that had seemed self-evident may strike others as a *non sequitur*. A friendly critic, by pointing out passages that seem unclear or illogical, and perhaps suggesting ways of remedying the difficulties, can be an invaluable aid in achieving the goal of adequate communication.

13

THE APPLICATION OF SOCIAL RESEARCH

Concern with Application During the Research

Presentation of Action-Oriented Research

Extending the Area of Application

Research and Social Policy

Unapplied knowledge is knowledge shorn of its meaning.
A. N. WHITEHEAD

U P TO THIS POINT, we have discussed problems and procedures common to all social science research, whether it be directed toward increasing general knowledge about human behavior or toward the solution of some practical problem. In this chapter, we shall discuss a problem specific to the latter type of research—that of increasing the likelihood that the findings will be used.

The immediate applicability of research findings to current social issues is largely a function of earlier decisions in the research process. To be sure, inquiries that have not been geared to immediate application from the outset may yield results that have practical significance. In the long run, they may have even greater social usefulness than a study undertaken with the goal of immediate application in mind. It is possible, for example, that modern theories of learning developed in the course of laboratory experimentation may one day revolutionize education, but, if this is to happen, someone must undertake the task of transforming theoretical concepts into realistic and relevant terms that will make possible the testing of their validity for concrete educational situations.

It is largely a question of preference whether a social scientist works with the goal of immediate or potential future application in mind, or whether he is completely indifferent to this issue. But the social scientist who is concerned with the immediate applicability of his work must keep this objective in mind at every stage of his study. The selection of the research problem, the choice of setting, the extent to which action personnel are involved, the manner in which the findings are presented—all may affect the likelihood of application.

Concern with Application During the Research

When an investigator is concerned with application of his work, planning for it must begin at the outset. One of the first things he must decide is the extent to which the people who may be expected to use the results should participate in planning and carrying out the research. Usually some minimum of cooperation is essential. Research intended to have immediate usefulness is frequently carried out at the request of an organization that hopes to solve some problem. Even if the investigator himself initiates the research, he is likely to want to carry it out in the setting of a functioning organization. Although a laboratory study, or a survey of individuals unconnected with any given organization, may sometimes be appropriate for research intended to have action implications, more often such work is carried out within a factory, an office, a housing project, a school, a community center. In order to conduct research in such a setting, the investigator must enlist the cooperation of the people in authority at least to the extent of securing their permission to go ahead with his plans.

Collaboration with an action agency may sometimes be necessary, or desirable, even if the investigator is not concerned with the application of his findings. Any study design that involves a functioning organization demands at least a minimum of collaboration on the part of the action personnel.[1] Much of the following discussion of sources of difficulty in such collaboration and of methods of reducing friction is relevant to any study conducted within an organizational setting, whether or not there is concern with application of the findings.

How much the action personnel should participate in the research, beyond the necessary minimum, is a matter for decision. Collaboration with lay people is time-consuming and does not always proceed without friction. Nevertheless, from the standpoint of application of research findings, the advantages of collaboration far outweigh its disadvantages.

---

[1] By *action personnel* we mean the members and staff of the organization within which the study takes place, whether this be a factory, a school, a religious organization, a labor union, a P.T.A., a boys' club. Similarly, the terms *action organization* and *action agency*, or simply *organization* and *agency*, are intended to refer to any such group in which research is being conducted.

There are two major ways in which collaboration with an action agency increases the likelihood that the research findings will be used. First, participation usually increases the agency's interest in the research and in its possible usefulness. It is a well-established psychological principle that the greater the degree of active participation in an endeavor, the greater the degree of involvement with its outcome. An agency that has been in close contact with a research project is more likely to act on recommendations emerging from the investigation than one that has had nothing to do with the development of the inquiry. Second, and equally important, collaboration with an action agency helps to ensure that the research is really relevant to problems as they appear in the daily operations of the organization and of others like it.

CONTRIBUTIONS OF THE ACTION PERSONNEL

Perhaps the most crucial step in determining whether the findings of a study will have immediate social usefulness is the selection of the research problem. Obviously, research concerned with the reasons housewives prefer one brand of scouring powder to another, or with the effects of different methods of supervision on production in a factory, or with the conditions under which race riots occur, is more likely to find immediate application than research on the mating behavior of chimpanzees. But the selection of a general area which is recognized as involving a practical problem or a matter for decision regarding social policy, no matter how urgent, is not in itself a guarantee of immediate applicability. The study of prejudice, for example, can lead to change in social practices, but it need not do so. Whether or not it actually does depends largely on the manner in which the research problem is conceptualized. If the problem is formulated so that the hypotheses bear on a possible or actual course of action that persons concerned with the situation envisage or perform, it may well lead to immediate application. This was demonstrated in the Deutsch-Collins housing study described in Chapter 1. Public housing officials had indicated that research results concerning the effect of occupancy pattern on race relations might be taken into account in making decisions about future policy; accordingly, the hypotheses formulated were directed at this question. A study focused on the relation between personality type and the nature of response to close personal contact with members of another ethnic group would be less likely to result in practical implementation. The formulation of research for immediate use requires a knowledge of the nature of decisions that are likely to be made by persons concerned in a practical way with the problem under investigation. This knowledge is best acquired in close collaboration with such persons and agencies in the early stages of an inquiry.

The final statement of the problem in terms that make it a workable starting point for research is, of course, up to the social scientist. He is the expert in the research process, and it is he who must take responsibility for the adequacy of the research procedure. The practitioner has a different kind of knowledge to contribute. Nothing but confusion is to be gained by mixing the functions of the two. Each is an expert, with a specialist's knowledge of the research matter, but one is concerned with advancing knowledge of a given phenomenon and the other with improving existing services. Sometimes friction occurs because of these disparate goals and standards. The practitioner may well become impatient with the experimenter's controls, and may wish to put new insights into effect immediately, whereas the experimenter may become exasperated with the practitioner's desire to enact changes when he has no solid evidence of their value.

Each partner makes his best contribution when it is highly specific to the function for which he has been trained. This division of labor is appropriate throughout the research, no matter how close the collaboration. The social scientist is the expert on research design, sampling, construction of measuring instruments. But the practitioner knows the specific situation. He can be of inestimable help in pointing out possibilities for "natural" experiments, such as comparing subgroups within the agency in which different practices are followed, or possibilities for setting up experimental manipulations in such a way that they will appear realistic to the subjects. Suppose, for example, that the research problem has to do with the effects of grouping high school students into classes that are relatively homogeneous or heterogeneous with respect to scholastic ability. If decisions on this matter have been left up to the principals of the various schools in the system, the superintendent of schools may be able to point out to the investigator schools which are similar in such matters as general socioeconomic level of the students, range of scholastic ability, and caliber of teachers, but which differ in the independent variable with which the research is concerned—the basis on which students are grouped. Or, if the existing situation does not contain arrangements that so neatly fit the research requirements, the superintendent may arrange to have homogeneous classes set up in some schools and heterogeneous ones in others, or to have some homogeneous and some heterogeneous classes within the same school.

The agency personnel can inform the investigator whether data needed for the study are available in records compiled in the course of the agency's regular operations, or they may be able to suggest ways in which the collection of data can be worked into on-going procedures. They can advise the investigator whether his proposed design or methods of data collection are likely to be feasible. For example, an investigator planning a study of street-corner gangs discussed his research plan with a group worker who had had experience with such gangs. The plan called for administering Rorschach tests to the gang members. The group worker predicted that it would be impossible to persuade the boys to respond to the Rorschach, and suggested that the investigator try to devise ways of getting the information he needed by means of participant observation. At times, action personnel, viewing the situation from their particular vantage point, may overestimate or underestimate difficulties; therefore the investigator should try to become sufficiently familiar with the situation to make his own estimate of the feasibility of his proposed procedures. Nevertheless, the practitioner may be an invaluable source of advice concerning resources and possible obstacles.

The action personnel may participate in carrying out the experimental manipulations or in gathering the data for the study. However, their participation in analysis of the data is likely to be limited, except in the case of studies set up as self-surveys and requiring only the simplest kind of analysis.[2]

---

[2] For a discussion of self-surveys, see Wormser and Selltiz (1951a and b).

SOME PRACTICAL PROBLEMS

Collaboration does not always run smoothly, nor are the recipients of research findings always eager to accept and act on them—even though they may have requested the investigation in the first place. Even if the organization has requested the study, this request may not represent a consensus on the part of all the relevant people or interest groups within the organization. One individual, or a few, in a central position, may have made the decision. There may be others who are not in favor of the research, and these may include people whose help is needed in carrying out the study or who will have some responsibility for applying the findings. Some of them may believe that no problem exists; others may recognize a problem but think that research cannot contribute to its solution; others may feel that the nature of the people or groups sponsoring the research is such that the study will inevitably lead to conclusions detrimental to their interests; still others may be sure that they know the solution and so consider research unnecessary. For example, the principal and board of trustees of a private school became concerned about the school's apparent lack of effect on the character of its students. They asked a research organization to undertake an exploratory study to evaluate whether there was, in fact, a discrepancy between the goals of the school and the outcomes in terms of the students' character and, if so, to identify possible reasons and suggest courses of action that might make achievement of the goals more likely. The plan of the study called for interviews with faculty, parents, and students. When the interviews with faculty members were started, it rather quickly became apparent that the faculty were antagonistic to the study. They saw the school's accomplishments as more nearly in keeping with its goals than did the principal and trustees. Moreover, to the extent that they recognized the results as falling short of what was desired, they held that the main source of the difficulty was their own low pay and heavy work schedule. In their opinion, the money spent for research might better have been used to increase their salaries. Several meetings with the entire group and with influential individuals were necessary to overcome their opposition.

In other situations, the relevant people may recognize a problem and believe that research can contribute to its solution, but some of them may feel that the specific experimental manipulations or other research procedures are in conflict with the goals of the organization or with its best functioning. Such a situation has been described and analyzed in considerable detail by Schwartz (1948). Two agencies cooperated in this study. One was engaged in the practice of group work on an interracial basis in a neighborhood child-recreation center; the other was established for the purpose of research in the area of interracial relations. On the basis of an "experience survey" (see Chapter 3) of workers in such neighborhood centers, the research agency formulated the following problem: What type of leadership behavior in an interracial group produces more favorable changes in the attitudes of children toward those of another skin color? Specifically, two practices were to be compared: (1) pointing out to the children at every opportunity that they were actually enjoying an experience in an interracial group, and (2) refraining consistently from mentioning the group composition. Another variable to be tested was whether emphasis on group achievement or on individual achievement was more conducive to good intergroup attitudes.

The research group, having formulated this problem, asked the director of the neighborhood center whether he and his staff would be interested in collaborating in such a study. The staff wanted to produce more favorable intergroup attitudes and believed that research could help them do a better job in this respect. They appeared to accept the formulation of the specific problem and the research design, and agreed to help carry it out.

The relationship between the two agencies in carrying out the study was very close. The maintenance of the experimental design—i.e., the following of strictly defined alternative practices in the designated children's groups—was completely dependent on the group workers themselves. However, it came to light several months after the initiation of the experiment that the group workers who had the assignment of emphasizing individual achievement were not doing so, because they regarded this as contradictory to their own professional standards.

This particular collaborative situation illustrated still another source of resistance. Quite apart from their feeling that one of the experimental variables required behavior out of keeping with their own standards, the group workers found other aspects of the research procedure a burden and an interference with their major task. The plans for data collection included use of a pictorial attitude test, the arrangement of test situations, and the recording of observations. The already heavy work load of the group workers was increased by demands that they record what they observed during each session; the introduction of test situations at periodic intervals interfered with their own spontaneity and that of their groups. Even though the research was designed to make group work more effective in the long run, situations arose where it seemed necessary for the group worker to sacrifice the research for the sake of carrying out his function in the group. It is also possible, of course, that the natural difficulty of deviating from habitual practices, rather than the requirements of the situation, interfered with the effort to introduce and study new methods.

Lack of understanding of the relevance of the research to solution of the problem at hand is another source of reluctance to cooperate in a study or to apply its findings. A large government agency once enlisted the help of a research team to conduct a content analysis of the output of its writers, in order to provide a basis for evaluating whether the material really conveyed the messages intended. In planning and carrying out the study, the social scientists worked only with the administrators of the program; the writers themselves were brought into the picture only when the report of the study had been completed. Many of the writers took exception to the study, especially to the method of analysis that had been used. Prolonged discussion and negotiations were required before they were able to see the value of the research.

This example suggests still another source of resistance to research: apprehension about the use to which findings may be put. Individuals may see the research as involving an evaluation of how well they are performing their functions; they may fear that possible negative evaluation will be used against them. In a work situation, for example, they may worry that evidence collected in the course of the research will be used as a basis for determining promotions or dismissals. Even where no such objective consequences are likely, people may be uncomfortable at feeling themselves "under the microscope." The chairman of a P.T.A. in which attendance at meetings has been declining may ask a social scientist for help in finding out the reasons for the decline and possible ways of reviving interest; but even though she has asked for the help research can give, she may be apprehensive that the findings will point to inadequacies in her performance as chairman.

One final source of resistance is especially likely to come into play at the stage of applying the findings: the reluctance to change accustomed ways of doing things. Application of research findings often implies doing something differently, in a way that will presumably be more effective. But ordinarily it is easier to keep on doing things as we have been doing them; inertia may lead to rejection of the research findings or of their implications for action. A dramatic example from medical research illustrates both this source of resistance and the one discussed immediately above—resentment of criticism. Beveridge (1950) recalls the fate of Semmelweis after he had discovered the origin of puerperal fever:

> . . . he instituted a strict routine of washing the hands . . . before the examination of the patients. As a result of this procedure, the mortality from puerperal fever in the first obstetric clinic of the General Hospital of Vienna fell immediately from twelve per cent to three per cent, and later almost to one per cent. His doctrine was well received in some quarters and taken up in some hospitals, but such revolutionary ideas, incriminating the obstetricians as the carriers of death, roused opposition from entrenched authority and the renewal of his position as assistant was refused.

METHODS OF REDUCING RESISTANCE TO RESEARCH[3]

The reader has probably noticed that in several of the examples above, opposition arose from persons who had not been consulted in the course of planning the research. This fact points to a basic principle in achieving successful collaboration with an action agency. Before a study gets under way, it should be discussed fully with all those who will be affected by the research, either through helping to carry it out

[3] For a more detailed discussion, see Likert and Lippitt (1953).

or through applying the findings.[4] This process is usually started with top administrators, whose support is ordinarily essential to carrying out research within an organization. However, cooperation on the part of other personnel can seldom be assured simply by orders from above, especially if the study makes heavy demands on them or extends over a long period of time. Therefore, the discussions should be extended to include all those who will be asked to help in the study or in applying its findings.

The more active the cooperation needed, the more essential it is that everyone concerned understand the nature and purpose of the research and be reasonably sympathetic toward it. It may be possible to eliminate reservations and objections through open discussion before the study is undertaken. If not, and if the objections come from a considerable number of people or from individuals who are in key positions to help or hinder the study, it may be better to abandon the plan rather than run the risk of finding the study blocked after it gets under way. In discussing the reservations and objections, the investigator must make it clear that he is willing to consider them seriously; he should not attempt simply to "talk down" the opposition. Frequently, arguments in favor of the research can be made more effectively by other members of the action agency than by the investigator himself. In any case, he must beware of promising, or of letting others promise, more than the study can realistically be expected to perform. Excessive promises are likely to boomerang.

Discussions with action personnel should not only give a clear picture of the nature of the research problem and the general procedures to be used; they should also state precisely what will be required in the way of collaboration. This statement should include not only a description of the kinds of things that may have to be done and how much time these tasks are likely to take, but an account of how the

---

[4] Sometimes, of course, the nature of the research problem is such that knowledge by the subjects of the specific details, or even of the fact that they are being studied, may affect the results. If the invesigator believes that this is the case in his study, he may make a conscious decision not to acquaint them with the research plan. However, it is often possible to discuss the research with the relevant personnel and still keep the actual subjects unaware of it. For example, in a study of leadership practices in a recreation center, the group workers can be given a full description of the study even though the children in their groups do not know that they are being observed.

research procedures may interfere with normal operations, to the extent that this can be foreseen. It may be possible to work out ways of making the research operation less of a burden on the action personnel; but research can seldom be completely unobtrusive, and this fact should be made clear. If the agency personnel are to be asked to undertake time-consuming duties in the conduct of the research, arrangements should be made with top administrators to release them from some of their other tasks. If the research design calls for some of the action personnel to behave in ways that are unusual or uncongenial, it may be preferable to hire persons who can be especially trained for the study. For example, in a study of the relative effectiveness of praise and criticism on scholastic achievement, many teachers who were sympathetic to the study might nevertheless be unwilling or unable to carry out the "criticizing" role. An experienced teacher with training in research, hired especially for the purpose of carrying out this role, might have less conflict about it because of her greater identification with the study.

The threatening aspect of research can often be reduced by stressing the aim of finding better ways of accomplishing the organization's goals—that is, by emphasizing the potential findings as a source of help rather than criticism. It should be made clear that the purpose of the study is not the evaluation of individuals, and that the findings will have no bearing on anyone's prospects for continued employment, promotion, etc. In this connection, it is appropriate to stress that what any given individual says will be kept in strict confidence by the research staff, and that no information will be reported in such a way that individuals can be identified. Such assurances should, of course, be given only if they can be rigidly adhered to.

Presentation of Action-Oriented Research

The way in which the research findings are presented, as well as the extent to which the action organization has participated in the research, helps determine whether the findings will be used. A special problem is created by the fact that there is little opportunity for collaboration during the stage of analysis. In the period between the end of data collection and the completion of the report, interest may wane.

INTERIM REPORTS

When data collection has been completed, many activities in which the sponsoring or collaborating agencies played a part come to a standstill. After the exciting events that so frequently occur during field work begins a period that, although it may be as eventful for the social scientist as any of the preceding stages of research, has little to offer his partner in the enterprise. This is inevitable. And it is also inevitable that this period should appear long to those who do not participate in the procedures of analysis and report-writing. What is more, their impatience is on occasion objectively justified when a practical solution of the problem under investigation cannot be postponed beyond a certain date. From this point of view, the selection of such a problem for research is, of course, always a risk.

In 1948, for example, when Israel became an independent state, an organization in the United States which was concerned with the maintenance of civil rights for the Jewish population of this country considered the possibility that this event might call for changes in its program. The organization wished to base its decision on a scientific inquiry into the effect of the foundation of the new state on the attitudes of non-Jewish Americans toward American Jews. Accordingly, a large-scale study was initiated. But the collection and analysis of data took a long time. In the meantime, the world did not stand still. Israel largely disappeared from the headlines; public attention became more and more absorbed in other matters. The agency, actively engaged in its large-scale activities and consulted daily about many problems of Jewish life, developed its strategy successfully without the benefit of the research. The study made an important contribution to research methodology and produced some interesting results, which were relevant to policy decisions. Yet from the point of view of its original purpose—to facilitate a decision on an acute problem of policy —the inquiry failed. The results came too late.

Even when the nature of a problem does not impose a time limit on application, the delay between data collection and presentation of findings may reduce the likelihood of application. This happens either because new problems arising within the agency absorb the energy and interest of the staff, or because the agency fails to understand the reasons for the delay. What can be done during this period to increase the probability that the findings will be applied?

One of the most effective ways to reduce, if not eliminate, tensions arising during this waiting period is to present an interim report. Such a report may contain either the first results of the over-all analysis or the final outcome of the analysis of some part of the investigation. It should be remembered that an interim report, however strongly its preliminary character is emphasized, is usually understood as a definite commitment. In this sense, it involve certain risks. If it is produced at too early a stage of analysis, the social scientist may, when he writes a final report, find himself in the position of having to change statements he has made—a situation that understandably reduces the collaborator's confidence. By and large, therefore, it is advisable to present interim reports, not on the full scope of a study, but on one completely analyzed section at a time. This possibility should be taken into account in planning the analysis, and those sections analyzed first that are most appropriate for separate presentation.

Whatever form the interim report takes, it fulfills a number of important functions, all of which help to increase the likelihood that the findings of the study will actually be applied. If the agency has to take action without waiting for the full report, the interim report may contain some findings relevant to such action. Its delivery may help to keep alive the agency's interest in the study and prevent misunderstandings about delays.

In addition, the interim report helps the agency to maintain realistic expectations with respect to social research. Frequently the level of expectation of what social science can do is unrealistically high. A collaborative research enterprise often arouses considerable enthusiasm in those who have not previously had close contact with social science. This enthusiasm can easily lead to the belief that now, at last, all questions and problems will be answered. A sample analysis presented as an interim report reduces such expectations to a more realistic level.

Furthermore, the interim report serves to spead over a longer period the time-consuming process of discussing research findings and their implications. The amount of time needed thoroughly to review a large-scale report is sometimes so great as to be forbidding, and may encourage a superficial examination which is detrimental to successful application.

It is, of course, not only the volume of a report that prolongs discussion and puts off application. Sometimes the results provoke resistance, and much time is needed to adjust to the findings and accept them. In extreme cases of unwillingness to accept results, the interim report will be of little help; in less extreme cases, it will provide time and occasion for a gradual readjustment to new ideas while other parts of the analysis are still in progress.

Finally, the interim report serves as a test of whether the social scientist has found the proper level for his communication; for instance, whether there is enough illustrative material. Difficulties spotted at this point may be remedied in the final report.

The preparation of an interim report and the ensuing conferences are, of course, time-consuming for the research staff; often they have not been anticipated in the budget. Yet the contribution they can make toward increasing the chances of application would seem to outweigh all other considerations.

The Final Report to the Collaborating Organization

In preparing both the interim reports and the final report to the collaborating organization or to others who are expected to act on the findings, the investigator must again remember that the main purpose of the report is to communicate to the audience. And this audience is quite different from the social scientists for whom technical reports are written. As a rule, the collaborators or the other persons who will apply the findings constitute a lay audience as far as the theory and methods of social science are concerned, but in the area of their activities they are experts, and their concrete knowledge of the specific situation being studied usually exceeds that of the social scientist. In reporting to them, the investigator must take into account the areas in which they are experts and those in which they are not.

A report to this audience usually starts with a formulation of the research problem in which the action aspects of the problem are emphasized. If formulations of the issues have been jointly arrived at in earlier collaborative efforts, these are presented in full. The formulation of the problem is best followed by a summary of the highlights of the findings; then by a detailed account of each of the findings. In addition, a special section on the implication of the results for concrete decisions is often included. Theoretical implications of the study, if there are any, are presented briefly, in such a way as to give the lay reader a sense of its general significance. The use of scientific terminology in such reports is generally inadvisable. Where such terms have to be introduced, they must be precisely and clearly defined. If statistical data are included, care should be taken to present them in such a way that they can be understood by an audience with little experience in dealing with such material.[5] In the written report, the research design and methods are usually described in an appendix, and tables other than those essential to an understanding of the findings are usually placed there also.

As far as the main body of a report to action personnel is concerned, however, the social scientist must remember that he is addressing experts. This audience should receive a comprehensive and detailed presentation of findings, qualifications and limitations of results, and possible alternative interpretations. In preparing and presenting a report for such an audience, the social scientist must be fully aware of the responsibility he carries in influencing social practices through his work.

In addition to submitting a written report, the social scientist often presents his findings orally to the collaborating agency. Many of the principles and procedures suggested in connection with reducing resistance during the course of the research apply also to the presentation of results. Ordinarily, the findings are reported first to the top officers of the organization, by the investigator himself. The findings may be reported to the other persons concerned either in a large meeting or in small groups, by the investigator himself or by members of the collaborating organization. Presentation to small groups provides

[5] For a detailed discussion of problems arising in the presentation of statistical data, see Zeisel (1957).

greater opportunity for discussion and for consideration of action implications for a specific unit or procedure.[6]

Successful application is facilitated if the results are presented to all those who will be expected to apply them, and perhaps also to those who will be affected by the changes. They should have a chance to ask questions, to make sure that they understand the findings. They should be encouraged to discuss the findings, to suggest alternative interpretations and additional possible applications. In fact, in pre-liminary reports the investigator may present only the bare findings, encouraging the action personnel to suggest interpretations and applications.

The threatening aspects of the findings may be reduced by emphasizing first those things the study shows are going well. Suppose that a survey among the students of a college shows that they are, on the whole, satisfied with the quality of teaching, the content of courses, and the library facilities, but that they have complaints about the living arrangements, the lack of help in securing jobs after graduation, and the scarcity of opportunities for meeting and talking with the faculty outside of class. In a report to the faculty, presenting first those aspects with which students are satisfied may reassure the faculty that the research has not been focused only on shortcomings. The explicit recognition that in many respects the college is doing a good job may make them less sensitive to the criticism of other aspects and more willing to consider whether the criticisms are justified and whether the unsatisfactory situations can be changed. Sensitivity to implied criticism may be reduced by focusing discussion on methods of remedying the shortcomings revealed by the research rather than dwelling on the evidence of their existence. However, it is sometimes necessary to stress such evidence in order to create an awareness that there are problems that need to be solved.

OTHER AUDIENCES FOR ACTION-ORIENTED RESEARCH

In addition to those who may make decisions and take action on the basis of the findings, there are two other audiences for action-

---

[6] Likert and Lippitt (1953) give a detailed account of a presentation following this sequence.

oriented research: social scientists and the general public. Preparation of reports for a scientific audience has been discussed in the preceding chapter; the presentation of action-oriented research to this audience does not introduce any new considerations.

Presentation of social research findings to the general public involves different problems altogether. Presentation to the lay public is rarely undertaken by the social scientist himself. As a rule, the mass media—press, radio, television, and motion pictures—employ specialists in the art of popularization. These middlemen fulfill an important function in the education of the public. Since they are usually responsible to those in charge of the mass communication media rather than to the social scientists who are their source of information, however, the success or failure of these men is often judged in terms alien to the concerns of science. The accuracy of their presentation is sometimes considered of secondary importance. Omitting qualifications of results, oversimplification, and, on the whole, greater claims for social science than are justified by the research are frequent by-products of this situation.

This state of affairs is particularly dangerous in the presentation of action-oriented research. The only way to deal with it satisfactorily lies in the hands of the social scientist. If he gives his consent to a popular presentation of his work, he should arrange to see the product before it is released for popular consumption. His main task in checking the presentation will usually be the introduction of appropriate qualifications about the generalizability of his findings.

Extending the Area of Application

So far we have discussed the manner in which the social scientist can encourage the application of his results by agencies that have collaborated in the research process. But if the collaborating agency is small, application solely by that agency means that use of the findings will be confined to a small group. The social scientist may want to concern himself with the possibility of extending the application of his findings beyond the situation in which they were obtained.

The problems in attempting to broaden the sphere of application beyond the collaborating agency are, in part, problems of *appropriate communication* with other potential users of research findings; in part they are related to the scientific problem of the justification for *generalizing* from one situation to another. We have discussed the question of generalization of research findings in Chapter 11 and shall consider it in another context in Chapter 14. In this chapter we shall examine some occasions where this becomes a practical problem.

The communication of research findings to other interested agencies can be carried out either by the staff of the agency collaborating in the original study or by the social scientist himself. Social workers, housing officials, union leaders, production managers, personnel of community organizations, and any other collaborators who may have been involved in a research project usually maintain organized and personal contacts with others in their professional fields. If their participation in the research project has been at all active, it is likely that they will spontaneously communicate their experience and stimulate others in their field to apply the findings of the study. For example, the Deutsch-Collins study of occupancy pattern in housing projects was widely discussed among housing officials and may have influenced policy formulation by housing authorities which had no firsthand contact with the inquiry. Wider application of the findings was also made possible by the publication of a series of articles in a housing journal. At least in the United States, virtually all professional groups who are likely to cooperate with social scientists publish periodicals. Such publications, in which problems of the profession are discussed, are a suitable medium through which the knowledge of relevant research can be spread and further application encouraged.

Not infrequently, the social scientist is asked to advise upon the application of his research in a new situation. In such cases, the question of whether what he knows can justifiably be transferred to a situation he has not investigated becomes a major one. In applying results beyond the original setting of the research, the social scientist shifts his role from that of a research worker to that of a consultant. The two roles differ in several ways. They involve different skills, activities, motivations, rewards, and responsibilities. If a research scientist temporarily assumes the role of a consultant, his performance in the new role will be better if the shift is made deliberately and of his own volition, rather than accidentally or in response to demands and pressures. It is not within the scope of this text to offer specific suggestions for the social scientist in his consultant role.[7] However, one cardinal rule can be presented: He should not make recommendations prior to full discussion of the features peculiar to the new situation. In conferences with the persons who have sought his advice, he will usually find it most helpful to recount the principal characteristics of his investigation and to ask in return for the essential elements of the problem being brought to him. Such conferences bring into the open both the potentialities and the inevitable risks involved in application of the research results to a new situation. In this process, the agency under whose auspices the research findings are to be applied becomes a full partner to the venture, and the reponsibilities for the outcome of the application are shared by both agency and consultant. It is the consultant's task to specify the conditions under which his original findings obtained; it is the agency's task to examine with him differences in conditions in the new situation. To weigh the importance of such differences is the combined task of both.

Research and Social Policy[8]

Both as a consultant and as a researcher, the social scientist may see his work become an influence in the determination of social policy. But he must be prepared for the fact that there are nonscientific considerations that enter legitimately into the decision-making process and interfere with or promote the application of his results. Much of his effort will be wasted unless he is prepared for this and learns to identify the realistic possibilities for application before becoming too deeply involved in encouraging it.

To take an example: An administrator had supported an investigation designed to diagnose a situation so that appropriate action could

[7] For a discussion of problems of consultation, see Likert and Lippitt (1953).
[8] For a more extended discussion of the relation between research and social policy, see Hyman (1955).

be taken. He sponsored the study in spite of some opposition from other persons in his department. At the time the study was completed, the administrator happened to be engaged in a general reorganization of his department, which aroused the opposition of the same members who had been hostile to the study. Although he was convinced of the value of the study, he realized that fighting two battles simultaneously might interfere with the proper functioning of his department. Since, at the time, he regarded the reorganization as more urgent than the action indicated by the study, he shelved the results until a more opportune moment.

Unforeseeable circumstances that interefere with application can always arise. But frequently it is unforeseen rather than unforeseeable circumstances that present such obstacles. The position of an agency in the community, its manner of arriving at policy decisions, and its ability to carry through program activities may all have an important bearing on the extent to which the findings of research will be applied. The social scientist can frequently make an appraisal of such matters before entering into a collaborative arrangement with the agency. If he is concerned with the immediate application of his findings, he will be well advised to do so.

This is not the place to discuss in detail the process of decision-making in social policy, a process about which all too little is known. One element in this process, however, must be mentioned because it has on occasion given rise to controversies among social scientists about the justification for encouraging application of results. It is sometimes argued that, since decisions on social policy involve social values as well as factual considerations, the social scientist should not attempt to participate in or to influence such decisions. Without doubt social values enter into the making of decisions about the application of research. It is a value question, for example, whether community efforts are to be directed toward eliminating or intensifying discrimination against minority groups. Is the social scientist, by virtue of his status as a scientist, compelled to ignore such values, or can he take sides? Leighton (1949) has answered the question thus:

> Within an area marked off for scientific investigation, the values of science reign supreme over each step in the process to-

ward conclusions and in the conclusions themselves. Moral values when pertinent dominate scientific values at three contiguous points: the selection of the problem to be investigated; the limitation of the human and other materials that may be used; and the determination of what shall be done with the results.

Much like the selection of a research problem (see Chapter 2), it is a matter of personal choice for the social scientist whether or not he will try to facilitate the application of his results. Scientific considerations are of no help here. They do, however, require that once the scientist takes a stand in favor of research implementation, he must point out qualifications and limitations of his research, and refrain from encouraging the application of findings in situations to which they cannot properly be generalized.

Application of research to social policy is not always dependent, of course, on assistance from a social scientist. Agencies reading a report of research that seems relevant to their problems may decide to apply the findings in their own situation, even though the investigator has done nothing to encourage this. There is also nothing to prevent agencies opposing the values of the social scientist and his collaborators from using published research for their own purposes. The real estate board of a southern city, for example, used the Deutsch-Collins study in a political advertisement to urge (unsuccessfully) the electorate to vote against public housing. They quoted the study:

> Our data clearly indicated that the *integrated* in contrast with the *segregated* bi-racial project creates more opportunities for close contact between races, a social atmosphere more conducive to friendly interracial relations and a more closely knit community project. . . .

To this correct quotation they added their appeal: "Public housing means an End of Racial Segregation in Savannah! . . . Vote 'No.' . . ." Thus, a scientific statement which was used in many cities as an argument for integrated occupancy patterns in public housing was used, within the value system of a city in which racial segregation prevailed, as an argument not only against integration but against public housing in general. Research findings, once published, become general property, like any other information. They do not in themselves indicate the desirability of one line of action or another. Rather, they indicate the probable consequences. People with different views concerning the desirability of given outcomes can use the same research findings as arguments for or against a given course of action.

14

RESEARCH AND THEORY

The Function of Theory

Theory as a Basis for Research

The Contribution of Research to the Development of Theory

Interrelation of Theory and Research—A Summary

Those who refuse to go beyond facts rarely get as far as facts.
T. H. HUXLEY

The Function of Theory

THROUGHOUT this book we have pointed to the limitations inherent in the results of a single study and the urgent need for systematic knowledge founded on a broader base. Without such broader knowledge, the insights of social science will necessarily be limited to the specific settings and problems in which investigations have been conducted.

From this point of view, the development of scientific laws and scientific theory has a very practical function. A *scientific law* is a summary of available knowledge of the relationship between properties in more general terms than the empirical findings on which it is based. Scientific laws are hypotheses considered to be true.

Braithwaite (1955) defines a *theory* as consisting of a:

... set of hypotheses which form a deductive system; that is, which is arranged in such a way that from some of the hypotheses as premisses all the other hypotheses logically follow. The propositions in a deductive system may be considered as being arranged in an order of levels, the hypotheses at the highest level being those which occur only as premisses in the system, those at the lowest level being those which occur only as conclusions in the system, and those at intermediate levels being those which occur as conclusions of deductions from higher-level hypotheses and which serve as premisses for deductions to lower-level hypotheses.

It is important to distinguish the modern scientific usage of the word *theory* from other meanings the word may have. In common parlance, *theory* is frequently identified with speculation; what is "theoretical" is unrealistic, visionary. Although it is true that in the early days of a science theories are often the result of armchair speculation and may have meager and weak support in empirical data, theory and observation become more and more closely connected as a science develops. In the present state of the social sciences, research and theory are not always closely linked, and theories are likely to contain speculative elements that go far beyond the evidence of available data. Thus, for example, some aspects of psychoanalytic theory have little confirmation in empirical investigation. Yet it has proved extremely useful as a basis for clinical work and as a source of new perspectives in considering human behavior. In general, however, the intention of a theory in modern science is to summarize existing knowledge, to provide an explanation for observed events and relationships, and to predict the occurrence of as yet unobserved events and relationships on the basis of the explanatory principles embodied in the theory.

One other characteristic of theories in modern science should be noted: this is their provisional character. In earlier times, a theory was considered a final explanation. Today, a theory is always held with some tentativeness, no matter how great the accumulation of findings consistent with it. It is considered as the most probable or most efficient way of accounting for those findings in the light of present knowledge, but it is always open to revision. It is not a static or a final formulation.

An Illustration of Theoretical Explanation

In the third century A.D., Tertullian observed a curious and apparently regular concurrence of events: "If the Tiber overflows into the city, if the Nile does not flow into the countryside, if the heavens remain unmoved, if the earth quakes, if there is famine and pestilence, at once the cry goes up: 'To the lions with the Christians.' "

Seventeen hundred years later, several social scientists (Raper, 1933; Hovland and Sears, 1940) reported another observation: If the per-acre value of cotton in the southeastern section of the United States is low, the number of lynchings of Negroes in that area is high.

Let us assume that the accuracy of both observations is beyond doubt.[1] The underlying similarity in the two statements—catastrophe leads to persecution—is all the more striking because they were made so far apart in time and referred to entirely different people and events. What is the explanation for this sequence of events?

According to Gibbon, the Roman populace had an explanation ready at hand: "The superstitious Pagans were convinced that the crimes and impiety of the Christians, who were spared by the excessive lenity of the government, had at length provoked Divine justice." Since the Christians were thus responsible for the fury of the gods, their death would "naturally" placate the gods, who would then order the Tiber back into its banks.

Let us consider whether this explanation accounts for the later event. Allowing for the change in superstitions throughout the centuries, the argument would run as follows: The Negroes have caused the fall of cotton prices; if they are killed, the cotton price will rise. Both explanations hinge upon the assumption that the Christians and the Negroes were guilty of a crime for which they deserved punishment. However, there are certain differences in the two sequences which make the explanation unsatisfactory for the second. Although we do not share the superstitions of the third century, we must admit that the behavior of the pagans had, at least, internal consistency; they acted on the assumption that punishment of the Christians would stop the pestilence. Lynch mobs, on the other hand, do not relate their actions to the cotton price; rather, they justify them in terms of an alleged or actual rape or a threatened or factual breach of the caste system. Cotton prices do not figure as a conscious motive. Nevertheless, the correlation exists.[2]

When two observations of a similar structure cannot be understood in terms of a given explanation, the social scientist is forced to one of two alternatives: either to demonstrate that the similarity was apparent rather than real, or to search for another explanation that does apply to both events. An explanatory theory is available that can

[1] Actually, this is not quite the case. The second has been challenged by Mintz (1946).

[2] As pointed out in Chapters 4 and 11, the existence of a correlation between two variables does not constitute proof that they are causally related. However, it does make reasonable a search for an explanation of why the two factors vary together.

account for both our examples. It involves the concepts of frustration, aggression, inhibition, and displacement.[3]

Like all concepts, these cannot be directly observed. They may, however, be inferred from events that can be observed. *Frustration* is defined by Dollard et al. (1939) as "that condition which exists when a goal-response suffers interference." *Aggression* refers to a class of acts that are designed to injure someone or something. *Inhibition* refers to the tendency to restrain acts because of the negative consequences one anticipates from engaging in them. *Displacement* refers to the tendency to engage in acts of aggression that are directed not against the source of frustration but against another target. These concepts are related to one another by a system of interlocking hypotheses called "the frustration-aggression theory" (see Dollard et al., 1939).

The major hypotheses of the theory are:

1. The amount of frustration is a function of three factors:
   (a) The strength of instigation to the frustrated goal-response;
   (b) The degree of interference with the frustrated goal-response; and
   (c) The number of goal-response sequences frustrated.
2. The strength of instigation to aggression varies directly with the amount of frustration.
3. The strongest instigation aroused by a frustration is to acts of aggression directed against the agent perceived to be the source of the frustration; progressively weaker instigations are aroused to progressively less direct acts of aggression.
4. The inhibition of any act of aggression varies directly with the strength of the punishment anticipated for its expression. Punishment includes injury to loved objects and being prevented from carrying out a desired act as well as the usual situations that cause pain.
5. The inhibition of direct acts of aggression is an additional frustration that instigates aggression against the agent per-

---

[3] For a discussion of the nature of concepts, see Chapter 2, pages 41–42. For a more detailed discussion of the concepts of frustration, aggression, inhibition, and displacement, and a more detailed presentation of the frustration-aggression theory, see Dollard et al. (1939). Our presentation of the frustration-aggression theory differs from theirs in a number of respects.

ceived to be responsible for this inhibition and increases the instigation to other forms of aggression. There is, consequently, a strong tendency for inhibited aggression to be *displaced* to different objects and expressed in modified forms.

6. The expression of any act of aggression is a catharsis that reduces the instigation to all other acts of aggression.

These interrelated hypotheses help to explain many diverse phenomena, all of which appear to be reflections of the same underlying process—namely, that when a person is frustrated and is inhibited from expressing his aggression directly toward the perceived source of frustration, he will displace his aggression.[4] According to this theory, the aggression against Christians by the Romans after the occurrence of natural catastrophes and the increase in lynchings of Negroes by southern whites after the fall of cotton prices both are explainable in the same terms. *Frustration*, produced by natural catastrophe or by fall in cotton prices (and, hence, in income), results in *aggression*, but the futility or fear of being directly aggressive against the gods or against society *inhibits* the direct expression of the aggression and results in its being *displaced* onto groups whose low social status prevents them from retaliating and hence from also inhibiting the aggression.

Thus, with the help of the concepts of frustration, aggression, inhibition, and displacement, an explanation can be offered not only for the observations about lynching and for the occurrences noted by Tertullian but also for many other events, such as the aggressive action of a child against a younger sibling following his frustration by his parents. This fulfills one requirement of theoretical explanation: It reduces a number of different phenomena to underlying general principles. The more diverse observations a theory can explain, the greater confidence we can have in using the general principles it embodies for the purpose of prediction.

[4] We hope the reader will understand that in presenting the frustration-aggression theory we do not mean to imply that it should be viewed uncritically. We have presented it for illustrative purposes. As a psychological theory, it has been subjected to a good deal of criticism (see Lewin *et al.*, 1944). Some of the major criticisms have centered upon the assumptions that frustration always instigates aggressive acts, that displacement is in a sense blind, and that expression of aggression is necessarily cathartic. Despite its limitations, the frustration-aggression theory was an important landmark in psychology.

RELATION BETWEEN OBSERVATION AND THEORY

Hempel (1952) has likened a scientific theory to a network, in which the terms or concepts are represented by the knots, and the definitions and hypotheses by the threads connecting the knots:[5]

> The whole system floats, as it were, above the plane of observation and is anchored to it by rules of interpretation. These might be viewed as strings which are not part of the network but link certain points of the latter with specific places in the plane of observation. By virtue of these interpretive connections, the network can function as a scientific theory: From certain observational data, we may ascend, via an interpretive string, to some point in the theoretical network, thence proceed, via definitions and hypotheses, to other points, from which another interpretive string permits a descent to the plane of observation.

The advantages of this two-way communication between the plane of observable phenomena and the plane of theory are obvious, provided we follow the rules governing traffic on either plane and between them. Awareness of this particular theoretical formulation of the relationship between frustration and aggression will suggest directions for the study of situations involving frustration. It explains otherwise puzzling situations. Applied to social problems of discrimination and persecution, it suggests that the attack on the actual cause of

[5] The reader may be puzzled by one feature of Hempel's model, the representation of definitions as well as of hypotheses by threads. Is not the definition merely a characterization of a knot, a specification of what a particular knot stands for? In one sense this is, of course, true. But it is easy to miss the fact that every definition that serves a scientific purpose conceals within itself a theoretical proposition— namely, that the things, processes, or events that are encompassed by the definition belong together in the sense that treating them as mutually equivalent under the definition facilitates the discovery of lawful relationships and the organization of data. We could, for example, define fish as creatures that live in water. By this definition, both whales and plankton would be fish. But scientists have found it more helpful to classify whales as mammals and to put plankton in still another category. The preceding definition of fish obscures important relationships. Similarly, if we were to define Negro in terms of degree of pigmentation of the skin, we would be putting together into one category groups of individuals who might better be distinguished and excluding others who might better be counted together with some of those we would have included under the definition (see Klineberg, 1935b). Is a given definition "good" or "correct"? That depends entirely on what it leads to. At issue is not the word, but the proposition that certain things are equivalent for certain purposes and that for these purposes those things that are excluded by the definition are not equivalent to the things that are included.

frustration may be a more successful means of preventing persecution than steps aimed directly at the persecution itself. It offers an alternative for the racist theory of discrimination, which states that the persecution of an out-group is a result of the out-group's attributes rather than of the needs of the in-group—a theory not dissimilar to the popular explanation which satisfied the Roman pagans.

However, as Zawadzki (1948) has pointed out, some observations of prejudice and discrimination raise questions for which the theory has no immediate answer, and thus reveal shortcomings in it as an explanatory principle. Why is aggression displaced most frequently onto the Negro in the American scene, where there are many other minorities that might serve the same function? Why do some people, such as the Comanche Indians whom Kardiner described, engage in aggression against their neighbors even though none of the ordinary frustrations are discernible either in their patterns of child-rearing or in their economic situation? What about the evidence presented by Freud, that frustration may lead to constructive activity as well as to aggression?

None of these questions is answered satisfactorily by the frustration-aggression theory without putting a strait jacket on facts or diluting the definitions of terms and theoretical postulates to such an extent that they lose their substance. In other words, the theory in its present form is inadequate because it cannot account for the variety of relevant phenomena.

This does not mean that the frustration-aggression theory is wrong. It does mean that it is insufficient, not specific enough and not adequate to cover all of the relevant observable phenomena, although it has done good service for a limited number. The limiting conditions under which it applies, however, have not yet been defined,[6] and this interferes seriously with its predictive value.

A survey of the state of theories in the social sciences will reveal that there are very few that can safely be used for explanation and prediction. Often, to speak in terms of Hempel's analogy, one discovers isolated knots with loose threads attached, awaiting the systematic effort needed to tighten them and to tie them together. And, most

---

[6] See G. W. Allport's comprehensive discussion (1950) of the frustration-aggression theory as it applies to the phenomena of prejudice.

frequently, even knots are not yet available. For example, in surveys conducted in 1948, 66 per cent of a sample of the American population agreed with the statement that "most people can be trusted," whereas in Germany only 6 per cent agreed with it (National Opinion Research Center, 1948). One feels intuitively that this is an important difference. But one searches in vain for a well-defined theory of national character or of the psychological impact of miltiary defeat and turbulent historical events in which the concept "confidence in other people" has a systematic place. Under these circumstances, the potentially important addition to knowledge on which these figures may bear remains hidden unless a relevant hypothesis is formulated and tested in a variety of situations.

Research and theory must proceed together toward increases of knowledge. Each has an important contribution to make to the other. Any social scientist may take either one as his starting point, but he has an obligation to consider at some point the bearing of his work on the interrelation of the two. If he concentrates on empirical research, he must examine its relevance to social theory if its potential contribution is to be realized. If his major interest is in the development of social theory, he must take into account ways of testing and expanding his theory by empirical research it it is to become more than interesting speculation.

Theory as a Basis for Research

Theories—even fragments of partially developed theory—provide an important guide for the direction of research by pointing to areas that are likely to be fruitful—that is, in which meaningful relationships are likely to be found. As Merton (1957) has put it:

> . . . if concepts are selected such that no relationships between them obtain, the research will be sterile, no matter how meticulous the subsequent observations and inferences. The importance of this truism lies in its implication that truly trial-and-error procedures in empirical inquiry are likely to be comparatively unfruitful, since the number of variables which are not significantly connected is infinitely large.

Cohen's attempt (1955) to formulate a theory that would account for the appearance of a "delinquent subculture" in certain sectors of American communities illustrates this function of theory for research stimulated by specific social urgencies, just as the frustration-aggression theory was stimulated by and served to guide clinical and experimental psychological research. In developing his theory, Cohen drew on the findings of prior research on delinquency, on his own experience with delinquent gangs, and on other theoretical formulations in psychology and sociology. Briefly, the development follows these steps:

1. All human behavior has the purpose of solving problems.
2. Although all individuals have problems, different kinds of problems are not randomly distributed throughout society; certain kinds of problems are more likely to be encountered by members of the working class than by professional people, by young people more than by older people, by boys more than by girls, etc.
3. A crucial condition for the emergence of new cultural forms is the existence, in effective interaction with one another, of a number of persons with similar problems of adjustment.
4. An important condition for an individual's adjustment is that he be thought well of by others who are important to him, and by himself.
5. For many working-class children, this condition is hard to fulfill. In school, in recreation centers, in all the activities of the larger community, they are judged in terms of middle-class standards, which many working-class children, for a variety of reasons, are not well equipped to meet.
6. The delinquent subculture deals with this problem by providing criteria of status which these children can meet.
7. Since most working-class children have been exposed to, and have partially internalized, middle-class standards, there is a conflict between these standards and those of the delinquent gang.
8. In order to eliminate this conflict, the delinquent subculture explicitly *rejects* (that is, it does not simply ignore) middle-class standards, particularly as they refer to the symbols and

actuality of achieved status; the criteria for status within the delinquent gang are the *opposite* of those held by "respectable" society.

Cohen points out that this theory suggests a need for data of a somewhat different sort than those that have usually been collected in research on delinquency. First, he suggests that more accurate data on the occurrence of delinquent acts are needed. Present statistics are based on official (police and court) records, or on quasi-official records of social agencies, neighborhood centers, etc. There is ample reason to believe that these statistics do not come anywhere near reflecting all the delinquent acts that occur. The problem is not simply, or even primarily, one of underestimating the extent of delinquency; there is no assurance that these records give an accurate picture of how delinquency is distributed in various sectors of society (in other words, there is no assurance that they constitute an unbiased sample of delinquent behavior). Studies comparing delinquent and nondelinquent children have typically selected their delinquent subjects from these official or quasi-official records, and their nondelinquents from among children, presumably comparable in other respects, who do not appear in such records. Cohen maintains that, in order to collect accurate statistics and to find unbiased samples of delinquent and nondelinquent children, it is necessary to start by selecting a random sample of the juvenile population of a given area and then to determine, through careful and sympathetic interviews, the actual occurrence of delinquency among this sample.

One may ask what it is about Cohen's theory that leads to this particular recommendation. Are not all students of juvenile delinquency aware of the limitations of present statistics, and would they not all agree with the desirability of an approach such as Cohen suggests? Perhaps so. But a test of Cohen's theory *requires* such data, since the theory rests explicitly on the assumption that delinquent gangs are more common in working-class neighborhoods than in other parts of the community. Although present official and quasi-official statistics show much higher incidence of delinquency in working-class neighborhoods, some investigators have suggested that this is a reflection of the social processes by which children come to the attention of official agencies rather than a reflection of the true incidence of delinquency. If it should prove to be true that the existence of gangs which are delinquent in relation to middle-class standards and symbols of achieved status is as typical of middle-class as of working-class neighborhoods, Cohen's entire theory would be invalidated.[7]

Second, Cohen recommends a changed emphasis in the kinds of information sought in studies of delinquent and nondelinquent children. Most such research has been concerned with correlates of delinquency—family background, personality, neighborhood characteristics, etc. Although recognizing that such data are useful, Cohen suggests that still more useful would be information about the delinquent behavior itself, and above all on the collective or individual nature of delinquent activity and on how delinquency differs in individual and group situations. Such information, in combination with information about the background factors that have typically been studied, would help to provide an understanding of how delinquent activity serves as a solution of the gang members' problems of adjustment.

Finally, Cohen's theory suggests a need for more research on delinquent groups as social systems—that is, on the structure, processes, history and subculture of delinquent gangs—rather than on the delinquent individual.

So far, this illustration has been concerned with ways in which a theory suggests fruitful research approaches to phenomena in the general area with which the theory is concerned—in this case, juvenile delinquency. But theory provides leads for research in still another way—by suggesting other kinds of phenomena that may perhaps be understood in the same general terms. The first four steps in Cohen's theoretical formulation, as given on page 488, constitute an approach to the understanding of how any subculture arises. Although Cohen does not elaborate this point, he suggests that such different subcultures as college fraternities and the world of jazz musicians may be understood in the same terms. Research on such groups would concentrate on discovering the common problems faced by the members and the

[7] Cohen recognizes the existence of delinquent gangs in middle-class neighborhoods and suggests conditions, in accord with his theory, which might account for them. However, the theory rests on the assumption that delinquent gangs occur primarily in working-class neighborhoods.

ways in which the particular patterns of these subcultures help the members to deal with them.

Closely related to this function of theory is another contribution it makes to research: increasing the meaningfulness of the findings of a given study by making it possible to perceive them not as isolated bits of empirical information but as a special case of the working out of a set of more abstract propositions. For example, if more adequate statistical studies confirm the assumption that delinquent gangs are more common in working-class than in middle-class neighborhoods, this fact in itself would not add greatly to our understanding of delinquency. But looking at gangs as an instance of a general tendency for people faced with common problems to work out a common solution helps to explain the association between working-class neighborhoods and delinquent gangs.[8]

This linkage of the specific empirical findings to a more general concept has still another advantage: It provides a more secure ground for prediction than do the findings by themselves. The prediction may be concerned with estimating whether a relationship between two variables which has been observed in the past will continue in the future, or it may be concerned with estimating whether changes in certain conditions will lead to changes in the observed relationship. To go back to the delinquency example: A variety of steps have been suggested as ways of reducing delinquency—more adequate recreational facilities, provision of counseling services in the schools, censorship of comic books, fining the parents of delinquents, increasing the number of police in high-delinquency areas, etc. Cohen does not discuss possible remedial measures, pointing out that there is not necessarily a direct link between understanding the "cause" of a phenomenon and finding a "cure." Nevertheless, his theory would seem to suggest that a measure intended to reduce gang delinquency is likely to be successful to the extent that it either changes the standards by which working-class children are judged in school and in the community generally, or helps them to meet those standards.

In summary: Theory increases the fruitfulness of research by providing significant leads for inquiry, by relating seemingly discrete findings by means of similar underlying processes, and by providing an

[8] This function of theory has been discussed in more detail in Chapter 2.

explanation of observed relationships. The more research is directed by systematic theory, the more likely are its results to contribute directly to the development and further organization of knowledge.

The Contribution of Research to the Development of Theory

The contributions between theory and research are not all in one direction. Theory stimulates research and enhances the meaning of its findings; empirical research, on the other hand, serves to test existing theories and to provide a basis for the development of new ones.

From a well-formulated theory, deductions can be drawn about what will happen in various situations under specified conditions. Thus, from Hull's reinforcement theory of learning, deductions can be drawn about such diverse matters as the rate at which different parts of a task will be learned, the effects of spaced versus massed practice, the effects of rewarding a given act regularly versus occasionally, etc. These deductions provide hypotheses for empirical research. If a given hypothesis is confirmed by studies planned to test it, the studies have contributed to verifying the entire theoretical structure from which the deduction was drawn. If, on the other hand, a hypothesis is not confirmed by research, the theory must be re-examined to consider whether it should be discarded as invalid or whether some modification would make it consistent with the research findings. In the latter case, of course, further studies are required to test whether deductions from the modified theory will be supported by empirical observation.

In the social sciences at the present time few theories are worked out in sufficient detail to suggest specific studies testing their validity. Thus research more often has the function of contributing to the *development* of theory than to its *testing*.

Contributions to the development of theory may be consciously planned for, or they may be more or less accidental. The social scientist who deliberately sets out to develop some aspect of theory is likely to follow one, or both, of two approaches. He may re-examine existing studies, or he may plan a program of related studies focused on the question in which he is interested. In either case, he is not likely to start completely from scratch; on the basis of earlier studies, or other theoretical formulations, or his own observations, he usually has certain concepts in mind, certain possibilities of alternative formulations, etc. His examination of existing studies, or his plan for studies to be carried out, will be made in the light of these concepts and these tentative formulations.

The development of theory on the basis of existing studies has been demonstrated by Merton and Rossi (1957) in "Contributions to the Theory of Reference Group Behavior." Merton and Rossi use as their material numerous researches in *The American Soldier* (Stouffer et al., 1949a) bearing upon the ways in which individuals select groups as reference points for the evaluation of their own status. Although *The American Soldier* studies were not *planned* in terms of the reference-group concept, a number of the studies concerned with morale and satisfaction were interpreted in these terms.

That people appraise their own status in comparison with that of others is not a new notion. Merton and Rossi, in their search for a theoretical formulation, examine efforts by other social scientists who have used this or similar concepts. Using all these available "knots" and "loose threads," the authors discuss the common elements in nine studies from *The American Soldier;* in each of these studies the attitudes of the soldiers are explained in terms of the relative deprivation they suffered compared with the reference group they used as a standard. The authors point out how the selection of a group for comparison varies from situation to situation. The soldiers evaluate their own situation sometimes with reference to members of their in-groups, sometimes with reference to another group. They may use as bases of comparison groups of the same status as their own, or of higher or lower status. Merton and Rossi see emerging from this re-examination of research results a question of:

> . . . central importance to a developing theory of reference group behavior: *under which conditions are associates within one's own groups taken as a frame of reference for self-evaluation and attitude-formation, and under which conditions do out-groups or non-membership groups provide the significant frame of reference?*

If that question were answered, we would have a reference-group theory instead of only the first steps toward its development. Such a theory would be an important tool in predicting and understanding morale in many situations.

In this example, Merton and Rossi have done what amounts to an *ex post facto* interrelation of separate pieces of research through the use of a single unifying concept—that of reference groups. In so doing, they have extended and clarified the reference-group concept, and have pointed out the direction in which further research is needed if the concept is to take its place in a theory of reference-group behavior.

The Yale Communication Research Program provides an example of the planning and carrying out of coordinated systematic research for the purpose of developing theory. The purpose and nature of this program have been described by Hovland, Janis, and Kelley (1953):

> A great deal of descriptive information has accumulated concerning persuasive communications—such as educational programs, publicity campaigns, advertising, and propaganda—and their effects on behavior and opinion. Most of this information comes from studies which focus on practical questions posed by communicators who make use of mass media. But for purposes of developing scientific propositions which specify the conditions under which the effectiveness of one or another type of persuasive communication is increased or decreased, the available evidence is extremely limited. Although applied research can be useful in suggesting tentative hypotheses and in posing theoretical problems for further analysis, the practical emphasis often results in the neglect of significant and provocative issues which do not appear to have immediate application. Hence basic research is greatly needed to supplement the findings derived from investigations of a practical nature. Such research, involving psychological experiments in a communication setting, can contribute to our understanding of the processes of memory, thought, motivation, and social influence.

The first phase of the program, as reported by Hovland and his colleagues, focused on relatively specific questions about factors and conditions influencing the effectiveness of communications in producing opinion change; for example, "How do differences in the credi bility of the communicator affect 1) the way in which the content and presentation are perceived and evaluated? 2) the degree to which attitudes and beliefs are modified?," "Under what conditions does overt verbal conformity facilitate or interfere with acceptance of the beliefs or opinions advocated by a communication?," etc. The initial studies provided at least tentative answers to many of these questions. At the same time, they suggested new ways of organizing the problem that seemed likely to be more fruitful in developing a unified theory of communication and opinion change. These new topics "cut across the usual categories of communication research," emphasizing the *processes* involved in opinion change rather than the *conditions* under which it occurs. They included study of internalization processes by which "outer conformity" is transformed into "inner conformity"; the relation between conflict and opinion change; and the relations among perception, judgment, and concept formation.

Research contributes to the development of theory also in less planned-for ways. It clarifies concepts; it initiates, it reformulates, and it refocuses theory.[9]

One of the most frequent contributions of empirical research is to the *clarification of the concepts* used in theoretical formulations. This occurs because research cannot proceed on the basis of concepts phrased in general terms; for research purposes, some *indicator* of the concept must be found.[10] In order to decide on an observable indicator of a concept, one must be clear about what he means by the concept. For example, if an investigator wishes to study the influence of certain features of community structure on mental health, he must have some way of estimating the mental health of his subjects. But in order to devise an appropriate measure, he must be clear about what he means by "mental health." The need for "working definitions" in carrying out research often points up a fuzziness in the concepts used in theoretical formulations and forces more precise definitions.

Research may also lead in unplanned ways to the *initiation* of

[9] In this section we have drawn extensively on the discussion by Merton (1957, Chapter 3).

[10] This is, of course, the process of establishing "working definitions" discussed in Chapter 2, pages 42–44.

theory. An investigation, whether it has its origin in some theoretical formulation or in a more trial-and-error approach, may yield an unexpected finding that seems surprising because it is incompatible either with existing theories or with other facts. In his search for an explanation, the investigator may formulate a new hypothesis, which then becomes the basis for subsequent research. Stouffer (in Merton and Lazarsfeld, 1950) describes in the following terms the incident which first led to the introduction of the concept "relative deprivation" in the interpretation of *The American Soldier* studies:

> In the Research Branch I well remember our puzzlement, which went on for months, over the finding that Northern Negroes in Southern camps, in spite of the fact that they said they wanted to be stationed in the North and that they resented discrimination in Southern buses and by Southern police, showed as favorable or more favorable responses to items reflecting personal adjustment in the Army than did those in Northern camps. Some of our analysts were almost in despair at this discrepancy. They actually held up the report on their study for over a month while they checked and rechecked in the vain hope of finding errors in the data or analysis to explain the paradox. When, eventually, it was suggested that the Northern Negro soldier in the South had very great advantages over Negro civilians in the South and that the advantages over Negro civilians in the North were much less, a clue to the paradox appeared. After a number of such experiences, it became evident that some concept like "relative deprivation" might be useful.

To be sure, the notion that people appraise their own status in comparison with that of others was not entirely new. It had been suggested earlier by George H. Mead, Herbert Hyman, and Muzafer Sherif. Nevertheless, the formulation made in *The American Soldier* had certain new elements and considerably extended the concept. It seldom happens that an unexpected finding leads, at one stroke, to the development of an entirely new theoretical concept.

On other occasions, research may lead to the *reformulation* or *extension* of theory by highlighting hitherto neglected facts. This function differs from the preceding one in that, in the present case, the facts are not inconsistent with existing theories or with other facts.

The need is not to find some new explanation, but to reformulate an existing theory which is capable of accounting for them.

For example, in the well-known "Hawthorne studies" (Roethlisberger and Dickson, 1939) the investigators started with the theory that physical conditions affect work output. This relationship had, in fact, been well established; the investigators were concerned with identifying the effects of specific changes, in order to find optimal conditions. At first they found what they had expected: improvement in physical conditions led to increased output. But then they found that changes in the direction of objectively poorer conditions were still accompanied by increases in output. This led to a re-examination of the initial theory. The difficulty appeared to be not that the theory was incorrect, but that it omitted important variables. Physical conditions *did* affect output, but this effect was overshadowed by the far greater effect of other changes accompanying the experimental manipulations. The workers in the experimental group knew that they were taking part in an experiment and were interested in its outcome; they had a different relationship with their supervisor than that which obtained in the regular departments of the plant; their being set apart as a small group led to an increase in cohesiveness among them. These social and attitudinal factors were so important that they obscured the effects of changes in physical conditions. The result was a significant broadening of the theory that output is influenced by factors within the work situation, to include social as well as physical conditions.

Empirical research may also *refocus* theory by shifting interest to new areas. This comes about chiefly through the development of new research procedures, which leads to a rapid growth of research on matters that can be investigated by these techniques. As research accumulates, theoretical interest shifts in the same direction, not because research findings automatically lead to theories, but because an abundance of empirical observations provides fertile ground for the development and testing of theoretical concepts. Consider, for example, the problem of the nature and organization of human abilities. Even before the days of what we now consider scientific psychology, this problem had evoked some interest. But the faculty psychologists and the phrenologists who were interested in aspects of the problem had no effective means of studying it; they were necessarily limited to speculative armchair theorizing and appeals to dramatic instances (or, as was often the case, dramatic coincidences). With the development of techniques for the measurement of abilities, reliance on dramatic instances could give way to systematically collected data; and otherwise sterile speculation could interact with these data, pose new problems for measurement, call for experimentation with factors affecting the outcomes of measurement, and thus grow into fruitful theory. It is not surprising, therefore, that Binet's response to the practical need for some dependable method of diagnosing feeblemindedness marked the onset of a new era in the history of psychology—an era in which the successes, failures, and abuses of the intelligence-testing movement not only led to the critical examination of basic premises and the growth of psychometric theory, but also served as a spur to efforts to meet the challenge of measuring other complex aspects of personality. And, of course, the extension of measurement into the domain of personality inevitably raised issues of conceptualization of personality variables, etc., etc.

Or, to take a less familiar example, the repercussions of which extended to a much narrower domain than those of the testing movement: When Zeigarnik decided to test an inference from Lewinian theory that subjects would remember better tasks which they were not permitted to complete than tasks which they carried through to completion, she introduced an experimental technique which lent itself to the testing of a wide variety of hypotheses. There occurred thereupon a proliferation of research and theory on the effects upon tension systems of such variables as success and failure, task versus ego orientation, carrying out substitute actions that differ from the interrupted ones in certain systematic respects, etc.[11]

Interrelation of Theory and Research—A Summary

The relation of theory and research is one of mutual contributions. Theory can point to areas in which research is likely to be fruitful, can summarize the findings of a number of specific studies, and can

[11] For an unusually complete account of the interaction of theory and research along these lines, see Lewin (1951), "Formalization and Progress in Psychology."

provide a basis for explanation and prediction. Research findings, on the other hand, can test theories which have been worked out, can clarify theoretical concepts, and can suggest new theoretical formulations or extend old ones. Moreover, the process of reciprocal contribution is a continuing one; research stimulated by theoretical considerations may raise new theoretical issues, which in turn lead to further research, and so on indefinitely. At whatever point in this spiral of activities a social scientist chooses to work, the significance of his contribution will increase with his insight into the processes that link the results of separate studies to theoretical formulations. To conduct research without theoretical interpretation or to theorize without research is to ignore the essential function of theory as a tool for achieving economy of thought.

APPENDICES

A. *Estimating the Time and Personnel
Needed for a Study*

B. *An Introduction to Sampling*

C. *Questionnaire Construction and Interview Procedure*

Appendix A

ESTIMATING THE TIME AND PERSONNEL
NEEDED FOR A STUDY

I N THE VERY earliest stage of planning, the investigator must consider what resources of time, personnel, and money will be needed to carry out the study he has in mind. This is equally important for the student planning a term paper, the doctoral candidate starting work on his dissertation, the social scientist applying to a foundation for support of a project, the consultant proposing a study to help in the solution of a a client's problem. Under some circumstances it is possible to secure the time, personnel, and money required by the tentative research plan; in others, it is necessary to adjust the plan so that it can be carried out within the available resources. In either case, it is important to have a realistic estimate of what will be required.

In this appendix, we shall make a few suggestions for estimating time and personnel requirements. Translating these requirements into appropriate salaries provides the basis for estimating that part of the budget. Additional costs, such as office rent, travel expenses, purchase or construction of equipment, etc., depend so much on the nature of the specific study that little can be said in the way of general guidance.

There is, unfortunately, no rule of thumb by which one can predict exactly how much time will be needed to carry out a study. Perhaps the most efficient way of going about the task is to list the various phases of the research procedure and estimate how much time and how many people will be required for each, rather than to attempt to arrive directly at an over-all estimate for the total project. The steps discussed in the various chapters of this book provide a basic outline of the steps that must be planned for: formulating the research question, defining concepts, planning the study design, developing the data-collection instruments, collecting and analyzing the data, writing the report. But many practical steps not discussed in detail in this book must also be considered; for example, the hiring and training of interviewers or observers, negotiations with agency personnel in the case of a field study, etc.

How does one estimate how long each operation will take? Primarily, one learns through experience—usually sad. It appears to be an almost universal rule that every operation takes longer than one would anticipate if everything went smoothly. The estimate must provide leeway for the snags that inevitably arise: the fact that the pretest shows that several interview questions need rewording, or that observers need additional training in order to use the data-collection instrument reliably; failure to find respondents at home on the first visit, and the need for several call-backs; the decision of the director of an action agency that he must consult his board of directors before giving permission to carry out research within the agency; the mistake in punching scores onto calculating machine cards, which leads to errors in several tables before it is discovered; and so on. One way of providing the extra time required by such contingencies is first to estimate how long each operation might be expected to take if it went reasonably smoothly, then to go back over these estimates, increasing them by 50 per cent or even more.

The amount of time needed for the different stages of the research process will depend to a considerable extent on the type of study. The following records of time and personnel actually used in three studies will illustrate both the wide range in total time and personnel that may be needed and the differences in the relative amount of time devoted to various operations.[1]

[1] It should perhaps be noted that each of these budgets underestimates the total period of time over which the study extended, since it includes only activities directly concerned with the study. Almost inevitably, however, there are some other demands on the time of the research staff, with the result that total elapsed time is greater than indicated by total time spent on the study.

Time Budget 1 is from the Deutsch-Collins study of intergroup relations in bi-racial housing projects, described in Chapter 1. The preliminary "experience survey" of housing experts, which took six months, is not included; the budget starts from the point of specific planning for the study of the effects of occupancy pattern. In this study, personal interviews were conducted with about four hundred white housewives (one hundred in each of four projects). The interview schedule contained more than one hundred questions; on the average, a single interview lasted about an hour and a quarter. In addition, about one hundred Negro housewives and a number of white children were interviewed. There were nineteen interviewers; the time shown in the "Interviewers" column refers to total man-days, not to actual elapsed time.

As we mentioned in Chapter 1, the study was preceded by an "experience survey" of housing experts, and began with rather definite hypotheses drawn both from this source and from the general body of literature on intergroup attitudes. Thus relatively little time was required for formulation of the problem and the research design or for analysis, compared with the large amount of time devoted to conducting and coding the interviews. The large amount of time needed for establishment of categories and coding stemmed from the fact that the interview consisted mainly of open-ended questions. In exploratory studies aimed at the development of hypotheses, analysis is likely to require a considerably greater proportion of time, since such studies, by their very definition, frequently have to proceed on a time-consuming trial-and-error basis.

Time Budget 2 applies to a small-scale exploratory study. Its purpose was to examine in systematic fashion the impressions left on twenty participants by a training workshop they had attended ten months prior to the study. These impressions were elicited in the course of intensive, relatively unstructured individual interviews. On the basis of the interviews, the investigator analyzed the probable effects of the workshop, deriving a number of hypotheses that could be tested in more rigorously designed subsequent studies. Since the participants in the workshop lived at some distance from one another, an exceptionally high proportion of the project time went into traveling

Time Budget 1
Study of Occupancy Patterns in Public Housing Projects
(The figures indicate working days)

Operation	Study Director	Research Associate	Consultant	Statistical Clerk	Interviewers	Coders	Secretary
Formulation and design	30	10	2				3
Negotiations, planning with housing officials	10	10	3				
Development of interview schedule (including pretest)	30	30	5				15
Selection of sample	3	3	1				1
Hiring and training of interviewers	3	3					
Interviewing	10	15			225		2
Establishment of categories	20	20	2				2
Coding	5	18				145	10
Statistical analysis	15	15	2	30			1
Conferences on interpretation	5	5	5				5
Report-writing (preliminary reports, several drafts, final report)	95	25					50
Editing	5	5	10				10
Misc. administrative work	20	20	5				20
Conferences and preparation of report for housing officials	25	15					5
Total working days*	276	194	35	30	225	145	124

*There are about 230 to 250 working days in a year, depending on vacation arrangements.

Time Budget 2
An Exploration of the Impact of a Workshop for Teachers
(The figures indicate working days)

Operation	Study Director	Consultant	Secretary
Formulation	3	3	1
Negotiations with workshop organizers		1	
Development of interview schedule	3	1	1
20 intensive interviews	15		6
Analysis and writing, draft	8	1	2
Editing and final report	1	5	2
Miscellaneous administrative and clerical work	3		
Total working days*	33	11	12

*There are about 230 to 250 working days in a year, depending on vacation arrangements.

Time Budget 3 refers to a study of the acceptability of answers to anti-minority remarks made in public. In this study, playlets in which one character made an anti-minority remark and another answered him in different ways were presented to groups of people. Some of the groups already existed for other purposes; others were composed of passers-by recruited on a busy street corner. Altogether, there were about one hundred groups, comprising some fifteen hundred individuals. Each group session lasted about half an hour. Data were collected primarily by means of short fixed-alternative questionnaires administered during the experimental sessions. In addition, approximately two hundred and fifty subjects were interviewed, each interview lasting approximately fifteen to thirty minutes.

The rather unusual nature of the problem and of the experimental stimulus (the playlets) led to a high proportion of time spent in the initial stages of problem formulation, research design, and development of the playlets. On the other hand, the fact that data were collected in groups, by means of short questionnaires and interviews, resulted in a relatively small proportion of time devoted to this aspect of the research operation. There is no "Interviewers" column because the interviewing was done by the staff members.

When research budgets are faulty, they almost invariably err on the side of underestimation. Often the social scientist simply does not realize how much work will be involved in his plans. Or, vaguely

Time Budget 3

A Study of Answers to Anti-Minority Remarks

(The figures indicate working days)

Operation	Study Director	Research Assoc. No. 1	Research Assoc. No. 2	Consultant	Actors	Coders	Statistical Clerk	Secretary
Formulation and design	45	45	45	30				10
Development of experimental stimulus (playlets)	30	30	30	15	10			5
Development of questionnaires and interview schedule	20	20	20	5				3
Data collection	25	25	25	1	125			3
Establishment of categories and coding	5	20	20			60		4
Statistical analysis	30	30	30				60	5
Conferences on interpretation	15	15	15	15				
Report-writing (several drafts and revisions)	60	40	40	10				25
Editing	2			10				10
Conferences with action agencies on results	6	5	4	6				
Miscellaneous administrative and clerical work	20	5	5	5				10
Total working days*	258	235	234	97	135	60	60	75

*There are about 230 to 250 working days in a year, depending on vacation arrangements.

recognizing it, he may still make a minimal estimate because he believes this will be more acceptable to his sponsors in the situation.

Sometimes the estimate is adequate for the work originally planned, but unforeseen possibilities for investigation emerge during the study. The social scientist may be carried away by zeal for collecting data or for following up these newly emerging leads. Many studies collect an enormous amount of irrelevant data, which are never used. To strike a happy medium between concern for scientific and financial economy and a flexibility of mind that permits a continuous development and refinement of ideas is an art that few people have mastered. It would be disastrous for the advancement of knowledge if the rigidity of the budget should restrict the flexibility of the mind. But it is no light matter either if flexibility of mind turns into undisciplined imagination and involves much unforeseen time and expense, thus endangering the continuity of the work because available resources have been exhausted.

Appendix B

AN INTRODUCTION TO SAMPLING

BY ISIDOR CHEIN

I N THIS APPENDIX we have not attempted to develop a manual of sampling procedures. Nor have we attempted to review statistical formulae and procedures appropriate for the handling of data obtained in sampling studies. We have aspired, without resorting to mathematical analysis and within the limits of available space, to give the reader some basis for an intelligent appreciation of the considerations involved in sampling.[1]

Some Basic Definitions and Concepts

A *population* is the aggregate of all of the cases that conform to some designated set of specifications. Thus, by the specifications "people" and "residing in the United States," we define a population consisting of all the people who reside in the United States. We may similarly define populations consisting of all the shop stewards in a

---

[1] For more comprehensive discussions of sampling and appropriate statistical treatments, see the chapters by McCarthy in Jahoda, Deutsch and Cook (1952, Volume 2), by Kish in Festinger and Katz (1953), and by Cochran in Snedecor (1956); also see Deming (1950), Cochran (1953), and Hansen, Hurwitz, and Madow (1953). For a very broad discussion of sampling theory and practice, including a review of empirical tests of sampling, see Stephan and McCarthy (1958).

factory, all the households in a particular city district, all the boys in a given community under sixteen years of age who are stamp collectors, all the case records in a file.

By certain specifications, one population may be included in another. Thus, the population consisting of all the men residing in the United States is included in the population consisting of all the people who live in the United States. In such instances, we may refer to the included population as a sub-population, a population stratum, or simply as a stratum (pl. strata). A stratum may be defined by one or more specifications that divide a population into mutually exclusive segments. For instance, a given population may be subdivided into strata consisting of males under twenty-one years of age, females under twenty-one years of age, males from twenty-one through fifty-nine years, etc. Similarly, we may specify a stratum of the American population consisting of white, male, college graduates who live in New England and who have passed their seventy-fifth birthday; or we may have some reason for regarding this group of individuals as a population in its own right—that is, without reference to the fact that it is included in a larger population.

A single member of a population is referred to as a population element. We often want to know how certain characteristics of the elements are distributed in a population. For example, we may want to know the age distribution of the elements or we may want to know the proportion of the elements who prefer one political candidate to another. A census is a count of all of the elements in a population and/or a determination of the distributions of their characteristics, based on information obtained for each of the elements.

It is generally much more economical in time, effort, and money to get the desired information for only some of the elements than for all of them. When we select some of the elements with the intention of finding out something about the population from which they are taken, we refer to that group of elements as a sample. We hope, of course, that what we find out about the sample is true of the population as a whole. Actually, this may or may not be the case; how closely the information we receive corresponds to what we would find by a comparable census of the population depends largely on the way the sample is selected.

For example, we may want to know what proportion of a population prefers one candidate to another. We might ask one hundred people from that population which candidate they prefer. The proportion of the sample preferring Mr. Jones may or may not be the same as the corresponding proportion in the population. For that matter, even the actual distribution of votes in an election may not correctly represent the distribution of preferences in the population. Unless there is a 100 per cent turnout, the actual voters constitute only a sample of the population of people eligible to vote. A very high proportion of the people who prefer Mr. Smith may be overconfident with respect to their candidate's chances and neglect to come to the polls; or they may be living in a rural area and be discouraged from coming to the polls by a heavy downpour. The election results may properly determine which candidate will take office, but they will not necessarily indicate which candidate is preferred by a majority of the population.[2] Similarly, the early returns in an election may be taken

[2] It has been a common practice to predict the outcome of an election on the basis of a pre-election sample survey which, at best, answered only the question of preferences. The results have occasionally been disastrous. The fiascos are by no means attributable simply to the failure of the samples to represent the distribution of preferences in the population at the time the polls were taken. In one instance (the presidential election of 1948), the pre-election surveys showed that a large proportion of people were undecided, and there are clear indications that an unanticipated consolidation of opinion in this group helped to confound the predictors. As already indicated in the text, the fact that different proportions of those who prefer different candidates may actually vote complicates the translation of preference estimates into election forecasts.

There are also measurement problems involved. Preferences measured one way may or may not correspond to preferences measured another way. Thus, behavior in the voting booth does not necessarily correspond to preferences expressed to an interviewer. The former is generally accepted at face value as the more valid measure, but we have no certainty that this is the case. A housewife, for instance, may follow her husband's preference rather than her own, at the last moment, and it is possible that there may be enough such instances to materially affect the outcome of an election; similarly, other kinds of subjectively felt pressures or momentary impulses may take effect in the election booth. Practical politicians seem to feel that the position of their candidate's name on the ballot affects his chances, as do the names of other candidates running for other offices on the same ticket; such effects may have bearing on voting behavior without affecting preferences.

Further complications arise from the gerrymandering of election districts and other factors (e.g., the electoral college system), which have the effect of giving different voters different weights in determining the outcome of an election. Perhaps the moral of this footnote will be clear: The usefulness of findings obtained from a sample may depend in large measure on factors which are extraneous to the sampling issues per se. Nor is it easy to draw a hard-and-fast dividing line between the

as a sample of the population of returns; and, as everyone knows, they can be thoroughly deceptive.

In the case of elections and in the case of early returns in a national election, there probably is not much we can do to guarantee that the samples will correctly represent their populations. The outcome of an election we must, perforce (barring some radical revisions of election procedures), accept on faith that it does reflect the popular will. And if we are misled by the early returns with respect to the final outcome, then, at least, our errors are soon corrected. There are, however, situations in which we can to some extent control the properties of the sample. In these situations, the way we go about drawing the sample can, if not guarantee, then at least increase the likelihood that the sample returns will not be too far from the true population figures for our purposes. We can never guarantee that the sample returns do reflect the population with respect to the characteristics we are studying unless we have simultaneously conducted a complete comparable census. We can, however, devise sampling plans which, if properly executed, can guarantee that, if we were to repeat a study on a number of different samples selected from a given population, our findings would not differ from the true population figures by more than a specified amount in more than a specified proportion of the samples.

For instance, suppose that we frequently want to know what percentage of a population agrees with certain statements. On each of these occasions we might put such a statement to a sample, compute the percentage who agree, and take this result as an estimate of the proportion of the population who agree. We can devise a number of sampling plans that will carry the insurance that our estimates will not differ from the corresponding true population figures by, say, more than 5 per cent on more than, say, 10 per cent of these occasions; the estimates will be correct within 5 percentage points (the *margin of error* or *limit of accuracy*) 90 per cent of the time (the *probability* or *confidence level*). We can similarly devise a number of sampling plans that will produce correct results within 2 percentage points 99 per cent

---

factors which are extraneous and those which are not. Thus, what is extraneous to the sampling of one population (e.g., eligible voters) may be intrinsic to the sampling of another (e.g., actual voters); the ambiguity arises when we sample one population with the intention of learning something about the other.

of the time; or within any other limits of accuracy and any assigned probability. In practice, of course, we do not repeat the same study on an indefinite number of samples drawn from the same population. But our knowledge of what would happen in repeated studies enables us to say that, with a given sample, there is say a 90 per cent probability that our figures are within 5 percentage points of those that would be shown by a census of the total population using the same measures. Having set our level of aspiration for accuracy and confidence in the findings, we would select from the available alternatives the sampling plan which can be most economically carried through. Needless to say, the higher the level of aspiration, other conditions being equal, the higher the cost of the operation.

A sampling plan that carries such insurance may be referred to as a *representative sampling plan*. Note that in this usage the word "representative" does not qualify "sample," but "sampling plan." What a representative sampling plan can do is to insure that the odds are great enough that the selected sample is, for the purposes at hand, sufficiently representative of the population to justify our running the risk of taking it as representative.

The use of such a sampling plan is not the only kind of insurance that can be taken out to decrease the likelihood of misleading sample findings. Another involves taking steps to guarantee the inclusion in the sample of diverse elements of the population and to make sure (either by controlling the proportions of the various types of elements or by analytical procedures in the handling of the data) that these diverse elements are taken account of in the proportions in which they occur in the population. We shall consider this type of insurance at greater length in our discussion of quota sampling and of stratified random sampling.

It should perhaps be emphasized that the dependability[3] of survey findings is affected not only by the sampling plan and the faithfulness with which it is carried out, but also by the measurement procedures used. This is one reason why sample surveys of a large population can,

---

[3] Throughout this appendix, the terms "accuracy," "dependability," and "precision" are used interchangeably. Although technical distinctions are sometimes made among these words, in most discussions of sampling they are used as synonyms.

in practice, produce more dependable results on some matters than can a census. There simply are not enough highly skilled interviewers available to get anything beyond the most superficial information in a national census; a survey on a smaller scale puts less of a drain on the available supply of interviewers and also more readily permits a relatively intensive training program. Similarly, a smaller-scale survey may make it economically feasible to spend more time with each respondent and, hence, make it possible to use measurement devices that could not be seriously considered (except on a sampling basis[4]) in connection with a census of a large population.[5]

The basic distinction in modern sampling theory is between *probability* and *nonprobability* sampling. The essential characteristic of probability sampling is that one can specify for each element of the population the probability that it will be included in the sample. In the simplest case, each of the elements has the same probability of being included, but this is not a necessary condition. What is necessary is that for each element there must be some specifiable probability that it will be included. This point will be considered more fully in connection with the discussions of simple random samples and stratified random samples. In nonprobability sampling, there is no way of estimating the probability that each element has of being included in

[4] It is not uncommon nowadays to collect certain items of information on a sampling basis in the course of conducting a census for other items of information.

[5] There is another reason why sampling surveys may produce more dependable information than censuses. In practice, no census ever reaches all the population elements; in effect, what is supposed to be a census is actually a sample, albeit a sample which includes a very high proportion of the population elements. If the unreached elements differ markedly from those that are reached, the result may be quite different from the true population value even though the unreached elements may be a relatively small proportion of the population. Not all of the unreached are unreachable; they vary along a continuum of accessibility, depending on the amount one is prepared to invest in trying to reach them. In a relatively small scale survey, one may be able to afford a greater relative investment in trying to reach the comparatively inaccessible elements. A census may also go after the known unreached on a sampling basis (e.g., by having interviewers return one or more times to dwellings where no one is at home on the first visit, or by sending more highly skilled interviewers to talk with respondents who have refused to give the desired information), but there is also an issue of the relative proportion of unknown unreached in the two procedures and this is a function of what one can afford to invest in exploring the terrain (e.g., discovering dwelling units in unsuspected places)

the sample, and no assurance that every element has some chance of being included.[6]

Probability sampling is the only approach that makes possible representative sampling plans. It makes it possible for the investigator to estimate the extent to which the findings based on his sample are likely to differ from what he would have found by studying the population. Conversely, if he uses probability sampling, he can specify the size of the sample (or the sizes of various components of complex samples) that he will need if he wants to have a given degree of certainty that his sample findings do not differ by more than a specified amount from those that a study of the total population would yield.

The major advantages of nonprobabiltiy sampling are convenience and economy—advantages that may outweigh the risks involved in not using probability sampling. Precise comparisons of the relative costs of the two approaches to sampling are, however, not available (see Stephan and McCarthy, 1958). Moreover, the comparative costs will vary depending on the number of surveys that are contemplated. Thus, if a number of surveys of the same population are to be carried out, the cost of preparing and maintaining lists from which to sample (generally a necessary step in probability sampling) can be distributed over all of them.

Major forms of nonprobability samples are: accidental samples, quota samples, and purposive samples. Major forms of probability samples are: simple random samples, stratified random samples, and various types of cluster samples.[7]

---

[6] If there is a class of elements that have no chance of being included, this implies a restriction on the definition of the population. If the nature of this class of elements is unknown, then the precise nature of the population is also unknown. If there is no assurance that every element has some chance of being included, this uncertainty implies that there can be no assurance as to the precise nature of the population that is being sampled.

[7] The reader should be warned that "accidental sampling" and "random sampling" are technical terms, as defined in the text. The words "accidental" and "random" may have quite different connotations in ordinary everyday usage. These meanings should not be confused with those assumed in the technical usage. Thus, it may be no "accident" (everyday usage) that a sampler picks the cases he does in an "accidental sample" (technical usage). In everyday usage a "random sample" may connote any nonpurposive sample or what is technically defined as an accidental sample. The justification of the technical usage would take us too far afield and will not be attempted here.

Nonprobability Sampling

ACCIDENTAL SAMPLES

In accidental sampling, one simply reaches out and takes the cases that fall to hand, continuing the process until the sample reaches a designated size. Thus, one may take the first hundred people one meets on the street who are willing to be interviewed. Or a college professor, wanting to make some generalization about college students, studies the students in his classes. Or a journalist, wanting to know how "the people" feel about a given issue, interviews conveniently available cab drivers, barbers, and others who are presumed to reflect public opinion. There is no known way (other than by doing a parallel study with a probability sample or with a complete census) of evaluating the biases[8] introduced in such samples. If one uses an accidental sample, one can only hope that one is not being too grossly misled.

QUOTA SAMPLES

Quota sampling (sometimes misleadingly referred to as "representative" sampling) adds insurance of the second type referred to above—provisions to guarantee the inclusion in the sample of diverse elements of the population and to make sure that these diverse elements are taken account of in the proportions in which they occur in the population. Consider an extreme case: Suppose that we are sampling from a population with equal numbers of males and females and that there is a sharp difference between the two sexes in the characteristic we wish to measure. If we did not interview any males, the results of the survey would almost certainly be an extremely misleading picture of the total population. In anticipation of such possible differences between subgroups, the quota sampler tries to guarantee the inclusion in his sample of enough cases from each stratum.

As commonly described, the basic goal of quota sampling is the selection of a sample that is a replica of the population to which one

---

[8] *Bias* refers to the difference between the average of the estimates of a population value that would be obtained from a very large number of samples selected by a given procedure and the actual population value, assuming identical measurement processes.

wants to generalize—hence the notion that it "represents" that population. If it is known that the population has equal numbers of males and females, the interviewers are instructed to interview equal numbers of males and females. If it is known that 10 per cent of the population lies within a particular age range, assignments are given to the interviewers in such a way that 10 per cent of the sample will fall within that age range.

The question of the kinds of characteristics that must be taken into account will be considered in more detail in the course of our discussion of stratified random sampling. It is enough, for the moment, to say that in the sampling of preferences, opinions, attitudes, etc., experience indicates that it is wise to take into account such bases of stratification as age, sex, education, geographical region of residence, socioeconomic status, and ethnic background. Not all these are equally visible; the usual practice is to set the quotas for the interviewers in terms of the more manifest traits and to get information in the course of the interviews on the less manifest ones. The latter information permits correction of the inadequacies of the sample by adjustments introduced during the analysis, a procedure that will be illustrated in the following paragraphs. It also calls attention to omissions, if any should occur, of important segments of the population.

It often happens, in practice, that the various components of the sample turn out not to be in the same proportions as the corresponding strata are in the population. The interviewers may not have carried out their instructions exactly; instead of interviewing equal numbers of males and females, 55 per cent of the people they interviewed may have been males. Disproportions between the sample and the population are most likely to occur, of course, in the less manifest traits which have not been included as part of the specifications for the interviewers' quotas. Suppose it is known that, in a given population, 40 per cent have not gone beyond grammar school; suppose, however, that only 20 per cent of the people interviewed fall in this category. The inadequacy in the sample can be corrected in the analysis by weighting the different strata in terms of their proportions in the population. This may be done by multiplying or dividing the obtained results by the appropriate figure.

Let us say that the total sample consisted of 1,000 persons, of whom 800 had attended high school, 200 had not. Suppose we asked this sample whether they had seen a certain television program, and the responses were as follows:

	No High School	High School	Total
Yes	20	400	420
No	180	400	580
Total	200	800	1,000

In other words, one-tenth of the people without high-school education and half of those with such education said they had seen the program. If we wished simply to report the figures for the educational groups separately, no adjustment would be needed. But if we wanted to estimate the proportion of the total population that had seen the program, our sample findings would be misleading. The program had been seen by 42 per cent of the people in our sample. But our sample underrepresented people in the lower educational category, overrepresented those with high-school education. To derive an estimate of the correct figure for the total population, we must calculate what the responses would have been if 40 per cent of the people in the sample had had only grammar-school education, 60 per cent had attended high school (the proportions we have assumed for the population). One way of doing this is to multiply the responses of the no-high-school group by 2 (to bring the 20 per cent in the sample up to 40 per cent), and of the high-school group by three-fourths (to reduce the 80 per cent to 60 per cent). This would give 40 "yes's" in the no-high-school group and 300 in the high-school group, or 340 for the total group; thus we would estimate that 34 per cent of the population had seen the program, rather than the 42 per cent we would have estimated if we had not weighted the strata in terms of their actual proportions in the population.

From this example it should be clear that the critical requirement in quota sampling is not that the various population strata be sampled in their correct proportions, but rather that there be enough cases from each stratum to make possible an estimate of the population stratum value, and that we know (or can estimate with reasonable accuracy) the proportion that each stratum constitutes in the total population. If these conditions are met, the estimates of the values for the various strata can be combined to give an estimate of the total population value.

However, despite these precautions in the selection of the sample, and the corrections in the analysis, quota sampling remains basically an accidental sampling procedure. The part of the sample in any particular class constitutes an accidental sample of the corresponding stratum of the population. The males in the sample are an accidental sample of the males in the population; the twenty-to-forty-year-olds in the sample constitute an accidental sample of the twenty-to-forty-year-olds in the population. If the instructions received by the interviewers and their execution of these instructions produce correct proportions of the compound classes (e.g., white males in the twenty-to-forty age range), the sample cases in these classes are still accidental samples of the corresponding compound strata in the population. The total sample is thus an accidental sample.

There is by now, however, enough experience with quota sampling to make it possible to minimize the risks of at least certain types of unfortunate accidents. It is known that interviewers, left to their own devices, are especially prone to certain pitfalls. They will interview their friends in excessive proportion. But their friends are likely to be rather similar in many respects to themselves. Now, consider the possibility that, in certain matters, people who do interviewing and others like them are atypical of the population at large. If these matters are involved in the survey, the sample results are likely to be inaccurate. Once we are aware of the danger, however, we can take steps to discourage the practice.

If interviewers fill their quotas by stopping passers-by and inviting them to be interviewed, they will tend to concentrate on areas where there are large numbers of potential respondents: the entertainment centers of cities, business districts, railway and air terminals, the entrances of large department stores. Such samples will overrepresent the kinds of people who tend to gravitate to these areas. A concentration on many varieties of such areas will presumably be better than a concentration on only one, but, even so, such samples will underrepresent the kind of people who seldom leave their immediate neighborhoods and especially those who seldom leave their homes. Often this will make no difference, but it is conceivable that, on some matters at some times, there may be sharp differences between the overrepresented and the underrepresented population segments. When this is the case, such a sample would, of course, yield misleading results. Again, to be forewarned is to be forearmed.

If the interviewers fill their quotas by home visits, they will tend to proceed along lines of convenience and striking appearance. Thus, concentrating on certain times of the day, they will tend to miss the kinds of people who are not at home at such times (e.g., working women during the daytime). Similarly, they will tend to avoid the upper stories of buildings without elevator service. They will tend to favor corner buildings and to avoid dilapidated buildings and buildings situated behind others. Such sampling tends to build in a systematic socioeconomic bias (i.e., in each residential area, to overrepresent the wealthier people) and possibly other biases as well.

The point to be noted about selective factors such as these is that they are not easily corrected during the analytical treatment of the data. For many populations we know in advance the true relative proportions of the two sexes and of the various age groups, and so can correct for disproportions in the sample, but what true proportion of what definable population is most likely to be found at a railroad terminal during the course of a survey? The major control that an investigator has available to him in connection with such variables is in the sampling process itself. He can try to assure that important segments of the population are not entirely unrepresented in his sample, try to benefit from his experience and sample in such a way that many possibly relevant variables are not too grossly distorted in his sample, and hope that whatever disproportions remain will not have any bearing on the opinions, preferences, etc., that he is interested in.

PURPOSIVE SAMPLES

The basic assumption behind purposive sampling is that with good judgment and an appropriate strategy one can hand-pick the cases to be included in the sample and thus develop samples that are satisfactory in relation to one's needs. A common strategy of purposive sampling is to pick cases that are judged to be typical of the population in which one is interested, assuming that errors of judgment in the selection will tend to counterbalance each other. Experiments on purposive sampling suggest that, without an objective basis for making the judgments, this is not a dependable assumption. In any case, without an external check, there is no way of knowing that the "typical" cases continue to be typical.

Purposive samples selected in terms of assumed typicality have been used in attempts to forecast national elections. One such approach is as follows: For each state, select a number of small election districts whose election returns in previous years have approximated the overall state returns; interview all the eligible voters in these districts on their voting intentions; and hope that the selected districts are still typical of their respective states. The trouble with the method is that when there are no marked changes in the political atmosphere, one can probably do as well by forecasting the same returns that obtained in previous years without doing any interviewing at all; when changes are occurring, one needs to know how the changes are affecting the selected districts in comparison with other districts.

Probability Sampling

Probability samples involve the first kind of insurance against misleading results that we discussed earlier—the ability to specify the chances that the sample findings do not differ by more than a certain amount from the true population values. They may also include the second kind of insurance—a guarantee that enough cases are selected from each relevant population stratum to provide an estimate for that stratum of the population.

SIMPLE RANDOM SAMPLES

Simple random sampling is the basic probability sampling design; it is incorporated in all of the more complex probability sampling designs. A simple random sample is selected by a process that not only gives each element in the population an equal chance of being included in the sample, but also makes the selection of every possible combination of the desired number of cases equally likely. Suppose, for example, that one wants a simple random sample of two cases from a population of five cases. Let the five cases in the population be A, B, C, D, and E. There are ten possible pairs of cases in this population: AB, AC, AD, AE, BC, BD, BE, CD, CE, and DE. Write each combination on a disc, put the ten discs in a hat, mix them thoroughly, and have a blindfolded person pick one. Each of the discs has the same chance of being selected.[9] The two cases corresponding to the letters on the selected disc constitute the desired simple random sample.

There are, in the tiny illustrative population of five cases, ten possible samples of three cases: ABC, ABD, ABE, ACD, ACE, ADE, BCD, BCE, BDE, and CDE. Using the same method, one can select a simple random sample of three cases from this population.

In principle, one can use this method for selecting random samples from populations of any size, but in practice it could easily become a lifetime occupation merely to list all the combinations of the desired number of cases. The same result is obtained by selecting each case individually, using a list of random numbers such as may be found in most textbooks of statistics. These are sets of numbers that after careful examination have shown no evidences of systematic order. Before using the table of random numbers, it is first necessary to number all the elements in the population to be studied. The table is then entered at some random starting point (e.g., with a blind pencil stab at the page), and the cases whose numbers come up as one moves from this point down the column of numbers are taken into the sample until the desired number of cases is obtained. The selection of any given case places no limits on what other cases can be selected, thus making equally possible the selection of any one of the many possible combina-

---

[9] In this illustration, each of the discs (i.e., each combination of two cases) has one chance in ten of being selected. Each of the individual cases also has the same chance of being selected—four in ten, since each case appears on four of the discs. There are, however, very many ways of giving each case the same chance of being selected without getting a simple random sample. For example, suppose we were arbitrarily to divide an illustrative population of ten cases into five pairs as follows: AB, CD, EF, GH, IJ. If we write the designations for these pairs on five discs, blindly pick one of the discs, and take as our sample the two cases designated on this disc, then every case has one chance in five of being picked but, obviously, not every possible combination has the same chance of being selected as every other —in fact, most of the combinations (e.g., AC) have no chance at all, since they have not been included on the discs.

tions of cases. This procedure is therefore equivalent to selecting randomly one of the many possible combinations of cases.[10]

Without going into the mathematical argument, it is possible only to illustrate the underlying principles of probability sampling. Consider, for this purpose, a hypothetical population of ten cases, as follows:

Case:	A	B	C	D	E	F	G	H	I	J
Sex:	F	F	F	F	F	M	M	M	M	M
Age:	Y	O	Y	O	Y	O	Y	O	Y	O
Score:	0	1	2	3	4	5	6	7	8	9

The first five cases are females, the last five males; the cases designated Y are younger and the O's are older. Age and sex will be considered

[10] The procedure of selecting a random sample should not be confused with the procedure of sampling from a list or a file of cases by taking every kth (for example, every fourteenth or every sixty-third) case. The latter procedure is called *systematic* sampling. Systematic samples may be either probability or nonprobability samples, depending on how the first case is selected. Suppose one wants to select every sixtieth case. To get a probability sample, the first case has to be selected randomly from the first sixty, and every sixtieth case thereafter is selected. If the first case is not selected randomly, the resulting sample is not a probability sample since most of the cases have a zero probability of being included in the sample. Although to the uninitiated systematic sampling seems to be the most natural and rational way to go about sampling from a list, it involves complications not present in a simple random sample. When the first case is drawn randomly, in a systematic sample, there is in advance no limitation on the chances of any given case to be included in the sample. If we are selecting a sample of 100 cases from a population of 6,000, before the first case is selected each case has one chance in sixty (100 in 6,000) of being included in the sample, whether we are using simple random or systematic sampling. But in a systematic sample, once the first case is selected, the chances of other cases are altered. Suppose the first case drawn is #46. Selecting every sixtieth case thereafter means that #106, 166, 226, etc., will be drawn; the cases between these numbers now have no chance of being included.

This means that a systematic sampling plan does not give all possible combinations of cases the same chance of being included; only combinations of elements 60 cases apart in the list have any chance of being selected for the sample. The results may be quite deceptive if the cases in the list are arranged in some cyclical order. Suppose, for example, that the 6,000 cases are houses in a community that was built according to a systematic plan, and that they are listed in order of streets and numbers. Corner houses would then appear at regular intervals throughout the list; say, the first house and every twentieth house thereafter is a corner dwelling. A sample consisting of cases 1, 61, 121, etc., would be made up entirely of corner houses; one consisting of cases 2, 62, 122, etc., would contain no corner houses. But corner houses are usually larger and more expensive than those within the block, and their occupants may accordingly differ systematically in certain characteristics. Thus any sample made up entirely of corner houses, or entirely lacking in corner houses, would give misleading results if the study concerned characteristics in which occupants of the two types of dwellings differ.

later, in relation to stratified sampling. The score represents some attribute of the individual, such as, his performance on a test of mechanical aptitude.

The mean score for this population of ten cases is 4.5. Assuming that this were not known, the problem would be to make an estimate of the population mean on the basis of the scores of the elements in the sample that is drawn. According to the definition of simple random sampling, the method of selecting the sample must give equal probability to every combination of the desired number of cases—in other

TABLE 1
MEAN SCORES OF SAMPLES FROM ILLUSTRATIVE
POPULATION OF TEN CASES WITH POPULATION MEAN SCORE
OF 4.5 (SIMPLE RANDOM SAMPLES)

	Number of Samples		
Sample Means[11]	Samples of 2 cases	Samples of 4 cases	Samples of 6 cases
.5	1		
1.0	1		
1.5–1.75	2	2	
2.0–2.67	5	10	2
2.75–3.25	3	25	10
3.33–4.00	8	43	52
4.17–4.83	5	50	82
5.00–5.67	8	43	52
5.75–6.25	3	25	10
6.33–7.0	5	10	2
7.25–7.5	2	2	
8.0	1		
8.5	1		
Total no. of samples	45	210	210
Mean of sample means	4.5	4.5	4.5
% of sample means greater than 4.00 and less than 5.00	11	24	39
% of sample means greater than 2.67 and less than 6.33	60	89	98

[11] With the small number of different scores in the illustrative population, there are only a limited number of possible sample means. Thus, for samples of two cases, there is no combination that can yield a mean of 2.25; but there are three samples of four cases (ABDF, ABCG, ACDE) with a mean of 2.25. Similarly, a mean of 2.67 is not possible for any sample of two or four cases, but is possible for one sample of six cases. For convenience of tabulation and in order to help bring out the characteristics of the sampling distributions, the means of the samples have been grouped.

words, over the long run, with repeated sampling, every combination should come up the same number of times. We can, therefore, figure out what will happen in the long run in our illustrative population by the simple device of considering all the combinations. That is, we take every combination of the desired number of cases and compute a mean for each combination. What results is a distribution of sample means—known as a *sampling distribution*. For example, there are 45 possible combinations of two cases in our hypothetical population of ten cases. One, and only one, combination (cases A and B) will yield a sample mean of .5; there are five combinations (A and J, B and I, C and H, D and G, E and F) that will yield sample means of 4.5; and so on. Similarly, there are 210 possible samples of four cases. One of these combinations (A, B, C, and D) will yield a sample mean of 1.5; one (A, B, C, and E), a sample mean of 1.75; and so on.

Table 1 shows the sampling distributions for sample means based on simple random samples of two, four, and six cases from our illustrative population.

Notice that for samples of any given size the most likely sample mean is the population mean;[12] the next most likely are figures close to the population mean; the more a sample mean deviates from the population mean, the less likely it is to occur. Also, the larger the sample the more likely is it that its mean will be close to the population mean.

It is this kind of behavior on the part of probability samples (not only with respect to means, but also with respect to proportions and other types of statistics) that makes it possible to estimate not only the population characteristic (e.g., the mean) but also the likelihood that the sample figure differs from the true population figure by any given amount.

One interesting feature of simple random sampling ought to be mentioned, even though it is hard for most people to believe it without mathematical proof. When the population is large compared to the sample size (say, more than ten times as large), the variabilities of sampling distributions are influenced much more by the absolute number of cases in the samples than by the proportion of the population that is

---

[12] Ths point is obscured in Table 1, for the case of samples of two, by the grouping of means. Actually, there are five possible samples of two cases with means of 4.5: there are four possible samples with mean of 4.0; etc.

included. That is, the magnitude of the errors that are likely depends more on the absolute size of the sample than on the proportion of the population that it includes. Thus, the estimation of popular preferences in a national pre-election poll, within the limits of a given margin of error, would not require a substantially larger sample than the estimation of the preferences in any one state where the issue is in doubt. Conversely, it would take just about as large a sample to estimate the preferences in one doubtful state with a given degree of accuracy as it would to estimate the distribution of preferences in the entire nation. This is true despite the fact that a sample of a few thousand cases obviously includes a much larger proportion of the voters in one state than the same-sized sample does of the voters in the nation.[13]

STRATIFIED RANDOM SAMPLES[14]

In stratified random sampling, as in quota sampling, the population is first divided into two or more strata. Again, the strata may be based on a single criterion (e.g., sex, yielding the two strata of male and female) or on a combination of two or more criteria (e.g., age and sex, yielding strata such as males under 21, males 21 and over, females under 21, females 21 and over). In stratified random sampling, a simple

[13] For the benefit of those who may have some knowledge of analytical statistics but who may nevertheless react with startled incredulity when explicitly confronted with the principle of the indifference of sample statistics to the *sampling fraction* (i.e., the proportion of the population included in a sample), it may be pointed out that the sampling fraction is not even mentioned in the relevant formulas given in most statistics textbooks. Thus, the familiar formula for the standard error of the mean is $\sigma/\sqrt{N}$, where σ is the estimated standard deviation of the population and N is the number of cases in the sample. This formula is derived from the mathematics of simple random sampling and, as given, omits a term. Correctly, the formula should be multiplied by $\sqrt{(1-f)}$, where f designates the sampling fraction. Obviously, the smaller the value of f, the less difference this multiplier makes. In sampling from an infinite population, f equals zero; in sampling from a finite population, it is never quite zero, but is generally too small to have any practical consequences and may hence be disregarded. This is the principle discussed in the text above. It should be remembered, however, that when a large proportion of a population is being sampled, taking account of the sampling fraction may considerably reduce the estimate of the probable margin of error of the sample findings. When the population is small, one must include a large proportion in the sample in order to achieve a small margin of error.

[14] For reasons of simplicity of presentation, some points already made in the discussion of quota sampling will be repeated here.

random sample is taken from each stratum, and the subsamples are then joined to form the total sample.

To illustrate how stratified random sampling works, we may return to the previously described population of ten cases. Consider samples of four with equal proportions of males and females (i.e., samples made up by combining subsamples of two males with subsamples of two females). To satisfy this last condition, many samples of four that were possible under the conditions of simple random sampling are no longer possible—for example, samples consisting of cases A, B, C, D or of cases A, B, C, F or of cases D, F, G, I—because they do not have two males and two females. In fact, there are now exactly 100 possible samples as compared to the 210 previously possible. As before, we have computed the mean score for each of the possible samples and thereby obtained the sampling distribution of the mean. Table 2 compares the sampling distributions for samples of four obtained on the basis of simple random sampling, stratified sampling using sex as a

Table 2

MEAN SCORES OF SAMPLES OF FOUR CASES FROM ILLUSTRATIVE POPULATION OF TEN CASES WITH POPULATION MEAN SCORE OF 4.5 (SIMPLE AND STRATIFIED RANDOM SAMPLES)

	Number of samples		
Sample Means[15]	Simple random samples	Samples stratified by sex	Samples stratified by age
1.50–1.75	2		1
2.00–2.50	10		7
2.75–3.25	25	3	8
3.50–4.00	43	25	26
4.25–4.75	50	44	16
5.00–5.50	43	25	26
5.75–6.25	25	3	8
6.50–7.00	10		7
7.25–7.50	2		1
Total no. of samples	210	100	100
Mean of sample means	4.5	4.5	4.5
% of sample means greater than 4.00 and less than 5.00	24	44	16
% of sample means greater than 2.50 and less than 6.50	89	100	84

[15] Again, the means of the samples have been grouped. See note to Table 1.

criterion for stratification, and stratified sampling using age as a criterion.

It will be noted that there is a marked improvement over simple random sampling when the sampling is based on a stratification of our hypothetical population by sex; with this kind of stratification we get a marked increase in the number of samples that give means very close to the population mean and a marked reduction in the number of sample means that deviate widely from the population mean. When the population is stratified by age, however, there is no such marked improvement in the efficiency of sampling; in fact, the means of individual samples are somewhat less likely to be very close to the population mean.

In general, stratification contributes to the efficiency of sampling if it succeeds in establishing classes that are internally comparatively homogeneous with respect to the characteristics being studied—that is, if the differences between classes (e.g. between males and females) are large in comparison with the variation within classes (e.g., among the males and among the females). In our illustrative population, the difference in scores between the sex groups is relatively large, that between age groups relatively small; that is why stratification by sex is effective in this case, stratification by age ineffective. The general principle is that, if one has reason to believe that stratifying according to a particular criterion or set of criteria will result in internally homogeneous strata, then it is desirable to stratify. If the process of breaking the population down into strata that are likely to differ sharply from one another is costly, then one has to balance this cost against the cost of a comparable gain in precision obtained by taking a larger simple random sample. The issues involved in the decision whether to stratify have, basically, nothing to do with trying to make the sample a replica of the population; they only have to do with the anticipated homogeneity of the defined strata with respect to the characteristics being studied and the comparative costs of different methods of achieving precision. Both simple and stratified random sampling involve representative sampling plans.

Except for a slight saving in arithmetic, there is no reason for sampling from the different strata in the same proportion. That is, even with respect to the criteria selected for stratification, it is not necessary that the sample reflect the composition of the population. Thus, in sampling from a population in which the number of males equals the number of females, it is permissible (and may sometimes be desirable) to sample nine, or five, or two, or some other number of females to every male. When this is done, however, it is necessary to make an adjustment in order to find the mean score (or the proportion of elements with a given characteristic, or whatever measure is desired) for the sample which will be the best estimate of the mean score of the total population of males and females. This is accomplished by "weighting" the figure for each stratum in such a way that it contributes to the score for the total sample in proportion to its size in the population, as in the quota-sampling illustration on page 518. When the various strata are sampled in constant proportion, one is spared this bit of arithmetic since the various strata are already properly weighted.

There may be several reasons for sampling the various strata in different proportions. Sometimes it is necessary to increase the proportion sampled from classes having small numbers of cases in order to guarantee that these classes are sampled at all. For example, if one were planning a survey of retail sales volume in a given city in a given month, simple random sampling of retail stores might not lead to an accurate estimate of the total volume of sales, since a few very large department stores account for an extremely large proportion of the total sales, and there is no guarantee that any of these large stores would turn up in a simple random sample. In this case, one would stratify the population of stores in terms of some measure of their total volume of sales (for example, the gross value of sales during the preceding year). Perhaps only the three largest department stores would be in the topmost stratum. The investigator would include all three of them in his sample; in other words, he would take a 100 per cent sample of this stratum.[16] Any other procedure in such a situation would greatly reduce the accuracy of the estimate, no matter how carefully samples were

[16] Note that in such a procedure, the cases in the total population do not all have the same chance of being included in the sample. Each of the three largest stores has a 100 per cent chance of being included, whereas each of the stores in another stratum may have only one chance in ten. But the probability of inclusion of each case can be specified, thus meeting the basic requirement for probability sampling (see pages 514–515).

taken from other strata. Again, of course, the figures from the various strata would have to be appropriately weighted in estimating the total volume of sales in the city.

Another reason for taking a larger proportion of cases from one stratum than from others is that one may want to subdivide the cases within each stratum for further analysis. Let us say that in our survey of retail sales we want to be able to examine separately the volume of sales made by food stores, by clothing stores, etc. Even though these classifications are not taken into account in selecting the sample (i.e., the sample is not stratified on this basis), it is clear that one needs a reasonable number of cases in each volume-of-sales stratum to make possible analysis of different types of stores within each stratum. If a given stratum has relatively few cases, so that sampling in the proportion used in other strata would not provide enough cases to serve as an adequate basis for this further analysis, one may take a higher proportion of cases in this stratum.

One of the major reasons for varying the sampling proportions for different strata cannot be fully explained without going into the mathematical theory of sampling, but the principle involved can be understood on a more or less intuitive basis. Consider two strata, one of which is much more homogeneous with respect to the characteristics being studied than the other. For a given degree of precision, it will take a smaller number of cases to determine the state of affairs in the first stratum than in the second. To take an extreme example: suppose that there is reason to know that every case in a given stratum has the same score; one could then determine how to represent that stratum in the total sample on the basis of a sample of one case. Of course, in such an extreme case one is not likely to have this information without also knowing what the common score is. But in less extreme cases one can often anticipate the relative degrees of homogeneity or heterogeneity of strata before carrying out the survey. For example, there may be a great deal of experience to suggest that, with respect to certain types of opinion questions, men will differ among themselves much more than will women; one would accordingly plan one's sample for a survey of such opinions so as to provide for sampling a larger proportion of men than of women. Because women may be expected to be more alike than men in these matters, they do not have to be sampled as thoroughly as do the men for a given degree of precision.

In general terms, one can expect the greatest precision if the various strata are sampled proportionately to their relative variabilities with respect to the characteristics under study rather than proportionately to their relative sizes in the population. A special case of this principle is that, in sampling to determine the proportion of cases possessing a particular attribute, strata in which one can anticipate that about half the cases will have the attribute and half will not should be sampled more thoroughly than strata in which one would expect a more uneven division. Thus, in planning a stratified sample for predicting a national election, using states as strata, one should not plan to sample each state in proportion to its eligible population; it would be wiser to sample most heavily in the most doubtful states.

One final point about stratified sampling: There may be reason to believe that certain criteria will provide very effective bases for stratification (ie., using these criteria, we would get strata which differ markedly from one another), but, as pointed out in the discussion of quota sampling, the relevant data may become available only in the course of the survey. In this case one cannot use the criteria in the sampling design, but one can apply the logic of stratified sampling theory in the analysis of the data. Thus, one can take a simple random sample, ascertain the information necessary for stratification during the course of the interviews, and use this information in grouping the cases according to their respective strata and weighting them appropriately in the analysis of the data.

For example, suppose that we want to survey the attitudes of the students in a certain school toward some issue and that we have some reason to believe that the proportions of "pro's," "anti's," and "undecideds" are likely to be different among the Negro and the white students. Suppose, further, that we have a complete listing of the student body but no identification of the race of the individual students, even though we know that 30 per cent of the students are Negro and 70 per cent are white. We could draw a simple random sample of the students and ascertain the race of each respondent while recording his views on the issue. The data might then come out as follows:

	No. in the School	No. that Turn up in the Sample	No. in the Sample Who Are		
			"Pro"	"Anti"	"Undecided"
Negroes	300	40	30	8	2
Whites	700	160	50	40	70
Total no.	1000	200	80	48	72
Percentage of sample	—	—	40	24	36

Projecting from the sample to the total numbers in the two racial groups, we would get:

	Estimated Number Who Are		
	"Pro"	"Anti"	"Undecided"
Negroes	225	60	15
Whites	219	175	306
Total no.	444	235	321
Estimated percentage of total student body	44.4	23.5	32.1

These figures are easily arrived at. Thus, three-fourths of the Negro sample are "pro," and three-fourths of 300 is 225. In this case, the corrected percentages are not dramatically different from the total-sample percentages, despite marked differences between the Negro and white groups. This results from the facts that the disproportion between the sampling fractions in the two groups is not very great (13 per cent of the Negroes are included in the sample as compared to 23 per cent of the whites) and that the Negro group constitutes a relatively small proportion of this population. Despite the relatively small differences in the results of the two procedures (i.e., the uncorrected and corrected percentage estimates) in this example, the assured precision is greater with the second.

From the viewpoint of the theory of probability sampling, it is essentially irrelevant whether the stratification is introduced in the sampling procedure or in the analysis of the data, except insofar as the former makes it possible to control the size of the sample obtained from each stratum and thus to increase the efficiency of the sampling design. It can be shown that any stratum of a simple random sample of a population is itself a simple random sample of the corresponding population stratum. Thus, not only is our total sample of the student body a simple random sample of the total population, but the 40 Negroes in the sample are a simple random sample of all the Negroes in the school, and the 160 whites are a simple random sample of the white students. In other words, our procedure of drawing a *simple* random sample and then dividing it into strata is equivalent to having drawn a *stratified* random sample using, as the sampling fraction within each stratum, the proportion of that stratum that turned up in our simple random sample. Thus, even though we were not in a position to stratify in advance, we can take advantage of the increased efficiency of stratified sampling.

CLUSTER SAMPLING

Except when dealing with small and spatially concentrated populations, there are enormous expenses associated with simple and stratified random sampling—for example, in the preparation of classified lists oi population elements and in sending interviewers to scattered localities. The more widely scattered the interviews, the greater are the travel expenses, the greater is the proportion of nonproductive time spent in traveling, and the more complicated—and hence expensive—are the tasks of supervising the field staff. There are also other factors that often make it difficult or impossible to satisfy the conditions of random sampling. For example, it may be easier to get permission to administer a questionnaire to three or four classes in a school than to administer the same questionnaire to a much smaller sample selected on a simple or stratified random basis; the latter may be much more disruptive of the school routines. For such reasons, large-scale survey studies seldom make use of simple or stratified random samples; instead they make use of the methods of cluster sampling.

In cluster sampling, one arrives at the ultimate set of elements to be included in the sample by first sampling in terms of larger groupings ("clusters"). The clusters are selected by simple or stratified random sampling methods; and, if not all the elements in these clusters are to be included in the sample, the ultimate selection from within the clusters is also carried out on a simple or stratified random sampling basis.

Suppose, for example, that one wants to do a survey of seventh-grade public-school children in some state. One may proceed as follows: Prepare a list of school districts, classified perhaps by size of community, and select a simple or stratified random sample. For each of the school districts included in the sample, list the schools and take a simple or stratified random sample of them. If some or all of the schools thus selected for the sample have more seventh-grade classes than can be studied, one may take a sample of these classes in each of the schools. The survey instruments may then be administered to all the children in these classes or, if it is desirable and administratively feasible to do so, to a sample of the children.

Similarly, a survey of urban households may take a sample of cities; within each city that is selected, a sample of districts; within each selected district, a sample of households.

Characteristically, the procedure moves through a series of stages—hence the common term, "*multi-stage*" *sampling*—from more inclusive to less inclusive sampling units until one finally arrives at the population elements that constitute the desired sample.

Notice that with this kind of sampling procedure it is no longer true that every combination of the desired number of elements in the population (or in a given stratum) is equally likely to be selected as the sample of the population (or stratum). Hence, the kinds of effects we noticed in our analysis of simple and stratified random sampling of our hypothetical population of ten cases (the population value being the most probable sample result and larger deviations from the population value being less probable than smaller ones) cannot develop in quite the same way. Such effects do, however, occur in a more complicated way,[17] provided that each stage of cluster sampling is carried out on a

---

[17] The complication arises from the fact that there are two sources of sampling error: the sampling of the larger sampling units and the sampling of population elements within the larger units. To illustrate the point that cluster sampling does have the same kinds of effects as simple and stratified random sampling, let us consider the simple case in which the second source of error is eliminated by studying all the population elements in the sampled larger units. Each larger unit has its score (consisting, say, of the mean score of its elements). But this leaves us with a simple or stratified random sample of the population of larger units—no different, in principle, from a simple or stratified sample of population elements. Hence, it is clear that the trends we noted in connection with random samples will tend to occur on this level. Now, if instead of taking 100 per cent samples of the elements in each larger unit, we were to take a simple or stratified random sample of the elements in each unit, the larger units become the populations from which these samples are drawn—and the tendencies we noted will again occur. Thus, these tendencies toward the greatest probability of achieving a sampling result that is the same as the population value, and toward progressively larger deviations becoming progressively less probable, will occur with respect to both sources of error that are involved in cluster sampling.

probability-sampling basis. One pays a price, however, in terms of sampling efficiency. On a per-case basis, effective cluster sampling is much less efficient in obtaining information than comparably effective stratified random sampling—that is, for a given number of cases, the probable margin of error is much larger in the former case than in the latter. Moreover, the correct statistical handling of the data is apt to be much more complicated. These handicaps are, however, more than balanced by the associated economies, which generally permit the sampling of a sufficiently larger number of cases at a smaller total cost. The comparison of cluster sampling with simple random sampling is somewhat more complicated. Stratified sampling principles may be used to select the clusters and what is lost in efficiency because of the clustering effects may be regained by this stratification. Depending on the specific features of the sampling plan in relation to the object of the survey, cluster sampling may be more or less efficient on a per-case basis than simple random sampling. But again, even if more cases are needed for the same level of accuracy, the associated economies generally favor cluster sampling in large-scale surveys.

Combinations of Probability and Nonprobability Sampling

If sampling is carried out in a series of "stages," it is, of course, possible to combine probability and nonprobability sampling in one design. That is, one or more of the stages can be carried out according to probability sampling principles and the balance by nonprobability principles. We shall consider two examples.

The investigator may select clusters by probability cluster sampling techniques but, at the final stage, select the elements as a quota sample. Thus, it is possible to select a probability sample of counties in a state; within each of these counties, a probability sample of neighborhoods; and within each of the selected neighborhoods, a quota sample controlled for, say, age and sex.

The advantage of such a design is that the major economies of quota sampling occur in obtaining the particular cases for the sample. It is relatively inexpensive to select the areas within which the final stage of sampling will take place by probability sampling, and one thereby gains the advantages of probability sampling, at least for the areas. There is some evidence, for instance, that quota samples built up in selected areas are more successful in controlling for such variables as socioeconomic status than quota samples in which the control of these variables depends on the judgments of the interviewers (Stephan and McCarthy, 1958).

It may be remarked, in passing, that quota samples are, in practice, nonprobability cluster samples. Our earlier description of quota sampling may have made it appear to be the nonprobability analogue of stratified random sampling; that is, it may have seemed that specified proportions of cases with given characteristics were selected from the total population. But in practice there are always restrictions on the geographical areas within which the sampling takes place. Hence, the traditional national quota sample has typically involved a nonprobability sample of areas as well as a nonprobability sample of elements within these areas. By using probability sampling to select the areas, however, one can gain an extra measure of security at relatively little cost.

The second example of combining probability and nonprobability sampling involves the opposite strategy. The investigator takes a probability sample of elements within a nonprobability sample of areas. The areas are selected as a purposive sample. For example, a number of counties may be selected on the grounds that they have, for years, tended to produce election results typical of their respective states; within each of the "typical" counties, the investigator selects a probability sample of eligible voters.

One way of looking at this kind of design is to regard the "typical" counties as defining a population. If a probability sample of this population is taken, the mathematical theory of probability sampling is completely applicable, and one can state the probable limits of error in the relation of the sample results to the true population values. One can then generalize the inferences regarding this restricted population to the national population, subject to the assumption that the "typical" counties are still typical of their respective states. So long as this assumption is valid, it seems likely that such a sampling plan will produce the most dependable sampling results at the least cost; but then, of course, with each application of this sampling design, one must hope that the assumption is in fact valid. The results of such a sampling plan can, however, always be stated in a form that makes it clear where the possibilities of error lie. Thus, a conclusion might read, "There is a nineteen-to-one likelihood that from 60 to 74 per cent of the eligible voters in these typical counties prefer Candidate A. If nothing has happened to make these counties atypical in this election, these results may be taken as reflecting the national distribution of preferences. If the actual distribution of votes follows the distribution of preferences at the time of the survey, it seems likely that Candidate A will be elected." The election post-mortem can establish how well the vote was predicted in the "typical" counties and whether they were indeed still typical.

Special Applications of Nonprobability Sampling

It has already been noted that the major advantages of nonprobability sampling are convenience and economy. It is likely, therefore, that many future sampling operations will be conducted according to nonprobability principles as long as researchers are convinced that these sampling procedures work reasonably well, despite the fact that they do not provide any basis for estimating how far the sample results are likely to deviate from the true population figures. Investigators, in other words, will continue to use nonprobability methods and to justify their use on the grounds of practical experience, even while conceding the superiority in principle of probability sampling. Moreover, many practical samplers will argue that, in many cases at least, this superiority exists only on paper. They will point out that there is a difference between the sampling plan and its actual execution; there can be many a slip in the carrying out of the plan which would nullify its theoretical advantages. Interviews, for instance, may fail to follow their instructions in selecting respondents, or they may omit some of the questions in interviewing some of the respondents (and, thereby, produce samples of somewhat different and not strictly comparable populations in relation to the various questions in the same interview schedule); some of the selected cases may refuse to be interviewed or not be available; compromises may be made by allowing interviewers to substitute other respondents when those designated for the sample are not found at home;[18] etc. The sample actually obtained may, hence, not be the probability sample it was planned to be.

Moreover, there are circumstances in which probability sampling is unnecessary or inappropriate. One such circumstance arises from the fact that one does not necessarily carry out studies of samples only for the purpose of being able to generalize to the populations that are being sampled. If one uses samples for other reasons, ability to evaluate the likelihood of deviations from the population values is irrelevant. For example, during the discussion of "experience surveys" in Chapter 3, it was pointed out that the goal is to obtain ideas, good insights, and experienced critical appraisals. One selects the sample—a purposive sample—with this in mind and not with the intention of assessing the status of opinion among practitioners. The situation is almost exactly analogous to one in which a number of expert consultants are called in on a difficult medical case. These consultants—also a purposive sample —are not called in in order to get an average opinion that would corre-

---

[18] It is sometimes claimed that one advantage of quota over probability sampling is that the former avoids the problem of refusals or unavailability. This is not correct. To be sure, the procedures of quota sampling may—and commonly do— by-pass the problem by ignoring such cases and allowing the interviewers to make substitutions. Ignoring a problem is not equivalent, however, to solving it. The existence of uninterviewable cases implies a restriction on the sampled population. Probability samplers generally acknowledge the restriction; quota samplers generally say nothing about it.

In probability sampling, when the restriction is accepted, the sound practice is either to not replace the drop-outs at all, or to replace them by selecting new cases by the same procedures that were used in selecting the original sample, rather than by, say, taking the nearest at-home neighbor of a not-at-home case. When the sound practice is followed, the resulting sample is a probability sample of the restricted population. This follows from the mathematically provable principle to which we have already referred: any segment of a probability sample is itself a probability sample of the corresponding segment of the population. If the restriction is not accepted, the sound practice is, of course, to make intensive efforts to recover the drop-outs.

Another expedient involves the use of data acquired in the course of the survey to transcend the restriction (see Politz and Simmons, 1949, and Simmons, 1954). Briefly, the logic of the Politz and Simmons procedure may be described as follows: Drop-outs resulting from the failure to find the selected respondent at home are consequential only if the probability of being at home has some bearing on the subject matter of the survey. Let us then find out from those who are at home what the probability would have been of the interviewer finding them at home if he had called at the same time of day during, say, the preceding five days. We can then relate this probability to the responses to the survey questions and correct the survey findings on the basis of this information.

spond to the average opinion of the entire medical profession. They are called in precisely because of their special experience and competence. Or the situation may be viewed as analogous to our more or less haphazard sampling of foods from a famous cuisine. We are sampling, not to estimate some population value, but to get some idea of the variety of elements available in this population.

Another example of sampling for ideas rather than for the estimation of population values is provided by the field of market research known as motivation research. The typical problem of motivation research is to find out something about motives, attitudes, associations, etc., that are evoked by certain products, brand names, package designs, etc., but that may not be obvious even to the respondents themselves. The results of such studies are turned over to advertising agencies which make use of them in developing advertising campaigns. Characteristically the motivation researchers are quite happy with accidental samples, or with purposive samples selected in such a way as to maximize the likelihood of differences among the elements in the sample. They are looking for ideas to transmit to the advertising men, not for correct estimates of population distributions. One might argue that they would be better off if they could establish, not merely the variety of motives that are likely to become involved with certain products, but also the precise distributions of these involvements. At present, however, it seems to be problematical whether the additional information would be worth the extra cost of getting it. At any rate, so long as these researchers deceive neither themselves nor their clients into believing that they are getting the second kind of information, no one can take exception to their application of accidental sampling.

Sometimes there is no alternative to nonprobability sampling. If one is trying to find out something, for example, about the attitudes of people on the other side of the "Iron Curtain," one has no realistic choice but to rely on informants who have recently spent some time there (each of whom reports on the accidental sample involved in his contacts), and on escapees, who are themselves far from typical. The choice here is between data that do not permit a statistical assessment of the likelihood of error and no data at all. Similarly, if one is trying to reconstruct a picture of a dying or recently deceased culture, one has no choice except to rely on relatively articulate informants for certain types of information. This does not mean that one is not concerned with the possibility of error; but one places one's reliance on the internal consistency of the data and its coherence with other things that one knows.

Another special case justifying the use of nonprobability samples arises from the fact that there are many important considerations in research in addition to the sampling design. It may be necessary to balance one consideration against another—for example, a better sampling design against a more sensitive method of data collection. Ackerman and Jahoda (1950), for example, studied the characteristics of patients in psychoanalytic treatment who had given expression to anti-Semitic sentiments. With complete protection of the anonymity of the patients, some forty analysts served as informants. The sample of psychoanalysts was, of necessity, an accidental one and, consequently, so was the sample of patients. Suppose that the investigators could have solved the problem of obtaining a probability sample of all psychoanalytic patients in a given area, should they have done so? Assume that this would have required giving up the psychoanalysts as informants and substituting a relatively superficial direct interview.

Similarly, in a study of factors related to the use of narcotics by boys in juvenile street gangs, Chein and his associates (see Wilner et al., 1957) used group workers as informants (also with complete protection of the anonymity of the individual gang member). These workers had spent months winning the confidence of the boys, convincing the latter that they were not confederates of the police, social reformers, or other things reprehensible in the eyes of the boys; and they had been working closely with the gangs for many more months— in some instances, for several years. Since these informants were available only for the gangs that were being worked with, the sample of gangs—and hence of gang members—was an accidental sample. Assuming that (1) it would have been possible to get a probability sample of gang members and that (2) the information obtained through the group workers was much more dependable than would have been information obtained through direct interview, what should the investigators have done?

The answer to such a question is not easy. The first thing to do, of course, is to assure oneself that the dilemma is real. If convinced that it is, one must then decide whether the problem is, under the circumstances, worthy of investigation at all. If the answer is still in the affirmative, one must decide, in terms of the research purpose, whether it would be better to gather more adequate information based on a not very sound sample or less adequate information based on a sounder sample.

We come, finally, to another special and controversial case of nonprobability sampling. Many studies in behavioral science are carried out on accidental samples of subjects. The data are treated, however, in a manner that is appropriate only to probability samples. For example, statistical tests of significance which presuppose random sampling are applied to the data.

One justification of this practice is completely spurious. The investigators argue that they are interested not in estimating population values, but in studying relationships among variables. For example, the question, "What are the effects of variations in routines of memorizing on the retention of the memorized materials?" does not seem to have reference to any population. Relationships, however, are subject to sampling error just as averages and proportions are. If a great many samples are taken from a given population, certain relationships may appear among some of the variables in some of the samples, and may not appear, or may appear in different degree, in others. Hence the results for a given sample may be quite misleading. If the samples are probability samples, we may legitimately estimate the probability of being in error by more than a specified amount; if they are not, we cannot legitimately make such estimates. Moreover, the answer to the question may be quite different for different populations of subjects (e.g., subjects differing in educational experience), for different populations of materials to be memorized (e.g., nonsense syllables vs. meaningful poems), and for different populations of associated conditions (e.g., presence or absence of distracting activities). Relationships never exist in a population vacuum.

A second justification of the practice is more subtle. The investigators, in effect, argue that they are not concerned with estimating true population values (of means, proportions, differences under different experimental conditions, correlation coefficients. etc.) for any particular population the characteristics of which are specified in advance. They may, therefore, postulate hypothetical populations of which the study samples are, to all intents and purposes, probability samples. For example, suppose that we wanted to study the effects of variations in routines of memorizing (under conditions of no distraction and with valued prizes offered for speed of memorizing) on the retention of poetry. We have available an accidental sample of the population of college sophomores and use this sample for our study. Now we postulate that the population elements in our sample are also elements of another population in which ease of access to the elements is uncorrelated with the relationships under study. Under this condition, our sample may be regarded as a quasi-probability sample of this hypothetical population.[19] When we apply statistical tests of significance to the findings of the study, we are, in effect, generalizing to this hypothetical population rather than to the population of college sophomores.

An implication of this line of reasoning should be spelled out. The relationships we have found by such a procedure (and let us assume, for the sake of argument, that they are very striking) hold for we know not whom. The defining properties of the hypothetical population are completely unspecified. One obvious characteristic is that the cases are readily available. Is the relevant characteristic of the population, then, that of being readily available? Elementary school children may also be easily accessible; so may residents of a home for the aged; so may workers in a factory. Would comparable studies of these groups produce the same results? Or is it possible that ease of access has

[19] For convenience, we have cast the present argument in terms of a population of persons. Actually, the issue is somewhat more complex. In the illustration cited, we have not mentioned the uncontrolled conditions of the experiment. Some of these involve attributes of the persons. In terms of the point made in the following paragraph, we will not know at the end of the experiment whether the findings hold for the entire population of sophomores, or for some subpopulation of sophomores (e.g., psychology majors who volunteer for experiments for some special reason), or indeed whether the attribute "sophomore" is at all relevant in the specification of the population. There are, however, invariably other uncontrolled conditions in an experiment which may or may not affect the outcome. Thus, we have not only an accidental sampling of sophomores, but also an accidental sampling of the conditions under which the experiment could conceivably be conducted. The true hypothetical population is, hence, not merely a population of persons, but a population of persons-under-conditions. The task of specifying the population prescribed in the following paragraph really applies to this "true" hypothetical population.

nothing to do with it? Suppose we were to change the conditions under which individuals make themselves available as the subjects of an experiment (e.g., by providing financial and other kinds of rewards), would we obtain the same findings on our new samples? It is only by the multiplication of such studies that we can begin to specify the properties of the population for which our findings hold. And, as we find samples for which the findings do not hold, we may begin to speculate about why they hold in some and not in others, formulate hypotheses, and select samples on bases that are relevant to the testing of these hypotheses. The point we are making is that the scientific quest does not end with the statement that a finding is or is not statistically significant. We still have the task of specifying the populations for which it is or is not significant. If we have no special reason for wanting to estimate the degree and character of relationships in an already specified population, it may be easier to begin the quest on nonprobability samples and to make use of the fiction of hypothetical populations of which our samples are quasi-probability samples to provide guide lines (e.g., statistical tests of significance) for the evaluation of the findings. But it is imperative for us to remember that at this point our scientific quest has barely gotten under way.

The application to accidental samples of statistical procedures appropriate to probability sampling highlights the issue that we do not, at the end of such a study, know the properties of the population to which we may legitimately generalize. Once the issue has been raised, however, it becomes apparent that we would not necessarily be much better off if we were to start with a probability sample of a well-defined population in the first place. Suppose, for example, that, instead of carrying out our study on an accidental sample of sophomores, we were able to use a probability sample of all of the sophomores at a particular college. To be sure, we would then be able to generalize to this population, within the limits of the estimated margin of error. But is this the population to which we really want to generalize? Do we not still want to know whether the specified characteristics of the population are relevant to the relationship we are studying? Do we not, for example, want to know whether the discovered relationship holds only for the sophomores at our particular college? Suppose that it does not. Does this not then point to the possibility of defining a more inclusive population for which the relationship holds, and would we not want to know the specifications of this more inclusive population? Suppose, on the other hand, that it does hold only for the sophomores at our particular college. Would we not then want to know what is so unique about our population of sophomores? And would not the tentative formulation of possible uniquenesses of our population suggest hypotheses that we would want to explore—hypotheses that might suggest population specifications that cut across our initial population and that include elements not included in our initial population? In either case, would we not want to press toward the discovery of the specification of a population within which the trend that we have discovered in our population to be statistically significant becomes a virtual certainty?

It should perhaps be added that we are not, in these last few paragraphs, preaching a paralyzing spirit of agnosticism that would prohibit anyone from coming to any conclusions. The progress of science and the scientific tenability of conclusions at any point in time are, after all, based on the coherence and consistency of many bits of fallible evidence, the articulation of theory, and the interlocking of the individually fallible bits of evidence with theory. It has been emphasized elsewhere in this book that science offers no possibilities of absolute proof. The scientist can, at most, aspire to the soundest conclusions that can be reached in the light of the best evidence that can be brought to bear on any issue. At the same time, science would only degenerate into dogma if one would not constantly remain alert to the sources of ambiguity and fallibility in the available evidence and the semantic gaps that may lie concealed in the generalizations that are drawn; if one would not attempt to weigh the possible alternatives that may be compatible with the evidence, particularly in the light of the sources of fallibility and ambiguity; if one would not attempt to pinpoint the gaps in knowledge; and if, even though one has dismissed some alternative on the ground that it is not sufficiently plausible to merit serious consideration or dismissed some manifest gap in knowledge as not sufficiently germane to merit intensive exploration, one would not be constantly prepared to reopen these issues and remain sensitive to the possibility of reopening them. In the light of these considerations, what we have attempted to do in these last few paragraphs is merely to look at a considerable body of contemporary research and research practice in the perspective of sampling theory. If there is any preachment implied, it is only another lesson in scientific humility.

Appendix C

QUESTIONNAIRE CONSTRUCTION AND INTERVIEW PROCEDURE

BY ARTHUR KORNHAUSER AND PAUL B. SHEATSLEY

Outline of Procedures in Questionnaire Construction[1]

EARLY IN PLANNING his research the investigator will weigh the merits of several techniques for collecting the desired data and decide whether to use a questionnaire[2] or some other method. If he chooses another method, he may still want to supplement it with a questionnaire. In deciding which part of the research job can best be handled by a questionnaire, the investigator must first discover the extent to which the desired data are already available in census volumes, in published or unpublished reports, or in collections of letters, diaries, etc. Then he must decide whether all or parts of the needed data can best be obtained through a formal questionnaire—or through "depth" interviews, long-continued case studies, standardized tests, refined observations and/or experiment.

[1] This section is a shortened and somewhat modified version of a discussion by Arthur Kornhauser which appeared in Volume II of *Research Methods in Social Relations*, edited by Marie Jahoda, Morton Deutsch, and Stuart W. Cook (The Dryden Press, Inc., 1951), pages 423–462.

[2] The term *questionnaire* is used throughout this appendix to refer to stand-ardized interview schedules as well as forms to be filled out by the respondent.

Let us assume, now, that the study director has decided to use a questionnaire. The entire process of its construction can be divided into the following six steps: deciding what information should be sought, deciding what type of questionnaire should be used, writing a first draft, re-examining and revising questions, pretesting, editing the questionnaire, and specifying procedures for its use.

Deciding What Information Should Be Sought

The first step in the research procedure—formulating the precise problem to be answered—provides the starting point for developing the questionnaire. Suppose that the purpose of a study is to determine the attitudes of the public toward the hydrogen bomb. Preliminary consideration of the problem may indicate the need for inquiry into beliefs and opinions about war, relations with the Soviet Union, the respondents' optimism or pessimism, their realism, fatalism, etc., as well as about the hydrogen bomb. The investigator must decide what aspects of the problem are to be dealt with in the particular study.

An excellent test of one's performance in this stage of questionnaire construction, and at the same time a valuable aid, is the preparation of "dummy tables" showing the relationships that are anticipated. By drawing up such tables in advance, the investigator forces himself to definite decisions about what data are required and how they will be used. He can even enter figures representing different possible findings, in order to visualize the bearing they would have on alternative hypotheses and to see what new hypotheses they suggest.

The research planner may well run through the possibilities represented by the headings in a classification such as the following, stopping at each point to decide what specific material his questionnaire should seek in the light of the specific purpose of his research.

Reports of "facts"

About the respondent:

Personal-history data, such as age, education, employment

Behavior data, such as newspaper reading, radio listening, church attendance, buying habits, voting behavior

About other persons known to respondent (family, employees, friends, etc.) :

Personal-history and behavior data as above
About events and conditions known to respondent:
Reports of accidents, home conditions, job surroundings, political meetings, wages received, etc.
Opinions, feelings, beliefs, etc.
"Reasons" for specified behavior and attitudes:
Objective factors: Influence of other persons, of conditions and events, of published communications, etc.
Subjective factors: Specific wants, underlying desires and dispositions, evaluations, meanings, etc.

DECIDING WHAT TYPE OF QUESTIONNAIRE SHOULD BE USED

The appropriate form of question depends on the mode of administration, the subject matter, the sample of people to be reached (educational and social level, etc.), and the kind of analysis and interpretation intended.

Each class of questionnaire content may suggest two markedly different kinds of item—those that ask *explicitly* for the information wanted, and those in which the desired information is *inferred* from responses directed to other matters. For example, instead of asking the respondent directly about his own social adjustment, he may be asked whether most people are hard to get along with. Questions of "fact" are often asked not to obtain direct information about the facts, which may already be known, but as indirect measures of knowledge or interests. *Opinions* about an issue may be sought because of research interest in the issue ("direct" questions) or in order to throw light on the personality of the respondent ("indirect" questions).

The investigator must also decide whether to use *closed* or *open-ended* questions. The relative advantages and disadvantages of the two types of question, and the use for which each is most appropriate, have been discussed in Chapter 7.

The use of *follow-up questions* or *probes* is advisable at many points in the ordinary interview, especially in connection with free responses. The questionnaire should anticipate where these are required and should provide the appropriate wording. Although sometimes a single, fixed follow-up question can be specified, usually several alternatives are needed, depending upon the preceding response. For example, if the answer is too general and indefinite, the follow-up may be: "In what way?," "Just how do you mean?," "Can you give me an example?," etc. If the answer is incomplete, the questions may be: "Any other reasons?," or "Would you tell me a little more about that?" Other follow-ups ask: "What makes you think this?," or "What was there about the picture that made you feel that way?," or "Where were you working at that time?," and so on through an endless variety of questions needed to clarify or amplify the initial response. To the extent that the improvisation of the follow-ups is left to the interviewer, to be adapted to the specific responses, we depart from a standardized questionnaire or interview and border on a "partially structured" interview.

The questionnaire planner also has to decide whether to use a set of *several questions* rather than a single question on particular points to be covered. Several specific questions covering different aspects of a topic often obtain more precise and useful information than does a more general question, even if it is open-ended and accompanied by follow-ups. (This point is discussed in more detail on pages 553–555).

First Draft of the Questionnaire

Probably the best way to begin is to outline or list the topics for the questionnaire, consider carefully what is likely to be the best sequence of topics (not the *logical* sequence, but the best *psychological* sequence from the standpoint of the respondent), and then write the questions.

In addition to the questions deemed essential, the questionnaire writer sometimes finds it wise to include a few extra ones aimed at checking the reliability of responses or measuring the influence of changes in wording. For example, two or more roughly equivalent or closely related questions, well separated in the questionnaire, may be asked in order to measure consistency of answers. The effect of different wording may be determined by constructing two parallel forms of questionnaire ("split-ballot technique"), to be used with equivalent samples of the population. The two forms have some of their questions in common, but certain other questions are worded in different ways in order that the effects of these differences may be measured.

At this stage of questionnaire construction, all available suggestions should be utilized. Questionnaires that have previously been drafted on the same or similar problems may prove most helpful. But the wise questionnaire writer will think the questions over and strive not only to improve them but to supplement or replace them in novel ways whenever this can be done to advantage. There are few places in social research where time-consuming, painstaking effort is more rewarding than in the preparation of questions.

Re-examination and Revision of the Questions

In the process of revision, it is invaluable to supplement one's own efforts by the critical reactions of individuals who are familiar with questionnaire methods and with the type of problem at hand. As far as possible, the experts should represent different approaches and reflect different social orientations. Few social research questionnaires will fail to benefit from forthright criticism by persons with different values and a different social outlook. In addition, the questionnaire should be scrutinized for technical defects that may exist quite apart from biases and blind spots due to personal values.

Pretesting the Questionnaire

The pretest is a try-out of the questionnaire to see how it works and whether changes are necessary before the start of the full-scale study. The pretest provides a means of catching and solving unforeseen problems in the administration of the questionnaire, such as the phrasing and sequence of questions, or its length. It may also indicate the need for additional questions or the elimination of others.

In general, the pretest should be in the form of personal interviews. In mail or telephone surveys, the interviewing pretest can be followed by a trial of the techniques actually to be used. The latter will detect any further problems peculiar to the procedure, such as lack of adequate instructions for filling out answers to questions. Ordinarily, if the preceding steps have been well performed, a few interviews suffice for the pretest. However, it is sometimes necessary to do many interviews in order to make sure that people differing in education, temperament, and opinion will understand the questions and give complete and pertinent answers. The people interviewed on the pretest should be similar in characteristics to those who will be interviewed in the final study.

Those who do the interviewing on the pretest must have a clear understanding of the purpose of the study. They must be informed of the over-all aim and the specific intent of each question, since they must note whether the question is understood and answered by the respondents in the manner intended. In conducting the interviews, they should be alert to every reaction and comment of the respondent and should record these verbatim. They should be instructed to try out alternative wordings of questions that are not clear.

A valuable part of the pretest interview is discussion of the questions with respondents after they have answered them. The respondent may be asked what the question meant to him, what difficulties he experienced in replying, what further ideas he had that were not brought out by the question, how he would ask the question, what his feelings were on questions to which he responded, "Don't know," etc.

It is also important to have the interviewer record his own observations, criticisms, and suggestions. What difficulties did he encounter in locating respondents and in interviewing them? What points seemed to cause embarrassment or resistance? Where did he have trouble maintaining rapport? Did the respondent become bored or impatient? On what questions did the respondent request further explanation? Was there enough space for recording answers? And so on.

If substantial changes are necessary, such as adding entirely new questions, a second pretest should be conducted. Sometimes, in fact, a series of three or four or even more revisions and pretestings is required.

Editing the Questionnaire and Specifying Procedures for Its Use

After all the preceding steps have been completed, the questionnaire should be ready for use. All that remains is a final editing by the research staff to ensure that every element passes inspection: the content, form, and sequence of questions; the spacing, arrangement, and appearance of the material; and the spelling out in detail of procedures for using the questionnaire.

The editorial job is directed primarily at making the questionnaire as clear and easy to use as possible. Directions for printing or mimeographing layout should be given precisely, with emphasis on legibility, ample space for replies, and the convenience of interviewers and respondents in following questions and writing answers.

The questionnaire itself should contain simple, clear directions telling the respondent (or interviewer) just what he is supposed to do—which questions are to be answered only by certain classes of respondents, which ones the interviewer is to explain, how fully and in what terms the response is to be recorded, where a list is to be shown to the respondent, and so on.

Guide for Questionnaire Construction[3]

What follows is essentially a check list of points to consider in formulating questions. The investigator may, for special reasons, decide to depart from the rules at various places. But he should move ahead cautiously, with full awareness of what he is and is not doing. The most troublesome errors in questionnaires do not arise from bad judgment after due consideration of doubtful points; they creep in unwittingly, even in "obviously simple" questions.

DECISIONS ABOUT QUESTION CONTENT

Is this question necessary? Just how will it be useful?

Does the subject matter require a separate question, or can it be integrated with other questions?

Is the point already sufficiently covered by other questions?

Is the question unnecessarily detailed and specific for the purposes of the study?

[3] For a more detailed and highly readable discussion, see Payne (1951).

EXAMPLES: Instead of asking the age of each child in the family, it is sometimes sufficient to get the number of children under 16.

Some studies of public opinion dispense with questions regarding respondents' income, since other information serves well enough for socioeconomic classification (rental level of district, occupation, etc.).

Are several questions needed on the subject matter of this question?

Should the question be subdivided?

EXAMPLES: Efforts to cut corners by combining two issues in one question must be avoided—for example, asking for a single answer about feelings toward Negroes and Jews; asking views about changes in wages and hours, instead of separating the issues; about nationality of "parents," instead of father and mother separately; etc.

Does the question adequately cover the ground intended?

EXAMPLES: If the investigator wants information about total family income, a question about the respondent's "earnings" may be inadequate, since it probably will not lead the respondent to mention "other income" or the earnings of others in the family.

A question simply asking people whether they are in favor of having more educational radio programs on the air would not reveal whether they wanted these for *themselves* or for the other fellow— that is, whether *they* would listen.

Is additional related material needed to interpret the answers?

EXAMPLES: Often replies to questions about specific social reforms can be understood better in the light of associated attitudes elicited by other questions—for example, questions that ascertain broad attitudes toward security and opportunity for the poor, antagonisms toward centralized authority, belief in need for social change, etc.

A question asking for the respondent's opinions about the characteristics of a particular racial group calls for parallel questions about other groups, in order to determine whether his opinions are specific to that group or reflect a more general view of out-groups or even of people in general.

In opinion questions, is further information needed about the intensity of the respondent's conviction or feeling?

EXAMPLES: In connection with questions on stereotypes, it may be important to find out not only whether the respondent has certain stereotypes but also what feeling tone, if any, is attached to these stereotypes. A person may think that the members of a certain group are "clannish," but he may feel that this is reprehensible, or admirable, or he may be indifferent about it. He may consider this trait admirable in one group and reprehensible in another.

Techniques for ascertaining intensity of opinion include "feeling thermometers," on which the respondent rates directly that he feels "very strongly," "fairly strongly," etc.; scales running from one extreme of intensity to the other (e.g., from "Don't care whether I vote for the candidate" to "Positively going to vote for him, even if I have to get out of a sickbed"); asking about the respondent's behavior (e.g., how much he has discussed the question or read about it, whether he has joined organizations, written to newspapers or congressmen, etc.).

Another procedure is to call attention to difficulties or sacrifices entailed in the respondent's position (e.g., higher taxes) to see whether and how this changes his opinion. Similarly, one may mention that many people hold a view opposite to his and then ask whether he thinks these people may be right.

One may ask the respondent to specify what sacrifices or penalties he would be willing to undergo if he could thus guarantee the outcome he wants—for example, how much money he is willing to pay a year to get television programs without advertising.

Is further information needed about how important the respondent considers the condition or issue asked about?

EXAMPLES: Free-answer questions may help to determine how significant the point in question is for the respondent, how much he emphasizes personal consequences, what concern he manifests over the social effects, etc. For example: What if there is another world war? What difference does it make if labor unions *have* (or are kept from having) a closed shop?

The respondent can be asked to give direct ratings of the relative importance of the issue in question compared with other issues, or to indicate which of different possible consequences he considers probable and whether a given condition "matters much" to him or not. For example, does he think a Republican victory in the next election will have important consequences, either good or bad; and what possible effects, as given in a check list, does he consider most important?

Do respondents have the information necessary to answer the question?

Is it a matter they can report on adequately?

Does the question call for answers the respondent either cannot give at all or cannot give reliably?

Is the point within the respondent's experience?

Is it too remote or nonvivid or difficult a memory?

Is it unanalyzed or unverbalized experience?

Is it subject to serious errors of observation and/or recall?

Does the question ask for opinions on matters so unfamiliar to the respondent that the opinion does not mean what it seems to?

Can the necessary background information be given to the respondent in the course of the questionnaire or interview, or should the question not be asked at all of respondents lacking the information?

If the question attempts to supply the needed background information, does it give an adequate and unprejudiced statement?

EXAMPLES: Does the question concern childhood behavior and attitudes, incidental recent experiences of no special interest to the respondent, or unanalyzed and inarticulate experiences? If so, and if the purpose is to obtain objective information rather than the respondent's subjective impression, official records, refined observations, and experiments should be used when possible. When questioning is used, the respondent should be aided in ways suggested on pages 556–557.

An opinion-poll question asking about who is to blame for a list of specific strikes found that from one half to four fifths of the respondents did not know enough about these strikes to express an opinion. In similar questions that did not directly ask whether people had the information, almost all the respondents expressed opinions regardless of their probable lack of information.

Can the desired information be supplied better by specific respondents other than the one first approached?

EXAMPLES: A mother may be able to report what books her youngster reads, but a child himself must be questioned to find out how he feels about reading these books.

Among people who were known to have redeemed war bonds, many denied that bonds had been cashed. Since the interviews were with either husband or wife, one cannot know whether the discrepancy was due to suppressed information or to lack of knowledge concerning the spouse's sale of bonds.

It is important in such instances to arrange to have the appropriate persons answer each set of questions—by using separate schedules, by having interviewers see the different individuals, by specifically requesting that the individual who receives the questionnaire have his colleagues answer certain of the questions, and so on.

Are alternative questions required on this subject matter to adapt it to different classes of respondents?

EXAMPLES: In radio research, those who listen to a radio program "regularly," "occasionally," or "never" have to be asked different sets of questions. The regular listeners may be queried about their attitudes toward the program; the occasional listeners may be asked, in addition, their reasons for not listening more often; the questions to nonlisteners ask whether they listen to other programs, whether they know of this program, etc.

Does the question need to be more concrete, specific, and closely related to the respondent's personal experience?

Is it asked in too general a form?

Can the information be obtained more easily by referring it more closely to the respondent's own behavior?

Does it utilize natural psychological aids to recall, such as having the respondent recall experiences in temporal sequence—working back from the present, or working up to the present from a specified time in the past?

EXAMPLES: It is often effective to use behavior indicators instead of, or along with, subjective expressions of feeling. For example, one can ask not only, "How well did you like the book?," but also "Have you recommended it to anyone else? Have you looked for other books by the same author?," etc.

An interview schedule used in an inquiry into women's morning radio listening, instead of asking what hours they usually listened and to what programs, first obtained a list of what they had listened to today, then the same for yesterday—and only then, as a final step, asked what programs they usually listened to during the morning hours.

Is the question content sufficiently general and free from spurious concreteness and specificity?

Ordinarily, the danger lies in questions that are too general; but on occasion the reverse is true, and a highly specific question is improperly used to tap general attitudes or to ascertain over-all facts.

Is the subject matter such that a specific question may elicit inaccurate or misleading responses?

EXAMPLE: At times, specific and recent instances may be unrepresentative. Since many activities vary seasonally, questions about what the respondent did today or last week may elicit a far less accurate report of his general activity than a question about his usual or average behavior during previous months (for example, amount of television viewing, miles of driving, or kind of breakfast food eaten).

Do the replies express general attitudes and only seem to be as specific as they sound?

EXAMPLE: This fault occurs most often in attitude or opinion questions. Suppose an investigator concerned with opinions about racial policies in a school system asks: "Do you feel that qualified Negro teachers have just as good a chance as qualified white teachers to be hired in the schools in this city?" Many people answer such a question on the basis of an assumption that, in general, Negroes are (or are not) treated fairly, rather than on the basis of any specific knowledge or opinion about practices within the school system. Thus, although the answers may seem to refer to the particular issue, this may be deceptive

In order to be sure, one must ask either a number of questions referring to different specific situations, or a general question in addition to the one concerning the specific situation in which he is interested.

Is the question content biased or loaded in one direction, without accompanying questions to balance the emphasis?

Is the question unfair in any way? Would the content be accepted as fair by informed persons with opposite views on the point under inquiry?

Is it likely to obtain answers that will unduly favor one side of the issue?

Does the question introduce unwarranted *assumptions* about the subject matter?

EXAMPLES: Opinion-poll questions often inquire into negative and vulnerable aspects of labor unions without accompanying questions about positive features, and without mentioning parallel negative aspects of business practices. By dwelling on what is wrong with unions, thinking is directed disproportionately to their disapproved features and an unfair picture is obtained.

Many single questions likewise reflect biased selection of subject matter; for example, a question about who pays the advertising costs of consumer goods, with no mention of the possibility that advertising makes it possible to sell the merchandise at a lower price.

Question content sometimes carries a bias simply because of the *timing* of the question. If a community has just experienced a race riot, questions on ending discrimination will give biased results. The same is true of questions on labor relations or international relations following upon some favorable or unfavorable event. Seasonal influences likewise may seriously bias answers to questions; for example, asking about favorite sports or recreational activities during the height of the football season.

Will the respondents give the information that is asked for?

Is the material too private, of an embarrassing nature, or otherwise likely to lead to resistance, evasion or deception?

What objection might a person have to answering?

Does the question "put him on the spot" or make him feel he is being quizzed?

Can one get the information in a manner which would not offend, or should it be omitted?

Do any special conditions exist at the time and place of the survey to augment suspicion or resistance?

EXAMPLES: There are obviously matters which people are reluctant to disclose; for example, family quarrels, receipt of charity, one's own limitations and difficulties, antisocial attitudes such as race and religious prejudices, "inside" information about a political or religious organization or labor union, etc. Such topics must either be avoided in interviews and questionnaires or forms of inquiry must be employed that will elicit the desired information without unduly disturbing the respondent.

One technique is that used to ascertain whether people read pulp magazines. The interviewer offered to buy any old magazines that might be lying around the house. This resulted in the report of a considerably larger number of low-prestige magazines than had been found by direct inquiry.

Much of the desired information, however, is subjective and essentially personal; it can be obtained only by questioning the respondent. Here the informal, free-answer type of interview sometimes succeeds where formal questions do not.

Special types of indirect and projective interview questions are sometimes used. Instead of asking a person how much he donated in a charity drive, why he gave, and why he did not give more, such questions might be made to refer to "people you know" or "people like you." This type of question assumes that what the person says about others is likely to be a projection of what is true of himself—a sometimes useful but not altogether safe basis for interpretation. Sometimes, a personal question will be answered more frankly if it follows a parallel indirect question about "most people": "And how do you yourself feel about this?"[4]

Even if direct questions are asked, skilled interviewers encounter

[4] See Chapters 7 and 8 for a more detailed discussion of questions of this type.

remarkably few refusals to reply. A great deal depends upon the interviewer's own attitude. If he is embarrassed or feels that the question is too personal, his doubts are readily transmitted to the respondent. If he confidently expects a reply, he is likely to get it.

Is the question likely to encounter emotional influences and desires that will lead to falsification of answers?

EXAMPLES: Many people answer even factual questions in a way that tends to exaggerate such matters as their income, education, and social status; reduces their actual age; ennobles their acts and motives.

One can also expect some replies to be thrown off by emotional influences that tend to exaggerate or minimize hardships. A pessimistic tendency has, for example, been noted in farmers' estimates of current crop damages. Where the content of a study is likely to suffer from such distortions, effort should be made to check or corroborate the information by different approaches to the matter within the questionnaire and by reference to outside sources when possible. Information about school and employment, for example, can be checked by seeing that dates and periods of time are consistent, by inquiring into courses of study and details of jobs, and by similar cross-checking techniques. In addition, when justifiable, efforts can be made to check with school authorities, previous employers, etc.

If the question content gives a clue as to who is sponsoring the study or what the purpose is, respondents often feel disposed to express appropriately favorable feelings, or at least, in a spirit of politeness, to withhold negative expressions. Hence the general policy of not revealing the sponsor or the specific purpose of the questions.

Another especially interesting influence to be mentioned here is the inclination of respondents at times to answer "for the record." Questions about labor relations are likely to be answered by both industrial and labor leaders with one eye on the possible effects of the opinion study. This "public-relations bias" may also affect the ordinary citizen. For example, when questioned about whether religion is declining in influence or whether religious or racial hatred is increasing, many respondents hesitate to acknowledge what they consider an evil trend lest they give comfort and encouragement to the "enemy."

In the examination of prospective questions, such influences have to be considered and, as far as is feasible, guarded against. The decision may be to omit the questions or to adopt indirect or free-answer methods or some other form of inquiry.

Decisions About Question Wording

Can the question be misunderstood? Does it contain difficult or unclear phraseology?

Are the words simple enough for the least educated respondent?

Are any terms used in a specialized way and, if so, is the meaning made clear by pictures or otherwise?

Is the sentence structure short and simple? Is there any looseness or ambiguity? What else *could* the question mean to a respondent?

Is the meaning clearly distinguished from other ideas the respondent may *think* the question asks—ideas that may seem more natural or important to him?

Could unintended emphasis on a word or phrase change the question meaning?

examples: Questions which ask for "nationality," "occupation," "marital status," and many other items of personal data often cause trouble unless spelled out in detail.

Such terms as "compulsory arbitration," "T.V.A.," "C.I.O.," "N.A.M.," "real wages," "closed shop," "advertising medium," and such academic expressions as "exclusion from employment" are encountered in questionnaires and interviews even though they convey no clear meaning to large sections of the American public.

Simple familiar words are often employed in a vague, ambiguous manner. For example, the simple question, "What kind of headache remedy do you usually use?" proved ambiguous, since to some respondents "kind" signified *brand* whereas to others it meant *tablets vs. powder.* Or, what does "Do you usually use pancake make-up?" mean? Every day? "Usually" whenever you use *any* make-up? "Usually" for special occasions? etc.

Long or difficult sentences are likely to be misunderstood by many respondents.

Sometimes, accenting particular words changes the meaning of a question. An unintended emphasis on the word "should" in the question, "Do you think the United States should accept Russian influence in Eastern Europe or not?" introduces a moral note and might well cause some respondents to answer in the negative, meaning we *should* not (although in the world of practical politics, it is the thing to do). A slight change in wording clearly reduces the likelihood of the moralistic accent on the word "should": "Do you think the United States should or should not accept Russian influence in Eastern Europe?"

If any suspicion of misunderstanding remains after questions have been worded as clearly as possible, good practice calls for follow-up questions by the interviewer to determine just what the respondent meant. The interviewer is instructed to ask such additional questions as, "Just how do you mean that? . . . Would you tell me a little more about what you have in mind there? . . . Will you give me an example of what you mean?"

Does the question adequately express the alternatives with respect to the point?

EXAMPLES: The safe rule is to make each of two alternatives explicit whenever there is the slightest ambiguity about the second alternative. Even when the implication is reasonably clear, a statement of the second alternative may serve to make it more vivid than it would otherwise be and hence to place the two possible answers on a more nearly equal footing. Payne (1951) gives a striking example of the effect of failing to state alternatives explicitly. To the question, "Do you think most manufacturing companies that lay off workers during slack periods could arrange things to avoid layoffs and give steady work right through the year?," 63 per cent said companies could avoid layoffs, 22 per cent said they could not, and 15 per cent expressed no opinion. A carefully matched sample of respondents was asked the question with an alternative explicitly stated: "Do you think most manufacturing companies that lay off workers in slack periods could avoid layoffs and provide steady work right through the year, or do you think layoffs are unavoidable?" When the question was asked this way,

35 per cent said companies could avoid layoffs, 41 per cent said layoffs are unavoidable, and 24 per cent expressed no opinion.

Is the question misleading because of unstated assumptions or unseen implications?

Is the frame of reference clear and uniform for all respondents?

Does the question bring out the basis for the respondent's reply—the frame of reference within which he is answering?

What consequences of the proposed action does he see?

Does the question distinguish between what he wishes to have true and what he thinks is true?

EXAMPLES: Many questions can be answered only on the assumption that certain other things are true, or the respondent may make certain assumptions in his answer. Unless questions designed to probe these assumptions are also included, the replies are subject to grave misinterpretation. The following are illustrations:

"Do you think the government should put a ceiling over wages?" (1942). Of people who answered in the affirmative, many doubtless took it for granted that prices were likewise to be controlled; perhaps also profits. However, since there were no follow-up questions to ascertain how extensively such assumptions were involved, answers could not be interpreted.

"To which of these groups do you feel you belong—the white-collar class, the working class, or some other class?" This question assumes that the person feels he belongs to a "class" based on occupation. One should first determine whether he feels any class identification and, if so, how he thinks of "class."

When questions are asked of the general public—whether on the veto power in the United Nations, the continued manufacture of the hydrogen bomb, or an anti-strike law—the investigator must consider the degree to which the implications of the action are seen, how far the opinions are offhand and superficial, and how far they reflect crystallized views based on public discussion. It is important to ask supplementary questions to ascertain the considerations the respondent has in mind in answering as he does. Free-answer questions may be used which ask for reasons, advantages of the course advocated, and arguments against it; or questions may ask the respondent to react to specific arguments for and against the measure; or questions of the following type may be used: "Are you in favor of (or opposed to) doing this *even if it means so and so?*"

Is the wording biased? Is it emotionally loaded or slanted toward a particular kind of answer?

Does it employ stereotypes? Does it contain prestige-carrying names? Does it employ superlative terms which push the answer one way or the other? (If such elements of bias are present, are they there intentionally—and does the research purpose justify their inclusion?)

Does the question tend to elicit replies that are more biased than those the respondents would give on the same point if they had an opportunity to answer freely and fully?

Would the wording be acceptable to persons with opposite views on the matter?

EXAMPLES: Two parallel opinion questions in 1939 asked whether the United States was likely to be involved in the war. The results show how greatly a difference in wording can affect responses when opinion is confused and undecided. One form asked, "Do you think the United States will go into the war before it is over?" The replies were: "Yes," 41 per cent; "No," 33 per cent; "Don't know," 26 per cent. The other form asked, "Do you think the United States will succeed in staying out of the war?" The replies were: "Yes," 44 per cent; "No," 30 per cent; "Don't know," 26 per cent. (Cantril, 1944.)

The influence of President Roosevelt's name caused an increase of about 5 per cent in the affirmative replies to the second of the following two questions:

"Do you like the idea of having Thanksgiving a week earlier this year?"

"Do you like President Roosevelt's idea of having Thanksgiving a week earlier this year?"

Is the question wording likely to be objectionable to the respondent in any way?

(See also pages 559–561.)

EXAMPLES: Instead of asking the respondent directly what the amount of his income is, a question such as the following makes it easier to obtain the information:

For the purpose of our survey, we need to have a rough indication of the income of your family. Would you mind telling me in which of these classes it falls:

Below $1,000 a year	From $3,000 to $4,000
From $1,000 to $2,000	From $4,000 to $5,000
From $2,000 to $3,000	Over $5,000 a year

The same use of lists and classifications may aid in questions about age, religion, etc.

A change in words may make a question more palatable. A question asking whether the respondent has "dealt on the black market" can be rephrased to ask whether he has "paid over-ceiling prices." Instead of "Did you graduate from high school?" the question can ask, "What grade were you in when you left school?" A good general rule is to avoid placing the respondent on the defensive; always leave him an easy "out."

Would a more personalized or less personalized wording of the question produce better results?

EXAMPLES: The investigator must judge in each instance whether a personal or an impersonal question will produce better results for the purposes of the particular survey. For example, a question may be asked in such different forms as the following:

"Are working conditions satisfactory or not satisfactory in the plant where you work?"

"Do you feel that working conditions are satisfactory or not satisfactory in the plant where you work?"

"Are you personally satisfied or dissatisfied with working conditions in the plant where you work?"

The most personal form of these questions probably elicits a more individual expression of feelings; the most impersonal, a judgment more tempered by what the respondent supposes other people think, or what he thinks the objective realities may demand. On the other hand, the impersonal form may, at times, prevent embarrassment and lead to franker replies.

Can the question be better asked in a more direct or a more indirect form?

EXAMPLES: Using the "indirect" procedure, questions are asked, for example, about how radical or conservative certain magazines or men in public life are. The respondent who calls them all conservative indirectly reveals his own "radicalism," and conversely with one who rates them all as radical.

Another type of indirect (or quasi-indirect) questioning is well illustrated in magazine-audience measurement. When respondents are asked directly to identify the articles and advertisements they have seen in a magazine, serious errors arise through false identifications occasioned by confusion and tendencies to exaggerate. Instead of asking the respondent directly to recall whether he has seen the pages, he is asked merely to say whether each item "looks interesting." This is followed by the question: "Is this the first time you have seen it?" By first focusing attention on interest, more satisfactory answers are secured regarding ads previously seen.

Other examples have to do with information and views which the respondent may be reluctant to give if he is asked about them directly. Veterans who evade (and resent) direct questions about their battle experiences sometimes report these memories with genuine interest if the questioner comes at them obliquely—for example, by asking how well army equipment held up in the field, whether enlisted men were sufficiently trained before going into action, etc.

No general recommendations are warranted regarding the use of indirect questions. Their possibilities and limitations have to be examined in each new setting and with the research purposes clearly in mind. Both technical and moral issues are involved: Whether the intended inferences can safely be drawn from indirect evidence; whether the particular type of indirection biases the response; whether the questions arouse suspicion of trickery or surreptitious prying—and whether such suspicion is justified.[5]

Decisions About Form of Response to the Question

Can the question best be asked in a form calling for check answer (or short answer of a word or two, or a number), free answer, or check answer with follow-up free answer?

EXAMPLES: When check answers are used, the alternatives are sometimes included as part of the question; sometimes they follow the question and serve merely for the convenience and guidance of the interviewer in recording responses. Ideally, the latter use of check answers should not have any effect on the responses; but in actual practice, it does exert a substantial influence. This may come about either through the respondent's seeing the printed blank or because the interviewer is influenced by the categories in his follow-up questioning and in his recording of answers. When the alternatives are contained in the question itself, they naturally exercise a more decided constraining influence.

Best results are often achieved by means of a combination of free-answer and check-answer methods or by compromises between them. Thus, single questions may consist of an initial check-answer part immediately followed by free-answer parts which inquire into the meaning of the check response and obtain examples, statements of the respondent's assumptions, the strength of his feelings on the point, etc. For example:

"Are people at the head of your company interested in their employees, or don't they care?" Interested———; Don't care———; Other answer——— "In what ways do they show that?"

If a check answer is used, which is the best type for this question—dichotomous, multiple-choice ("cafeteria" question), or scale?

EXAMPLES: The simple yes-no response (and similar dichotomous choices such as agree-disagree, do or do not) are appropriate for many

[5] For a more detailed discussion of indirect questions, see Chapter 8.

questions dealing with points of fact and with issues which are clear-cut and on which well-crystallized views are held. Even on direct yes-no questions and simple two-way comparisons, however, it is usually found desirable to include an intermediate response of "doubtful," "undecided," "same," "no difference," "both," etc. The inclusion of such responses is sometimes considered inadvisable because it provides too easy and attractive an escape for respondents who are disinclined to express a definite view. On the other hand, forcing replies into two extreme categories (particularly if the interviewer is not even supplied with a space for checking an intermediate answer) is likely to cause difficulty for many respondents and to yield results that are less realistic and more misleading than is true when an intermediate reply is provided for.

A graded series of response possibilities frequently gives the investigator additional or more accurate information than a dichotomous response and presents the question more adequately and acceptably to the respondent. The most common multiple-choice responses utilize three, four, or five gradations, but larger numbers are sometimes appropriate. A widely used special form of multiple choice (the so-called "cafeteria" question) asks the respondent to choose from a list of assorted words or statements one or more that best represent his own view. The items may or may not be arranged in order from high to low, good to bad, favorable to unfavorable, etc., to constitute a crude scale. Examples of several of these forms follow.

> Suppose a person is asked by a close friend to do something that requires a personal sacrifice. In your country, how strong an obligation would a person of your age feel to help his friend?
>
> _____ not strong at all
> _____ not very strong
> _____ rather strong
> _____ very strong
> _____ extremely strong

Put a "1" in front of the thing that is most important to have or do in order to get ahead in the world. Put a "2" before the next most important, etc.

_____ pull   _____ brains
_____ good luck   _____ hard work

Of course, you want ALL these things—but which will influence you most when it comes to choosing your next car? Check three items.

_____ Appearance   _____ Operating Economy
_____ Comfort   _____ Pick-up
_____ Dependability   _____ Safety
_____ Ease of Control   _____ Smoothness
_____ First Cost   _____ Speed
                          _____ . . . . ?

> *If a check list is used, does it cover adequately all the significant alternatives without overlapping and in a defensible order? Is it of reasonable length? Is the wording of items impartial and balanced?*

EXAMPLES: Poor check lists constitute one of the most common faults in questionnaire construction. The "cafeteria" type of question seems to offer special temptations to careless listing of miscellaneous alternatives.

Many check lists consist of loose and ambiguous qualitative terms—*usually, sometimes, rarely, frequently, occasionally, good, fair, poor.* The difficulty with these terms is that respondents have different standards in mind, so that two persons may report the same facts under different categories. When feasible, it is better to use concrete and objective terms for the different degrees.

Another frequent fault of check lists is that they are incomplete. As noted in Chapter 7, several studies have shown that replies may be seriously changed by the omission of one or more significant alternatives from the check list. Many check lists are defective because they contain alternatives that appear equally true or that are not mutually exclusive; items that do not fit into the continuum formed by the other items (the list does not remain in one dimension); items that are loaded in wording, ambiguous, or too extreme; items that contain more than one idea; items that influence responses by being over-specific; items that overrepresent or underrepresent one side of an issue. The following examples illustrate some of these faults:

> Which one of these four statements comes closest to what you yourself think about advertising on television?
> a. I'm in favor of advertising on television because it tells me about the things I want to buy.
> b. I don't particularly mind advertising on television. It doesn't interfere too much with my enjoyment of the programs.
> c. I don't like advertising on television, but I'll put up with it.
> d. I think all advertising should be taken off television.
>
> (What if the respondent is in favor of advertising on television but not "because it tells me about the things I want to buy"? He is almost forced by such lists to say things he doesn't mean.)

> Why do you think the government wants to keep prices from going higher? Which one of these comes closest to your opinion?
> a. So some people won't be able to get too much while others get too little.
> b. So people won't worry about prices going higher and start to hoard.
> c. So there won't be any necessity for raising wages and salaries.
> d. So there won't be a lot of profiteering.
>
> (Most respondents regarded the alternatives here as equally compelling and were at a loss to choose only one.)

To the question, "To what social class do you belong—middle class, or upper, or lower?" almost nine tenths of the respondents answered "middle class." But when psychologically more realistic alternatives—middle class, lower class, working class, upper class—were offered in a different question, only 43 per cent said "middle class"; 51 per cent chose "working class."

The sequence of items in a check list also deserves attention. The first and last items tend to be favored; when the list is read to the respondent rather than shown to him, the last item tends especially to receive a disproportionate number of responses. It is good practice to have the interviewers rotate the order in which items are presented, or to have alternate forms of the questionnaire containing different ordering of the items.

Is the form of response easy, definite, uniform, and adequate for the purpose?

EXAMPLES: Many ways of making answers easy and definite have been referred to under preceding points. Among the most important are the use of check categories instead of asking for precise estimates (as with income, age, etc.) and the obtaining of raw figures rather than averages, percentages, or other derived figures. Thus it is better not to ask what percentage of income is spent for rent but to get the figures for income and rent separately; to ask not the average distance of recent automobile trips but the distance of each recent trip. It is also becoming standard practice to show the respondent a card with the alternative replies whenever the check list is at all lengthy or difficult to hold in mind.

Whenever a question schedule contains a long series of blanks for check answers or numerical entries, it is desirable to have clearly indicated columns and to use guide lines or extra spaces to reduce the chances of error in locating responses.

One of the methods that make for easy tabulation is precoding. The answers are anticipated; the code is set up and included on the questionnaire; and the interviewer or respondent merely checks or circles the coded answer. For example:

	Col. No.	Yes	No
1. a. Do you have a radio in working order?	5	1	2
b. Do you usually read a daily newspaper?	6	1	2
c. Do you usually read a weekly newspaper?	7	1	2
d. Do you read any magazine regularly?	8	1	2

This method can be used for all or part of the questionnaire. Its advantage is that a further coding operation is unnecessary and the information can be machine-punched immediately.

The disadvantage of this method is that there may be a tendency to force answers into a code. Some questions are better left as free-answer questions; precoding them would mean inaccuracy and a possible sacrifice of information.

DECISIONS ABOUT THE PLACE OF THE QUESTION IN THE SEQUENCE

Is the answer to the question likely to be influenced by the content of preceding questions?

Do earlier questions create a certain set or expectation that might influence answers to this question?

Do preceding questions aid the recall of ideas that bear on this question?

Does this question become inappropriate if certain answers were given previously?

EXAMPLES: When both general and specific questions are to be asked on a topic, it is usually advisable to have the general ones come first. Thus, if people are to be asked what improvements they desire in their working relations and also how they like their foreman, the first question must be placed before the second; otherwise, better supervision will be disproportionately emphasized as a desired improvement simply because it has been freshly called to mind.

Earlier questions may also create a generally favorable or unfavorable mental set toward the topic considered—as when a series of questions about strikes and labor troubles precedes questions about attitudes toward unions and their regulation.

A final example illustrates a simple and fairly common pitfall. The second of the following questions obviously becomes inappropriate and awkward if the respondent has given an affirmative answer to the first:

a. Do you think the government is giving the public as much information as it should about our military strength as compared with Russia's?

b. What aspects would you especially like to know more about?

Is the question led up to in a natural way? Is it in correct psychological order?

EXAMPLES: People are often more willing to answer objective questions about situations and behavior than about attitudes, preferences, and motives. Moreover, they may find it easier to formulate their attitudes or motives after the situation or behavior has been clearly specified. Thus it is usually best to start with simple objective questions. Once the respondent has been drawn into the interview, he may be more willing to answer questions about his feelings, motives, etc. Thus, an interview that was designed to ascertain how people felt about living in a trailer camp began by asking when the respondent had moved to this camp, where he had lived before, how he happened to come to this place, and then how he liked it in the camp, etc.

Questioning "along the time line" may be helpful. The respondent can more readily recall objective facts and report reasons and attitudes if he is helped to remember them in their original sequence. For example, in a study of the development of occupational interests, rather than asking simply "When did you first decide you wanted to be a _____?" and "Why did you choose that occupation?" one might start by asking the respondent if he remembers whether as a small child he had any ideas about what he wanted to do when he grew up, what they were, why the occupations he favored at that time seemed attractive, and so on, specifying various periods in his life.

People often find it easier to answer if questions proceed from the more familiar to the less so, from the more important aspects to those of minor importance, from the relatively specific or immediate to the more general or remote. For example, an inquiry into points of satisfaction and dissatisfaction in work can move smoothly from such matters as the activities involved in the job to surrounding conditions, fellow workers, employment terms (hours, wages, etc.), and on to life outside the plant and to economic and social conditions.

Does the question come too early or too late from the point of view of arousing interest and receiving sufficient attention, avoiding resistance, etc.?

EXAMPLES: Some suspicion may be aroused if a home interview with workers opens abruptly with the question: "Where do you work? In what department?"

An opening question such as, "Do you think the government is giving the public as much information as it should about the hydrogen bomb?" is likely to arouse some resistance, since the respondent may hesitate to criticize the government to a stranger. The same question would probably be answered much more readily at a later point in the interview.

An opening question that was found rather uninteresting to many respondents read: "Would you say that housing conditions for defense workers around here are satisfactory, only fair, or poor? How about transportation conditions (bus service, etc.) for defense workers?" An opener such as this is to be contrasted with simple, definite, interesting ones such as: "What was the last movie you saw?" "How many times have you moved since Pearl Harbor?" "Have you ever been up in an airplane?" "Do you have a radio in working order?"

It is usual to place questions asking for personal and identifying data about the respondent at the end of the question form. He is ordinarily more willing to tell his age, education, marital status, income group, etc., by this time—and in case he is not, at least the replies to the previous questions have not been interfered with by the suspicion or resentment that personal questions occasionally arouse.

The Art of Interviewing[6]

This section, like the preceding one, is concerned with stand-ardized interviews, containing either closed or open questions. A few of the points apply also to unstructured and partially structured inter-views, but for the most part such interviews require greater skill and a quite different interviewing procedure (see Chapter 7, pages 263–268).

The quality of interviewing depends first upon proper study de-sign. Even the most skilled interviewers will not be able to collect valid and useful data if the schedule of questions is inadequate to the survey's objectives or has been put together clumsily. On the other hand, if they are properly selected and trained, a staff of ordinary men and women using a well-designed standardized questionnaire can elicit the required information.

Within the limits of survey design, however, there is ample room

[6] This section is taken, with slight modifications, from a discussion by Paul B. Sheatsley which appeared in Volume II of *Research Methods in Social Relations*, edited by Marie Jahoda, Morton Deutsch, and Stuart W. Cook (The Dryden Press, 1951), pages 463–492.

for "the art of interviewing" to come into play. The interviewer's art consists in creating a situation wherein the respondent's answers will be reliable and valid. The ideal usually sought is a permissive situation in which the respondent is encouraged to voice his frank opinions without fearing that his attitudes will be revealed to others and without the expression of any surprise or value judgment by the interviewer.

The first requisite for successful interviewing, therefore, is to create a friendly atmosphere and to put the respondent at his ease. With a pleasant, confident approach and a questionnaire that starts off easily, this is usually not difficult to achieve. From then on, the interviewer's art consists in asking the questions properly and intelligibly, in obtaining a valid and meaningful response, and in recording the response accurately and completely.

CREATING A FRIENDLY ATMOSPHERE

The interviewer's introduction should be brief, casual, and positive. The study's interest lies in the actual questions, and the interviewer should get into them as quickly as possible. Lengthy introductions or explanations only arouse the respondent's curiosity or suspicion. The best approach is: "Good morning. I'm working on a local public-opinion survey and would like to get a few of your ideas. For instance . . ."—and read the first question. Frequently the respondent will answer that question and go right ahead with the entire interview with only the most cursory inquiries about the objectives of the survey.

The interviewer's aim should be to interview everyone eligible for the sample. A small proportion of respondents will be suspicious or hostile, and a larger number may require a little encouragement or persuasion; but the good interviewer will find that hardly one person in twenty actually turns him down. Many people are flattered to be singled out for an interview. The interviewer should answer any legitimate questions the respondent has and should, if necessary, produce his credentials and explain that names are not recorded, that the interview is not a test (there are no "right" or "wrong" answers), and that in a democracy it is important to find out how people feel about important issues—and the only way to find out is to ask them.

The interviewer's manner should be friendly, courteous, conversational, and unbiased. He should be neither too grim nor too effusive; neither too talkative nor too timid. The idea should be to put the respondent at ease, so that he will talk freely and fully. A brief remark about the weather, the family pets, flowers, or children will often serve to break the ice. Above all, an informal, conversational interview is dependent upon a thorough mastery by the interviewer of the actual questions in the schedule. He should be familiar enough with them to ask them conversationally, rather than read them stiffly; and he should know what questions are coming next, so there will be no awkward pauses while he studies the questionnaire.

The interviewer's job is fundamentally that of a reporter, not an evangelist, a curiosity-seeker, or a debater. He should take all opinions in stride and never show surprise or disapproval of a respondent's answer. He should assume an interested manner toward his respondent's opinions and never divulge his own. If he should be asked for his views, he should laugh off the request with the remark that his job at the moment is to get opinions, not to have them.

The interviewer must keep the direction of the interview in his own hands, discouraging irrelevant conversation and endeavoring to keep the respondent on the point. Fortunately, he will usually find that the rambling, talkative respondents are the very ones who least resent a firm insistence on attention to the actual business of the interview.

ASKING THE QUESTIONS

Unless the interview is unstructured or only partially structured, interviewers must be impressed with the importance of asking each question exactly as it is worded. Each question has been carefully pretested to express the precise meaning desired in as simple a manner as possible. Interviewers must understand that even a slight rewording of the question can so change the stimulus as to provoke answers in a different frame of reference or bias the response.

Any impromptu explanation of questions is similarly taboo. Such an explanation again may change the frame of reference or bias the response, and it is easy to see that if each interviewer were permitted to vary the questions as seemed best to him, the survey director would have no assurance at all that responses were in comparable terms. If any respondent gives evidence of failing to understand a particular question, the interviewer can only repeat it slowly and with proper emphasis, offering only such explanation as may be specifically authorized in his instructions and, if understanding is still lacking, note this fact on the schedule.

For similar reasons, the questions must be asked in the same order as they appear on the questionnaire. Each question sets up a frame of reference for succeeding questions, and it is assumed that each respondent will be exposed to the same stimulus. Frequently the answer to a later question will be influenced by facts called to mind in an earlier one; to ask the later question first, even though to the interviewer there seems sound reason for doing so, will destroy the comparability of the interviews.

The interviewer, finally, must ask every question, unless the directions on the questionnaire specifically direct him to skip certain ones. It may sometimes seem that the respondent has already, in answering a prior question, given his opinion on a subsequent one, but the interviewer must nevertheless ask the later question in order to be sure, perhaps prefacing his inquiry with some such phrase as "Now you may already have touched on this, but . . ." Similarly, even if the question seems foolish or inapplicable, the interviewer must never omit asking it or take the answer for granted. Again, he may preface the inquiry with some such remark as, "Now I have to ask . . ."

Obtaining the Response

It might be thought a simple matter to ask a respondent the required questions and to record his replies, but interviewers will soon find that obtaining a *specific, complete* response is perhaps the most difficult part of their job. People often qualify or hedge their opinions; they answer "Don't know" in order to avoid thinking about the question; they misinterpret the meaning of the question; they launch off on an irrelevant discussion; they contradict themselves—and in all these cases, the interviewer usually has to *probe*.

Alertness to incomplete or nonspecific answers is perhaps the critical test of a good interviewer, and since no cne can foresee all the possible replies which may call for probes, each interviewer must understand fully the over-all objective of each question, the precise thing it is trying to measure. Both the written instructions and the oral training should emphasize the purpose of the question and should give examples of inadequate replies which were commonly encountered during the pretest. By the time he is actually out interviewing, the interviewer should have formed the automatic habit of asking himself, after each reply the respondent gives him: "Does that completely answer the question I just asked?"

When the first reply is inadequate, a simple repetition of the question, with proper emphasis, will usually suffice to get a response in satisfactory terms. This is particularly effective when the respondent has seemingly misunderstood the question, or has answered it irrelevantly, or has responded to only a portion of it. If the respondent's answer is vague or too general or incomplete, an effective probe is: "That's interesting. Could you explain that a little more?" or "Let's see, you said. . . . Just how do you mean that?"

Throughout, the interviewer must be extremely careful not to suggest a possible reply. People sometimes find the questions difficult, and sometimes they are not deeply interested in them. In either case, they will welcome any least hint from the interviewer which will enable them to give a creditable response. Interviewers must be thoroughly impressed with the harm which results from a "leading probe," from any remark which "puts words in their mouth." To be safe, the interviewer shouid always content himself with mere repetition of all or part of the actual question, or with such innocuous nondirective probes as are suggested in the preceding paragraph.

The "Don't know" reply is another problem for the interviewer. Sometimes that response represents a genuine lack of opinion; but at other times it may hide a host of other attitudes: fear to speak one's mind, reluctance to focus on the issue, vague opinions never yet expressed, a stalling for time while thoughts are marshaled, a lack of comprehension of the question, etc. It is the interviewer's job to distinguish among all these types of "Don't know" response and, when appropriate, to repeat the question with suitable assurances. In one case, for example, he might say, "Perhaps I didn't make that too clear. Let me read it again"; in another, he might say, "Well, lots of people have never thought about that before, but I'd like to have your ideas on it, just the way it seems to you." Or, again, he might point out, "Well, I just want your own opinion on it. Actually, nobody really knows the answers to many of these questions."

Qualified answers to questions that have been precoded in terms of "Yes-No," "Approve-Disapprove" or similar dichotomies are an interviewing problem which is actually in the domain of the study director. As far as possible, the most frequent qualifications of opinion should be anticipated in the actual wording of the question. If very many people find it impossible to answer because of unspecified contingencies, the question is a poor one. Most qualifications can be foreseen as a result of the pretest, and those that are not taken care of by revisions of the wording should be mentioned in the instructions to interviewers, with directions on how to handle such answers. In some cases, special codes may be provided for the most frequent qualifications; in other cases the interviewer may be instructed to record them as "Don't know" or "Undecided." In avoiding many qualifications inherent in the response to almost any opinion question, the interviewer may find it helpful to use phrases such as, "Well, in general, what would you say?" or "Taking everything into consideration," or "On the basis of the way things look to you now."

REPORTING THE RESPONSE

There are two chief means of recording opinions during the interview. If the question is precoded, the interviewer need only check a box or circle a code, or otherwise indicate which code comes closest to the respondent's opinion. If the question has not been precoded, the interviewer is expected to record the response verbatim.

On precoded questionnaires, errors and omissions in recording are a frequent source of interviewer error. In the midst of trying to pin the respondent down to a specific answer, keep his attention from flagging, remember which question comes next, and the many other problems that engage the interviewer's attention in the field, it is not surprising that he will sometimes neglect to indicate the respondent's reply to one of the items, overlook some particular question, check the wrong code on another, or ask some other question when it should be skipped.

The better the interviewer, the fewer the mistakes he will make, but even the best interviewers will occasionally be guilty. The unforgivable sin is to turn in the interview as complete when it contains such errors and omissions. The only certain way for the interviewer to avoid this is to make an automatic habit of *inspecting each interview*, immediately after its completion, before he goes on to another respondent, to make sure that it has been filled in accurately and completely. If he is lacking any information, he can go back and ask the respondent for it; if his questionnaire contains any errors or omissions, he can correct them on the spot; if his handwriting is illegible in places, or if he has recorded verbatim replies only sketchily, he can correct the weakness right there. If he waits until later in the day, or until he returns home at night, he will have forgotten many of the circumstances of the interview, or perhaps the prospect of editing the whole day's work will seem so forbidding that he will skip the matter completely.

The importance of clerical errors and omissions can be impressed upon the interviewer during training by pointing out that the questionnaire is designed as an integral whole, and that the omission or inaccurate reporting of a single answer can make the entire interview worthless. Thus, if for each question the responses of persons with different amounts of education are to be shown separately, and the interviewer neglects to record the amount of schooling the respondent has had, that whole interview must be discarded in that part of the analysis.

In reporting responses to free-answer questions, interviewers should be aware of the importance of *complete, verbatim* reporting. It will often be difficult to get down everything the respondent says in reply, but aside from obvious irrelevancies and repetitions, this should be the goal. Interviewers should be given some idea of the coding process, so that they can see the dangers of summarizing, abbreviating, or paraphrasing responses. Unless the coder can view the *whole* answer, just as the respondent said it, he is likely to classify it improperly or lose some important distinctions that should be made.

Interviewers should be instructed to quote the respondent directly, just as if they were news reporters taking down the statement of an important official. Paraphrasing the reply, summarizing it in the interviewer's own words, or "polishing up" any slang, cursing, or bad grammar not only risks distorting the respondent's meaning and emphasis, but also loses the color of his reply. Frequently the verbatim responses of individuals are useful in the final report as illustrations of the nuances of attitudes, and they should not be abbreviated or distorted.

Although it is frequently difficult to record responses verbatim without using shorthand,[7] a few simple techniques can greatly increase the interviewer's speed and the extent to which he succeeds in the verbatim recording of responses. It is perfectly permissible to ask the respondent to wait until the interviewer gets down "that last thought (that's pretty interesting)," but in order not to slow up the interview, the following devices will be found helpful for speedy recording. First, an interviewer should be prepared to write as soon as he has asked a question and to write while the respondent talks, not waiting until the entire response is completed. (Experienced interviewers often finish their recording of the prior response while they ask the next question and the respondent is considering his reply.) Second, the interviewer should use common abbreviations. Third, he should not bother to erase, but should cross out instead. Fourth, he may depart from the ideal of verbatim recording to the extent of using a telegraphic style; omission of "a", "the," and such parenthetical expressions as "well," "you know," "let's see," will ordinarily not lead to loss or distortion of meaning. But the interviewer should not speed up his recording by merely jotting down key words here and there. The connecting words and phrases are easily forgotten, and the recorded answer, even if it means something to the interviewer, may prove incomprehensible to the coders.

It is generally helpful if, on precoded questions, the interviewer reports verbatim anything the respondent says to explain or qualify his coded response; but he should not solicit such comments. The volunteered remarks of respondents often help the study director later

[7] Shorthand recording, although it has the advantage of more easily achieving a verbatim report, has the disadvantage of requiring later transcription, which may be very time-consuming and thus expensive.

in evaluating the meaning of the results and warn him of any com monly held qualifications or differences in intensity of opinion.

SAMPLING

Sampling is an essential part of the interviewer's job. No matter how precise and detailed the original sampling design, its execution will depend upon the training and competence of the interviewers who carry it out. Although the interviewer's responsibility is much greater under quota-sampling conditions, in which he himself selects the respondents to be interviewed, even under probability sampling, where he has no freedom of choice, he must be careful to avoid error and bias.[8]

If the sample is predesignated by name, for example, the interviewer should be given advice on how best to make contact with the assigned individuals and how to overcome any hostility he may encounter. If a system of substitution is provided for cases in which the originally designated respondent cannot be interviewed, the circumstances in which substitutions are allowed should be described carefully so that the sample will not be biased by too free an exercise of this provision.

If the sample is of an area type—that is, if it involves selection of dwelling units within a given area according to some prearranged plan—interviewers must be thoroughly trained in its execution. It has been found, for example, that biasing errors may easily creep into the listing of dwelling units, and into the supposedly random selection of households and of individual respondents within those households.

As pointed out in Appendix B, biases are particularly likely under quota sampling, in which the interviewer selects the subjects. It is especially likely to occur when quotas are assigned in terms of economic levels, the definition of which is largely subjective. Unless some restraint is exercised upon the interviewers, they will generally tend to pass up persons who look unpleasant, uninterested, or inarticulate, and to seek out individuals they think will give them "good" answers. There is also the danger that unless area controls are introduced, too many interviews will be concentrated in one neighborhood, with consequent

---

[8] Different types of samples are discussed in Appendix B.

overrepresentation of particular religious, occupational, or national groups.

It is generally helpful, when a quota-type sample is used, to give interviewers informal quotas in terms of education and to keep a check on this factor as the interviews are returned. Such an additional informal control will ensure some effort on the part of interviewers using quota samples to avoid the usual tendency of including too few respondents in the lowest educational and socioeconomic groups, and will permit the study director to caution any members of the staff who seem to be guilty of sampling bias of this type.

BIASING FACTORS INTRODUCED BY THE INTERVIEWER

Interviewer "bias"—that is, systematic differences from interviewer to interviewer or, occasionally, systematic errors on the part of many or even all interviewers—may enter not only in the selection of the sample, but also in the asking of questions and the eliciting and recording of responses. Interviewer bias is not simply a matter of prejudiced or untrained interviewers exerting influence on their respondents and deliberately or carelessly distorting the answers they receive. The dangers of bias cannot be overcome simply by hiring "impartial" interviewers. The fact that an interviewer has strong opinions on the subject under survey does not necessarily mean that his work will be biased, nor does the fact that he has no strong stand of his own necessarily make his work free from bias.

Much of what we call interviewer bias can more correctly be described as interviewer *differences* which are inherent in the fact that interviewers are human beings and not machines and that they do not all work identically or infallibly. The fact that respondents, too, are human beings, with differing perceptions, judgments, and personalities, simply compounds the differences that would occur even if the interviewers were engaged in evaluating physical instead of human materials. It is not to be expected, therefore, that interviewers will unfailingly bring back complete, comparable, and valid reports. Although a large number of the more obvious types of error and bias can be overcome by appropriate methods of interviewer selection and training, some are bound to remain. Fortunately, however, it is easier for the study director to become aware of the biases of interviewers, and thus to discount their effects in his interpretation of the data, than it is for the clinician, the experimenter, or the participant observer to detect his own bias when he himself collects the data.

Assuming an unbiased selection of respondents, bias in the interview situation appears to come about through (1) the respondent's perception of the interviewer, and (2) the interviewer's perception of the respondent. We use the term *perception* here in the broad sense, which emphasizes the manner in which the relation between interviewer and respondent is influenced and modified by their wishes, expectations, and personality structure.

There is an abundance of experimental evidence to prove that bias may result, under certain conditions, regardless of anything the interviewer may do to eliminate it. In one study, 50 per cent of a sample of non-Jewish respondents told non-Jewish interviewers that they thought Jews had too much influence in the business world, whereas only 22 per cent of an equivalent sample voiced that opinion to Jewish interviewers. Similar experiments have shown that Negroes will frequently answer differently when interviewed by white people, and that working-class respondents are less likely to talk freely to middle-class interviewers. Such effects can occur no matter how conscientiously the interviewer attempts to be "unbiased."

The magnitude of these effects naturally varies with the way in which the respondent perceives the situation. Thus, in one study, it was demonstrated that Negroes spoke more frankly with white interviewers in New York than they did in Memphis, Tennessee. The interviewing situation was "objectively" the same in both cities, but respondents perceived it differently. By altering the respondent's perception of the situation (for example, by assuring him that his name will not be recorded), these biasing effects can often be reduced, but they can seldom be eliminated.

The study director should keep these matters in mind when he selects his interviewers, and the staff should be warned of the dangers. It is for reasons of this type that interviewers are usually instructed, for example, to dress inconspicuously so that their clothes and appearance will not influence lower-class respondents; to interview the respondent privately so that his opinions will not be affected by the presence of some third person; and to adopt an informal, conversational manner in an effort to achieve the best possible rapport.

Not all interviewer effects operate through the respondent's perception of the interviewer, however. Indeed, some respondents appear to be totally immune to even the most flagrant biasing characteristics of the interviewer. Fully as important a source of bias are the interviewer's perceptions of his respondent. No matter how standardized the questionnaire may be and no matter how rigidly the interviewer may be instructed, he still has much opportunity to exercise freedom of choice during the actual interview, and it is often his perception of the respondent that determines the manner in which he asks the question, the way in which he probes, his classification of equivocal responses to precoded questions, and his recording of verbatim answers.

Interviewers do not approach each new respondent in an unstructured fashion: indeed, they often have strong expectations and stereotypes, which are more and more likely to come into play as they continue interviewing. On the basis of their past judgments, or of prior answers received from other respondents, they may, for example, quite unconsciously come to associate lack of education with ethnic or religious prejudice; or they may come to anticipate a large number of "No opinion" responses from the Negroes they interview. Such expectations will almost inevitably affect their performance.

Thus, given the same "No opinion" response from a wealthy businessman and from a Negro housewife, they may probe the former's reply, in the belief that an opinion must be lurking there somewhere, whereas they will routinely accept the latter's reply without probing and go on to the next question. An experimental study has shown that when the same equivocal answer regarding aid to Europe was embedded first in an "isolationist" context of previous responses and then in an "internationalist" context, only 20 per cent of the interviewers classified it in internationalist terms in the first context, but 75 per cent of the same interviewers classified it as internationalist in the second context. Experiments on verbatim recording have also shown that interviewers tend to select from long answers those parts that most nearly conform to their own expectations or opinions and to discard the rest.

A final source of bias arises from the interviewer's perception of the *situation*. If he sees the results of the survey as a possible threat to his interests or beliefs, for example, he is likely to introduce bias. Or if he regards his assignment as impossible, he is almost bound to introduce bias. Such difficulties can best be overcome by proper motivation and supervision.

Since interviewers are human beings, such biasing factors can never be overcome completely, but their effects can be reduced by standardizing the interview, so that the interviewer has as little free choice as possible. Thus, the use of a standard wording in survey questions aims to prevent the bias that would result if each interviewer worded the question in his own fashion. Similarly, if interviewers are given standard instructions on probing procedure, on the classification of doubtful answers, and so on, their biases will have less chance to operate.

It should be noted, however, that as the interviewer's freedom is restricted, the opportunities for effective use of his insight are correspondingly restricted. Conversely, the more responsibilities the interviewer is given for probing and evaluating his respondent's opinion, the more bias is likely to result. A compromise must generally be made. In a study whose results are to be analyzed statistically and quantitatively, and in which large numbers of inexperienced or hastily trained interviewers are relied upon, it is wise to reduce the interviewer's freedom of choice to a minimum by standardizing, so far as possible, every aspect of the interview situation.

Since bias, in the sense that different interviewers will not always bring back the same answers from equivalent respondents, can never be entirely eliminated, the study director's main responsibilities are so to select, train, and supervise his staff that any net effect of bias will be at a minimum, and to be aware of the possibilities of bias at various points so that he can discount their effects in his analysis.

Many critics tend to exaggerate the significance of "interview bias"—overlooking the fact that social scientists are universally dependent upon data that have been collected by means of oral or written reports, and that these reports, no matter how collected, are invariably subject to essentially the same sources of error and bias as are those collected by survey interviewers. The clinician and, frequently, the experimenter depend upon oral reports of feelings, perceptions, behavior, etc.; and they, as well as the sophisticated "participant observer" in another type of investigation, are just as likely to bias their subjects' responses as are the interviewers participating in an attitude survey. The major difference is that when the social scientist has to depend upon the reports of interviewers whom he selects and trains, he becomes more aware of the dangers and difficulties involved.

BIBLIOGRAPHY

ABT, L. E. and L. BELLAK, 1950. *Projective psychology*. Knopf.

ACKERMAN, N. W., and M. JAHODA, 1950. *Antisemitism and emotional disorder: a psychoanalytic interpretation*. Harper.

ACKOFF, R. L., 1953. *The design of social research*. University of Chicago.

ADORNO, T. W., E. FRENKEL-BRUNSWIK, D. J. LEVINSON, and R. N. SANFORD, 1950. *The authoritarian personality*. Harper.

ALLPORT, G. W., 1942. *The use of personal documents in psychological science*. Bulletin 49, Social Science Research Council.

ALLPORT, G. W., 1950. *Prejudice: a problem of psychological and social causation. J. Social Issues*, Supplement Series No. 4.

AMERICAN PSYCHOLOGICAL ASSOCIATION, 1953. *Ethical standards of psychologists*.

AMERICAN PSYCHOLOGICAL ASSOCIATION, 1957. *Publication manual* (revised).

ANDERSON, H. H., and G. L. ANDERSON, 1951. *An introduction to projective techniques and other devices for understanding the dynamics of human behavior*. Prentice-Hall.

BAEHNE, G. W., 1935. *Practical applications of the punched card method in colleges and universities*. Columbia University.

BALDWIN, A. L., 1950. *Statistical problems in the treatment of case histories. J. Clinical Psychology, 6*, 6–12.

BALES, R. F., 1950. *Interaction process analysis*. Addison-Wesley.

BALES, R. F., and H. GERBRANDS, 1948. *The "interaction-recorder." Human Relations, 1*, 456–463.

BARKER, R., T. DEMBO, and K. LEWIN, 1941. *Frustration and regression: an experiment with young children.* Studies in topological and vector psychology II. University of Iowa Studies in Child Welfare, *18*, No. I.

BARTLETT, F. C., 1932. *Remembering.* Cambridge University.

BEERS, C. W., 1935. *A mind that found itself: an autobiography* (8th ed., 1953, Doubleday). National Committee for Mental Hygiene.

BELL, J. E., 1948. *Projective techniques: a dynamic approach to the study of the personality.* Longmans Green.

BENNE, K. D., and G. E. SWANSON, eds., 1950. Values and the social scientist. *J. Social Issues, 6,* No. 4.

BERELSON, B., 1952. *Content analysis in communication research.* Free Press.

BERKOWITZ, L. and H. GUETZKOW, 1949. *Manual for overall observers.* Naval Conference Research, University of Michigan. Mimeographed.

BETTELHEIM, B., and M. JANOWITZ, 1950. *Dynamics of prejudice.* Harper.

BEVERIDGE, W. I. B., 1950. *The art of scientific investigation.* Norton.

BEYLE, H. C., 1932. A scale for the measurement of attitude toward candidates for elective governmental office. *American Political Science Review, 26,* 527–544.

BLANKENSHIP, A. B., 1946. *How to conduct consumer and opinion research.* Harper.

BLANKENSHIP, A. B., et al., 1947. Survey on problems of interviewer cheating. *International J. Opinion and Attitude Research, 1,* 93–107.

BOGARDUS, E. S., 1925. Measuring social distances. *J. Applied Sociology, 9,* 299–308.

BOGARDUS, E. S., 1928. *Immigration and race attitudes.* Heath.

BOGARDUS, E. S., 1933. A social distance scale. *Sociology and Social Research, 17,* 265–271.

BRAITHWAITE, R. B., 1955. *Scientific explanation: a study of the function of theory, probability and law in science.* Cambridge University.

BROWN, J. F., 1947. A modification of the Rosenzweig picture-frustration test to study hostile interracial attitudes. *J. Psychology, 24,* 247–272.

BRUNER, J. S., 1941. The dimensions of propaganda: German shortwave broadcasts to America. *J. Abnormal and Social Psychology, 36,* 311–337.

BRUNSWIK, E., 1955. Representative design and probabilistic theory in functional psychology. *Psychological Review, 62,* 193–217.

BRUNSWIK, E., 1956. *Perception and the representative design of psychological experiments* (2d ed.). University of California.

BÜHLER, C., 1934. Drei Generationen im Jugendtagebuch. *Quellen und Studien zur Jugendkunde, 11.*

BURWEN, L. S., and D. T. CAMPBELL, 1957. The generality of attitudes toward authority and nonauthority figures. *J. Abnormal and Social Psychology, 54,* 24–31.

CAMPBELL, D. T., 1950. The indirect assessment of social attitudes. *Psychological Bulletin, 47*, 15–38.

CAMPBELL, D. T., 1957. Factors relevant to the validity of experiments in social settings. *Psychological Bulletin, 54*, 297–312.

CAMPBELL, D. T., and D. W. FISKE, 1959. Convergent and discriminant validation by the multitrait-multimethod matrix. *Psychological Bulletin, 56.*

CANTER, R. R., JR., 1951. An experimental study of a human relations training program. *J. Applied Psychology, 35*, 38–45.

CANTRIL, H. A., JR., A. AMES, JR., A. H. HASTORF, and W. H. ITTELSON, 1949. Psychology and scientific research. *Science, 110*, 461–464, 491–497, 517–522.

CARTER, H., 1945. Recent American studies in attitudes toward war: a summary and evaluation. *American Sociological Review, 10*, 343–352.

CATTELL, R. B., 1952. *Factor analysis: an introduction and manual for the psychologist and social scientist.* Harper.

CATTELL, R. B., A. B. HEIST, P. A. HEIST, and R. G. STEWART, 1950. The objective measurement of dynamic traits. *Educational and Psychological Measurement, 10*, 224–248.

CATTELL, R. B., and L. B. LUBORSKY, 1950. T-technique demonstrated as a new clinical method for determining personality and symptom structure. *J. General Psychology, 42*, 3–24.

CATTELL, R. B., E. F. MAXWELL, B. H. LIGHT, and M. P. UNGER, 1949. The objective measurement of attitudes. *British J. Psychology, 40*, 81–90.

CHAPIN, F. S., 1947. *Experimental designs in sociological research.* Harper.

CHAPPLE, E. D., 1949. The interaction chronograph: its evaluation and present application. *Personnel, 25*, 295–307.

CHEIN, I., 1956. Narcotics use among juveniles. *Social Work, 1*, 50–60.

CHEIN, I., A. F. CITRON, M. H. WORMSER, and W. SCHWARTZ, 1952. *Basic issues in Jewish education and group work.* American Jewish Congress (New York). Mimeographed.

CHURCHMAN, C. W., 1948. *Theory of experimental inference.* Macmillan.

CITRON, A. F., I. CHEIN, and J. HARDING, 1950. Anti-minority remarks: a problem for action research. *J. Abnormal and Social Psychology, 45*, 99–126.

CLARK, K. B., and M. P. CLARK, 1939. The development of consciousness of self and the emergence of racial identification in Negro pre-school children. *J. Social Psychology, 10*, 591–599.

CLARK, K. B., and M. P. CLARK, 1950. Emotional factors in racial identification and preference in Negro children. *J. Negro Education, 19*, 341–350.

COCHRAN, W. G., 1953. *Sampling techniques.* Wiley.

592 BIBLIOGRAPHY

COCHRAN, W. G., 1956. Design and analysis of samplings. In *Statistical methods*, by G. W. Snedecor, 5th ed. Iowa State College.

COCHRAN, W. G., and G. M. Cox, 1957. *Experimental designs* (2d ed.). Wiley.

COHEN, A. K., 1955. *Delinquent boys: the culture of the gang*. Free Press.

COHEN, M. R., and E. NAGEL, 1934. *An introduction to logic and scientific method*. Harcourt.

COLLIER, J., JR., 1957. Photography in anthropology: a report on two experiments. *American Anthropologist, 59*, 843–859.

Confessions of St. Augustine, 1948. (F. J. Sheed, trans.) Sheed & Ward.

COOK, L. A., 1950. *Intergroup relations in teacher education*. College Study in Intergroup Relations, Vol. II. American Council on Education (Washington, D.C.)

COOK, S. W., 1949. *The role of social values in social-psychological research*. Mimeographed. Research Center for Human Relations, New York University.

COOK, S. W., J. HAVEL, and J. R. CHRIST, 1957. *The effects of an orientation program for foreign students*. Mimeographed. Research Center for Human Relations, New York University.

COOMBS, C. H., 1948. Some hypotheses for the analysis of qualitative variables. *Psychological Review, 55*, 167–174.

COOMBS, C. H., 1950. Psychological scaling without a unit of measurement. *Psychological Review, 57*, 145–158.

COOMBS, C. H., 1953. Theory and methods of social measurement. In *Research methods in the behavioral sciences*, ed. by L. Festinger and D. Katz. Dryden.

COTTRELL, L. S., JR., ed., 1957. *Public reaction to the atomic bomb and world affairs*. Cornell University.

CRISWELL, J. H., 1937. Racial cleavages in Negro-white groups. *Sociometry, 1*, 87–89.

CRISWELL, J. H., 1939. Social structure revealed in a sociometric retest. *Sociometry, 2*, 69–75.

CRONBACH, L. J., 1949. *Essentials of psychological testing*. Harper.

CRONBACH, L. J., 1951. Coefficient alpha and the internal structure of tests. *Psychometrika, 16*, 297–334.

CRONBACH, L. J., 1953. Correlations between persons as a research tool. In *Psychotherapy: theory and research*, ed. by O. H. Mowrer. Ronald Press.

CRONBACH, L. J., and P. E. MEEHL, 1955. Construct validity in psychological tests. *Psychological Bulletin, 52*, 281–302.

CRUTCHFIELD, R., and D. H. GORDON, 1947. Variations in respondents' interpretations of an opinion-poll question. *International J. Opinion and Attitude Research, 1*, 22–31.

DAVIDSON, D., P. SUPPES, and S. SIEGEL, 1957. *Decision making: an experimental approach.* Stanford University.

DAVISON, W. P., 1947. An analysis of the Soviet-controlled Berlin press. *Public Opinion Quarterly, 11,* 40–57.

DEAN, J. P., 1954. Participant observation and interviewing. In *An introduction to social research,* ed. by J. T. Doby. Stackpole.

DEMING, W. E., 1950. *Some theory of sampling.* Wiley.

DERI, S., D. DINNERSTEIN, J. HARDING, and A. D. PEPITONE, 1948. Techniques for the diagnosis and measurement of intergroup attitudes and behavior. *Psychological Bulletin, 45,* 248–271.

DE SALES, R. R., ed., 1941. *My new order.* Reynal.

DEUTSCH, M., 1949. An experimental study of the effects of cooperation and competition upon group process. *Human Relations, 2,* 199–232.

DEUTSCH, M., and M. E. COLLINS, 1951. *Interracial housing: a psychological evaluation of a social experiment.* University of Minnesota.

DIXON, W. J., and F. J. MASSEY, JR., 1957. *Introduction to statistical analysis.* (2d ed.). McGraw-Hill.

DOLLARD, J., L. W. DOOB, N. E. MILLER, O. H. MOWRER, and R. H. SEARS, 1939. *Frustration and aggression.* Yale University.

DU BOIS, C., 1944. *The people of Alor: a social-psychological study of an East Indian island.* University of Minnesota.

DUDYCHA, G. J., 1943. A critical examination of the measurement of attitude toward war. *J. Social Psychology, 39,* 846–860.

DURKHEIM, E., 1951. *Suicide.* (J. A. Spaulding and G. Simpson, trans.) Free Press.

ECKERT, J. W., 1940. *Punched card methods in scientific computation.* The Thomas J. Watson Astronomical Computing Bureau, Columbia University.

EDWARDS, A. L., 1950. *Experimental design in psychological research.* Rhinehart.

EDWARDS, A. L., 1957a. *Techniques of attitude scale construction.* Appleton-Century-Crofts.

EDWARDS, A. L., 1957b. *The social desirability variable in personality assessment and research.* Dryden.

EDWARDS, A. L., and K. C. KENNEY, 1946. A comparison of the Thurstone and Likert techniques of attitude scale construction. *J. Applied Psychology, 30,* 72–83.

EDWARDS, A. L., and F. P. KILPATRICK, 1948. A technique for construction of attitude scales. *J. Applied Psychology, 32,* 374–384.

EYSENCK, H. J., and S. CROWN, 1949. An experimental study in opinion-attitude methodology. *International J. Opinion and Attitude Research, 3,* 47–86.

FERGUSON, L. W., 1935. The influence of individual attitudes on construction of an attitude scale. *J. Social Psychology, 6,* 115–117.

FERGUSON, L. W., 1957. More measurement than validation. *Contemporary Psychology*, 2, 237–238.

FESTINGER, L., 1947. The treatment of qualitative data by scale analysis. *Psychological Bulletin, 44*, 149–161.

FESTINGER, L., and D. KATZ, eds., 1953. *Research methods in the behavioral sciences.* Dryden.

FESTINGER, L., H. W. RIECKEN, and S. SCHACHTER, 1956. *When prophecy fails.* University of Minnesota.

FESTINGER, L., S. SCHACHTER, and K. W. BACK, 1950. *Social pressures in informal groups.* Harper.

FISHER, R. A., 1951. *The design of experiments* (6th ed.). Oliver and Boyd.

FLESCH, R. F., 1949. *The art of readable writing.* Harper.

FLESCH, R. F., 1954. *How to make sense.* Harper.

FLESCH, R. F., and A. H. LASS, 1955. *The way to write* (2nd ed.). McGraw-Hill.

FRANK, L. K., 1939. Projective methods for the study of personality. *J. Psychology, 8*, 389–413.

FRANZ, J. G., 1940. The place of the psychodrama in research. *Sociometry, 3*, 49–61.

FREEMAN, F. S., 1955. *Theory and practice of psychological testing* (rev. ed.). Holt.

FREUD, S., 1939. *Moses and monotheism.* Knopf.

FROMME, A., 1941. On the use of certain qualitative methods of attitude research: a study of opinions on the methods of preventing war. *J. Social Psychology, 13*, 425–459.

GARDNER, B. B., and S. J. LEVY, 1955. The product and the brand. *Harvard Business Review, 33*, 33–39.

GETZELS, J. W., 1951. The assessment of personality and prejudice by the method of paired direct and projective questions. Unpublished doctoral dissertation, Harvard University.

GOLDSEN, J. M., 1947. Analyzing the contents of mass communication: a step toward inter-group harmony. *International J. Opinion and Attitude Research, 1*, 81–92.

GOOD, C. V., 1941. Effective reporting of research. *Phi Delta Kappan, 24*, 178–184.

GOODE, W. J., and P. K. HATT, 1952. *Methods in social research.* McGraw-Hill.

GOODMAN, M. E., 1952. *Race awareness in young children.* Addison-Wesley.

GOTTSCHALK, L., C. KLUCKHOHN, and R. ANGELL, 1945. *The use of personal documents in history, anthropology and sociology.* Bulletin 53, Social Science Research Council.

GRANNEBERG, R. T., 1955. The influence of individual attitude and attitude-intelligence interaction upon scale values of attitude items. *American Psychologist, 10,* 330–331. Abstract.

GREEN, B. F., 1954. Attitude measurement. In *Handbook of social psychology,* Vol. I, ed. by G. Lindzey. Addison-Wesley.

GREENWOOD, E., 1945. *Experimental sociology.* King's Crown.

GROSS, N., W. S. MASON, and A. W. McEACHERN, 1958. *Explorations in role analysis: studies of the school superintendency role.* Wiley.

GUETZKOW, H., 1950. Unitizing and categorizing problems in coding qualitative material. *J. Clinical Psychology, 6,* 47–58.

GUILFORD, J. P., 1954. *Psychometric methods* (2d ed.). McGraw-Hill.

GULLIKSEN, H., 1950. *Theory of mental tests.* Wiley.

HAIRE, M., 1950. Projective techniques in marketing research. *J. Marketing, 14,* 649–656.

HALBWACHS, M., 1930. *Les causes du suicide.* Felix Alcan (Paris).

HAMMOND, K. R., 1948. Measuring attitudes by error-choice: an indirect method. *J. Abnormal and Social Psychology, 43,* 38–48.

HAMMOND, K. R., 1955. Probabilistic functioning and the clinical method. *Psychological Review, 62,* 255–262.

HANSEN, M. H., W. N. HURWITZ, and W. G. MADOW, 1953. *Sample survey methods and theory.* Wiley. 2 vols.

HARDING, J., and R. HOGREFE, 1952. Attitudes of white department store employees toward Negro co-workers. *J. Social Issues, 8,* 1, 18–28.

HARTLEY, E. L., 1946. *Problems in prejudice.* King's Crown.

HARTLEY, E. L., and S. SCHWARTZ, 1948. *A pictorial doll play approach for the study of children's intergroup attitudes.* American Jewish Committee (New York). Mimeographed.

HEBB, D. O., and W. R. THOMPSON, 1954. The social significance of animal studies. In *Handbook of social psychology,* Vol. I, ed. by G. Lindzey. Addison-Wesley.

HELGERSON, E., 1943. The relative significance of race, sex, and facial expression in choice of playmate by the pre-school child. *J. Negro Education, 12,* 617–622.

HEMPEL, C. G., 1952. Fundamentals of concept formation in empirical science. *International Encyclopedia of Unified Science,* Vol. II, No. 7. University of Chicago.

HENRY, W. E., and H. GUETZKOW, 1951. Group projection sketches for the study of small groups. *J. Social Psychology, 33,* 77–102.

HINCKLEY, E. D., 1932. The influence of individual opinion on construction of an attitude scale. *J. Social Psychology, 3,* 283–296.

HOMANS, G. C., 1950. *The human group.* Harcourt.

HOROWITZ, E. L., 1936. The development of attitude toward the Negro. *Archives Psychology,* No. 194.

HOROWITZ, E. L., and R. E. HOROWITZ, 1938. Development of social attitudes in children. Sociometry, 1, 301–338.

HOROWITZ, R. E., 1939. Racial aspects of self-identification in nursery school children. J. Psychology, 7, 91–99.

HORWITZ, M., and D. CARTWRIGHT, 1953. A projective method for the diagnosis of groups. Human Relations, 6, 397–410.

HOVLAND, C. I., I. K. JANIS, and H. H. KELLEY, 1953. Communication and persuasion: psychological studies of opinion change. Yale University.

HOVLAND, C. I., A. A. LUMSDAINE, and F. D. SHEFFIELD, 1949. Experiments on mass communication. Studies in Social Psychology in World War II, Vol. III. Princeton University.

HOVLAND, C. I., and R. R. SEARS, 1940. Minor studies in aggression: VI. Correlations of lynchings with economic indices. J. Psychology, 9, 301–310.

HOVLAND, C. I., and M. SHERIF, 1952. Judgmental phenomena and scales of attitude measurement: item displacement in Thurstone scales. J. Abnormal and Social Psychology, 47, 822–832.

HUNT, J. McV., 1941. The effects of infant feeding-frustration upon adult hoarding in the albino rat. J. Abnormal and Social Psychology, 36, 338–360.

HYMAN, H. H., 1955. Survey design and analysis: principles, cases, and procedures. Free Press.

HYMAN, H. H., et al., 1954. Interviewing in social research. University of Chicago.

INFORMATION AND EDUCATION DIVISION, U. S. War Department, 1947. Opinions about Negro infantry platoons in white companies of seven divisions. In Readings in social psychology, ed. by T. M. Newcomb and E. L. Hartley. Holt.

JAHODA, M., and S. W. COOK, 1952. Security measures and freedom of thought. Yale Law Journal, 61, 297–333.

JAHODA-LAZARSFELD, M., and H. ZEISL, 1932. Die Arbeitslosen von Marienthal. Hirzel (Leipzig).

JANIS, I. L., 1943. Meaning and the study of symbolic behavior. Psychiatry, 6, 425–439.

JASPERS, K., 1950. Is science evil? Commentary, 9, 229–233.

JENNINGS, H. H., 1943. Leadership and isolation (2d ed. 1950). Longmans.

JONES, E., 1953–1957. The Life and work of Sigmund Freud. Basic Books. 3 vols.

JONES, E. E., and R. KOHLER, 1958. The effects of plausibility on the learning of controversial statements. J. Abnormal and Social Psychology, 57, 315–320.

KAPLAN, A., 1943a. Content analysis and the theory of signs. Philosophy of Science, 10, 230–247.

KAPLAN, A., 1943b. *Reliability of "favorable" and "unfavorable" symbol classification in newspaper headlines.* Document No. 42, Library of Congress, Experimental Division for the Study of War Time Communications.

KAPLAN, A., and J. M. GOLDSEN, 1943. *Reliability of certain categories for classifying newspaper headlines.* Document No. 40, Library of Congress, Experimental Division for the Study of War Time Communications.

KATZ, D., 1951. Social psychology and group process. *Annual Review of Psychology,* ed. by C. P. Stone. Annual Reviews, Inc. (Stanford, Calif.).

KATZ, D., and H. H. HYMAN, 1947. Morale in war industries. In *Readings in social psychology,* ed. by T. M. Newcomb and E. L. Hartley. Holt.

KATZ, I., J. GOLDSTON, and L. BENJAMIN, 1958. Behavior and productivity in bi-racial work groups. *Human Relations, 11,* 123–141.

KELLER, H. A., 1903. *The story of my life.* Doubleday, Page.

KELLEY, H. H., C. I. HOVLAND, M. SCHWARTZ, and R. P. ABELSON, 1955. The influence of judges' attitudes in three methods of attitude scaling. *J. Social Psychology, 42,* 147–158.

KELLY, E. L., and D. W. FISKE, 1950. The prediction of success in the VA training program in clinical psychology. *American Psychologist, 5,* 395–406.

KENDALL, P. L., and P. F. LAZARSFELD, 1950. Problems of survey analysis. In *Continuities in social research,* ed. by R. K. Merton and P. F. Lazarsfeld. Free Press.

KERR, M., 1943. An experimental investigation of national stereotypes. *Sociological Review, 35,* 37–43.

KINSEY, A. C., et al., 1948. *Sexual behavior in the human male.* Saunders.

KISH, L., 1953. Selection of the sample. In *Research methods in the behavioral sciences,* ed. by L. Festinger and D. Katz. Dryden.

KLINEBERG, O., 1935a. *Negro intelligence and selective migration.* Columbia University.

KLINEBERG, O., 1935b. *Race differences.* Harper.

KORNHAUSER, A., 1951. Constructing questionnaires and interview schedules. In *Research methods in social relations,* Vol. II, first ed., ed. by M. Jahoda, M. Deutsch, and S. W. Cook. Dryden.

KRAMER, B. M., 1949. Dimensions of prejudice. *J. Psychology, 27,* 389–451.

KRECH, D., and R. S. CRUTCHFIELD, 1948. *Theory and problems of social psychology.* McGraw-Hill.

LAMBERT, R. D., and M. BRESSLER, 1957. *Indian students on an American campus.* University of Minnesota.

LANDIS, K. M., 1948. *Segregation in Washington.* National Committee on Segregation in the Nation's Capital (Chicago).

LaPiere, R. T., 1934. Attitudes vs. actions. *Social Forces, 14,* 230–237.

Lasswell, H. D., 1942a. *Analyzing the content of mass communication: a brief introduction.* Document No. 11, Library of Congress, Experimental Division for Study of War Time Communications.

Lasswell, H. D., 1942b. The politically significant content of the press: coding procedures. *Journalism Quarterly, 19,* 12–23.

Lasswell, H. D., 1946. Describing the contents of communications. In *Propaganda, communication, and public opinion,* by B. L. Smith, H. D. Lasswell and R. D. Casey. Princeton University.

Lasswell, H. D., N. Leites, and associates, 1949. *Language of politics.* George W. Stewart.

Lazarsfeld, P. F., 1935. The art of asking why. *National Marketing Review, 1,* 26–38.

Lazarsfeld, P. F., 1944. The controversy over detailed interviews—an offer for negotiation. *Public Opinion Quarterly, 8,* 38–60.

Lazarsfeld, P. F., 1957. *Latent structure analysis.* Bureau of Applied Social Research, Columbia University. Mimeographed.

Leahy, A., 1931. Punching psychological and sociological data on Hollerith cards. *J. Applied Psychology, 15,* 199–207.

Lee, A. M., 1949. A sociological discussion of consistency and inconsistency in intergroup relations. *J. Social Issues, 5,* 12–18.

Lee, A. M., and N. D. Humphrey, 1943. *Race riot.* Dryden.

Lee, R. S., 1957. *The family of the addict: a comparison of the family experiences of male juvenile heroin addicts and controls.* Unpublished doctoral dissertation, New York University, Graduate School of Arts and Science.

Leighton, A. H., 1949. *Human relations in a changing world.* Dutton.

Levine, J. M., and G. Murphy, 1943. The learning and forgetting of controversial material. *J. Abnormal and Social Psychology, 38,* 507–517.

Levy, D. M., 1943. *Maternal overprotection.* Columbia University.

Lewin, K., 1951. Formalization and progress in psychology. In *Field theory in social science: selected theoretical papers,* ed. by D. Cartwright. Harper.

Lewin, K., C. E. Meyers, J. Kalhorn, M. L. Farber, and J. R. P. French, Jr., 1944. *Authority and frustration.* Studies in topological and vector psychology III. University of Iowa Studies in Child Welfare 20.

Lewis, H. B., 1941. Studies in the principles of judgments and attitudes: IV. The operation of "prestige suggestion." *J. Social Psychology, 14,* 229–256.

Likert, R., 1932. A technique for the measurement of attitudes. *Archives Psychology,* No. 140.

Likert, R., and R. Lippitt, 1953. The utilization of social science. In

Research methods in the behavioral sciences, ed. by L. Festinger and D. Katz. Dryden.

LINDGREN, E. J., 1935. Field work in social psychology. British J. Psychology, 26, Part 2, 174–182.

LINDQUIST, E. F., 1953. Design and analysis of experiments in psychology and education. Houghton Mifflin.

LINDZEY, G., and E. F. BORGATTA, 1954. Sociometric measurement. In Handbook of social psychology, Vol. I, ed. by G. Lindzey. Addison-Wesley.

LOEVINGER, J., 1947. A systematic approach to the construction and evaluation of tests of ability. Psychological Monographs, 61, No. 4.

LOEVINGER, J., 1948. The technic of homogeneous tests compared with some aspects of "scale analysis" and factor analysis. Psychological Bulletin, 45, 507–529.

LOWENTHAL, L., 1943. Biographies in popular magazines. In Radio research 1942–43 ed. by P. F. Lazarsfeld and F. N. Stanton. Duell, Sloan.

LUNDBERG, G. A., M. KOMAROVSKY, and M. A. McINERY, 1934. Leisure: a suburban study. Columbia University.

McCARTHY, P. J., 1951. Sample design. In Research methods in social relations, Vol. II, first ed., ed. by M. Jahoda, M. Deutsch, and S. W. Cook. Dryden.

McCLELLAND, D. C., 1951. Personality. Dryden.

MACCOBY, E. E., and N. MACCOBY, 1954. The interview: a tool of social science. In Handbook of social psychology, Vol. I, ed. by G. Lindzey. Addison-Wesley.

MacCRONE, I. D., 1937. Race attitudes in South Africa. Oxford.

McGRANAHAN, D. V., 1951. Content analysis of the mass media of communication. In Research methods in social relations, Vol. II, first ed., ed. by M. Jahoda, M. Deutsch, and S. W. Cook. Dryden.

McGREGOR, D., 1935. Scientific measurement and psychology. Psychological Review, 42, 246–266.

McNEMAR, Q., 1940. Sampling in psychological research. Psychological Bulletin, 37, 331–365.

MARGENAU, H., 1950. The nature of physical reality: a philosophy of modern physics. McGraw-Hill.

MEAD, M., 1946. Research on primitive children. In Manual of child psychology, ed. by L. Carmichael. Wiley.

MEREI, F., 1949. Group leadership and institutionalization. Human Relations, 2, 23–29.

MERTON, R. K., 1947. Selected problems of field work in the planned community. American Sociological Review, 12, 304–312.

MERTON, R. K., 1957. Social theory and social structure, (rev. ed.). Free Press.

MERTON, R. K., M. FISKE, and A. CURTIS, 1946. *Mass persuasion.* Harper.

MERTON, R. K., M. FISKE, and P. L. KENDALL, 1956. *The focused interview.* Free Press.

MERTON, R. K., and P. F. LAZARSFELD, eds., 1950. *Continuities in social research.* Free Press.

MERTON, R. K., and A. S. ROSSI, 1957. Contributions to the theory of reference group behavior. In R. K. Merton, *Social theory and social structure,* (rev. ed.). Free Press.

MERTON, R. K., P. S. WEST, and M. JAHODA, forthcoming. *Patterns of social life: explorations in the social psychology and sociology of housing.* Part of this work, entitled *Social facts and social fictions: the dynamics of race relations in Hilltown,* is available in hectographed form from the Bureau of Applied Social Research, Columbia University.

MINTZ, A., 1946. A re-examination of correlations between lynchings and economic indices. *J. Abnormal and Social Psychology, 41,* 154–160.

MORENO, J. L., 1934. *Who shall survive?* (rev. ed. 1953, Beacon House) Nervous and Mental Disease Publishing Co., Series No. 58. Washington, D. C.

MORGAN, J. J. B., 1945. Attitudes of students toward the Japanese. *J. Social Psychology, 21,* 219–227.

MORRIS, R. T., and O. M. DAVIDSEN, forthcoming (probably 1959). *The two-way mirror: a study in cross-cultural education* (tentative title). University of Minnesota.

MOWRER, O. H., 1953. "Q technique"—description, history, and critique. In *Psychotherapy: theory and research,* ed. by O. H. Mowrer. Ronald Press.

MÜNSTERBERG, H., 1908, 1923. *On the witness stand: essays on psychology and crime.* Clark Boardman.

MURPHY, G., and R. LIKERT, 1938. *Public opinion and the individual.* Harper.

MURPHY, G., L. B. MURPHY, and T. M. NEWCOMB, 1937. *Experimental social psychology.* Harper.

MURRAY, H. A., et al., 1938. *Explorations in personality.* Oxford.

MURRAY, H. A., and C. D. MORGAN, 1945. A clinical study of sentiments. *Genetic Psychology Monographs, 32,* 3–149; 153–311.

MUSSEN, P. H., 1950. The reliability and validity of the Horowitz faces test. *J. Abnormal and Social Psychology, 45,* 504–506.

NATIONAL OPINION RESEARCH CENTER. *Opinion News,* Aug. 1, 1948.

NEWCOMB, T. M., 1931. An experiment designed to test the validity of a rating technique. *J. Educational Psychology, 22,* 279–289.

NEWCOMB, T. M., 1943. *Personality and social change: attitude formation in a student community.* Dryden.

NEWCOMB, T. M., 1946. The influence of attitude climate upon some determinants of information. *J. Abnormal and Social Psychology, 41,* 291–302.

NEWCOMB, T. M., 1947. Some patterned consequences of membership in a college community. In *Readings in social psychology,* ed. by T. M. Newcomb and E. L. Hartley. Holt.

NORTHROP, F. S. C., 1947. *The logic of the sciences and the humanities.* Macmillan.

OGBURN, W. F., 1947. On scientific writing. *American J. Sociology, 52,* 383–389.

OSGOOD, C. E., G. J. SUCI, and P. H. TANNENBAUM, 1957. *The measurement of meaning.* University of Illinois.

PACE, C. R., 1939. A situations test to measure social-political-economic attitudes. *J. Social Psychology, 10,* 331–344.

PACKARD, V., 1957. *The hidden persuaders.* McKay.

PARSONS, T., 1937. *The structure of social action.* McGraw-Hill.

PARTEN, M. B., 1950. *Surveys, polls, and samples.* Harper.

PATON, M. R., 1935. Selection of tabulation method, machine or manual. *J. Marketing, 6,* 229–235.

PAUL, E., and C. PAUL (trans.), 1921. *A young girl's diary.* Preface with a letter by Sigmund Freud. Thomas Seitzer.

PAYNE, S. L., 1951. *The art of asking questions.* Princeton University.

PEAK, H., 1953. Problems of objective observation. In *Research methods in the behavioral sciences,* ed. by L. Festinger and D. Katz. Dryden.

PEASE, K., 1949. *Machine computation of elementary statistics.* Chartwell House.

PINTNER, R., and G. FORLANO, 1937. The influence of attitude upon scaling of attitude items. *J. Social Psychology, 8,* 39–45.

POFFENBERGER, A. T., 1942. *Principles of applied psychology.* Appleton-Century.

POLITZ, A., and W. SIMMONS, 1949. An attempt to get the "not at homes" into the sample without call-backs. *J. American Statistical Association, 44,* 9–31.

PROCTOR, C. H., and C. P. LOOMIS, 1951. Analysis of sociometric data. In *Research methods in social relations,* Vol. II, first ed., ed. by M. Jahoda, M. Deutsch, and S. W. Cook. Dryden.

PROSHANSKY, H. M., 1943. A projective method for the study of attitudes. *J. Abnormal and Social Psychology, 38,* 393–395.

PROSHANSKY, H. M., 1950. Projective techniques in action research. In *Projective psychology,* ed. by L. E. Abt and L. Bellak. Knopf.

RAPER, A. F., 1933. *The tragedy of lynching.* University of North Carolina.

RAPKIN, C., E. GRIER, and G. GRIER, 1957. *Group relations in Newark— 1957.* Urban Research (New York).

REMMERS, H. H., ed., 1934. Studies in attitudes. Purdue University studies in higher education, 26. *Bulletin of Purdue University, 35*, No. 4.

ROBINSON, W. S., 1957. The statistical measure of agreement. *American Sociological Review, 22,* 17–25.

ROETHLISBERGER, F. J., and W. J. DICKSON, 1939. *Management and the worker.* Harvard University.

ROGERS, C. R., 1945. The non-directive method as a technique for social research. *American J. Sociology, 50,* 279–283.

ROGERS, C. R., and R. F. DYMOND, 1954. *Psychotherapy and personality change.* University of Chicago.

ROGERS, C. R., and B. F. SKINNER, 1956. Some issues concerning the control of human behavior: a symposium. *Science, 124,* 1057–1066.

ROHDE, A. R., 1946. Explorations in personality by the sentence completion method. *J. Applied Psychology, 30,* 169–181.

ROSENBERG, M., W. THIELENS, and P. F. LAZARSFELD, 1951. The panel study. In *Research methods in social relations,* Vol. II, first ed., ed. by M. Jahoda, M. Deutsch, and S. W. Cook. Dryden.

ROSENFELD, E., 1958. The American social scientist in Israel: a case study in role conflict. *American J. Orthopsychiatry, 28,* 563–571.

ROTTER, J. B., 1951. Word association and sentence completion methods. In *Projective techniques,* ed. by H. H. Anderson and G. L. Anderson. Prentice-Hall.

ROTTER, J. B., and B. WILLERMAN, 1947. The incomplete sentence test as a method of studying personality. *J. Consulting Psychology, 11,* 43–48.

ROWNTREE, B. S., 1941. *Poverty and progress.* Longmans.

SACKS, J. M., 1949. The relative effect upon projective responses of stimuli referring to the subject and of stimuli referring to other persons. *J. Consulting Psychology, 13,* 12–21.

SAENGER, G., and E. GILBERT, 1950. Customer reactions to the integration of Negro sales personnel. *International J. Opinion and Attitude Research, 4,* 57–76.

SAENGER, G., and H. PROSHANSKY, 1950. Projective techniques in the service of attitude research. *Personality,* Symposium No. 2, 23–34.

SAFFIR, M. A., 1937. A comparative study of scales constructed by three psychophysical methods. *Psychometrika, 2,* 179–198.

SANFORD, F. H., 1950. *Authoritarianism and leadership: a study of the follower's orientation to authority.* Institute for Research in Human Relations (Philadelphia).

SANFORD, F. H., and J. ROSENSTOCK, 1952. Projective techniques on the doorstep. *J. Abnormal and Social Psychology, 47,* 3–16.

SARGENT, S. S., and G. SAENGER, 1947. Analyzing the content of mass media. *J. Social Issues, 3,* 33–38.

SARTRE, J. P., 1948. *Portrait of the anti-Semite.* Secker and Warburg (London).

SAYLES, L. R., 1954. Field use of projective methods. *Sociology and Social Research, 38,* 168–173.

SCHUTZ, W. C., 1952. Reliability, ambiguity, and content analysis. *Psychological Review, 59,* 119–129.

SCHWARTZ, W., 1948. *Action research in a group work setting: a record of a co-operative experience.* Unpublished master's thesis at the New York School of Social Work, Columbia University.

SCOTT, W. A., 1955. Reliability of content analysis: the case of nominal scale coding. *Public Opinion Quarterly, 19,* 321–325.

SEELEMAN, V., 1940–1941. The influence of attitude upon the remembering of pictorial material. *Archives Psychology, 36,* No. 258.

SEEMAN, M., 1947. Moral judgment: a study in racial frames of references. *American Sociological Review, 12,* 404–411.

SELLTIZ, C., 1955. The use of survey methods in a citizens campaign against discrimination. *Human Organization, 14,* 19–25.

SELLTIZ, C., A. L. HOPSON, and S. W. COOK, 1956. The effects of situational factors on personal interaction between foreign students and Americans *J. Social Issues, 12,* 33–44.

SELLTIZ, C., and associates, 1950. The acceptability of answers to anti-Semitic remarks. *International J. Opinion and Attitude Research, 4,* 353–390.

SHEATSLEY, P. B., 1951. The art of interviewing and a guide to interviewer selection and training. In *Research methods in social relations,* Vol. II, first ed., ed. by M. Jahoda, M. Deutsch, and S. W. Cook. Dryden.

SHERIF, M., and C. SHERIF, 1953. *Groups in harmony and tension.* Harper.

SIEGEL, S., 1956. *Nonparametric statistics for the behavioral sciences.* McGraw-Hill.

SIMMONS, W. R., 1954. A plan to account for "not-at-homes" by combining weighting and call-backs. *J. Marketing, 11,* 42–54.

SMITH, G. H., 1954. *Motivation research in advertising and marketing.* McGraw-Hill.

SMITH, J. G., and A. J. DUNCAN, 1945. *Sampling statistics and applications.* McGraw-Hill.

SNEDECOR, G. W., 1956. *Statistical methods.* 5th ed. Iowa State College.

SOLOMON, R. L., 1949. Extension of control group design. *Psychological Bulletin, 46,* 137–150.

SPITZ, R. A., and K. M. WOLF, 1946. Anaclitic depression: an inquiry into the genesis of psychiatric conditions in early childhood, II. *The Psychoanalytic Study of the Child,* Vol. II.

STAR, S. A., and H. M. HUGHES, 1950. Report on an educational campaign: the Cincinnati plan for the United Nations. *American J. Sociology, 55,* 355–361.

STEIN, M. I., 1947. The use of a sentence completion test for the diagnosis of personality. *J. Clinical Psychology, 3,* 47–56.

STEINZOR, B., 1949. The development and evaluation of a measure of social interaction. *Human Relations, 2,* 103–122.

STEPHAN, F. F., and P. J. McCARTHY, 1958. *Sampling opinions: an analysis of survey procedure.* Wiley.

STEPHENSON, W., 1953. *The study of behavior: Q-technique and its methodology.* University of Chicago.

STEVENS, S. S., 1946. On the theory of scales of measurement. *Science, 103,* 677–680.

STEVENS, S. S., 1951. Mathematics, measurement, and psychophysics. In *Handbook of experimental psychology,* ed. by S. S. Stevens. Wiley.

STEVENS, S. S., 1957. On the psychophysical law. *Psychological Review, 64,* 153–181.

STOUFFER, S. A., 1949. An analysis of conflicting social norms. *American Sociological Review, 14,* 707–717.

STOUFFER, S. A., et al., 1949a. *The American soldier: adjustment during army life.* Studies in Social Psychology in World War II, Vol. I. Princeton University.

STOUFFER, S. A., et al., 1949b. *The American soldier: combat and its aftermath.* Studies in Social Psychology in World War II, Vol. II. Princeton University.

STOUFFER, S. A., et al., 1950. *Measurement and prediction.* Studies in Social Psychology in World War II, Vol. IV. Princeton University.

Technical recommendations for psychological tests and diagnostic techniques, 1954. Prepared by a joint committee of the American Psychological Association, American Educational Research Association, and National Council on Measurements Used in Education. Supplement to *Psychological Bulletin, 51,* No. 2, Pt. II.

THELEN, H., and J. WITHALL, 1949. Three frames of reference: a description of climate. *Human Relations, 2,* 159–176.

THOMAS, W. I., and F. ZNANIECKI, 1918. *The Polish peasant in Europe and America.* Badger.

THOMSON, G. H., 1946. *The factorial analysis of human ability* (2nd ed.). University of London.

THORNDIKE, R. L., 1949. *Personnel selection test and measurement techniques.* Wiley.

THURSTONE, L. L., 1927. The method of paired comparisons for social values. *J. Abnormal and Social Psychology, 21,* 384–400.

THURSTONE, L. L., 1928. An experimental study of nationality preferences. *J. Genetic Psychology, 1,* 405–425.

THURSTONE, L. L., 1929. Theory of attitude measurement. *Psychological Bulletin, 36,* 222–241.

THURSTONE, L. L., 1931. The measurement of social attitudes. *J. Abnormal and Social Psychology, 26,* 249–269.

THURSTONE, L. L., and E. J. CHAVE, 1929. *The measurement of attitude.* University of Chicago.

TORGERSON, W. S., 1958. *Theory and methods of scaling.* Wiley.

TRYON, R. C., 1955. *Identification of social areas by cluster analysis.* University of California Publications in Psychology, 8, No. 1.

TRYON, R. C., 1957a. Communality of a variable: formulation by cluster analysis. *Psychometrika, 22,* 241–260.

TRYON, R. C., 1957b. Reliability and behavior domain validity: reformulation and historical critique. *Psychological Bulletin, 54,* 229–249.

UNDERWOOD, B. J., 1957. *Psychological research.* Appleton-Century-Crofts

UNIVERSITY OF CHICAGO PRESS, 1949. *A manual of style* (11th ed.).

WALKER, H. M., and J. LEV, 1953. *Statistical inference.* Holt.

WARNER, W. L., and associates, 1941–1947. *Yankee City series.* Yale University. 4 vols.

WATSON, G. B., 1925. *The measurement of fair-mindedness.* Teachers College, Columbia University Contributions to Education No. 176. Teachers College, Columbia University.

WEITZ, J., and R. C. NUCKOLS, 1953. The validity of direct and indirect questions in measuring job satisfaction. *Personnel Psychology, 6,* 487–494.

WESCHLER, I. R., 1950. An investigation of attitudes toward labor and management by means of the error-choice method. *J. Social Psychology, 32,* 51–67.

WEHL, H., 1949. *Philosophy of mathematics and the natural sciences.* Princeton University.

WHITE, B. W., and E. SALTZ, 1957. Measurement of reproducibility. *Psychological Bulletin, 54,* 81–99.

WHITE, R. K., 1949. Hitler, Roosevelt, and the nature of war propaganda. *J. Abnormal and Social Psychology, 44,* 157–174.

WHITING, J. W. M., and I. L. CHILD, 1953. *Child training and personality: a cross-cultural study.* Yale University.

WHYTE, W. F., 1951. Observational field-work methods. In *Research methods in social relations,* Vol. II, first ed., ed. by M. Jahoda, M. Deutsch, and S. W. Cook. Dryden.

WHYTE, W. F., 1957. On asking indirect questions. *Human Organization, 15,* 21–23.

WILNER, D. M., E. ROSENFELD, R. S. LEE, D. L. GERARD, and I. CHEIN, 1957. Heroin use and street gangs. *J. Criminal Law, Criminology and Police Science, 48,* 399–409.

WILNER, D. M., R. P. WALKLEY, and S. W. COOK, 1955. *Human relations in interracial housing: a study of the contact hypothesis.* University of Minnesota.

WOLFENSTEIN, M., and N. LEITES, 1950. Two social scientists view "No Way Out"—the unconscious vs. the "message" in an anti-bias film. *Commentary, 10,* 388–391.

WOOLLEY, E. C., and F. W. SCOTT, 1944. *College handbook of composition* (4th ed.). Heath.

WORMSER, M. H., and C. SELLTIZ, 1951a. Community self-surveys. In *Research methods in social relations,* Vol. II, first ed., ed. by M. Jahoda, M. Deutsch, and S. W. Cook. Dryden.

WORMSER, M. H., and C. SELLTIZ, 1951b. *How to conduct a community self-survey of civil rights.* Association Press.

WRIGHT, Q., and C. J. NELSON, 1939. American attitudes toward Japan and China, 1937–38. *Public Opinion Quarterly, 3,* 46–62.

WRIGLEY, C., 1957. Electronic computers and psychological research. *American Psychologist, 12,* 501–509.

ZANDER, A., 1951. Systematic observation of small face-to-face groups. In *Research methods in social relations,* Vol. II, first ed., ed. by M. Jahoda, M. Deutsch, and S. W. Cook. Dryden.

ZAWADZKI, B., 1948. Limitations of the scapegoat theory of prejudice. *J. Abnormal and Social Psychology, 43,* 127–141.

ZEISEL, H., 1957. *Say it with figures* (4th ed.). Harper.

ZEVIN, B. D., ed., 1946. *Nothing to fear* (Addresses of Franklin D. Roosevelt). Houghton.

ZOBER, M., 1956. Some projective techniques in marketing research. *J. Marketing, 20,* 262–268.

INDEX

INDEX

Abstractions, high-level, 41
Abt, L. E., 281n.
Accidental sampling, 515n., 516, 541–544
Ackerman, N. W., 62, 540
Act, in structured observation, 226
Action agency, 457
  final report to, 469–471
  interim report to, 466–469
Action-oriented research, 457–466
  audiences for, 471–472
  presentation of, 466–472
  and social policy, 474–477
Action personnel, 457
  contributions of, to research, 458–460
  resistance of, to research, 461–464, 470–471
Adorno, T. W., 184, 284, 295, 357
Advertising, motivation research and, 539
"After-only" experiments, 108–112
Age, as variable, 136
Agency, action, 457, 466–471
Aggression, 483, 486
  and prejudice, 62
Allport, G. W., 235, 323n., 324, 327, 486
Alor, 284–285
Ambiguity, in check lists, 569
American Documentation Institute, 450
American Jewish Congress, 58n.
American Psychological Association, 218n., 453
American Sociological Society, 54
American Soldier, The, 493
Ames, A., Jr., 28
Analysis
  anticipatory, 387–390
  factor, 379n.
  raw data as aid to, 432–440
  symbol, 340
  of variance, 124–125
  (See also Categories)

Anderson, G. L., 281n.
Anderson, H. H., 281n.
Angell, R., 323n.
Animals, social behavior of, 202
Anomie, 319
Anonymity, in questionnaire, 240
Anthropologists, observation by, 202, 203–204
Anti-Defamation League of B'nai B'rith, 54
Anti-Semitism, measures of, 184–185, 357–358
Application, practical, of research, 457–466
Applied research, 4–5
Argument-completion test, 290
Army, integrated units in, 138
Attitudes
  definition of, 146
  of foreign students, 33–35, 37, 41–42
  toward minority groups, 295, 297
  scales, 357–383
  semantic differential as test of, 381
  social, projective methods for study of, 285–299
  social, structured disguised tests of, 299–310
  test of, and social pressures, 151
Audio-introspectometer, 229
Aussage test of perception and memory, 304
Authoritarian Personality, The, 184–185, 295, 312
Authority figures, and family experiences, 161–162
Average deviation, 412–413

Baehne, G. W., 408n.
Baldwin, A. L., 409n.
Barker, R., 115, 347
Battle of Britain, 111, 118–119
"Before-after" design, offset, 116

609